# THE SECRET TEACHINGS OF ALL AGES
## VOLUME 2

# THE SECRET TEACHINGS OF ALL AGES VOLUME 2

MANLY P. HALL

# Contents

Adultbrain Publishing is dedicated to breathing new life into timeless literary works by resurrecting old classics for the modern age. We meticulously curate and convert these masterpieces into high-quality digital and audio formats, making them accessible to a new generation of readers and listeners. Our commitment to preserving the essence of these works, while enhancing them with today's technology, allows us to offer immersive experiences that retain the authenticity of the original texts. Whether rediscovering a beloved classic or experiencing it for the first time, our editions invite readers to start using their Adultbrain today.
Published by Adultbrain Publishing.
ISBN: 978-1-998704-64-4
eISBN:978-1-998704-65-1
Title: The Secret Teachings of All Ages Volume 2: Lectures on Ancient Philosophy and the Foundations of Esoteric Wisdom
Start using your adultbrain today.
For more information, visit: www.adultbrain.ca

"We are the gods of the atoms that make up ourselves but we are also the atoms of the gods that make up the universe."

"To repress rebellion is to maintain the status quo, a condition which binds the mortal creature in a state of intellectual or physical slavery. But it is impossible to chain man merely by slaving his body; the mind also must be held, and to accomplish this, fear is the accepted weapon. The common man must fear life, fear death, fear God, fear the Devil, and fear most the overlords, the keepers of his destiny."

"We can only escape from the world by outgrowing the world. Death may take man out of the world but only wisdom can take the world out of the man. As long as the human being is obsessed by worldliness, he will suffer from the Karmic consequences of false allegiances. When however, worldliness is transmuted into Spiritual Integrity he is free, even though he still dwells physically among worldly things."

Manly P Hall

# I

## Publisher's Preface

When Manly P. Hall published The Secret Teachings of All Ages in 1928, he offered the world not just a book, but an intellectual Rosetta Stone—an atlas of forgotten mysteries, a cathedral of symbols in print. The original volume remains one of the most comprehensive and symbolically layered treatises on ancient wisdom ever assembled. It bridged East and West, science and spirit, myth and metaphysics, offering an ambitious vision of an eternal philosophy hidden beneath the creeds, rites, and rituals of all cultures.

Yet, as expansive as it was, The Secret Teachings was never intended as a conclusion. It was an invitation.

Volume II continues that invitation—taking readers deeper into the initiatic structure that underpins Hall's great work. In this continuation, we witness Hall as philosopher and teacher, not just compiler. These lectures and essays present the inner curriculum, the esoteric architecture behind the symbols—a mystical scaffolding of philosophy, psychology, cosmology, and ethical discipline meant not merely to inform, but to transform.

In these pages, readers will discover how the gods of mythology represent spiritual principles and psychological forces; how initiation mirrors the soul's evolution; how sacred alphabets conceal cosmological structures; how Tarot reveals the journey of consciousness; and how the Rosicrucians encoded their wisdom in allegory and symbolism that transcends the bounds of language and time. Just as Francis Bacon suggested in Wisdom of the Ancients, the myths of old were not idle stories, but philosophical truths veiled in poetry—messages encrypted for minds prepared to decode them.

To that end, we have carefully restored and compiled several of Hall's rare and often overlooked essays—many drawn from his elusive journal The All-Seeing Eye—and interwoven them among his public lectures. These writings include The Esoteric Structure of the Alphabet, The Symbolism of the Tarot, What the Ancient Wisdom Expects of Its Disciples, The Rosicrucian Mysteries, and more. They act as bridges between doctrines, reflections upon mysteries, and meditative pauses in the unfolding narrative of Hall's thought. Each section reveals another facet of a vast metaphysical mosaic.

Together, these lectures and essays outline what Hall considered the path of the true seeker—not a dogma to be swallowed, but a discipline to be lived. For Hall, ancient wisdom is not a set of beliefs, but a way of being. The disciple is not one who believes most fervently, but one who strives most earnestly to know. In this tradition, truth is not granted; it is earned. The ancient schools demanded mental clarity, moral integrity, and philosophical maturity from their initiates. Hall carries that standard forward and challenges modern readers to do the same.

This edition is not a casual read. It is a guidebook for the spiritually serious, the philosophically curious, and those who sense that behind the veil of the ordinary lies a greater order—waiting not to be worshiped, but understood. Whether you are stepping into Hall's universe for the first time or returning after years of study, Volume II will reveal a new layer of insight and possibility.

We at Adultbrain Publishing are proud to present this newly typeset and curated edition of The Secret Teachings of All Ages, Volume II, designed with care for both new initiates and seasoned philosophers. We believe that Hall's voice—clear, compassionate, and unshakably grounded in perennial wisdom—deserves to be heard by each new generation.

May this volume serve as torch and trail, illuminating your path toward the center of the mystery.

— Adultbrain Publishing

2025

"PHILOSOPHY IS THE SCIENCE OF ESTIMATING VALUES. THE SPIRIT OF TRUE PHILOSOPHY IS NOT TYRANNICAL, BUT GENTLE AND PERSUASIVE. ITS AIM IS THE PERFECTION OF MAN, AND ITS KEYNOTE IS BALANCE AND MODERATION."

— MANLY P. HALL

# II

⚜

# A Note to the Reader

This volume is not arranged for casual consumption. It is a curated journey through the structure of ancient philosophy—layer by layer, symbol by symbol. Each lecture builds upon the next, and the interspersed essays serve not as distractions, but as keys and mirrors—illuminating the ideas just presented, or preparing the mind for what lies ahead.

Though originally delivered as individual addresses, these lectures form a coherent initiatory curriculum. Taken together, they reflect Manly P. Hall's lifelong vision: that philosophy is not mere intellectualism, but the very pathway to spiritual regeneration.

We encourage readers to move through this volume deliberately and reflectively. Many of the ideas presented here will seem familiar to those acquainted with Hall's Secret Teachings, but here they are given greater depth, structure, and philosophical grounding.

You may find it useful to read a single lecture, pause with the following essay, and sit with the material before continuing. The wisdom of the ancients does not yield itself to hurried eyes. It requires stillness, humility, and effort.

This book is for those who would not only understand the mysteries—but live them.

# III

## Preface to the First Edition

Although complete in itself, this book is primarily designed to complement and amplify the larger volume on Symbolical Philosophy published last year. During the spring and fall of 1928, I delivered two series of lectures on Symbolism and the Ancient Mysteries—one in San Francisco and the other in Los Angeles—to groups largely composed of subscribers to An Encyclopedic Outline of Masonic, Qabbalistic and Rosicrucian Symbolical Philosophy. These lectures were carefully taken down in shorthand, and form the basis of the present work.

A considerable portion of my larger book is devoted to the rituals and figures of the Greek Mysteries, and this treatise is an effort to clarify the subject of classical pagan metaphysics. In his Miscellanies, published at the beginning of the last century, Thomas Taylor, the eminent Platonist, predicted that the "sublime theology which was first obscurely promulgated by Orpheus, Pythagoras, and Plato, and was afterwards perspicuously unfolded by their legitimate disciples; a theology which, though it may be involved in oblivion in barbarous, and derided in impious ages, will again flourish for very extended periods, through all the infinite revolutions of time."

Our civilization has not yet learned to value appreciation for the beautiful as the very foundation of an enduring culture. Unless we respond to the harmonious, the elegant, the symmetrical, and the rhythmic, we are recreant to past good, a menace to present integrity, and an obstacle to future effort. This truth is well made in The Merchant of Venice:

"The man that hath no music in himself
Nor is not moved with concord of sweet sounds,
Is fit for treasons, stratagems and spoils."

For lack of aesthetics, man lives the life of a Caliban, and in death receives the reward of a Thersites. It is not enough that our codes be true; they must also be beautiful. If learning does not teach us to love, we learn without understanding.

We have shackled the Titans and bound the elements to our service. Like proud Bellerophon we have bridled Pegasus, but already the gadfly of Zeus is at work. By concentrating all our energies upon temporal concerns, we have builded an empire, moving each stone into place at terrific cost. We have heaped up institutions as the Pharaohs piled up pyramids, yet our monuments, like those along the Nile, shall become the tombs of their own builders. We have paid a frightful price for our boasted success, for our strength has taught us to hate, our power to kill, and our thought to reason away our souls.

We must seek for that sufficient code which guided the wise through every generation. We must again establish those perfect Mysteries through which alone, as Plato declared in the Phaedrus, man becomes truly perfect. Ares was burned up by his own flame, and his host of evil spirits consumed with him. Man, tired of vain wrangling and contending for power, longs for those quiet groves where olden sages communed with their familiars.

Neoplatonism forms the basis for this exposition. Never in the history of metaphysics, since that great Alexandrian day, has the mind of man contemplated so rationally and lucidly the riddle of Abiding Destiny. The fruitage of noble endeavor can never die, nor is truth to be lightly cast aside. Unmoved by the calumny of ungrateful ages and the anathemas of a bigoted theology, the Platonic philosophers sit upon their golden thrones, awaiting with philosophic patience the day when an unbelieving world shall comprehend.

MANLY PALMER HALL

Los Angeles, California,

June 1, 1929.

# IV

The Voice of the World

"But since the generated world is a collective whole, if we apply the ears of our intellect to the world, we shall, perhaps, hear it thus addressing us:

'There is no doubt that I was produced by Divinity, from whom I am formed perfect—composed from all animals, entirely sufficient to myself, and lacking in nothing; for all things are contained in my ample bosom: the nature of all generated beings, gods both visible and invisible, the illustrious race of daemons, the noble army of virtuous souls, and men rendered happy by wisdom and virtue.

Nor is the earth alone adorned with an endless variety of plants and animals, nor does the power of the universal soul alone diffuse itself into the sea and become bounded by its circumfluent waters, while the wide expanse of air and aether remains destitute of life and soul; but the celestial spaces are filled with illustrious souls, supplying life to the stars and directing their revolutions in everlasting order.

Add, too, that the celestial orbs, in imitation of Intellect—which seeks after nothing external—are wisely agitated in a perpetual circuit around the central sun.

Furthermore, whatever I contain desires the Good—collectively considered, and in particulars according to their peculiar ability; for that general Soul by which I am enlivened, and the heavens, the most illustrious of my parts, continually depend on the Good for support, together with the gods who reign in my parts, every animal and plant, and whatever I contain which appears to be destitute of life.

While some things are seen to participate in being alone, others in life, and others, beyond this, are endowed with sentient powers; some possess the still higher faculty of reason, and lastly, others are all life and intelligence. For it is not proper to require equality among such as are unequal, nor to expect that the finger should see—but rather to assign this as the province of the eye, while another purpose is desired in the finger, which can, I think, be no other than that it remains a finger and performs its peculiar office.'"

— Plotinus, On Providence

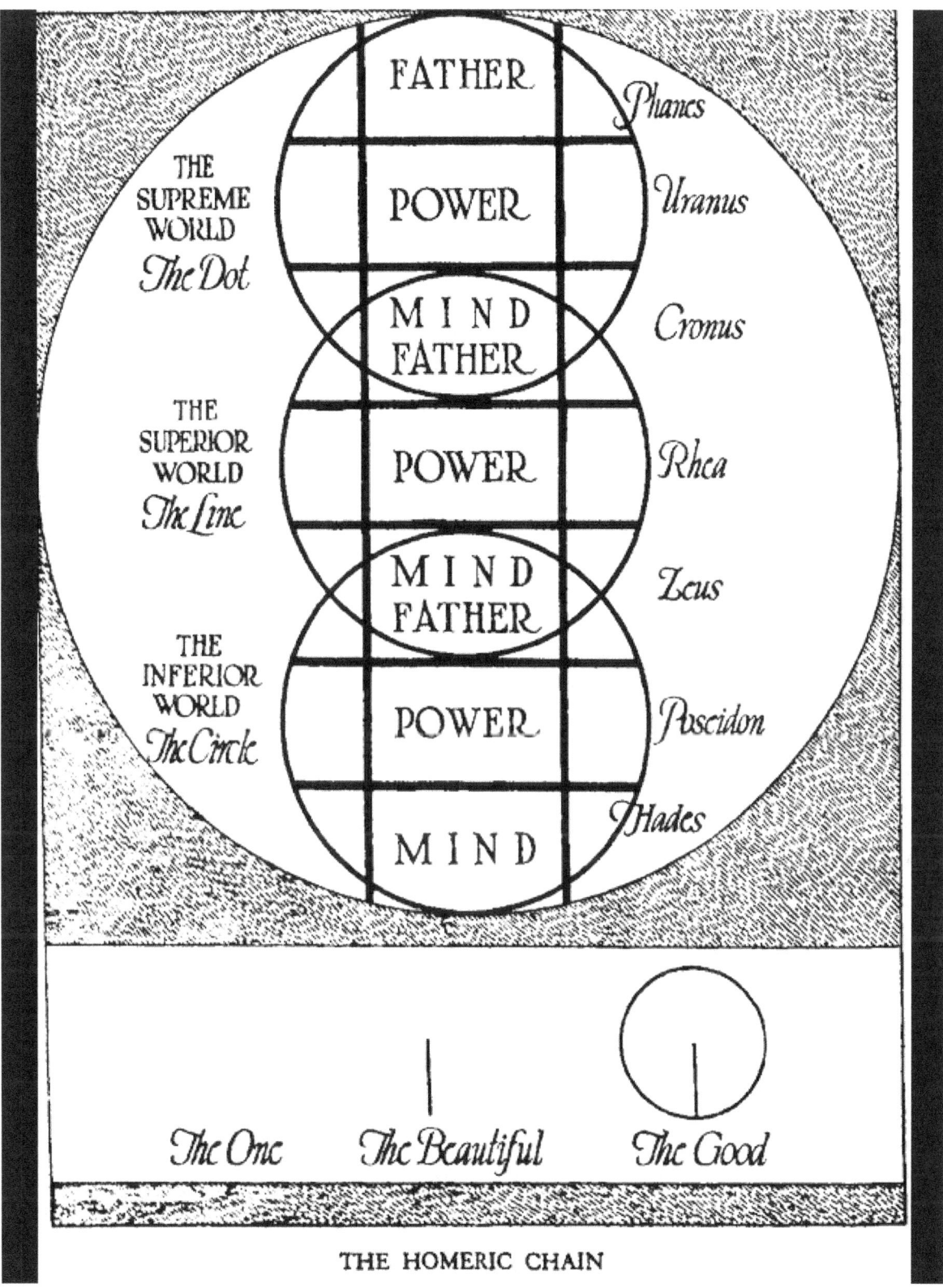

FATHER — *Phanes*

POWER — *Uranus*

THE SUPREME WORLD *The Dot*

MIND FATHER — *Cronus*

THE SUPERIOR WORLD *The Line*

POWER — *Rhea*

MIND FATHER — *Zeus*

THE INFERIOR WORLD *The Circle*

POWER — *Poseidon*

MIND — *Hades*

*The One*  *The Beautiful*  *The Good*

## THE HOMERIC CHAIN

The order of the gods of the three worlds, grouped in Chaldean triads, is here set forth according to the doctrines of Orpheus. This mystery was concealed by the first symbolists under the figures of the dot, the line, and the circle. To the mystic, the fables of the ancients are indeed resplendent with unsuspected truths.

# V

## The Nature of the Absolute

TO define adequately the nature of the Absolute is impossible, for it is everything in its eternal, undivided, and unconditioned state. In ancient writings it is referred to as the NOTHING and the ALL. No mind is capable of visualizing an appropriate symbolic figure of the Absolute. Of all the symbols devised to represent its eternal and unknowable state, a clean, blank sheet of paper is the least erroneous. The paper, being blank, represents all that cannot be thought of, all that cannot be seen, all that cannot be felt, and all that cannot be limited by any tangible function of consciousness. The blank paper represents measureless, eternal, unlimited SPACE. No created intelligence has ever plumbed its depths; no God has ever scaled its heights, nor shall mortal or immortal being ever discover the true nature of its substance. From it all things come, to it all things return, but it neither comes nor goes. Figures and symbols are pollutions drawn upon the unblemished surface of the paper. The symbols, therefore, signify the conditions that exist upon the face of SPACE or, more correctly, which are produced out of the substance of SPACE.

 The blank sheet, being emblematic of the ALL, each of the diagrams drawn upon it signifies some fractional phase of the ALL. The moment the symbol is drawn upon the paper, the paper loses its perfect and unlimited blankness. As the symbols represent the creative agencies and substances, the philosophers have declared that when the parts of existence come into manifestation the perfect wholeness of Absolute Being is destroyed. In other words, the forms destroy the perfection of the formlessness that preceded them. Symbolism deals with universal forces and agencies. Each of these forces and agencies is an expression of SPACE, because SPACE is the ultimate of substance, the ultimate of force, and the sum of them both. Nothing exists except it exists in SPACE; nothing is made except it is made of SPACE. In Egypt Space is called TAT.

SPACE is the perfect origin of everything. It is not God; it is not Nature; it is not man; it is not the universe. All these exist in SPACE and are fashioned out of it, but SPACE is supreme. SPACE and Absolute Spirit are one; SPACE and Absolute Matter are one. Therefore SPACE, Spirit, and Matter are one. Spirit is the positive manifestation of SPACE; Matter is the negative manifestation of SPACE. Spirit and Matter exist together in SPACE. SPACE, Spirit, and Matter are the first Trinity, with SPACE the Father, Spirit the Son, and Matter the Holy Ghost. SPACE, though actually undivided, becomes through hypothetical division Absolute (or Ultimate) Spirit, Absolute (or Ultimate) Intelligence, and Absolute (or Ultimate) Matter.

The most primitive and fundamental of all symbols is the dot. Place a dot in the center of the sheet and what does it signify? Simply the ALL considered as the ONE, or first point. Unable to understand the Absolute, man gathers its incomprehensibility mentally to a focal point—the dot. The dot is the first illusion because it is the first departure from things as they eternally are—the blank sheet of paper. There is nothing immortal but SPACE, nothing eternal but SPACE, nothing without beginning or end but SPACE, nothing unchangeable but SPACE. Everything but SPACE either grows or decays, because everything that grows grows out of SPACE and everything that decays decays into SPACE. SPACE alone remains.

Philosophically, SPACE is synonymous with Self (spelled with a capital S), because it is not the inferior, or more familiar, self. It is the Self which man through all eternity struggles to attain. Therefore the true Self is as abstract as the blank sheet of paper, and only he who can fathom the nature of the blank paper can discover Self.

The dot may be likened to Spirit. The Spirit is Self with the loss of limitlessness, because the dot is bound by certain limitations. The dot is the first illusion of the Self, the first imitation of SPACE, even as Spirit is the first limitation of Self. The dot is life localized as a center of power; the blank paper is life unlimited. According to philosophy the dot must sometime be erased, because nothing but the blank paper is eternal. The dot represents a limitation, for the life that is everywhere becomes the life that is somewhere; universal life becomes individualized life and ceases to recognize its kinship with all Being.

After the dot is placed on the paper it can be rubbed out and the white paper restored to its virgin state. Thus the white paper represents eternity, and the dot, time; and when the dot is erased time is dissolved back into eternity, for time is dependent upon eternity. Therefore in ancient philosophy there are two symbols: the NOTHING and the ONE—the white paper and the dot. Creation traces its origin from the dot—the Primitive Sea, the Egg laid by the White Swan in the field of SPACE.

If existence be viewed from the Self downward into the illusion of creation, the dot is the first or least degree of illusion. On the other hand, if existence be viewed from the lower, or illusionary universe, upward toward Reality, the dot is the greatest conceivable Reality. The least degree of physical impermanence is the greatest degree of spiritual permanence. That which is most divine is least mortal. Thus, in the moral sense, the greatest degree of good is the least degree of evil. The dot, being most proximate to perfection, is the simplest, and therefore the least imperfect of all symbols. From the dot issues forth a multitude of other illusions ever less permanent. The dot, or Sacred Island, is the beginning of existence, whether that of a universe or a man. The dot is the germ raised upon the surface of infinite duration. The potentialities signified by the blank paper are manifested as active potencies through the dot. Thus the limitless Absolute is manifested in a limited way.

When considering his own divine nature, man always thinks of his spirit as the first and greatest part of himself. He feels that his spirit is his real and permanent part. To the ancients, however, the individualized spirit (to which is applied the term was itself a little germ floating upon the surface of Absolute Life. This idea is beautifully brought out in the teachings of the Brahmans,

Buddhists, and Vedantists. The Nirvana of atheistic Buddhism is achieved through the reabsorption of the individualized self into the Universal Self. In Sir Edwin Arnold's Light of Asia, the thought is summed up thus: "Om, mani Padme, hum! the daybreak comes and the dewdrop slips back into the shining sea." The "dewdrop" is the dot; the "sea" the blank paper. The "dewdrop" is the individualized spirit,

or I; the blank paper that Self which is ALL, and at the achievement of Nirvana the lesser mingles with the greater. Immortality is achieved, for that which is impermanent returns to the condition of absolute permanence. The dot, the line, and the circle are the supreme and primary symbols. The dot is Spirit and its symbol in the Chaldaic Hebrew—the Yod— is actually a seed or spermatozoon, a little comma with a twisting tail representing the germ of the not- self. In its first manifestation the dot elongates to form the line. The line is a string of dots made up of germ lives—the monadic lives of Leibnitz. From the seed growing in the earth comes the sprig—the line. The line, therefore, is the symbol of the dot in growth or motion. The sun is a great dot, a monad of life, and each of its rays a line—its own active principle in manifestation. The key thought is: The line is the motion of the dot.

In the process of creation all motion is away from self. Therefore there is only one direction in which the dot can move. In the process of return to the perfect state all motion is toward self, and through self to the Universal Self. Involution is activity outward from self; evolution is activity inward toward self. Motion away from self brings a decrease in consciousness and power; motion toward self brings a corresponding increase in consciousness and power. The farther the light ray travels from its source the weaker the ray. The line is the outpouring or natural impulse of life to expand. It may seem difficult at first to imagine the line as a symbol of general expansion, but it is simply emblematic of motion away from self—the dot. The dot, moving away from self, projects the line; the line becomes the radius of an imaginary circle, and this circle is the circumference of the powers of the central dot.

Hypothetically, every sun has a periphery where its rays end, every human life a periphery where its influence ceases, every human mind a periphery beyond which it cannot function, and every human heart a periphery beyond which it cannot feel.

Somewhere there is a limit to the scope of awareness. The circle is the symbol of this limit. It is the symbol of the vanishing point of central energy. The dot symbolizes the cause; the line, the means ; and the circle, the end. The AINSOPH of the Hebrew Cabalists is equivalent to the Absolute. The Jewish mystics employed the closed eye to suggest the same symbolism as that of the blank sheet of paper. The inscrutable NOTHING conveyed to the mind by the closing of the eyes suggests the eternal, unknowable, and indefinable nature of Perfect Being. These same Cabalists called spirit the dot, the opened eye, because looking away from itself the Ego (or I AM) beholds the vast panorama of things which together compose the illusionary sphere. However, when this same objective eye is turned inward to the contemplation of its own cause, it is confronted by a blankness which defies penetration.

Only that thing which is permanent is absolutely real; hence that unmoved, eternal condition so inadequately symbolized by the blank sheet of paper is the only absolute Reality. In comparison to this eternal state, forms are an ever-changing phantasmagoria, not in the sense that forms do not exist but rather that they are of minor significance when compared to their ever-enduring source.

While through lack of adequate terminology it is necessary to approach a definition of the Absolute from a negative point of view, the blank sheet of paper signifies not emptiness but an utter and incomprehensible fullness when an attempt is made to define the indefinable. Therefore the blank paper represents that SPACE which contains all existence in a potential state. When the material universe—whether the zodiac, the stars, or the multitude of suns dotting the firmament— comes into manifestation, all of its parts are subject to the law of change. Sometime every sun will grow cold; sometime every grain of cosmic dust will blossom forth as a universe, and sometime vanish again. With the phenomenal creation comes birth, growth, decay, and the multifarious laws which have dominion over and measure the span of ephemerality. Omar Khayyam, with characteristic Oriental fatalism, writes:

"One thing is certain and the rest is Lies;

The Flower that once has blown forever dies."

The illusions of diversity—form, place, and time—are classed by the Orientals under the general term Maya . The word Maya signifies the great sea of shadows—the sphere of things as they seem to be as distinguished from the blank piece of paper which represents the one and only THING as it eternally is. The mothers of the various World Saviors generally bear names derived from the word Maya, as for example, Mary, for the reason that the various redeeming deities signify realization born out of illusion, or wisdom rising triumphant from the tomb of ignorance. Philosophic realization must be born out of the realization of illusion. Consequently the Savior«Gods are bom out of Maya and rise through many tribulations into the light of eternity.

The keys to all knowledge are contained in the dot, the line, and the circle. The dot is universal consciousness, the line is universal intelligence, and the circle is universal force—the threefold, unknowable Cause of all knowable existence (the three hypostases of Atma). In man the spirit is represented by the dot and conscious activity or intelligence by the line. Conscious activity is the key to intelligence, because consciousness belongs to the sphere of the dot and activity to the sphere of the circle. The center and the circumference are thus blended in the connecting line—conscious activity or intelligence. The circle is the symbol of body and body is the limit of the radius of the activity of mind power pouring out of the substance of consciousness .

In ancient philosophy the dot signifies Truth, Reality, in whatever form it may take. The line is the motion of the fact and the circle is the symbol of the form or figure established in the inferior or material sphere by these superphysical activi- ties. Take, for example, a blade of grass. Its form is simply the effect of certain active agents upon certain passive substances. The physical blade of grass is really a symbol of a degree of consciousness or a combination of cosmic activities. All forms arc but geometric patterns, being the reactions set up in matter by mysterious forces working in the causal spheres. Conscious activity, working upon or brooding over matter, creates form.

Matter is not form, because matter (like SPACE, of which it is the negative expression) is universally disseminated but, as stated in the ancient doctrine, the activity of life upon and through its substances curdles (organizes) matter so that it assumes certain definite forms or bodies. These organisms thus caused by bringing *the elements of matter into intelligent and definite relationships are held together by the conscious agent manipulating them. The moment this agent is withdrawn the process of disintegration sets in. Disintegration is the inevitable process of returning artificial compounds to their first simple state. Disintegration may be farther defined as the urge of heterogeneous parts to return to their primitive homogeneity ; in other words, the desire of creation to return to SPACE. When the forms have been reabsorbed into the vast sea of matter, they are then ready to be picked up by some other phase of the Creative Agencies and molded afresh into vehicles for the material expression of divine potentialities.

In its application to the divisions of human learning, the dot is the proper symbol of philosophy in that philosophy is the least degree of intellectual illusion. It is not to be inferred that philosophy is absolute truth but rather that it is the least degree of mental error, since all other forms of learning contain a greater percentage of fallacy. Nothing that is sufficiently tangible to be susceptible of accurate definition is true in the absolute sense, but philosophy, transcending the limitations of the form world, achieves more in its investigation of the nature of Being than does any other man-conceived discipline. The more complex the form, the farther removed it is from its source. As more marks are placed upon the white sheet of paper a picture is gradually created which may become so complicated that the white paper itself is entirely obscured. Thus the more diversified the creations, the less the Creator is discernible. Taking up the least possible space upon the paper, the dot detracts the least from the perfect expanse of the white sheet.

Philosophy per se is the least confusing method of approaching Reality. When less accurate systems are employed, a cobweb of contending and confusing complexities is spread over the entire surface of the blank paper, hopelessly entangling the thinker in the maze of illusion. As the dot cannot retire behind itself to explore the nature of the paper upon which it is placed, so no philosophy can entirely free itself from the involvements of mind. As man, however, must have some code by which to live, some system of thought which will give him at least an intellectual concept of ultimates, the wisest of all ages have contributed the fruitage of their transcendent genius to this great human need. Thus philosophy came into being. Like the dot, philosophy is an immovable body. Its essential nature never changes. When the element of change is introduced into philosophy it descends to the level of theology, or rather, it is involved and distorted by the disciplines of theology.

Theology is a motion, a mystical gesture as it were; it is the dot moving away from itself to form the line. Theology is not a fixed element like philosophy; it is a mutable element subject to numberless vicissitudes. Theology is emotional, changeable, violent, and at periodic intervals bursts forth in many forms of irrational excess. Theology occupies a middle ground between materiality and true illumined spirituality which, transcending theology, becomes a comprehension, in part at least, of divine concerns.

As has already been suggested, the line is the radius of an imaginary circle, and when this circle is traced upon the paper we have the proper symbol of science. Science occupies the circumference of the sphere of self. The savant gropes in that twilight where life is lost in form. He is therefore unfitted to cope with any phase of life or knowledge which transcends the plane of material things. The scientist has no comprehension of an activity independent of and dissociated from matter; hence his sphere of usefulness is limited to the lower world and its phenomena. The physical body of what man calls knowledge is science; the emotional body, theology; and the mental and supermental bodies, natural and mystical philosophy respectively. The human mind ascends sequentially from science through theology to philosophy, as in ancient days it descended from divine philosophy through spiritual theology to the condition of material science which it now occupies.

Consider the great number of people who are now leaving the church at the behest of science. Most of these individuals declare their reason for dissenting to the dictates of theology is that the dogma of the church has proved to be philosophically and scientifically unsound. The belief is quite prevalent that nearly all scientists are agnostics, if not atheists, because they refuse to subscribe to the findings of early theologians. Thus the mind must descend from credulity to absolute incredulity before it is prepared to assume the onus of individual thinking. On the other hand, the scientist who has really entered into the spirit of his labors has found God. Science has revealed to him a super theology. It has discovered the God of the swirling atoms; not a personal Deity but an all-permeating, all-powerful, impersonal Creative Agent akin to the Absolute Being of occult philosophy. Thus the little tin god on his golden throne falls to make way for an infinite Creative Principle which science vaguely senses and which philosophy can reveal in fuller splendor.

The primitive symbols now under discussion bring to mind the subject of alphabets. The ancient Alphabet of Wisdom is symbolism, and all the figures used in this supreme alphabet are taken out of the dot, the line, and the circle; in other words, they are made up of various combinations of these elementary forms. Even the Arabic numerical systems and the letters of the English alphabet are compounded from these first three figures. In Oriental mysticism there are certain objects considered peculiarly appropriate for subjects of meditation. One of the most important of the native drawings is that of a lotus bud carrying in its heart the first letter of the Sanskrit alphabet, the letter usually made resplendent by gold leaf. This letter, as the first of the alphabet, is employed to direct the mind of the devotee toward all things which are first, especially Universal Self which is the first of all Being and from which all Nature emerged, as all the letters are presumed to have come forth from the first letter of the alphabet. Thus from one letter issue all letters, and from a comparatively small number of letters an infinite diversity of words, these words being the sound symbols which man has employed to designate the diversified genera of the mundane creation. The words were originally designed as sound-names, and were so closely related to the objects upon which they were conferred that by an analysis of the word the mystical nature of the object could be determined. St. Irenaeus describes the Greek cosmological man as bearing upon his body the letters of the Greek alphabet. The sacredness of the letters is also emphasized in the New Testament where Christ is referred to as the Alpha and the Omega, the first and the last, the beginning and the end. The letters of the alphabet are those sacred symbols through the combinations of which is created an emblem for every thought, every form, every element, and every condition of material existence. Like the very illusional world whose phenomena they catalog, words are slayers of the Real, and the more words used the less of the nature of Reality remains. In the introduction to The Secret Doctrine, H. P. Blavatsky gives several examples of the ancient symbolic alphabets in which the Mystery teachings arc preserved. Writing was originally reserved for the perpetuation of the Ancient Wisdom. Today the Mysteries still have their own language undefiled by involvement in the commercial and prosaic life of the unillumined. The language of the initiates is called the Senzar, and consists of certain magical hieroglyphical figures by which the wise men of all lands communicated with each other. In the primordial symbols of the dot, the line, and the circle, are also set forth the mysteries of the three worlds. The dot is symbolic of heaven, the line of earth, and the circle of hell— the three spheres of Christian theology. Heaven is represented by the dot because it is the first world or foundation of the universe. In its mystical interpretation the word heaven signifies a "heaved up" or convoluted area, and may be interpreted to mean that which is raised above or elevated to a state of first dignity. In a similar manner the origin of the word salvation may be traced to saliva, though the kinship of the two words has long been ignored. Thus salvation signifies the process of mixing gross substance with a spiritual fluidic essence which renders it cosmically digestible and assimilable. Heaven is a figure of the superior state or condition of power, and consequently is the proper symbol of the supreme part of the Deity out of whose substances (or, more correctly, essences) the lesser universe is composed. Heaven is the plane of the spiritual nature of God, earth the plane of the material nature of God, and hell that part of existence in which the nature of God (or good) is least powerful; the outer circumference of Deity. The Scandinavian hel-heim —the land of the dead—is a dark and cold sphere where the fires of life burned so low that it seemed as though they might at any moment flicker out. Thus hell may be defined as the place where the light fails, or in which divine intelligence is so diluted by matter as to be incapable of controlling the manifestations of force. In the ancient Greek system of thought Hades, or the underworld, simply signifies the physical universe in contradistinction to the spiritualized and illumined superior worlds. The Greeks conceived the physical universe to be that part of creation in which the light of God is most obscured, and darkness not as primordial Reality but rather the absence of divine light. Darkness in this sense represents the privative darkness as distinguished from the darkness of the Absolute which includes the nature of light within its own being.

So-called physical life begins at the point where matter dominates and inhibits the manifestations of energy and intelligence. Spirit, so-called, is only one-fifth as active in the physical world as it is in its own plane of unobstructed expression. Therefore the physical plane is simply a sphere in Nature wherein arc blended four-fifths of inertia and one-fifth of activity. This does not mean that the inhabitants of this sphere are composed four-fifths of material substances but rather that the greater part of their spiritual natures can find no medium of expression, and consequently are latent. Thus the spiritual nature signified by the dot is inclosed or imprisoned within matter signified by the circle, the result being the various ensouled forms evolving through the material sphere.

It may be well to summarize in the simple terminology of the Alexandrian Neoplatonists, to whom die modern world is indebted for nearly all the great fundamentals of philosophy. If you will turn to the diagram at the beginning of this chapter you will note three circles in a vertical column and each horizontally trisected and overlapped. The upper circle signifies the power of the dot, the central circle the power of the line, and the lower circle the power of the circumference. Each of these circles contains its own trinity of potencies, which were called by the Chaldeans the Father, the Power, and the Mind. The three circles each trisected give nine hypothetical panels or levels which signify the months of the prenatal epoch and also the philosophical epoch as given in the nine degrees of the Eleusinian Mysteries. By this symbolism is revealed much of the sacredness attached to the number 9. By the method of overlapping, however, the 9 is reduced to 7, the latter number constituting the rungs of the Mithraic or philosophic ladder of the gods—the links of the golden chain connecting Absolute Unity above (or within) with Absolute Diversity below (or without).

The first trinity (the upper circle) consists of God the Father and the nature of his triple profundity; the second trinity (the middle circle), God the Son in his triple sphere erf intellection; the third trinity (the lower circle), God the Holy Spirit, the Formator with his formative triad which is the foundation of the world. God the Holy Spirit, the third person of the Christian triad, is synonymous with Jehovah, the racial god of the Jews; Shiva, the destroyer-creator of the Hindus; and Osiris, the Egyptian god of the underworld. A study of the form and symbols of Osiris reveals that the lower portion of his body is swathed in mummy wrappings, leaving only his head and shoulders free. In his helmet Osiris wears the plumes of the law and in one hand clasps the three scepters of the underworld—the Anubis-headed staff, the shepherd's crook, and the flail. As the god of the underworld, Osiris has a body composed of death (the material sphere) and a living head rising out of it into a more permanent sphere. This is Jehovah, the Lord of Form, whose body is a material sphere ruled over by death but who himself, as a living being, rises out of the dead not-sclf which surrounds him. In India Shiva is often shown with his body a peculiar bluish white color.

This is the result of smearing his person with ashes and soot, ashes being the symbol of death. Shiva is not only a destroyer in that he breaks up old forms and orders, but he is a creator in that, having dissolved an organism, he rearranges its parts and thus forms a new creature. As the bull was sacred to Osiris, was offered in sacrifice to Jehovah, and was also a favorite form assumed by the god Jupiter (consider the legend of Europa), so Nandi is the chosen vahan of Shiva. Shiva riding the bull signifies death enthroned upon, supported by, and moving in harmony with law; for the bull is the proper symbol of the immutability of divine procedure.

It is now in order to consider the subject of recapitulation. The vision of Ezekiel intimates that creation consists of wheels within wheels, the lesser recapitulating in miniature the activities of the greater. In the diagram under consideration it is evident that by trisecting each of the smaller worlds or circles they are capable of division according to the same principle that holds good in connection with the three major circles. Thus as the first large circle itself is synonymous with the dot, so the upper panel of each of the trisected circles is also symbolic of the dot. Hence the upper panel of each circle is its spiritual part, the center panel its intellective or mediatory part, and the lower panel its material or inferior part. The entire lower circle ruled over by Zeus was designated by the Greeks as the world, because it was wholly concerned with the establishment and generation of substances. The upper panel of the inferior world, partaking of the same analogy as the first world or upper circle (which it recapitulates in part) is termed the spirit of the world. The central panel, likewise recapitulating the central circle, becomes the mind or soul of the world, and the lower panel, recapitulating the lower circle, the body or form of the world. Thus spirit consists of a trinity of spirit, mind, and body in a spiritual state; mind of a spirit, mind, and body in a mental state; and form or body of a spirit, mind, and body in a material state. While Zeus is the God of Form, he manifests as a trinity, his spiritual nature bearing the name Zeus.

The intellective nature, soul or mediatory nature of Zeus is termed Poseidon, and his lowest or objective material manifestation, Hades. As each of the Hindu gods possessed a Shakti (or a feminine counterpart signifying their energies), so Zeus manifests his potentialities through certain attributes. To these attributes were assigned personalities, and they became companion gods with him over his world.

The Zeus, Poseidon, and Hades triad of the Greeks is the Jupiter, Neptune, and Pluto triad of the Romans. Jupiter may be considered synonymous with the spiritual nature of the sun which, according to the ancients, had a threefold nature symbolic of the threefold Creator of the world. The vital energy pouring from the sun and one of its manifestations becomes Neptune, the lord of the hypothetical sea of subsolar space. In Neptune we have a parallel with the hypothetical ether of science, the super-atmospheric air which is the vehicle of solar energy. Pluto becomes the actual gross chemical earth, and his abode is presumed to be in dark, subterranean caverns where he sits upon his ancient throne in impenetrable and interminable gloom. The analogy to the dot, the line, and the circle again appears. Jupiter is the dot, Neptune the line, and Pluto the circle. Thus die life body of the sun is Jupiter; the light body of the sun, Neptune; and the fire body of the sun, Pluto ruling his inferno. It should be continually borne in mind that we are not referring to great universal realities, but simply to those phases of cosmogony directly concerned with matter, which is the lowest and most impermanent part of creation. Over this inferior world with its form and its formative agents sits Jupiter, lord of death, generator of evil, the Demiurgus and world Formator, who with his twelve Titanic Monads (the Olympic pantheon) builds, preserves, and ultimately annihilates those things which he fashions in the outer sea of divine privation.

It is noteworthy that the astronomical symbol of the sun should be the dot in a circle, for as can be deduced from the subject matter of this lecture the dot, the circle, and the hypothetical connecting line give a complete key to the actual nature of the solar orb. When Jupiter, or Jehovah, is called the lord of the sun, it docs not necessarily mean the sun which is the ruler of this solar system; it means any one of the millions of universal suns which are functioning upon the plane or level of a solar orb. Jupiter manifests himself as a mystical energy which gives crops, perpetuates life, and bestows all the blessings of physical existence, only to ultimately deprive mankind and his world of all these bounties. Jupiter is the sun of illusion, the light which lights the inferior creation but has nothing in common with that great spiritual light which is the life of man and the light of the world.

According to the Gnostics, the Demiurgus and his angels represented die false light which lured souls to their destruction by causing them to believe in the permanence of matter and that life within the veil of tears was the true existence. According to philosophy, only those who rise above the light of the inferior universe to that great and glorious spiritual luminescence belonging to the superphysical spheres, can hope to discover everlasting life. The physical universe is therefore the body of Jupiter, Jehovah, Osiris, or Shiva. The sun is the pulsating heart of each of these deities, and sun spots are caused (as H. P. Blavatsky notes) by the expansion and contraction of the solar heart at intervals of eleven years. In the Greek and Roman mythologies, Zeus, or Jupiter, is the chief of the twelve gods of Olympus. Olympus was a mythical mountain rising in the midst of the world. It is the dot or sun itself, for it is written that the tabernacle of the gods is in the skies. From the face of this sun shines a golden corona whose numberless fiery points are the countless gods who transmit the life of their sovereign lord and who are his ministers to the farthest corners of his empire. In the Hebrew philosophy the rays of the sun are the hairs of the head and beard of the Great Face. Each hair is the radius of a mystical circle, with the sun as the center, and outer darkness as the circumference. It is curious that in Egypt the name of the second person of the triad—the mani- fester—should be Ray or Ra, and his title, "the lord of light." Ra bears witness, however, to his invisible and eternal Father, for the light of the sun is not the true sun but bears witness to the invisible source of the effulgence. Thus, as the beams of the physical sun become the light of the physical body of existence, so the rays of the intellectual sun are the light of the mind, and all power, all vitality, and all increase come as the result of attunement to the fiery streamers of those divine  beings to whom has been given the appellation of "the gods."

A few words at this time concerning the symbolism of Neptune. While Neptune is popularly associated with the sea, occultly he signifies the albuminous part of the great egg of Jupiter. In certain schools of Orphic mysticism, the inferior universe (like the supreme, all-inclosing sphere) is symbolized by an egg. This lesser egg has Jupiter for a yolk, Neptune for the albumen, and Pluto for the shell. It is therefore evident that Neptune is not associated with the physical element of water, but rather with the electrical fluids permeating the entire solar system. He is also associated with the astral world, a sphere of fluidic essences and part of the mirror of Maya, the illusion. As the connective between Jupiter and Pluto, Neptune represents a certain phase of material intellect which, like the element of water, is very changeable and inconstant. Like water, Neptune is recognized as a vitalizer and life-giver, and in the ancient Mysteries was associated with the germinal agents. The fish, or spermatozoon, previous to its period of germination, was under his dominion. Descending from the sphere of cosmology to the life of the individual, it is important that certain analogies be made between Jupiter as the lord of the world and the microcosmic Jupiter who is the lord of each individual life. That which in our own nature we call / is, according to mysticism, not the real I or Self but the Jupiterian or inferior I—the demiurgic self; it may even be said to be the false self which, by accepting as real, we elevate to a position greater than it is capable of occupying. A very good name for Jupiter is the human spirit as differentiated from the divine spirit which belongs to the supermaterial spheres. In man Jupiter has his abiding place in the human heart, while Neptune dwells in the brain, and Pluto in the generative system. Thus is established the formative triad in the physical nature of man. As the physical universe is the lowest and least permanent part of existence, so the physical body is the lowest and least permanent part of man. Above the lord of the body with his Aeons or angels is the divine mind and all-pervading consciousness. The body of man is mortal, though his divine parts partake, to a certain degree, of immortality. Over the mortal nature of man rules an incarnating ego which organizes matter into bodies, and by this organization foredooms them to be redistributed to the primordial elements. As Jupiter had his palace on the summit of Mount Olympus, so from his glorious cardiac throne on the top of the diaphragm muscle he rules the body as lord of the human world. Jupiter in us is the thing we have accepted as our true Self, but meditation upon the subject matter of this lecture will disclose the true relationship between the human self and the Universal ALL of which it is a fragmentary yet all-potential part.

Recognizing Jupiter to be the lord of the world, or the incarnating ego which invests itself in universal matter, it then becomes evident that the two higher spheres of trinities of divine powers constitute the Hermetic anthropos, or nonincarnating overman. This majestic and superior part, consisting of the threefold darkness of Absolute Cause and the threefold light or celestial splendor, hovers above the third triad consisting of the threefold world form, or triune cosmic activity. The highest expression of matter is mind, which occupies the middle distance between activity on the one hand and inertia on the other. The mind of man is hypothetically considered to consist of two parts: the lower mind, which is linked to the demiurgic sphere of Jupiter, and the higher mind, which ascends toward and is akin to the substance of the divine power of Kronos. These two phases of mind are the mortal and immortal minds of Eastern philosophy. Mortal mind is hopelessly involved in the illusions of sense and substance, but immortal or divine mind transcending these unrealities is one with truth and light. Here we have a definite key to several misunderstood concepts as now promulgated through the doctrines of Christian Science.

Since intelligence is the highest manifestation of matter, it is logically the lowest manifestation of consciousness, or spirit, and Jupiter (or the personal 7) is enshrined in the substances of mortal mind where he controls his world through what man is pleased to term intellect. The Jupiterian intellect, however, is that which sees outward or toward the illusions of manifested existence, whereas the higher or spiritual mind (which is latent in most individuals) is that superior faculty which is capable of thinking inward or toward the profundities of Self; in other words, is capable of facing toward and gazing upon the substance of Reality. Thus the mind may be likened to the two- faced Roman god Janus. With one face this god gazes outward upon the world and with the other inward toward the sanctuary in which it is enshrined. The two-faced mind is an excellent subject for meditation. The objective or mortal mind continually emphasizes to the individual the paramount importance of physical phenomena; the subjective, or immortal mind, if given opportunity for expression, combats this material instinct by intensifying the regard for that which transcends the limitations of the physical perceptions.

Subservient to Jupiter who, bearing his thunderbolt and accompanied by his royal eagle is indeed the king of this world, are Neptune and Pluto. The god Neptune, or course, is not to be regarded as either the planet or as an influence derived from the planet, but as the lord of the middle sphere of theinferior world. In man the middle sphere between mind and matter is occupied by emotion or feeling. The instability of human emotion is well symbolized by the element of water which is continually in motion, the peaceful surface of which can be transformed into a destroying fury by forces moving above its broad expanse. The emotional nature of man is closely associated with the astral light or magical sphere of the ancient and mediaeval magicians. In this plane illusion is particularly powerful. As one writer has wisely observed, "It is a land of beauty, a garden of flowers, but a serpent is entwined about the stem of each." Among the Oriental mystics this sphere of the astral light is considered particularly dangerous, for those who are aspiring to an understanding of spiritual mysteries are often enmeshed in this garden of Kundry, and believing they have found the truth are carried to their destruction by the flow of this astral fluid.

Riding in his chariot drawn by sea-horses and surrounded by Nereids riding upon sporting dolphins, Neptune carries in his hand the trident, a symbol common to both the lord of the illusion and the red-robed tempter. Neptune is the lord of dreams, and all mortal creatures are dreamers; all that mankind has accomplished in the countless ages of its struggle upward toward the light is the result of dreaming. Yet if dreams are not backed up by action and controlled by reason they become a snare and a delusion, and the dreamer drifts onward into oblivion in a mystic ecstasy. You will remember that according to Greek mythology there was a river called the Styx which divided the sphere of the living from that of the dead. This river is the mysterious sea of Neptune which all men must cross if they would rise from material ignorance into philosophic illumination. This Neptunian sea may be likened to the ethers which permeate and bind together the material elements of Nature. The sphere of Neptune is a world of ever-moving fantasy without beginning and without end, a mystical maze through which souls wander for uncounted ages if once caught in the substances of this shadowy dreamland.

The lowest division of the Jupiterian sphere is under the dominion of Pluto, the regent of death. Pluto is the personification of the mass physical attitude of all things toward objective life. Pluto may be termed the principle of the mortal code, in accordance with which Nature lives and moves and has her being. Pluto may also be likened to an intangible atmosphere permeated with definite terrestrial instincts. Unconsciously inhaling this atmosphere, man is enthused by it and accepts it as the basis of living. The individual who is controlled by the Plutonic miasma contracts a peculiar mental and spiritual malaria which destroys all transcendental instinct and spiritual initiative, leaving him a psychical invalid already two-thirds a victim of the Plutonic plague. As Plato so admirably says, "The body is the sepulcher of the soul," and whereas Neptune is symbolic of the astral or elemental soul (which is a mysterious emanation from elementary Nature) Pluto is the god of the underworld, the deity ruling the spheres of the mysterious circle of being and therefore represents the lowest degree of Jupiterian light, which is physical matter. Hades, or the land of the dead, is simply an environment resulting from crystallization. Everything that exists in a crystallized state furnishes the environment of Hades for whatever life is evolving through it. Thus the lower universe is ruled over by three apparently heartless gods—birth, growth, and decay. From their palaces in space these deities hurl the instruments of their wrath upon hapless humanity and elementary Nature. But he who is fortunate enough to escape the thunderbolts of Jove will yet fall beneath the trident of Neptune or be torn to pieces by the dogs of Father Dis (Pluto). The ancient Greeks occasionally employed a centaur to represent man, thus indicating that out of the body of the beast which feels upon its back the lash of outrageous destiny rises a nobler creature possessed of God- given reason, who through sheer force of innate divinity shall become master of those who seek to bind him to a mediocre end.

While on the subject of the dot, the line, and the circle, there is one very simple application of the principle which we insert in order to emphasize the analogies existing through the entire structure of human thought. Take a simple problem in grammar. The noun, which is the subject of the sentence, is analogous to the dot; the verb, which is the action of the subject, is analogous to the line; and the object, which is the thing acted upon, is analogous to the circle. These analogies may also be traced through music and color and through the progression of chemical elements. Always the trinity of the dot, the line, and the circle has some correspondent, for it is the basis upon which the entire structure of existence and function—both universal and individual—has been raised. Consider this fundamental symbolism, philosophize upon it, dream about it, for an understanding of these symbols is the beginning of wisdom. There is no problem, whether involved with the simple mechanism of an earthworm or the inconceivable complex mechanism of a universe, that has not been constructed upon the triangular foundation of the dot, the line, and the circle. These are the proper symbols of the creative, preservative, and disintegrative agencies which manifest the incomprehensible Absolute before temporary creation. The three worlds we have outlined are the supreme, the superior and the inferior worlds of the Orphic theology as revealed by Pythagoras and Plato. The supreme world is the sphere of the one indivisible and ever-enduring Father; the superior world is the sphere of the gods, the progeny of the Father; and the inferior world is the sphere of mortal creatures who are the progeny of the gods. "Therefore," says Pythagoras, "men live in the inferior world, God in the supreme world, and the men who are gods and the gods who are men in the intermediate plane." You will recall that it was said of Pythagoras by his disciples that there were of two-footed creatures three kinds: gods, men, and Pythagoras. It should be inferred that the dot represents the gods, the circle men, and the line connecting them Pythagoras, or the personification of that superhuman wisdom which binds cause and effect inextricably together, and which is the hope of salvation for the lesser. The Deity dwelling in the supreme world and which the Platonists termed the One, was, according to the Scandinavians, All- Father, the sure foundation of being. In India it was Brahma and in Egypt, Ammon. The line always represented the Savior- Gods, they being the eldest sons or first-born of intangible Deity. The line bears witness of the dot as the light bears witness of the life. All this gives a clue to the statement in the New Testament, "Whoso hath seen the Son, hath seen the Father, for the Son is in the Father and the Father in the Son." In other words, whoso hath seen the line, hath seen the dot, for the dot is in the line and the line is in the dot. In the ancient Jewish rites the line was Michael, the archangel of the sun; in Scandinavia, Balder the Beautiful. It is to the lower world of men that the light (the dot pouring into the line), personified as the Universal Savior, descends to redeem consciousness from the darkness of a living grave (the circumference of the circle). The Mystery God who lifted souls to salvation through his own nature thus represents the line, the divine symbol of the way of achievement, for it is written that none shall come unto the Father save by the Son and none of those creatures dwelling in the circumference can reach the center or dot save by ascending the hypothetical line of the radius. The line is the bridge connecting cause with effect. In Immanuel Kant's philosophy we find the dot designated the noumenon and the circumference the phenomenon; the former the Reality, the later the unreality. The line (the human mind) must ever be the agency that bridges the void between them. In the Platonic philosophy there are three manners of being:

(1) gods, or those most proximate to the Absolute, who dwell within the nature of the dot;

(2) men, or those who are most distant from the Absolute, who dwell in the circumference of the circle;

(3) the heroes and the demigods, who are suspended between Divinity and humanity and who dwell in the sphere of the line.

So, according to philosophy, the line is a ladder up which man ascends to light from his infernal state and down which he descends in his involution. The fall of man is the descent down the ladder from the dot to the circumference; the resurrection or redemption of man is his return from the circumference to the dot. Of such importance are these primary symbols that we have felt it absolutely necessary to devote the introductory lectures of this series to the subject of the dot, the line, and the circle. It should ever be borne in mind that the veneration for symbols is not idolatry, for symbols are formulated to clarify truths which in their abstract form are incomprehensible. Idolatry consists in the inability of the mind to differentiate between the symbol and the abstract principle for which it stands. If this definition be accepted, it can be proved that there are very few truly idolatrous peoples. Philosophically, the literalist is always an idolater. He who worships the letter of the law bows down to wood and stone, but he who comprehends the spirit of the law is a true worshiper before the measureless altar of eternal Nature upon which continually burns the Spirit Fire of the world.

THE VEDIC TRIMURTI

Is it proper that the Leader of the Universe should be regarded as the head of the world and that its three complexions should be symbolized by faces. Speaking its word of power, each face causes to issue from its mouth a sacred syllable, by which the surfaces of the three worlds are agitated and caused to assume the semblance of creation.

# VI

⁓⁓⁓

# Concerning the Nature of God

Realizing that a man's conception of God is his God, let us consider further the mystery of Deity. Remember that it is not really God whom we define—it is merely our own conception of the highest expression of Wisdom, Beauty, and Truth. Colonel Robert Ingersoll did not realize the magnitude of his statement when he said, "An honest God is the noblest work of man." Our God must be the God of the 20th century, for we see It through the eyes of our generation. Our God must march with us, sharing our problems, or we cannot know It. God is always our God, for we can never realize or understand the God of another man.

The Deity is always an omnipresent, omniscient, omnipotent, and omniactive agent—expressing in full the ideals which we express in part, attaining in full that which we attain only in part, and understanding clearly that great mystery called life which we understand not at all.

Not so long ago a man said to me, "Do you believe in God?" What he really meant was, "Do you believe in my concept of God?" This man had attended some of our lectures and, hearing us discuss the various religions of the world but not especially emphasize the one with which he was most concerned, came to the conclusion that, like the benighted heathen of old, we were following "false gods" and worshipping "graven images."

If this same friend had chanced to see our collection of Javanese gods, Hindu, Japanese, and Chinese Buddhas, Egyptian Osirises, and Chaldean deities, he would have been absolutely certain that we were outside the pale of salvation. This man was sincere, true, honest, and, according to his own light, consistent and well-meaning. But to us his concept of God seemed so pitifully small. It lacked the dignity and serenity of a noble conception; it was puny and hopelessly inadequate; it was the God of a race, a family, or a clan—it was not the God of a great universe.

It had both friends and enemies; it neglected some and favored others, and was even so small that it descended to the level of human wrangling and petty faultfinding. It didn't like the Chinese and had permitted two-thirds of the world to live in darkness while it fostered a small group of chosen people. It ordered suffering, permitted crime, advocated sacrifice, and fought with men against men upon the field of battle.

Therefore, we were forced to say to this man, "We do believe in God—but not in your God!" And he went away as dissatisfied and fearful as before, firmly convinced that we were not only idolatrous but, since our last statement, pantheistic in that we had affirmed a plurality of Deity.

Meditating upon the question of this sincere individual—"Do you believe in God?"—we organized our concepts of Divinity and, having had the same question put to us on another occasion, have decided to present for your consideration the God we have found. Please remember that this is only our God, and foolish is that man who follows the Gods of others; each must find his own God for himself and, having found It, build upon that spot a tabernacle.

In ancient days when man found his God, he carved an image of It in wood or stone or molded It in clay. This was a fatal mistake, for the God in clay or stone could not grow, and age after age while the image remained the same, the minds of men had grown. Therefore the Gods of our forefathers seem crude to us, for we are not our forefathers. We are the past plus the present and our Gods are the Gods of the present.

The Navajo Indian will not make images of his deities, lest he fall into idolatry. When he desires to represent his God, he does so with colored sand and as soon as the image has served his purpose, destroys it with a sweep of his hand. Each day the God of the wise man changes as his own wisdom increases, for the wise man realizes that the Supreme One never changes and is always the sum of everything. The mind of man is growing and each day it learns a little more concerning the mystery of being, and as the mind grows the knowledge of God grows. But only the perfect man, complete in every way, full of understanding, unlimited by any shadow of ignorance, can behold the Deity in the full glory and splendor of Its Being. And that man does not live today, nor will he exist until the endless millenniums of time bring the human race back again into the living presence of its Divine Source.

We conceive God to be an eternally-existing Principle: unborn—therefore incapable of death; uncreated—therefore incapable of dissolution. The most appropriate designation of this Principle is the Good. The full and unconditioned state of Good is the Absolute, beside which there is nothing else and outside of which there is no existence. All things are created out of the substance of the one and eternal Good; therefore are themselves part of the Good, partaking of the immortality of the Good, subsisting upon the nature of the Good, and at dissolution returning again into the perfect nature of the Good.

The Good is both the source and ultimate of all existence, and the highest form of Good is the knowledge and understanding of the true condition of Good. As the Good is eternal, so all creatures composed of It and subsisting upon It are, like itself, eternal, indestructible, and incorruptible. The only ignorance is the ignorance of the Good, and death can only exist in that mind which has not yet discovered its fundamental oneness with the eternal and never-changing Good.

We conceive God to be One and incapable of division, for although a multiplicity of manifestations apparently diversified are perpetually manifesting within Its nature, It remains the sum of all Its parts and members. To man the universe appears as unity in diversity, but to the One the universe is diversity in unity.

God being the Only Cause of all manifestation and expression, it must naturally follow that all manifestation and expression is Good. Therefore equality is established by the common benignity of cause. Difference may, and does, exist in the material sphere, this difference being based upon the proximity of manifestation to its own cause. That which is closest to cause unconsciously is youngest; that which is closest to cause consciously is oldest. Youth is proximity to beginning;

age, proximity to end. But as beginning and end are one, age excels youth only in terms of understanding.

We conceive God to be One manifesting through a multiplicity, the foundation of that multiplicity being the threefold nature of the One. All the attributes of power cognizable by man may be reduced to three. These three are therefore termed the Trinity, or three persons of the Godhead.

The three persons are not the One, for the One cannot be divided, but are rather expressions of the One. When the One expresses Will, it is termed the Father, because the Will is the first after the One. When the One expresses Wisdom, it is called the Son, for it is the second after the One. When the One expresses Activity, it is called the Holy Spirit, for it is the third after the One. All three are in the One, are potentialities of the One and are called the faces, or attributes, of the eternal and unconditioned One. The One by Its Will created the heavens; by Its Activity, the lower worlds; and by Its Wisdom It bound them together that they should be one even as It is One. Therefore the height of wisdom is the recognition of the One, for wisdom binds the parts together, and man calls heaven the Father God and the lower worlds Mother Nature. Man places himself between the above and the below, for the wisdom of God is in his soul and his duty is to reconcile the above and the below, uniting them within himself.

We conceive God to manifest Itself through a multiplicity of powers emanating from the three, and this multiplicity we denominate the Gods. Thus we establish pantheism in monotheism, with monotheism supreme. The parts of the One are the Gods; the One formed of the parts is the God. The Gods are an illustrious chain of graduated divinities, uniting cause with effect. These divinities are merely the intelligent attributes of the One Intelligence. Man himself is a God but not the God, for man is a part, but God is the sum of the parts. The Divinity in man is God and therefore worthy of libation and offering. How much more so, then, the greater divinities who partake in greater degree of Divinity! God is all of man, but man is not all of God. Therefore the part is inferior to the whole to the same degree that it is less than the whole, yet all are ultimately One and ultimately inseparable.

We conceive God to exist in all creatures in accordance with the individual comprehension of the creature. In other words, Divinity is present to the degree that it is recognized. The more of God man finds, the more of God is present in him. All growth is the process of increasing capacity to cognize Good and to apply the newly-cognized power to the problem of existence. Therefore all creatures, animate and inanimate, are ensouled by the Good and their power is commensurate with the expression which they are capable of giving to the Good. The grain of sand contains the Good, for it is a unit of the Absolute Life. But man considers the grain of sand inferior to himself inasmuch as it manifests the Good in a lesser degree than he. The planets are individual intelligences, being unfoldments of the Divine Life on a level greatly superior to that of man. For this reason the planets are denominated Gods, they having so greatly unfolded the Divine Power within themselves that they are capable of controlling not only animate forms like those of man but also of furnishing environments for races and species inferior to themselves. These races and species then offer libations to the unit of power which gives them the opportunity for individual expression. The result is the worship of the planetary Gods. But while these tutelary deities are honored, the intelligent worshipper is in reality making offering to the Absolute and Eternal One, for it is the presence of this Absolute and Eternal Power in the constitution of the tutelary deity that is the true cause of its existence.

We conceive God to be absolutely impersonal, for being a universal and all pervading essence.

It is within the nature of every creature and substance regardless of whether we term that creature or substance good or bad. This point is well illustrated by an ancient Eastern fable. Once there was a Hindu mendicant who was told that God was in everything. So, walking down the street, he said to himself, "God is in the dog, God is in the tree, God is in all things. Therefore nothing can hurt me."

A few moments later an elephant ambled down the street, but the Hindu mendicant made no effort to avoid the animal, because he believed that God was in the elephant and therefore it would not hurt him. The man on the elephant's head cried out a warning, but the holy man did not heed it. The elephant, reaching him, twisted his trunk around his body and threw the amazed devotee over a nearby fence.

Returning to his Master, the sorely injured Hindu complained that although he had affirmed God to be in everything, the elephant had cruelly injured him. After hearing the details of the story, the aged sage replied, "You did well, my son, save in one particular: you failed to hear the voice of God in the warning of the elephant-driver!"

We cannot conceive of a God less universal than the universe itself.

You will remember the story of the flattered king who, to silence the meaningless babbling of his courtiers, ordered his throne to be set up on the seashore, declaring that if he were—as his nobles affirmed—greater than God, he would order the tide not to come in and wet his feet. He quickly demonstrated, however, that the tide knew no master among men.

The God we worship must be as great, at least, as the tide which through the ages follows its predestined course. We can worship no anthropomorphic deity controlling the universe as fretfully and inconsistently as King James ruled England.

God is infinite power—grand enough to whirl uncounted universes through millenniums inconceivable, yet minute enough to evolve with endless consistency the tiniest forms of microscopic life.

This God has no time for religious wranglings and creedal dissensions. The immutable laws of Nature are Its ministers. He who serves the Good is rewarded by that harmony which must exist between the Principle and Its servant. He who departs from the way of the Good suffers not from the jealousy of God or the revenge of an irritated Deity, but rather his suffering is caused by the very act of departing from the way of the Good.

What matters it the faith a man belongs to if he serve the Good, or what does it profit him if he serve the evil? When all substances and creatures are of the nature of God, then all words used to describe them are synonyms of God. Consequently, what matters it what God be called? It is the understanding of Good—and not the name applied to it—which constitutes true reverence and veneration.

We conceive the three primary attributes of God to be the three fundamental paths also by which Deity may be approached. Therefore, man may know God by Will, by Wisdom, or by Action. For man, action means service, and he who serves God will realize that no one can long serve his Master without gaining a knowledge of the One he serves. God is revealed to Its servants by their very services, and he who is in doubt as to what to do to glorify his Creator can never go wrong if he dedicates his life to constructive and humanitarian labor.

By Wisdom, man is enabled to glimpse in part the Divinity of his Maker, for Wisdom organizes effects until the cause of those effects is hypothetically estimated. The wise man knows God because he alone realizes how necessary God is. The world could get along very well without the God that most men worship, but the wise man's God is the very mechanism of the universe. The wise man's God is the fuel, the machine, and the product all in one.

By Will the Mysteries accomplish the union of man with his Divine Source, for Will is the divine urge to accomplishment, and once that urge is awakened, the ultimate result is certain though untold ages may intervene.

We conceive God to be without the human concept of revenge. We believe in no vengeful God, for upon what can It wreak vengeance but upon Itself? If there be a hell, it also must be part of God, and what true man or woman can conceive a Deity within whose nature an Inferno can exist?

Hell is the condition of ignorance and can only exist in the soul that has never found the Universal Good. Heaven is light, and he who dwells in the light dwells in the consciousness of Good and is immortal.

There is no mortality except for those who believe in death. There is no immortality save that which man discovers when he recognizes his unity with his Creator. The universe is Life. Life thrills through every part of it. Life pulsates through every atom of it. Life stretches out boundlessly before everything.  Yet in the midst of all this pulsating life, man believes that he can die. There is no death but ignorance; there is no life but wisdom. But wisdom is supreme; therefore life is supreme. Among the ancient peoples there were some who believed that good and evil were eternally-existing principles which should combat themselves forever. This conception is founded upon man's limitations of sense perception. Seeing what he believes to be evil, man therefore assumes that which he believes to be true, failing to realize that his narrow-nearsightedness has caused him to perceive only an infinitesimal part of a plan which, could he comprehend it all, would reveal its absolute goodness.

We conceive God to be the inward parts of all beings and things and that, having this divine all-powerful potentiality within, each one may accomplish any worthy motive which inspires him. The Divinity within man means infinite capacity, but only through ages of growth and development may he bring to flower these divine potentialities within himself. The Divinity within man is a seed that is sown in the ground of his material nature. Whether this seed shall blossom forth depends upon the quality of the soil (his body) and the presence of sunlight (his mind), for without water (the body) and fire (the mind) the seed of the spirit cannot grow. Therefore it must remain through the ages awaiting an environment suitable for its expression.

You will remember the grains of wheat found clasped in the mummified hand of an Egyptian Pharaoh. After 5,000 years they were planted and produced a harvest. Like these grains of wheat is the spiritual Self in man, which, though it lies long in the tomb, will bring forth its kind in abundant harvest when planted in the proper soil.

So we believe in a God of infinite power, unlimited by mortal concept, unimpeded by the limitations of human fancy; a God in all, of all, through all; a common parent, a common father, and a common urge to accomplishment. We believe ourselves to be part of that Supreme One, sharing a common birthright of immortality and omnipotence. We believe all temples to be Its house, all hearts Its shrine, all hands Its hands, all ideals Its ideals, all dreams Its dreams, and all accomplishment unity with Itself.

## Man

To the eye of vulgar Logic, says he, what is man? An omnivorous Biped that wears Breeches.
To the eye of Pure Reason what is he? A Soul, a Spirit, and divine Apparition. Round his mysterious ME, there lies, under all those woolrags a Garment of Flesh (or of Senses), con-textured in the Loom of Heaven; whereby he is revealed to his like, and dwells with them in UNION and DIVISION; and sees and fashions for himself a Universe, with azure Starry Spaces, and long Thousands of Years. Deep-hidden is he under that strange Garment; amid Sounds and Colors and Forms, as it were, swathed-in, and inextricably overshrouded: yet it is sky-woven, and worthy of a God. Stands he not thereby in the centre of Immensities, in the conflux of Eternities?
—Sartor Resartus

# VII

❦

# God, the Divine Foundation

FROM the preceding lecture it is evident that any description or definition of unknowable ultimates is possible only in the terms of negation. In other words, every definition so-called must be eliminative, and that which remains when all else is taken away must necessarily be the only thing incapable of removal. When considering the nature of primordial substance, the average school of philosophy postulates an active First Cause; otherwise it is wholly at a loss to explain how creation can be the product of a passive power. Activity is accordingly postulated as a fundamental attribute of Being. To me, however it is inconceivable that the First Cause (or more correctly the Causeless Cause) should be either positive or negative.

Rather it seems more fitting to posit a permanent condition which is neither positive in an "active" sense nor negative in a "passive" sense, but which is power in absolute suspension. For lack of a better defining term we might conceive of Eternal Being as an enduring neitherness, partaking of neither the presence nor the absence of any tangible force or condition.

The condition of the Absolute can only be suggested by a suspended neitherness of both activity and inertia. To attempt an analysis of the fabric of even the groundwork of SPACE far exceeds the capacity of any human intellect. Never in the history of philosophy has there been evolved a mind capable of grasping all the multitudinous elements of Being. The world is filled with people who foolishly try to teach or seek to be taught the length, breadth, and thickness of ultimates, when but a moment's true thinking would demonstrate the fallacy and futility of such effort. Since the groundwork of SPACE—the ultimate abstraction—transcends every faculty and every dimension, it can never be comprehended by a reasoning organism that must necessarily arrive at its conclusions on the basis of faculty and dimension. For the human mind to understand that which is greater than itself is as impossible as for a mere man to swallow the ocean. The effort of the human mind to circumscribe the entirety of manifestation is comparable to a mollusk trying to enclose the sea within its shell Realizing, therefore, how apropos is the ancient statement that to define Deity is to defile it, we are forced to accept the inevitable conclusion of the ages: namely, that the ultimates of beginning and end are alike unknowable. These conclusions arc in harmony with the deductions of both Socrates and Buddha.

The gods may be conceived of in either the singular or the plural sense; in the singular if we consider the deities as fractional parts of one Creative Agent; in the plural if we look upon the various parts as separate vehicles of cosmic intelligence. Thus in many ancient doctrines we have evidence of a fundamental monotheism manifesting through a complex polytheism. For example, the Elohim, or secondary gods of the ancient Jews who, as the Creative Demiurgi, moved upon the face of the deep and together constitute a single cosmic deity. In the same way the elaborate pantheon of the Hindus is a mosaic of gods, who in combination form the nature of the supreme and all- powerful Brahma. The gods may be considered as symbolic of the individual states of consciousness continually unfolding within the nature of Absolute Being. The concept of a single personal Deity who was prudent enough to fashion himself without eyelids lest he fall asleep from that exhaustion which must necessarily result from an eternal vigil is hardly adequate to meet the evident needs of existence. Up to the present time the advocates of monotheism have advanced no concept of Deity adequate to control creation without the assistance of a privy council or celestial parliament. A few moments of serious consideration will reveal that a fundamental monotheism manifesting through an elaborate polytheism is by far the most noble concept of cosmic government, and is the basis of all the successful governments maintained by man upon earth. The modern world is inclined to look askance at the elaborate pantheons of the Greeks, Egyptians, and Hindus, and rather prides itself that it has outgrown such theological crudities. Even now, however, there is a definite reversion to the pantheistic cults of antiquity, and when properly understood the Orphic theogony will enjoy a glorious renaissance.

The subject of philosophic polytheism deserves further attention. Polytheism must not be considered synonymous with the blind adoration of an infinitude of imaginary superhuman beings, but rather as the recognition of a concatenated progression of evolving creatures, each influencing and to a certain degree controlling those inferior to itself, and in turn controlled by those superior to itself. The gods should not be considered as personally directing the destiny of individuals. Rather they are vast centers of radiant force consciously or unconsciously influencing anything that exists or subsists upon their sphere of manifestation. For example, a city does not wilfully mold the character of its inhabitants; nevertheless it is an active factor in determining the character of each individual unit of its population. This simile, while possibly not apparent at first thought, is particularly apt, for as cells exist in the human body, so man is but a cell in a larger organism which he pleases to term a god. The cells of the human body may feel a similar veneration for man, who in the light of cell intelligence must be a boundless and infinitely powerful deity.

Polytheism therefore may be best defined as a veneration for causal agencies. Obedience to the will of the gods was regarded as the basis of human happiness and simply meant that only those who lived in harmony with natural law could hope for a tranquil existence. To the ancients it seemed essential that intelligence should manifest from an intelligent Creator; in other words, the manifesting thought proved the existence of the unmanifested Thinker. Intelligence exists in every department of creation. The entire universe is controlled by definite laws that evidence the omniscience of the Eternal Thinker.

From the fountainhead of immeasurable Mind the cogitations of Deity stream forth to make fertile with thought the whole area of Being. Broken up by creations as upon a prism, the Mind-Light of Deity becomes manifest as an infinite order of separate and specialized intelligences. Thus upon the surface of the sea of Universal Mind appear numberless foci, each controlling a definite phase of cosmic activity. The gods are such foci; so are men, but to a more limited degree. The sum of all these individual minds is the one Universal Mind, so that in the last analysis gods, men, and worlds are each fragments of the whole. The philosophers of all ages have realized that the achievement of perfect wisdom lies in the elevation of the power of comprehension to that state where it is able to grasp the relation of die parts of existence to the sum of existence, which the Buddhists designate the Self.

All great systems of religious philosophy agree that anterior to the gods is the One and Undivided, who is the very foundation of manifested existence or the first limitation of Absolute Being, and who may properly be designated the Father of gods and men. We shall now turn our attention to a consideration of the powers and attributes of this first of all mortals, the chief of those who die, the first-born of Absolute Self. In seventy-two languages men call this first power God, the first and most perfect of creations, the eldest of the old, and the Most Ancient of the Most Ancient. God is best defined as the first manifestation of Infinite Existence, the limitation of Limitlessness. In his adoration of Deity man is prone to consider God as synonymous with ALL in that God is synonymous with all that man can hope to comprehend. But behind comprehension is that which is incomprehensible, the thrice-black darkness which exists unhonored and unsung through the unmeasured duration of eternity, and upon whose placid surface time comes and goes, and beginnings and ends are but incidental. To return to the symbolism of the preceding lecture, God is the dot, the first island floating in and upon the permanent depths of Unlimited Existence. God is therefore capable of definition in the terms of the Dervish, by whom as chief of beings he is denominated the Axis of the world, or that immovable center about which all revolves.

Before it is possible to approach Deity through philosophy, it is necessary to nullify the traditional practice prevalent throughout Christendom of referring to Deity as a masculine potency and ascribing to him most human vices, which, however, become virtues by reason of his unquestioned position as despotic arbiter of right and wrong. The modern religious thinker is no longer inclined to venerate a deity who is simply a highly glorified King George III. In that now vanishing picturesque period of absolute monarchies when fretful and senile princes, arrayed in ridiculous periwigs, ruled by "divine right", God was invested with all the propensities of the "blood royal", and the celestial hierarchies were metamorphosed into landed gentry. In spite of the repeated emphasis upon our age of enlightenment, the majority of people still continue the age-honored practice of molding God into a likeness of themselves. The reason for this probably lies in the fact that man, possessing a spark of Divinity within himself, feels his kinship with God and believes himself privileged to rush in where angels fear to tread, and give definition to the undefinable. God being, as Ingersoll so well expressed it, "the noblest work of man," we find in the attributes of the God people worship, a definite key to their own ethical and philosophic status. It is noticeable that people with puerile intelligences and petty concerns conceive God to be localized as a neighborhood sprite who spends most of his time eavesdropping, and who can afford to ignore universal concerns while he heaps maledictions upon some poor, benighted wretch who did not keep his eyes closed during grace! On the other hand, those who have learned to know something of the greater verities of life worship a growing God. This does not presuppose that God is necessarily increasing, but rather that man's increasing capacity to comprehend ever reveals more of the stupendous nature of Divinity. As a person approaches a physical object, the object apparently increases in size. The same is true of the mind as it approaches the subject of its consideration. Hence, to the philosopher God extends through the infinitude of time, distance, and thought, and to him it is inconceivable that even for a second Deity should descend into a state less dignified than the all-inclusiveness of its intrinsic nature.

Among many ancient peoples God was considered as being androgynous, and referred to as the Great Father-Mother.

When the Creator was represented by an image, various subtle devices were employed to indicate its hermaphroditic nature. The Isufara of the Hindus is depicted with one side of his body male and the other female. In Greek and Roman statuary frequent examples are found of a masculine divinity wearing feminine garments and vice versa, or a heavily-bearded god may have his hair arranged in a distinctly feminine coiffure. Again, the structure of the face of such deities as Bacchus and Dionysus often shows a sensitive, feminine countenance disguised by a beard or some article of masculine adornment. In other cases the feminine counterpart of the deity is considered as a separate individuality. For this reason each of the gods was declared to have had his consort or feminine aspect of his own being.

Thus Mithras, the Persian Light-Savior, is considered to be masculine, but a certain portion of himself divided from the rest becomes Mithra, a feminine and maternal potency. As previously noted, in India each god has his shaJ(ti, or feminine part.

Among some peoples Diety has been considered for ages as primarily feminine, as the Brahmans who refer to God as "the Great Mother." In Roman Catholicism there is also a definite tendency to idealize the feminine principle of God through the person of the Virgin Mary, who is elevated to a most exalted position as "Queen of Heaven " The custom of depicting God either as male or female is the outgrowth of man's oldest form of worship: phallicism. Masculine and feminine properties are presumed to be positive and negative respectively. Hence God, being an active or positive agent, was conceived to be masculine; nature, being a passive or negative body, was regarded as feminine in that it received into itself and nurtured to maturity the germinal essences of Divine Life. The proponents of a masculine God declare that in the beginning was activity, the positive cause of existence. On the other hand, the proponents of the pre-eminence of the feminine principle declare that activity first issued from a universal matrix; consequently that which comes forth from the matrix is subor- dinate to its own origin. To a certain degree the Madonna expresses this concept, for the man child is creation born out of the womb of SPACE—the Holy Mother of Ages.

To the philosopher, God, as the first manifestation of unmanifested and incomprehensible ALL-ness, contains both the potencies of the mother and the father in equilibrium. Material existence is the result of the hypothetical division taking place within the nature of this androgynous Deity, from whose higher (or masculine) nature is created the superphysical universe, and from whose inferior (or feminine) nature is divided the world of form. From this point of view God does not act upon an extraneous body, but action and reaction are simply the interaction of the parts of one universal Deity. The English language lacks a proper term with which to designate Deity. The word God is comparatively meaningless, as it gives no hint of the gender or dignity of Divinity other than merely signifying "good." Since either a masculine or a feminine term is inappropriate and obviously incomplete, and a neuter term entirely too negative, a word is needed which wall express the undivided potencies of both positive and negative in equilibrium.

When the terms masculine And feminine were used in philosophic symbolism the ancients gave a certain supremacy to the masculine principle for two reasons: (1) as the male was endowed with greater physical endurance, among primitive peoples physical strength was considered the most necessary attribute of Divinity; (2) as the tribal or state government was a patriarchate, it necessarily followed that God as the Supreme Ruler became dignified as a masculine entity. Those races, however, which elevated woman to a high social status were more prone to endow Deity with distinctive feminine characteristics than were those peoples where woman was regarded as little better than a slave. As time went on man thus became the personification of the positive principle and woman of the negative. This viewpoint, however, will not bear close philosophic scrutiny. The so-called inferiority of the female is simply a symbolic figure, having no reference whatever to either the political or ecclesiastical status of woman. It is surprising, however, the extent to which the stigma of this little-understood symbolism has influenced both the racial and individual life of woman. It is still not uncommon to meet people who, while they can give no definite explanation for their feelings, are convinced that the feminine organism lacks some peculiar psychical or soul quality which has been reserved exclusively for masculine expression. The popular misconception (presumably promulgated by the Moslems) that heaven was a place accessible to woman as the result of special intercession on the part of her husband, while not publicly taught in Christendom, is nevertheless painfully evident to those able to analyze accurately the mental and emotional reactions of the average man. Woman's responsibilities as the mother of humanity afford ample evidence to the profound thinker that she is far from being a "negative" creature. The maternal principle was elevated by the Greeks to first place, and the Mater Deorum (Mother of the Gods) was esteemed worthy of universal veneration.

The relative superiority or inferiority of either the positive or negative principles leads to one inevitable conclusion: namely, that all manifestation being ordered by Divine Providence,

it is impossible to determine intelligently the ultimate importance of conditions, each of which is essential to all. God as the Father impregnates SPACE with his seed; God as the Mother receives this seed into herself and protects it through the ages necessary for its unfoldment; and God as the Child is himself the very seed which as God the Father he sowed. Thus is explained the ancient Rosicrucian adage: "All is in All; All is All."

The commentaries of the Cabalists upon the early Hebrew Scriptures contain lengthy dissertations upon the nature of God as the first being or power to manifest itself upon the surface of AIN SOPH, the limitless and boundless Sea of Eternal Potentiality. According to the Cabalistic version, there appeared upon and in AIN SOPH a great, gleaming, jewel-encrusted crown. This John Heydon calls the wise man's crown set with suns, moons, and stars and ornamented with archangels. Ten sparkling sapphires sent streamers of celestial splendor from their faceted surfaces, and the great crown, Kether, which was the foundation of the world, rested upon the intangible but immovable foundation of the Absolute Divinity. From the crown issued forth the multitudes of divine and elementary beings who people the forty spheres comprising the Cabalistic universe.

Thus, to a certain degree, the crown is an ark which, resting upon the hypothetical Ararat of Limitless Being—the Mount of Eternity—caused to issue from itself by twos and by sevens all that pageantry of life which had been preserved within it through the pralaya, or deluge of cosmic oblivion. Kether, the Ancient of Ancients, the Long Face, the Opened Eye, the Holy One, and the Father Foundation, enthroned in the midst of Being, wills creation and it is. Kether has neither shape nor form imaginable to us, but in an effort to conceive in part its dignity we ascribe to it the noblest forms within the vista of our comprehension. The sphere is the most perfect of all bodies and was therefore chosen by both Pythagoras and Plato as the most perfect symbol of "Him who shall remain." It is evident, however, that this Being does not actually resemble a crown, an opened eye or, as the Cabalists affirm, a bald head. These figures of speech in no way limit or change the enduring nature of this first power. Whether we call It Father or Mother or Son; whether we consider It as androgynous or sexless, human or composite, personal or impersonal. It remains forever itself, the first manifestation of unmanifested power. It was in the beginning, for Its appearance marks the term of beginning and end, and Time has its inception with the establishment of this first Divinity. God is as enduring as Time, but Time and God are both servants of Infinity.

The meditation of the mystics upon the nature of the first God revealed to them that Deity occupies a position somewhat analogous to a focal point. In God the unknowable potentialities of Absolute Existence were concentrated, and through the nature of Deity pass downward and are distributed as active potencies throughout the negative sphere or field of manifeststion. Infinite Being thus flows through God into creation, and existence ascends through God to its Infinite Source. God is therefore the least material and the most spiritual of all created things; of all beings the eldest; of all things the newest. Yet,being differentiated from Immortal Being, Deity is mortal and subject to ultimate reabsorption into Universal SPACE. In the most abstract sense, God is a hypothetical point established in the midst of Absolute Self through which It (Absolute Self) manifests forth into tangibility and consequent impermanent existence. God is the All made One; the universe is the One made All.

Of all the terms with which Deity has been invested there is none more simple and yet more consistent with the nature of ALL than that used by Plato, who defines God as the unmoved, self-moving Mover. God is unmoved in the sense that It is the sure foundation which will remain as long as time. God is self-moving in that activity is its innate quality.

God is the all-mover in that it is the life-giving principle animating all the structures which combine to form the inferior universe. God is the seed in the field of SPACE. From the dark philosophic earth of Infinite Being it draws all that it manifests. In the symbolism of the Far East, God comes as a lotus bud upon the surface of the Great Sea which, after living its appointed span, dies back into the infinite Ocean of Chaos. God is the first-born, the infinite Monad so well described by Democritus in his development of the atomic theory.

Now comes the legitimate question: If Absolute Being is unlimited and unconditioned with all its forces in a state of suspension, what causes these periodic centers or deities to come into being and what law governs their continuance and ultimate dissolution? In other words, if the Absolute possesses neither will nor activity in a centralized or manifesting state, how is the genesis of gods and worlds to be explained ? Why does not the Absolute remain throughout duration in the same unknowing and all-pervading state?

It is difficult to conceive of a perfect state giving birth to an imperfect state, and yet, according to philosophy, this is exactly what occurs when Universal Being supports ephemeral creation upon the surface of itself, or, as the Hindu mythologist would say, Varaha (the boar incarnation of Vishnu) elevates cosmos upon its tusks. The answer to the problem of First Cause has confounded several otherwise excellent systems of theology, and the solution advanced by mystical philosophy is one of the most daring postulates of the human mind. Yet for man with his limited intelligence to ponder too deeply upon such abstract mysteries is highly dangerous, for the solidarity of thought itself is jeopardized.

Sir Francis Bacon, one of the greatest thinkers of the modern world, realized how fatal to the success of the seeker after truth is the assumption of knowledge. Knowledge he declared to be the end, not the beginning, of the rational quest after facts. Much of the body of truth, however, is ascertained by the aid of certain fundamental postulations which must then run the gauntlet of observation and experimentation. Unable to delineate the boundaries or profiles of Universal Cause, the mind must necessarily reduce cosmic phenomena to terms apprehensible to human reason. To cope with the problems of the abstract the mind must first discover in the concrete the analogy of the abstract. Having found a simple natural analogy, the philosopher employs the most basic of all the Hermetic axioms: namely, that which is below is like unto that which is above.

The law of analogy is the most powerful weapon ever placed in the hands of man with which to solve the riddle of the Unknown, for by analogy he is able to classify the orders of invisible life, and chart that vast interval between the limitation of human nature and the limitlessness of Divine nature With the assistance of the law of analogy, let us then approach the problem of First Cause. Sleep is a state somewhat resembling death; in fact St. Paul definitely relates them to each other. Death, moreover, is analogous to the state of the Absolute in that it is the cessation of that activity which destroys the tranquillity of infinite duration. Again, no sense of time, place, or condition is apparent during sleep. A few seconds of a distorted dream may represent a lifetime in which persons and places come and go with kaleidoscopic speed. Speed also partakes of the nature of the Absolute in that the objective world disappears; the sleeper rests in an unknowing state and an almost Nirvanic trance-like condition controls the functioning parts. During sleep there is neither will nor rational activity in the objective world; oblivious to the entire panorama of existence, the objective soul lies in a state which is neither light nor darkness and which defies intelligent definition.

Sleep, however, does not override the claims of habit. If a person is accustomed to awake at a certain hour, when that hour arrives consciousness seemingly rises out of unconsciousness with no apparent motivation other than the subtle, innate urge of habit. The individual wakes, and grasping with drowsy fingers the sense perceptions, assumes the labors of the day.

The mind was never told to rouse the sleeper, nor did he have any realization that some intangible agent would at a certain time dissipate the state of dreaming and force the life back into wakeful activity. The sleeper suddenly opens his eyes and discovers it to be the usual rising hour. Habit is seemingly stronger than the state of sleep, for it is something that awakens the sleeper even when he cannot wake himself. Therefore, says the Ancient Doctrine, the comings and goings of creation upon the surface of infinite expanse are the impulses of the law of periodicity . Thus periodicity may be defined as the habit of Infinite SPACE . Habit causes the unknown elements and agencies comprising the Absolute periodically to spawn forth worlds and to draw them back again into itself periodically.

Habit causes the sleeping universe to awaken after the Seven Nights of Rest, and after its Seven Days of Labor habit and necessity again cause the tired creation to sink back into the arms of SPACE. Though not a thinking substance, SPACE contains the potentiality of thought. Thought is simply one of the numerous limited expressions of SPACE and does not come into manifestation until the creative processes have limited the ALL to that condition known as intelligence. That is the reason why the law of periodicity, or the spontaneous awakening of life, is necessary, in that SPACE possesses no tangible urge or force other than habit, which is itself a purely hypothetical term.

It is the supreme and eternal habit of Absolute Being to create and also to take creation back again into itself. Thus the outpouring and the inflowing may be likened to the ebb and flow of an eternal sea. Creation sinking into SPACE is no better able to conceive of the Absolute than is man to conceive of the substance of sleep. Nor do the Seven Sleepers upon awakening from their ages of slumber have any more concept of the condition from which they have emerged than has man when he rises from his slumbers. It is a daring thought to define cosmic law as the habit of SPACE, but the urges which immutably direct all things to their predestined end are thus explained.

Periodically upon the face of Not-Being (which is ALL Being) there appear centers of life—the chakras or seeds of future worlds. The swastika is their proper symbol, for it is the whirling across that represents the centralizing motion of the Eternal ALL. This first all-inclusive bubble, a magnificent iridescent sphere floating gracefully through eternity, is called God, and within its transparent shell creation lives and moves and has its being. Its purpose finally fulfilled, the bubble bursts and disappears, its parts are reabsorbed into the surrounding apparent nothingness.

All that man is or can ever hope to he depends upon his concept of God. No individual is greater than the God he worships, nor is he capable of worshipping a concept of God greater than himself. Thus is established a vicious circle. The noble concept of Baron von Leibnitz that the universe is made up of monads or metaphysical germs all contained within one great Monad may be contrasted with the theological concept of the last century which conceived the Deity to be a married man who took strange delight (as Voltaire has noted) in watching his creation eat the body of his beloved Son at the sacrament. Mans concept of God must pass through three definite states symbolized by the dot, the line, and the circle, which received so much consideration in the preceding lecture. The lowest concept of God is as a personality, a physical entity, whose symbol is the circumference of the circle. Superior to this concept is that of God as an individuality, a mental entity, whose symbol is the line. The third and highest definable concept is that of God as a spiritual entity, a permeating and diffusing life-giving principle, whose symbol is the dot. But above all these concepts and superior to God even as a spiritual entity is that concept of Absolute SPACE—formless and definitionless—whose only symbol is the blank sheet of paper.

In every philosophic system God is either the beginning or the end of the chain of thought. We may invest our concept of Deity with certain qualities and conditions and, accepting that as a starting point, seek to grasp the necessary process involved in the creation of the phenomenal sphere. Or we may posit as our working formula certain divine manifestation in the material universe, and by induction seek to understand the nature of a Deity capable of producing such phenomena out of its own nature. Thus in our investigation we either begin with the dot and travel toward the circumference, or we begin with the circumference and travel toward the dot. On the one hand we posit a Deity and then, imagining ourselves to be that Deity, construct a universe; on the other hand we posit a minute atom and through an infinite series of combinations and unfoldments trace manifesting life back to its spiritual source. Antiquity posited Divinity and then constructed the universe; the twentieth century first posits the universe and then looks for God. As God, however, is not obvious to the crass materialist, he is often entirely eliminated in the findings of that particular type of scientist. You will remember that upon reading Laplace's great work upon astronomy Napoleon made the remark, "But you make no mention of God," to which the great scientist haughtily replied, "Sire, I have no need for that hypothesis."

Generaly speaking, the elimination of God by the scientist is only a passing symptom. It occurs at that stage where the scientist, like the precocious child, upon reaching the summit of Fool's Mountain decides that he himself is sufficient to postulate a cause for the universe and is qualified to manipulate it according to his own whims. Upon essaying the role of general manager of cosmos, man invariably discovers that the task is far too arduous, and so eventually returns to God his universe. Modern thought, which is basically skeptical, declares God to exist only when discovered. As yet, however, none has discovered Deity. The only discovery thus far made is the absolute necessity of a First Cause, and this paramount need for such a Supreme Activity is conclusive proof of the existence of such a force or being.

To summarize, the modern world bases its entire philosophy of life upon the reality of the visible, whereas the ancient world conceived the invisible to be the real. Thus we have two diametrically opposing viewpoints. In the final analysis it is evident that the viewpoint of antiquity is correct. In the first place, the visible is actually such a small part of existing Nature, it is inconceivable that it should be accorded a position of first importance. All bodies float in a vast sea of SPACE, forming but a fractional part of the contents of this great sphere of Being. The invisible life must be superior to its vehicle of manifestation. Therefore the great Reality—life—cannot actually be considered a part of the phenomenal universe. It is a strange but fundamental truth that the least permanent thing in the universe is a rock, and the most permanent is so-called empty space; for the time will come when the rock will cease to be, but space will never pass away. Form can be destroyed and is ever changing, but space, by its very nature, is indestructible and forever the same. We now come to the nature of emptiness . Emptiness merely implies the absence of form; but the formless active agent, being all-permeating, fills all existence. You may pour the water out of a glass and then declare the glass to be empty because apparently it contains nothing. Any scientist, however, will assure you that the empty glass contains a sufficient number of atoms to blow the earth out of its orbit if their combined energy could be properly directionalized. Emptiness, therefore, is paradoxically an incomprehensible fullness. Philosophically considered, the absence of form means impossibility of destruction. That which has no form cannot have the form taken away. Emptiness, so-called, is consequently more permanent than fullness. In its conventional sense, fullness means that the container is filled to capacity with physical elements.

The true fullness, however, is that area which is completely filled with spiritual and eternal agencies. Of such a nature is SPACE which, far from being empty, may be likened to a spiritual solid, whereas the physical world may be best described as a spiritual vacuum.

According to the Platonists, all the creations manifesting outward from the nature of God are arranged in the order of their proximity to First Cause. Those nearer the source of life partake more of the celestial effulgence than those more distant; in other words, the light radiating from a flame more closely resembles the flame at the source than at the extremity of its rays. The order of the gods is therefore determined by their proximity to the central creative fire of the universe, which is termed the Altar of Vesta or the Tower of the All-Wise Father. The gods arc not to be considered as independent entities or forces, but rather as monads with numerous subordinate powers and intelligences dependent upon them. Each deity is, in turn, a dependency of a superior being, until at last all unite in a common dependency upon the benevolence of First Cause. Thus each individual deity may be symbolized by the dot, the line, and the circle. As a dot, each god is the central monad of a host of inferior dependencies; as a line, each god is a streaming radiance nourishing its subordinate parts; and as a circle or circumference each god is a fractional part of a still greater monadic entity. The majesty of these divinities is therefore established by the law of relativity. Each god is the father of a multitudinous progeny which exists within its own nature and which must unquestioningly obey its dictates. Each deity is, in turn, part of the progeny of a still higher and more exalted power to which it renders homage. Thus each deity is both a creator and a creation in one. As man ascends the ladder uniting effect with cause, he approaches ever closer to conscious realization of Source. He therefore passes through the angelic choirs described by Dante in his Paradisw. These choirs in concatenated circles about the flaming throne of the Eternal Father represent the orders of divine emanations. Thus the central flame is ever surrounded by a many-ringed nimbus of subordinate lights supporting all creation.

Let us approach the problem of macrocosmic interdependency through a consideration of certain microcosmic realities. The human body may be considered either as a single unit or as a host of minute living organisms combining in accordance with certain definite laws. Each individual cell is a living and immortal creature and it also has been definitely established that various organs of the human body possess at least a selective intelligence. Yet all these separate, living parts are suspended, as it were, from the single monad of the human heart. The heart is to the body what the sun is to the solar system and First Cause to existence. If one of the cells within the body dies, the body still lives, but if the chief governing monad ceases to function, then all the cells or dependent parts partake of the general dissolution. As the life of the body is centralized in the heart even though a general life is diffused throughout the body, so, while life may be discovered in every creature existing in the manifested sphere, all these subordinate lives are swept to a common destruction if the Great Monad upon which they depend be removed. The lesser lives have their origin in the greater and must always remain its dependents. Deity as the first Monad of the world is the foundation of the universe, the Sacred Island, sometimes analogous to Shamballah, the City of the Gods. Upon this Monad is erected all creation; with its dissolution the far-reaching and diversified phenomena collapse like a house of cards. Therefore God may be defined as that upon which a lesser part depends; our God is the Monad from whose nature we as lesser monads hang by hypothetical threads. Hence there are many gods, for all beings, both great and small, hang as dependencies upon the natures of superior forms of life.

Next we must consider the philosophic principle of priority. Of a number of things related to each other, that which is fundamental is primary or first, and the rest are dependencies.

For example, a ship may carry a large and diversified cargo. If any part of the cargo be thrown overboard, the safety of the ship is not necessarily endangered. If, however, the ship should sink, all its cargo goes down too. Thus the cargo depends upon the ship for its preservation, but the ship does not depend upon the cargo. The priority of either a science or a living organism is established by the degree of its fundamental importance to all other sciences and organisms. The destruction of priority automatically annihilates all its dependencies. If you destroy that which is first, that which is secondary also ceases.

If you destroy that which is secondary you in no way injure chat which is first; you simply limit some phase of its manifestation. Pythagoras used the science of mathematics to illustrate the principle of priority. Remove mathematics and you destroy every form of human knowledge which is in any way dependent upon numbers or the theory of mathematics. For example, consider the relationship between mathematics and music. The science of harmonics is wholly dependent upon mathematics. If you remove the knowledge of music from the world, you destroy a certain phase of mathematics, but the body of numbers is left uninjured. On the other hand, if you remove mathematics from the world, the entire theory of harmonics perishes. Of the two, mathematics is primary and music secondary. Another simple illustration: The tree has one trunk and many branches. The branches are dependencies of the trunk, for if one of the branches be removed the life of the tree is not seriously impaired and the other branches remain unaffected. Destroy the trunk, however, and all the branches die together. In the search for knowledge the highest wisdom is first to learn those things which have priority. To learn mathematics, for example, is to possess already a certain knowledge of all sciences, because it is the first among the sciences. For this reason the Greeks and Egyptians demanded of all disciples seeking initiation into the Mysteries an understanding of mathematics.

The identity of first things can be determined by applying the principle of priority. Things are considered of greater or lesser importance according to what they depend upon and what is dependent upon them. Man is master over those forms of life dependent upon him, but a slave to that infinity of forces which he depends upon for every expression and manifestation. The gods are merely symbolic representations of states of relative dependency. The gods are greater than man because they represent the members of existence upon which man depends. Such a chain of dependency is well represented by the institution of feudalism. A country was divided among a group of nobles whose relative importance depended upon the extent of their individual domains. A certain number of baronies constituted an earldom, and a group of earldoms, in turn, formed a dukedom. Above the dukedom was the principality, and over all the king, who on a smaller scale was the god of his nation. Greatness depends upon constructive and destructive power—destructive in the sense of changing rather than annihilating.

A further thought concerning the term dependency . Our hands and feet are dependent upon us for their animating principle; we are dependent upon them for the expression of certain innate desires and attitudes. Our hands and feet protect us, but they are obviously less than that which they protect. They may be likened to vassals or stewards. In the days of knighthood, when knights went into battle they were attended by- esquires or stewards who rode behind their masters to free them from their heavy armor in the event they were unhorsed, or to arrange for a ransom with their conqueror. In ancient philosophy the gods represent the hands and feet and vital members of the cosmic body. Like the cherubim of the Jews, they run back and forth in the whirlwinds, executing the orders of the Most High even as our busy fingers carry out the dictates of our brain. The one Supreme Power manifesting throughout the cosmic organism should be considered as manifesting throughout all created things, each of which is a faculty or member of minor or major importance.

An interesting story came to our attention of an East Indian pundit who was trying to explain to a rather bigoted Christian missionary the reason for the great number of heads appearing upon the shoulders of certain Hindu divinities. "My dear sir," exclaimed the missionary, "yonder many-headed image is a ghastly caricature of a god, and how can any people who have risen above an aboriginal state worship such a grotesque and unnatural concept of God?" the pundit smilingly replied: "You do not understand our method of symbolizing divine agencies.

In your own scriptures it is plainly implied that God is all there is and that in him we live and move and have our being. God is the heavens and the earth and all the creatures that inhabit them. You have a head, I have a head, all human beings have heads. Has God, therefore, not as many heads as there are heads, as many hands as there are hands, and as many feet as there are feet? Are not all minds his mind, all thoughts his thoughts, and all works accomplished for him done by him through his manifested parts? Therefore, my dear sir, our failure is not for lack of comprehension but because no artist alive is able to carve enough heads to adequately represent the nature of the Creator."

Philosophy is not solely an intellectual reasoning process whereby certain definite conclusions are reached concerning macrocosmic and microcosmic realities. Philosophy utterly fails in its mission unless that mystical elixir—understanding—tinctures the whole. Understanding is the rarest of all faculties. It is a subtle power which adds to the intellectual concept a definite stimulating realization or intuitive grasp of the fundamental elements involved in any problem and their relationship to each other. Understanding is the ultimate stage of knowledge; it is the perfect realization of the purpose and meaning of things. For two thousand years the men of the church have been studying Christianity; orators have shouted its precepts from the housetops; the Crusaders carried the message with the sword, the monk with the crucifix, and the Holy Inquisition with the firebrand. For nearly two thousand years men and women of devout spirit have prayed and fasted and meditated; they have even died as martyrs that the spirit of their faith might go on. Of this host of propagandists of Christianity, most had either an intellectual or an emotional concept of the Master Jesus and his mission. Only here and there was one who understood, and too often his fate was to fall before the mob of enthusiastic but misunderstanding zealots.

Today there are innumerable truths which remain unrevealed to the seeker after knowledge because he does not possess the philosophic open-sesame. To the understanding mind all doors open; to those without understanding life must ever remain a tormenting enigma. At the beginning of this chapter is a diagram showing the god Brahma as the creator of the universe. From his three heads, representative of the triune nature of First Cause, extend three streamers of force outward to form the foundations of the three worlds. In modern Hindu mysticism Brahma is generally represented with four heads and occasionally with five, one of which is supposed to have been cut of by Shiva. The fourheaded Brahma is a demiurgic god, being the foundation of the four elements. The three-headed Brahma here referred to signifies the abstract Creative Logos, or the dot, manifesting as primitive potencies the threefold darkness of the Absolute, from whose incomprehensibility Brahma is but one degree removed. The three mouths of Brahma breathe forth the sacred whirlwinds of cosmic breath, which become incarnate in the universe as the creative Trimurti of Brahma, Vishnu, and Shiva, and which correspond to the first trinity of all peoples. From one mouth issues the breath which is to become spirit, which, after passing through numerous modifications, manifests as the causal agent throughout the worlds. From the second mouth streams that force which is to be the intermediary state throughout the universe. This state is most tangible as mind or that mysterious thinking air which, permeating the objective thinking structure, manifests as continuity of reason, perception, and ultimately apperception. The third head breathes forth the Maker of worlds and his angels, and from these outpouring essences are fashioned the objective spheres and their diversified genera.

In mystical philosophy the dot, or first emanation, is presumed to have three faces. The key to their meaning is at once apparent if the word phases is substituted for faces . The dot contains three phases of one power, yet in an undifferentiated state. Thus God in mystic Christianity is the dot, while the Father, Son, and Holy Ghost are his phases, or the first manifested Trimurti. The three phases or faces are sometimes referred to as the three modes of Being. From these primary modes manifests an infinitude of complex organisms. Between this cosmological mystery and the allegory of Noah's ark there is a certain analogy. Noah is the dot, his three sons are the faces, and their wives are the shakti, or negative expressions of these faces. As from the positive pole of Being there is manifested this triad of agencies, so from the negative pole of Being is manifested the quaternary of demiurgic forces. The two combine to form the sacred septenary so appropriately symbolized in the Masonic apron with its triangle rising out of or falling into (according to the degree) the square. The descent of the 3 into the 4 properly symbolizes the ensoulment of the world by its spiritual cause; the ascent of the 3 out of the 4, the resurrection of life from its sepulcher of form.

The process by which the entire objective universe is caused to issue forth from the first monadic dot can be likened to that process by which the oak tree emerges from the acorn. It is unreasonable to assume that the oak tree manifests any qualities that were not originally in its seed, yet that so much should have come from apparently so little is indeed a mystery. The oak tree is in the acorn in potentiality, yet when these potentialities come into objective existence they seem vastly greater than their source. According to the Oriental mystics, the universe is an inverted tree. The seed is the dot from which springs forth the World Tree whose branches are the gods and whos leaves are creation. This is the great tree of the Cabalists and also the illusional banyan of the Hindus, for it exists but a moment upon the substances of Eternity and then falls back again into SPACE. From the three mouths of the first Trimurti issue powers: spiritual, intellectual, and material; divine, human, and animal; also die creative elements of air, fire, and water, air being symbolic of the intangible Father, fire of the radiant Son, and water of the Demiurgus who seeks with material impulses to quench the fire of spiritual light. These three are personified as the Builders of the world. The Father is King Solomon, the Son is Hiram Abiff, and the Holy Spirit is Hiram of Tyre, who furnishes the materials.

Having thus established the fundamental nature of the dot, we now pass to the constitution of the line wherein is revealed the mystery of the Savior-God of all ages and the second Principle of existence.

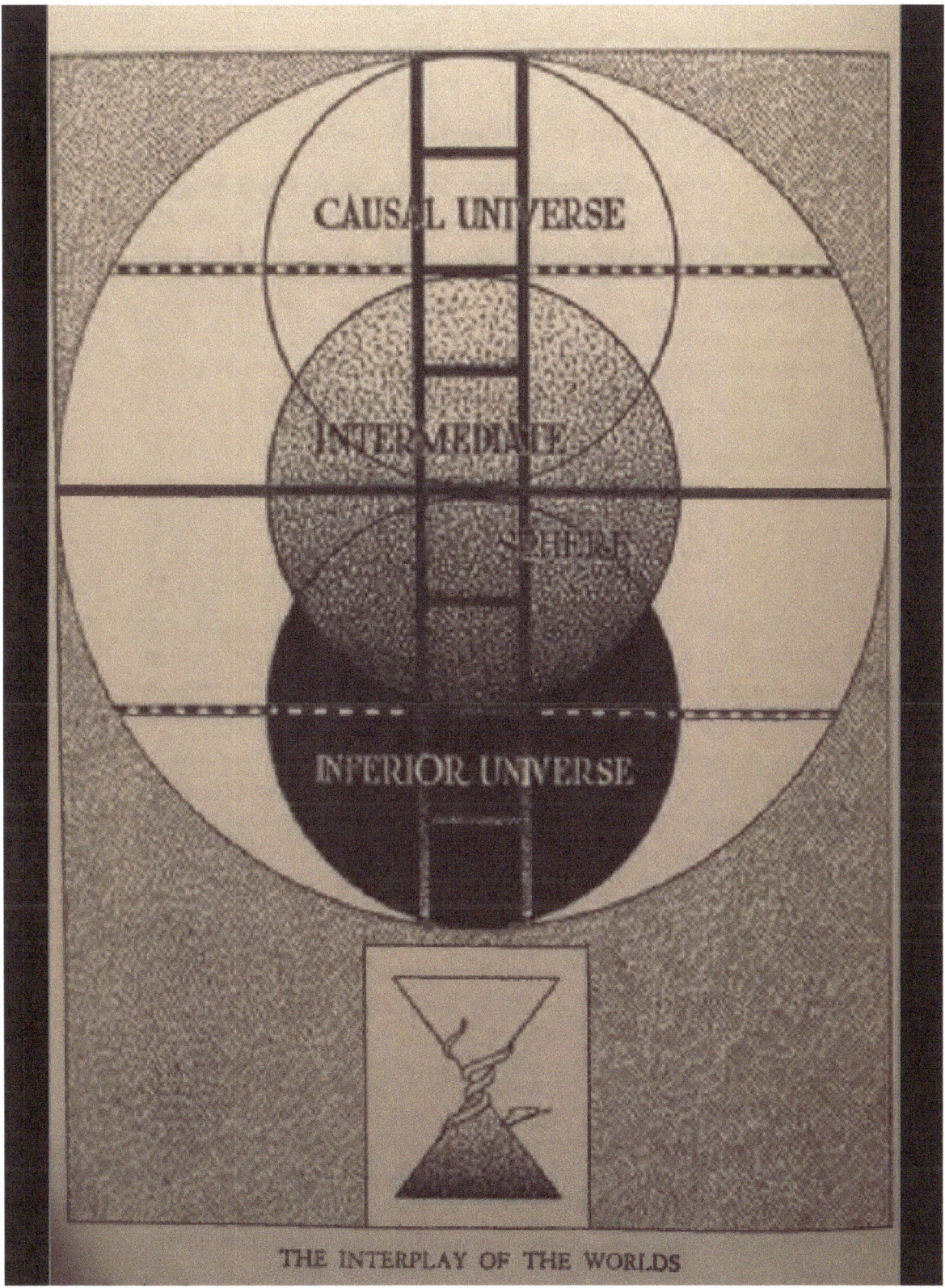

THE INTERPLAY OF THE WORLDS

This figure sets forth the constitution of the Intermediate Sphere, by which the extremes of Spirit and Matter are reconciled and the harmony of the universe preserved. The ancients unite in the recognition of three worlds existing within one eternal and unlimited state. Philosophy is the science of the relationships of these worlds.

# VIII

꧁꧂

# Illumined Mind, the Universal Savior

LIGHT is the most appropriate symbol of manifesting spirit because it is the inherent nature of light to radiate, and this outpouring is represented by a simple vertical line drawn downward from the dot, or heart of existence. An analysis of the flame reveals its threefold constitution and their correspondence to the three phases of the dot considered in the preceding lecture. The blue (or nearly colorless) heart of the candle flame signifies the dark, hidden Father; the golden radiance surrounding this area is the bright, flaming Son who bears witness before the worlds of his unknowable Father; and at the circumference is a reddish, smoky flame representative of the Demiurgus, or Lord of the World. Because of its triune nature, fire for ages has been employed as the symbol of the threefold God. Pyrolatry is one of the oldest forms of religious expression.

Light can also be symbolized by a globe, the outer surface of which is the hypothetical point where the rays of light terminate. In reality, light is a rate of vibration pouring off, or outward, from the heart of the vibratory ray or cause of vibration, which must be symbolized by the flame. For the sake of the analogy, the heart of the flame can be compared to the dot; the radiant light pouring from the flame to the line; and the outer darkness which absorbs the light, to the circumference or outer limit of manifestation. Consider for a moment the relationship of the ray to its source. The true flame is invisible and superphysical, but it is made discernible to the eye through a rate of vibration called light, and to other sense perceptions through a rate of vibration called heat. Life, light, and heat are the trinity, with life as the Father, light as the Son, and heat as the Demiurgus. It may well be said, therefore, that no man hath seen the Father, for the transcendency of Being is concealed behind a flaming ring which blinds all who gaze upon it.

Radiance is the ceaseless effort of a central force to expand; it is the continual pouring off of sparks from an endless supply. The dot may be likened to a tube through which a mysterious spiritual fluid ever pours. The moment this fluid is free from the restraining pressure of the tube it has a tendency, like water, to expand and spread out in the form of a huge fan. Activity is continually manifesting throughout the universe. There is a never-ending battle between the effort of all life to expand and the effort of substance to resist expansion. A concrete example of this particular point may be helpful. By means of experimental balloons it is possible to estimate atmospheric conditions above the earth's surface. As the toy balloon ascends it expands until at an altitude of approximately eleven and one-half miles it will explode, in spite of every precaution that may be taken. The reason for this is that the outside pressure decreases as the atmosphere grows less dense, until finally the expanding quality of the gas inside the ballon meets with so little outside resistance that the walls of the ballon are unable to support the pressure. We have present in Nature, therefore, a continual expansion from within which is offset by a continual pressure from without. Thus the physical nature of every organism is particularly adapted to the pressure of its environment. Man's entire evolutionary progress has fitted him to sustain the atmospheric pressure at the earth's surface. The moment he leaves this atmospheric environment he must readjust himself, and beyond a certain point he cannot exist.

The aviator has felt every part of his body racked with this effort to meet the ever decreasing pressure of higher altitudes. For similar reasons explorers climbing lofty mountains frequently suffer from bursting blood vessels. The pressure at the earth's surface is not as great, however, as that beneath the ocean, where the most powerful apparatus is required to withstand the pressure of the water. As man's physical existence is confined to a certain stratum of air pressure, so spiritually he is likewise limited to a definite plane of cosmic activity.

The denser the substances surrounding the individual, the greater the pressure from without. Hence materiality continually checks the natural expansion of the spiritual and intellectual self. The less material the environment, the greater the opportunity for the spiritual nature to expand, until finally at the gate of the Absolute the little globe of individual consciousness—like the toy balloon—reaches the point where there is no outward pressure whatsoever. The shell itself is symbolic of a degree of external pressure, but when all pressure has been removed, consciousness now freed from limitation is diffused again throughout the nature of existence. Hence the Absolute represents the vanishing point of external pressure. The circumference of the sphere of being is the plane established by the inward pressure of substance and the outward pressure of consciousness. As the scope of consciousness is enlarged the power of expansion increases and the walls of substance are pushed farther back. Conversely, as consciousness is denied expression and its impulses become weaker, the circle of substance approaches ever closer to the center of consciousness.

Philosophically defined, growth is the struggle of life to control its environment or, rather, to include more and more of its environment within the area of its own self-knowing. Perfect freedom of expression is the goal of all life. All things, both animate and inanimate, are striving for that freedom which lies in perfect expression. It naturally follows that there is but one freedom—perfection. Every creature is a slave to those parts of itself as yet unresponsive to the impulses of its internal life principle. Every individual consequently is a slave to his own material constitution; he is a prisoner held in by walls of unresponsive substance. Thus the natural expression of the inner life principle is to refine and improve the qualities of its outer vehicles that it may the more easily control and direct them. It is evident that die more refined the substance, the more easily it is influenced by subtle forces. By a certain definite organization, consciousness equips its outer nature with organs of responsiveness, so that the lower self comes ever more nearly en rapport with its own Cause. A common example is the radio, which is a mechanical contrivance constructed according to definite scientific principles which enable it to pick up vibratory rates of sound inaudible to even the delicate mechanism of the human ear.

Returning to the symbolism of the line, the line is a potential cosmic nerve ray designed to confer consciousness upon the area covered by its tiny threadlike fingers. Man is slowly acquiring control over his physical body by ever increasing the acuteness of his nervous organism, for by his nerves the various parts of his body are tied together. The nerve is an impulse carrier which gives man consciousness over a certain area of otherwise unresponsive substance. Man's nerves function far more acutely now than in ages past; they are becoming much more sensitive and bring to man much knowledge concerning the nature of the substance composing his world. As the result of this increasing sensitiveness, nervous disorders arc increasing, for the finer the mechanism the greater the likelihood of derangement. The Romans termed the line Mercury, the messenger of the gods. Like the lines of the telegraph and telphone, the nerves bring the distant parts of the organism into direct contact with the central station of the brain. The nerves do not necessarily end at the outer circumference of the physical body, but in the form of etheric streamers extend outward into the aura, or intangible atmosphere surrounding the physical body. Here they continue to function in a limited degree as impulse carriers. These etheric nerve ends arc continually contacting forces and forms both visible and invisible, and conveying certain indefinite impulses back to the brain. Many of our so-called "hunches" and unaccountable antipathies or affinities are the result of curious reactions set up by these etheric nerve threads which bind every part of the lower organism of man, visible and invisible, into one solid body. The line or ray coming out of the dot may be likened to a primitive nerve giving to the dot a consciousness of the nature of its environment. It thus becomes the messenger between the center and the circumference of life. The line is the outpouring of cause into effect. The line permeates its environment with the qualities of the first innate life principle of the central dot; it is the effort of the center to include the circumference within itself. The phenomena of growth represent the gradual effort of life, which is innately perfect, to objectify its perfection and blend itself with the perfection of all. In this manner the subjective potentialities of life gradually become objective potencies or powers. Growth is really the bringing of the inside of life to the outside; a gesture from within outward; the unceasing effort of the active agent to communicate its conscious qualities to its unconscious environment The ultimate of growth is the bringing into conscious expression all of the seed germs of power lying latent in every atom of existence. The dot contains within itself all potentialities as the symbolic acorn contains the oak tree. Every leaf that in the future will grow upon the oak tree exists as a potential power in the germinal essences of the acorn. Growth merely brings these latent potentialities into active manifestation by building into them material elements which make them apparent to physical sense perceptions. The fundamental reason for this growth is the active urge to express the potencies of self and escape the imprisonment of limited vehicles.

Pythagoras said that when the triangle is once established any problem is already two-thirds solved. The foundation of all existence is triangular. We are a threefold creation; the triangle of man consists of his spirit, his body, and the link connecting them. In its macrocosmic sense there is a divine creation, an elemental creation, and the link connecting them. Life is a divine, eternal principle; matter (except in its absolute sense) is a temporal and transitory thing. These two are separated by the whole interval of being. They are the opposites, and between them is a neutral field where one acts upon the other, for in their self-sufficient states the two have little in common. Divine nature is essentially a part of the divine creation; physical nature a part of the material creation. In ancient symbolism it was declared that the two seas—the ocean of Divinity above and the ocean of Nature below—were divided, "the waters which were under the firmament from the waters which were above the firmament."

The universe of divine energy above and the universe of material energy below are the substances from which are extracted respectively the spirit and the body of man. The spirit is an atom of divine substance, the body an atom of material substance, and the higher vests itself in the lower and the product is a living thing. Presuming spirit to be the actuating part and matter the part worked upon, it will be evident that the spirit cannot control the body without the assistance of a connecting tissue wherein the irreconcilable opposites are blended. Thus in order that the abstractly spiritual may affect the concretely material, a great hierarchy of mediatory agencies must be established. In certain of the ancient Mystery schools it was taught that there were eighty thousand degrees of intelligence intervening between absolute consciousness and absolute unconsciousness, each degree representing a mediatory element or condition. Considered as a unit, these degrees represent the middle or neutral field. In alchemy mercury, or quicksilver, is used to symbolize this blending element, because mercury accepts into its own nature other metals. In mythology the god Mercury was the mediator or neutral power serving as the messenger between the gods above and mortal man below.

Still another pair of opposites must be considered: divine truth and human ignorance. Above (in the sense of proximate to cause) is divine Reality, the one great need of all creation; below (in the sense of distant from Source) is man, who may achieve salvation only through the attainment of Reality. Here are both the living water and the empty bowl waiting to receive it. But absolute truth and ignorant humanity are divided by a vast interval of understanding. Truth knows no man; man knows no truth. Truth is that mysterious, infinite, boundless Reality; man a mere worm existing in minutes, hours, and days, and spending most of them foolishly. Here the sum of the knowable is the dot, gross ignorance the circumference of the circle. That which is necessary to unite these two and thus blend them into the perfection of type is the line, the mediator between cause and effect.

A simple analogy of the dot, the line, and the circle with the processes of knowledge may be traced in the following manner. In the center of the circle is the dot representing a fact; at the circumference of the circle stands a student desirous of learning this fact; between these two is an interval filled with a number of agencies, any one of which (in many cases the sense perceptions) may become the mediator between the knowable and the one capable of knowing. In order to gain a more extensive understanding of existence with its vast number of physically apparent facts, the interval is occupied by an elaborate educational system, and thus between knowledge and the student body stands the professor who acts as mediator and assists in the dissemination of the subject matter.

Everywhere in Nature is to be found a mediating principle which is capable of contacting both extremes simultaneously, or at least intermittently. If is most difficult to unite the abstract and the concrete in a single nature, consequently you may hear such remarks as "Genius is eccentric," "A wonderful man, but—", etc. Those who possess abstract knowledge can seldom clothe it in words understandable to others. As man attempts to elevate himself spiritually he gradually separates himself from his material environment. To have a stature great enough to raise its head to heaven and still keep its feet upon the earth is the proof of true enlightenment. If wisdom is to instruct ignorance, it must be capable of appreciating the state of ignorance as truly as the state of knowledge. If the mind has raised itself above the consciousness of ignorance, it will never be able to impart wisdom to the ignorant. To instruct the minds of others it is necessary to approach them along the lines of the familiar; they must be reached on a thought level commensurate with their own, otherwise they cannot grasp the problems presented.

Since in the universal scheme the divine mediator must have the consciousness of both the upper and the lower, philosophy postulates three manners of beings: gods, who are great centers of intelligent power; men, who are little centers with marvelous potentialities; and god-men or man-gods who act as mediators between the superior and the inferior. Thus is revealed the meaning of that enigmatic statement of the Pythagoreans that there were three kinds of creatures: gods, men, and Pythagoras, the latter being representative of the mediator who was able to bind together the superior and the inferior creations. In a similar manner the identity of Jesus (according to the Gnostic traditions) is clarified, for in some places he is referred to as the Son of God and in others as the Son of man. As the Son of man he ascended out of the earth to the inheritance of a heavenly state (heaven in the sense of accomplishment); as the Son of God he veiled his sense of knowing in a mortal vehicle and descended from the mysteries of the higher aeons into the state of human ignorance, and was thus able to converse with mortals upon the level of their own understanding. In the words of an ancient philosopher: "He who has not even a knowledge of common things is a brute among men. He who h as an accurate knowledge of human concerns alone, is a man among brutes. But he who knows all that can be known by intellectual energy is a God among men."

Man's status in cosmos is determined, therefore, by the quality of his thinking. Quality, as applied to mental processes, is not necessarily intensity but rather refinement and delicacy. The trained scientist may reach a very high degree of intellectuality and yet lack that beautifying element which is indispensable to true understanding. Unless the inner nature transcends the limitations of both the flesh and the mind, the self can never attain to a full measure of expression. Whether a man be a beast or a god does not depend upon his outward appearance but rather upon the clarity of his inner perceptions. Many of the most respected citizens of every community arc actually ravaging beasts concealing their primitive instincts under a thin veneer of culture. On the other hand, some whom the world regards as failures possess an innate beauty which elevates them far above the level of their fellows.

The gods may be defined as those in whom the state of knowing has reached a degree of relative perfection, and beasts those creatures in whom the state of knowing is asleep. Between these two extremes is man, who wanders about in a state of partial knowing, united to the bestial creation by his ignorance and to the higher orders of divinities by his dawning rationality. Between the states of knowing and not-knowing the Greeks postulated the middle distance, a point where consciousness and unconsciousness are blended in semiconsciousness. Between the light of spirit above and the darkness of matter below there is the twilight zone which is the proper sphere of mind and where creatures endowed with minds seek to read the book of their destiny by the all-too-insufficient light. This central twilight zone is divided by a hypothetical median line into two hemispheres. The upper hemisphere, partaking most directly of the supreme effulgence which is proximate to it, is the dwelling place of the Sons of God—the Ben Elohim of the Hebrews—or those beings fundamentally divine but who partake somewhat of the qualities of the middle distance and therefore descend to the hypothetical median line dividing the upper and lower hemispheres of the middle distance . The lower hemisphere is proximate to the dark sphere of ignorance, but partaking, to a certain degree, of the superior light, becomes the abode of the redeemed souls—the Ishim of the Hebrews. Inferior creatures rising out of the darkness of their mortal night, though they be of the earth earthy, may ascend into the middle distance and at this hypothetical median line contact the demigods who descend from the superior spheres. Thus in the middle distance are to be found both the demigods who have descended from above as instructors of mankind, and the supermen who, rising from the insufficiency of matter, converse with the demigods through the hypothetical median line.

It follows that the ancients conceived the instructors of humanity to be of two kinds: (1) those who descended from the light aeons of the internal causal world, and, brooding over humanity, spoke through oracles and oracular souls or prophets; (2) those who through the peculiar culture of the Mysteries were elevated to a state of sensitiveness wherein they became ready pens in the hands of the heavenly writers. Knowledge likewise is twofold: that knowledge which, having its origin among the celestial beings of the light world, is communicated to man and constitutes the revealed or sacred writing; and that knowledge which is evolved by man himself during his ages of struggle in the inhibiting environment of the mortal world. The wisdom imparted by the demigods partakes of that higher knowledge which belongs to the sphere of consciousness and causation, while that wisdom imparted by the superhuman (or illumined human) souls, being further removed from cause, lacks the definiteness and authority of the divinely-given code. The demigods teach the celestial or inner body of knowledge; the superman, the terrestrial or outer body of knowledge. Therefore, the initiates and the prophets bear witness of the light, though not directly partaking of its power to the extent of the demigods.

According to the esoteric doctrines of Platonism, the demigods can never become men or descend to the level of mortality because they are of a different and higher order of creation. On the other hand, though man through discipline and enlightenment rises to a state approaching deification, he can never actually become one with the gods, for he must continue in the life stream of which he is a part. This does not mean that man will not ultimately attain to the state of Divinity but rather that he will create his own genus of gods, for the life of one creation can never become identical with the life of any other creation but must evolve its own vehicles of manifestation. The same law that prohibits man from becoming like the gods also prohibits the gods from becoming like man, even though they control and direct his destiny. In spite of its magnificent power and divine abundance of wisdom and understanding, the demigod is unable to build a physical body and hence must borrow one already prepared for its use. Such a body then becomes its oracle or shrine, and through it the demigod reaches the dwellers in the dark sphere of matter.

Thus when one of the demigods, or great Devas, desires to communicate with mankind it descends to the median line where, working through the plane of mind (the mediating principle), it overshadows a mortal who has raised himself to this exalted state, and through the higher vehicles of such a mortal contacts humanity. By thus overshadowing the mind of the mortal initiate, the Deva causes him to think, speak, and act according to the celestial will. The demigods must not be considered as personalities but rather as individualities, in that they function in substances too rarefied (free of gross physical elements) to permit the existence of personal organisms. The demigods are units of knowing, relatively superior to mortal men but incapable of molding physical matter except through the medium of mind. Supermen are personal beings who are gradually outgrowing personality. Though still limited by mortal bodies, they have learned to separate consciousness from form and function (temporarily at least) in the same substances that constitute the attenuated organisms of the demigods. Various Greek philosophers are said to have been overshadowed by gods or daemons .

Thus Pythagoras was declared to be overshadowed always by the spirit of the Pythian Apollo, and Socrates likewise by a mysterious creature which he referred to as his "god." Bringing with it certain great truths otherwise inaccessible to man, such a deity elevates the one so overshadowed to a position of unusual philosophic dignity.

At this point it is necessary to remind the reader that the demigods, since they are part of the causal agencies which together constitute the spiritual world, are themselves in and of the spiritual natures of all creatures. Thus man's own spirit is a demigod hovering over his lower organisms, which are as disciples receiving the instruction necessary to right living from the god within. In Oriental art Arjuna is frequently shown receiving instruction from Krishna on the battlefield of Kuru- shetra. Arjuna, the son of Kunti, the mortal man, is often represented as a diminutive figure while above him in all the splendor of his azure radiance stands the blue Krishna. Here Arjuna represents the personal or mortal / and Krishna the demigod or oversoul upon whose instruction the mortal man depends for his inspiration to right action.

Occasionally the spiritual and the material worlds are symbolized by two pyramids, one inverted with its base in the heavens and the other upright with its base upon the earth.

The two pyramids meet at their apexes. The pyramid with its foundation in heaven decreases in size as it descends, and is the proper symbol of the decreasing choirs of celestial beings (forces and intelligences) that descend in concatenated order from the effulgence of the Twenty-fourth Mystery which is the First Mystery from above. The upright pyramid with its foundation in matter indicates by its converging sides the gradual decrease of materiality until at its apex materiality vanishes.

Occasionally a serpent is wound about the point where the two apexes meet, thus indicating the mystery of mind and the astral light which is the blending of the superior and the inferior Aeons. This concatenated order of decreasing materiality and increasing spirituality forms the many-runged ladder rising from the darkness of oblivion below and the perfect light of celestial splendor above, and was the ladder that the angels ascended and descended in Jacob's vision. Man painfully climbs the many steps leading to the summit of the pyramid of material attainment, and upon reaching the apex finds himself at the foot of an incalculable flight of steps that leads upward to the very source of Being. Upon this upper flight of steps stand the demigods, above them the gods, and around about the winged spirits who dwell in the middle distance and are the divine messengers. This entire picture must be considered, however, as a symbolic representation of the states and conditions of consciousness, intelligence, and force, which by their orderly combinations bring all phenomena into manifestation.

The figure accompanying this chapter sets forth in a diagrammatic manner the interplay of the three worlds forming the basis of Greek and Hindu philosophy. Once this point is comprehended, the entire structure of ancient thought is revealed. The circles, of course, merely represent vast areas of spiritual activity occupying the same place at the same time but separated from each other by the vibratory rates of their atomic particles. The white sphere represents the causal nature, the black sphere the material universe. It will be noted that the third, or intermediate sphere consists of a dotted area, the dots increasing in number below and decreasing in number above the horizontal line. The entire diagram is divided horizontally by a heavy line which represents the definite point of separation between the causal universe and the universe of effects. This diagram should be considered as applicable not only to cosmos but to every organism in the universe, which by its very existence demonstrates that it is composed of spiritual and material agencies combined as shown in the drawing. The ladder rising through the three worlds signifies the path of attainment that leads from darkness into light. That part of the ladder occupying the space below the central dividing line represents the mystery of water, which is purification; that part of the ladder above the central dividing line represents the mystery of fire, which is the baptism of the spirit. Here is the key to the two baptisms of the Christian Gnostics, for John the Baptist is made to say, "I indeed baptize you with water unto repentance: but he that cometh after me shall baptize you with the Holy Ghost, and with fire."

In this figure is thus set forth the entire purpose of the ancient Mysteries and the processes of human regeneration. Here also is set forth a still greater mystery—the mystery of the dying god —with which we must now concern ourselves.

The Augustinian, or outer, interpretation of the dying god mythos declares the martyr Savior to be the line descending from the dot to the circle which, falling into the darkness of the circumference, is swallowed up (or allegorically dies) by becoming immersed in the irrational sphere of matter. Man is declared to have two souls, or rather, two hypothetical phases of one soul consciousness. The first and superior is the rational soul; the second and inferior, the irrational soul. The rational soul is that part of man which is ever in awareness of divine and eternal self. The irrational soul is that part which, being incapable of retiring into the mysteries of self, mistakes the outer nature for the inner and assumes the objective man to be the real. The qualities of the rational soul are apperception, realization, comprehension, and other higher mental and supermental faculties. The qualities of the irrational soul are external perception, ignorance, selfishness, lust, greed, and kindred vices. The rational soul is necessarily unselfish because it conceives self to be distributed throughout the entire substance of Being. Glimpsing the universal ultimates of life, the rational soul is not hypnotized by the illusion of a personal self and therefore does not urge toward personal aggrandizement and accumulation. The irrational soul is fundamentally selfish because it conceives self to be isolated, and the service and preservation of self therefore becomes an all-important consideration. Sin and death are the masters of the irrational soul. Realizing the kinship of one with the All, the rational soul, however, attains immortality and omnipotence. Socrates defines man as a self-knowing being immersed in a not-knowing body. This is the outer mystery of the dying god slain for the sin of the world or, more correctly, by the sin of the world. Descending from the spiritual Aeons and dying by reason of immersion in the unknowing nature of the inferior creation, the self-knower becomes the motif of many allegories. A well-known example is that of Jonah being thrown overboard and swallowed by the hippocampus or mythological whale. Jonah (the knower) is immersed in the sea of illusion (life) and swallowed by cetus (the leviathan or monster of mortality).

St Augustine explains the allegory differently, declaring the whale to symbolize God who, when the prophet was cast by men into the sea of tribulation, was accepted into the body of God and carried safely to shore. The three days that Jonah remained in the whale's belly, however, links the allegory definitely to the dying-god myth, for according to the Mysteries the rational soul is immersed for three days in the nature of the inferior sphere. Again, the irrational universe (the not-knowing part) is divided into twelve sections which are symbolized by the signs of the zodiac and called the Twelve Holy Animals. These are the twelve parts of unreality. In the Greek Mysteries they are called the Titans or primordial giants who took the body of Bacchus (the rational soul) and tearing it to pieces devoured the flesh. This signifies, in the terms of the Pythagoreans, that the one knower—the real part of every creature and the rational soul of the universe—is destroyed and its integrity dissipated by multitude, represented by the Titans.

Paracelsus calls man a composita, or a being composed of man and beast, a concept symbolized in the Mysteries by the centaur who had the head and shoulders of a man and the body of a horse. Man is twofold: a rational nature rising out of an irrational nature—hence, the mystery of the dying god. The rational soul is the eternal martyr who awaits the day of his liberation, which can only be accomplished when man elevates himself above the level of material impulse. Bacchus torn to pieces by the Titans, Atys gored by the wild boar, Adonis dead at the foot of the pine tree, Orpheus slain by the Ciconian women—all these ancient martyrs represent the rationality of man falling a victim to the inconstancies of his inferior nature. Chiron, the centaur instructor of Achilles, has a different significance however, for here the centaur represents the god-man with its head in the supreme world and its body in Nature. The centaur is therefore one of the demigods overshadowing a highly evolved human soul. The irrational nature of man is well symbolized by the Cretan labyrinth where rules the Minotaur, the bull-headed lord of matter, the creature which most mistake for their own true self. Into this irrational sphere descends Theseus, who prevents himself from being lost in the tortuous passageways by unraveling behind him Ariadne's thread. The rational soul thus slays the beast-man and becomes king of the country of its own life. So much for the exoteric significance of the dying-god allegory.

In the secret teachings it is written that mind itself is the Savior-God. Mind is the martyr of the ages, the eternal and universal Prometheus sacrificed upon the altar of human necessity. Mind is the willing sufferer upon the tree. Mind must destroy itself that that which is greater than mind may endure. According to the Mysteries, there comes that time in the quest of consciousness when man discovers the mind to be the slayer of the Real. Then as he sloughs off his evil nature, he must slough off his mind that his consciousness may be disentangled from the infinite complex of the mental web. The mind is incapable of ascending to the state of consciousness. The mind can never completely annihilate the sense of separateness, for it depends upon comparison for its function and differentiation for its very existence. Consequently, though the mind is ever the link between consciousness and unconsciousness, it too must be ultimately sacrificed in order that the Great Work be accomplished. By the death of the mind consciousness is released to complete perfection, but woe unto him who slays the mind without that understanding which must be given out of the Mysteries.

The mind must not die until its own work has been completed and its function has reached the highest possible degree of perfection. As the mind increases in power and rationality, it grows gradually to realize that there is something beyond thought. The mind is capable of realizing this power but is never able actually to contact it. There is a supermental state which is synonymous to a certain extent with the causal sphere. The Buddhist sees consciousness as a universal sea. Consciousness is therefore something that is moved only by a divine ebb and flow, by a realization of itself. This universal, all-penetrating sea is the true substance of everything, for consciousness (or Self) was before the beginning and consciousness (or Self) is after the end. Beginning and end are illusions, but Self is eternal. Consciousness is therefore union with Self. Consciousness knows no separateness. As long as me and thee exist, consciousness is not perfected. Life and death, good and evil, light and shadow—these are the illusions of mind. But in consciousness diversity is totally annihilated and all things are one in reality and in essence. The bond of brotherhood is proved by the mind to be good, but the realization of brotherhood is not consciousness. The bond of friendship is demonstrated by the intellect to be necessary, but friendship is less than consciousness. There is no consciousness until the / in each is one and indivisible from the / in All. Until we are everything that we in our ignorance believe surrounds us, there is no complete consciousness. We may study the star intellectually, but we have never attained consciousness until we are the star, the stone, the heavens, and the earth. When our consciousness is perfect we extend from the heights of height to the depths of depth; we permeate the whole nature of existence; we are in everything, we are through everything, we are the whole nature of everything.

The difference between intellect and consciousness is therefore the difference between a mental concept of an object and an actual mingling of our consciousness with the consciousness of the object itelf. This latter state is realization. The intellectual concept, however, must to a certain degree precede the consciousness. As the mind is higher than the body, and the body must ultimately accept the thinking organism as its master, so consciousness is higher than mind, and the mind must ultimately give way to it. The mind is a bridge connecting consciousness and unconsciousness, but having crossed the bridge, it is left behind, its usefulness past. As a bridge, however, the mind is a vital necessity, and he who depreciates it is as false as he who permits himself to become the servant of its whims. The Buddhist priest entering into Nirvana, and the Brahman bridging the chasm between mortal consciousness and samadht, both cast aside mind as a snare and a delusion; yet without it the very principles upon which they work would be incomprehensible to them. The Eastern mind, endeavoring to annihilate the unreal and mingle itself with the

Real, depends first upon the intellect to reveal the processes of illumination and the reasonableness of their abstract conceptions. The Western schools of philosophy differ from the Eastern in that they teach the perfection of the mind before its rejection, whereas the Eastern schools are prone to regard the mind as a hindrance, to be discarded at the very beginning of spiritual growth. Thus the Eastern mystic with his own nature slays the mind, while the Western philosopher, by elevating the mind to a realization of its own insufficiency, causes the intellect voluntarily to offer itself as a willing sacrifice upon the altar of spirit.

The ability to feel with rather than for is the essential difference between consciousness and emotion. When we feel for things we are emotionally moved. Pity, sympathy, and kindred feelings stirs, and yet they seldom give any definite impulse that is of value in the adjustment of any chain of circumstances. When we feel with things we are so much a part of them that we understand the innermost elements of their being. Thus understanding comes with consciousness, and knowledge with intellectual comprehension. According to the ancient doctrines, perfect consciousness—the ability to feel with everything as part of everything—was regarded as the ultimate state of so-called human unfoldment, and he who had achieved this had attained to godhood in his own right. The gods are simply emblematic of varying degrees of consciousness in that vast interval between ignorance and realization. At present humanity is semiconscious—conscious over the area of the known and unconscious over the area of the unknown. We have reached a degree of consciousness that enables us to study the exoteric, or outer constitution of things. We will never know the urges, however, that cause the diversified phenomena of existence until we are united with the inner nature that animates the outer body.

Consciousness is gauged, therefore, by our ability to unite ourselves with the soul urges of those creatures that surround us, and true greatness is measured by the power to come en rapport with the causes of objective manifestation. Many centuries ago there was founded in Korea a group of Eastern thinkers of Buddhist persuasion who developed the science of realization to a higher degree than any group since Gautama himself. The story is told that to one of the monasteries of this order in Japan there came a disciple who dedicated his life to the attainment of this inner consciousness. Year after year he struggled to master the illusions of his outer nature and find the infinite and all-pervading self within. His patience

was tireless, his devotion unwavering. Yet the passing years found no apparent improvement in his spiritual condition; he was never able to be one with all the life that surrounded him. After having spent the best part of a lifetime in wandering and meditation without reward, he finally returned to the little monastery, having decided that if he could not attain to consciousness life was useless and he would destroy himself. Just inside the monastery grounds was a tall tower, and climbing to the top the monk cast himself off with a silent hope that his search would end in the peace of death. While in the act of falling, consciousness came to him, and with it the realization that the earth below was so surely a part of himself that it would not injure him when he fell upon it. The result of this realization was that he landed on his feet uninjured after a fall which would have killed the ordinary man. His face radiant with the inner conviction that had come upon him, he rushed to the abbot of the monastery who had been his friend for many years, and bowing before the aged man exclaimed, "At last I know, Master; at last I know!" Seeing the look

of divine understanding upon the face of the mendicant, the abbot smilingly asked, "What do you know?" "I cannot tell you what I know, Master. There are no words, no thoughts that can express it. If you know, you must know as I know.
 I can make no revelation of it to any man." The abbot looked at him for a moment and then replied, "It is evident, my son, that you know. The fact that you cannot tell it is the proof that you possess it. Nothing of which we may speak can transcend the world of illusion, for words themselves were created to describe unrealities. Therefore the unutterable is the real and the un-thinkable is the true; the utterable is the false and the thinkable is the phantom of a dream."

In this renaissance of the metaphysical we hear much of consciousness and understanding and spiritual realization. But one thing is certain and to be depended upon he who possesses con-sciousness will make no effort to reveal it, for the very achievement brings with it a realization of the hopelessness of attempting to communicate the wonders of the Self to a world that knows nothing of the contemplative life. People talk glibly of cosmic consciousness and unity with Ab-solute Being, but their very words belie the fact. A great Buddhist monk was once brought into the presence of the Emperor of China, and the Emperor addressed him thus: "Anwser me, O servant of the enlightened, one question." And the saffron-robed sage replied, "Noble sire, what is your question?" The Son of Heaven answered, "I would know the end of things, the ultimate state." Daruma gazed upon him for a moment with a strange expression of mingled sadness and amusement—amused that any man should dare to ask in words that which no words can explain, sad that anyone should know so little as to ask so much. Finally the sage answered, "O Emperor, bring me a potted plant" A servant brought one in and the monk, looking at it for a second said, "This is a rare porcelain, is it not?" "It is worth a fortune," replied the Emperor. Thereupon the sage dashed the potted plant to the hard floor where it was shattered to bits. Filled with wrath the Emperor cried out, "Foolish one, what have you done ?" "I have answered your question con-cerning the ultimate of things," the sage rejoined. "Words fail, thoughts fail, but in this way I can give you evidence of that which must be evidenced by the self alone." For a time the Emperor was buried in thought, and then shook his head.

"I do not understand," he said. "Alas," replied the sage, "alas, sire, I can do no more!"

During the progress of our lectures we have been asked again and again to describe those spiritual processes by which the mystery of the Self is to be revealed. If those who asked knew or realized the nature of their question they would know that it is unanswerable by mortal man, and that he who even attempts to give an answer thrice proves his unfitness to possess the answer. Many are the paths of Dharma by which the law is revealed, and more than this of the law cannot be said: He who would know and comprehend must learn to think and dream and feel in the rhythm of universal concerns, leaving behind him the pettiness of personal affairs. To achieve to the end of Tao he must exchange the rhythm of the senses for that vast ebb and flow of measureless eter-nity, for only when man ceases to be man is he not man. When he ceases to be a creature; when he ceases to think or to feel or to know; when he ceases to feel his kinship with the earth or the sky; when he is no longer mortal or immortal; when he is neither one with the grain of dust nor with the gods; when all conditions have passed away; when dimension and time have disap-peared; when nothing remains except the all-pervading Universal Self, unthinkable, unknowable, transcendent, and perfect; when the interval between the self and the Self in all has been annihi-lated—when all these things are one and I-am-that-one and yet 1 am not, then the soul has ceased to be a soul and is Self. Nirvana is reached when each finds himself to be all and rests forever in the state of Not-Being, which is All-Being, indivisible and perfect.

In Japan the Tango no Sekku, or Festival of the Boys, is a very important one, and is celebrated annually early in May. Among the important symbols in evidence at this time is the paper flag or kite cut in the shape of a great fish. This banner is hollow and the wind blowing into it causes the carp to become inflated and swim about in the air in a very lifelike manner. The ceremony of flying the carp had its origin in the ancient Chinese legend of the dragon carp, This fish, which swims with great resolution against the current, is considered in the Orient to be a fitting em-blem of the soul of man swimming against the stream of illusion and striving to reach perfection despite the opposition of time and circumstance. The dragon carp, according to the legend, de-sired to swim against the Dragon Gate rapids, and again and again threw its body into the air, only to be beaten back by the strength of the angry current. The gods, beholding the struggle of the carp, marveled at its patience and endurance, for it returned from each new defeat with fresh courage and determination to conquer the rapids. At last, with a supreme effort the carp achieved its end, and when it reached the haven of the placid waters above the rapids, the body of the great fish glowed with a celestial splendor and became the symbol of the accomplishment of perfec-tion. The gods gave the fish the life span of a thousand years, and at the end of this period it was transfigured. Surrounded by streamers of divine radiance, it ascended into the heavens and be-came one of the immortals. In Buddhist symbolism, the achievement of the dragon carp, fittingly symbolizes the attainment of Nirvana. Again and again the human soul seeks to stem the tide of mortal fate. Heedless of wordly ridicule and misunderstanding, the mystic patiently continues his effort to clear the rapids of his own lower nature. At last, passing through the maelstrom of the lower self he finds peace, and being transfigured ascends into the heavens to be united in Nirvana with all creatures and all ages. The difference between the intellectual concept and consciousness lies in certain indescribable realities too deeply imbedded in the nature of Being to permit de-scription. In the East, consciousness is likened to the lotus bud which, gradually opening, reveals more and more of itself to a wondering world until at last the golden heart in all its splendor is disclosed.

Perfect consciousness to man is perfect realization of the nature and relationship of parts to the fundamental unity in which they exist. The ability to understand the actual order of Being, and to see everything correctly, is to be conscious. To see things as they seem to be is to be subject to the illusions of the lower mind.

An example of consciousness may be briefly summed up in the statement that to know the nature of all things is to realize that all things are good. To intellectually achieve this attitude is very sim-ple, for it is only necessary to affirm continually that the thing is good, and after a while the mind, following the line of least resistance, accepts the affirmation as a fact and no longer questions the reality of that good. But there is a vast difference between convincing oneself intellectually of the goodness of things, and becoming really conscious of the goodness of things. Consciousness is not the result of the mind convincing the Self; consciousness is the result of the Self convincing the mind. The mind incarnated in the Christos speaks of consciousness personified in the Father in these words: "The Father is greater than I." Consciousness is greater than mind, which is born out of and is a limited expression of the Supreme Parent.

What then did the Emperor Julian infer when he spoke of the sacred Mysteries of the Seven-Rayed God who lifted souls to salvation through his own nature? Simply this: No more can Reality descend to the level of ignorance than can the lesser of anything contain the greater. If man would grasp the Infinite, it is therefore necessary for him to raise himself to the level of the Infinite, and as he ascends the mystery becomes ever more clear. Universal Mind is the Seven-Rayed Savior-God through which man must ascend from the primitive state of darkened mindlessness to the perfect state of all-knowing mindlessness. Thus mind is indeed the Savior-God who leads the soul to the comprehension of Self. But, as was true of Moses, the Lawgiver of Israel, it is not written that mind shall enter into the Promised Land. Having led the children of Israel (the parts of the inferior nature) through the Wilderness of Sin to the portals of the Gates of Peace, the mind lies down among the bleak hills of Moab, its work accomplished, and rests in the Law. His face illumined by the celestial radiance reflected from the sphere he can never fully understand, mind, the Universal Savior, dies at the gate of Nirvana while the souls he has redeemed pass on to perfection.

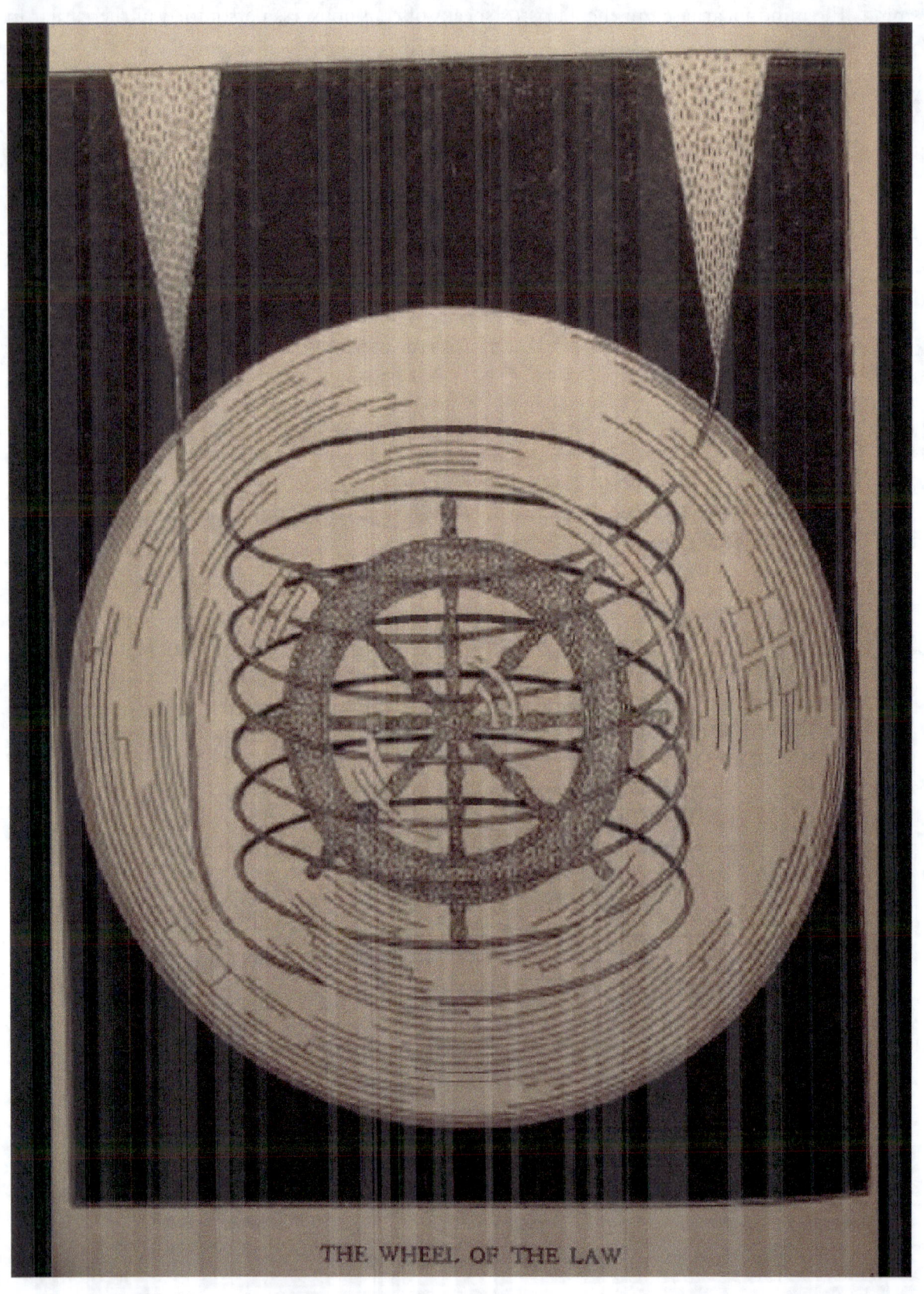

THE WHEEL OF THE LAW

The pathway of the generating soul is here represented by a converging line of force which, piercing the wall of the Auric Egg, descends—as is shown on the left—into the Demiurgic sphere. The soul then begins the ascent of the seven spirals, by which it is ultimately liberated and diffused back again into First Cause, as shown on the right.

# IX

The Mystery of Initiation

During the last few years a great wave of mysticism has swept over the world. The heart of mankind is hungry for greater knowledge, the soul, yearning for fuller understanding, has sought to tear away the veil which forever drapes the figure of Wisdom. Man has sought to learn those mystic truths so long lost to the world, and in his study and search he has found that there are strange and mysterious beings known to the world as Initiates.

Among the ancient works and the mystery schools of those peoples now dead, strange ceremonies called initiations were given in some mysterious way, and the popular mind has come to believe that there is a mystic rite—an initiatory ceremonial—which makes man one with the immortals. And in the name of this wonderful and mystic concept, terrible crimes have been committed against the spiritual and occult teachings.

There is probably no word in the English language that has been so abused, so misused, so often used, and so little understood as the word "Initiation." Every dream, every phantom form, every unusual happening, has been called the initiation, and all over the world temples have sprung up in the name of the mystery schools to initiate candidates into the Wisdom teachings—some of them without cost, but in the majority of cases, a heavy fee accompanies the initiation, in which, for say $25.00, the candidate is dubbed "Sir Somebody" or made a leading luminary in some mystic shrine.

The result of this perversion is that the sacredness, the beauty, and the true realization of the meaning of initiation has been lost to the world, for it is very true that there are none who can so damage a religion or an idea as those who claim to be its followers. How long it will take the world to learn that initiations are not ceremonials, it is difficult to say, but sometime each individual must realize that swinging robes and incense burners and other trimmings do not constitute initiation, and that no one on the face of the earth could buy it for the fortune of Croesus, nor in any way receive it until he himself, by his life, has become worthy of its mystic blessing.

There are few in this world who know what real initiation is, and there are fewer still who, having discovered it, really want to so live that this mystic rite may be unfolded within their souls. The true initiate is a very wondrous and mysterious being, and any words that we can say concerning such a one are very poor indeed. Those who have not already walked the path can have but a feeble idea of what an initiate really is, for such a one has unfolded within himself or herself, as the case may be, certain principles of which the average layman knows nothing.

The powers of life and death, the powers of destruction and construction, the mystic principles of integration and disintegration—all these are in the hands of the Great Ones of God. The knowledge of life is the mystic power of the Initiate, for only those who have walked the ways of many can ever know what the laurels of initiation mean.

Only when his heart is filled with love for humanity and with the great suffering and great peace of those who know, can he so express the powers within himself that he is of use in so great a plan. The Initiate has the mindless mind of Spirit, which thinks only the thoughts of life, to the source of which he each day draws nearer; he is filled with the understanding of nature's plan for her children, and only this knowledge holds in check a heart that would otherwise break with sorrow.

He knows that strange, sweet melancholy—that mystic feeling few have ever realized—such as must have filled the soul of Jesus as He wept o'er Jerusalem.

The true initiate is initiated by God and not by man, and he will give his life, his soul, his very being, to lift the suffering in the name of the Father. It is only those who have a heart great enough to enfold all creation, a consciousness.

# X

The Inferior Creation and its Regent

IN THE Platonic system of philosophy the dot is called the *One . The early mystics held that Being should be considered the first, in that One is a being. Plato, however, maintained that the One is All-Being, because being is a condition of the One and consequently dependent upon it. The fallacy of terms is again apparent. Being in this sense has no connection with the thought of to be or exist, but signifies that which is without existence in that it has neither a positive nor a negative state, Thus while Plato assails the term, he still maintains in his philosophic writings the existence of a universal state preceding the One but denies that this universal state should be called Being, intimating that it should always be assumed by the mind but no effort ever made to denominate it. The moment denomination is given, this abstract quality becomes the One, in that definition cannot possibly be applied to the Absolute, the One being the highest definable state. The line out of the dot, or the One, is called the Beautiful : the circle, or radius of the line, the Good. In this manner is established the great Platonic triad: the One, the Beautiful, and the Good. The Pythagoreans conceived the number 1 to be before all numbers. It is called the capstone of the pyramid of numbers.

All other numbers are simply aggregations of l's. Two is two Ts; three, three l's; a million, a million l's. Remove the 1 and you destroy all numbers. Therefore it is the first and has absolute priority. The power and dignity of the number 1 are expressed in permanence, stability, immovability. In philosophy beauty is a form of motion or emotion. The Beautiful is an eternal flow; it is the One in motion. The Good, which is the third and lowest aspect, contains or accepts into itself the nature of the Beautiful; it is the manifestation of the Beautiful in the sphere of creation. For example, he who has the Beautiful within his own soul radiates the Good and is called the Good. It may be said that to be beautiful is good; also that to be good is beautiful. Consquently that is good which contains beauty. From this Platonic definition it is apparent why the Savior- Gods of all nations have been symbolized as Beautiful. Aesthetically considered, Beauty is the redeeming power. When the human soul opens itself to the reception of Beauty it is then transmuted. Beauty is a force into the presence of which none can come and remain unmoved. Beauty is an internal force symbolic of supersubstantial harmony manifesting through goodness. In its final analysis Good is symmetry, or the harmonious coordination of parts. In other words, that is good in which the parts work together. That individual is good in whom the natural forces function naturally. It also follows that a symmetry of parts is harmonious and harmony of parts produces a concord which is termed beautiful. According to the ancients, the world is the receptacle for the Beautiful, which in turn manifests the all-knowing of the One. This lecture is to be devoted to a consideration of the world that is called Good, and how, through the continual Adversary, it ultimately effects the perfection and liberation of the rational nature. The world is a form, and forms arc molded from matter.

Matter ranges from an unrecognizable state of crystallization to an unrecognizable state of vitalization, both extremes alike intangible because of the inability of our sense perceptions to cognize any ultimate. Form exists not only in things that can be seen but in such as can be perceived through the senses of hearing, touch, taste, and smell. Form therefore is not merely a physical body that can be seen; it may be a subtle emanation as light or sound. A word cannot be seen and yet a word is a form. Under certain conditions drug addicts can see words coming out of people's mouths, their supersensitiveness being the result of a low form of drug-invoked psychism. A thought is not visible nor can it be held between the fingers, and yet a thought is as truly a form as is a piece of stone. The inferior universe therefore includes every conceivable state or condition of form. Form is the inferior nature of everything manifesting being. Form includes not only every part of the universe from the mental level downward but, ultimately, up through the higher spiritual spheres; in fact every plane upon which differentiation exists. But the planes of consciousness above that of thought, and the entities dwelling therein, have a term other than form applied to them. The circle, or circumference, is therefore the symbol of feelings, thoughts, and bodies in all their infinite ramifications.

The ancients symbolized form and the laws controlling the organization of matter into bodies by a reaping skeleton, the emblem of death. Form has ever been regarded as the parent of ignorance. Throughout the inferior creation consciousness lies buried in form. Form is the confusing, resisting, limiting, inhibiting, and imprisoning part of existence. Nothing in whose nature even a trace of form remains is capable of absolute consciousness. Form is the graveyard of consciousness. Since all life is thus inhibited by form, no creature controlled by the form part is rational. Philosophically speaking, absolute form—that is, the ultimate degree of form—is ultimate negation, because it is the absence of all that is necessary to the greatest good. In its most enmeshed state life is at its lowest ebb. Therefore, in philosophy form is termed the Eternal Adversary. In Egypt form was called Typhon, and as a symbol of his disrepute he was pictured with the head of a crocodile and the body of a hog— sometimes the wings of a bat were added. Form is always the destroyer. In India form is known as Shiva, or Rudra, the lord of destruction, or rather, the principle behind the form is so defined. In the realm of philosophy form is one of the unsolved problems of the ages, for it is in reality simply an inferior life inhibiting the manifestation of a superior life. In this sea of confusing form elements men live and move and have their being, and out of the ever-changing substances of form all mortal creatures build their bodies, which are thus destined to return to the elemental spheres from which they were derived.

The universe of matter that extends throughout the infinite vistas of unmeasured space and includes within itself the heavenly bodies functioning through space and bearing with them an indescribable diversity of flora and fauna, is all part of what the ancients termed the underworld.

Even the apparent vacuum in which these mighty bodies exist, and the host of invisible agencies that order sidereal dynamics, form part of a vast but inferior creation manifesting through the realm of form. This world of form—suns, moons, and stars—is called hades, or the land of death. It is the world of darkness. It is called dark because in it the light of spirit is swallowed up and creatures move in the haze of uncertainty. Darkness, however, does not imply evil, but simply the lack of light. In the sphere of form all creatures lack the full brilliance of consciousness or awareness. In this dark world, which is the circumference of the circle of existence, man is at his greatest degree of separateness from spiritual Source, and the sphere in which he functions is the lowest degree of divine agency. All through mythology the gods of light and life fight the demons of darkness and death. In the Babylonian mythology Merodach slays the dragon, and in the Christianized version of the myth St. George is the hero. The dragon of matter, a foul, flame-breathing monster, must be slain by Siegfried in order that the treasure of the Nibelung may be recovered. Every creature struggles against the inertia of its immediate personal environment, Inertia is the characteristic attribute of form. It must be realized that this is inertia in a relative sense, for if matter be reduced to its ultimate it will be found to consist of life particles vibrating at incredible rates of speed. In comparison to the consciousness of man, however, matter is unconscious; in comparison to the active principles of the universe, matter is negative. On the other hand, in comparison to orders of life undoubtedly existing, but unknown to us, matter may very well be considered positive. Matter, or form, simply represents the unconquered environment that surrounds every life struggling for existence. As the world of life and consciousness represents the spiritual nature of Deity, so the vast ocean of matter, continually changing and manifesting an infinitude of forms, is the inferior part or body of Deity. As all creatures are made in the image of their Universal Creator, it follows that each has a spiritual nature which is part of and harmonious with the spiritual nature of the universe, and also a material nature which is part of and harmonious with the cosmic body. When the emphasis of the life is upon its spiritual part we term the individual idealistic, but when the emphasis is upon the material part we term him materialistic. Character is determined by the plane of his own nature upon which the emphasis of the individual's life is placed. Every human being has moments when he rises above his own level; also moments when he sinks below that level. This level may be termed in music the keynote of the individual, with the sharp as its higher and the flat as its lower phase. In Chaldean philosophy there is the wonderful legend of Ishtar and Tammuz. The story deals particularly with the descent of Ishtar through the seven worlds into hades, the inferior sphere. The allegory simply signifies the incarnation of the rational soul in the substances of the irrational world. The irrational world is divided into seven strata by the rings of the planets upon which sit, according to the Mysteries, the Seven Governors of the World, each of whom bestows upon the incarnating soul one of the seven limitations of matter called veils by Hermes. However, in the myth of Ishtar, instead of the soul being veiled or having certain adornments given to it, the allegory sets forth the limitation of spiritual power through the removal of certain divine attributes. These attributes signify the functioning of certain spiritual forces, which functioning is rendered impossible by the involvements of the soul in matter. The spiritual properties of the rational self are symbolized by a crown, jewels, breast and body adornments, and sandals. As Ishtar descends through the seven gates of the seven Governors, each takes from her one of her spiritual qualities until, deprived of all the evidence of her royal birth (spiritual origin), she arrives in the "house of no return," the dark and gloomy precincts of death.

Each human soul entering into mortal incarnation has thus been robbed, by the seven worlds of matter, of the manifesting proofs of its divinity until, helpless and impotent, the all-knowing spiritual man appears in the physical world as a wide-eyed babe incapable even of self-preservation. Thus the immortal assumes the dream of mortality, and clouded by the veils of the seven planets takes up the humdrum of mortal existence, all oblivious to the godhood within. Robbed of her adornments, Ishtar must patiently accept the infirmities heaped upon her by the irate goddess of death. After many tribulations Ishtar is at last rescued from her infernal prison through the intercession of the deities, and ascending once more through the heavenly gates receives back the symbols of her royal rank and dignity. Then, speeding her wings, she soars upward to the spheres of light Philosophically considered, the descent of the rational nature of man into its irrational body is involution ; the resurrection of the rational nature from this condition of immersion, evolution. The physical universe is the sphere of ignorance where each creature is at its worst in that it has forgotten the best within itself. So thick and numerous are the veils of the rings that the light of spirit is obscured until but a dim haze bears witness of its effulgence.

It naturally follows that accomplishment in the physical world is the greatest of all accomplishments, for it is under the most difficult of all situations. Here is a key to the story of the prodigal son, who represents the incarnating soul. The pigsty where he must eat and sleep with the hogs represents one ancient patriarch's concept of the physical universe. When at last the prodigal, having repented of his iniquities and having seen the folly of material existence, returned to the house of his Father (the light-world), the fatted calf was killed in his honor, for his accomplishment was great. Jealous of the attention bestowed upon the improvident youth, the elder brother made his dissatisfaction known to his Father, who replied that there was ample cause for rejoicing in that the lost had been found and the dead lived again.

The story carries the same thought permeating Egyptian philosophy: namely, that life in the mortal sphere without a realization of the Divine Plan is the true death; that resurrect don from this state is the most desired of all attainments. Yet to rise victorious from the dark world of hopeless involvement is an accomplishment so noble that it elevates the conquering soul to a dignity exceeding that of the angels who are never confronted with this problem.

The stupefying effect of matter (rather its organizations into form) is appropriately symbolized by cold. Those of you who have been out when it was sixty degrees below zero know what it means when the mercury freezes and the air is filled with a continuous crackling sound. Huge logs split from end to end with a sound like the report of a great gun, and even the nails seem to ooze out of the wood. It is hard to fight cold because it discourages the effort to resist its influence. Over the nature gradually comes a feeling of comfort and peace accompanied by an overwhelming desire to rest. No prospect seems so pleasant as to go to sleep in the snow; no effort seems so unnecessary as to fight against the innate urge to drift off into the sleep of death. Cold fights you by taking away your desire to resist. This is the most insidious of all foes, and is comparable to the way in which form destroys spiritual initiative.

Materiality does not attack the body or the conscious functioning of the mind; it assails the will power and destroys the morale. As long as there is the desire to fight ignorance and degeneracy, as long as there is the inner urge to resist evil and the illusions of matter, it is possible to attain liberation with reasonable effort. Form, however, fights in an underhanded way by taking away the desire to master its elements, and substituting therefore the lethargy of indifference which prefers to leave things just as they are and go along with the rest of the world, enjoying its momentary pleasures and suffering as resolutely as possible the concurrent ills of life. When the material urge of physical environment has so benumbed the inner nature that every spiritual aspiration is anesthetized, the individual is reduced to the level of that mediocre throng who are content to struggle along in the age-old ruts. Such have hypnotized themselves into the false belief that existing conditions are inevitable and unchangeable.

When the desire to do right for the sake of right is smothered by matter, there is left but one power capable of dealing with the problem of inertia: namely, pain, either mental, physical or emotional. Through suffering, the insufficiency of material accomplishments is demonstrated. The desire to do good for the sake of good is an urge far too subtle to survive the stifling influence of matter. Hence to counteract man's incessant effort to forget his own spiritual needs is his continual proclivity to hurt himself. Man's effort to control his own life without intelligence invariably demonstrates its futility. He strives to live without the help of consciousness, with the result that he exists in pain and tribulation. Because of his suffering he acquires a great incentive toward knowledge for its own sake in order to save himself from the pain resulting from ignorance. Thus the law of self-preservation is ever forcing the way. ward feet back into the path that leads to light. Physical suffering first led man to ponder the mysteries of his own being. In the last analysis, however, the pain of the body is the least poignant. Then came emotional suffering—the pain in the heart- much more desperate and difficult to endure. Lastly came mental suffering, in which the entire constitution is torn and racked by that gargantuan conflict when the faculties of the mind hurl thought missiles at each other. Looking at the average individual, we see a consciousness that is impotent in the grasp of form which, like cold, has benumbed its sensibilities. Cold is the proper symbol of the circumference of the sphere of Being.

The word hell, derived from the Scandinavian hel, means cold, though its has long been associated with its opposite term, heat. This discloses a certain consistent inconsistency characteristic of the works of man. Some missionaries visiting the Far North described in "glowing" terms the sulphurous nature of hell. As a result the Eskimos were immediately interested, for the underworld was thereby made particularly inviting to a race that found extreme difficulty in keeping heat in their chilled organisms. Obviously, any intimate description of hell depends for its effectiveness upon the equation of longitude and latitude. Just as life, light, and heat are associated with the quality of expansion, since the natural impulse of life is to expand, so death, darkness, and cold are related to the quality of contraction, since the natural impulse of death is to contract.

Realizing (according to the ancient Mysteries) that the physical universe was the sphere of death and that there was no death so real as immersion in form, let us now consider the nature and structure of this great dark sphere as it was taught to the philosophers of ancient days, and is still preserved among those groups who are perpetuating the Ancient Wisdom. The material universe considered as a unit is the body of the Lord of Form or the Master of the World. This World Lord, whose consciousness is of the nature of mind, is the Jehovah or IHVH of the Jews, the Zeus of the Greeks, and the Jupiter of the Romans. In the philosophy of the Gnostics and the Neo* platonists he was called the Demiurgus. The original interpretation of this word is difficult to ascertain, but it may be rendered in its philosophic sense as the false urge. The Demiurgus is therefore to be defined as the composite material universe considered as a personal being or power.

The emanations from this Lord are called his powers, and are sometimes referred to as the princes of the world. You will remember that Jesus warned his disciples that the princes of this world would never understand him, and that they had nothing in common with him. The princes of the world arc the divisions of the forces controlling the form universe, these forces being considered as gods. Philosophically, the Lord of the World is the great autocrat, for autonomy is a principle nonexistent in the universal sense. This despot, who is conceived as using the earth for his footstool and the heavens for his throne, is presumed to control his universe through the inexorable justice of law, which because of man's ignorance breeds fear, hate, and death. When you think of the philosophic trinity, remember that the third person of this triad is the Lord of the World, called the Heartless One because he is the slave- driver of the Cycle of Necessity. He is the terrible ogre or giant of hate, so-called, who grinds our bones to make his bread. The ancients were divided in their opinions concerning the real nature of the Demiurgus. Some affirmed him to be a devil because he is an agency that is ever destroying, but does he not wreak destruction in order that reconstruction may follow upon a higher level of manifestation? He is the Lord of Death because he controls birth and death, for these phenomena exist nowhere except in the world of forms. Again, some have attributed to him the diabolical genius of a madman who created a nightmare universe where everything is as it should not be. He is the power that binds man to the world of illusion, and in the terms of the early Church Fathers is the enemy of the eternal God (Good).

Paraphrasing, however, the statements of Omar, the question may be asked: If he be evil, who placed him there? In Faust, Mephistopheles—the agent of the Demiurgus—is made to say, "I am the spirit of negation, part of the power that still works for good while ever scheming ill." Accordingly, the second group of ancient philosophers declared the Demiurgus to be ever adding to the glory of God by demonstrating the insufficiency of the form-world. He is therefore not the enemy of good but the eternal contrast to good necessary that man may realize the perfection of right. Who would know or appreciate good if he had not experienced the lack of it? The Lord of the World is therefore the master who whips man until, unable longer to bear the lashes of unkind destiny, the sufferer revolts against his own insufficiency and thus is directed into the way of light. In antiquity the Lord of the World was well symbolized as the master of the whip and the wielder of the flail.

The Egyptian Pharaohs carried three scepters symbolic of their authority from the Demiurgus: The Anubis-hcaded staff, symbolic of the sagacity of the World Lord; the shepherd's crook, symbolic of the priesthood and the authority of the World Lord over the souls of men; and the flail, symbolic of the mastery which the Demiurgus exercises over the bodies of all creatures.

Returning to our primitive symbolism, the Anubis-hcaded staff is symbolized by the dot, the shepherd's crook by the line, and the flail by the circle. These are representative respectivel of rulership through wisdom, rulership through faith, and ruler- ship through force. Thus the dot is now termed government. It was once the crown, but now so large a part of government is administered by the people that the crown can only be used in its abstract sense. The dot, however, signifies government by the state. The line is the tiara, or government by the church, and the circumference is the people who are the beneficiaries of government. Thus we find three tremendous forces continually focussed upon the objective life of man, and the perversion of these forces constitutes the threefold fountain-head of evil as opposed to the threefold fountain-head of light. Through the perversion of government we have ignorance; through the perversion of the church, superstition; and through the perversion of the people, fear. Thus come into existence the great Masonic trio of evils: ignorance, superstition, and fear, the murderers of human liberty and the destroyers of understanding.

Although we conceive ourselves to exist in a world amply lighted physically by the sun, and adequately illumined mentally and ethically by philosophy, religion, and science, we actually dwell in a sphere as dark as Egypt's night. There is but one true light in the universe: namely, the light of understanding, a trait in which humanity is woefully deficient. The presence of hope, belief, and fear is definite proof that the world lacks knowledge and adequate spiritual perceptions.

The darkness of this underworld is so dense that we cannot perceive the hearts of our fellowmen. We cannot sense the motives that inspire our neighbor to action, nor can we pierce the surrounding gloom and see that which lies but a few steps ahead. While humanity sojourns in this underworld of mortal light and spiritual darkness, it is actually passing through an embryonic state. Within the womb of matter fetal man is being prepared for birth into the greater universe of divine realities. The physical universe may therefore be termed the antechamber of Cosmos, the little room with the hole in the floor referred to in the Mysteries. As infant man must be carried for the nine months of the prenatal epoch before his organisms are able to bear exposure to external conditions, so the world must carry within the darkness of its own nature for nine philosophic months that mortal who is to be born into life and unfoldment through the substance of higher spheres. In ancient philosophy this physical universe is referred to as a great egg wherein all manners of creatures are passing through prenatal epochs. People have the mistaken idea that when they come into physical existence they are born. In their egotism they have forgotten that all mortal things are embryo gods who cannot achieve to Divinity until they have transcended every vestige of mortality. Every living thing is an embryo. In some previous embryonic state we lost our gills and caudal appendage. The webs of our fingers and toes were also cut, and our tongues loosened, but even with these evidences of progress we come into this world imperfect and incomplete; or, as the theologian would say, "we are conceived in sin and born in iniquity." This statement has no reference to indiscretions of our ancestors but to the philosophic fact that the mortal universe, when compared to the transcendency of the higher worlds, is a sphere of sin and death. By physical birth we have merely exchanged the amniotic fluids of the womb for the somewhat less dense atmospheric fluids of the world. We are still bound to the earth by an umbilical cord of sense, interest, and desire, and not until through the development of our discerning faculties we acquire the power to sever this bondage to the inferior nature can it be said that we are really born.

This great egg surrounding the material sphere has for its inner surface that canopy of the heavens which man vainly seeks to explore with high-powered telescopes. With each improvement in equipment he is enabled to penetrate a little farther into the blue haze of SPACE. He always reaches a point, however, where vision fails and impenetrable SPACE goes on. The moment man arrives at the limit of his own faculties, he reaches the walls of a hypothetical sphere that hem him in and isolate him from the rest of Being.

The Hermetist likened the physical universe to a glass globe in which were contained numberless vapors and seething forces. As the agonies of chemical change may be viewed through the walls of the test tube, so, like the Bunsen burner, that mysterious power called cosmic urge unceasingly agitates the chemicals contained within the globe of physical existence. While enclosed within this impenetrable shell man cannot conceive of a universe beyond; of a state nobler or more enduring than his present state.

Life is thus composed of a host of creatures, seemingly like atoms in SPACE whirling round and round forever within this crystalline shell of the Universal Egg. At last, however, comes the great day, "Be With Us," when the Egg of the Universe is broken and the substances therein imprisoned flow back once more into their first and primitive Absoluteness.

Thus, floating upon the face of Absolute Being is a finite globe destined to remain for a little while. This globe is the vast material universe of countless worlds and suns which overwhelms us with its immensity but which, when compared with the absolute limitlessness of SPACE, is of pigmy proportions. Though but an atom within the tortured body of this globe, humanity cherishes its dream of existence, striving with the feeble fingers of its mind to grasp the threads of Universal Wisdom by which the globe is held suspended from its unknown source.

Although this globe filled with the contents of material existence is being hurled through space to ultimate destruction, the secret philosophy of the ancients taught that it was possible for the individual to free himself from the swirling mass and by right of his own divinity break through the shell of the World Egg and thereby achieve individual liberation. Upon this hypothesis nearly all the Mysteries of antiquity were established, a notable exception being the Jewish which taught that there was no liberation for one apart from all. Alchemy offers an excellent symbolic description of the processes of spiritual liberation. At this point it is apropos to consider the philosophical definition of the word spirit . This has nothing in common with its accepted theological meaning. In philosophy spirit is not the divine part of every nature considered as an individuality, but rather this divine part considered as one undivided causal nature permeating all life. In the Buddhist philosophy spirit and soul are considered part of the illusion of matter in the sense that an individual who speaks of his spirit or his soul speaks without realization of the fact that there is but one spirit in the universe and all so-called divisions of it are purely hypothetical. Hence, though there may be an infinity of bodies existing in the sphere of maya there is but one consciousness, which the Oriental mystic pleases to term the Self . Of not-selves there are myriads; of Self, but ope.

To think of spirit as divided into a host of individual units, each embodied in a separate form, is to think in terms of error. To the mystic the idea of the growth of his own spirit apart from the growth of the spirit of all is inconceivable. That which grows to the point where it bursts through the Egg of Existence is consequently not the spirit but what the Greeks termed the rational soul, or the mental power, which represents the highest form of individuality. It therefore follows that it is as impossible for one individual to have a spirit more highly evolved than another as for one area of the sea to be wetter than another. The degree of development is thus measured first by the extent to which the parts of the lower nature have been synchronized, and secondly by the interval of quality between them and their spiritual cause. No one has a consciousness higher than another, for there is but one consciousness in the universe. He who is presumed to have a higher consciousness is simply one whose organisms are fine enough to manifest more completely the potentialities of this single consciousness. Mankind may be considered as a vast organism with one Spirit or Self manifesting through an infinite number of intellectual and physical organisms, the latter deluded into the belief that they are free and independent. On a still higher level this composite Spirit of all mankind, which is merely an expression of the Universal Spirit of all things, is deluded, in turn, by the concept that mankind is different and separate from the rest of Universal Being. Such terms as old and young, highly evolved and less evolved, spiritual and material, should be applied only to personalities and individualities, for in the sphere of consciousness they do not exist. As the Absolute is ageless, being all age, no part can technically be older than another. Hence difference is an illusion of the mind, but necessary however to the present evolution of life, yet without foundation in Divine Reality.

To return to alchemy, Self or Spirit is the universal gold, the king of the metals. Gold exists in every element of the universe; even the sunlight and the atmosphere contain minute quantities of this precious metal. The base substances surrounding this universal or spiritual gold, are referred to as the lesser metals. The purpose of alchemical experimentation was to germinate that seed of universal gold, which when properly nurtured would take unto itself and tincture the base metals, absorbing them all into its own glory. Ultimately Self, the only enduring state, thus absorbs into its own Being all the phases of the not-self. Touching them with its transmuting power it causes them to become one with its own effulgence.

According to the Greek terminology the gold is the rational soul, and the transmutation process that of distilling the golden elixir from the base substances of ignorance and perversion.

When you have gathered your proper elements, says the alchemist, you place them in a retort and hermetically seal it.

You then begin the cycles of distillation, causing the chemicals to pass through an orderly sequence of increasing intensity until finally a point is reached where the elixir thus distilled seeps through the glass without injuring it and passes off like a hot oil, there being no container in the world sufficiendy strong to hold it. The allegory is evident. The hermetically sealed vessel is the lower world, the way in and out stopped by the mysteries of birth and death. The chemicals are the heterogeneous mass of created things thrown together in a mysterious fashion.

The cycles of distillation are the processes of evolution, so-called, by which the life is given ever fuller expression through regenerated vehicles and gradually released from irrationality. When the cycles of intensification have reached a certain stage, those beings who have attained to this point can no longer be held within the globe of the inferior creation, and the soul seeps through the wall of the Egg of Existence or, as the Buddhist might say, enters Nirvana. This is the rebirth out of the Womb of Necessity; this is the time when man releases himself from the bonds that bind him to the Wheel of Birth and Death. He who has attained this end is rightly termed no longer a man but the Philosophers Stone.

According to the concept of mystical philosophy, every individual passes through two births and two deaths. At the time of the first, or lesser birth, man is born into the irrational sphere where he becomes an objective manifesting creature but loses contact with the subjective spiritual spheres. Technically, therefore, this birth into the outer universe results in the death of the higher self which must remain asleep in the tomb of material organisms until the Great Day of Liberation. The second birth is, in reality, the death of the lower nature.

When it occurs the rational part reawakens, and rising triumphant from its rational sheath, mingles itself with the victorious and illumined Aeons. At the first birth the self dies out of Eternity and enters into the illusion of Time; at the second birth, the self ascends out of the illusion of Time and diffuses its being throughout the substances of Eternity. Everything that is born into material existence passes from a greater to a lesser state. After the elementary birth, which is the immersion of the rational soul into the irrational universe, the soul enters upon what is called the Cycle of Necessity. The Cycle of Necessity is simply the Wheel of Births and Deaths. During this cycle the temporarily individualized soul passes from one condition of unreality to another. The intervals between these conditions are the lesser births and deaths which take place within the World Egg. There is first the birth into the great egg, then the cycles of birth and death within the egg (referred to as reincarnation or metempsychosis), and finally the philosophic death out of the irrational nature forever. At the time of the philosophic death, which is also the second birth, the soul escapes from matter forever, and having pierced through the hypothetical wall of existence returns to the ever-enduring state of the Absolute.

By way of degression, let us consider a little more in detail the subject of reincarnation. There is a popular misconception concerning the continuity of identity throughout the cycle of incarnations. People are heard to say, "I wish I knew who I was in my last incarnation," or "I think I must have been a Hindu in my last life." According to the most profound systems of thought, the so-called personalities which come forth out of the "Silent Watcher" are all pendent from this single cause but are not directly related to each other. Among the potentialities of the self is the power of projecting a host of individualities into temporary existence. After existing their appointed span, these individualities are reabsorbed into the Self from whose essences they were originally differentiated.

Thus the spiritual causal nature of man is capable of objectifying periodically a chain of personalities, each a separate and individual creation endowed with separate and individual faculties. For example, John Doe is a personality, being objectified from an impersonal and transcendental nature, itself neither personal nor individual. When John Doe has finished the span of his physical existence, he is absorbed back into his own spiritual causal nature, which is not John Doe nor does it know John Doe, but which is an all-pervading superphysical life.

When John Doe has been returned to this universal state, he simply ceases to exist. He will never reincarnate again, nor will his characteristics and traits be perpetuated. The universe will never again know of John Doe. After a period of inaction, however, the spiritual causal nature which gave John Doe being will create a new personality. This personality will neither remember John Doe nor associate its life in any way with that of John Doe, and yet certain qualities will be manifested in the new personality which could not have come into expression had they not passed through certain definite stages of growth while in the personality of John Doe. Therefore, the incarnating individuality of one incarnation never incarnates again, but out of the spiritual origin in which this incarnating life was individualized new individualized lives will be formed which will come into manifestation, and then in turn vanish. Thus the Self gives birth to an infinite number of personalities, but it is the Self—not the personalities—that endures. This Self does not actually incarnate or reincarnate, but from itself it individualizes incarnating organisms.

Consider for a moment the diagram at the beginning of this chapter. The large circle represents the Egg of Existence—the cosmic sphere, or aura, of the Demiurgus,—whose outer circumference is termed the "Ring Pass Not," or the extremity of manifestation. The line descending and piercing the wall of the great Egg is consciousness emerging from the Self and merging into the substances of the Egg. The point where the descending line breaks the wall of the circle and enters into the limitation of existence is the first birth—the true philosophic death,—for the Egg is the sepulcher in which consciousness is buried. Having penetrated the wall of the Egg, the line of consciousness begins the spiral path of the Wheel of Necessity.

This spiral path is made up of lives and deaths, which are termed incarnations. At last, having through philosophy learned of the true mystery of existence, the consciousness breaks through the wall in the second death, or philosophic birth, and reascends to the sphere of Universal Consciousness which is its true dwelling place. It will thus be seen that while the Buddhist theory differs in minor details from the philosophic atheism of the Greeks, its essential nature is the same. In Buddhism (which, as you know, considers Deity only in the form of Self, or Absolute Existence, and has no concept of a personal God) reincarnations occur within the lower spheres of the Egg of Being, those spheres being considered as the ground wherein is set up the Wheel of Necessity. Accordingly, one great Buddhist philosopher is declared to have said: "Of births and deaths there are a countless number, but one Great Death and one Great Birth is the measure of accomplishment." Thus are differentiated the greater and the lesser cycles.

By divine prerogative, by the impulses controlled by law— which is the habit of SPACE—life is periodically immersed in creation, where it continues its spiral progress in the smaller cycle until finally it escapes through the wall of being and finds perfection in its own source. Thus we have physical existence contrasted with divine existence. The physical birth and death of man is a minor mystery. As sleep is a little death, so birth and death are miniature cycles of existence, but the Great Death and the Great Birth are the supreme cycle of existence and the grand mystery of life. Although its physical nature is alone susceptible of analysis, there is within each so-called material creature a spiritual, or superphysical, part. Whether we term it spirit, soul, higher mind, or consciousness it is that something within the shell of matter which is superior to and must eventually become master of the irrational universe. The only reason that this higher part is confined within the lower world is that man as an individual neither appreciates this inner strength nor understands how to directionalize it in order that it may achieve liberation and carry with it to perfection the lesser parts which are under its domination. The rational soul, or spiritual life of man, has a higher origin, and is predestined to attain a far more noble end than is appreciable to the mortal mind with its limited comprehension. Now comes a legitimate question: "Just how can man escape from the crystal ball of matter with its limiting materializing agencies and return to the Dawn Land from which he originally came?"

Liberation is to be attained most simply (according to the Eastern school) through the projection of consciousness. We have already intimated that man lives upon the level of his thoughts; the universe that is real to him is simply that world with which his thinking has attuned him. When man causes his consciousness to accept the reality of the illusionary universe, he is swallowed up in the illusions he has thus affirmed. The moment consciousness rises above the level of illusion man is freed from its limiting influences.

Man is composed of three major parts: a divine part which may be correlated to the dot of primitive symbolism; a superhuman part correlated to the line; and a human or natural part correlated to the circle. When he lives upon the level of the physical plane and is controlled by his physical propensities, man is necessarily cn rapport with the physical universe and subject to the inconsistencies and incongruities of matter. When he lifts his consciousness above material things and lives in the world of his higher mind, man then dwells in the intellectual sphere. This is a much broader vista but still is limited to certain fallacies of thinking, for even the higher mind with its magnificent grasp of the problems of lower existence is necessarily imperfect and to a great degree immersed in the maya of physical existence. When ultimately he lifts his consciousness above mind and thought to spiritual realization, man then lifts his entire nature from the intellectual to the spiritual world. The consummation of this elevation is the goal of human effort, and here and there among the elect of the earth one, like the great Buddha, achieves to perfect realization and absolute liberation. The path of liberation, however, is too difficult for the majority to travel, for few will give up the lesser self with its likes and dislikes in exchange for an abstract Reality which has neither desire nor feeling but which dwells in unbroken contemplation throughout eternity.

The world in which we live is simply the sphere wherein we have centered our activities. The higher our ideals, the higher are our activities, and consequently the higher is our world. Selfishness is the key to the inferno, for the inferno, or inferior universe, is ruled by selfishness. The physical world is that sphere controlled and directionalized by selfish urges, and every soul that is selfish is bound to the physical universe. Qualities within us bind us to forces outside which are like those qualities. As long as selfishness endures within our own souls it holds us to the sphere of selfishness without. As we transmute qualities within our own natures we ascend into new worlds of corresponding consciousness outside.

Man is held by his materiality to the material sphere, by his intellectuality to the intellectual sphere, by his ideality to the ideal sphere. But regardless of his own viewpoints or activities, man is eternally bound by his innate Reality to the Absolute, which is the fullness of Reality. When he has extricated himself from the instincts and impulses of materiality, man is philosophically free from the material world. When the intellect within him is transmuted into idealism, man passes from the world of thought to that supermental sphere for which there is no adequate name. The philosophic ascension of the soul is simply the process of raising motives and activities to ever higher levels of idealism.

Having lifted his mind to the contemplation of cosmic realities, the philosopher is no longer moved by the considerations of immature materialistic intellects. Having mastered material ambition, the philosopher is incapable of stooping to the petty accomplishments of physically-minded people. Having lifted himself out of the physical life, he no longer lives to

gratify the whims of his physical nature. The true philosopher is free from material bondage because he ceases to desire material power or material possession. Incapable of desire, he is incapable of the sense of loss; having outgrown unimportant things, he is not disappointed if he does not possess them. He has learned with the Buddha that possession is a curse, desire a snare, and selfishness an illusion. Of such a sage it may be said that he has climbed up from the valleys of worldliness to the high mountains of clear thinking where the panorama of the greater life spreads out before him. Dwelling in his world of thought, the philosopher gradually achieves to the realization that the mind which lifted him out of matter has also been outgrown. The mind which made him a man will prevent him from becoming a god; the stone upon which he raised himself thus far has now become a millstone about his neck. Thus as the philosopher first casts off worldliness to dwell in the broader vista of the mind, so ultimately he casts off mindfullness that he may enter into the newer and greater vision—the rulership of intellect by spirit. He casts aside the thinker as he would a worn-out body, and rises from the mountain tops into the free air of SPACE to vanish gradually as an inconceivable speck in the vast expanse of ALL.

As the sage sits upon his mountain about to cast aside mind and rise into the Nirvanic reaches of Eternity, the world passes in panoramic review before his enlightened vision. He secs

the great inferno spread out below him; about him on the mountain tops the gods of the world—the Keepers c^f the Vale of Tears. The illumined sage beholds the ways and byways

of the earth, a great crisscrossed labyrinth of complexities wherein immortal creatures mistakenly struggle not to prove their own immortality but rather to establish the evidence of mortality. He sees life as a vast chamber with two doors, with birth as the entrance to and death the exit from this mortal span. He then understands the allegorical rituals through which he passed as a neophyte in that day when he himself was "raised" to light. He realizes that the world of mortal man is a gloomy subterranean sphere peopled with distorted imps who, like the Nibelungen, hoard up treasures in ancient crypts in obedience to the dictates of their crafty king. The philosopher then grasps the import of the mystical allegory of the rope that is lowered into the pit that those who can cling to it may be drawn up to life. The rope is the secret doctrine and those who catch hold of the swinging cable may be drawn up into the light of Reality and Truth, In the life of every struggling creature there comes a time when the insufficiency of life within the narrow confines of matter is apparent.

By the disciplines of illumination the soul learns how to cast aside the inadequate coil of mortal limitation and ascend into the sphere of reason, there to dwell in the luminosity of divine proximity. The words of Milton concerning the fall of Satan then become profoundly significant: Him the Almighty Power Hurled headlong flaming from the ethereal sky, With hideous ruin and combustion, down To bottomless perdition, there to dwell In adamantine chains and penal fire, Who durst defy the Omnipotent to arms.

Satan, who signifies worldliness and self-sufficiency, is rewarded for his effort to establish a kingdom in opposition to the kingdom of good by being forced to dwell in the state of separateness which he himself conceived. In the East the illusion of separateness is looked upon as the cause of all suffering and sorrow. The great work of primitive Buddhism was to emphasize the fundamental unity of life through the doctrine of the one Universal Self. In the Western world where competition is held to be the only sound basis of commercial progress there is a continual wrong emphasis, for the parts are then arrayed against each other and no effort made to emphasize the common ground of Being in which all exists as parts of a tremendous whole.

The next chapter will be devoted to a consideration of the Eastern philosophy of perfection as accomplished by conscious reunion with Absolute Being through the Dharma of realization. The mortal sphere of competitive endeavor is hell indeed, wherein creatures exist in servitude to their own desires, while over them the Regent of the World, grim and unrelenting, sits with folded wings upon His throne raised on the dais of the Seven Heavens.

## THE MYSTERY OF REALIZATION

The Oriental mystic is here diagrammatically shown seated in the midst of his own area or consciousness. Through the disciplines of his order, he is enabled to so withdraw himself from the concerns of the outer life as to dwell in a samadhic felicity. Thus the aspiring soul seeks Self in the selflessness of the Great Law.

# XI

❧

# The Tree of the Sephiroth

THE Tree of the Sephiroth may be considered an invaluable compendium of the secret philosophy which originally was the spirit and soul of Chasidism. The Qabbalah is the priceless heritage of Israel, but each year those who comprehend its true principles become fewer in number. The Jew of today, if he lacks a realization of the profundity of his people's doctrines, is usually permeated with that most dangerous form of ignorance, modernism, and is prone to regard the Qabbalah either as an evil to be shunned like the plague or as a ridiculous superstition which has survived the black magic of the Dark Ages. Yet without the key which the Qabbalah supplies, the spiritual mysteries of both the Old and the New Testament must remain unsolved by Jew and Gentile alike.

The Sephirothic Tree consists of ten globes of luminous splendor arranged in three vertical columns and connected by 22 channels or paths. The ten globes are called the Sephiroth and to them are assigned the numbers 1 to 10. The three columns are called Mercy (on the right), Severity (on the left), and, between them, Mildness, as the reconciling power. The columns may also be said to represent Wisdom, Strength, and Beauty, which form the triune support of the universe, for it is written that the foundation of all things is the Three. The 22 channels are the letters of the Hebrew alphabet and to them are assigned the major trumps of the Tarot deck of symbolic cards.

Eliphas Levi declared that by arranging the Tarot cards according to a definite order man could discover all that is knowable concerning his God, his universe, and himself. When the ten numbers which pertain to the globes (Sephiroth) are combined with the 22 letters relating to the channels, the resultant sum is 32--the number peculiar to the Qabbalistic Paths of Wisdom. These Paths, occasionally referred to as the 32 teeth in the mouth of the Vast Countenance or as the 32 nerves that branch out from the Divine Brain, are analogous to the first 32 degrees of Freemasonry, which elevate the candidate to the dignity of a Prince of the Royal Secret. Qabbalists also consider it extremely significant that in the original Hebrew Scriptures the name of God should occur 32 times in the first chapter of Genesis. (In the English translations of the Bible the name appears 33 times.) In the mystic analysis of the human body, according to the Rabbins, 32 spinal segments lead upward to the Temple of Wisdom--the skull.

The four Qabbalistic Trees described in the preceding chapter were combined by later Jewish scholars into one all-inclusive diagram and termed by them not only the Sephirothic but also the Archetypal, or Heavenly, Adam. According to some authorities, it is this Heavenly Adam, and not a terrestrial man, whose creation is described in the opening chapters of Genesis. Out of the substances of this divine man the universe was formed; in him it remains and will continue even after dissolution shall resolve the spheres back into their own primitive substance. The Deity is never conceived of as actually contained in the Sephiroth, which are purely hypothetical vessels employed to define the limits of the Creative Essence. Adolph Franck rather likens the Sephiroth to varicolored transparent glass bowls filled with pure light, which apparently assumes the color of its containers but whose essential nature remains ever unchanged and unchangeable.

The ten Sephiroth composing the body of the prototypic Adam, the numbers related to them, and the parts of the universe to which they correspond are as follows:

| No. | THE SEPHIROTH | THE UNIVERSE | ALTERNATIVE |
|---|---|---|---|
| 1 | Kether--the Crown | Primum Mobile | The Fiery Heavens |
| 2 | Chochmah--Wisdom | The Zodiac | The First Motion |
| 3 | Binah--Understanding | Saturn | The Zodiac |
| 4 | Chesed--Mercy | Jupiter | Saturn |
| 5 | Geburah--Severity | Mars | Jupiter |
| 6 | Tiphereth--Beauty | Sun | Mars |
| 7 | Netsah--Victory | Venus | Sun |
| 8 | Hod--Glory | Mercury | Venus |
| 9 | Jesod--the Foundation | Moon | Mercury |
| 10 | Malchuth--the Kingdom | Elements | Moon |

It must continually be emphasized that the Sephiroth and the properties assigned to them, like the tetractys of the Pythagoreans, are merely symbols of the cosmic system with its multitude of parts. The truer and fuller meaning of these emblems may not be revealed by writing or by word of mouth, but must be divined as the result of study and meditation. In the Sepher ha Zohar it is written that there is a garment--the written doctrine-which every man may see. Those with understanding do not look upon the garment but at the body beneath it--the intellectual and philosophical code. The wisest of all, however, the servants of the Heavenly King, look at nothing save the soul--the spiritual doctrine--which is the eternal and ever-springing root of the law. Of this great truth Eliphas Levi also writes declaring that none can gain entrance to the secret House of Wisdom unless he wear the voluminous cape of Apollonius of Tyana and carry in his hand the lamp of Hermes. The cape signifies the qualities of self-possession and self-reliance which must envelope the seeker as a cloak of strength, while the ever-burning lamp of the sage represents the illumined mind and perfectly balanced intellect without which the mystery of the ages can never be solved.

The Sephirothic Tree is sometimes depicted as a human body, thus more definitely establishing the true identity of the first, or Heavenly, Man--Adam Kadmon--the Idea of the Universe. The ten divine globes (Sephiroth) are then considered as analogous to the ten sacred members and organs of the Protogonos, according to the following arrangement. Kether is the crown of the Prototypic Head and perhaps refers to the pineal gland; Chochmah and Binah are the right and left hemispheres respectively of the Great Brain; Chesed and Geburah (Pechad) are the right and left arms respectively, signifying the active creative members of the Grand Man; Tiphereth is the heart, or, according to some, the entire viscera; Netsah and Hod are the right and left legs respectively, or the supports of the world; Jesod is the generative system, or the foundation of form; and Malchuth represents the two feet, or the base of being. Occasionally Jesod is considered as the male and Malchuth as the female generative power. The Grand Man thus conceived is the gigantic image of Nebuchadnezzar's dream, with head of gold, arms and chest of silver, body of brass, legs of iron, and feet of clay. The mediæval Qabbalists also assigned one of the Ten Commandments and a tenth part of the Lord's Prayer in sequential order to each of the ten Sephiroth.

Concerning the emanations from Kether which establish themselves as three triads of Creative Powers--termed in the Sepher ha Zohar three heads each with three faces--H. P. Blavatsky writes: "This [Kether] was the first Sephiroth, containing in herself the other nine ספירות Sephiroth, or intelligences. In their totality and unity they represent the archetypal man, Adam Kadmon, the πρωτ◇γονος, who in his individuality or unity is yet dual, or bisexual, the Greek Didumos, for he is the prototype of all humanity. Thus we obtain three trinities, each contained in a 'head.' In the first head, or face (the three-faced Hindu Trimurti),

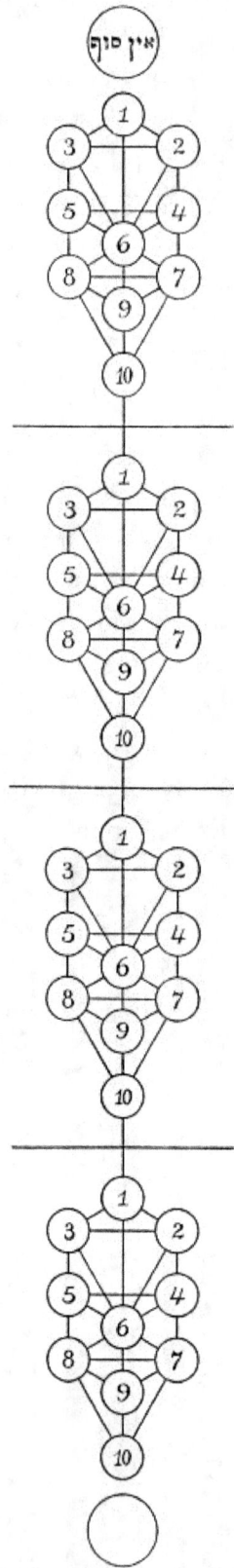

we find Sephira [Kether], the first androgyne, at the apex of the upper triangle, emitting Hachama [Chochmah], or Wisdom, a masculine and active potency--also called Jah, יה--and Binah, בינה, or Intelligence, a female and passive potency, also represented by the name Jehovah יהוה. These three form the first trinity or 'face' of the Sephiroth. This triad emanated Hesed, הסד, or Mercy, a masculine active potency, also called El, from which emanated Geburah גבורה, or justice, also called Eloha, a feminine passive potency; from the union of these two was produced Tiphereth טפארת, Beauty, Clemency, the Spiritual Sun, known by the divine name Elohim; and the second triad, 'face,' or 'head,' was formed. These emanating, in their turn, the masculine potency Netzah, נצה, Firmness, or Jehovah Sabaoth, who issued the feminine passive potency Hod, הוד, Splendor, or Elohim Sabaoth; the two produced Jesod, יסוד, Foundation, who is the mighty living one El-Chai, thus yielding the third trinity or 'head.' The tenth Sephiroth is rather a duad, and is represented on the diagrams as the lowest circle. It is Malchuth or Kingdom, מלכות, and Shekinah, שכינה, also called Adonai, and Cherubim among the angelic hosts. The first 'Head' is called the Intellectual world; the second 'Head' is the Sensuous, or the world of Perception, and the third is the material or Physical world." (See Isis Unveiled.)

Among the later Qabbalists there is also a division of the Sephirothic Tree into five parts, in which the distribution of the globes is according to the following order:

(1) Macroprosophus, or the Great Face, is the term applied to Kether as the first and most exalted of the Sephiroth and includes the nine potencies or Sephiroth issuing from Kether.

(2) Abba, the Great Father, is the term generally applied to Chochmah--Universal Wisdom--the first emanation of Kether, but, according to Ibn Gebirol, Chochmah represents the Son, the Logos or the Word born from the union of Kether and Binah.

(3) Aima, the Great Mother, is the name by which Binah, or the third Sephira, is generally known. This is the Holy Ghost, from whose body the generations issue forth. Being the third person of the Creative Triad, it corresponds to Jehovah, the Demiurgus.

(4) Microprosophus, or the Lesser Face, is composed of the six Sephiroth--Chesed, Geburah, Tiphereth, Netsah, Hod, and Jesod. The Microprosophus is commonly called the Lesser Adam, or Zauir Anpin, whereas the Macroprosophus, or Superior Adam, is Arikh Anpin. The Lesser Face is properly symbolized by the six-pointed star or interlaced triangles of Zion and also by the six faces of the cube. It represents the directions north, east, south, west, up, and down, and also the first six days of Creation. In his list of the parts of the Microprosophus, MacGregor-Mathers includes Binah as the first and superior part of the Lesser Adam, thus making his constitution septenary. If Microprosophus be considered as sexpartite, then his globes (Sephiroth) are analogous to the six days of Creation, and the tenth globe, Malchuth, to the Sabbath of rest.

(5) The Bride of Microprosophus is Malchuth--the epitome of the Sephiroth, its quaternary constitution being composed of blendings of the four elements. This is the divine Eve that is taken out

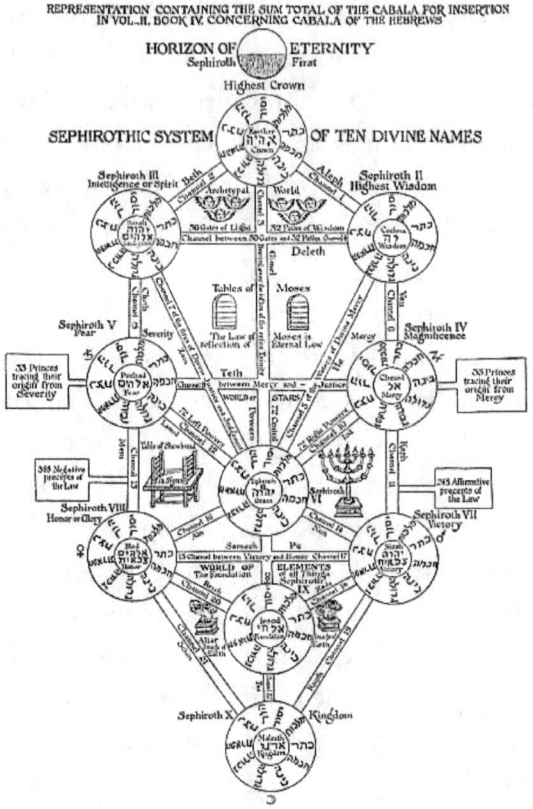

According to the mysteries of the Sephiroth, the order of the Creation, or the Divine Lightning Flash which zigzags through the four worlds according to the order of the divine emanations, is thus described: From AIN SOPH, the Nothing and All, the Eternal and Unconditioned Potency, issues Macroprosophus, the Long Face, of whom it is written, "Within His skull exist daily thirteen thousand myriads of worlds which draw their existence from Him and by Him are upheld." (See The Greater Holy Assembly.) Macroprosophus, the directionalized will of AIN SOPH, corresponding to Kether, the Crown of the Sephiroth, gives birth out of Himself to the nine lesser spheres of which He is the sum and the overbrooding cause. The 22 letters of the Hebrew alphabet, by the various combinations of which the laws of the universe are established, constitute the scepter of Macroprosophus which He wields from His flaming throne in the Atziluthic World.

From this eternal and ancient androgyne--Kether--come forth Chochmah, the great Father, and Binah, the great Mother. These two are usually referred to as Abba and Aima respectively--the first male and the first female, the prototypes of sex. These correspond to the first two letters of the sacred name, Jehovah, יהוה, IHVH. The Father is the י, or I, and the Mother is the ה, or H. Abba and Aima symbolize the creative activities of the universe, and are established in the creative world of Briah. In the Sepher ha Zohar it is written, "And therefore are all things established in the equality of male and female; for were it not so, how could they subsist? This beginning is the Father of all things; the Father of all Fathers; and both are mutually bound together, and the one path shineth into the other--Chochmah, Wisdom, as the Father; Binah, Understanding, as the Mother."

There is a difference of opinion concerning certain of the relationships of the parts of the first triad. Some Qabbalists, including Ibn Gebirol, consider Kether as the Father, Binah as the Mother, and Chochmah as the Son. In this later arrangement, Wisdom, which is the attribute of the Son, becomes the creator of the lower spheres. The symbol of Binah is the dove, a proper emblem for the brooding maternal instinct of the Universal Mother.

Because of the close similarity of their creative triad to the Christian Trinity, the later Qabbalists rearranged the first three Sephiroth and added a mysterious point called Daath--a hypothetical eleventh Sephira. This is located where the horizontal line connecting Chochmah and Binah crosses the vertical line joining Kether and Tiphereth. While Daath is not mentioned by the first Qabbalists, it is a highly important element and its addition to the Sephirothic Tree was not made without full realization of the significance of such action. If Chochmah be considered the active, intelligent energy of Kether, and Binah the receptive capacity of Kether, then Daath becomes the thought which, created by Chochmah, flows into Binah. The postulation of Daath clarifies the problem of the Creative Trinity, for here it is diagrammatically represented as consisting of Chochmah (the Father), Binah (the Mother, or Holy Ghost), and Daath, the Word by which the worlds were established. Isaac Myer discounts the importance of Daath, declaring it a subterfuge to conceal the fact that Kether, and not Chochmah; is the true Father of the Creative Triad. He makes no attempt to give a satisfactory explanation for the symbolism of this hypothetical Sephira.

According to the original conception, from the union of the Divine Father and the Divine Mother is produced Microprosophus--the Short Face or the Lesser Countenance, which is established in the Yetziratic World of formation and corresponds to the letter ו, or V, in the Great Name. The six powers of Microprosophus flow from and are contained in their own source, which is Binah, the Mother of the Lesser Adam. These constitute the spheres of the sacred planets; their name is Elohim, and they move upon the face of the deep. The tenth Sephira--Malchuth, the Kingdom--is described as the Bride of the Lesser Adam, created back to back with her lord, and to it is assigned the final, ה, or H, the last letter of the Sacred Name. The dwelling place of Malchuth is in the fourth world--Assiah--and it is composed of all the superior powers reflected into the elements of the terrestrial sphere. Thus it will be seen that the Qabbalistic Tree extends through four worlds, with its branches in matter and its roots in the Ancient of Ancients--Macroprosophus.

Three vertical columns support the universal system as typified by the Sephirothic Tree. The central pillar has its foundation in Kether, the Eternal One. It passes downward through the hypothetical Sephira, Daath, and then through Tiphereth and Jesod, with its lower end resting upon the firm foundation of Malchuth, the last of the globes. The true import of the central pillar is equilibrium. It demonstrates how the Deity always manifests by emanating poles of expression from the midst of Itself but remaining free from the illusion of polarity. If the numbers of the four Sephiroth connected by this column be added together (1 +6 +9 + 10), the sum is 26, the number of Jehovah. (See chapter on Pythagorean Mathematics.)

The column on the right, which is called Jachin, has its foundation on Chochmah, the outpouring Wisdom of God; the three globes suspended from it are all masculine potencies. The column at the left is called Boaz. The three globes upon it are feminine and receptive potencies, for it is founded in Understanding, a receptive and maternal potency. Wisdom, it will be noted, is considered as radiant or outpouring, and Understanding as receptive, or something which is filled by the flowing of Wisdom. The three pillars are ultimately united in Malchuth, in which all the powers of the superior worlds are manifested.

The four globes upon the central column reveal the function of the creative power in the various worlds. In the first world the creative power is Will--the one Divine Cause; in the second world, the hypothetical Daath--the Word coming forth from the Divine Thought; in the third world, Tiphereth--the Sun, or focal point between God and Nature; in the fourth world it is twofold, being the positive and negative poles of the reproductive system, of which Jesod is the male and Malchuth the female.

In Kircher's Sephirothic Tree it should be especially noted that the ornaments of the Tabernacle appear in the various parts of the diagram. These indicate a direct relationship between the sacred House of God and the universe--a relationship which must always be considered as existing between the Deity through whose activity the world is produced and the world itself, which must be the house or vehicle of that Deity. Could the modern scientific world but sense the true profundity of these philosophical deductions of the ancients, it would realize that those who fabricated the structure of the Qabbalah possessed a knowledge of the celestial plan comparable in every respect with that of the modern savant.

The Tetragrammaton, or the four-lettered Name of God, written thus יהוה, is pronounce Jehovah. The first letter is י, Yod, the Germ, the Life, the Flame, the Cause, the One, and the most fundamental of the Jewish phallic emblems. Its numerical value is 10, and it is to be considered as the 1 containing the 10. In the Qabbalah it is declared that the a Yod is in reality three Yods, of which the first is the beginning, the second is the center, and the third is the end. Its throne is the Sephira Chochmah (according to Ibn Gebirol, Kether), from which it goes forth to impregnate Binah, which is the first ה, He. The result of this union is Tiphereth, which is the ו Vau, whose power is 6 and which symbolizes the six members of the Lesser Adam. The final ה, He, is Malchuth, the Inferior Mother, partaking in part of the potencies of the Divine Mother, the first He. By placing the four letters of the Tetragrammaton in a vertical column, a figure closely resembling the human body is produced, with Yod for the head, the first He for the arms and shoulders, Vau for the trunk of the body, and the final He for the hips and legs. If the Hebrew letters be exchanged for their English equivalents, the form is not materially changed or the analogy altered. It is also extremely significant that by inserting the letter ש, Shin, in the middle of the name Jehovah, the word Jehoshua, or Jesus, is formed thus:

יהשוה

In the Qabbalistic Mysteries, according to Eliphas Levi, the name Jehovah is occasionally written by connecting together 24 dots--the 24 powers before the throne--and it is believed that the name of the Power of Evil is the sign of Jehovah reversed or inverted. (See Transcendental Magic.) Of the Great Word, Albert Pike writes: "The True Word of a Mason is to be found in the concealed and profound meaning of the Ineffable Name of Deity, communicated by God to Moses; and which meaning was long lost by the very precautions taken to conceal it. The true pronunciation of that name was in truth a secret, in which, however, was involved the far more profound secret of its meaning. In that meaning is included all the truth that can be known by us, in regard to the nature of God." (See Morals and Dogma.)

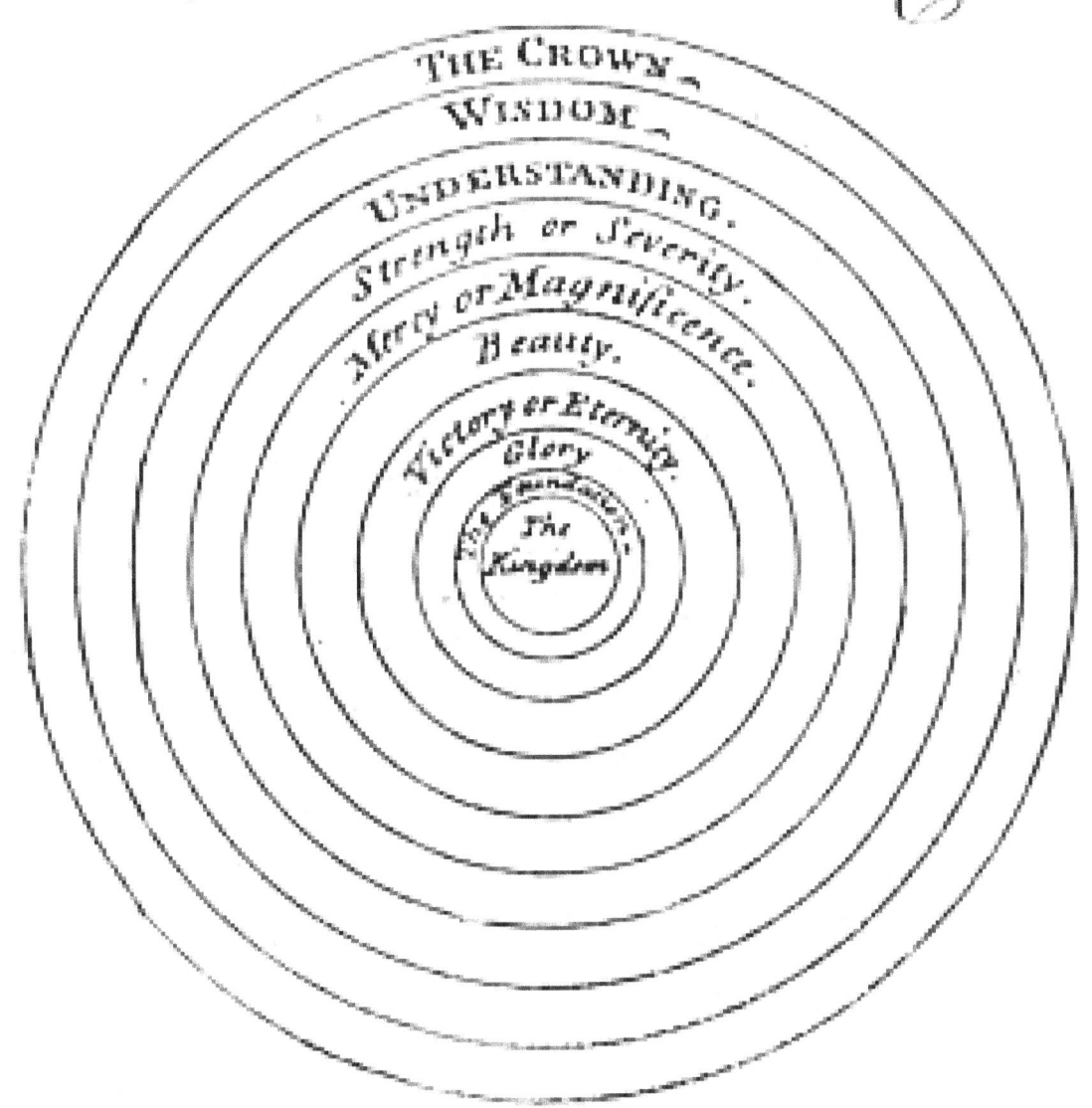

Table of the SEPHIROTHS in Circles.

# XII

〜〜〜

# The Annihilation of the Sense of Diversity

The gods have already been defined as personifications of divine attributes, that is, they signify conditions of Universal Consciousness. Whereas the Absolute signifies All Consciousness in suspension, the gods are differentiated phases of Universal Consciousness. While the ignorant venerate the gods either as personalities or divine beings, the philosopher recognizes them as cosmic planes or modes of, realization. Thus Buddha is to be regarded primarily as the condition of perfect illumination rather than as a personality.

A subtle point is contained in the fact that he who attains to Buddhahood is not a Buddha but the Buddha. In other words Buddha, like light, is an all-pervading state, and he who becomes luminous shines not with a separate light but rather is merged with the one light whose radiance is diffused throughout all worlds. In its ascent to source, consciousness is merged sequentially with ever higher universal aspects of itself, becoming one with each level or plane with which it is temporarily blended. These planes or levels, representing the various phases of expanding consciousness, form the concatenated order of the gods. Hades, for example, was the Greek god of death or, more explicitly, materiality. Accordingly, Hades represents the consciousness of materiality. Whoever moves and feels in terms of materiality is materiality, for we are what our consciousness is. The modern thinker would term the material-minded person a materialist. The esoterist, however, would say that the material-minded person is materiality. Again, the western scholar considers a lawbreaker a criminal, whereas the Oriental thinks of the lawbreaker as crime. If, therefore, the Eastern sage conceives of crime as an individualized monster, then each criminal becomes not an individual expression of that monster but the actual monster itself. Hate, for example, can hardly be thought of as an individual, and yet it is definitely a state of consciousness (more correctly, unconsciousness). The Eastern mind cannot conceive of a number of entities each a separate condition of hatred, because the moment hatred is born in the human heart the person who permits this condition to exist within himself becomes the embodiment of the plane of universal hatred.

In other words, a universal condition is made manifest in that individual. Several men may hate at the same time in different parts of the world, yet there is but one consciousness of hatred with which they all hate. Hence this demon of hate may exist in more than one person simultaneously, During a great war millions may hate at the same time, yet each is neither a fraction of hatred nor simply manifesting hatred. Each is himself hate, and all who indulge this passion are identical with the nature of hatred.

The multiform images of the Buddhists all signify extensions and modes of consciousness. As realization increases and the unfolding self grasps more and more of the infinite span, the symbols become ever more complex while the principles for which they stand become ever more simple. Frequently a number of arms are used to represent the metaphysical potencies. Thus the consciousness of right judgment may be depicted as a hand holding some legal instrument. Similarly, the consciousness of priestly protection by another arm sustaining some implement of the priestcraft; the consciousness of rulership by still another arm elevating a crown or scepter; the consciousness of the good and just physician by a hand holding some instrument of surgery or healing herb; the consciousness of all-knowing by a hand holding a short staff or a scroll; and the consciousness of the divine avenger by a closed fist shaking a thunderbolt. A plurality of arms and heads thus becomes a method highly appropriate to symbolize the invisible but all-powerful qualities which the chela during his development expresses through the depth of his own being. Whenever through self-unfoldment an individual attains to the state of consciousness symbolized by a certain god, then that god is declared to be incarnate in that personality and to actually walk the earth. Thus the god of joy is incarnate in the joyful man, the god of mercy in the merciful, the god of truth in the truthful, and the god of war in those who fight. Being divine attributes, the gods thus become flesh in those mortal creatures who have unfolded and given expression within themselves to those godlike attributes.

In the Temple of Ten Thousand Buddhas at Kyoto, Japan, are to be found numberless images of the Buddha and the attendant Bodhisattvas, or disciples of the Lord of Enlightenment. Perfection is represented in the form of the Buddha, and the disciplines or ways of perfection in the forms of Bodhisattvas. The latter are the stages of enlightenment, the symbols of the sure and eternal path which winds through the illusion and leads ultimately to the attainment of perfect good.

Dear to the heart of the East is the beloved Kwan-Yin, or Kwannon, the great Bodhisattva Avalokiteswara, the Oriental Madonna, commonly called the Goddess of Mercy. For centuries the Buddhist monks have striven in their meditations to blend their consciousness with this divinity of compassion—the Merciful, Enduring One. The artists-priests have loved to depict upon silk or carve in stone, wood, or ivory the form of this compassionate "Consciousness of Protection.'

Kwan-Yin was originally a masculine figure, probably based upon an historical Buddha (presumably the second of the great line), but through the centuries the compassionate nature of Avalokiteswara is responsible for the gradual metamorphosis of the figure into a feminine divinity. In China and Japan Kwan-Yin is usually a standing figure robed in graceful flowing gradients with the face set in compassionate repose. Often the figure has only two arms, although a favorite number is six. When shown with six arms, Kwan-Yin is generally seated with her head resting upon the palm of her hand. In Japan there are figures of the Kwan-Yin with as many as a thousand arms to symbolize the universal scope of the Kwan-Yin consciousness. In Tibet the figure is often shown with eleven heads. Certain late Buddhist writings give definite philosophical meaning to numbers, so the multiplicity of members is of particular import.

The poses of the various hands give a key to the exalted nature of Eastern mysticism. The mudras, or hand postures of the Buddha, constitute a secret science of which little is known to those not initiated into the Buddhist Mysteries. The hand may be extended in an attitude of giving, which then signifies the consciousness of giving, and which, when free from all terrestrial taint, gives an exquisite pleasure to the inner self. The joy of giving is a commendable state of consciousness, as is also the joy of receiving. All these joys are finally discarded, however, until but one remains: namely, the perfect bliss of contemplation of Self. In Japan there is a lovable Buddhist divinity usually shown with a bald head and a benign countenance. This is Jizo, the god of little children. Because of his great love for helpless child souls, Jizo has become their patron and protector. When a baby dies, according to the Japanese legend, it wanders in a gloomy cavern awaiting rebirth, where it has for its only task the heaping up of little piles of stones. In his Glimpses of Unfamiliar Japan Lafcadio Hearn describes the cave of the children s souls where flows the legendary fountain of milk from which the dead children drink and where in the gloom sits the smiling Jizo. When the evil spirits frighten them the loving Jizo extends his arms and the childrens souls all run and hide in the sleeves of his kimono.

It is evident that Jizo signifies not only the consciousness of the love of children but also, in a more lofty sense, that consciousness which, having elevated itself to the heights of realization and gazing down upon unknowing humanity, realizes all creatures to be but little children piling up heaps of stones. Whether these piles be in the distant Japanese cave of Kaka or the stone heaps of a great city, Jizo gazes with boundless compassion upon infant humanity. When the monsters of war, greed, and lust frighten the ignorant and immature, he then extends his arms, and like the Master Jesus brooding over Jerusalem longs to gather the weak and helpless under the protection of his flowing robes. The god Jizo is incarnate in those in whom love for the weak and desire to serve the helpless springs from a true realization of that which must be accomplished. Jizo is a principle, and those possessing and manifesting this principle are one with him in his labor of love.

In the Tushita heaven of the Lamas dwells the radiant consciousness of Maitreya, the loving one, the desired of all nations—the Buddhist Messiah who is yet to come. This Bodhi- sattva is the personification of man's hope of ultimate achievement. He signifies the eternal tomorrow, the time of all accomplishment. Robed in futurity, he is the consciousness of noble destiny. At the Lama temple in Peking is to be seen a gigantic figure of Jam-pa (Maitreya), whose gilt lacquered body dazzles the beholder with its brilliance and whose expressionless face gazes down upon the altar seventy feet below. Maitreya gives a definite key to the world-wide belief in a coming Savior whose advent will be marked by miracles and who shall lead his people to spiritual and temporal victory. Maitreya is the consciousness of hope and he comes to those who can sense, even abstractly, the existence of a nobler and more illumined state. According to popular superstition, the advent of Maitreya, like the tenth avatar of Vishnu, will be a particular and definite occurrence. In reality, however, Maitreya is continually manifesting as the circumstances that lead worlds, nations, and individuals up along the path of the law to final absorption with the Absolute. Maitreya saves the world by revealing to the world that it is capable of salvation; for out of the realization of possible perfection is born the hope and strength to persevere. Maitreya is therefore the embodiment of Dharma, and he who accepts the Law shall be saved by the Law. Jesus, another personification of the Law, assured his followers that those who believed in him should not perish. Maitreya is the way, the truth, and the life which, coming to every life, redeems all who accept it.

In dealing with the subject of consciousness, it is possible to conceive of Reality as permeating the entire area of space and gradually contracting itself toward the center, thereby limiting itself in the establishment of unreality. Or, on the other hand, consciousness may be regarded as occupying a central point from which it radiates itself throughout all Being, pouring its effulgence into the Abyss of the not-self, which is thereby redeemed. The Cabalists reconciled both these viewpoints by affirming that AIN SOPH (the Absolute) first retired from the circumference to the center to establish the illusion and then diffused itself over the area privated by its first withdrawal, thus re-establishing Reality. The Ptolemaic system of astronomy, though untrue from a scientific point of view, clarifies one of the esoteric teachings of ancient learning so long misconstrued by modern scholars.

By placing the earth in the center of the solar system and dividing the interval between the earth and the inner wall of the heavens by a number of planes corresponding to the orbits of the planetary bodies, a diagrammatic figure of consciousness and its extensions is created. Outside the orbit of the earth were the spheres of the Moon, Mercury, Venus, Sun, Mars, Jupiter, and Saturn in the order noted. Beyond the sphere of Saturn was the plane of the constellations which formed the inner surface of the zodiacal globe. Outside this globe was the Empyrean, or dwelling place of the gods. The Mysteries taught that man must ascend in realization from the earth through the rings (or planes) of the planets to the circle of the zodiac. Having reached the wall of heaven, he was then to break through and enter the supreme universe. After realization has pierced the crystalline shell of Being, it then ceases to be under the jurisdiction of the Governors of the seven planets and the vast body of cosmic agencies controlling all mundane creations. The student, however, should not conceive of his consciousness as rising but rather of his inferior self ascending through various levels of consciousness to ultimate union with the All-Knowing.

This idea requires further amplification. What man pleases to call his spirit is, in reality, the level of Self to which he is attuned by the quality and completeness of his realization.

The Oriental symbolizes Universal Self as an immense sunburst, its inconceivably magnificent center surrounded by innumerable rings of petal-like emanations, which decrease in brilliancy as they recede from the center. This sunburst fills all conceivable space, extending from up to down and from in to out, and each of its petals, or rays, supports (in the sense of being the causal nature of) a definite genus of so-called evolving life. Thus the infinite diversity of manifestation reflects the infinite potentialities of the causal nature. The question may properly be asked how the Self, though an absolute unity and hence incapable of diversity, can still exist in a number of apparently different states. To employ a simple analogy, let us take two goblets, one containing wine and the other water. The wine will symbolize Self; the water, the illusionary universe of privation of the Self (the Abyss of the German mystics). If a small quantity of the wine be poured into the water, the wine will undergo no actual change, yet it will be so diluted as to be apparently different from its original state. Then imagine all the wine to be divided into single drops which are allowed to fall into the water one at a time. Each drop will cause a minute but definite difference in the degree of dilution and, consequently, the wine will exist in as many conditions as there are degrees of dilution. Yet the wine will actually undergo no change, and regardless of how much water is added it will still remain a single substance. Thus the infinite diversity of manifestation has its origin not in separate spiritual agencies but in the conditions which the Self is capable of assuming in relation to its own absence.

In East Indian philosophy the human figure is substituted for the earth; otherwise the Ptolemaic system of the planets is preserved, the outermost orbit becoming the boundary of limitation that separates the individual from the universal state. Sitting in meditation in the midst of his little universe, the philosopher by definite projection of the faculties of realization annihilates one by one the walls that enclose him until finally with one supreme effort he shatters the globe of his individuality and achieves Nirvana. Let us try to conceive the process whereby the mystic transcends all environment and becomes en rapport with universal principles- Recognizing in the orbits of the planets certain major levels of realization, it soon becomes evident that the mind perse in unable to cope with the situation, for in spiritual concerns the intellect is well-nigh powerless. In an effort to explain simply the theory, let us presume that the earth in the center of the Ptolemaic chart represents the state of absolute ignorance, and the Empyrean beyond the circle of the zodiac, absolute wisdom or consciousness.

Humanity numbers in its ranks many so-called worldly-wise men—powerful intellects thickly encrusted with the catalogued notions and superstitions of others. Since all material knowledge is added on from without, under the stress of desperate need the inner nature is discovered to be incapable of sustaining the intellectual conceits thus foisted upon it. On the other hand, realization is a power which has its source within the inner nature itself. Like the balm of Gilead it brings with it peace, courage, and understanding. It tinctures the outer nature with a spiritual comprehension, giving an intuitive grasp of facts and the power to discern Reality. It may therefore be stated that the fundamental difference between knowledge and understanding lies in the direction of the flow of power, knowledge flowing in from without and understanding flowing out from within. Realization is consequently a problem of the inner life and can receive little assistance from the outer nature. The mind creates elaborate theologies and intricate systems of reasoning which are without other than intellectual foundation, and in moments of dire need it is all too apparent that these adumbration's lack the substance of sufficiency. Hence, to convert an individual by outer means is useless, for true conversion can only come through the inner realization of certain divine or natural facts. To affirm oneself to occupy a certain position in the universe means nothing, but to realize the nature of a certain position or condition is to be one with that condition or to occupy that position.

While Ptolemy knew that the earth was not the center of the solar system, he also knew that earthiness was the beginning point of all achievement and that each struggling creature rising from its own earthiness must ascend through the circles of realization to eventually achieve complete liberation from the grossness of inferior nature. Seated in the midst of the circles and separated from the Universal Self by seven great walls of limitation of consciousness, the unillumined nature dwells in a state of isolation, accepting in its ignorance the illusion of diversity and regarding all creation as conspiring to bring about its destruction. Man must attain the realization necessary for his liberation by one of two paths: (1) He must follow the apparently endless spiral of life which leads in and through creation and eventually brings him to realization through experience. This experience is largely the essence of the reactions of joy and sorrow together with the recognition of the sequence of cause and effect in all the incidents of life. (2) By the Dharma of Realization the disciple may so intensify his attitudes through philosophic discipline as to achieve in a comparatively brief period of time that which the mass of humanity must attain by the slower and more circuitous route of natural processes.

Through realization alone can the Great Work be consummated. Only he who possesses realization is able to dispel the illusion of diversity. The true magnitude of an individual is measured by both the intensiveness and extensiveness of his realization, for the individual extends in every direction as far as his realization is capable of penetrating. For example, in his least illumined state man is but a mere speck in the midst of universal expanse. In his most illumined state, however, man has so increased in rational magnitude that universal expanse becomes a mere speck within his realization. In his ignorance man conceives the universe as including him, only to ultimately discover that his divine potentialities are so boundless that, when adequately manifested, the universe and countless vistas unmeasured are but infinitesimal parts of his own being. In Pythagorean terminology, man in his relapsed states conceives himself to be one of many, only to find upon arrival at the fullness of understanding that he has encircled the many and resolved them into his own unity. The figure seated in the rings represents the mystic directionalizing his realization upon the Eternal. By this process he recapitulates the entire scheme of universal unfoldment, and reveals the causal urge behind all racial and individual development. In the diagram the rings are numbered from 1 to 7.

The first ring immediately surrounds the seated form of the sage, and the area thus enclosed by it, being the smallest division, signifies the most limited state of realization. Those whose poverty of realization restricts them to this level of consciousness may be considered ignorant to the degree of the savage. Here the life is ruled by fear and hatred—fear of the unknown and hatred for that which possesses superior knowledge. With crude implements and cruder instincts these unknowing ones seek to fulfill Nature's first law, self-preservation.

The finer emotions and sentiments are entirely absent, and the organic quality of the body is so low that the capacity for physical pain is thereby reduced to a minimum. Understanding is totally lacking, but in its place is a certain primitive cunning which warns of danger and instructs in the rudiments of physical survival. Little or no effort is made by this type to communicate its attitudes or feeling to others. It does not establish any definite communal life, but lives by itself and for itself alone, and finally creeps away to die leaving its unburied bones to bleach upon some wind-blown crag.

Though civilization has reached practically every corner of the earth and savage tribes are fast vanishing before its advance, it is possible to veneer the exterior and still leave the interior nature as primitive as ever. The addition of a Prince Albert coat or a pair of spats does not necessarily result in a highly advanced degree of culture, for many people suspected of considerable refinement are still innately barbaric. In fact, all who advocate isolated individualism are reverting to aboriginal type. Whenever the activities of life are centered exclusively upon the aggrandizement of the lesser self, such an attitude is unfailing evidence of the survival of Crookbone traits. Where the individual is completely wrapped up in himself, feels himself sufficient for himself, and regards all humanity as legitimate prey for exploitation, we have definite proof that his consciousness is still limited to the narrow confines of the first ring. The universe beyond means nothing to him, for beyond his realization it has no existence.

When the meditating sage elevates his realization until it recognizes the insufficiency of such a code and can no longer live in this sense of utter separateness, then the first ring is said to be annihilated and the realization sweeps outward to meet the limiting confines of the second ring. The circle of realization has thus been considerably enlarged and the self has taken the first step to escape from the not-self. As growth is synonymous with increasing inclusiveness, the individual functioning upon the level of consciousness of the second ring accepts into himself a limited number of external objects. In the dawn of civilization the family was lifted to a certain degree of equality with the individual who constituted himself its head. Such an individual still viewed the world as hostile, but out of it he chose a few and these he accepted on a parity with himself.

His sense of protection included them; his love of self regarded them as part of himself and consequently legitimate objects for his affection. To a certain degree he viewed the members of his family as possessions, but psychologically he possessed them because his realization included them; for nothing can be actually possessed unless it is enclosed by the realization of possession. There is to be found in human nature an inherent trait which causes each individual to feel himself to be different from any other living thing and consequently superior to and free from the laws governing the body of creation. In this ring the individual rises to that state of consciousness where he decides that those of his immediate circle upon whom he confers his affections are likewise composed of this superior substance and, like himself, differ from the rest of society. However, the fact that even one or two are included with self demonstrates that the annihilation of the sense of diversity has begun, for as the self accepts into itself that which was previously a stranger to it, the cosmic march toward unity begins and continues until all existence has thus been absorbed.

Today there are millions of people whose spiritual natures are the substance of the second ring. They will cheat the world that they may lavish their ill-gotten gains upon their own family circle. Humanity at large is still a stranger to them; their realization fails to recognize in all mankind the common heritage of similar loves, hopes, fears, and aspirations. This particular thought brings to mind the plea of Shylock in the third act of the Merchant of Venice for scattered and downtrodden Israel. By taking a few liberties with Shylock's speech, a truth is established beyond the conception of those whose realization limits them to the consciousness of the second ring. "Have not all men eyes; have not all men hands, organs, dimensions, senses, affections, passions; are not all men fed with the same food, hurt with the same weapons, subject to the same diseases, healed by the same means, warmed and cooled by the same summer and winter as you are? If you prick them, do they not bleed; if you tickle them, do they not laugh; if you poison them, do they not die?"

To summarize, the consciousness of the second ring covers blood relations and those upon whom particular affections are lavished: the mother, father, husband, wife, and child. These are accepted as parts of self and the work of unification has been inaugurated; for while in the first ring these are five separate people, in the second ring they are included as members of the one in whom the realization of their proximity has been established.

When realization increases to the point where it includes the stranger without the gate, the spirit of friendship is born. A friend is one to whom we are related by consciousness rather than by blood. Pythagoras declared his friend to be his alter ego —his other self. At another time he stated friendship to be that condition in which one soul existed in two bodies, thereby elevating this relationship far above that of the ties of blood.

Until realization reaches the third plane friendship is impossible because up to that point egotism is so dominant a motive that man's love for himself precludes all other affections.

When realization annihilates the substances of the second ring and flows through into its enlarged field of expression, the tribal (later the national) spirit is evolved. A certain clannishness is manifested, for though the great world without is still excluded, nevertheless the sense of inclusiveness has been increased to take in those having a similar origin or living in close proximity. Having one leader, the tribe is simply an enlarged family, the chief or head symbolizing the father; for nearly all tribal forms of government are patriarchies.

Eventually the tribe grows into the nation and there is born a curious mental attitude termed patriotism . Patriotism is merely an accentuated egotism which embraces the members of the tribe or nation to which the egotist himself belongs. Fundamentally it is based upon the belief that that of which the individual is a part, is, like himself, incapable of wrong. Consequently all examination of motive is regarded as superflous, and the attitude that "I and mine are right and you and yours are wrong" is an attitude to be assumed and maintained at all costs. Long regarded as a virtue, patriotism will yet demonstrate itself to be a most pernicious attitude, for it can be and has been controlled and directionalized by personal interest, frequently to tragic ends.

To affirm that an individual can do no wrong merely because he is of the same blood or clan as oneself, and to defend him because of such relationship is a fault, and contributes to his own moral delinquency and the destruction of the nation. There can be but one true patriotism: namely, patriotism to principle. But those dwelling in the consciousness of the third ring are as yet unaware of principle, and to them their tribe or nation is elevated to a position approximating Deity. Yet with all his faults and blindness, the one who has attained to this degree of consciousness, has gone far in the mastery of diversity, for his realization has increased until in part, at least, it has included an entire nation within the range of common interest. True, it has not yet learned to understand the structure and consciousness of nations, but this comes later. Here is the man who will die for his friend but cannot possibly understand his friend; for he serves not the consciousness of his friend but rather his own preconceived standard of friendship. It may therefore be said, regardless of the actual integrity of the friend himself, that he dies nor for his friend but for his own concept of friendship. Man creates standards and later serves them as though they were divine creations, only to discover ultimately that Deity had no hand in their fashioning.

When the sage, seated in the midst of his rings of consciousness, elevates his realization to the sphere of the fourth ring, he passes from national to racial concerns. His ever increasing vista of understanding has revealed to him that the inhabitants of earth are not merely isolated individuals nor even families and tribes, but rather can be classified under a few racial headings. It naturally follows that the mind establishes comparisons between the relative superiority of these races; also that the unillumined man should upon some pretext or other elevate the particular race of which he is a part to the position of superiority. If at the time of making the comparison his own nation occupies a position that is evidently inferior, he will philosophize upon their past glory or dream of their future ascendancy. Such an individual, however, continues to annihilate diversity, for in his analysis of peoples he no longer conceives of a billion and a half separate units but rather of a score of major segments, each composed of a vast number of lesser parts from this attitude is born the racial spirit: we have "chosen" peoples and "rejected" peoples, racial gods, racial attitudes, and racial prejudices. Practically all civilized humanity is now in the throes of racial upheaval. The white man regards the black man as his inferior. Throughout the Southern States there is a definite color line drawn which in some cases is incalculably unjust. There are schools in the United States where the pupils, encouraged by parents of puerile intelligence, have risen in a body and refused to admit the enrollment of colored children in their classes. While the white man views with contempt the black man, he considers with ever increasing alarm the machinations of the yellow man and the brown man. The lot of the red man apparently gives his white brother little concern, for the latter feels that the work of extermination goes on apace. It is interesting to note at this stage the effort man makes not to be inclusive; for he seems to fear lest he should learn to love everything so much that he would have nothing left to hate.

The question of sex equality becomes an issue during this period and man has undertaken to determine whether woman really has the consciousness of a human being or whether she must depend upon man for rational intelligence. We sec people everywhere who function upon this level of the fourth ring. They are called broad-minded, charitable citizens with progressive ideas. In many instances they foster foreign missions and believe in spreading the white man's light throughout the dark and gloomy areas where the benighted non-Aryans reside. As Charles Erskine Scott Wood has noted, they discuss the holy war of Christendom and the unholy wars of the barbarians! They are more or less patronizing and condescending in their attitudes, feeling that by reason of their exalted status they can well afford to be "nice" to their less fortunate younger brothers. Such people do not compare favorably with those few outstanding examples of intelligence produced by the world. If contrasted, however, with the primitive attitudes of the first ring, their progress is apparent. These people arc trying to be big, but are bound to their littleness by precedent, environment, education, and fear. They dread to be on the unpopular side of any issue, yet sincerely wish that the popular side might occasionally be the right side.

In ancient astrology the fourth plane—that of the sun— was regarded as a middle point dividing the inferior or sub- solar planets from the superior orbs moving outside the solar orbit. It naturally follows that when the realization has been lifted to the consciousness of the fifth circle it should concern itself with greater verities. He who has reached this stage is capable of understanding the immortal words of Thomas Paine: "The world is my country, and to do good is my religion." The only defect in the slogan is the lack of definite understanding regarding the word good. The ideal is an excellent one but its fulfillment is very difficult, for good can never be discovered as long as the individual considers himself its true criterion.

Having thus pierced all the rings of consciousness to the fifth, realization has now reached that point where it begins to recognize the magnitude of the plan behind manifesting life. The concerns of nations and the politics of men then recede into insignificance; for from this comparatively exalted level of realization humanity is viewed as a single unit.

At this stage there also comes the realization that human life is not the only rational manifestation of Deity. Consciousness and intelligence are recognized in the lower kingdoms, and brotherhood extends to all corners of the earth, including all races and species without distinction. The vastness of the whole and the infinitesimal smallness of the part we call the world begins to be apparent. Upon this level philosophy begins,—that is, philosophy as apart from the individualistic codes established by primitive man with no thought for that which was beyond the vista of his own comprehension. The principles of justice emerge from the codes of primitive retribution. Power becomes thoughtful of weakness and might considerate of that which is less than itself. From the code of the survival of the fittest comes the realization that it is possible to make fit the unfit that all may survive. The subtler virtues are elevated above the grosser propensities and grace and beauty are regarded as superior to strength.

Although truth is still but a concept, the increasing realization gives the sense of magnitude which overawes and causes the half awakened faculties to glimpse the immeasurable that lies beyond. The sage within is coming into himself; the sky wanderer is casting off the bonds which bind him to earth; the voices of the Seven Spheres are calling and something far down in the depths of man's nature is tugging at its fetters, crying out for freedom to join in the ecstatic dance of life. Having raised himself to the contemplation of the world and its mystery, the sage finds himself one with the world and its mystery, his heart merged with the heart of the world, his mind teeming with the thoughts of the world, his whole being filled with the longings of the world. He ultimately reaches the state where he may truthfully say that he understands the world, for man understands what he is and is what he understands.

When realization pierces the sixth ring and blends itself with the consciousness of that plane, it is declared that the individual transcends individual concerns and becomes a citizen of the universe. His kinship with the sun, the moon, and the stars is established; for the consciousness that was formerly individual discovers individuality to be a limiting and binding illusion. Of such souls as have attained to this exalted state are the Bodhisattvas,—those who stand at the very gateway of liberation. These exalted ones may still turn back and as Elder Brothers walk the dusty roads of the lower worlds; but before them the swinging veils of Eternity are very thin and the voice of the great sea of Reality calls to them to immerse their lesser selves in its limitless expanse. To describe the consciousness of those so proximate to Reality is a futile undertaking for any one not so illumined. It can only be said that such as these brood over mortality, and leaning from the casements of heaven regard with solicitude divine this mundane sphere. These are the Great Ones who walk from star to star, whose souls are so vast that the whirling bodies of the firmament are encircled by them. These are the ones who gaze straight into the face of the sun unblinded.

The Oriental mind conceives these illumined and perfected ones to be vast beings whose statures extend from earth to heaven, whose feet rest upon pink lotus buds, and whose flowing draperies reveal in their grace the innate perfection of the wearer. Nowhere in all the mighty figure is a single incongruity to be found. The long, slender fingers either assume

the mudras with perfect rhythm or hold the symbols of divine accomplishment. Surrounded by its blazing nimbus, the noble head is set in absolute repose, yet in the awesomeness of its grandeur there is nothing to inspire fear, for the perfected ones are not terrible in power but rather beautiful in humility.

Though the great face of the Bodhisattva blazes like burnished gold, there is in it that sweet repose which makes all who behold it cease their strivings and enter into meditation. The jewels in the crown gleam and glisten with a holy light, and the clanking rings upon the mendicant's staff sound the music of the spheres. With his feet rising from the earth in lotus cups and his head blended with the heavens, the Bodhisattva thus stands as the embodiment of those redeeming graces which, latent in most men, have been awakened and brought to full expression through the aeons of preparation. The lips of the illumined are as lotus buds, for they have been perfected through ages of perfect speech and from them issue the words of perfect wisdom. The half-closed eyes contemplate the measureless vistas in whose depths resides the perfect Buddha, and toward this ultimate that lies beyond the seventh ring the Great One thus directs the ageles: chant of the Law:

I take my refuge in Thy Name and Thee! I take my refuge in Thy Law of Good!

I take my refuge in Thy Order! OMI It is not written that the lesser shall include the greater in its scope of awareness. It is impossible, therefore, to trace the magnitude of that illumination which, standing at the threshold of Reality, already glimpses the Endless. Of this consciousness all that can be said is that, robed in its own exaltedness, it awaits the day when it shall be merged with the All.

At last for the aspiring soul there comes the Great Day "Be With Us," which is indeed the end of all beginnings. This day, that has a dawn but no sunset, begins in time and lasts throughout eternity. Diversity has been completely absorbed and naught remains save the meditating saint and the Absolute. The iridescent bubble of being now floats upon the great Ocean from whose primordial spray it was fashioned.

For one breathless, unmeasurable second of time the bubble hangs suspended, an opalescent sphere. Against its confining walls the imprisoned sage hurls the blazing thunderbolt of his will. The bubble bursts and instantly disappears except for a fine mist that settles back into the endless sea. Thus is accomplished the annihilation of the last ring of illusion, when realization becomes so exalted as to be incapable of further qualification; when nothing but All is sufficient and the multitude of illusions—including the dream of existence— have been dissipated. The leering Yama (the god of illusion) who sought to grasp the bubble and its holy contents, retires discomfited, for the perfected one has escaped into the Refuge that endures. No more will the illumined one walk with man; his last discourse has been given; for the last time he has taken upon himself the veil of sorrow, for he has now merged himself with the Law that is his Refuge. Those who seek the perfected one must search for him in perfection, for he has become one with all the good which he sought. He is identical with the beauty that he served; he is the truth whose actuality he conceived; he is the sure foundation that is the absolute necessity.

To the disciples left behind, the Master who passes into Nirvana is one who has passed out of the world which shall cease, into the world which ceases not. He has become one with all the permanence that is and through all the manifestations of Infinite Law he is revealed. He has become one with the finger that traces the sunsets upon the western sky; one with the god of morning who, parting the curtains of night, ushers in the day; one with the winds and the rains. He gazes down from the blue mists of heaven and up from the dark mystery of the earth; his voice is heard in the mantra and his eloquence in the booming of the temple gong; his strength is made manifest in the Law and his meekness in the humility of the mendicant. The one gone has ceased to be somewhere but has grown to be everywhere , for he has found Reality and is himself one with that which all men seek. One by one the aspiring soul has discarded the limiting rings of consciousness. From the least to the greatest he has risen, and this he has accomplished by becoming the least among the least. With one supreme effort of realization he has renounced death and become deathless; he has willingly surrendered life and become lifeless. So, lifeless and deathless, he remains immovable in Eternity.

Climbing up the ladder of the stars he has followed the path to perfection; he has walked the Middle Road which has been established since the beginning of the world; he has followed in the footsteps of the sages gone before, and after him will come myriads yet unborn, until sometime the way to Nirvana shall be the royal road by which all humanity passes from the ephemerality of mortal existence to the unchangeableness of divine existence.

He who attains the Absolute is himself the Absolute; for while all men contemplate some world to which their consciousness has attuned them, he who has attained the Absolute contemplates only the inconceivable perfection of the Absolute itself. United with that which eternally endures, the perfected soul is freed forever from the illusion of change, of difference, of time, and of distance. It is useless, however, to attempt an analysis of the consciousness of the one in whom consciousness has thus been merged with Reality. While we struggle impotently with the tangled skein of life, such a one has gathered all its strands together and rewound the line of life to its own beginning. While we are borne upon its surface, powerless to stem its currents, such a one has reversed the waters of the river of life and caused them to flow back to their own source. Having revealed to all men through his life the fulfillment of the Law and having preached his farewell sermon that all might understand, the great Buddha entered Nirvana. Having by his resurrection demonstrated to all mankind the illusion of death, the Master Jesus ascended into the aeons to be united with his heavenly Father. Having demonstrated that justice alone shall survive, Socrates drank the hemlock and with perfect realization exchanged the death of life for the life of death. Certain of the Reality that lies beyond, and given courage by ever increasing vistas of consciousness, the aspiring soul proceeds to the annihilation of the unreal by hurling himself voluntarily through the wall of his prison into the embrace of the Law which is his Refuge and his End.

Having thus considered, in diagrammatic fashion at least, the principle involved in the unfoldment of realization, let us view the subject from the standpoint of the philosopher. If asked to describe the sensations through which he passes as he projects his realization inward toward the Self, the Oriental mystic would reply that he first seats himself in the midst of the bustle and confusion of the world. Then, having established his physical body in the posture and state prescribed by the Law, he begins the conscious withdrawal of himself from his outer life. Gradually the turmoil around him ceases until the physical world seems to sink away into space, leaving him alone immersed in a quasi emptiness which is permeated, however, by the sense of protection and well-being.

In its ascent realization passes through various states or conditions where, if right-mindfulness is not employed, the mystic wanders off into a phantasmal world which the European magicians of the Middle Ages chose to call the sphere of the astral light. Here the sense of emptiness is no longer present, for space seems filled with strange and exotic perfumes, and the one in meditation beholds flowers falling from space upon him until he is literally buried beneath a mass of sweet-smelling blossoms. Over him then steals a bliss unalloyed and the compelling urge to drift off into the astral gardens which have thus suddenly materialized into being. As Eliphas Levi says, however, the serpent of evil is entwined about each flower, and he who tarries here will never find the Real. But, resolute in his defiance of the phantasms thus conjured up by Mara, the realization of the mystic rises above all these through spheres of light and color, through planes where endless music peals as from a heavenly organ. At length all phenomena cease; light and darkness cease; the realization of the personal self ceases.

Slowly over the entire being descends an absolute peace and the mystic is swept into infinite realization. At this point the sage will end his description, for here description fails. Realization is the power by which the great achievement is rendered possible. Realization, as previously stated, must not be confused with intellectual acquiescence in, or concept of an idea. Realization is the measure of accomplishment. Realization is the product of right-thinking, right-feeling, and right-acting. Realization is not attainable except as the reaction of right-doing; only experience, renunciation, compassion, love, service, and ideality can build realization, and only realization is capable of elevating man through the various spheres of consciousness. Thus are definitely set forth the way, the means, and the end; but no man can take this path for another. Diversity is the paramount illusion. Only realization can overcome the concept of diversity. A great soul is obvious from his instinctive effort to synthesize the elements of life. Take, for example, the so-called body of knowledge. That which man believes he knows he has divided into a host of subdivisions, each of which is served by intellects naturally segregative and separative. The physicist, the biologist, and the anthropologist all live in worlds apart, each seeking with his own particular fragment of the body of knowledge to solve the riddle of it all. However, as consciousness reveals more and more of Reality to man, all these man made divisions disappear and the multitude of streamlets converge to form the three great rivers of science, philosophy, and religion. These, in turn, eventually empty into the one great ocean of Truth. Never will knowledge be possible, however, until we realize that each part is helpless without all the others; that all branches of learning are useless until merged in a single science representing the sun} of human thought, feeling, and belief.

It is sad but true that with few exceptions what man thinks he knows actually stands between him and knowledge, for he who is rich in beliefs is usually a pauper in facts. The theorist is too involved in his own irrational complexities to recognize rational simplicity. Barring the individual from the path of attainment are not only the unrecognized absurdities of his own life, but also the cumulative prejudice, bigotry, and false emphasis of generations. The theology of his fathers, the philosophy of his ancestors, and the stupendous scientific institutions of his contemporaries all tend to overawe the individual into acceptance of the unreal. The gods are so silent and man so bombastic that ignorant mortals may well be excused if they regard the dogmatic utterances of man as more authoritative than the silence of the gods. Only after much experience with the pyrotechnics of discordant isms is the eloquence of divine silence discernible. The world is largely composed of people whose smugness is impervious—people who are orthodox in their orthodoxy and orthodox in their heterodoxy. With equal facility they defend both their plethora of beliefs and their paucity of them. Exhibiting the keenest pleasure, they conduct one through the many chambers of their minds, woefully unaware that all this vast mental establishment represents a prison and not a palace. He who would tread the path that leads to light and liberation must first cast aside not physical possessions—which, at best, are but gew-gaws—but the so-called treasures of the mind, which are actually a hodgepodge of notions.

Divorced from all bias and assumption, stripped of the garments of pomp and ceremony, and exchanging the robes of self-satisfaction for the simple saffron garment of humility, the mendicant soul achieves by the Middle Road. His reliance is neither upon God nor man but upon the Law. In full realization that the Law of all things is ultimate perfection, the seeker after Reality takes his stand upon that eternal urge which moves all to this ennobled end.

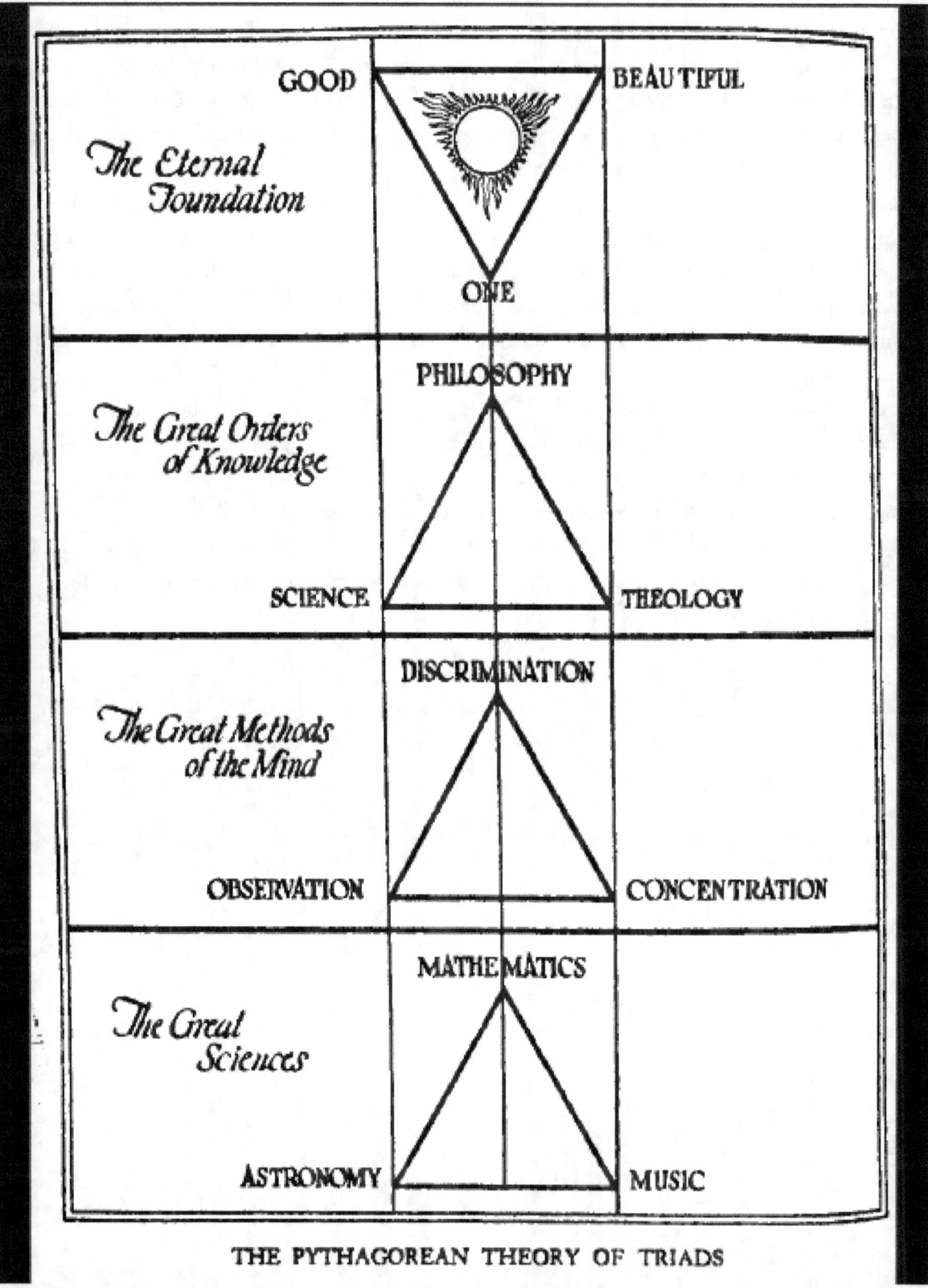

**THE PYTHAGOREAN THEORY OF TRIADS**

The fundamental motion of the One toward the Two, and from their sum the Triad is established. The triangle is the skeleton of the universe, the whole diversity of life being erected upon a threefold foundation. The complicated order of manifestation may cause the uninformed to lose sight of the unchanging Three, which is indeed the God of the wise.

# XIII

### ❦

# The Seven Days of Creation

Science and theology are widely at variance on the subject of the Creation Myth. The scientist is surrounded by ample evidence that all things grow slowly and naturally from a seed or germ containing potentially all of the parts and members which issue forth from it. The scientist firmly maintains that "nothing from nothing comes," whereas the theologian as emphatically declares that in the beginning there was "nothing" and from it came "everything!" When the enthusiastic clergyman announces that God reached out His right hand and made the sun and, grasping a handful of space with His left hand, molded it into the moon, the scientist is on the verge of nervous prostration.

In the first place, the prosaic man of letters has not the same conception of God as that which Michelangelo visualized while ornamenting the Sistine Chapel. Science refuses to take seriously the theological concept that God is a man, being convinced that if there were such a gigantic being floating around in space juggling constellations, the Mt. Wilson telescope would have discovered him ere this. On the other hand, the theologian is sorely distressed lest the soul of the savant earn for itself a brimstone pit as the retribution for its heresies. "God is spirit," announces the minister confidently. "What is spirit?" thunders back the scientist. "There is no use discussing it with you," replies the theologian, "you are not in the right frame of mind." "God is energy," proclaims the savant, a profoundly wise look upon his face. "What is energy?" retorts the minister. "That's a point that has been bothering us," answers the scientist complacently, "but we are making rapid progress towards the discovery of its constituents."

After carefully measuring the whale's throat, science announces that it was physically impossible for Jonah to have passed through it, and further investigation also has demonstrated that no whales are to be found in that part of the world. Experts in hygiene, after due consideration, announce that sanitary conditions on the Ark left much to be desired and that to ventilate a structure containing from two to seven of every known creature with one window less than two feet square was setting a very bad example for the younger generation. The natural history expert then proclaims that if the Ark landed on Mt. Ararat, the original snails haven't reached home yet.

While such statements may seem utterly ridiculous, they are the greatest single cause why hundreds of thousands of persons are leaving the Christian churches annually. They explain the vast number of agnostics and atheists among the younger people, for the juvenile mind, if not mature, is at least too logical in its function to ignore such religious absurdities. We still occasionally hear the term "old-time religion," and desperate efforts have been made to convince the modern world that this form of faith has a practical value. Such efforts have proved decidedly unsuccessful. In olden times it was possible to force people to declare allegiance to something they did not believe or accept. Possibly the "persuasive" measures used at that time had something to do with the alacrity with which people saw the error of their ways. We no longer live, however, in those good old days when people were converted with the thumbscrew and the fires of their zeal kept bright by burning visions of a torture chamber.

With the passing of physical torture as a method of demonstrating the love of God, there followed a period of mental torture. The thumbscrew gave place to the bogey of hell and the individual who for one reason or another was late to prayer meeting or missed communion was paralyzed with fear for the safety of his immortal soul. The day of the hell-fire and damnation sermonizing, when little children left church with ashen faces and trembling lips and strong men feared the dark, has also passed away except in a few outlying districts. These are the elements of the old-time religion: God was an autocrat, a tyrant, a despot; man a serf, who must enter the presence of His Maker groveling and dissembling piety.

The day that man fears his God is over. It may be true that now he fears nothing and consequently goes to excess in evil. Yet fear and love cannot exist together in the same heart. He who fears God does not love Him; he who loves God cannot fear Him. So there is coming into the world a new-time religion, which is nothing more nor less than a DEFENSE OF THE DEITY. Righteous men and women are rising up, declaring, "We know not who God is but something within our own souls tells us that He or It is God, impartial, just, true, and filled with mercy." Whereas in the past man's God was handed to him, man is now going forth in quest of a God, in search of a Deity noble and exalted enough to be a true ideal and an eternal inspiration. Thus, while the old-time religion may be defined as an acceptance of a man-made God, the new-time religion is a search for an eternally-existing Deity in no way subject to the limitations of human consciousness.

Where shall man search for a knowledge of His God? There are three places he may look: in his own heart, in his world, and in his sacred books. There was once a man who entered a temple to pray to his God and the priest of the temple came forward to receive his homage. And the man said to the priest, "Whose house is this?" and the priest answered, "This is the house of God." And the man who had come to pray turned to the priest, saying in a stern voice, "Then out of my way, MAN!"

God's dwelling is the heart of man; God's dwelling is His world. This is the doom of the church, for the wise man knows that every house is a church, every home an altar, every creature a shrine, and he himself a priest ordained since the beginning of the world.

The 20th century man and woman has reached a point in mental unfoldment which enables him or her to consider, with at least reasonable intelligence, the problem of individual salvation. The ever-increasing knowledge possessed by the race as a mass is also a great factor in man's growth. Excavations are bringing to light more complete records of the ancient world and gradually it is dawning upon the individual that the faith which he is serving is not properly understood—that he has been following vain superstitions and soulless illusions. He discovers that his Christianity is not the Christianity of the first century of the Christian Era. He realizes that he has been the victim of a great deceit; that the doctrines he has received were not those which would liberate him from the bondage of ignorance but rather false dogmas which would involve him ever more deeply in dependence.

Some day the religions of the world will be separated from the excrescences of superstition and their true purport revealed to humanity. The Scriptures are far greater than the interpretations given to them. They are ancient things, these Holy Books, and they have been preserved from generation to generation for uncounted thousands of years. Each nation has bequeathed to its successor a legacy of sacred writings and philosophic lore.

The Scriptures constituting the King James Bible have been gathered from every part of the world, from the very pagan nations to which it is shipped back in carloads for purposes of their "conversion." Do you realize that in nine cases out of ten the missionary who converts a pagan to the Bible is merely teaching him his own pagan cult under a new name? The missionary in India does not realize that his own Bible contains much Hindu mysticism. If he did, his mortification would know no bounds.

One of the most curious doctrines set forth in the Old Testament is that of the seven creative days described in the opening chapter of Genesis. It has been a never-failing source of amazement to me how it is possible for Christian ministers to discourse upon the opening verses of Genesis year after year, generation after generation, and never discover that they have misinterpreted and mistranslated the entire volume. Yet probably within the radius of a few miles may be found Hebrew scholars belonging to the Jewish faith who could in a very few moments show the Christian minister that he hadn't the faintest idea of the Creation Myth in the true light of Judaism. Jewish scholars know that the Christians have little or no comprehension whatsoever of the philosophical profundity of the Old Testament. Yet for centuries eminent divines have waxed eloquent on this most important subject, of which they nothing know.

In the same category with the Creation Myth is that endless source of ecclesiastical uneasiness—the Adam and Eve episode. For several hundred million years according to science and about four thousand years according to theology, this old planet has been struggling along attempting to live down the fatal mistake of our first and common parents who chanced to partake of a certain piece of fruit which all modern dietitians declare to be a most nutritious product especially if eaten in the forenoon. For this offense all humanity is supposed to pass through its mortal span with a hangdog look, ever mindful that the sins of its ancestors were grievous indeed.

While we cannot blame the agnostic for shunning a cult which seriously affirms that the salvation of billions of human beings can be endangered by an apple, we believe that a sincere investigation of the meaning of these ancient allegories as preserved in their original tongues would prove both profitable and inspiring and also supply material for the most profound reflection. There is a meaning to these ancient stories, a meaning unconsidered, yes unsuspected, by the great masses who year after year have accepted the inane explanations advanced by minds wholly disqualified to interpret their hidden meanings.

If we would interpret aright the allegories and parables of our Scriptures, we must turn to the source of those allegories and parables, namely the Jewish faith. But here again we are confronted with an almost insurmountable difficulty, for the Jew of today has forgotten his own philosophy and his race . Having mingled itself with all the peoples of the earth, he has lost its sublime heritage of spiritual ethics.

Most Jews today are satisfied with the Talmud, and the scholars among their people are chiefly concerned with interpreting the religious code therein contained. While the Rabbis may understand in part the Tora, or the body of the law, they have ceased to consider those more mystical writings that reveal the true spirit of Judaism. Ignorant of the profundity of the subject, all too many of the younger Rabbis find it easier to ridicule than to learn. Therefore, concerning himself with modern psychology, he seeks to supplant the secret doctrine of Israel with modernism—an almost meaningless and totally inadequate spiritual code.

Centuries of intercourse with adherents of other creeds and doctrines have had their effect upon the Jew. Especially does this appear to be true today, for it is very apparent that the Jew is assuming much of the culture and philosophy of Christendom. We lament this tendency, for while undoubtedly an ever-increasing understanding between these two great religions will result in good, we fear that it may cause the Jewish scholar to interpret his own archaic lore more and more in the light of the absurdities advanced by Christian divines, thus making it ever more difficult to discover the true meaning of these ancient doctrines.

The Mishna and the Qabbalah are the keys to true Jewish mysticism, and the Sepher Yetzirah and the Sepher ha Zohar, when properly interpreted, reveal the very essence of the original Rabbinical knowledge. Like all other great faiths, Judaism is twofold, its lesser part to be revealed to the many and its greater part concealed from all but the few. The same is true in Christianity. That part which we have so long revered is really chaff, for we have not learned as yet to thresh our doctrines as we do our grain. Remembering that Scriptures have always been written to conceal rather than to reveal, let us briefly sketch over the Creation Myth of the ancients in the light of the Qabbalistic teachings of the Hebrews and the secret doctrine of the Brahmins and the Greeks.

Before doing so, let me warn you that the order of the verses in the first chapter of Genesis is incorrect and not according to the original meaning; that many of the words are improperly translated and consequently must not be accepted as having any meaning like that now assigned to them. A few examples will clarify the subject. The first chapter of Genesis in Hebrew reads: ALEIM BRA BRAChIT AT EChIM UAT EARTz. This has been interpreted to mean "In the beginning God created the heaven and the earth," but from it may be extracted the following more amplified description: "The Forces, or Makers, of the world carved, or sculptured, as a beginning of existence the substances of the celestial firmament and the starry heaven and the substances of the lower, or arid, earth."

Again, where it is written that the ALEIM made man in their own image, it should be interpreted "in their shadow." Of course, the gravest error by far is that of interpreting ALEIM as meaning "God." In fact, the word "God" itself is a poorly chosen term with which to designate Divinity. The ALEIM are the ancient "Builders," the "Fabricators" of the world. They are not one but many, and they move or "brood" upon the face of unfinished being. Again, where it is written that "the earth was without form and void," the word "void" should be translated "an egg, or ovoid," for it signifies the Egg of Kosmos which the Egyptian deities are so often shown turning upon a potter's wheel.

According to the ancient Hebrews, in the beginning there was a complete and unconditioned state of eternal existence which stretched throughout and permeated the entire area of Being. This first and unconditioned potentiality they denominated AIN, or the Boundless. This Boundless and Limitless Existence, while actually indescribable, was hypothetically divided into three parts: AIN, the ALL; AIN SOPH, the Limitless One; and AIN SOPH AUR, the Limitless Light. These three together as one constituted THE ABSOLUTE. To define it was to defile it. It was the sure foundation of all existence, and the universe was an inverted tree with its roots in the ALL and its branches descending through the different gradations of existence. To AIN SOPH the ancient Qabbalists gave many names in an effort to dignify it and exalt it above all creatures and forms. Its symbol was a closed eye, and it in no way partook of existence other than to contribute its eternal life to be the spirit of existing things.

Qabbalism is a doctrine of emanations, and according to its exponents there emanated from the Eternal Condition, AIN SOPH, a bright and shining point—the Open Eye, the first of the Gods, the Ancient of Days, the Eternal Crown, the One from whom comes forth the many. This was denominated Kether, or the most ancient of the Fathers. In Kether, the Universal Seed, was contained the Universal Tree, which evolved out of it according to a fixed and immutable law. Kether corresponds to the "Father" in the Christian Triad, who not only gives birth out of Himself to the Great Mother, Aima, which is called Understanding, but also to the Great Father, Abba, called Wisdom. Through the union of the Great Father and Great Mother is produced the Child—Creation.

The various schools of Qabbalism have different methods of evolving the first triad out of AIN SOPH. To some, Kether is the Father and Binah the Mother, with Chochmah, or Wisdom, as the Son. To others, Chochmah is the Father, Binah the Mother, and Tiphereth the Son. To still a third group, Chochmah is the Father, Binah the Mother, and a mysterious hypothetical point called Daath is the Son. However the division may be effected, there is always a triune foundation consisting of Three revealing the One, thus establishing the triangular foundation of the world. At this point, please consider the accompanying diagram which sets forth the principles of Creation according to what the Qabbalists call "The Universal Tree," or "The Tree of the Sephiroth." This Tree consists of ten globes joined together by 22 lines, or paths. The ten globes represent the ten numbers from 1 to 10 as shown, and the 22 paths are the letters of the Hebrew alphabet. Taken together, these constitute the 32 paths of wisdom, the 32 degrees of Freemasonry, and the 32 teeth in the Divine Head.

The Tree consists of three vertical columns, those on the right and left being the pillars of Jachin and Boaz respectively, and the one in the center the sacred column of Equilibrium, which is dedicated to the Deity Himself. Thus positive and negative are revealed with equilibrium in the midst, and the true order of the universe is made manifest. Like the Pythagoreans, the Hebrews depict the universe as issuing in ten stages from the Absolute, these stages being shown as globes upon the branches of the Sephirothic Tree. This great Tree descends through four worlds and finally in the lowest consists of the ten divisions of the sidereal system in the following order:

| No. | The Sephiroth | The Universe |
|---|---|---|
| 1 | Kether—The Crown | Primum Mobile |
| 2 | Chochmah—Wisdom | The Zodiac |
| 3 | Binah—Understanding | Saturn |
| 4 | Chesed—Mercy | Jupiter |
| 5 | Geburah—Severity | Mars |
| 6 | Tiphereth—Beauty | Sun |
| 7 | Netsah—Victory | Venus |
| 8 | Hod—Glory | Mercury |
| 9 | Jesod—The Foundation | Moon |
| 10 | Malchuth—The Kingdom | Elements |

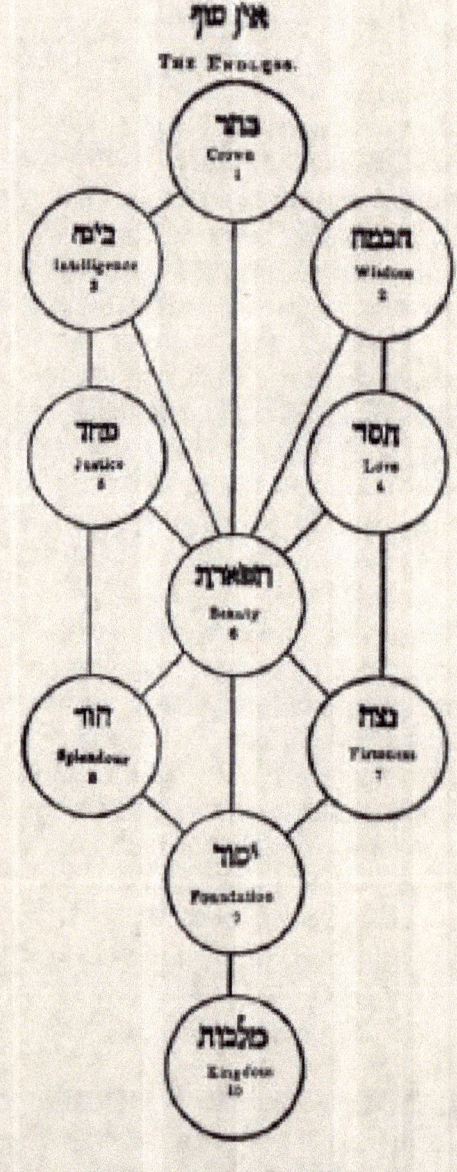

## The Tree of the Sephiroth

To each of these spheres or globes the Hebrews assigned one of the ten great Names of God, one of the ten archangels, one of the ten angelic powers, one of the ten parts of the sidereal world, and one of the ten demons of the underworld. They also divided the Ten Commandments, assigning a Commandment to each of the Sephiroth, and later the Christian Qabbalists assigned a tenth part of the Lord's Prayer to each of these globes. At this time it is important to make clear the true meaning of the Sephirothic globes. They are to be considered as planes of Nature, of which each includes all less than itself and is included in all greater than itself. Thus, Kether, the first globe, actually contains within itself potentially the energies of the nine inferior spheres emanating from it. For this reason, the Sephiroth are often shown as a series of concentric rings, with Kether at the outer edge of the circle and Malchuth in the center. The first three Sephiroth constitute the Triad, which is the foundation of the world. The remaining seven parts are divided into the six "Days" of Creation and the "Sabbath" of rest. Thus, Creation is the process of the Divine Life descending according to the order of the numbers from Kether to Malchuth.

The accompanying diagram shows the ten parts of Creation—the Sephiroth—assigned to the various sections of a great human body. The human figure is the Celestial Adam—the Great Man—in whose "image" the human man was created. Here we see Kether, the Crown, representing the spiritual center of the upper brain, possibly the pineal gland. Chochmah and Binah—the Father and Mother—are the two hemispheres of the cerebrum. Chesed and Geburah are the arms—the active parts of the Great Man. Tiphereth is the heart and, more generally, the entire trunk of the great body. Netzach and Hod are the two legs, or the supports of the universe. Yesod is the male generative power, and Malchuth both the feet and the female generative power. Thus the Cosmic Androgyne is in reality the Grand Man of Nebuchadnezzar's dream, with head of gold and feet of clay. In his History of Magic, Eliphas Levi thus describes the Creation of the world according to the ancient Jewish concept as embodied in the Sepher ha Zohar:

"That synthesis of the world, formulated by the human figure, ascended slowly and emerged from the water, like the sun in its rising. When the eyes appeared, light was made; when the mouth was manifested, there was the creation of spirits and the word passed into expression. The entire head was revealed, and this completed the first day of creation. The shoulders, the arms, the breast arose, and thereupon work began. With one hand the Divine Image put back the sea, while with the other it raised up continents and mountains. The Image grew and grew; the generative organs appeared, and all beings began to increase and multiply. The form stood at length erect, having one foot upon the earth and one upon the waters. Beholding itself at full length in the ocean of creation, it breathed on its own reflection and called its likeness into life. It said: Let us make man—and thus man was made. There is nothing so beautiful in the masterpiece of any poet as this vision of creation accomplished by the prototype of humanity. Hereby is man but the shadow of a shadow, and yet he is the image of divine power. He also can stretch forth his hands from East to West; to him is the earth given as a dominion. Such is Adam Kadmon, the primordial Adam of the Kabalists. Such is the sense in which he is depicted as a giant; and this is why Swedenborg, haunted in his dreams by reminiscences of the Kabalah, says that entire creation is only a titanic man, and that we are made in the image of the universe.

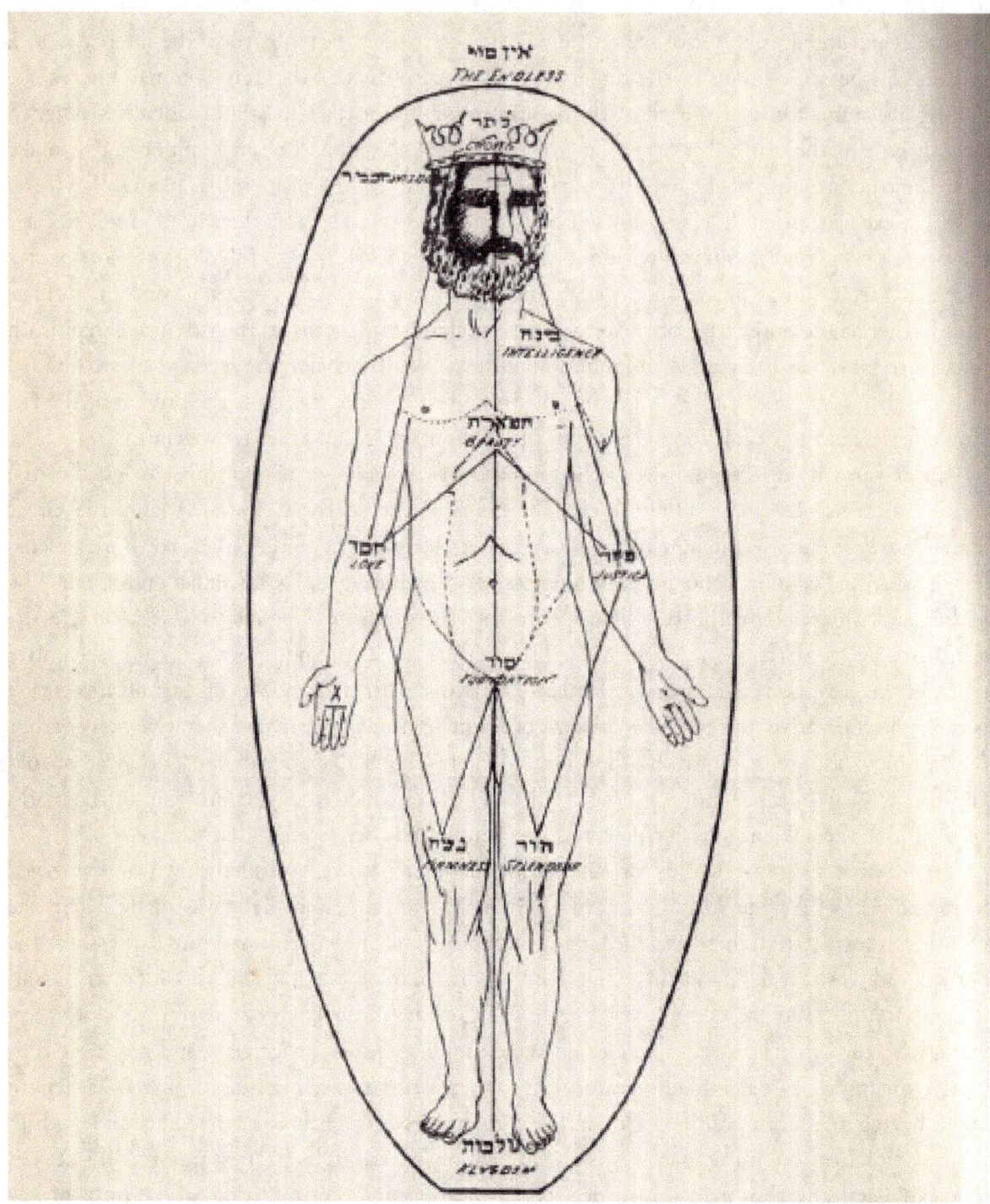

Thus, the incarnation of the Grand Man resulted in environments suitable for the unfoldment of the multitudes of creations, which in their sum constitute the Universal Being. According to the teachings of the Zohar, the Sephirothic Tree is divided into five parts or divisions.

The terms applied to these parts are quite familiar to students of philosophy and comparative religion, but few understand their exact meaning. In the Zohar, Kether, the Crown—which is literally the objectification of AIN SOPH, the Limitless and Eternal Being—is called Macroprosophus: the Great Face, the Long Face, or the Immense Countenance. Many chapters are devoted to a minute description of the parts of the Great Face. It is described as having no eyelids, for "the God of Israel neither slumbers nor sleeps." Its hair and beard are divided into a vast number of parts, and its brain is filled with the divine dew. From its mouth issue the sacred letters and numbers by which the universe is established, and its power is without limit.

The second of the five primary divisions is Chochmah, Abba, the Father—the term applied in the Qabbalah to the principle of Wisdom, a positive emanating power, flowing forth into the third division, Binah, or Aima, the Mother, termed in the Zohar "Understanding."

The fourth division is Microprosophus, the Short Face, the Lesser Face, the Smaller Countenance. This is composed of the six Sephiroth—Chesed, Geburah, Tiphereth, Netzach, Hod, and Yesod—and is commonly called Zauir Anpin, or the Lesser Adam, whereas Macroprosophus is designated Arikh Anpin, or the Superior Adam. The Lesser Face, consisting of six parts, is appropriately symbolized by a cube, which body consists of six surfaces. It is also the double interlaced triangles of Zion—the signet seal of Solomon. It represents the cardinal directions: north, east, south, west, up, and down, and the evolution of life through its globes constitutes the six Days of Creation.

The tenth sphere, Malkuth, constitutes the fifth division, and its designation is "The Bride of Microprosophus." Malkuth is composed of the four elements, and being the physical sphere, is an epitome of all the divine planes which are involved in its existence. It is the foundation—or the feet—of the world and is the sphere alluded to in the Lord's Prayer where it is written: "For thine is the kingdom, the power, and the glory."

According to both the Greek and Hermetic schools, as well as that of the Hebrew Qabbalists, the spirit of man, entering into the mystery of birth, descended through the supermundane spheres from the birthplace of souls—the Milky Way, or the sphere of the fixed stars. The ladder used in the Mithraic initiations signifies by its seven rungs the spheres of the seven planets which, according to the ancients, constituted the sidereal world.

In coming into physical manifestation, the soul first reached the sphere of Saturn. Here, the Governor of the Saturnian ring gave man a divine principle—in fact, a certain part of the power of Saturn actually entered into the composition of man. From the ring of Saturn the soul descended to that of Jupiter, where it was further clothed. From the sphere of Jupiter it descended into that of Mars, where a third garment or veil was given to it. From Mars it descended into the Sun, where the light and intelligence of the divine globe was imparted to the descending soul. From the sphere of the Sun the soul descended to that of Venus, where the fifth veil was cast over it. From here it descended to the sphere of Mercury, where it was invested with the sixth veil. From Mercury it descended to the sphere of the Moon, where the seventh veil was added, and from there it descended into the Earth, bringing with it the septenary constitution imparted to it by the Governors of the supermundane spheres.

In the various schools the order of the planets differs somewhat, but in every case the principle involved is the same. The seven Days of Creation are not "days" or "years," but are the seven stages through which the soul must pass in order to reach perfection.

The spirit of man, stripped of its vehicles and the bequests of the Governors, is a radiant spiritual center of power and force. The Lord of the first ring imparts its power, and the spirit of man becomes limited by the vestments with which it is enswathed. These vestments become its invisible bodies, and when it assumes material form, they are the causal forces which result in certain peculiarities in the physical constitution and nature.

In the evolution of this physical globe, the Lord of the first ring gave to the spirits of the Earth chain the bodies of stones, and this constituted "the first Day." Then the Lord of the second ring gave the mineral the power of growth and it became a plant, and this constituted "the second Day." Then the Lord of the third ring gave to the plant the power of motion and emotion, and it became an animal, and this constituted "the third Day." Then the Lord of the fourth ring—the golden globe of the sun—gave to the animal the power of thought and the animal became a man, and this constituted "the fourth Day." In the fifth "Day," the fifth Lord will give to man a new and spiritualized faculty which will make him a superman, a true Ben-Elohim, and on the sixth "Day" the Lord of the sixth ring will also bestow his gift, and the superman will then become what to us must appear a demigod. Upon the seventh "Day," the seventh power will be added, but it is called a "Day of Rest," because the power is not a new faculty but rather the gift of coordination, wherein all the parts are brought under the control of one divine power—the spiritual Ego.

One of the subtlest shades of meaning concealed within the above description of the involving soul is that the nature of man serves as a point for the incarnation of the Lords of the rings of the various planets. In other words, the powers and faculties with which man expresses himself are in reality the energies or hierarchies constituting the septenary body of the Solar Lord. Therefore, man is not one but seven in one. Of this seven, three are primary and four secondary. The three primary are the invisible or causal nature, and the four secondary are the visible or reflective nature. The seven powers, represented by the lower seven Sephiroth, are the colors of the spectrum—the three primary being the superior, and the four secondary the inferior. The three primary powers have their musical analogy in the first, third, and fifth notes, and the four secondary powers in the remaining notes of the octave.

From the above a glimpse may be obtained of the real involvements to be met with in a study of the Old Testament. Thousands of pages of Qabbalistical writings must be culled, and the legends and allegories of a score of nations must be fitted together if the Biblical student is really to gain an understanding of the documents given to him out of antiquity.

# XIV

⚜

# The Disciplines of Salvation

ASSUMING realization to be the product of definite philosophic disciplines, we now turn to a consideration of the sciences and procedures which are most valuable in the unfoldment of the rational intellect and the directionalization of the conscious Knower. Initiated into the mysteries of contemplative philosophy by the Brahman initiates of Ellora and Elephanta, Pythagoras set forth three disciplines as essential to salvation through unity with Universal Cause. Supreme in his contemplative genius, Pythagoras differs from his Eastern mentors in that he conceived the universal state to be attained through elevation of the mind rather than annihilation of thought procedure. As the first step toward realization, he accordingly taught the training of the mind so as to make it capable of sustained logical activity. The misconception is quite general that a common school education equips the mind for the profession of living, and, if supplemented by university training the individual is thereby qualified to question and debate intelligently the dictums of eternity. Modem education, is not founded upon strict rational procedure; hence the mass of humanity is not educated but rather supports its notions by the vain mumblings of archaic dogma. Unless first subjected to definite disciplines, the mind is incapable of rational functioning. There are few, alas, who, like the young Dalai Lama of Tibet, are able to rise in their cribs on their natal day and recite the Sutras in a convincing manner I If a man should approach us and say, "I am a human being and a biologist simply because I am a born biologist," we would consider him ridiculous, knowing that many years of definite application must be spent in equipping the reason to cope with the issues of biology.

Yet if someone else equally lacking in fitness comes along and says, "I am free, white, and twenty one; my thoughts, consequently, are as good and my conclusions concerning life as sound as those of any other man," we would smile benignly and exclaim, "Ah, vive la democratie!"

Since few people regard thinking as an exact science, an intellect such as Socrates' could in a few moments literally rip to shreds the entire fabric of human notions. To learn to think intelligently requires more time and effort than any other profession known to man, and is only to be realized through the most exacting disciplines. Most wordly-wise men are in the same position as the young patrician, Alcibiades, who because he wrestled well and played the lyre not too badly considered himself qualified to sit in the Athenian Senate. But all are not fortunate enough to have Socrates, the plebeian, barking at their heels, continually reminding them in no uncertain terms that not on a single count could they qualify.

With the same delightful inconsistency characteristic of human procedure, when Socrates revealed to the Athenians their ignorance they corrected the condition by poisoning the man who had the audacity to confront them with it.

Pythagoras invariably demanded of his disciples a familiarity with the principles of three sciences: mathematics, music, and astronomy. These sciences are today capable of filling the same ends which they served in ancient days, for they not only reveal to those familiar with their principles certain cosmic verities, but also instill the principles of order, rationality, and comparative values. The curse of the twentieth century is the superficiality of its thought and the resultant insufficiency of the foundation upon which the structure of life is erected. What does it mean to become proficient in mathematics, music, and astronomy? Remember, we do not refer to the utilitarian aspect of these sciences which too frequently realizes its ideal in the creation of the bookkeeper, the jazz pianist, and the elderly prognosticator who determines the annual precipitation from observation of the size of the sun-spots.

Those who approach life with the Oriental attitude—namely, that matter is a vast sea of illusion—may rightly question he advisability of devoting years to the mastery of sciences wholly concerned with the substances of the illusion. Such individuals, however, must learn to regard a certain rational grasp of the tangible as prerequisite to a conception of the intangible. It is not what man actually learns that is of value to him, but rather the mental and spiritual activities within his own nature that necessarily precede and follow learning. Like the carpenter building a chair, the accomplishment is not the production of the chair but the ability to build chairs. Thus thought in itself should not be regarded as an accomplishment or necessarily valuable, for only the ability to think represents a definite degree of unfoldment within the nature of the thinker himself.

When the student realizes that the entire fabric of creation is permeated by certain exact elements and principles, he unconsciously begins to figure and think in terms of exactness. The philosophy of salvation is nothing if not exact. According to both Pythagoras and Plato, mathematics is the father of the sciences—the first and greatest of the mystical disciplines of exactness. Without mathematics as a foundation, nothing can endure; upon its exactitude is raised the entire structure of order and sequence. All other arts and sciences are dependencies of mathematics, for into each enters the element of precision that manifests the unchangeable nature of number.

Referring to our fundamental symbolic triad, mathematics is the dot, music the line, and astronomy the circle. The mysteries of the invisible causal sphere are to be approached by the principles of mathematics; the mysteries of the intermediate sphere are revealed by the profundities of aesthetics and harmonics; the mysteries of the inferior sphere are disclosed

by the study of astronomy. Thus these sciences are the first triad of knowing and he who masters them is equipped to face the universe with a definite assurance that he is part of a

scheme whose principles are inflexible, whose agencies are beautiful, and whose results are exact. Many people with whom we have discussed these Pythagoric disciplines complain that life is so short and its problems so numerous that time does not permit the mastery of such complicated studies. The inconsistency of such an attitude is primarily one of wrong emphasis. He who does not start because he fears he will not live to finish will never live to start.

A certain friend approaching his eightieth year is on the verge of commencing the study of Spanish because he feels that it will be an important language during his next incarnation.

An individual with such an attitude has surmounted a great obstacle. Too many live in the past and as the years roll by consider the future as an ever-diminishing quantity. The realization of infinite futurity is indispensable to accomplishment, but it is useless unless accompanied by a definite impulse to make now the starting-point of achievement.

Pythagoras was well aware that inconstancy and inconsistency render valueless the greater part of human rumination,— hence he regarded the quality of exactness as essential to true mental functioning. He knew that a mind trained to recognize but one right answer to any problem in mathematics would likewise recognize that there is but one right solution to any problem in life. Yet Pythagoras was not fundamentally a mathematician; he was a philosopher, but mathematics was the first and sharpest of his tools. Mathematics is the supreme discipline in the science of knowing. More mystics have come into an understanding of the unseen side of life and realized the unfoldment of their inner perceptions through mathematics than through any other science known to man.

Mathematics is the Pythagorean symbol of what the Buddhist terms the Law—the procedure of Being. Through numbers the intricate mechanism of divine will is disclosed, for nothing else reveals so patently the exactness of cosmic method and the immutability of cosmic ends. The vast field of manifestation is shown to be an orderly chain of emanations issuing from the incomprehensibility of First Cause, and after passing through definite phases of change returning to that from which they were temporarily separated. Through mathematics a hypothetical framework is established by means of which the natures of all manifestations are analyzed and the modes of their directionalization determined. He who understands mathematics can never conceive of himself as existing in an unorganized universe nor regard himself as an exception to the immutable laws of Being. Thus is established the realization of participation in all the activities of Cosmos, and the glory of the whole is augmented as mathematics unveils the magnificence of the Eternal Plan.

In music the Real and the ideal are blended. The mathematical basis upon which the science of harmonics is founded insures preservation of the principle of exactness. At the same time music stimulates lofty emotional reactions and thus ameliorates the austerity of numbers. While mathematics emphasizes the exactness of Deity, music reveals the moods of the Causal Nature. Like a flowering vine twining itself about the harsher outlines of mathematical procedure, music softens and beautifies the angles of cosmic discipline. Many dream of the beauty of things as they could be, but only the philosopher can recognize the beauty of things as they are. To such as are able to lift themselves above the personal concerns of life, the concord of the All is apparent. When Pythagoras taught that men should depend not upon their ears but upon mathematics for the determination of harmony, he emphasized a subtle verity: namely, that the exactness of divine procedure is the absolute standard of harmony, and the order of universal flow is the perfect pattern of all rhythm. These are also the salient points of the philosophy of Taoism, and the ascetics of every age have striven to unite their own lesser natures with the harmonic procedures of divinity.

Worlds, like atoms, are in a state of ceaseless vibration, and this vibration shared by all manifestations is the mysterious dance of life. From the inner nature the study of music causes to issue forth a love for life in all its diversity. While mathematics inspires awe for the immutability of divine jurisprudence, music reveals the all-knowing Lawmaker as tempering justice with mercy. Astronomy strangely supplements both mathematics and music, and in turn is completed by them. The author of the Merchant of Venice causes one of his players to say:

There's not the smallest orb which thou beholdst, But in his motion like an angel sings, Still choiring to the young-eyed cherubims. By the science of astronomy the magnitude of Reality is established, for if the unreal stretches from time to timelessness, how much greater must that perfection be of which creation is the inferior past? Gazing out into the infinite from the nanthill he calls the earth, man comes to realize the insignificance of his personality; but as the eyes of his inner reason open he beholds the Reality within through the transcendency of which he is made to partake of the glory of both the manifested and the unmanifested. In an effort to catch a possible glimpse of any stray gods who might be prowling about the fringe of creation, astronomers are fashioning ever larger and more efficient equipment with which to scan the heavens. A new telescope is now under construction by which stars of the twenty-fifth magnitude will be brought within the range of human vision. Thus, of all forms of human learning none possesses the power of astronomy to impress the individual with the realization of cosmic magnitudes. The contribution of astronomy to the attitude of toleration is incalculable; for from the time when Giordano Bruno gave his life that the heavens might be saved for astronomers, the insufficient god of theology was doomed. Equipped with the realization awakened by contemplation of the profundities of mathematics, music, and astronomy, the candidate after spiritual understanding may fearlessly knock at the portals of the House of Wisdom and demand admission to the hidden house of the Mysteries.

To those just beginning to awaken to the immensities of life, philosophy is a very hard religion. At first philosophy seems to be faith without sentiment, for it is not concerned with emotion in the ordinary acceptance of the term. Having no time for the petty interests which constitute the life of the average individual, philosophy, because of its concern over infinities and ultimates, seems distant and austere. Most individuals live in a universe of trivialities, spending their entire appointed span in the struggle for worthless trinkets. Such naturally desire and create a God concerned with trivialities, for their Deity is presumed to be interested in the effect of early frosts upon the crops or the probability of the leghorns escaping the roup; He must also be invoked at conferences and haled willy-nilly into court to act as sponsor for the integrity of those who testify. On Sunday he is likewise obligated to be in attendance at all the churches, not to mention the Wednesday evening prayer-meeting.

When philosophy attempts to dissipate this puerile conception of the Causal Agent, a great hue and cry goes up and those who never had a God other than themselves, cry out, "You have destroyed our faith; you have blasphemed our Creator and you strive to take away our God!"* To such mediocre minds philosophy is assuredly a monster who demands a degree of intelligence requisite for attainment which would require time and application far beyond their willingness to sacrifice for such an end. In reality, however, philosophy has a heart greater than all the hearts of the world, and it is most loving and most kind because it is most just. Philosophy, like a wise parent, occasionally finds it necessary to chastize its children, not in anger but in the realization that man himself has no enemy like his own uncorrected vice. The truly great philosophers have been men and women whose hearts overflowed with love and understanding; but also they have been strong, and their strength lay in their recognition of that which was necessary for the good of all. Out of philosophy is born the camaraderie of the spirit.

Philosophy does not grind the masses down to a state of bondage in order that it may elevate a few. On the contrary, philosophy is a mental democracy. Thought is not turned
to the disqualification of one another, but directed by all to the common end of wisdom. The humanity of today opposes the mind that generalizes, for we live in an age of specialization. The fact that philosophers think in terms of cosmic immensity causes the conservative intellect to view them askance. While minds of small caliber arc concerned with the issues of ward politics, the philosopher contemplates that camaraderie which he has discovered among the sparks of infinite Being that fill the endless vista of beginnings and ends. The philosopher is a wanderer through the fields of space; to him the earth is a tiny oasis in a vast wilderness. Two or three palm trees, a little fountain, and a winding road—these constitute the caravanscry where he rests between his daily journeys.

To people who are selfish; who seek prestige and demand attention; who are superior to others; who feel that in their veins courses a noble blood; who believe that when God molded them he breathed upon them twice while upon less fortunate mortals he breathed but once—to these and all other varieties of hypocrites philosophy is not pleasing, for it is the creed of honest men and can never come into its own until there are honest men.

Philosophy stands for something infinitely superior to physical honesty; something far more difficult of attainment: it stands for mental honesty. It is the fellowship of those who understand; a brotherhood of as many orders as there are degrees of understanding. It is strange that in modern times those who espouse philosophy are prone to grow either unfeeling or eccentric. They are inclined to become mentally lazy.

Trusting themselves to the laws of which they have but an insufficient concept, they cease that individual struggle which, after all, is the only measure of true greatness. They have not discovered that while law governs the universe, love is its administrator in the hearts of men. Hence, the knowledge of law is not sufficient. To such knowledge must be added the realization that we are the administrators of that which we know, and that within ourselves we have the privilege of tempering the blast of eternal glory so that the shorn lamb may not be destroyed thereby.

Observation, discrimination, and concentration are prerequisites of knowing. It is first necessary to observe the infinite diversity of phenomenal being; then to discriminate between that which is primary in importance and that which is secondary. Having determined that which is most worthy of consideration, it is then necessary to concentrate the attention upon the task of discovering the recondite truths therein contained.

When these three faculties arc properly combined they result in a very high degree of rational penetration. Only such individuals as have learned to observe, discriminate, and concentrate arc qualified to occupy executive positions in any walk of life. If, for example, these faculties had been possessed to even a reasonable degree by the early translators and editors of the Bible, what a different aspect would be taken on by the Scriptures; for instead of words, words, words, the spirit of Holy Writ would have been preserved.

In what particular does observation differ from seeing? We prefer to think of observation as the perfection of seeing, and the perfection of seeing is not the mere beholding of an object but rather the instant discernment of its inner constitution.

Observation is not the mere seeing of things but rather the ability to see through things, making transparent, as it were, their outer nature so that the causal agencies precipitating them may be estimated. Observation, therefore, not only envisages the inherent nature of an object but also its relationship to that which precedes it as cause and follows it as consequence.

Readers of the works of Sir Arthur Conan Doyle are familiar with the fascinating deductions of Sherlock Holmes which he was forced to explain in all their detail to the ever bewildered Dr. Watson. Into the mouth of Sherlock Holmes his creator puts an excellent description of the powers of observation, for it is true that a man's shoes, the manner in which

he holds his hands, his air and carriage all reveal to the trained observer the characteristics of the inner nature which must manifest through these physical peculiarities. The range of human vision is able to take in a comparatively immense area of manifestation, and yet comparatively little of that which is seen is recorded in such a way that it can be evoked by the reasoning processes. Only when the consciousness itself is focused upon the organs of sight is their record preserved.

We arc most likely to behold and preserve the memory of that which is related to some major interest of life. Thus, a plumber will instinctively turn his attention to water pipes, while the artist will scrutinize the lower corner of the canvas for the painter's signature.

In great measure, therefore, observation is directionalized by interest, for man sees first that which interests him. Only after ages of mental unfoldment does man learn that in the last analysis all things are of equal interest. Interest is generally unjust in that it focuses the attention upon some fractional part before the panorama of the whole has been taken into consideration. At this point the problem of philosophic indifference should be considered. The philosopher is indifferent not in the sense that he ignores or refuses to concern himself with the diversity of being, but rather that he refuses to become biased by directionalizing his interest primarily upon any single phase of life to the exclusion of the remainder.

We study observation first because of its generalizing effect.

If particularity precedes generality, the result will be mental intolerance and injustice. If however, specialization follows generalization, then the mind-familiar with all—may justly choose one phase of existence and develop it with rationality. But when the individual, having first conceived generality and estimated its profundity, chooses to continue dealing with and thinking in terms of generality, he truly remains a philosopher.

In his introduction to An Essay on the Beautiful by Plotinus, Thomas Taylor writes: "But surely the energies of intellect are more worthy our concern than the operation of sense; and the science of universal, permanent and fixed, must be superior to the knowledge of particulars, fleeting and frail. Where is a sensible object to be found which abides for a moment the same; which is not either rising to perfection, or verging to decay; which is not mixed and confused with its contrary;

whose flowing nature no resistance can stop, or any art confine?

Since then there is no portion of matter which may not be the subject of experiments without end, let us betake ourselves to the regions of mind, where all things are bounded in intellectual measure; where every thing is permanent and beautiful, eternal and divine. Let us quit the study of particulars for that which is general and comprehensive, and through this learn to see and recognize whatever exists."

Observation may be considered as the process of seeing with the mind rather than with the eye. It involves an analysis of the object beheld and the effort to sense or conceive its intrinsic nature. The end of observation is the ability to cognize the life behind the form, the fact behind the fancy, the truth behind the symbol, and the Self behind the not-self. Through observation one is able to discover wisdom in the words of fools and foolishness in the words of most wise men. Observation, furthermore, is the ability to comprehend the pervading wholeness. He who sees may see the parts, but he who observes closely may glimpse the divine cement that binds the fractions together. We live in a world of men who see in part and are seen in part; who think in part, hope in part, fear in part. The universe is regarded as fragmentary or partitive because we lack the faculty of seeing the wholeness of things.

Observation is that transcendent faculty which is able to grasp the wholeness of things in its span of comprehension, whereas ordinary sight is simply the ability to analyze the fragments. Thus sight differs from observation as widely as analysis differs from synthesis.

The inherent danger of observation is that when the man of ordinary vision begins to observe the vastness surrounding him and to realize that even the most minute particle of that vastness is itself immeasurably great, bewilderment ensues. There is an overwhelming sense of inadequacy to cope with the enormousness of the scheme. Then it is that the faculty of discrimination comes to the rescue, emphasizing the fact that if man is not capable of knowing all now he must compromise by devoting himself to a consideration of only the best. We all realize that in one short span of physical life we cannot do everything, we cannot know everything, we cannot have everything, we cannot be everything—the major part of accomplishment must be left in the keeping of futurity. So, contemplating the heterogeneous mass of phenomena, the rational soul establishes itself upon the surface of phenomena and directs its attention to the specific task of choosing from all that which is next and most necessary to the unfoldment of the faculty of realization.

He who possesses discrimination is master of the science of values. Discrimination is the value sense; It is the ability to look upon a number of objects apparently equally important, and instantly, instinctively, unerringly recognize that which is chief among them. Recognizing the whole to be of paramount value, it is then necessary to determine the nature of those parts which contribute most to the whole, or that part of the tangible proximate to the intangible.

According to the Greek philosophers discrimination is that faculty which organizes things into their value sequence, placing that which is primary first, that which is secondary second, and so on ad infinitum . Discrimination is one of the most valued possessions of the inferior man, for it enables him to conserve energy and thus evade the illusions of time, distance, and quality that he himself has established. Discrimination reveals to man that he has what he saves and loses what he wastes in the realm of the physical. By concentrating the energy upon that which is primary, and hence superior, discrimination results in the proper conservation of life. The length of life is not to be estimated by the number of years that we plow blindly through the mire of matter. Not time but accomplishment is the true measure of existence. The attainment of true wisdom in all its phases—spiritual, aesthetic, and ethical—is the supreme accomplishment. By directionalizing all the energies upon these more important matters, discrimination liberates the mind from the hopeless drudgery of the mediocre.

There arc three forms of discrimination. The first has for its goal the discovery of that part of visible and sensible things which is primary. It is limited to the form sphere and deals with the problems of multitude and magnitude. For example, in the human body this form of discrimination determines the heart to be the chief part of the body. The second form of discrimination is that concerned with the relative integrity or excellence of innate characteristics. It is limited to the comparison of mental and moral excellences. This type of discrimination would elevate the idealist above the realist, the generous above the penurious, the unselfish above the selfish, the beautiful above the so-called practical; for it conceives the greatest good to occupy always the highest place. The third and highest form of discrimination is the power to differentiate between permanence and impermanence, Reality and unreality. It is limited to an estimation of the degrees of spiritual permanence. Through this type of discrimination is established the philosophic fact that the spiritual, or invisible man is the real man. Only the one in whom the faculty of discrimination is highly evolved is brave enough to elevate to the position of first importance and greatest solidarity that which to most men is an intangible mystery.

Discrimination is essential to success in every department of life—spiritual, mental, and physical. Men and women in the physical world must choose means and methods of solving the problems of livelihood, and through the use of right discrimination the material activities can be chosen so as to produce definite benefit in the superphysical nature. Discrimination differentiates between people and what they do; between the thinker and his thought; between the spirit and its body; between the innate Divinity within and the objective materiality without. Discrimination gradually elevates the consciousness of the individual until it is prone to seek out the good as that which is most worth-while. The height of discrimination is the recognition of the best. Evil is recognized as the least degree of good; matter, the least degree of spirit; the not- self (which is the personality), the least degree of the real Self (which is the principle). Discrimination has for its arch-enemy human selfishness.

Because of its innate dishonesty, humanity deprives itself of the right to know good and evil. Justice is symbolized as blindfolded so that its personal attitudes may not influence its decisions. If discrimination is to be of value, it must also be applied with a strictly impersonal attitude; for the instant the mind is personally involved in its problem, the sense of true perspective and relationship is lost. Most people sit in one end of the scales when they weigh a problem. We are prone to live not according to our knowledge of right and wrong but according to our prejudices and whims. Things have an unpleasant way of looking not as they actually are but as we want them to, all because we cannot divorce the personal equation from our problem. Thus we make the decision fit our own desire and try to resolve the universe into a facsimile of our own notions. Many people who would scorn to be dishonest in the physical sense are dishonest mentally. The one who possesses true discrimination realizes only too well that he can never be just while he is personally involved in the question on which he must pass judgment.

A slight digression may not be out of order for the purpose of considering two terms which modern psychology has popularized: namely, the inferiority and superiority complexes. In reality, these two types are each twofold in character. The inferiority-inferiority complex is that mental attitude which causes the individual to picture himself as a groveling, squirming worm of the dust, predestined to be blind, to live in darkness, and eternally to be trodden under foot. This attitude paralyzes initiative and is a never-ending blasphemy against the Divinity innate in every creature.

The inferiority-superiority complex is the index of the hopeless egotist. Its victims have full confidence in their own integrity and excellence and in every act evince the realization of their self-importance. They make themselves heartily obnoxious, however, by assuming airs of modesty and inferiority in order to adduce evidence that they are not what they know they are. They have heard that great people are invariably distinguished by their modesty,—hence their assumption of the virtue!

The superiority-superiority complex manifests itself as boundless self-assurance. Such an individual, like the character of the story book, "can achieve the impossible, do the un-do-able, and un-screw the inscrutable!" The pages of history teem with the exploits of these colossal egotists who, however, backed their egotism up with achievement. Such achievements, though, are almost invariably of a temporal nature. Several philosophers also exhibited this moral obliquity, but arc remembered chiefly for more worthy accomplishments. The superiority-inferiority complex is usually borne by an individual who is an inveterate but unconscious liar. Such a person gives an external exhibition of consummate nerve while internally recognizing himself unable to cope with the situation. In other words, he is the high-pressure bluffer, the "personality plus" product of modern pseudo-psychology. If it were possible for such a person to be honest with himself but for a single instant, his courage would ooze out like a cold sweat and leave him a moral bankrupt. Discrimination is not only the ability to choose wisely from the mass of mental and physical phenomena around us, but is also the ability to analyze the elements of our own thinking, feeling, and acting for the purpose of unfolding that which is good and eliminating that which is unnecessary. A very good way to approach this particular problem is to make an inventory of our assets and liabilities—mental, emotional, and physical. While so engaged we might choose as our motto: What is man that the Lord should be mindful of him? What do we know that our opinions should be of vast pith and moment? By what right do we sit in judgment upon the world and its Maker? During such self-examination we are lost without honesty or, more correctly, integrity. It is well that we differentiate between honesty and integrity. Honesty gives sixteen ounces to the pound because of law, while integrity gives sixteen ounces to the pound because sixteen ounces make a pound.

Having decided to judge yourself with absolute integrity, make a list of the virtues you possess, together with the degree of their opposites which manifest in your nature. If you are kind, to what degree are you unkind? If you are generous, to what degree are you penurious? If you are just, to what degree are you unjust? Perfections are determined by the degree of imperfections.

Thus truthfulness is determined by the degree of untruthfulness. This is doubtless the reason one is so prone to see faults in others, for faults are the basis upon which the degree of faultlessness is to be estimated. Possibly for the same reason few people are congratulated for their virtues with either the fervor or the frequency that they are criticized for their vices. Having arrived at a reasonable estimate of the proportions of ignorance intervening between your present state and the desired state, next list the arts, sciences, and crafts with whose principles you have some degree of familiarity. Then ask yourself what is the percentage of your understanding of them as compared to that which is knowable concerning them. Discrimination will assist you to judge accurately the relation occupied by what you know to that which can be known. It logically follows also that your capacity to understand is measured by that which you understand, and by the understanding with which you understand you arc most likely to be understood.

Since it reveals man's incompleteness, discrimination is therefore a continual urge toward completion. Man is not perfect until he knows all and is united in consciousness with all.

Until this state is reached there can be no cessation of activity without disaster. We all have mental faculties that are weak; sense perceptions uncertain in the quality of their acuteness. Discrimination assists us to develop rationality by balancing the faculties until all the parts involved in the process of knowing are equilibrated. The result is a balanced and rational attitude toward the various conditions of life. Discrimination inspires tolerance in that it reveals the relationship which man as a spiritual condition bears to the body which he occupies. Discrimination proves that while the spirit is willing, the flesh is weak. Criticism should therefore be directed against these inconsistencies existing in the relationship of the parts. In this way the sting of personality is removed.

The spirit of man is ever composing beautiful melodies, but by the time they reach physical expression they are mostly reduced to discords. Such was the dilemma of the young man learning to play the cornet, who, turning to his teacher, exclaimed: "Why is it that when I blow the music in it is so sweet, but when it comes out it is so sour?" Discrimination helps man to recognize the melodies of the spirit and ignore the inharmonies of the flesh. Hence, discrimination is a forgiving faculty, not in the general acceptation of the word but in the sense of understanding; for the moment we fully understand people we have forgiven them.

Spirit is intrinsically beautiful, and those who raise their consciousness to the recognition of universal life dwell in the sense of beauty. Discrimination reveals the beautiful in that it chooses to gaze upon the face of Reality and to ignore the seething ocean of illusion. The realization of Self is synonymous with the recognition of Divinity, and he who beholds with his inner perception the radiant face of the One has reached the vanishing point of enmity and animosity. Discrimination also dispels the illusion of relationships. Relationship is a man made concept of proximities; it is an effort to give expression to the interval—mental or physical—by which things are separated, for relationship is not estimated by the proximity of one part to another but rather by the distance one part is away from another. Through believing that by the concept of relationship he unites life, man's efforts in this respect all too often contain only the sense of increasing separateness; for when we take that which is already synonymous with ourselves and relate it to ourselves we are really dividing it from ourselves.

Discrimination finally reveals to us that relationships are illusions of the mortal mind and that since all things are one in essence they are consequently indivisible and incapable of existing in any relationship of proximity one to the other. Even the ideal of friendship, though the loftiest of man's illusional attitudes, is thus revealed as insufficient. But even as wisdom is merely the vanishing point of ignorance, so illusion exists in a state of orderly concatenation, with friendship as the last, and consequently the least degree of the illusion of relationship.

Having through discrimination attained to a state of right- mindfulness, it is necessary to maintain such state and project it to perfection through the aid of concentration. Having discovered the purpose of life through observation and discrimination, man consummates that purpose through concentration of his faculties upon that single end. To concentrate means simply to focalize all the energies upon an appointed task. The mental activities of most people are scattered like spray when they are confronted by the solid wall of that which is to be known.

Individuals read books while their minds are concerned with other interests. When the intellect is laden with responsibilities which it cannot cast off, it ceases to function with the acuteness necessary for philosophic perception. The true thinker realizes that his mind is capable of fatigue, and while this fatigue may not be apparent in the grosser activities it precludes the possibility of exactness in fine thinking. The normal mind works on the union basis of an eight-hour day with time and a half of? for over-time. For every period of intense effort the mind must he compensated by a similar period of relaxation. The immature intellect of the average person must work slowly and orderly if it is to accomplish, for only a genius such as Julius Caesar can do a dozen things at once with any degree of success. It may truthfully be said that half an hour of profound mental activity is a day's work for the mind and he who accomplishes this is entitled to be termed industrious in things of the intellect. We presume ourselves to be mentally active during the entire period of wakefulness, but in reality we wander in a sort of mental delirium in which the elements of concetion and reflection tumble over each other in hopeless disorder. Only when confronted by some actual crisis does the mind rise to organized activity, and after the crisis is past the resultant mental exhaustion is far greater than the average person realizes. About fifteen minutes of unremitting mental concentration will exhaust the ordinary man. Only by special training can the intellectual faculties be elevated to the stage of prolonged, orderly functioning. As exercise scientifically chosen will strengthen an otherwise deficient physical member, so definite and proper mental exercise will increase mental capacity. In the field of mental culture the Greeks enjoyed a supremacy never approached by any other race. They built gymnasiums not only for the culture of the body but also for the mind, the result being their overwhelming superiority in the realm of creative thought.

In its philosophic aspect concentration implies that all the life activities are centered upon the noblest goal and held in this state of fixation until the goal is achieved. Consecration of life to definite purpose is indispensable to accomplishment.

Philosophy assures its disciples that when man, through discrimination, has discovered the desired end and is willing to sacrifice every other interest to the attainment of that end, he will ultimately arrive at indissoluble union with the object of his desire. This is, of course, a superphysical truth. If a man devotes a lifetime of effort to amassing a million dollars, he will not ultimately take upon himself the actual appearance of money. He will, however, gradually deteriorate until his life is susceptible of complete expression in terms of money. Through concentration the life energies are co-ordinated upon the path of achievement, and success is in direct proportion to the power or degree of concentration. As the sun's rays concentrated by a burning glass are able to generate a high degree of heat, so man's mental and physical energies when properly focussed give expression to potencies never dreamed of.

In order to find the solitude considered essential to concentration, the hermits of old retired from the world of men and immured themselves in the depth of the forest or in caves high upon the mountain side. Surrounded by the tranquillity of Nature they dreamed their lives away, finding in their solitary retirement a certain measure of peace. Of course, such an environment made the act of concentration comparatively easy, but for the same reason also made its efficacy less potent. By thus isolating himself from the social body—though never able to sever the physical bonds which still related him to it the ascetic sought to approach Divinity by retiring from a world which he mistakenly assumed to be the antipode of Deity.

Having through discrimination attained to a state of rightmindfulness, it is necessary to maintain such state and project it to perfection through the aid of concentration. Having discovered the purpose of life through observation and discrimination, man consummates that purpose through concentration of his faculties upon that single end. To concentrate means simply to focalize all the energies upon an appointed task. The mental activities of most people are scattered like spray when they are confronted by the solid wall of that which is to be known.

Individuals read books while their minds are concerned with other interests. When the intellect is laden with responsibilities which it cannot cast off, it ceases to function with the acuteness necessary for philosophic perception. The true thinker realizes that his mind is capable of fatigue, and while this fatigue may not be apparent in the grosser activities it precludes the possibility of exactness in fine thinking. The normal mind works on the union basis of an eight-hour day with time and a half off for over-time. For every period of intense effort the mind must be compensated by a similar period of relaxation. The immature intellect of the average person must work slowly and orderly if it is to accomplish, for only a genius such as Julius Caesar can do a dozen things at once with any degree of success.

It may truthfully be said that half an hour of profound mental activity is a day's work for the mind and he who accomplishes this is entitled to be termed industrious in things of the intellect. We presume ourselves to be mentally active during the entire period of wakefulness, but in reality we wander in a sort of mental delirium in which the elements of conception and reflection tumble over each other in hopeless disorder. Only when confronted by some actual crisis does the mind rise to organized activity, and after the crisis is past the resultant mental exhaustion is far greater than the average person realizes. About fifteen minutes of unremitting mental concentration will exhaust the ordinary man. Only by special training can the intellectual faculties be elevated to the stage of prolonged, orderly functioning. As exercise scientifically chosen will strengthen an otherwise deficient physical member, so definite and proper mental exercise will increase mental capacity. In the field of mental culture the Greeks enjoyed a supremacy never approached by any other race. They built gymnasiums not only for the culture of the body but also for the mind, the result being their overwhelming superiority in the realm of creative thought. In its philosophic aspect concentration implies that all the life activities are centered upon the noblest goal and held in this state of fixation until the goal is achieved. Consecration of life to definite purpose is indispensable to accomplishment. Philosophy assures its disciples that when man, through discrimination, has discovered the desired end and is willing to sacrifice every other interest to the attainment of that end, he will ultimately arrive at indissoluble union with the object of his desire. This is, of course, a superphysical truth. If a man devotes a lifetime of effort to amassing a million dollars, he will not ultimately take upon himself the actual appearance of money. He will, however, gradually deteriorate until his life is susceptible of complete expression in terms of money. Through concentration the life energies are co-ordinated upon the path of achievement, and success is in direct proportion to the power or degree of concentration. As the sun's rays concentrated by a burning glass are able to generate a high degree of heat, so man's mental and physical energies when properly focussed give expression to potencies never dreamed of.

In order to find the solitude considered essential to concentration, the hermits of old retired from the world of men and immured themselves in the depth of the forest or in caves high upon the mountain side. Surrounded by the tranquillity of Nature they dreamed their lives away, finding in their solitary retirement a certain measure of peace. Of course, such an environment made the act of concentration comparatively easy, but for the same reason also made its efficacy less potent. By thus isolating himself from the social body—though never able to sever the physical bonds which still related him to it— the ascetic sought to approach Divinity by retiring from a world which he mistakenly assumed to be the antipode of Deity. He overlooked the obvious fact that he who finds not God among men will find him nowhere else.

Rabindranath Tagore once expressed his aversion for the life of the ascetic by declaring that without love and companionship the path of perfection was not worth walking at all.

Concentration is not necessarily promoted by isolation; in fact, the acid test of concentration is to be found in the environment of confusion. If the mind can be deflected from its goal by the phantasm of surroundings, it is incapable of concentration; for when concentration is perfected all the faculties are united in the performance of a definite task and no sense perceptions are left unoccupied with which to register external impressions.

While concentration seems a herculean effort to the mind that has not learned to co-ordinate its own parts, it is accomplished without effort by the trained thinker; in fact, many possess the faculty without the slightest knowledge of its existence. The musician lost in some rhapsody, the artist spellbound before his unfolding creation, the philosopher oblivious to the world as he ponders the immensity of space, the tragedian buried in his part, the financier frenziedly watching the blackboard of the stock exchange—all these not only exemplify the power of concentration but also its application to various ends, worthy or unworthy, according to die clarity of discrimination present.

Regardless, however, of the factor of worthiness, wherever we find true concentration we find excellence. The faculty of concentration also manifests through continuity, the least developed faculty of the American people. Continuity means the sequential unfoldment of a project from germinal beginning to final consummation, or the resolution not to relinquish the task until it is completed. This faculty is frequently lacking in children and seriously interferes with their efficiency in later life. When work seems arduous we quickly tire of it; or because we are not sure whether we really want the thing for which we strive we soon doubt our desire to gain it. When we are certain of our own minds, and carry labor to its legitimate end, our undertaking will be crowned with success.

We are then confronted with the problem of whether the finished product is an aid or a hindrance to us in our quest for Reality. We should never concentrate upon any desired end until discrimination has revealed it to be the supreme ideal; for the universe avenges itself for the misuse of its agencies by forcing us to abide by our own decisions. The ultimate ideal of concentration is attained when all the external parts are turned inward toward the contemplation of Self. When all the forces of the outer nature are thus united, then is generated the strength with which to achieve perfection.

The diagram at the beginning of this chapter sets forth in the figurative terms of Platonism the relationship of the elements under discussion The threefold Divinity—the One, the Beautiful, and the Good—manifests out of itself an inconceivable number of secondary triads. The secondary triad pertaining to absolute knowledge is composed of the rational principles now incorporated in the all-too-inadequate vehicles of philosophy, religion, and science. Thus it is demonstrated that philosophy partakes of the indivisible nature of the One and hence serves as the reconciling, unifying agent, being symbolic of the point of absolute intellectual convergence.

Theology likewise reflects to an imperfect degree the nature of the Beautiful, a postulate substantiated by the emphasis placed upon the fine arts by nearly all religious systems.

Science, in turn, imperfectly manifests the nature of the Good, and those who minister at its altars lay special stress upon utilitarianism. Descending to the level of method we find a new triad established: namely, discrimination, concentration, and observation. Discrimination may be conceived to be the goal of philosophy, concentration the goal of theology, and observation the goal of science. On the mental plane these three may also be considered as indispensable factors in the acquisition of knowledge. Observation is the sharpest tool of science; concentration is essential to the esoteric doctrines of theology; discrimination is the secret of philosophic insight.

In the world of physical arts and sciences, the One becomes mathematics, the first and most exact of all the sciences, which partakes of the powers of the One through the succession of philosophy and discrimination. The Beautiful becomes music, which partakes of the primal Beauty through the succession of theology and concentration. The Good becomes astronomy, which partakes of the original Good through the succession of science and observation. Thus is demonstrated the soundness of the ancient Pythagorean doctrine that the establishment and relationship of triads is the true basis of philosophic procedure.

If the diagram be considered from the standpoint of the Socratic school, we have an invaluable key to the unfoldment of the inner nature. Socrates affirmed the possibility of stimulating the superphysical nature by familiarizing the objective nature with those tangible arts and sciences that had their correspondences in the superphysical. For example, the study of astronomy increased the power of observation. Through its development observation in turn produced the scientist, and the scientist plying his scientific pursuits ultimately achieved to a knowledge of the Good. Thus unfoldment of the inferior stimulated unfoldment of its analogy in the superior, and step by step in such indirect fashion the highest was ultimately attained.

A question frequently asked by metaphysical students is how it is possible to stimulate the spiritual nature, and herein will be found the answer. Each part of the objective nature manifests some potentiality of the subjective life principle. The refinement and perfection of any part of the objective nature is a direct stimulus to its correspondence in the causal nature from which it was originally objectified. Thus the physical activity of thinking, when properly directionalized, develops the entire mental nature or body. Similarly, the proper directionalization of physical emotion results in the unfoldment of the emotional body which, being invisible and intangible, can only be contacted through its pole in the outer nature. Eventually man will be able to definitely relate all his physical parts and members with their incorporeal causal agencies. He can then at will stimulate his superphysical organisms through right directionalization of their corresponding physical organisms.

The purpose of this chapter is to give a brief outline of what constitutes a rational beginning of the philosophic life. He who would achieve to the highest must realize that without the systematic culture of the entire organism, even a relative degree of perfection is unattainable. The general metaphysical practice of platitudes, affirmations, and denials is unsound in theory and barren of results; for the organization of the life is only possible through certain definite, exact, and unchanging disciplines that have been preserved to the present generation as the priceless heritage of antiquity.

Many people possess to varying degrees so-called psychic powers. Such powers may be considered as natural to them; in other words, they have not been acquired by any definite effort. But regardless of how remarkable these natural endowments may seem to both their possessor and the world at large, they are a liability rather than an asset unless they are reduced to order through philosophic discipline. Nearly all so-called natural mystics have missed the goal for which they strove because they were satisfied to accept intangibles and indefinite attitudes as the lodestar of life. With few exceptions such natural psychics conceive themselves to be very highly evolved souls, unmindful of the fact that the lowliest canine possesses psychic powers far exceeding their own; but incapable of rationally directing its powers the animal must live and move and have its being in bondage to man. The psychic who has not through rational discipline become master of these psychic endowments is in no way superior spiritually to the brute, and will ultimately suffer some brutish end for his irrationality. The fond illusion that perfection comes "naturally" to such people must go if true consciousness is to be attained.

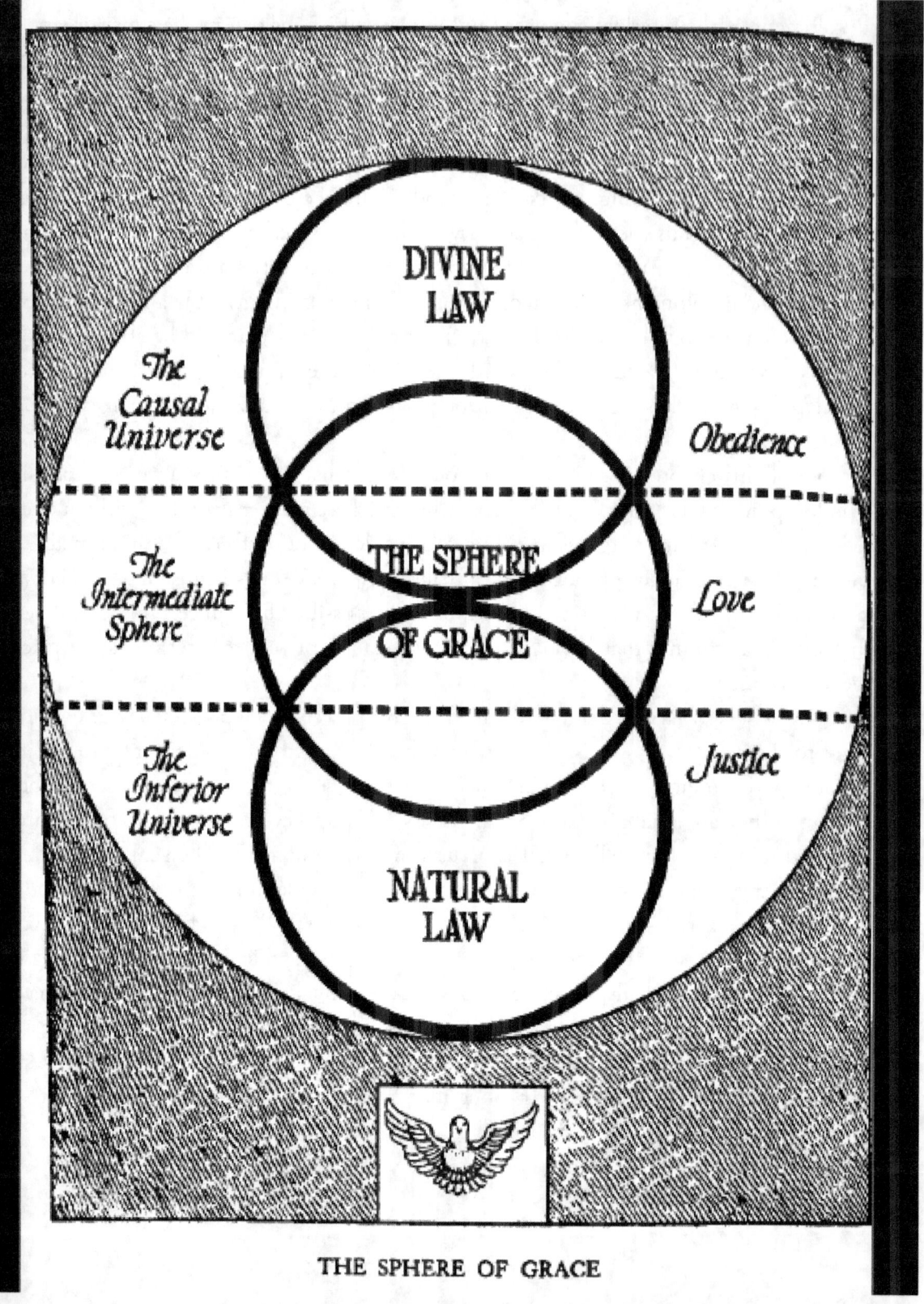

The Causal Universe

The Intermediate Sphere

The Inferior Universe

DIVINE LAW

Obedience

THE SPHERE

Love

OF GRACE

Justice

NATURAL LAW

THE SPHERE OF GRACE

Herein is revealed the mystery of the Universal Soul and the redemption of man through the doctrine of grace. When atonement is understood in its Platonic interpretation as an at-one-ment, or reconciliation of the not-self and the Self through the disciplines of philosophy, we come to sense the magnitude of spiritual redemption.

# XV

※

# What the Ancient Wisdom Expect of Its Disciples

A STUDY CONCERNING THE MYSTERY SCHOOLS
MANLY P HALL

This publication was originally written to protect sincere persons from the confusion of conflicting beliefs which came to be known as popular metaphysics. This was a conglomerate of European psychology, Asiatic mysticism, and New England psychism. Most of the dialogue was well intended, but the public in general was not qualified to judge the merits or demerits of teachers or their teachings. It was assumed that spiritual education could be communicated in easy lessons; however, it soon became obvious that the situation was out of hand. The only practical solution was to restate the original teachings of those esoteric orders which have descended to us from the ancient world—that enlightenment must be earned by personal dedication to an enlightened code of conduct.

In the ancient system of initiation, the truth seeker must pass through a second birth, and those who attained this exalted state were known thereafter as "the twice born." Only one who has been born again can understand the mysteries of heaven. This new birth, however, is not attained by merely joining a sect. It must be personally earned through a complete regeneration of character and conduct.

It is a mistake to assume that all persons whose actions are mysterious, or who claim to be members of secret orders are adepts or initiates in the true meaning of these words. There has been a vast amount of pretension and only discrimination can protect the truth seeker from imposture. If we can free our minds from the glamour which surrounds the esoteric sciences and attain a solid knowledge of the principles of true philosophy, we will not be long deceived. Legitimate teachers in the field of mystical religions are known by their works and not by their claims.

The commercialization which is currently disfiguring most fields of human endeavor is undermining the integrity of modern religions. The exploitation of the spiritual emergency in human affairs is contributing to the popular feeling that theological institutions are exploiting the sorrows of our time. Scarcely a day goes by in which we are not asked to pass judgment upon some sect or belief. There is an old saying that it is very hard to cheat an honest man. Many would-be joiners are not strictly honorable in their intentions. Some are escapists seeking to avoid the consequences of their own misconduct. Others seek the keys to prosperity and a dominant personality, while still others are asking for strength to live with character defects which they do not wish to correct. There also are certain persons who long to become members of a spiritual aristocracy with power to influence the lives of relatives and friends. Such individuals are proclaiming their willingness to be deluded and exploited.

In the last few years, there has been a strong emphasis on psychic phenomena. Well qualified exponents are sincerely trying to explore the field of extrasensory perception and to discover if possible the latent faculties of the mind and soul. There is greater dependence upon consultation with professional psychics and in some instances a more or less troubled person today by accepting advice from six or seven psychics at the same time. By degrees, therefore, many lose the power of using their own minds to ar- rive at personal decisions. The result is a weakening of faculties we are all here to strengthen. It is important to remember that we must each of us become more adequate if we wish our life patterns to be more constructive. There was an old Greek fable to the effect that even the most wealthy man must eat his own food. If he hires another to do his eating, the one he hires will gain the nourishment.

We sincerely hope that the accompanying essay will prove useful and helpful. Many thoughtful readers have found it to be a practical guide for those who wish to have a safe journey along the road leading to the understanding of life's purpose.

Manly Hall.


GREAT as is the number of present-day religious movements, both heterodox and orthodox, few of them inspire their followers to serve their fellow men along practical and intelligent lines. One by one the various cults are being involved in materialism and commercialism, among which by necessity they have been established. This is not to be wondered at, for it is difficult to separate our religion from our daily lives. We may call it by many different names, but it still reflects the thoughts and moral character of those who form its organization.

Modern attitudes on life are not healthy, and organizations built up by unhealthy people cannot be normal. Commercial- ism has attacked every plane of society. It has entered into all the walks of life. Our race is money mad. It is insane on the subject of personal gain. It will give nothing to serve others, but will give everything to gain the knowledge which will make it possible for the mediocre to become a commercial power over- night. The struggle inseparable from the ethics of competition is largely responsible for this condition. Graft has appeared in almost every walk of life. Nearly every existing institution is overrun by some mild form of moral dishonesty, and if every walk of life is commercialized and perverted, we cannot expect religion to escape.

History records no graft or prostitution equal to the grafts that today masquerade under the names of "psychology" and "new thought." The art of duping the public has evolved from the disreputable buffoonery of the Middle Ages to the polished pharisaism of the twentieth century. As seagulls follow a ship, so this curse has followed in the wake of that great wave of selfishness and moral perversion which is the product of our commercial age.

When correctly understood and properly used for the ser- vice of humanity, psychology, meta-physics, and new thought are highly commendable and their truths are sorely needed by ignorant humanity today. But what has happened? These names have been used to conceal all forms of mental, moral, spiritual, and physical infamy until everything we know of them today is a pros-titution and commercialization of the truths for which they once stood. Their success is based upon the assumption that the people with whom they work are too ignorant to realize the injury that is being done.

We are not attacking the principles underlying these cults and philosophies nor the true thing for which the names stand. Neither are we attacking those sincere people who seek to assist others to build and unfold their characters. We are attacking perversion of truth and those persons who, shielding their crimes under the cloak of wisdom, deliberately and consciously mislead the public for the aggrandizement of self.

In the 14th chapter of St. John, 30th verse, Jesus states: "Hereafter I will not talk much with you; for the prince of this world cometh, and hath nothing in me." The Ancient Wisdom is not of this world; it belongs to an entirely different sphere. It is not interested in improving the mater-ial condition of the individual from the standpoint of placing him in executive positions or sur-rounding him with opulence. The Ancient Wisdom seeks to build the character of man, knowing that if he can be made right with himself, far more is accomplished than when he is made a ruler over many men.

Truth expresses the synthesis of the Divine Wisdom. Truth is the eternal reality of things. Psy-chology and metaphysics as taught today are not true, and the things taught under the guise of Truth are no better than those who disseminate them. An intellectual fact is not necessarily a truth; the misapplication of it is a falsehood.

If an individual wishes to take a course in business efficiency at the expense of others; if he wishes to attend a night school class in order to learn how to become a moral pickpocket, he is privileged to do so as long as he is willing to accept the Karmic consequences. You will remember that when Lucifer decided to rebel against God, the Deity allowed him to do so. It is demoral- izing to a community for people to believe that God either gives or authorizes classes in slick salesmanship, shrewd bargaining, and mortgage foreclosing, or that He advocates sitting in the silence to get rid of an undesired marriage partner. Modern psychology has made God appear to be as dishonest as the persons who promulgate these doctrines. All this has a destructive effect on the life and health of the race. Let us consider a few points toward which the Ancient Wisdom was adamant and modern religion is lax. We can pick them from things going on around us all the time without going into abstractions.

1. In all things involving the acquirement of knowledge, the Ancient Wisdom says, "First purify your own life." This means literally what it says. Until selfishness is removed from the soul of a student he can never hope to gain any knowledge that will serve him for any purpose more lofty than as a mental stimulant. The modern psychological cults overlook this entirely, failing to em-phasize any virtue essential for the human nature outside of endless desires for things not nor-mally attainable. Once men died for Truth, but now Truth dies at the hands of men.

2. The Apostles who died for their faith, the Christians who sang in the arena while the lions

were turned loose upon them, or who hung coated with tar as living torches in Nero's gardens—these furnished vivid demonstrations of the sincerity, humility, honesty, and devotion of the early followers of Christ. The Master himself was led up into the mountain by the demons and tempted by a vision of the cities stretched out in the plains below. The ancient initiates were tempted by the things of this world. Buddha, standing beside the crib in which lay his infant son, chose between all the things which life held dear and the wandering life of an ascetic. But the great need of humanity filled his soul, and he sacrificed all to his great, unselfish love.

Again and again students are tempted by the voice of the world, and only if they are strong, will they gain that wisdom which they seek. The true occultist wants nothing but wisdom. When Solomon raised his hands to his God, Jehovah spoke from the heavens asking him what he would have, and he answered, "God give me the gift of wisdom." Jehovah asked him if there were not other things he desired, but Solomon answered, "No, only wisdom." And God told Solomon that because he had asked only for wisdom that all the other things should be added unto him and that from this day to the end of the world there would never be another king so rich, so great, or so blest. These are facts well worthy of consideration in the light of modem psychology.

As we listen to the words of the modern exponents of things divine, we see them making converts by offering to the ignorant the very things by which the ancient Masters were tempted by the demons of the air. Again and again the new cult leader promises his disciples the cities of the plains. His credulous fol- lowers fall over each other to study at his feet and learn how, through magnetic personalities or mental gymnastics, they can acquire the earthly possessions which he promises them. The crime does not lie in desiring the things of this world, for to a certain degree they are both necessary and good. Man would not be placed in his present environment unless he were expected to study and benefit by his experiences. The great crime lies in claiming these perverted doctrines to be spiritually inspired and representing God's chief desire to be making people financially independent.

3.   Compare the initiates of days gone by, fighting a people who could not understand, struggling with idolatry and supersttion and seeking to mold out of these things a truer and nobler concept of life, wandering day after day over the blistering sands like Moses in the wilderness—compare those master minds with the self-termed master minds of today and then ask yourself if you should follow them. The human race has never desired that which was best for it, but like a child it reaches out its hands and cries for the moon. Today the race does not know what is good for it, and individuals, instead of seeking to unfold their constitutions symmetrically, have gone mad over a system of philosophical hocus-pocus which promises something for nothing and exchanges divine wisdom for a moderate fee.

4.   Without labor, there is no inspiration, and none can do our work for us but ourselves. The Ancient Wisdom demanded many years of purification and preparation before the adepts were willing to instruct in even the simplest things. Many modern occultists are glibly teaching Pythagorean mathematics and numerology, and if you come every afternoon for a week you will be greatly amazed how little you will discover. They wonder why it is that many of the keys of the Pythagorean mysteries have been lost to the world. The answer is simple. Pythagoras never instructed his disciples in any of his philosophical concepts until after they had passed through five

years of the strictest discipline, among other things one provision being that during the entire time they were not to speak a word, in order that afterwards they might know how to hold their tongues. We would have much less trouble if our psychologists refrained from speaking for the first five years, for most of them are preaching with no more foundation for their eloquence than two weeks' study with someone no better informed than themselves.

5. There is another class of people who go about discussing the Infinite with ease and fluency who as yet have never acquainted themselves with the finite. A most interesting rule of the Ancient Wisdom is that none of its initiates discuss the Absolute. They explain the hypothesis of First Cause, but state finally that no human being, themselves included, know sufficient concerning it to give an intelligent opinion or definition; and no wise man presumes to discuss that about which he knows nothing.

When Buddha was asked concerning the Absolute, he declined to discuss the subject. He was also silent concerning the gods, feeling that they were beyond the range of human intelligence. As a result, it has been said that he was an atheist, or at least a pantheist, when in reality it was his respect and reverence for Deity that led him, in his sublime wisdom, to refrain from giving utterance to words whose very inadequacy would but defile. When the disciples of Socrates questioned him concerning the Absolute, he also refused to discuss it, stating that it was beyond his wisdom and that it played no practical part in everyday life. But again and again fools dash in where angels fear to tread. While the greatest minds ever evolved by the human race dare not speak for fear they will desecrate that which is too sacred for words, some person, with neither record of accomplishment nor prospect of anything better, seeks to impress the uninformed by glibly discussing things he knows nothing about.

6. There is only one series of true occult exercises in the world—namely, esoteric exercises. Every nation has adopted these exercises with certain modifications to meet the needs of race, color, and organic qualities. The Christians took theirs from the Jews, the Jews from the Egyptians, the Egyptians from the Brahmans, and so on ad infinitum. When Buddha gave his faith to India he merely gave a doctrine for the consideration of the common people, for, being a Brahman himself, he followed the Brahman culture of esoteric exercises. The so-called occult exercises are those formulas given by word of mouth by the initiates to their disciples under the pledge of absolute secrecy, in order that these disciples may use the exercises in spiritualizing, etherizing, and purifying their bodies.

One of the most reprehensible crimes perpetrated today is the teaching by present-day occultists of crazy, homicidal, and suicidal practices under the guise of esoteric instructions. If followed persistently, these practices will result in the death of those who attempt to follow them. The redeeming feature is that the average Western mind is incapable of concentrating long enough or consistently enough upon anything to be seriously harmed. All the esoteric instructions in the hands of unqualified people today are the result of treason and broken vows among the lower degrees of initiates. In order to receive them from such sources the recipient must become a party to the crime. Not only this, but when the student permits himself to listen to instructions gained falsely, he nullifies any good which he might otherwise gain.

Having obtained the instructions without the necessary preparation and apprenticeship ordered by the Great School, he cannot receive the spiritual insight that he desires. It breaks the hearts of the Masters to see people who know better dabbling with so-called esoteric exercises, gathering in circles to go into the silence, rolling their eyes into the tops of their heads and sitting in darkened rooms hoping to see something. It is not the mere fact that the student does these things which hurts the Teachers; it is the fact that the disciples have grown so little in discrimination that it is possible for them to become parties to such absurdities. We do not mean that they will not see things, hear voices, and gain certain mediumistic powers. We mean that they will be less useful after they have secured those powers than before, for they will have to unlearn again all those things and habits which they learned unwisely.

7. The Masters are ever waiting to entrust their disciples and students who show desire to receive with that wisdom which the world so sadly needs. If the student desires to go forth and teach, he will be given a work to do—that is, if he will honestly, sincerely, and intelligently prepare himself for his labors. The reason why so many false doctrines are being taught is that people who have an idea do not ask themselves, "Is this theory which I have, true? Am I living the sort of a life that would permit me to receive real truth into my soul? Am I unselfish, open, obedient, humble, and consecrated? Have I developed my mind so that it can think? Have I opened my heart so that it can feel? If I have not, then the thing which I have received is distorted by the glass through which it shines, and all I can give the world is a distorted image, a dishonest representation of truth. Have I actually consecrated my life and all that I am, unselfishly and without reservation, or am I only an intellectual dabbler? Am I a success or a failure in life? Am I surrounded by friends or by enemies of my own making? Am I respected by my community? Do I allow other people to live their own lives, or am I trying to force my beliefs upon all with whom I come in contact? Have I, or have I not, consciously and beyond all possibility of mental exaggeration, received personal instruction from the inner schools? I and I alone know that. The rest of the world, except the enlightened few, must believe what I say. If I have not received such instructions, am I big enough to admit it and say, with respect to my doctrines, that they are only my own opinions; or am I palming off these opinions as cosmic truths upon no firmer ground than the fact that I believe them?"

All these questions the student must ask himself, for he alone can answer them; but he is capable of injuring many if he is not honest in his statements concerning these fundamental truths. If every teacher and student would thus interrogate himself, endless sorrow could be avoided, for he would realize that as an evil tree cannot bring forth good fruit, neither can a sin-filled body nor a perverted mind be the channel for the transmission of wisdom. Like begets like; the eccentric individual thinks eccentric thoughts, while the sane mind views all things sanely.

8. Psychologists today teach how one person may influence another to do things otherwise foreign to his nature. Let each student of the Mystery School be careful, therefore, when he studies with psychologists that the psychologist does not turn the tables on him. If he teaches you how to gain some advantage over another and twist that individual to your own ends, take care that he does not discover your gullibility and capitalize on you by way of demonstrating the application of his own philosophy. These things work both ways, and if you expect to psychologize others you must expect to be psychologized in turn; for it is a poor rule that does not work both ways. It is,

however, a good rule which most people are willing to have turned around and applied to them. Psychology has psychologized the public and, like the children of Hamlin town who followed the Pied Piper, immature minds have followed false teachings until they have disappeared into the unknown.

9.    Among the so-called students of truth we see the fruitage of the delusions from which the world suffers. Sickly, nervous, no longer capable of solving their own problems, they sit around treating each other, waiting like spiritual Micawbers for some- thing to turn up. These people were once useful, intelligent members of their community, but they are now so involved in mental absurdities that they are useless both to themselves and to society in general. Most of all, they are like gaunt scarecrows who frighten others from the paths of wisdom.

10.    The Ancient Wisdom is sane. It seeks to solve the problems with which we are surrounded today. It is spiritual and reasonable, in the highest sense of the word. It is seeking to develop better men and women to meet the problems of future generations. It is based upon the law of cause and effect. It has no patented formulae, no shortcuts, but builds firmly and solidly the characters of those who unite themselves with its work. It is not led by mountebank teachers, but by great minds that have dedicated themselves since the beginning of the world to the promulgation of the sacred truths. It speaks with the experience of eternity, for it has led a thousand nations into being and buried as many when they turned from its course. The nations of antiquity which still exist are the ones which have preserved its laws, while those that have fallen are the ones that have ignored its commandments.

There is no greater honor than to be called to the service of this eternal Wisdom which was before the beginning and which will ultimately become the visible exoteric ruling body of the planet. Through the doors of its temple man passes from the temporal to the eternal, from ignorance to wisdom. It is strong and great, this Ancient Wisdom. It is the earth moistened with the waters of life in which are planted the seeds of doctrines, faiths, and religions. All these are dependent upon it for nourishment and growth. They blossom forth and are glorified, but the dark and mysterious soil in which they all grow is the Ancient Wisdom. From it they come; to it they will again return. They are temporal; it is eternal.

Since earliest times, the belief in a superior and supreme Being manifesting in totality what man manifests only in part has been the common property of human creatures. The mindless man struggling up through the muck and mire of the Paleozoic fens beat his hairy breast with long, misshapen arms and raised his cry to an unknown God. Even the hairy anthropoids of today have certain rudiments of religious worship. Soulless but aware, they turn their half-formed faces to the sky and clasp their hands as though in prayer. No one knows whence came the spirit of worship—the great desire to express thankfulness for the mere privilege of existing—but it is as old as history. The first writings are of the gods. Probably the first buildings were temples, for we are realizing more day by day that every structure in Nature is a sanctuary built without the voice of workmen or the sound of hammers. It is not only a sanctuary but also an altar. It is not only the altar, but also the offering laid upon the altar. There is no voice, no people that does not bear witness to some God, some presence felt in the silence, some power seen in heaven.

All human beings are divided into four general classes, but each one lives in only one part of himself; or rather he minimizes all other portions and emphasizes this one above the rest. The lowest of these divisions is the physical nature, and those who dwell therein are of the earth, earthy; they live only for the gratification of their physical natures. Their idea of heaven is a place where there is food, feasting, and little or no work. They are the Brahmanic Sudras who, born in chains, are doomed to live and die in shackles of low organic quality. The very structure of the bones and flesh prohibits fineness in texture either of body or soul. Their minds are only partly active. Their bodies resemble prisons more than dwelling places. They differ from the finer temperaments as the dray horse differs from the Arabian thoroughbred. Like the former, they live to labor, plodding along to a mediocre destiny. They are the laborers who must in truth earn their bread by the sweat of their brows. Give them opulence and they cannot retain it. Give them luxuries, and they do not appreciate them. They are the dark earthy ones who must ever bow before intelligence. They do not love God, for they cannot know Him. They are like the hairy anthropoids, raising their hands to unknown elements.

The second division is made up of the artisans and those who labor both with mind and hand. They are the brown men of the Indian myth. They buy, sell, and exchange. To their basic dullness has been added a certain cunning and some intelligence. Having a mind, they control the mindless. They are the petty shopkeepers and those of a similar class who are gradually ex- changing the labor of the hand for the labor of the head. Not having the mental organism with which to reason, they fill the places of worship where thinking is done for them. They are the ones who allow their clergy to decide all spiritual problems for them, feeling themselves incapable of assuming the onus of heavy thinking. As a result, their ideas of eternity are rather abstract and their credulity is utilized as a commercial asset by certain types of minds who consider it legitimate to capitalize on the ignorance of others.

The third class is made up of the scientists. With microscope, telescope, and other apparatus still more complex, they attack the boundary lines of the known and wage war upon the limit- less chaos. Those who wage this war in the cause of science are mostly concrete thinkers who follow as far as their instruments will lead them and then must wait for instruments still more powerful. Most of these minds are atheistic or at least agnostic— that is, of course, unless they have two standards, one to last six days in the laboratory and the other to be assumed Sunday morning in church. The miracles of theology are incapable of chemical analysis and are consequently taken cum grano salis by the scientific world. Therefore the controversy between science and theology is bequeathed as a legacy to have and to hold upon that helpless posterity who come into the world to inherit the debate.

The fourth and highest group embraces philosophers, musicians, and artists, all living in an abstract mental world sur- rounded by dreams and visions wholly unrecognizable by the other types. They have reached beyond the world of academic education to the world of creative idealism, which is at present the highest function of the human mind. This world is the dwelling place of genius, of invention, and of the things which lower mentalities can only accept but never analyze. Religiously, these minds are deistic. Most of them are monotheists—believers in one God. Many of them are mystics or occultists, and, although possibly not yet sufficiently advanced to recognize their doctrines, yet belong to that finer type of mind capable of piercing the veil which divides the shadow from the substance.

In all human nature there is a certain expression of primitive instinct. With the desire for food which expresses the hunger of the material nature and the desire for freedom which expresses the hunger of the intellectual nature is also found that appreciation for the unknown—that aspiration which bears witness to the slumbering germ of a spiritual nature which somewhere in the constitution of all living things lies dormant and apparently lifeless.

As soon as man was capable of thought his mind turned upon himself. He sought to find a solution to the mystery of his own existence, which his unfolding intelligence was reveal- ing to him in greater fullness every day. " What am I? Why am I here? What lies beyond the horizon line of futurity?" These were the great problems which confronted the primitive man, and these are also the great problems which confront the men and women of today.

Religions have gradually been evolved as man sought to explain himself. Once they were few and simple; now they are many and complicated. This in itself shows the ever-unfolding faculty range of the human mind. The primitive man could count up to only the number of his own fingers. Since then, however, the human mind has conceived mathematics, and by this science can now deal in infinite computations of numbers with at least some degree of intelligence. The greatest proof of the evolution of the human mind is found in the development of man's handiwork. The hollowed log of the primitive savage has become the great steamship of today. This great develop-ment which has gradually been brought about through the ages is not the result of the miraculous trans- formation of natural substances but the gradual growth of the human mind, which is mold-ing all it contacts into ever more complicated forms as the result of its ever-increasing senses and functions.

Religion is the outgrowth of many ages of spiritual hunger, when the soul of the primitive man, finding itself insufficient, turned in awe to the immensity of Nature, in whose endless pageantry it saw a power far greater than itself. The savage turned to the winds and found in them some-thing superior to himself. He trembled in fear at the voice of the thunder; fell prostrate in ter-ror as great storms swept through the primitive world and volcanic craters belched forth red-hot stones and ashes. He offered sacrifice to the gods of the air that they should spare him; he cried from the tops of the mountains and offered incense to the stars. He could not find God any-where, so offered sacrifice to Him everywhere. He saw his crops burn for lack of water, his chil-dren sicken about him. His hopes were dashed to the ground by an unknown, unnamed thing which, though he could not understand, was the determining factor in every thought and action of his life. This was undoubtedly the origin of religion as man knows it. We remember the words of Pope: "Lo, the poor Indian! whose untutored mind sees God in clouds, or hears Him in the wind."

Man is small; Nature is great. Man is finite; Nature is infinite. Man struggling against Nature is like a tiny boat buffeted by the waves. In the endless grinding wheels of Nature ancient man recognized power. He realized that there was something greater than himself—a power that was supreme. He longed to exercise it, and through millions of years struggled, like Hiawatha and the Maize King, to extract from unknown power the secret of its greatness. Like Isis, he conjured Ra to tell his name and sought again and again to raise the veils of the World Virgin. He found that some things which he did destroyed him, while others brought him happiness and peace. He sought to learn which was which, and why, realizing that his very existence depended upon the wisdom of his choice.

Finding at last that he could not master Nature by force, he sought to master it through obedience. Our religious codes are largely the outcome of primitive experiments as the human mind, struggling for survival, gradually learned the will of Nature and molded itself into that will.

Today we are privileged to look back upon the history of the race and profit by the experience of the ages. Saints, sages, and saviors unnumbered have lived and died grappling with the problem of human destiny. The fruitage of their labors is preserved to us in the scriptures and philosophies of all nations. What are the so-called sacred books? Are they not merely the contributions to the knowledge of the world made by those who, devoting their lives to the problems of humanity and learning to solve them, have wandered alone yet unafraid in those causal worlds which man calls Nature?

Gradually man has built the body or institution he calls religion. It is a mental temple, its dome upheld by a number of columns, each of these columns one of the faiths of men. The East, the West, the North, and the South have contributed either to the strength or the beauty of that structure. The entire building, however, is a material thing. It is the offering of man to the Unknown. As the spirit enters the human body when the embryo reaches a certain degree of unfoldment, so will the spirit of Truth enter the religious body when that structure has adequately prepared itself for such a coming.

The world knows many religions, but Nature has but one Truth. All so-called faiths and doctrines are contributing to the knowledge of that one Truth. All are expressing one ideal through a multitude of tongues. There is a babel on the earth, but there is only one voice in the heavens. All faiths are seeking to answer one question: "What is the purpose of existence?" Each answers it differently. When all are gathered together in their diversities, Truth is established, for Truth is the sum of all these things. Reality is all things unto all men.

The Ancient Wisdom is the invisible, spiritual side of religion which quickens the body of religion. It is the one spirit which speaks through a multitude of tongues. It is that presence which enters in when its temple has been built by the body of its work- men. It vivifies the body of faith, making it alive and not merely a series of empty shells. Like the gods of India, it has many arms and many heads, but only one heart.

In the very early period of human differentiation, man was incapable of self-government, but was ruled by those appointed by Nature to preserve him and unfold him to the point when he would be capable of taking care of himself. We are told that when our solar system began its labors, spirits of wise beings from other solar systems came to us and taught us the ways of wisdom that we might have that birthright of knowledge which God gives to all His creations. It was these minds which are said to have founded the Mystery Schools of the Ancient Wisdom, for this Wisdom was the knowledge of the will of Nature for Her children.

The greatest art in all the world is the art of being natural, for that which is natural shall survive. For ages religion has been founded upon a false hypothesis. It has sought to fill the world with miracles and unnatural things. It has sought to dictate and dogmatize. For this reason it is failing.

Religion is a body, but today it is a soulless body. It has not built its tabernacle according to the law. It is not serving intelligently and honestly the needs of the human race, but rather is involving itself and its members in endless dissensions of creed, doctrines, and codes, forgetting entirely the spirit of Truth. As a result, one of the most important elements of human life is gradually removing itself from the world; and for lack of an honest, intelligent, fair-minded, and progressive religion we have an age of extreme materialism when the God of man merely changes from a gilded figure of an unknown God to a gilded coin with distinctly practical uses.

The Ancient Wisdom tells us that there is but one religion and that its seed was planted in the souls of things with the beginning of the world. It became a mighty tree with its roots in heaven and its branches on earth, like the sacred banyan of India. As all the branches depend upon one trunk, so all faiths and religions depend upon one source, one light for all that they have been, are, or ever shall be. Some branches are large and strong, while others are small and weak, but through all of them courses one life. That life is light, and that light is the life of men.

The Ancient Wisdom knows neither heathen, nor Christian, nor pagan. It recognizes only many branches on one tree, each branch in itself incomplete but each part of the Tree of Faith. The Tree asks nothing of the branches, other than that they shall be true to the Tree and bear true witness of the life coursing through the Tree. The Ancient Wisdom is the life in the Tree of Faith. We do not see the life. We see only the leaves and branches which bear witness to the life, but in due season the miracle of the tree is accomplished. The life of the tree is glorified in the bud and in the flower. The life of the tree is consummated in the fruit of the tree. The glory of the life of that tree is in the new seed which bears full witness to the creative power of all that has gone before.

This tree is indeed a Tree of Life, for without the higher and finer sentiments man does not live; he merely exists. If any branch of that tree does not bear fruit, the Master tells us that it shall be cut off and cast into the fire. It is the duty of all living things to produce some truly constructive labor as recognition of the divine life which is within them. God is most glorified when His children glorify His spirit within themselves.

In the remote past the gods walked with men and while the instructors from the invisible planes of Nature were still laboring with the infant humanity of this planet, they chose from among the sons of men the wisest and the truest. These they labored with, preparing them to carry on the work of the gods after the spiritual hierarchies themselves had withdrawn into the invisible worlds. With these specially ordained and illumined sons they left the keys of their great wisdom, which was the knowledge of good and evil. They ordained these anointed and appointed ones to be priests or mediators between themselves (the gods) and that humanity which had not yet developed the eyes which permitted them to gaze into the face of Truth and live.

Overshadowed by the divine prerogative, these illumined ones, founded what we now know as the Ancient Mysteries. These were schools of religious truths, religion being here used in its sense of implying divine wisdom. To these spiritual universi- ties were admitted the most worthy and most capable of the sons of men. At first these schools were publicly recognized. Great temples were built to house the priests and serve as chambers of initiation. The record of the mystical arcane was in the form of carvings, baked clay tablets, and papyrus rolls. Generation after generation was illumined by the wisdom secreted in these sacred repositories.

Gradually a separation took place among the schools of the Mysteries. The zeal of the priests to spread their doctrines in many cases apparently exceeded their intelligence. As a result, many were allowed to enter the temples before they had really prepared themselves for the wisdom they were to receive. The result was that these untutored minds, slowly gaining positions of authority, became at last incapable of maintaining the institution because they were unable to contact the spiritual powers behind the material enterprise. So the Mystery Schools vanished. The spiritual hierarchy, served through all generations by a limited number of true and devoted followers, withdrew from the world; while the colossal material organizations, having no longer any contact with their divine source, wandered in circles, daily becoming more involved in the rituals and symbols which they had lost the power of interpreting.

An interesting and concrete example of the deterioration of the Mystery Schools and their rituals is found in the children's Punch and Judy play. For hundreds of years the frivolous of all Western nations have laughed at the strange antics of these little figures. The world has long forgotten that this play originated among the early Christian mystics, where Punch was Pontius Pilate and Judy was Judas Iscariot. The little club which Punch carries is a degeneration of the ancient scepters which were carried by Roman dignitaries in the Holy Land. It is also quite probable that the famous scene between Punch and the baby is taken from the early Christian story of the Slaughter of the Innocents.

It is really remarkable how down through the ages, by word of mouth, by allegory and symbol, and by natural example, the truths revealed to the ancients have been perpetuated to our own day and yet have ever been concealed from the eyes of the profane. It has been said that wisdom lies not in seeing things but in seeing through things. For the occultist at least, this is doubly true.

During the Atlantean periods of which Plato dreamed, the work of gathering and arranging the Ancient Wisdom went on apace, for the people of Atlantis were the greatest exponents of concrete thought the world has ever known. The Atlanteans never fully understood the wisdom that was theirs, for even in those early times the gods had withdrawn from the mass of humanity, and spoke to man only through appointed priests and oracles. The method of communication used by the spiritual powers is faithfully set out by Josephus in his description of the Ark of the Covenant and the priests who served it. This ark was an oracle, and the gods spoke to the high priest by means of the language of symbolism. From the Atlanteans, with their ancient Tabernacle Mysteries, we have secured nearly all that we know concerning the Ancient Wisdom and its Mysteries. According to the Sacred Book, they were the keepers of the spiritual records which had been given to them by their progenitors, the Serpent Kings, who reigned over the earth.

It was these Serpent Kings who founded the Mystery Schools which later appeared as the Egyptian and Brahman Mysteries and other forms of ancient occultism. The serpent was their symbol, for they taught man the use of the creative energy which courses through Nature and his own bodies as a serpentine line of force. They were the true Sons of Light, and from them have descended a long line of adepts and initiates duly tried and proven according to the law. These have kept alight the divine truths through many generations of ignorance and thoughtlessness. The later Atlantean world crumbled because it wavered from the law. It forgot that Nature was the ruler of all things, and in attempting to survive unnaturally it was destroyed. Before its disintegration, however, the Ancient Wisdom passed into the new Aryan world, where from the heart of the lofty Himalayas its adepts and initiates began the process of building a new people to be the living tabernacles of the gods among men.

Man has not always been a material being. Eternities ago he was a spiritual creature, of radiant and glorious powers. Gradu- ally he assumed the coats of skins which we call bodies, and his radiance was darkened by the sheaths of clay. Little by little he lost touch with his Fathers, the Sons of Light, and began to wander in darkness. At the time when the third eye closed in man, during the period of the ancient Lemurian world, the hu- man race lost contact with its invisible teachers. Gradually even the memory of them faded out until only myths and legends remained. Mythology is the authentic record of those periods of transition when the diviner sparks were gradually assuming the bodies of mortality.

But man was never left to wander alone in ignorance. When the ties connecting him to the unseen worlds were broken, certain methods were established whereby the will of the gods could be made known. To this end, a certain number of men and women were instructed how to bridge the chasm which then separated the gods from men. The method of establishing this communication was the greatest of all the secrets of ancient occultism. This secret has been preserved for the race, for at a later time all human beings will be able to communicate directly with the gods once more. During the great interval of ages, this wisdom has been perpetuated in the Mystery Schools, and a few chosen disciples in each generation have been given the sacred privilege of knowing the gods. This wisdom and the power and knowledge they have gained they in turn impart to a few chosen and beloved disciples. Thus the work is carried on.

The ability of the Mystery Schools to communicate with the invisible worlds is the basis of their power; for all the creative hierarchies dwell in the unseen worlds, and there the disciple must go in order to consult them. The reason for this is that the human race is the only one in our scheme of things that is equipped with both a physical and a mental body. The gods, so-called, have never descended into physical substance. Consequently, having no body composed of dense chemical elements, they are incapable of manifesting here. In order to communicate with them, man must, therefore, learn to function consciously in his own invisible bodies. When he is capable of doing this, he can communicate with the spiritual beings who dwell in similar superphysical substances. Thus, while religion deals only with fancies, theorems, and beliefs, the initiates of the Ancient Wisdom go straight to the fountainhead of wisdom and, learning the will of the gods, make that will the law of their lives. The initiate does not guess, wonder or soliloquize; he labors with facts for he is one with the truths of Nature.

The secret path of spiritual illumination is the way which the planetary Logos has established that His children might learn to know of Him and accomplish His ends. The Logos is surrounded by a hierarchy of superhuman beings and also by a group of great initiates who may be called the fruitage of the human world period. These great initiates, with their divinely- inspired minds, are established as mighty pillars in the House of their God. They are the supports of the Temple of Human Progress. These great minds were called by the ancient Jewish mystics "The Cedars of Lebanon." These are the trees which Solomon is supposed to have cut from the forests of earth to use as the mainstays of his divine temple. From north, east, south, and west the secret truths of these initiated minds have been gathered. The adepts and mystics of all nations have given to their disciples the fruitage of their investigations while functioning in the invisible worlds. The Mysteries Schools, fulfilling the ancient law, are fashioned in the pattern of Nature, and we know them today as the seven Great Schools of the Mysteries. All these are branches of one tree which grows in the center of the Garden of the Lord, watered by the four rivers (the wisdom of the four worlds). As every ray of light breaks into seven colors when it strikes a prism, so this ancient truth, striking the prismatic body of the material world, appears in a septenary body. This body is called the seven-headed serpent, for although it speaks with seven mouths it has but one brain, one life, one origin.

The priests of the Mysteries were symbolized as a serpent, sometimes called Hydra. From this word we have secured our common word, hydrant. As the hydrant carries water, so through the hydra-body of the initiate pass the waters of life. He is, there- fore, a tube or channel through which they are disseminated like water from the nozzle of a hydrant.

These seven schools, each composed of twelve initiates and their disciples surrounding a thir- teenth exalted brother, are the God-ordained perpetuators of the Ancient Wisdom as it has come from the dawn of the world when the gods descended from the nebula of the sun and took up their dwelling place on the sacred island at the north polar cap.

As this document is not intended for propaganda purposes, we shall not name any of these schools, but they represent the seven planets and the seven great paths. They represent also the seven vital organs of the human body and the seven vials which pour out their contents upon the world. All disciples seeking to gain knowledge concerning the laws of Nature must secure that wisdom through one of these seven channels appointed by the Infinite for the furtherance of His peculiar work. Every one of these Mystery Schools is invisible and unknown. They can only be found after long searching and repeated disappointment. In recognition of the dignity of these schools and the sanctity of the wisdom which they represent, this treatise has been prepared to give in a simple way some of the marvelous truths for which they stand.

Every hundred years the voice of the Great School is heard, and into the world comes one to bear witness to the unseen. He speaks with the voice of wisdom, and he is overshadowed by the seven lights. Gradually the Mystery School (the seven branches considered as a unit) is leavening the entire loaf of hu- man thought. Today as never before men are turning to search for their gods; or we should say they are rather turning away in disgust from our age of materiality which is slowly crushing the beauty and spirituality out of life. Our materiality is destroying the souls of men; it is breaking the heart of the world; it is sti- fling the finer side of every nature, and something within man is revolting against this unnatural oppression. Many who have never given it thought before are now wondering what the end of it all will be, how far the human race can involve itself without bringing the entire structure of modern ethics crashing down in ruins.

Within the last fifty years, thousands have become spiritual pilgrims and taken up their search for truth, seeking amid the hills and valleys of the human soul for the answer to the riddle of des- tiny. They are seeking for those mystic Masters of Wisdom known to legend but of whom history bears no record. Through- out all this searching there is a great uncertainty, but one or two facts stand out very clearly. First, the majority of people do not know what they are looking for. If they should meet truth, they would not recognize it. The Masters they seek are about them every day; but like Sir Launfal they journey into distant lands, seeking for those things which are upon their own doorsteps. Secondly, they would not accept wisdom if they should find it. They would all be glad to have the power that the Masters have, but few would labor unselfishly and untiringly for ages to secure that power and then consecrate it unreservedly to the good of humanity.

Before passing on to our next subject, let us sum up a few points to be remembered concerning the Great Work and its workers in the world.

1. The instinct of reverence for the Unknown is implanted in all human life. It seems that even many of the higher animals must have it, for as they sit at the feet of their beloved masters their animal souls speak through upturned eyes filled with love and tenderness. The love of the dog for its master and the love of the disciple for his teacher are closely allied. The dog asks for nothing but kind words and will lay down its life for its master.

Such is true devotion. From the savage upward, reverence and devotion to the gods form part of the moral code of all humanity. Many may deny it, but in the form of either faith, fear, or superstition it persists.

2. The Maker of the great plan which we call life, the Being from which we have been differentiated, has given man certain potentialities; these when awakened to dynamic powers will give to each the faculties whereby he may know that plan. By learning it himself and applying his wisdom, he may then reach the position where he can assist others to harmonize their lives with the same law.

3. For the purpose of disseminating this wisdom wisely among all the nations of the earth, the Schools of the Ancient Mysteries have been established, not by the will of man but by the gods themselves laboring through channels chosen from the most highly evolved children of earth.

4. Having established these schools, the superior intelligences became the central invisible powers of these schools and are still in actual communication with the Adepts and Masters who at the present time manipulate the destinies of these secret orders.

5. All growth spiritually must take place through one of the seven channels appointed by Nature for that purpose, and at some stage in his spiritual growth each disciple will enter the planetary path best fitted to evolve the qualities that lie dormant within himself.

6. These seven schools, together with their branches in all parts of the earth, constitute the Great White Lodge. This is the divine institution appointed to give the Ancient Wisdom to our planet. It is composed of all of the initiates and adepts of the White Path and forms the invisible government of the earth.

7. The Ancient Wisdom contains the true and accurate knowledge of the plan whereby the gods, man and the universe were established, are being maintained, and will later be dissolved into eternity. It is the knowledge of all things in their relation to God, Nature and themselves, and it is the only guide by which man can be shown the path he must follow if he would liberate himself from the ignorance and darkness of materiality.

8. Anyone may walk that path who will accept and live up to the obligations which the Ancient Wisdom places upon all who would learn the mysteries of life and death. If they will live the life which it points out, they shall know not only the doctrine which it preaches but also the Great

Ones who have been chosen by their own virtues to teach their younger brethren the Ancient Wisdom.

In all the schools of the Ancient Wisdom the members are divided into three general classes or groups. Every seeker after truth is in one of these divisions, whether conscious of it or not. The esoteric teachings of all religions are the same. The ends to be attained are identical in every case. The only difference between them is that each school is especially fitted to reach and work with the type of mind and body of the people among whom it is established. In other words, we may say that the Mystery Schools interpret truth along the lines of the familiar, clothing wisdom in symbol and allegory familiar to those who are sup- posed to receive it. All the schools demand the same inflexible standards of consecration and virtue, teaching that each student and candidate must build his own character, unfold his own spiritual powers, and control his own lower nature before he can receive assistance from any superior source.

When little children come into this world they are sent to our public and private schools in order to prepare themselves intelligently for their period of activity here. While they are young and un-informed, their parents protect them, but when they reach maturity they are expected to assume the responsibilities of life and help others as they themselves have been assisted. No one is born without responsibility. Each living thing is responsible for itself, and when it fails to assume its individual responsibilities others must suffer as well as the thoughtless one.

As growing children are instructed in the laws governing their environments in order that they may intelligently assist in molding the destiny of the race, so the Mystery Schools are instructing those children of men who desire to know the laws that govern the unseen world. These laws, al-though entirely unknown to the average individual, play an important part in everyday life. The Mystery Schools are universities where the spiritual nature is unfolded and trained, and man is prepared to become an active worker in the great plan of cosmic progress.

The world we live in is a world of effects. Around us, but invisible, are the worlds of causation. They are the realities, while the visible, which lives through the power of the invisible, is the il-lusion. No matter how deeply we study the material arts and sciences, we can never find out the real cause of anything. Science is still seeking and will continue to search indefinitely for a real foundation upon which to work.

The four great questions upon which all knowledge should be based remain unanswered, and sci-ence is forced to admit that they are beyond the scope of modern mentality. What is life? What is consciousness? What is force? What is mind? None can answer, for these are invisible things, incapable of being measured or analyzed, consequently no material mind incapable of reason be-yond the point of concrete vision will ever solve their riddle.

If we would step across the line which divides the true from the false, the spiritual from the ma-terial, the eternal from the temporal, we must realize that the Mystery Schools were established in the world so that this transition might be possible. Through the special instruction and un-derstanding gained by membership and graduation from these institutions, man is enabled to be-come a citizen of two worlds, for the schools themselves are of two worlds. Their gateways are in the mate- rial world, otherwise none would know that they exist; but the temples themselves are in the spiritual substances of Nature. In order to reach these temples, candidates must learn to function in the so-called invisible substances. The worlds of causation are invisible only because they are beyond the range of our sense perceptions. By certain forms of culture, however, it is possible to develop sense perceptions at present latent in the average individual. These senses, being more highly evolved than those we ordinarily use, are capable of studying and exploring the so-called causal worlds.

As power is given to man commensurate to his wisdom and understanding, it is not safe at the present time to reveal to the world at large the methods whereby entrance to the invisible world is possible. If this knowledge were given to selfish people unprepared for their responsibility, they would be able to destroy the universe, either through perversion or ignorance. In order to protect this sacred wisdom obstacles have been placed in the way of its attainment which only the sincere and courageous would be strong enough to overcome. Years of service, self-purification and self-mastery must be passed through before any candidate will be admitted to the path of wisdom.

Three steps (degrees) lead up to the temple door, and all who wish to enter, whatever their race or their religion, must climb them. There is no other legitimate way of gaining wisdom. Those who seek to enter the Temple of the Mysteries by any way other than the gate appointed by the Masters, the same are thieves and robbers. Man is willing to spend from ten to fifteen years on his material education in order that he may surpass his fellow man in some pursuit. Should he, then, expect to attain his spiritual wisdom in any shorter time?

The position a person occupies in the Mystery Schools is not the result of choice, ballot or election; it is his life and the way that he lives it that is the determining factor in all his spiritual studies. He is automatically placed upon the path of wisdom according to his vices and virtues. The rapidity of his advancement depends wholly upon his own  merits—the sincerity, integrity, and devotion which marks his daily life. He may remain many years in one grade or pass like a comet through many grades in a few years. This depends entirely on how sincerely and honestly he has labored and how completely he has mastered the temperaments and failings which hold him back.

The three divisions into which disciples of the Great Work are divided are given to us out of great antiquity. They are the same divisions that we find among the priests of the tabernacle of the Jews; they are the same as the caste divisions of India, and many others. We may consider them under three headings, as follows:

The first degree is that of Student. This is the lowest of the three grades of the Mystery Schools, and is composed of persons of either sex who have accepted the Masters of Wisdom and their work of unfolding human consciousness as the greatest reality in life and who have, of their own free will, joined themselves to the cause of human progress. This does not mean that they have sworn adherence to any individual or material organization. It means that they have sanctified their lives and dedicated their efforts to humanitarian service, which is the true path of mastery and the only road which escapes the pitfalls of egotism and commercialism.

Service is a great word. It means a devotion to the needs of the masses which is so strong, perfect, and unselfish that wealth, honors, and all things this world holds dear, will be given up instantly, gladly, and without the sense of sacrifice in the service of the ideal it has espoused. The class of student includes all who think, read, study, and aspire along the lines of the Ancient Wisdom. In its ranks are all so-called independent occultists, various kinds of untrained psychics, mediums, psychologists and others who have no direct connection with the teachers from any division of the Great School but who are seeking according to their own light to understand the initiates words as they have heard them or found them recorded in literature.

In this group we also find many student teachers who, while not initiated into the Mysteries, are seeking to assist others on the path of wisdom. Such a one was Socrates, who, while himself ignorant concerning many things, gave to the world two of its greatest initiates, Plato and Aristotle.

The student is generally without any actual proof of the thing he believes. Some intuitive voice within, however, tells him that the studies he is laboring with are true. He must so accept them. The privilege of knowing the reason for the things that he does, is not given to him as yet. He must obey blindly the great laws as they are revealed to him and await the pleasure of the Elder Brothers. During these years of spiritual darkness he must spend his life in self-improvement along those lines which he normally recognizes as virtuous and true. He must consecrate himself to the labor of preparing his nature for the greater responsibilities that are to come.

Over a hundred years ago a great disciple of alchemy and magical philosophies compiled a series of suggestive rules for those who desire to become true students of wisdom. We have extracted from the writings of Francis Barrett the following thoughts (not quoted in full):

Lesson I. Learn to cast away from thee all vile affections ... and in constancy of mind let all thy dealings be free from deceit and hypocrisy.

Lesson II. Keep thine own and thy neighbor's secrets; court not the favors of the rich; despise not the poor, for he who does will be poorer than the poorest.

Lesson III. Give to the needy and unfortunate what little thou canst spare; for he that has but little, whatever he spares to the miserable, God shall amply reward him.

Lesson IV. Be merciful to those who offend thee or who have injured thee; for what shall the man's heart be who would take heavy vengeance on a slight offense? Thou shalt forgive thy brother until seventy times seven.

Lesson V. Be not hasty to condemn the actions of others, lest thou shoulder, the next hour, fall into the very same error; despise scandal and tattling; and let thy words be few.

Lesson VI. Study day and night and supplicate thy Creator that He would be pleased to grant thee knowledge and under- standing.

Lesson VII. (Omitted as irrelevant.)

Lesson VIII. Avoid gluttony and all excess—it is very pernicious, and from the Devil: these are the things that constantly tempt man, and by which he falls a prey to his spiritual adversary; for he is rendered incapable of receiving any good or divine gift.

Lesson IX. Covet not much gold, but learn to be satisfied with enough; for to desire more than enough is to offend the Deity."

These rules for spiritual propriety are as good today as when they were first written, and should be deeply considered by all students, for all things come to man by attraction and if seeds of wisdom and virtue are not within himself, the gods can bestow nothing upon him. The duty of every student of the Ancient Wisdom is to make himself valuable to his fellow men, for when he does this he makes himself valuable to the plan of Nature.

The student must always realize that he is preparing himself to become the hands and feet of Wisdom, for when Wisdom enters into the soul of man the wise becomes its servant. The student must always bear witness to the divine urge of progress. He must train his mind, control his appetites, and make him- self a well-balanced example of human growth. His intellectual pursuits should be largely along lines which will assist him in his judgment of human nature. He should study both people and things. He should not become a recluse, for if he loses touch with the world and the things of the world he cannot efficiently serve that which he has given up.

His study is to view life as a place and a time for learning, realizing that wisdom is the jewel to be extracted from material existence. He must always keep in mind that he is not studying for himself alone but is building for the day when, his long years of preparation finished, his wisdom will be used by still greater powers to assist in those great problems which ever confront the world.

Every student should seek to develop talents. He should try to make two blades of grass grow where one has grown before. He must become a creative genius, an outstanding example of intelligence in the highest sense of the word. But it should always be unselfishly. He should never become attached either to the work he is doing or to the positions that he occupies, for the Master may call him to other labors at any moment. If he can legitimately and honestly become a power in the community wherein he dwells, he should assume such responsibilities, for they offer greater opportunities for the accomplishment of the greatest good to the greatest number.

It is not expected that a student should have clairvoyant powers or any personal spiritual abilities. In fact, it is better that he should not, lest in his unenlightened ignorance he pervert them. Students seeking to gain various forms of mediumship and psychism by occult exercises and mantrams, should take warn- ing. (One of the Masters of wisdom has distinctly stated that all forms of phenomenalism are to be rejected by the student). He must build a spiritual, mental nature, and not merely allow his emotional palate to be tickled by weird phenomena. No true student of any legitimate Master should ever attempt to converse either with the living or the dead through mediumistic powers. Some schools have made it clear that students will forfeit their right to instruction by seeking to communicate with the departed or by indulging in similar forms of psychism).

The student is not expected to be a great occultist or a great mystic. Such aspirations belong only to the higher grades. It is, however, demanded by the Masters of the student that he shall be simple, humble, honest, and patient, struggling daily to gain mastery with the true virtue over the undesirable traits of his own nature.

He is not in a position to dictate what the Masters will have him do. He must accept unquestioningly the responsibilities that are given to him of the great Unknown, and fulfill each of them as honestly and thoroughly as lies in his power. At this period of probationship the student is gaining mastery over the little things. Let him make sure that he is successful. Let him struggle to control the sharp tongue, the critical mind, and the abnormal viewpoints, that they shall not later bring dishonor upon the Spirit of Truth when it shall come to dwell within his nature.

The true student is cutting out a finer character from the rough ashlar that has been given him. He is struggling to im- prove each day just a little, asking not for power or light but for strength to shape his destiny more truly to the standards of Wisdom. These are the labors of the student.

His worthiness to receive greater knowledge is tested by long years of ignorance, often by much suffering. Through all he must be obedient, patient, and true, realizing that each sorrow is an opportunity, each misfortune a lesson in disguise. These lessons he must learn; when this task has been done, they vanish to return no more.

When he offers himself to the Master's service, the student is filled with unworthy thoughts and elements. Behind him stretch many ages of thoughtlessness and crime. His higher bodies are a mass of bad Karma, and he is totally unfitted for his labors. Before wisdom can be given to him, it is necessary that his evil nature be cleansed. So the Masters give him the labor of purifying himself as the first test of his sincerity. All that follows depends on how that first work is accomplished. Thus his consecration often results in years of sorrow for the student; but everything has its price in Nature, and a cleansed soul is the price of wisdom, for it is only a balanced and hon- est nature that can honestly think or honestly analyze. All the perversions of the past present their bills and demand payment. A great spiritual housecleaning follows, for all these bills must be paid. No true religion teaches a student that these debts can be escaped. A man does not avoid his responsibilities by becoming spiritual. He is merely given the privilege of paying his debts sooner. In this great truth Christianity has been false to its founder, for Christianity as we have it today is a religion of vicarious atonements, until in referring to the spiritual status of the average Christian, one of the Masters stated: "The pauper angels of the Christian heavens." If the student takes up the Ancient Wisdom to escape his sins, he fails before he begins; for the Masters want only honest men and women in their service and all honest people shoulder their own responsibilities.

As the result of this unexpiated Karma, the path of student- ship is often beset with infirmity and suffering, but these things are the tests which prove the character of the candidate. He will be accepted by the Masters only if his character survives these misfortunes and comes through them deepened and mellowed by the experiences. The student must labor year after year, waiting in patience and perfect trust until he has so far succeeded that he is found worthy to receive instruction from one of the Masters of their disciples.

No student knows when that moment will be, nor should he desire it to be hastened. His present labor is to serve to the best of his ability. In the hands of those wiser than himself he has entrusted his destiny and his immortal spirit, and in patience he awaits their pleasure. His province is to do; theirs to judge the doing.

The second degree is that of Disciple. In this grade are the acepted chelas "students" of an Initiate, Master or Guru. For them the veil is beginning to lift. They have placed their feet firmly upon the winding path that leads to the Temple of one of the seven Great Schools. Instead of wandering far in the search for wisdom, they gather at the feet of their appointed Master and learn from him.

Today in occult work there is too much wandering from one place to another, too much uncertainty in the soul of the student. Let him choose one path and, having established the integrity of the teacher and the teaching, remain with that.

One day while the student was laboring in the vineyard of life, tired but faithful and patient withal, the Master came that way and stopped to watch the student at his work. The student was singing at his toil. Each thing he did was accomplished with love and sincerity. Trust, hope, and consecration were his tools. He was laboring not for himself but for his brother and his God. Accompanying every act was a prayer—a silent consecration of the work of his hands and the meditations of his heart to that great invisible Thing in whom he lived and moved and had his being. The heavier the load, the greater his joy, for he was doing good. All this and other things the Master saw. But the student did not see the Teacher, for the sweat from the laborer's brow ran down into his eyes and blinded him. The Master stepped over to the student, saying, "Leave now your labors and follow me." The vineyard vanished, the dirt fell from the hands of the worker, and for a moment he dwelt in space, while before him was the shining figure of his Master. He sank on his knees at the feet of the Master and kissed the hem of his robe. Again the Master spoke: "You are my disciple. You have not chosen me; I have chosen you. You have been faithful unto a few things; now you shall have power over more and greater things."

Thus is the disciple chosen by his Master and brought into personal contact with the Teacher, his cosmic benefactor. Each Master has a number of disciples, usually twelve. They are his chosen sons. He becomes their father, and they leave all else and cling unto him. As our physical fathers and mothers bring us into the physical world and help us build our bodies here, so the Masters give us birth into the unseen spiritual worlds and assist us to build our superphysical vehicles so that we may function there. For this the Master is both father and mother, and more; for he gives us eternal birth while our material parents bring us only into the illusion.

The disciple does not choose his Master; it is the Master who calls his disciples from their various labors to follow him. None not actually and actively engaged in the vineyard of life will ever be called to the greater work. For the disciple the day of book-learning is over. The day of personal investigation is at hand. He has been accepted, and now the spiritual worlds centralize upon him and help him in every possible way. We may say that the disciples are the esoteric students. They are those who, having been weighed in the balances, have been found not wanting. They have reached that point when the discerning eye of the Initiate notes their sincerity and they are accepted as beyond the liability of failure.

The Master, after making a personal examination of the auric bodies of his disciples, gives them individual instruction concerning the preparation through which they must go before they can be admitted into the Great School itself.

It is this Teacher, the beloved Guru, and this one alone, who has the power and right to prescribe any form of occult exercises such as meditation, concentration, breathing, chanting, visualizing, and so forth. Students show very poor discrimination when they allow strangers interested only from a commercial standpoint to prescribe any form of spiritual exercise for them. They prove by their ignorance that they cannot be trusted with greater responsibilities. With his clairvoyant knowledge the Master will discover the exact spiritual status of the student and instruct him accordingly, assisting him to strengthen the weak points and round out the invisible side of his nature. The work for each disciple is absolutely individual and hence differs from that of all other disciples. In all this world there are no two people constituted exactly alike. The physical body merely bears witness and molds itself into the pattern of the spiritual organ-ism. Therefore this individuality merely proves the absolute individuality of each spiritual organism.

No one but a moral murderer or an unmitigated ignoramus would attempt to prescribe one medicine for all cases. Anyone who writes a book for general circulation telling an individual how to develop his spiritual sight must remember that thou-sands of people, no two of them alike, will read it, and many will destroy themselves in seeking to follow instructions which were not intended for them. Such an individual would thus prove conclusively that he was mentally unfitted to receive the instructions in the beginning or he would certainly have retained sufficient intelligence to use them more wisely.

The true Masters never appear in public teaching large classes or groups concerning occult exercises, but come privately to their disciples and instruct each one individually. The ability to inform the disciple concerning the steps to be taken before his actual initiation is the result of the high degree of development reached by the Adept. None who is not an Adept is able to prescribe for the spiritual needs of students without assuming heavy Karmic responsibilities. The disciple will probably be visited at night by his Teacher, who will come in a superphysical body. The student will feel certain that he is fully awake, and in a spiritual sense of the word he is, but he will recognize the Master only through superphysical vision. If he has not developed his spiritual nature by right living, right thinking and right feeling during his probation as a student, he will be unable to recognize the Master when he comes.

The work of the disciple is to learn unquestioning obedience. As the child obeys its father, so must he obey his Master once that Master has proven his authority and his virtue. To disobey the Master in even the slightest particular is to be separated from him possibly for the rest of his life. The student must obey unquestioningly the instruction which he receives. To deviate from it in even the slightest detail may prove fatal to himself. His work as a disciple is to prepare his embryonic superphysical bodies so that when he is an Initiate he may use them as vehicles of consciousness.

The third degree is that of Initiate. In this grade are the accepted and proven disciples who, while out of the physical body, under the direction of their Teachers, have actually and consciously taken one or more initiations in the invisible Temple of a true Mystery School. There are no spiritual initiations given in the physical world. All the true initiations must take place in the invisible worlds, for that is the only place where there can be found those authorized and fitted to give them. The forms and rituals used here are all exoteric and only symbolic of the true spiritual rituals used in the Mystery Temples. Today even the rituals mean very little, for in the majority of cases the student has not only lost the meaning of the symbolic services, but he has also forgotten that they had an inner significance. As Eliphas Levi, the great transcendentalist, has well said, the tests and obli-gations of the Mystery Schools are no longer given because none are sufficiently illumined to understand their inner significance. Therefore, none are willing to go through their hardships only to find that their ignorance will remain unenlightened. This is the great fault which mystics find with the religions in the world today. In the majority of cases they are pageantries of empty words.

On the threshold between the visible and the invisible worlds stands the Dweller, which Lord Bulwer-Lytton has so well described in his great Rosicrucian novel, Zanoni. This sphinx-like creature, which each must pass on his way to the Temple of Light, represents the lower nature of the candidate himself. While the consciousness is within the bodies, it cannot see this demon, but when outside it gets a detached view of itself, the lower animal nature made visible through a composite astral body is seen and recognized for the first time. This spectre the candidate must pass as he steps across from one world to the other. In order to accomplish this feat successfully, he must gain complete control over the forces in his own nature which since his first differentiation from the animal consciousness have been building the lower side of his nature. If mentally and spiritually he has mastered those elements he is strong enough to pass unmoved and unafraid before this phantom of his own perversions and enter with strength and courage into the invisible worlds.

When he is able to do this, the candidate shows that he has taken the first step toward self-mastery. Having accomplished this and learned to control his own complex organisms, he is now ready to be given power over greater things.

There are many grades of initiates, and no matter how far a seeker may pass on the pathway of understanding there is always something more for him to accomplish. We may compare it to a man walking toward the horizon. As rapidly as he approaches it, it recedes from him. No one but the Absolute itself is all- wise, all-powerful, all-knowing, or all-complete. Wisdom and ignorance are comparative terms, not only in the material world but in the spiritual world as well. The mere fact that he has been

accepted by one of the Ancient Schools does not mean that the student has become all-wise. It merely gives him a little more exalted view. He merely sees life with slightly broadened vision, but he is still subject to the laws of Nature. He is still subject to faults and failings, he is still capable of failure.

With his initiations the disciple gains certain occult powers that ever increase as he advances along the pathway of adept- ship. As the schools in the material world are divided into many grades, so the spiritual school in the Mystery Temple is divided into many stages and degrees. The disciple gradually passes from one initiation to another as he becomes more efficient in the labors which the invisible world expects him to accomplish. As he passes ever higher he gradually increases in power, wisdom, and understanding. Not, however, until the initiate reaches a very high degree does he become independent of the bonds that curb the ordinary human being. We may say he does not become superior to law until he becomes part of the law itself, and then he is above breaking it. Even after many initiations all the laws of human limitation hold good. Initiates are subject to birth, growth, and old age. Sickness and sorrow still confront them at every turn. They must return to this life again like other normal beings until their development carries them to a state of consciousness much higher than that which the average individual can hope to reach in one lifetime.

There are no initiates who are not clairvoyant, at least to a certain degree, for they cannot receive their spiritual ordination until they are capable of functioning consciously out of the physical body. Neither are there any true initiates who do not know their true position. Many people come and say, "I had a strange experience in my sleep. Was it an initiation?" The answer in nearly every case is negative. The initiate is in doubt neither as to what he has accomplished nor what he has been through. The average student can ask himself, "What am I here and now? Am I worthy to be picked for greater responsibility? If I were a Master, with all the world to choose from, would I choose myself for great and responsible works? If I would not, with my narrowed sight, would the Master be deceived by the slender virtues I possess and choose me when there are others much more fit?"

There are no Adepts or Masters in this world or upon the invisible planes who have not passed through all the sorrows and uncertainties of human experience. They have reached their present position because they have mastered those uncertainties and have risen above the circumstances which chain most people to the selfish side of life. All of the Great Ones have passed sequentially and gradually from ignorance to wisdom. None was made overnight. Each was tempted and each was strong through the moments of temptation. All were persecuted. Many died for their ideals, preferring wisdom above all treasure and truth above all power. Each initiate who now sits in session with the Elder Brothers has earned his position by consecration, intelligence, and sincerity. These are the magic keys which open the gates of the Mystery Schools.

Again and again the question is asked, "How can we know an initiate if we come in contact with one?" We can only answer, "By their works shall ye know them." After analyzing the lives and habits of those initiates whom we are able to recognize with our limited vision, we find that they all adhered to a general series of rules. Conditions are altered by the needs of the moment, but among the ancient manifestos we find hints as to the conduct of adepts and mystics.

For many hundreds of years the true Adepts and Initiates shrouded themselves in an impenetrable veil of mystery. This procedure served many ends. First, it protected the Initiates from the endless inconveniences to which they would be subjected by the curious and the credulous. It also permitted them to live quietly and silently, to study and pray, unknown and unsuspected even by their next door neighbor. Then, again, it multiplied the power which they had over a world which could not oppose them because it could not discover them. And, lastly, it enabled these schools and their disciples to escape the persecutions of religious bigotry and intolerance that have always been felt when man sought to discover God without benefit of clergy.

The Egyptian Sphinx is supposed to have pointed out the initiate's code of conduct by the symbolic interpretation of the four creatures composing it. The body of the bull with its great strength was interpreted to mean the process of labor, "to do." The legs and tail of the lion speak of courage and are interpreted as meaning "to dare." The wings of the eagle bespeak of loftier things, so they are interpreted as "to aspire." The human head, with its sealed lips, means "to be silent." Of all these rules, the last is the most important.

One of the ancient occult axioms was, "If ye know it, be si- lent." Today in both the orthodox and occult worlds of religious thought there is entirely too much talking. There are too many claiming powers and virtues which they do not possess. Places of worship have become institutions of debate, while cliques and clans are breaking off in all directions because idealism has been wrecked on the rocks of petty personality. There is a surfeit of initiates, but little wisdom. There is a multitude of pedagogues and demigods, but all together cannot keep peace in their own ranks, let alone convert the Gentiles. Nearly all this comes from too much talking, and making light of serious matters. The names of the Masters have been dragged in the mud. The Mystery Schools have merely become part of the paraphernalia with which to juggle commercial psychology, and the spirit of reverence and love which the ancient world felt for its initiates has been lost in our day because of the host of false initiates and fraudulent psychologists. A true occultist, be he student, disciple, or initiate, never discloses his position to any except those equally interested and equally sincere along similar lines. He should do his work incognito, veiling the truths he has learned in the simple language of the street, telling men what they should do, not what he himself is; urging, suggesting, but never forcing either his opinions or his philosophies upon others; neither is he puffed up by applause nor disheartened by criticism. He should labor quietly in the field where he finds himself. He should always be inconspicuous, silent, and unobtrusive. He should labor diligently, allowing his work and not his tongue to speak for him.

An initiate or disciple should never state his position publicly, nor should he discuss his spiritual aspirations. If he has been privileged to view spiritual phenomena in his own life, if he has been taken out of his body or is developing clairvoyant powers, those are the most sacred things in his life. They should never be spoken of in public, for they are sacred to him and his Master. To discuss personal powers is the worst breach of etiquette conceivable in the occult world.

Looking back over the lives of Initiates we note several things concerning which they were most exacting. We are sorry to find that students of today are rather lax in these things. Therefore, we suggest for your consideration the following:

(a)   All true occultists abide by the laws of the nations and the community in which they dwell. While in many cases they recognize these laws as imperfect, they abide by them lest by their moral example they should teach the less intelligent to break the restraining bonds of law and order. It is said that laws are made for those who break them. We may add that laws were not made for Initiates, but there is a very small minority of people intelligent enough to live together honestly without the assistance of law. No matter how bad these laws are, they are far superior to the lawlessness which would exist when the mental hazard of punishment is removed from the untrained and unregenerated man.

From time to time occultists are dragged into court because they have failed to set a good example to their fellow creatures. There is no doubt that the element of persecution which existed in the Middle Ages is still to be found in places and that many are unjustly persecuted. But still there are entirely too many who, feeling that their spirituality is superior to that of their fellow creatures, deliberately ignore the law. Especially is this true with the wildly fantastic soul-mate and free-love institutions. These things are not sanctioned under any conditions by the Ancient Wisdom, for the Mystery Schools themselves instituted the legal bond of matrimony. Anything which suggests the breaking of existing laws without first preparing a better law for the mass of the uninformed is outside the pale of the Ancient Wisdom.

(b)   True occultists break no laws, regardless of how unjust they may be. If they see injustice, they labor to introduce more just legislation. A notable example of this is found in the life of Abraham Lincoln. Many times slaves came to him before the Civil War begging him to assist them to escape from their lives of servitude. This Lincoln refused to do, because it was against the law, but he told them that while he would never break the existing statutes he would consecrate his life to making a better law. It is in this spirit that all occultists must work with injustice, for in this way truth is established without the rioting and Bolshevism of lawlessness.

(c)   All occultists and initiates should assume the dress and customs of the nation or people among whom they dwell, lest any departure from that custom shall cause them to be unduly conspicuous. This was one of the strictest rules of the Ancient Wisdom teachers, and is found among the old manifestoes of the Rosicrucian brotherhood.

(d)   The true Adept and Initiate shall reveal his identity to no man, unless that one is worthy to receive it. The secret work which they have been permitted to have is a two-edged sword. When they had prepared themselves to receive it, it was good for them, but by promiscuously giving it to others they could do great harm. Therefore, they reveal to no man the secret instructions they have received nor the source from whence it came, being satisfied to disseminate it quietly and inconspicuously. When questioned concerning these things, they state their position and then remain silent. This privilege to remain silent they defend with their lives.

(e)   The true Initiate and disciple shall never be boisterous or declamatory in his statements, nor radical in his viewpoints, nor encourage such conditions among those with whom he comes in contact, nor speak for his organization or his Masters. The true Initiate has no will but the will of his Masters, nor does he palm off his own judgment as having any more important origin than his own brain. He must take no radical steps unless commanded to do so by the Great Brothers who have the lives of men in their care.

(f)   When dwelling in a community, Initiates shall be peace- loving, simple, kindly, charitable, and not critical of those about them, making themselves invaluable through their intelligence and their integrity. They shall watch their conduct day and night that it may in no way reflect against the exalted organization of which they bear witness. They shall be humble in all things, willing and glad to do the most menial labor if it will add to the welfare and progress of their fellow creatures. It shall be said of such a one, as of the Master Jesus that he went about doing good.

(g)   Under no conditions shall they use any of the spiritual powers which they may possess for their own aggrandizement or protection, unless such is for the unselfish good of others. It is against all the laws of occultism to apply any knowledge which is of a supernatural nature for the salvation, preservation, or improvement of self. As stated of the Master Jesus, others He could help but Himself He could not save. For this reason modern psychology and mental magic of various kinds are contrary to the orders of the Ancient Wisdom; for by modern psychologists the student is taught these spiritual gifts that he may use for his own aggrandizement.

(h)   Under no condition is the teacher warranted in exacting pay for the spiritual instructions which he gives, for no money was paid to receive them nor is any coin of the realm a payment for them. The student assumes his share of responsibility, and ingratitude is one of the major sins of occultism. When a student who is in a position to assist retards, through his miserliness, the work of the Master, such a one assumes all the Karmic debts incurred as the result of his failure to cooperate. No student should study occultism with the object of using it as a commercial enterprise. Such will never see either the Masters or the Temple.

The foregoing may throw some light on the reason why it is so difficult to determine the position of the ancient initiates. Their reticence and humble spirit have seldom found a place on the pages of history, and yet they are the real molders of the destinies of nations. They are the invisible powers behind the thrones of earth, and men are but marionettes, dancing while the invisible ones pull the strings. We see the dancer, but the master mind that does the work remains concealed by the cloak of silence.

A follower of the Master or of any of the seven Great Schools which they have established in order to disseminate the Ancient Wisdom, is not privileged to call himself a member of any occult order or school until he has passed one or more actual initiations in the spiritual Temple of the order to which he has been drawn by his planetary lights. The reading of literature, the payment of fees, or the signing of pledges does not make the student an occultist or a member of any of the true spiritual orders. Only by the first initiation in the spiritual Temple is he made a true member. He may join this society, that organization or the other brotherhood, and so state, but he is thus affiliating himself with only an exoteric order. His true membership comes with his entrance into the Temple which contains the spiritual hierarchy that animates and vivifies the outer material institution.

Time and time again we find students, disciples, and even initiates of the lower orders who, through a certain remnant of egotism still remaining in their natures, have brought disgrace upon the thing which they truly love. This usually results from some ignominious failure which they make and which, because they have incessantly emphasized their spiritual position, is laid at the door of the school which they claim to represent. With a slight revision of Scriptural phraseology, today many people say, "What good thing can come out of occultism?" This attitude is the result of the great spiritual schools being humiliated again and again by the abject failure of some of their disciples. This condition is largely the result of egotism, for the disciple was unable to stand a little dignity without making sure that everyone knew about it. Egotism is one of the most serious of human failings that the occultist has to overcome, for it makes him insensible to his own worthiness, of which no true disciple should ever lose sight.

In this day of religious thought, most people desire to be- long to something. Like barnacles they attach themselves to the ship of human progress and finally, when a sufficient number of these crustaceans have attached themselves with their hard- shelled opinions, the ship either sinks under the weight, or, like some of our occult organizations, must go into drydock and have its incrustations removed. When you claim membership in anything, ask yourself whether that institution is as proud of having you as a member as you are of claiming membership in it. Most people join spiritual movements to gain something for themselves. They become parasites, living off a Tree of Wisdom which another man has planted and cultivated. True people affili- ate themselves with the Mystery Schools not to better themselves but to serve that institution faithfully and well. Until they feel that they are a credit to it in every sense of the word, they do not wish to have their name linked with that of which they are not a worthy representative.

Instead of claiming membership in this, that or the other and thus casting reflection upon the integrity of the Masters, let us take another of the ancient rules for our standard and in this way uphold the dignity of the superior thing. Let us suppose that you have just joined the ancient religious order which was called Gnosticism.

We have said that there were three divisions—students, disciples and initiates. Let us see how we should state our position if we were to attain any one of those three degrees in the ancient religion of the Gnostics.

If a student, we would say, "I am a student of the Gnostic philosophy." If a disciple, we would say, "I am a disciple of the Gnostic path of wisdom." If an initiate admitted into the spiritual Temple of the Gnosis, we would say, "I am a Gnostic." In this last simple statement we have distinctly affiliated ourselves with the spiritual hierarchy manipulating the Gnostic order. We would never say that we were anything unless actually initiated into the esoteric organization, which, concealed behind the exoteric order, is in every case the true institution of which the exoteric structure is but the symbol.

Every member of an occult organization should make his position unmistakably clear. He owes this not only to the order but also to himself, for daily misunderstandings arise because students are not honest enough to admit themselves to be merely seekers and not adepts in disguise. The Ancient Wisdom demands honesty and would have in its ranks none without sufficient love for the order to defend it from every calumny and bear upon their own shoulders, if necessary, its honor and integrity.

Why should people try to be virtuous when they see others pass on to wisdom with all their sins? The high standards of the Wisdom Schools are discredited by persons who, while full of faults, claim to be initiated members in good standing of an organization which stands for all that is high and noble. In the name of the Great Work, it is wise to admit that all we have of virtue we owe to the Masters and their instructions, while for our vices we are indebted to our own lower natures. This attitude will serve the Great Work far better than you will ever know.

# XVI

❦

# The Doctrine of Redemption Through Grace

THE Christian theory of redemption is unique in that it emphasizes salvation as attainable in spite of vice rather than because of virtue; in fact, the prime saving virtue for the Christian is acceptance of the divinity of Jesus Christ. That a viewpoint so philosophically unsound could have gained so firm a foothold in the number and power of its adherents is more than passing strange.

The early Christian theologians condemned nearly every normal attitude of mankind, advocating extreme practices and austerities that have produced a full measure of religious neurotics and worse. Regarded as sanctified souls, these abnormals engrafted upon the main body of their faith attitudes and disciplines which, being the products of irrationality, only added to the general confusion. It is philosophically inconceivable, for example, that Deity should advocate flagellation as a means by which the flesh could be mortified into a state of piety.

Nor has any utilitarian value, divine or human, yet been demonstrated to result from sitting like St. Simeon Stylites for thirty years upon the top of a pillar sixty feet in the air. It is a theory, ingenious but unconvincing, that to be born was a disaster because of the indiscretions of our first parents; that to live was a crime to be expiated only by living miserably; and that to die was simply a transition by which the members of the church militant were reborn into the choirs of the church triumphant.

For the individual living in the cosmopolitan religious atmosphere of North America it is difficult to realize the influence wielded by theology over the devout in those countries where religion still dominates almost every phase of individual and community life. Out of such a theological autocracy have risen organizations differing widely in attitudes and standards. On the one hand we find the Misericordia, whose hooded members—often men of distinction and culture—unhesitatingly served the needy of every class in the hour of plague or disaster. On the other hand we find the Ignorantine Friars—men of sincere motive but benighted vision—who boast of their illiteracy and consider a knowledge of even the fundamental principles of life as detrimental to the plan of salvation. While not actually requiring austerity of some kind, several great world religions openly encourage the practice among the members of their various orders. Even today most people view with a marked reverence one who has made of his physical body a broken and emaciated sacrifice in the effort to atone for his participation in humanity's heritage of sin.

The God of joy is dead, and in his stead rules the God of tears. Man, unillumined, cannot achieve tranquillity. He struggles impotently against a universe which, to his myopic vision, seems bent on his annihilation but which is really molding him into a future god. In his ignorance of the plan the suffering human creature conceives all being to be ruled by the scepter of sorrow.

In that supreme dramatic achievement, Lazarus Laughed, Eugene O'Neil enunciates the gospel of joy, a gospel which must some day supplant grief-stricken theology and lead man from the worship of death to the worship of life. Lazarus is made to say: "Man's loneliness is but his fear of life I Lonely no more! Millions of laughing stars there are around me!

And laughing dust, born once of woman on this earth, now freed to dance! New stars are born of dust eternally! The old, grown mellow with God, burst into flaming seed! The fields of infinite space are sown—and grass for sheep springs up on the hills of earth 1 But there is no death, nor fear, nor loneliness There is only God's Eternal Laughter! His Laughter flows into the lonely heart!"

Springing up during the decline of classical pagandom, Christianity felt itself divinely called to save the world from the insufficiency of previous doctrines. Witnessing with holy horror what it termed the perversions of the barbarians, the church finally arrogated to itself the office of sole mediator between the spirit of righteousness on the one hand and a wayward world on the other. Arbitrarily seating itself in the chief place, with one imperious gesture it dissolved the body religious, consigning all previous knowledge and beliefs of man into the limbo of decadent cults. Discovering that, like man, no faith can live by itself alone, Christianity was later forced to borrow from the pagans the very fundamental principles upon which its own philosophy is erected. It accordingly accepted the concept of heaven and hell as disseminated by the Egyptians and Greeks, but changed the personnel of the doorkeepers. The angelic hierarchies with which the Jews populated the celestial spheres were appropriated en masse and thereupon ceased their Hebrew chants to sing hymns in ecclesiastical Latin. With one fell swoop Christendom thus became master of all the spheres which the enraptured vision of pagan cosmologists had perceived. The church not only sought to stamp out heathenism from the earth but, invading even the uttermost parts of the invisible universe, drove the illustrious souls of pagandom from their own heavens and hells to make room for the proselytes of Christianity.

In its religious philosophy Christianity was thus truly eclectic, placing its mark of approval on isolated fragments of thought in such a haphazard manner that it is now impossible to find any thread of consistency which will bind the whole together. Hence, its articles of faith must be considered individually except in the few isolated cases where a common denominator is present. According to the churchmen, this weight of disagreement is not to be regarded as detracting from the sanctity or validity of the articles, since each is the direct revelation of a Deity who revealed what he wanted to when it pleased him, and whose reasons therefor transcended human estimation. Whatever profundity is found in Christian philosophy is due primarily to this infusion of pagan ideas. Conversely, the shallowness of Christianity is the direct result of the clumsy efforts made to improve upon the ancient doctrines. The integrity of the individual was the keystone of pagan idealistic philosophy. The unfoldment of the triune nature of man—spiritual, mental, and physical—was based upon the foundation of personal integrity. Even the most bigoted church historian must admit that the magnificent edifices of pagan learning were raised upon the solid rock of personal virtue.

Their philosophy emphasized to both the Egyptians and the Greeks the indispensability of right-thinking and right-living as prerequisites of right-being. Though the standards of ancient integrity may appear curious and obscure to this genertion, they unquestionably produced an ethical type surpassing in many ways the products of what we conceive to be our more enlightened code. While the pagans are now regarded as a superstition-ridden people because of their offerings to their Lares and Penates, it remained for Christianity to present the human race with the most indefensible and at the same time the most vicious of all superstitions, namely, the doctrine of vicarious atonement —the redemption of a sinful world by the supreme sacrifice of one just man. While the myth of the dying god is to be found in many religious systems, Christianity was the first and only cult to construe the mythical incident as a literal atonement. Christ becomes, so to speak, a scapegoat, the sacrifice offered up that the people might go free.

According to the church, the Passion abolished the old order of approach to Divinity and supplanted it with a brand-new modus operandi of salvation. Heaven, earth, and hell were all dislodged from their time-honored foundation lines, and the sins of all creation were wiped out by the blood of the Lamb.

Even the impassive sternness of Deity relaxed at the spectacle of this sublime and supreme ordeal. The incident of the crucifixion monopolized the stage in the drama of Christianity, for it speedily overshadowed any and all other dogmas to such a degree that mere admission of the universal import of Christ's incarnation and death became the sole prerequisite of spiritual redemption.

Thus a new standard of integrity was created which, however, still conveyed to the enlightened few its cryptic message of mystical ideality, but which could not fail to be interpreted by the unenlightened masses as evidence of the supremacy of words over works, of affirmation over action. Whereas the criers of the pagan Mysteries, according to Celsus, declared the superior worlds to be attainable only by men and women of outstanding intellect and lives consecrated to individual regeneration, the criers of the Christian Mysteries offered heaven with its eternal bliss to anyone who would confess his sins and affirm the divinity of Jesus Christ.

Twenty centuries of application have demonstrated the danger of the doctrine of vicarious atonement. Undermining the morale of Christendom, this concept has resulted in a philosophy of special privileges and exceptions which has infected church and state alike. This doctrine has caused the history of Christendom to be written in letters of blood. Nearly all who have enjoyed its privileges have donned the garments of sorrow, and kneeling in sackcloth and ashes cried for liberation from the bondage of its dogma. An emperor of China once said: "Wherever Christians go they whiten the soil with human bones; and I will not have Christianity in my empire."

How can anyone who has sensed the dignity of the Universal Plan reconcile the eternal justice of divine procedure with the right of excommunication in which the body religious ejects into outer darkness some offending hand or foot, enjoining such a soul forever from further participation in the goodness of God? How insignificant must be the power of that heaven or that hell which mortal man so easily manipulates at will! Where in the realm of all that is noble and just is there place for the concept that the souls of millions of babes are doomed to wander in the black vistas of the lost because they died in infancy without baptism? A faith cruel enough to espouse such doctrines inevitably inspires cruelty in its followers; for if it will damn its own with such unfeeling malignancy, how can it be expected to show mercy to the stranger without the gate?

The survival of the church, therefore, is contingent upon its own realization of how it has misinterpreted both the real mission of its founder and the symbolism of the pagan cults from which it derived the subject matter of its creed. Christianity will never be a great religion until its adherents recognize that it is merely a new body serving as the vehicle of an old idea; that when it departs from the original concepts to wander in the maze of theological absurdities, it defeats the primary purpose for which it was conceived. These unnatural attitudes of theologians toward life have resulted in the establishment of an unnatural faith wherein the lofty principles of the ancient philosophers have been distorted out of all semblance to their true import. Christianity as the only true religion is worthless. If the faith, however, be regarded as a definite step in religious evolution, it is then possible to estimate its importance with a reasonable degree of accuracy. Christianity is not the sole revelation of God to man. It is but a fractional part of the body religious. It is simply a crutch upon which the genus homo leans until he learns to stand and walk alone. It is something he believes in before he is capable of believing in himself with understanding. Like all external things it will finally pass away and be remembered only for that which it contributed to the inner realization of its devotees.

The three major doctrines concerning the plan of redemption are: (1) redemption through mass effort; (2) redemption through individual effort; and (3) redemption through the vicarious atonement. The Jews, as a "chosen" people, are an example of the first concept; Platonic philosophy, with its repeated emphasis upon individual achievement, is example

of the second; and Christianity, with its World Martyr, is the outstanding example of the third.

The rough out the entire structure of Western thought there is a definite emphasis upon the factor of individuality. In the Orient, however, perfection is considered possible only through the annihilation of individuality. Without much careful examination of their underlying principles, these divergent systems of philosophy are apparently irreconcilable.

To the trained thinker the attainment of perfection as the result of individual effort is by far the most rational viewpoint toward the problem of redemption; for it is natural to presume

that in an orderly universe each element must diligently work out its own salvation. In things spiritual, humanity in general realizes all too well the insufficiency of its own knowledge, and only because of its fatuous belief that it can reap where it has not sown is the situation rendered bearable.

The doctrine of the vicarious atonement opens the gates of heaven to millions who in their own right are not entitled to admission. It is surprising the tenacity with which this idea retains its hold upon the public mind, even after modern educational facilities have dissipated the theory of a personal God. The palpable inadequacy of the literal interpretation of the vicarious atonement is almost conclusive proof that it has a more subtle significance only to be discovered by the most searching analysis of the philosophic elements involved.

The doctrine of the vicarious atonement is based upon the debatable question of the precedence of love over law. It is written, "For God so loved the world that he gave his only begotten Son, that whosoever believeth in him should not perish, but have everlasting life." (John iii:16). If the postulate of a personal Deity is accepted, then it is not unreasonable that a just Creator should send his representative into the world to make known his will to man. It is not philosophically sound, however, that God should love the world more because that selfsame world had crucified his only begotten 1 In the early writings of the Church Fathers it is declared that Christ, by virtue of having died for mankind, appeared before the throne of his Father to intercede for the world for which he had sacrificed his life. Like his prototypes Bacchus and Dionysus, Christ was a personification of Divine Love—the inexplicable emotion. Since the dawning of his rational faculties, man has striven to understand the position occupied by spiritualized emotion in the Universal Plan. He is able to classify the entire procedure of life and postulate the laws by which the universe is governed, but the riddle of love has proved more elusive than even the riddle of life itself. Since man invests Deity with feelings akin to his own, so God was considered to be not only the Lord of judgment and order, but also the Lord of love. Since man loved those who were close to him in the world, so he visualized the Deity as likewise bestowing his affections upon those "chosen" peoples who obeyed his laws and made proper sacrifice. As the outgrowth of this man-made concept, the God of antiquity was ever swayed by caprice. At one time he would exalt his people and prosper their efforts; at another time he would scourge them with his wrath and wreak his vengeance upon them. Like Zeus on Olympus, the Creator was subject to inconstant moods, at one moment minded to scatter with his divine lightnings all his fashionings and the next to elevate them to a parity with himself.

Since God had created man, it was assumed by theologians that he must also to some degree remember and love these imperfect products of his handiwork. Hence, to redeem an inconstant creation from its own inconstancy, the Word took upon itself flesh, and being fashioned in the image of man dwelt among men, preaching the law and giving those who accepted the law an opportunity to survive the Armageddon which would sweep away the unbelieving. After that event the earth, it was presumed, would then become once more an Edenic garden where the elect would dwell in unbroken felicity throughout the uncounted eternities of futurity. The inner realization of the truth of this concept was redemption, and insured membership in the body of the redeemed.

To the scientist and the philosopher, however, it is evident that God is not a man nor in any way limited in his manifestation by the laws governing the inferior creation. In spite of all theological argument to the contrary, it is unthinkable that the Universal Spirit—whose dwelling is immeasurable space and in whose vast nature suns, moons, and stars are infinitesimal atoms—could have localized itself in a little Syrian town and been born in the image of a man. In our search for fundamental truths we must discard the notion that the various elements in this mysterious drama are personalities, and thus restore them to their true dignity as universal principles.

For many centuries it has been believed that to destroy the personality of God was to detract from his magnificence, when in reality to invest him with a personality is to degrade him to the estate of man. Impersonality is a divine attribute; it is a state inherent in the nature of God, and a condition to which man must attain in the quest of his own divinity. If the personality—yes, even the individuality—of God is discarded as an illusion of the human mind, Deity is thereby elevated to its true philosophic estate, namely, an all-pervading, universalized essence. It naturally follows that this essence is without either footstool or throne; it does not hover over either communities or individuals but is distributed without partiality throughout the entire substance of space.

But, the orthodox Christian will exclaim, how did the prophets and saviors of old have face-to-face interviews with such a Deity? The answer is simple: They didn't. Wherever such conversations are recorded they are symbolic references to the inner experiences of the spiritual life. They come under the same general heading of what psychologists now term the "mystical experience," and are concerned solely with extensions of consciousness and degrees of realization. The phenomena accompanying these experiences are simply allegorical descriptions of mystical conditions couched in language suitable for the moral instruction of those in whom this inner nature is still dormant.

The impersonalizing of all the host of spiritual agencies introduces an entirely new aspect into the problem of the vicarious atonement, for it is quite evident that the cause of humanity could not be pleaded before a tribunal composed merely of symbolic figures of universal agencies. Archangels could scarcely be present when archangels are emblems of spiritual forces. And that God should appear in wig and robe is as inconceivable as that the Holy Ghost is actually a dove. At first glance the whole idea may savor of sacrilege, but upon sober reflection the reader will realize that it is the first step toward the elevation of Deity to an estate worthy of the Universal Parent A consideration of the problem of the vicarious atonement,

if confined purely to the present superficial and conventional lines of treatment, must inevitably subject the doctrine to honest doubt and ridicule. Hence, the student of theology must cast about for the fountainhead in which the doctrine had its real inception. Christianity borrowed so much from the Orphic philosophy that the student should not be criticized but rather commended if he turns in that direction. Nor will he be disappointed. The Neoplatonism of Alexandria also furnishes a clue, and Gnosticism (especially the Alexandrian branch) is permeated with valuable suggestions.

The diagram at the beginning of this chapter should be studied carefully in connection with this subject. The three intersecting globes—designated the Causal Universe, the Intermediate Sphere, and the Inferior Universe —are representative of the threefold universe. The Causal Universe is the universe of spirit and is ruled over by the law of the spirit, which is absolute and unchanging. The Intermediate Sphere—which signifies the World Soul—is governed by its own laws, which laws are inconceivable to mortal man but whose mysterious synchronizing urge man defines as love . The dark Inferior Universe below also has its own laws by which it was created, is maintained, and will ultimately be dissolved. These are called the natural laws of life, but have been elevated by theology to the dignity of divine laws. Consequently, when we speak of those natural laws which we regard as the manifestations of God, we refer to those causal agencies governing the Inferior Universe, which in their entirety are termed in ancient philosophy the will of the Demiurgus, or Lord of the World. The keynote of the Inferior Universe is law. Those whose consciousness does not elevate them above its limitations have not learned as yet to temper justice with mercy; they still live in the concept of an eye for an eye and a tooth for a tooth, and boast of the inexorable quality of these universal laws.

The keynote of the Intermediate Sphere is love, which is also a law moving in perfect concord with the principles of the soul, its true vehicle. The apparent inconsistencies of physical affection are referable to two sources: (1) the principle of love is often confused with animal emotion, a physical propensity; <2> where love does manifest in its true nature, its manifestation—like all spiritual functions in man—is intermittent; for meeting with the obstacle of matter it is distorted and its consistency usually broken up.

The keynote of the Causal Universe is divine law as opposed to the natural law of the Inferior Universe. Divine law is not comparable with natural law in that it is the power directionalizing consciousness. It never manifests in the physical universe in a manner sufficiently detached to be susceptible of analysis. In the famous play by that name, "Mr. Wu," the Chinese mandarin, is made to say when describing the customs of his people: "The law by which we live is the law by which we die."

Tersely stated, such are the laws or forces manipulating the Inferior Universe. In the Causal Universe, however, are found only the laws by which things endure, for there neither life nor death exists.

By some eminent authorities Christianity is maintained to be an Oriental cult in that it emphasizes the necessity of the contemplative life and regards the visible universe as an illusional sphere from which man cannot escape save through the spiritual nature of Jesus Christ. Christ here is regarded as the channel or mediatory power by means of which it is possible to emerge from the dark underworld and become one with the sphere of Reality. St. Paul lays special emphasis upon the effectiveness of belief and, conversely, the ineffectiveness of accomplishment. He says: "For by grace are ye saved through faith; and that not of yourselves: it is the gift of God: Not of works, lest any man should boast." (Eph. ii:8-9).

The "works" here mentioned signify outward activities, regardless of the degree of their constructiveness. According to this view it is—strictly speaking—useless to engage even in virtuous endeavor, for all endeavor (virtuous or otherwise) is simply an illusion. The outward nature of the individual is regarded as incapable of good in that it is a part of the world and stained with the sin common to mortality. All of the outer life with its endless diversity of interest must consequently be cast aside and sole emphasis be placed upon the spiritual nature, which alone is capable of approach to Reality. This viewpoint (in which the best life is a failure unless accompanied by an unquestioning faith in the infallibility of the church) was the natural outgrowth of, and became most powerful in, an age of physical insecurity where life and property were in constant jeopardy. Investment in things physical had slight appeal where an entire community might be swept away to gratify a besotted emperor's whim, or where tens of thousands might perish to furnish sport for a Roman holiday.

With the twentieth century, however, new attitudes and new scenes occupy the world stage. Chief emphasis is now placed upon physical existence. Every effort of inventive and legislative genius is concentrated upon the improvement and security of this existence in order that at least a relative degree of comfort (if not happiness) may be enjoyed by the masses. When defeat in war or the distemper of his superiors brought to man no alternative other than that of slavery, he had but one hope: namely, that he might speedily die. Where social inequity thus decreed unhesitating obedience to the dictates of tyrants, there inevitably resulted a philosophy which emphasized as the only conceivable freedom the state beyond the grave. But the modern man and woman do not regard this earth as such a forbidding place that immediate escape therefrom is a pleasing prospect. Science is ever devising conveniences which, while they may ultimately result in deterioration of our more rugged racial virtues, are fast becoming the common enjoyment of nearly every stratum of society. Man's chief struggle is now for leisure in which to improve himself, and in the mechanical trend of his civilization he visualizes a world which will some day be maintained by automata so that the present slaves of industry may have opportunity to acquire the cultural benefits of art, science, and philosophy.

In every walk of life the necessity for finer mental functioning is keenly recognized. The world of St. Paul has disappeared forever, and with the passing of the old regime has

gone that concept of the world as merely a highly magnified Roman Empire, with the Demiurgus, or fabricator of it, as a dissipated Caesar served by a degenerate court. The spirit of democracy prevalent in the realm of government has even invaded the domain of spirit, and in a certain sense the Lord of the world is now elected by the popular vote of the citizenry. Little by little the universe has assumed so many of the features of democracy that it begins to display the inconsistencies of a democratic system. Not many centuries ago man bowed stolidly before the doctrine of the divine right of kings, and if deep in his heart he resented the intolerance of his rulers he dared not breathe that criticism. It has been but a similar short time since man first dared to speak the name of God; when those few who had the temerity to discuss matters of religion hid themselves in attic or cellar lest the world should learn of their lesc-majeste.

Today, however, if we do not like our magistrates we summarily impeach them; if our kings annoy us we dethrone them, while to ridicule and caricature their slightest eccentricity is

an open-field diversion. In his unfoldment of self-expression man finally grew bold enough to question the dictates of theology; nay even to debate publicly the infallibility of dogma

and challenge the God of antiquity to destroy him with his ire. Today man no more hesitates to dispute so-called divine mandates than he does to find fault with the conclusions of petty politicians.

To deal with such a complete reversal of attitudes requires an entirely new interpretation of divine law. Man no longer kneels when he worships; he stands up and faces his Creator unafraid. While at first this may savor of rank heresy, it will yet prove to be the solid foundation of a newer and truer criterion of conduct. By almost imperceptible degrees the Creator has come to be regarded as synonymous with the agencies controlling creation. He no longer makes laws and later breaks them; he is now an integral part of the great scheme itself, bowing before the same immutable principles that sway the whole of Being. The philosophic code for this age will emphasize obedience to Nature's laws, for he who follows most closely Nature's example will become the most virtuous and estimable member of society.

Primitive man innately worshipped that of which he was most afraid. The Demiurgus, or Lord of the Inferior Universe, was an imminent autocrat by whose thunderbolts all the achievements of man were shattered. This wielder of destiny, who arbitrarily dictated the end of things and who even molded the act of Providence according to his fancy, was regarded as part God, part demon. He was a God of every imaginable wrath and horror, whose voice was heard in the thunderclap, whose throne was the tempest, and who rocked the earth with his displeasure. According to this view laws were but divine whims to be changed at divine pleasure, and as diversified as divine moods. None dared to question the right of Deity to elevate one man an debase another for the same deed. The universe was run at the pleasure of an erratic agent who moved individual and nations like pawns upon a chess-board, and when he tired of the game simply brushed them all away with a gesture of his hand. While entire races languished in the benighted state of savagery, this God concerned himself particularly (as Voltaire has noted) with the number of bells on the petticoats of his high priest! In terms of modern psychology, this Demiurgus functioned in the "detail" mind.

While the Demiurgus was an important figure in all ancient philosophy, it remained for Christianity to elevate him to chief position among the gods of the universe. To the Greeks he was known as Zeus, who, though father of the gods and lord of the world according to popular concept, was in the enlightened eyes of the sage a subordinate deity who might thunder at his pleasure without ruffling the disposition of the wise; for only such as accepted the reality of ignorance, fear, and death could be controlled by the Demiurgus. As philosophy annihilated these three superstitions and liberated man from bondage to his own terror, those who drank of its life- giving waters escaped from the sway of the Demiurgus and became citizens of a greater and nobler world.

It is not difficult to understand the misconception that elevated the Regent of the physical universe to chief place among the gods. We understand best that which is most like ourselves, and the Demiurgus partakes so abundantly of human frailties that we can almost truthfully declare that we understand him. When he casts down a rebellious people who insist on making altars round in form when he desires them square, he is simply treating us to that arbitrary exhibition of power which most men would like to exhibit if they possessed it. This God is therefore very close to the human heart; as close in fact as human concepts of hate, revenge, and destructiveness. The Divine Spirit, superior to all this petty bargaining for favors; in whose nature virtue is supreme, and who with infinite "mildness" and perfect compassion broods over the destiny of Cosmos, is so unlike benighted humanity that man cannot estimate its qualities other than by intellectual means.

Hence, the first person of the ancient triad of gods was the recipient of little veneration. Ammon is said to have had but one temple in Egypt, whereas Ra and Osiris (the lesser members of the Creative Triad) had sanctuaries to the number of many thousands. In India the shrines of Vishnu and Shiva dot the landscape on every hand, but where are the temples of Brahma? Throughout Christendom where are the altars of God the Father? His Son has churches unnumbered and even the Virgin and the saints all have niches in conspicuous places, but God, the sole Creator, is apparently forgotten, or rather absorbed in the glory of his own emanations. God the Father will thus remain without place of worship until men become capable of comprehending the principle for which Divinity stands. When the spirit of God the Father takes up its abode in their lives, then will his symbols representative of understandable principles be present in the world. The new religion to come will worship God in his creative aspect as being superior to his preservative (the Christos) and his destructive (the Jehovistic) aspects.

When the true relationship existing between the various members of the Creative Family (the Trinity) has been established, the real significance of the doctrine of salvation through grace is at once apparent. Ancient philosophy concerned itself with this problem of the Demiurgus, and the method of evading the doom awaiting those caught in his net of illusion. Hence, philosophy was, primarily, a discipline evolved to elevate man above the Demiurgic level and enable him to dwell in the realm of spirit over which the Lord of Form was powerless. In other words, salvation was achieved by escaping from the material self; by liberating the eternal Knower from its noneternal sheath. Christendom believes that this escape was made possible through the incarnation, death, and resurrection of Jesus Christ, who by rolling away the stone from his sepulcher liberated all mankind from bondage to the concept that death was the finale to life. Only such as believe in death can actually die and they alone are actually in slavery to the world and its Regent. Thousands of years, however, before the birth of Jesus Christ, pagandom "liberated" man from servitude to his inferior self, creating by means of the Mysteries that "royal road" leading upward to permanence from impermanence. By an infinite grace the door between the dark world below and the bright spiritual sphere above was thus left ajar, and through this mystic portal passed the illumined of the ages.

When Jesus Christ as the personification of the qualities of the rational soul is made to say: "I am the way, the truth and the life: no man cometh unto the Father, but by me" (St. John xiv:6), it is abundantly evident that he spoke in a figurative sense and that the saving principle thus referred to is not to be understood as a personality. The "way" here signifies the spiral path of attainment established in the world coincident with creation itself. This way—which is in truth the plan of salvation itself—• can scarcely be regarded as a man, even though a highly illumined one. Nor can "truth" be conceived of as an individual, for truth is the unchanging nature of things as they actually are—a concept transcending the comprehension of mortal creatures. Finally, the mystical "life" by which the regeneration of the individual is wrought is unrelatable to any personality, since it obviously exists as an all-pervading principle. In this enigmatic fashion is set forth the fact that Christ (the Christos) signifies the procedures and qualities of that cosmic rationality which, according to the Greeks, had its seat in the rational soul of all men but which manifested itself only in those who through the disciplines of philosophy had lifted their irrational selves to a state of participation in the effulgence of the rational soul. In the Greek Cabala, the numerical value of Christ (Christos) is 888 which means the higher mind, and which the Greeks conceived to be the spiritual Knower complemented by rationalized, or regenerated, intellect.

As rationality is at first latent in all irrational things, new light is thus thrown upon the statement, "Christ in you, the hope of glory." In other words, the rationality in you is the saving "grace." The word grace has two distinct shades of meaning. It may be considered as the mercy of God by which he chooses to pardon those parts of himself which momentarily displease him. In its aesthetic sense, however, grace becomes an actual attribute of the internal nature itself. Sometimes we use words better than we know. The ninth definition of grace in Webster's New International Dictionary reads:

"Attractiveness; charm; esp., the aesthetic value shown in suppleness and ease, spontaneity, and tactful harmony; the charm of congruity, harmony, and pliancy in beauty as distinguished from sublimity or force; beauty as displayed in free flowing curves, easy and natural contours, fluent color, or felicitous and musftal diction; as applied to persons, manners, etc., easy and natural elegance; in a weakened sense, propriety; seemliness; comeliness." It is thus evident that the grace by which man is saved may be considered not only as an attribute of Deity but also as an attribute of man himself. From the latter point of view man works out his own salvation through aesthetics, in which his own innate grace actually becomes his redeeming virtue. If we correlate the triune nature of God to the One, the Beautiful, and the Good, the quality of grace in the light of the definition quoted at once becomes synonymous with the Beautiful. Thus, microcosmically, grace is the rhythm in the human soul, and macrocosmically, the universal harmony by which the divine beauty of the Plan is revealed as coessential with the divine order of the Plan. It will yet be philosophically established that the grace which man himself develops in his relationship to the manifold problems of life will be the grace by which his salvation is assured.

The popular concept that belief in the divinity of Christ is a prerequisite to virtuous living may be interpreted in a way which casts considerable light upon an otherwise obscure subject. In this case all depends upon the interpretation of the word belief. If belief is regarded as merely an intellectual acceptance of the truth of a statement, then the entire subject simply resolves itself into another theological absurdity. If, however, belief takes the form of an inner realization of the spiritual truths involved, then indeed it is a spiritual power. Belief in immortality must precede knowledge of immortality. That faith upon which man establishes his philosophy of life and which gives him the courage to sacrifice all in the quest of that which is the greatest good, is indeed a sustaining faith. For example, the neophyte entering the House of Wisdom assumes the disciplines of philosophy because he has faith in the efficacy of philosophy; he believes that the path he has chosen will ultimately lead him to where faith will be exchanged for understanding, and belief for knowledge. Belief, then, in the reality and faith in the attainability of achievement—these are indispensable to accomplishment. Faith in self and belief in the divinity of self—these must precede perfection. But faith without works is dead, and belief is valueless unless it inspires to the attainment of the thing believed in.

According to the vicarious atonement, one just man expiated the sins of an unjust world. In the Orphic philosophy a mysterious agency—which men indiscriminately call love, beauty, or harmony, but which the Greeks termed the rational soul —descended out of the perfection of Deity where it had existed in an undivided state and was scattered like seed throughout the substances of the inferior world. As the Demiurgus could control only matter, these seeds from a higher sphere were of too exalted a nature to be dominated by his edict. These seeds remained apparently lifeless, however, through the dawn period of the world, the Demiurgus molding the substances of matter at his pleasure and ignoring the germs lying dormant therein. Worlds and men were thus gradually fabricated until the whole genera of life appeared, but still the seeds remained inactive. Man wandered hopelessly in the gloom of mortality, living and dying without light or understanding in his servitude to the Demiurgus and his host of spirits. At last the spirit of rebellion entered creation in the form of Lucifer, who in the guise of a serpent tempted man to revolt against the mandates of Jehovah (the Demiurgus). In Greece this character was known as Prometheus, who brought from the gods the impregnating flame that would release the life latent in this multitude of germlike potentialities. In Christianity, Christ (the Christos) is the divine fire which, striking the latent germs of immortality, liberates them from their ages of impotency.

As man emerged from barbarism and began to cultivate what may be called the intuitional, or soul qualities, an environment of beauty was thereby created wherein the germ of the rational soul could be stimulated and made to grow to the point where it would completely remold the life of man in terms of the beautiful and the true. In a purely technical sense there are three definite methods by which man may impregnate this germ of spirituality within himself. The first method is known as worlds and in antiquity was symbolized by the soldier who went forth to "fight the good fight." The age of chivalry was the natural product of the ideal that the greatest good could be accomplished by destroying the forces of evil and thus attempt to re-establish the golden age upon earth. The second method is love , under which heading is included the factors of faith, belief, and service. Through prayer and devotion to noble ideals a certain glorification is awakened in the life.

Love is elevated and impersonalized until it becomes a great spiritual urge stimulating all that is true and noble within the soul. The third method is philosophy. The venerable sage, contemplating the wisdom of the ages, thus sought to elevate his rational nature until it could gaze unafraid upon the vastness of Being, The understanding thus created excites a noble intellectual passion which brings with it the stimulation of the soul qualities. In all three methods there is a crowning state—a condition of apotheosis or ecstasy in which for a moment man actually dwells upon the plane of his ideals. The knight in deadly combat rose to heights of heroism wherein he gladly gave his life for principle. Those in whom faith is the dominant factor are elevated to a condition of overwhelming proximity to Deity, as testified to by the enraptured visions of the mystic. To the philosopher there comes the gradual realization of cosmic immensities; and at length the sublime spectacle of it all picks him up and sweeps him into the philosopher's heaven —a state where all thought is clarfied and the rational faculties become momentarily able to cope with the riddle of existence.

Regardless of the means by which this clearer and larger vision is attained, its purpose is ever the same. The ecstatic state becomes like a bolt of fire which, striking the germ of rationality within the physical nature of man, causes them to burst open and release that universal redeeming and rationalizing power which was mixed with primordial matter before it was molded into worlds. Thus what Jacob Boehme calls "the tree of the soul" has its beginning. Its roots are in the dark earth of mortality, but gradually the tiny shoot—whose very nature is Divinity—grows upward to blossom forth into a beautiful and noble plant. When once this seed of Divinity has been quickened the power of the Demiurgus is broken. The Lord of the world may thunder his displeasure. Though he slay man a thousand times, yet shall that man live, for life has been awakened within him. Though all the furies of creation may attempt to destroy that tiny soul-plant, yet shall it prevail against them, for it is composed of the substances over which death and destruction are powerless. Through the disciplines of the Mysteries this redeeming plant—which the Christians have called Christ —is caused to increase in power and magnitude until in its perfected state it absorbs into itself all of the irrational nature upon whose substances it was formerly maintained. When it is realized that antiquity postulated a period called the golden age during which the rational soul so controlled universal manifestation that all things lived together in a state of harmony, beauty, and goodness, all the elements necessary to complete the world drama of salvation are at hand. The rational soul is therefore the beloved of the Father, dwelling with God (the One) in a state of absolute felicity. Again, the spirit of beauty and truth is symbolized as the beloved son of the Universal Spirit through whose rhythmic principles the immeasurable dignity of the First Cause is most adequately manifested. Then came the symbolic "fall" of man foreshadowed in the incarnation, death, and resurrection of the spirit of universal harmonics. As Bacchus was torn to pieces by the Titans and his dismembered parts scattered throughout the universe, so the principle of redeeming beauty (or love) was disseminated as the aforementioned seeds throughout the irrational sphere. When man reawakens (resurrects) this spirit of universal love, it ascends into the presence of the Creator, there to intercede for that regenerated one.

The newly unfolded realization that beauty is the most powerful of all agencies is itself the redeeming grace, and the vicarious atonement merely signifies that there is a spirit of beauty resident in mortal man which can accomplish for mortal man what he cannot accomplish for himself. Two natures reside in every individual: one, as Goethe says, to the heavens aspires, the other in the earth aspires. The heaven-man (the Christos in us) is not born of woman but is conceived of the Holy Ghost. This spiritual agent becomes our redeemer when of our own free will we elect it to be the master and director of our activities. Thus the just man in us redeems his own sinful shadows. He descends into hell and forever abolishes the power of evil; he ascends into heaven and pleads our cause in the firmament. Through him we partake of Divinity even as through our outer natures we partake of humanity.

As man increases in rationality the spirit of the beautiful begins its ministry of transmuting the baser elements of the not-self. The uncouthness of the nature gradually disappears and tinctured with the grace of the indwelling Divinity the outer nature is transformed. The rationality within permeates the entire structure causing it to sing with a new harmony and establishing a more perfect symmetry between its component parts. Thus mortal man who is nothing of himself, is brought into proximity with the sky-man, who is the spirit of life and truth. When the union of the two is effected and the animal nature—the relapsed heretic of the ages—is at last converted to the true faith, then the miracles so eloquently described in Scripture take place. Those who are mentally and spiritually crippled are healed; those who are blind to the greater realities of life are made to see; those driven frantic by the seven devils of worldly desires are freed from their bondage to the senses; and those tainted with the leprosy of ignorance are cleansed. Furthermore, those who hunger for the food that satisfies the inner self shall be fed by that inner knowledge which is the true bread of life.

When rationality—not in the sense of intellectuality but of true and beautiful knowing in the sense of identity with spirit— assumes the reins of human life, then that life becomes beautiful and happy in the fullest and truest sense. From this and other evidence it can be established with philosophic certainty that Christ is indeed the spirit of truth, which few recognize but which when recognized becomes the redeemer of the life. He who desires to recognize this truth must realize that it is the supreme goal of all endeavor. He who would succeed in his quest for it must first of all develop one peculiar faculty which we will term appreciation.

It has often been said that appreciation touches off endeavor, but here again is a word with two meanings. We ordinarily conceive appreciation to mean the esteem felt by others for ourselves, but what it actually means is the esteem we feel for others. The heart that is receptive to the beautiful in life will achieve unity with the object of its desire. Man possesses the power to appreciate and recognize the goodness and beauty of existence. This power which makes realization possible is itself the blood of the divine Bacchus—the god-soul—who through its blood in man shall redeem the world, There is in us a certain spiritual capacity: the power to be more than we are, the power to be more than simply a crawling worm bowing humbly before the despotic Regent of the world. This power to transcend our mortal selves is symbolized by the blood of the god-man that, freed by the spear of necessity, pours down into the cup of matter, there to remain as the cleansing blood.

Age after age finds mankind soaring to nobler heights, and each passing generation shows some marked progress in the realization of new ideals. Let us then realize that this power to increase; this power to elevate us so high that even the stars cannot restrain us; this power to be magnified until the very universe becomes a confining wall; this power which enables us to face our Creator unafraid; this rational Knower who is limitless—this is the Universal Savior, the Christ, which in the magnificence of itself ultimately atones for all that has gone before and by right of its very existence makes man partaker of all good things to come. Man cannot be destroyed by his gods because his gods are within himself. By his incarnation, Christ (the rational soul) infuses into all creation a quality as immortal as the gods themselves. By right of this capacity for divinity within himself man may not be cast aside, but is entitled to infinite opportunity and divine protection. Thus is the symbolism preserved whereby a man through the Christ in him shall arrive at the condition of that glorified perfection which is now the object of his faith. Each of us is struggling to be free from the bondage of his mortal sepulcher. The Sky-man yearns for the stars, and if he be lifted up to his true estate of first place in the constitution of man will draw all the rest unto him that all good works may be brought to speedy consummation. The science of redemption may be said to embrace any and all means by which the dormant germ-like potentialities of Divinity resident within all human nature are first awakened and then stimulated to divine perfection through aspiration. In summing up it follows, therefore, that such diversified elements as beauty, belief, grace, faith, love, appreciation, labor, and thought—all being expressions of rationality—are indispensable to the perfection of the whole.

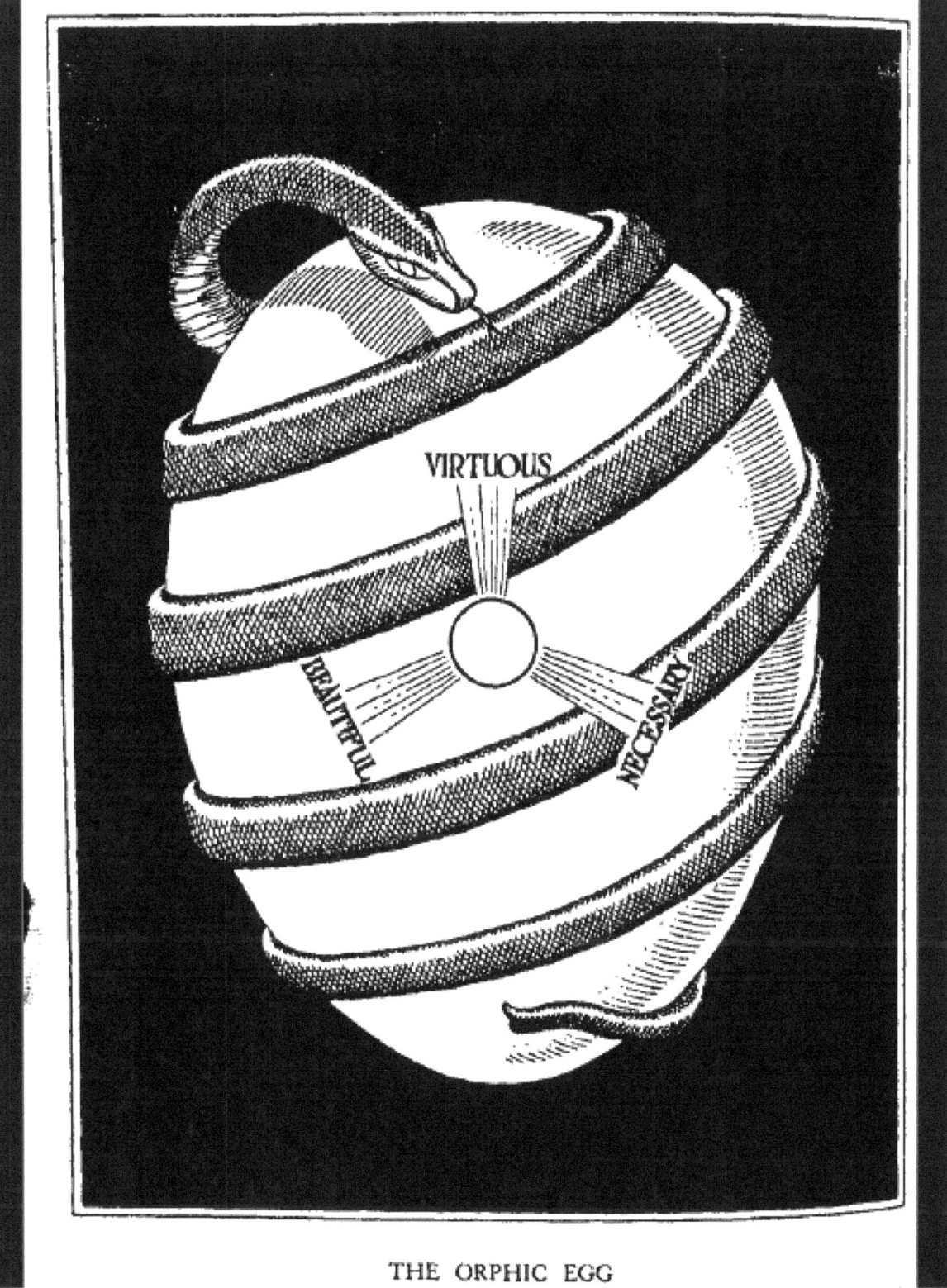

## THE ORPHIC EGG

The Universal Germ, stirring within the Egg of Creation, established the worlds and generations by three "gestures." It fashioned the souls of things according to Virtue, the bodies of things according to Beauty, and the laws by which souls and bodies are maintained according to the Necessary. Together, these comprise the Work which is called The Good.

# XVII

❧

# The Mission of Aesthetics

ESTHETICS is that branch of philosophy concerned primarily with the intrinsic nature of beauty, its place in the Divine Plan, and the processes whereby beauty can be created or caused to manifest where previously it did not exist in a tangible state. That beauty produces a profound effect upon the entire nature of man is too well established to be questioned. Just what constitutes beauty, however, and why it wields so profound an influence is still a subject of controversy. Is environment the basis of an aesthetic standard; that is, does the familiar become the standard of aesthetic propriety? In a limited sense this must be true. On the other hand, man has been surrounded for ages with such familiar themes as war, disease, and decay; yet he has never come to regard these as beautiful, at least not in his lucid moments. Beauty, declared the ancients, results from the harmonious correlation of parts; the spectacle of the mutual agreement of all the elements involved in a common pattern creates a pleasant reaction in the sensory organism of man. That the urge toward what man terms the beautiful is universally present in Nature was also asserted. Certain natural processes were cited in support of this belief. For example, vines and creepers rapidly grow up to hide the gaunt outlines of a rotted tree, and flowers in profusion blanket the shell-torn fields of Flanders once made horrible by the unleashed fury of man.

Standards of beauty vary with the evolutionary status of races and individuals. The preference displayed by the nobility of Hawaii for stoutness of figure proved rather embarrassing to the court of Queen Victoria. The hennaed whiskers of the Rajput gentry, while very chic in Rajputana, arc a striking incongruity to Western standards of aesthetics. The quaint African custom of distending the lips and ears by the insertion of loops of bone or pliable wood is productive of a type of beauty totally beyond our Occidental comprehension. Furthermore, though our poets wax eloquent over the graceful lines of a swan's neck, die Burmese belles (who achieve the literal effect by stretching their necks with iron rings) find our modern verse-mongers strangely unresponsive to their charms.

It is difficult—perhaps impossible—for the individual to view life with any aesthetic standard other than his own. If it were possible to analyze the sensory organism that can see symmetry in the bound and distorted foot of a Chinese lady, one great mystery of aesthetics would be well-nigh solved. The gradual evolution of man's concept of beauty seemingly depends upon both the power of observation and the sense of proportion.

For example, the child recapitulates, in some measure at least, the racial evolution of which it is a product. Children, while fond of drawing, are generally incapable of recognizing perspective, and among primitive types nearly all art is two-dimensional. When a child designs a crude little house the size of a postage stamp and draws a man beside it several inches high, it senses no inconsistency in the possibility of the man to enter the house. In a similar way the little girl regards her doll as alive and intelligent, although well-aware that its head is made of porcelain and its body of sawdust. Great battles are fought with little tin soldiers on a nursery floor, and both the little chinchilla bear and wooden horse are endowed by their juvenile owner with all the qualities of their living prototypes. The sculptor of the Stone Age, probably likewise unaware of the crudity in his technique, evidently viewed his art as a striking reproduction of the person or principle he sought to portray.

When the mediaeval artist drew upon canvas faces which were as expressionless as eggs he endowed them, so he believed, with all the beauty and vividness of his model. The evolving standards of symmetry, however, have outgrown his ideal, making the products of his brush now valuable for their oddity rather than their merit. Thus, while we are able to estimate the inconsistencies of the past when contrasted with the apparent consistencies of the present, we are wholly unable to realize how inconsistent the present will appear in the light of future standards. Some may still recall the time when Dame Fashion decreed bustles and leg-of-mutton sleeves for milady, and when gentlemen had the creases pressed out of their trousers lest they be suspected of buying ready-made clothes. While all admit the revolutionary changes of fashion, the mental process that justifies these changes and ridicules that which it previously justified is more difficult of analysis. The average individual believes that beauty in style is established by the caprice of the modiste and fashionable tailor, who find it lucrative to cater to the love of novelty innate in human nature. While this may be the superficial explanation for these cycles of change, the definite trend of the centuries is produced by certain psychological tendencies. In discussing such problems of aesthetics as simplicity and complexity, a modern writer has arrived at some remarkable deductions. Simplicity has long been accepted as the chief prerequisite of beauty. This is definitely opposed to the barbaric tendency toward adornment. It is reasonably certain, for instance, that clothing (except in the most frigid zones) is the outgrowth of the desire for ornamentation rather than the dictate of utility. The theory is also now advanced that complexity is used to conceal weakness, and simplicity to reveal strength.

The evolutionary trend of aesthetics is obviously toward simplicity, for complexity invariably creates the sense of discord by scattering the faculties of comprehension. Man originally conceived ornamentation as complementing his personal dignity; he considered adornment a setting wherein he might be shown to better advantage. Illustrative of the degree to which this element has eclipsed the personality is the story of two ladies watching a third go by wearing a very expensive ermine cloak. Turning to the second lady, the first remarked; "Did you see that magnificent cape that just passed by?" Thus, in the effort to be beautiful, humanity has become a race of mannequins, hopelessly enslaved to fads and styles which, if not actually detrimental, are at least unnecessary. Greek supremacy in aesthetics is based upon the fact that they achieved the objectification of the beautiful while at the same time preserving utter simplicity. Never did they permit principles and ideals to become involved in complicated forms of manifestation so that they were even partly obscured. In Greek art the idea was ever apparent, and with the objectification of that ideal labor forthwith ceased, for beauty was recognized to be a principle so elusive that it invariably escaped if the means to capture it were unduly stressed. Apropos of this truth is the saying that it requires two men to paint a great picture: the first is the artist; the second, a near friend whose duty it is to shoot the artist at the psychological moment.

The plea of Greenwich Village, "Art for art's sake," while it expresses a theoretical ideal, is often misapplied. There is a tendency to produce technicians who become so skilled in the manipulation of various mediums that they overlook the fact that all mediums are useful simply for the expression of an idea. The great artist is not necessarily a great technician; he is rather a man with a great idea. It is a curious, but nevertheless noteworthy fact that those with the best knowledge of grammar and composition seldom write the best books. Those who become slaves to means or methods are prone to lose sight of ends. Words are sound mosaics which by their combinations create pictures in the mind of the one who hears them. It is the ability of the speaker to create this picture in the mind of his audience that is of prime importance. His greatness is measured by the sublimity of that picture.

What words are to the orator, pigments are to the artist. Through their infinite combinations eternal and intangible verities are expressed in a language comprehensible to the understanding soul. All the arts and sciences are such mediums of expression, fulfilling their purpose when they are developed not for their own sake but for the sake of those inner convictions which through them alone can be shadowed forth to become an impulse or urge in the external life. It is his own shortsightedness which invariably thwarts the ends of the technician. A certain thrill which accompanies the possession of an intricate and adequate mechanism of expression has a tendency to fascinate the mind and hold it as in a hypnotic spell. The fact that words, like colors, are susceptible of such a variety of combinations often intrigues the mind from pursuit of an ideal to lose itself in the maze of approaches to that ideal. The desirable knowledge of method is thus acquired, but the chief purpose has been frustrated: namely, arrival at the true goal.

The result is a wasted life in the sense that self-expression has failed to be objectified. To the ancients, the arts and sciences were all sacred to the gods, and upon being admitted to apprenticeship the future craftsman dedicated whatever proficiency he might later acquire therein to the service or expression of eternal truths. Man studied that he might not only learn but that he might use intelligently. And what may be termed intelligent use? The answer is: a use that is beautiful, virtuous, and necessary, since these are the true characteristics of Divinity; for God was regarded as the most beautiful, the most virtuous, and the most necessary of all things.

In its truest sense, therefore, aesthetics may be considered a philosophic discipline by which the consciousness of man is equipped to estimate the degree of beauty, the degree of virtue, and the degree of utility inherent in the nature of an object; also the power to discern how these qualities may be increased to ultimate perfection. The first work is to establish the nature of beauty, virtue, and utility in their most comprehensible sense. Before beauty is cognizable in other than its transitory and inconsequential sense, the consciousness must be elevated to that level of rationality on which the principle of beauty exists, dissociated from the clumsy efforts of man to express its qualities. Upon the basis that only the beautiful is capable of recognizing the beautiful, the assumption of the philosophic life is regarded as indispensable to the recognition of the aesthetics of Divinity.

Socrates would have conceived beauty as expressing itself in the social fabric as utility and in the moral fabric as virtue. To be beautiful is the natural state of all that is good, in that good must manifest good; and beauty most adequately expresses, and is the inevitable attribute of the good. One of the primary axioms of geometry—that things which are equal to the same thing are equal to each other—may be profitably applied to this Socratic triad. So, in answer to the question, What is the most beautiful of all things? philosophy says that which is the most virtuous and the most necessary. What is the most virtuous of all things? That which is the most beautiful and the most necessary. What is the most necessary of all things? That which is the most beautiful and the most virtuous.

The truth of these assumptions is self-evident. Never has the world realized more clearly the utilitarian value of beauty or how necessary virtue is to the survival of the whole. Much of the crassness with which modern civilization is cursed has resulted from the divorce of beauty and utility, in which the spirit of aesthetics has been sacrificed to what we foolishly term the "practical." Some years ago I visited a state prison, and upon being taken into that section reserved for those commonly called "lifers" I was struck with the pathetic effort of

the convicts to preserve the spirit of beauty behind the drab stone walls of their penal institution. The men had built little wooden flower boxes, fastening them to the foot of the grating of their cell doors. In these boxes were planted creeping vines which, growing upward, entwined themselves about the gratings and made of the iron bars a trellis. Also in the tenement districts of large cities where thousands are huddled together in an atmosphere of squalor and vice, the little potted geranium on the fire escape is a familiar spectacle, bearing witness to that spark of aesthetics which the Lord of the Whole hid deep within each human heart.

Although to a certain degree an intangible asset, beauty is the molding factor in racial and national life. As long as the spirit of the beautiful shines forth through the bodily structure of peoples and institutions, these increase in power and glory; but when aesthetics dies, the very structure of society deteriorates and begins its march toward inevitable oblivion. Beauty is a soul quality, and like the soul is visible only in its tincturing effect upon its immediate environment. When life is actuated by the spirit of the beautiful, the entire organism—social as well as individual—^is the beneficiary of a definite grace and charm which render a relatively imperfect body not only endurable but even attractive. It is not given that all human beings should have beauty or symmetry of form and features. As we pass through the Hall of Fame where the likenesses of the world's illustrious are preserved for the admiration of posterity, if mere physical symmetry be regarded as the sole criterion of excellence many of these geniuses were but rude caricatures of men and women. Carved deeply in the marble of immortality we find the crude and distorted face of Socrates, a little farther down the gaunt figure and aquiline features of Dante, while from his niche stares great Milton whose sightless eyes could yet envision paradise. More recent additions to the immortals are the lank and raw-boned Lincoln and the crippled Steinmetz. Why have the beautiful so often mounted to power through tyranny and oppression, while the deformed have nobly and unselfishly served mankind ? The answer seems evident. Beauty has regarded its own existence as a substitute for merit, and fascinated by its reflection in the mirror of vanity has therefore passed into oblivion. On the other hand, those of unsightly mien have struggled for that transcendent internal beauty which has elevated them to chief place in the hearts of men.

That man has a compound nature is difficult for most people to understand. In other words, man is not merely an individual; he is many individuals considered as one. With similar propriety we might refer to an army as a single entity, disregarding the fact that an army is really an aggregation of entities. The brain of man is actually composed of over forty lesser brains, each a specialized organ of thought. Each of these complete thinking organisms vies with every other to dominate the entire organism of thought, and through this competition of parts the compound mental attitude is established. Unaware of what may be termed the ethical code in the relationship of these brain parts to each other, man believes himself to be the master of his thinking processes, when in reality he is frequently the victim of their machinations. Throughout the entire constitution of man there is a continual plotting for precedence. To a certain degree each part victimizes its associates, with the result that the organism is a seething maelstrom of biological intrigue. In similar fashion the social order—which is really a vast body—may be likened to the fabulous dragon whose seven heads are continually biting at each other.

While the interdependence of parts prevents an open outbreak, there are few bodies in which even a comparative degree of harmony can be said to exist. The compound human organism may be fair to gaze upon but this does not necessarily prove that the various strata of its microcosmic social system are on amicable terms with each other. The human body is one of many examples of the failure of the democratic theory, for nothing could be more tragic than the picture of man's hands or feet liberated to work out their own destiny irrespective of the welfare of the rest. Only because there is within each of us an autocrat who binds the various members to the accomplishment of its own ends can even a semblance of order be maintained. When it is further realized that this autocrat is itself capable of error (in fact, almost incapable of anything else!) we may better grasp the problem presented by the government of man's functions. The wonder is not that man manages his affairs so poorly, but that he manages them at all! An individual whose own internal parts are so bady disorganized as to make rational functioning impossible cannot but reflect his own indecisions into the social order of his civilization. The codes by which he lives, being the product of his own internal disquietude, thus engender national and international friction with their resultant crime, war, and disease.

Like individual power, racial power must result from the autocratic usurpation of authority by some figure—no matter how despotic and arbitrary—who grasps the reins with a strong hand and drives the whole toward the consummation of its own desires. Men like Alexander the Great, Caesar, Genghis Khan, and Napoleon, represent the personification of a racial urge which Nietzsche might call "the will to power." These men gathered up the belligerent elements which had previously expended themselves in a guerrilla-like warfare of factions and directed them toward the goal of world conquest. While this procedure proved most distressing to the strangers without the gates who were its luckless victims, it alone preserved the political integrity of the exploiting powers.

The moment either an individual or a nation ceases to struggle against external obstacles, internal dissensions arise. As soon as the Christian Church stopped fighting the pagans, it began fighting itself. As rapidly as nations reach the point where they are strong enough to maintain an isolated individualism, they arc destroyed by civil war. It is sad, but nevertheless true, that up to the present time conquest has been the only force strong enough to surmount national prejudices and cement them into national alliances. There is undoubtedly a certain relationship between this fact and the well-known adage that the devil finds mischief for idle hands to do. As the individual is likewise a nation in miniature, he is only capable of maintaining the efficiency of his separate organisms while these organisms as a whole are directed toward the achievement of a definite end. Though the lodestar of both nations and individuals, ambition has also proved to be their undoing; for, having outdistanced their resources, they were unable to maintain the positions they had gained. An ancient philosopher once said, "If you want to humble your adversary, give him power." Power may be defined as the privilege of self-expression. Only the wise, however, can express themselves and still be great; the remainder reveal their own ignorance and thereupon tumble from their gilded thrones. To the question, what is the most powerful thing in all the world? the financier would answer, money; the general, guns and men; the religionist, the church; the scientist, knowledge; the philosopher, reason; the mystic, love; the aesthetician, beauty.

Money, while not inherently evil, has been the motivating principle behind nearly every form of crime known to man. Guns and men, as we know all too well, have become the elements of a gigantic destructive science which may hurl millions of living things to a horrible death in order to establish a diplomatic technicality.

The church, founded originally for the worship of God and the service of man, has now become an arrogant institution, looking with contempt upon those who supply it with the where- withall of its very existence. Knowledge has deteriorated until it is simply a dust-covered stack of dry and worthless notions.

Reason has degenerated into debate, wherein minds which should be directionalizing their efforts toward the good of the whole, huddle together under the cloak of learning and mumble their absurdities. Love, the most sacred of all emotions, has been dragged from its lofty pedestal, and crimson-robed lust seated in its stead. As for beauty, it has sunk to depths so low as to be considered the vicarious atonement for irrationality. That beauty is a power is undeniable, but the magnitude of that power is as yet unsuspected. As the proper directionalization of beauty is a potent factor in the civilizing of races, so the misuse of this agency results in a corresponding degree of depravity. External beauty combined with the insolence of internal pride produced a Lucrezia Borgia who, with a face as beautiful as that of a saint, poisoned without a qualm of conscience all who stood in her way. Yet it is written of Lucrezia Borgia that despite her surpassing beauty there was an intangible something about her which filled everyone in her presence with indescribable fear and loathing. Thus the internal nature is impossible of total concealment, and where the outer beauty does not complement the grace within the soul, an incongruity surrounds the personality like an intangible miasma.

The warring segments of a personality, as has been suggested, can only be unified by a common purpose which will enlist the sympathetic co-operation of all. Right motive —one of the eight noble paths of Buddhism—can be made to unite all the diversified faculties and members of the nature and directionalize them toward achievement of the greatest good.

The consciousness that steadfastly contemplates only good through all its diversified perceptions may be said to have united its various parts into a pattern worthy to be designated beautiful. Co-operation only can be conceived of as beautiful, for competition must ever manifest as a grotesque absurdity. Only a propaganda-ridden world could possibly imagine war to be beautiful, and competition is merely a bloodless war in which the soul and not the body is slain.

While contemplating the nature of the Supreme Good, the Neoplatonists of Alexandria also philosophized with rare lucidity upon the nature of the beautiful. Plotinus writes concerning the order of the beautiful as it emerges from the first Beauty: "And in the first rank we must place the beautiful and consider it as the same with the good; from which immediately emanate intellects as beautiful. Next to this we must consider the soul receiving its beauty from intellect; and every inferior beauty deriving its origin from the forming power of the soul, whether conversant in fair actions and offices, or sciences and arts. Lastly, bodies themselves participate of beauty from the soul, which, as something divine, and a portion of the beautiful itself, renders whatever it supervenes and subdues, beautiful, as far as its natural capacity will admit."

Beauty, existing independent of form and as a divine principle, is likened to the fountainhead of existence, from which streams of beauty flow forth to permeate and beautify the whole inferior creation. Furthermore, the beauty of the inner nature greatly transcends the beauty of the outer, for the spiritual essences constituting the supersubstantial man, being more proximate to Cause, partake more fully of the nature of Cause, which is true Beauty. Hence, as Plotinus also observes, there are those who "on perceiving the forms of gods or daemons, no longer esteem the fairest of corporeal forms."

The quest of the truly beautiful is therefore identical with the quest of Self, for Self in its perfect and universalized sense—the all-pervading Consciousness postulated by the sage—is the perfect source of all beauty and therefore partakes in perfect measure of all that which is manifested from itself. That this supreme truth was taught by the sacred institutions of antiquity is further evidenced by Plotinus, who continues: "Just as those who penetrate into the holy retreats of sacred mysteries are first purified, and then divest themselves of their garments, until some one, by such a process, having dismissed everything foreign from the God, by himself alone, beholds the solitary principle of the universe, sincere, simple, and pure, from which all things depend, and to whose transcendent perfections the eyes of all intelligent natures are directed, as the proper causes of being, life, and intelligence. The Neoplatonists did not confine themselves solely to a theoretical consideration of mystical truths; they deemed it also essential that the disciple learn to actually partake of the verities disclosed by intellectual contemplation. If perfect beauty was synonymous with perfect good, then the achievement of perfect participation in its effulgence was of first importance. As the ephemeral beauties of the outer (or material) world were sensed chiefly through the eyes, so the eternal beauties of the inner (or spiritual) world could only be sensed through a mystical perception which they termed the "eye of the soul." "We must enter deep into ourselves," again says Plotinus, "and leaving behind the objects of corporeal sight, no longer look back after any of the accustomed spectacles of sense. For it is necessary that whoever beholds this beauty should withdraw his view from the fairest corporeal forms, and convinced that these are nothing more than images, vestiges, and shadows of beauty, should eagerly soar to the fair original from which they are derived. For he who rushes to these lower beauties, as if grasping realities where they are only like beautiful images appearing in water, will doubtless, like him in the fable, by stretching after the shadow, sink into the lake and disappear.

For by thus embracing and adhering to corporeal forms he is precipitated, not so much in his body as in his soul, into profound and horrid darkness; and thus blind, like those in the infernal regions, converses only with phantoms, deprived of the perception of what is real and true."

While the Alexandrian mystics shared the Oriental attitude concerning the attainment of Reality through rejection of the illusions of sense, they had more definite conclusions as to the method whereby the Causal Beauty was to be realized. Their instructions read thus: "Recall your thoughts inward, and if, while contemplating yourself, you do not perceive yourself beautiful, imitate the sculptor; who, when he desires a beautiful statue cuts away what is superfluous, smooths and polishes what is rough, and never desists until he has given it all the beauty his art is able to effect. In this manner must you proceed, by lopping what is luxuriant, directing what is oblique, and by purgation illustrating what is obscure; and so continue to polish and beautify your statue until the divine splendor of Virtue shines upon you, and Temperance, seated in pure and holy majesty, rises to your view."

To the ancients aesthetics was not only the science of beauty, but that discipline whereby each individual in his quest for truth might elevate his own level of functioning so as to become luminous with the reflected light of Universal Beauty, and ultimately identical therewith. Two forms of beauty were postulated: that which is intrinsic to the nature of a body, and that which is extrinsic or communicated from some external source. In man, for example, beauty was the natural attribute of the spiritual nature, but the material nature partook thereof only by reflection. Being a rational creature manifesting through an irrational animal organism, man has the capacity to recognize and estimate the excellence of order, symmetry, and grace. Even as that which is base finds response in the baseness of the material nature, so that which is beautiful a- wakens a pleasant reaction in the rational part. As Bacchus was dismembered by the Titans and his parts strewn throughout the irrational sphere, so the rational soul of man is scattered throughout the substances of his irrational animal nature. To the presence of this element of confusion is referable the inability to recognize or appreciate such soul qualities as harmony and beauty.

The pleasurable sensation which beauty awakens in the beholder was said by the Greeks to arise from an internal symmetrical nature beholding an external body with qualities similar to its own. As the internal nature dwells in perfect order, it thus rejoices in order and recoils from disorder. To a certain degree beauty is order, and as such is compatible with that internal orderliness which inevitably follows the liberation of rationality from the disorganizing effect of matter. Beauty rejoices in its own nature and even the faintest shadow of it awakens a glad response. The infinite diversity of standards by which beauty is measured result from the various combinations of rationality and irrationality present in the soul. That which is beautiful to one is not necessarily beautiful to another, and yet beauty as a principle is common to all. We consider that to be beautiful which approaches most closely the symmetry of our own internal natures; and as the inner nature evolves more perfect harmonies we become more discriminating in our responsiveness to external stimuli. Gradually symmetry of form gives place to symmetry of thought, and the beauties of the inner nature are then revealed as surpassing the beauties of the outer form.

The Neoplatonic theory of beauty may be summed up as the rationality of the beholder rejoicing in the evidence of rationality in the thing beheld. Grace, symmetry, harmony, and order are unquestionable evidence of a rational consciousness, and we rejoice in this evidence to the same degree that we possess the ability to recognize them. That is most beautiful, therefore, which elicits most perfect response from our inner perceptions. Through philosophy we ascend from that beauty communicated from an external source to the recognition of that beauty identical with Source itself. Having ultimately attained through right thinking, right feeling, and right living to the condition of the beautiful within ourselves, with enraptured vision we can respond in perfect measure to the eternal beauty which flows from the inexhaustible fountain of the one Good.

In the present century two great opposing systems of thought are struggling for supremacy. On the one hand is idealism, which declares that to be practical which is beautiful; on the other hand is realism, which asserts that to be beautiful which is practical. It is difficult to estimate the profound effect caused by this simple interchange of the words practical and beautiful. Practicality must be interpreted to imply the greatest good to the greatest number, and there is no question that, if so interpreted, that which is of the greatest good to the greatest number is the beautiful necessity. However, we may well ask if what we now term practical is actually fulfilling this ideal. Much of the structure of modern civilization is revolting to the finer sentiments of humanity. Elbert Hubbard can hardly be censured for defining civilization as "a device for increasing human ills; a machine for the perpetuation of the weak; an ingenious contraption for spreading disease and hunger." Men and women of vision all realize that modern civilization is doomed to collapse under the weight of its own infirmities.

Like the mighty Juggernaut, it is rumbling down the hillside of Time to vanish ultimately in the vale of oblivion below. The reason civilization must crumble is because it is not beautiful; and lacking the order, harmony, symmetry, and grace which collectively constitute beauty, it will be disintegrated by the friction of its own individual parts. Like the scaled, fire-belching dragon of mythology, it is the jealous guardian of the tree upon whose branches hangs the Golden Fleece. Even today the Argonaut sets forth. Man in his quest for happiness—which alone makes life endurable—is determined, like Jason, to wrest the highest prize from the clutches of the monster he himself has created. The future dragon-slayer is first born in the human soul as the spirit of revolt against the crushing weight of the artificial world which man in his folly has raised, Babel-like, to rival the glory of the heavens. Man has built a house whose bricks are made of mud and held together by slime. Indifferent to the laws of social architecture, he has raised this mighty edifice upon shifting sand, and now its walls of their own weight threaten to collapse about the heads of the foolish builders.

Seated on their golden thrones the Titans of finance gaze down, like the huge stone Memnons of Egypt, upon a devastated land. Like the Pharaohs of the ancient Nile their sandals are pounded from the golden crowns of vanquished kings.

Wall Street may be likeneft to that gloomy ravine which led down to the depths of Dante's Inferno. Here souls lost in the maze of their own greeds and passions wander in the dim
light that finds its way down between the towering skyscrapers that rise cliff-like on either hand. Wall Street is a most appropriate symbol of the path of glory which General Wolfe declared leads but to the grave; for at one end of that short but awful thoroughfare lay the murky and polluted waters of the river; at the other stand the crumbling and moss-covered headstones of Trinity's churchyard. There is a common saying upon the "Street" that those who succeed are laid away in pomp to the chime of old Trinity's bells, while those who fail are found floating upon the turbid breast of the river.

As one gazes downward upon the teeming world maelstrom of human endeavor where millions of creatures in ant-like confusion struggle to survive, with no time, no strength, no opportunity to dream, to hope or to aspire, he can better sense the incubus of civilization. To what end all this cyclopean struggle in which destruction is ever the victor? As one regards this seething cauldron where, like the witches of Macbeth, the three sisters—ignorance, superstition, and fear—brew their poisonous broths, he cannot but recall the prophetic words of Prospero
in The Tempest :

The cloud-capped Towers, the gorgeous Palaces, The solemn Temples, the great Globe itself, Yea, all which it inherit, shall dissolve, And like this insubstantial Pageant faded
Leave not a rack behind: we are such stuff As dream are made on; and our little life Is rounded with a sleep.

When the Bishop of Ripon suggested to the British Association for the Advancement of Science that it take a ten-year vacation for the good of the human soul, this venerable churchman precipitated a storm of protest. "The very greatness of his [man's] recent achievements," declared the Bishop, "would seem to make his ruin more certain and more complete." While any cessation of man's effort to improve his own status would undoubtedly prove disastrous, there is no doubt that the Bishop has sensed an impending catastrophe—that ever-widening gap between the spiritual and the material life of man.

Man's internal progress has failed to keep abreast with the growth of his conveniences. With the advent of the washing machine it cannot be said that we have registered corresponding improvement in our standards of beauty, ethics, and aesthetics. The popular superstition that if the body is comfortable the spirit will take care of itself has not been justified by experience. Although too many churchmen wander in a maze of theological complexities, still for the most part they recognize the need of spiritual education. If his inner nature fails, man perishes; and while in the last analysis failure can only be temporary, still to disregard the sciences of the higher life is but to prolong the agonies of the unillumined state.

The enlightened theologian does not desire to tear down the achievements of science or belittle the blessings that it has conferred upon mankind. The true spiritual thinker merely affirms the necessity of elevating the sciences of the soul to a parity with those of the body. He regrets that man should learn to live so well only to ultimately die as badly as before. Whereas, according to the theologian, man may live in this world but a few score years, he is predestined to endure in a transcendental state throughout all eternity. If he is willing to spend so great a part of his life equipping himself for the little span of earth life, should he not, argues the Bishop, also give some consideration to that greater life of which the present is but the vestibule?

A just criticism against modern science is that as it magnifies by its repeated emphasis the importance of terrestrial concerns, it belittles in like measure the still nobler concerns of the spirit. Savants are too prone to solve the problem of the after-death state by disdainfully rejecting the concept of immortality as but another survival of primitive superstition. Thus the day of greatest physical light bids fair to become the day of greatest spiritual darkness. It is questionable if science will ever be able to make the earth such a desirable locale that world-worn souls will not ultimately be glad to escape from its stifling environment.

The goal of science apparently is perpetuation of the physical life, which seemingly is the only life of which it is sure. Since woman is devoting more of her time to consideration of world problems she may be gratified to learn that one scientist assures us that within the next century babies will be manufactured in the laboratory to meet any and all specifications. Physical immortality, therefore, may be regarded as the ultimate goal of science, which can conceive of no other form of immortality. Thus, the modern scientist actually seeks that same elixir of life which he ridicules the mediaeval alchemist for declaring to be a reality.

The church very properly opposes this so-called practical attitude, since if physical immortality be the real goal of existence the universe is without integrity, for how can the dead past share in the immortality of the unborn future? The mystic also realizes the insufficiency of this new physical urge which worships a word and pays homage to its own achievements as summed up in the term practical. To him the word is a synonym for the prosaic in whose presence the finer qualities of life must inevitably languish and die. No sane man would block the progress of human thought or condemn any real contribution to the life, happiness or efficiency of the race. Men and women with vision would, however, rejoice if they could see growing up in the world an institution both vast and beautiful which would serve the aesthetic needs of the individual, and would insure that life would be not only efficient but also beautiful; that man would enjoy not only health of body but be possessed of healthy emotions and ideals. The population of earth is sufficient to assure science that it will never be without a body of informed men and women to carry forward its ideals. There are enough also to form another group as strong, as noble, and as true to preserve those aesthetic principles which existed long before the dawn of modern thought and without which science as an institution could never have existed.

When by some joyous exception of Nature we find the scientist in whom the beautiful is an awakened and radiant force, there results a type of mind as constructive as any modern society can produce. It will yet be demonstrated that no scientist can achieve to the highest in his chosen field until he acknowledges the existence of a superphysical nature which survives the dissolution of its temporal parts. Even as men in primitive times fashioned crude images and then bowed humbly before their own creations, so the scientist of today has but elevated his superstitions to a more dignified level; for having fashioned with his own reason the entire body of science, he now contemplates with an awe approaching blind adoration the craftsmanship he has wrought. Without doubt the prosaic attitudes of scientific men have done much to turn thinking minds from the contemplation of aesthetics to the more utilitarian themes of biology and physics. Science has the unquestioned advantage of tangible evidence of its utilitarian value.

We are ever surrounded by the examples of scientific accomplishment, while the accomplishments of aesthetics, being largely limited to the internal nature, make no showing impressive to the uncultured. With its emphasis solely upon the practical, the realistic interpretation of life over-justifies existing conditions; for it assumes that because deformity exists it must be necessary and, being necessary, it must be beautiful. Dr. Will Durant has defined the true offices of realism and idealism. Existing conditions, he declared, should be analyzed in the terms of realism and reconstructed in the terms of idealism. There is an element of precocity among civilized peoples today which is most unseemly; sophistication is everywhere. The surfeit of advantages which we have enjoyed has brought in its train the state of boredom. Nothing pleases, nothing suffices, nothing intrigues. The race has an inclination to sit around and await dissolution as the one remaining experience that may contain the element of novelty. College youths finds it necessary to murder in order to create a passing thrill. Externally we arc simply over-civilized; internally we are morons. The very people who suffer most keenly for this chronic ennui, who are satiated with the entire subject of life, have never really experienced in their thoughts, feelings or actions any of the more profound verities of existence.

Turning from the sordidness of realism, let us look at the world through the eyes of those dreamers who have dared to believe that the good in human nature would ultimately blossom forth and regenerate the entire social system. Beauty, declared the ancient philosophers, was the only offering acceptable to the gods. Furthermore, beauty being the environment of Divinity, God himself was present in every manifestation of the beautiful. In the Scriptures it is written that if the temple is built according to the Law, the living God will dwell therein. The Greek Dionysiacs symbolized the establishment of world harmony by the erection of a temple to the Unversal Creator. Upon the theory that like attracts like they philosophized that when the world was made beautiful, souls of the nature of beauty would incarnate to people it. Because of their belief in reincarnation, the Greeks taught that rational souls incarnated in harmonious environments, whereas discordant areas were populated with irrational creatures whose own internal discord attracted them to a discordant sphere.

The remarkable physical symmetry for which the Greeks are justly famed is ascribed to a peculiar practice. Prospective mothers were isolated from the confusion of the community life and spent their days in secluded gardens filled with statuary representative of the ideals of grace and beauty. They were not permitted to look upon any asymmetrical object lest it mark the coming child. In some communities they went so far as to destroy at birth the crippled or unsightly. This was done not only to prevent the suffering resultant from such affliction but also that society might not through the sight of such malformations perpetuate that which was not beautiful.

Much of our crime and degeneracy can be traced to home environment. Mystical philosophy declares heredity in its conventional sense to be a fallacious doctrine. We do not actually inherit the traits of our ancestors; rather, these traits are environments which call into incarnation souls of a like degree of rational development. A home in which dissension reigns attracts to itself a soul equally discordant. When upon reaching maturity such a soul exhibits the traits of its parents, such traits are erroneously ascribed to the previous generation by such as do not realize that each evolving consciousness has its own definite temperament and does not receive its temperamental bias from another.

The collective attitudes of nations, generations, and races result in their drawing into objective manifestation all subjective qualities consistent with their own. When a nation gives itself over chiefly to problems of finance, souls who conceive money to be of primary importance incarnate therein until ultimately the entire fabric of that people is permeated with this common attitude. Souls in whom corresponding interests do not exist depart from such people and either appear in other races or else in anticipation of a better day resign themselves to patience.

If we truly wish to beautify our present civilization we must realize the necessity of creating an environment which will draw into objective manifestation the nobler souls whose rational faculties have been unfolded to a comprehension of the harmonious and the good. This same environment will further stimulate to rationality those who have not yet fully achieved to this exalted state. Philosophy was the dominating passion of ancient Greece and so intense was its attractive power that it drew into incarnation the greatest number of noble thinkers the human race has ever produced. If we would endure as a great people, we too must realize that as qualities increase in excellence they also increase in permanence, and that a civilization established upon virtue, beauty, and utility will endure long after the structures erected upon the foundations of finance and war have vanished from the earth.

Today the philosopher in search of reality must retire deep into the recesses of his inner self and thus escape from the discordances of the outer life. If he would think, he must depart from the mob which in its non-productive scrambling scatters the faculties of the mind and robs man of his most precious gift—the power of thought. It should not be necessary for man to leave the world in order to find himself, for his world should be a place where his true nature may mingle in concord with the true natures of all other beings.

The sham of civilization is apparent when we realize that it forces the majority of people to assume false lives, to live in conflict with their inner convictions. The idealist must keep silent or be reviled; the thinker must hold his peace or be persecuted; the mystic dares not share his vision with the world which, though aware that he is right, will crucify him if not in body at least in soul. Hence, those with little knowledge babble continuously and their words become the laws of men, while those of nobler vision must remain unknown, unhonored, and unsung. Never can we rise to the true heights seen by the eyes of the idealist while we are in servitude to the inferior part of ourselves.

Man does not realize the weight of that curse by which he was cast forth from the light of truth to wander in the darkness of his own making. He feels helpless in the presence of the vast industrial mechanism which has required centuries for its perfection and which has now assumed an appearance so formidable that even those who consider themselves its masters tremble and are afraid. Philosophy knows that before man can really live, the machine must go; and if humanity is incapable of self-emancipation it must wait until the mechanism grinds itself to pieces.

It is predestined that the golden age shall come again; that men shall live together in love and understanding, and the earth shall become once more a garden of surpassing beauty as it was in the beginning. In that time men shall learn all that they learn now. There shall be great institutions for research and record; the arts and crafts shall flourish. But unlike preceding generations this era shall not pass away; for the God of it shall be Beauty and where Beauty in its various aspects rules a people, that people shall remain as permanent as eternity. It is not necessary that we tear down the entire structure of our present system or revert to some savage type and start anew. It is merely necessary that we tincture utility with beauty; that we add the soul qualities of symmetry and grace to the products of our schemings.

Beauty is the deadly enemy of every excess, for into its constitution enter the elements of grace, proportion, symmetry, and harmony. A thousand means have been suggested by which the injustice of men may be offset, but all these must ultimately fail unless aesthetics becomes an integral part of our social fabric. Until the soul reaches that degree of rationality wherein it is able to recognize the supreme importance of the beautiful, it cannot withstand the urge of selfishness and greed which ever lure nations as well as individuals to their destruction. When we love the beautiful as we now love the dollar we shall have a great and enduring civilization. When we adore the God of harmony as we once worshipped the God of vengeance, we shall know the inner mystery of life. When we create with symmetry, preserve with integrity, and release with joy, then only are we good. Never until we have become one with the good can we be happy, for happiness is the realization of internal beauty which joyously goes forth to mingle itself with the beauty that dwells in space.

## THE LADDER OF LIFE

**Man is ever ascending from an inferior to a superior state according to a law which was established coeval with the foundation of generation. This law is the philosophic ladder, which is treated more in detail in Chapter Seventeen. It is likewise the mysterious Masonic ladder—that ancient symbol of the Secret Work.**

# XVIII

❦

# The Great Pyramid

Supreme Among the wonders of antiquity and unequalled by the achievements of subsequent architects and builders, the Great Pyramid of Gizeh stands a mute witness to an unknown civilization that, having endured its predestined span, passed into the dim oblivion of prehistoric times.

Who were the illumined mathematicians who planned its parts and dimensions; the master craftsmen who supervised its construction; the cunning workmen who trued its stones?

Imposing in its silence, inspirational in its majesty, divine in its simplicity, the Great Pyramid is indeed "a sermon in stone!" Its awesomeness beggars description, its magnitude overwhelms the puny sensibilities of man, and among the shifting sands of time it stands as a fitting emblem of eternity itself.

The Great Pyramid is the unsolved riddle of the ages. Years have been devoted by eminent scholars to the study of its many marvels. But no matter how profound these intellects have been, the Pyramid has proved itself to be still more profound. One learned Egyptologist, after devoting the best years of his life to its study, declared that a complete understanding of the monument's true purpose would require a perfect knowledge of not only every known science now possessed by mankind, but also many others of which present humanity is unaware.

Our race has turned to the goal of objective attainment. It is conquering the visible, tangible universe which surrounds it and of which it is a part. It is flying through the air and sailing under the sea. It is exploding electrons and projecting magnificent units of electrical energy through the invisible ethers of space. It is manufacturing guns that will hurl tons of metal seventy or eighty miles. It is reaching out into the unknown elements of Nature in search of destructive forces which, if discovered, will jeopardize the destiny of the planet itself. Yet with all this knowledge man is hopelessly ignorant of himself. He is ignorant of the cause which brought him into being, the reason why he is a manifesting creature, and the ultimate towards which he is being swept with irresistible force.

Whereas we explore the visible, antiquity explored the invisible. Whereas we construct machines to do our labor, they called upon the elements and with that power possessed by primitive peoples controlled the air, the earth, the fire, and the water, and made servants out of the winds.

What is more, they accomplished all this without following that circuitous route by which modern civilization seeks to attain the same end.

We declare the Great Pyramid of Gizeh to be the imperishable monument of ancient achievement—a divine legacy from an unknown past, constructed at the cost of infinite labor and infinite patience that all posterity may know the will of the gods and the path of attainment. In its measurements

*The Initiation in the King's Chamber*

man may read, as in a book, that secret doctrine which the first civilizations of antiquity bequeathed to their heirs, successors, and assigns.

Inasmuch as numerous eminent authorities have written concerning the physical dimensions and composition of the Great Pyramid, it does not seem advisable to spend much time on ground already so thoroughly covered. We will therefore merely touch on a few highlights of its construction and then pass on to a consideration of its philosophical significance.

While not the tallest of structures, the Great Pyramid is undoubtedly the largest building in the world. It has a ground area of a trifle less than 13 acres, covers nearly three times as much space as the Vatican at Rome, and towers 150 feet higher than St. Paul's Cathedral. The base line of each side is over 750 feet in length and its vertical height is about 482 feet.

The weight of the Great Pyramid is estimated to be somewhere in the neighborhood of 5,273,834 tons, while the weight of the earth is estimated at 5,273,000,000,000,000,000,000 Pyramid tons. It is noteworthy that the significant figures in each calculation are the same.

The age of the Great Pyramid has been the subject of much speculation and debate. Up to recent years, it would have been stark heresy to declare the building to be more than 7,000 years old at the utmost, because science—controlled by theology—dared not disagree with the orthodox findings of man's theological historians. But as that day has passed and estimates now place the age of the earth at over 300,000,000 years, it is possible to approach somewhat closer to the probable facts than it was in the last century.

The prevalent idea that the Great Pyramid was built a few thousand years B.C. is now outmoded by all the evidence at hand. Distinct marks of erosion are now to be seen high up on the sides of the Great Pyramid, which ipso facto proves that at some time in the infinite past the waves of a great sea nearly 300 feet in depth broke against its ancient walls. There is no record of any such flood in historic times. Even Biblical historians are prone to admit that the Great Pyramid was erected before the Flood and that it was the Deluge of Noah that left the erosion marks upon its walls.

The Great Pyramid is at least 25,000 years old; it is much more likely to be from 60,000 to 100,000 years old. It stood long before the Egyptians established their post-Atlantean empire. It was the House of God. One artist, after estimating with great care the intricacies of its construction, bowed his head and said: "None but God Himself could have built it. It was not the work of man."

We affirm that man, however, did build it, but we declare it was not the man that modern science advances as representative of the human race 100,000 years ago. It was no Pithecanthropus or Piltdown man, no Neanderthal or Cro-Magnon with brain capacity but little in advance of the anthropoid, who trued its stones or calculated its relationship to the motion of the heavenly bodies! No Stone-Hatchet man worked out its mathematical equations, no cave dweller mixed its indestructible mortar! Its achievements were the achievements of a race of supermen excelling in pursuits of which modern civilization is comparatively ignorant.

Is it possible that somewhere in the dim past this earth was peopled by a mighty race as resplendent in scientific achievement as it was profound in philosophic precept? A myopic science will most likely answer, "Absurd! Impossible!" Yet the fact remains that the builders of the Great Pyramid were well acquainted with both the mysteries of universal dynamics and the nature of the human soul.

All the wisdom possessed by the ancients seems to have been epitomized in the structure of the Great Pyramid, and he who solves its riddle must necessarily be as wise as he who contrived it!

The Great Pyramid is the perfect emblem of Divinity, the absolute symbol of humanity, the complete type of Nature, and the image of time, eternity, and existence. In one simple geometrical figure, constructed according to an eternal principle, is set forth the secret of all things—all processes, all laws, and all truth.

Using the Pyramid measurements as a basis, Mr. William Petrie computed the distance of the sun from the earth as 91,840,000 miles, which was about three and one-half million miles less than the accepted mean distance. Several years later the distance was recalculated by an international gathering of astronomers, who estimated the true mean distance to be 91,500,000 miles. In all probability, the Great Pyramid measurement is more accurate than even these later findings. It is therefore evident that the men who built the Great Pyramid were not only astronomers but that their skill in computing celestial distances was at least equal to our own.

While it is undoubtedly true that many of the pyramids were used as tombs, it is quite certain that the Great Pyramid of Gizeh was never intended as a sepulchral vault. No mummified body was ever found in it, and the sarcophagus in the King's Chamber is suspected of having been constructed for any one of a dozen purposes, ranging from a baptismal font to a grain bin.

Leaving the materialist to flounder in the midst of incalculable sums and endless contradictions, let us examine the form and composition of the Great Pyramid in the light of Egyptian esotericism—the secret doctrine of the priests.

The Great Pyramid stands with its four faces to the four cardinal angles. The entrance, partway up the side, is in the north and so cleverly concealed that it is practically invisible from below. The entrance consists of a square surmounted by a triangle, thus signifying that the earth is surmounted by spirit. The entrance is hidden to signify that the way of light is difficult to find, and narrow is the gate that leads to eternal life, and none may enter except he bow his head to the inevitable.

The square base of the Pyramid in the Mysteries signifies its sure foundation upon the earth, for Nature is the base upon which must be raised the Divine House—the structure of wisdom must have a solid foundation in the laws of Nature. As the word pyramid signifies light and fire, it is a material edifice built in the symbolic form of a flame, with its point upward. This point may be considered as an indicator that wisdom is above and ignorance is below. The square base further represents the four elements, and the sides the four spirits which guard the angles of the world.

Among the ancient Egyptians, the triangle, or pyramid, was symbolic of immortality, for it was a point rising out of a square, thus signifying the resurrection of spirit out of matter—the 1 out of the 4. The 5 points are the number of the priest and also the secret Pythagorean emblem of man. The 5 is the Initiator—the Dragon-Slayer—He who attains to Self by the destruction of the Not-Self.

In substantiation of our belief that the Great Pyramid was the Sacred House of the Mysteries, we quote from that eminent authority on Masonic symbolism, Albert Churchward: "We contend that the Great Pyramid of Gizeh was built in Egypt as a monument and lasting memorial of this early religion on true scientific laws, by divine inspiration and knowledge of the laws of the universe.

Indeed, we may look on the Great Pyramid as the first Masonic temple in the world, surpassing all others that have ever been built.

This thought opens up a great field of speculation. Was the Great Pyramid the one House of SOL-OM-ON? Was the architect of that House the mysterious Hiram Abiff, whose name means

"Our Father CHiram," or the Sun Fire? Were the stones for the Great Pyramid cut by bronze saws, their teeth made of diamonds, or were they cut by means of cosmic fire or the shamir with which Moses cut the jewels for the breastplate of the High Priest? What was the shamir, the sacred stone, which disintegrated anything it touched? Was it the Great Magical Agent of the universe focused upon a point prepared according to the secrets of the Mysteries? We favor the idea that the Great Pyramid was the real Solomon's Temple. We know that history has been sadly distorted and, while to the modern Mason it may seem incredible that the Great Pyramid could be the birthplace of his Craft, we would ask him to answer two questions: What building greater than the Pyramid has any architect designed or any craftsman executed upon the face of the Earth? For the administration of the three degrees of Blue Lodge Masonry what structure more fitting than the Great Pyramid could be found, with its three appropriate chambers and a sarcophagus ready at hand in the King's Chamber for the giving of the Master Mason's degree?

Egypt has always been regarded as the land of mystery. She surpassed all other nations in her knowledge of architectonics, chemistry, and astronomy. She is looked upon as being the cradle of science and philosophy and while we know comparatively little concerning the exact nature of Egyptian culture, we are continually confronted by evidence of its superiority. In fact we know a great deal less about Egypt than we care to admit, and being fundamentally materialists, most Egyptologists have given little consideration to the religious equation—the supreme element in the history and civilization of all ancient nations.

In spite of all evidence to the contrary, we shall yet discover that the Rosetta Stone is not the key to the Egyptian hieroglyphics. We shall yet realize that the true meaning of the Egyptian ideographs has never been revealed. We are totally ignorant of the knowledge possessed by the better minds of the ancient Egyptian world for a very simple reason: The Egyptians, like all other enlightened races, divided their knowledge into two parts: exoteric and esoteric. The exoteric was that portion of learning revealed to the many and the esoteric that part reserved for the illumined few and never reduced to writing save in the form of hieroglyphics and symbols which were meaningless without that key which was the treasured possession of the initiated priestcraft.

The Egyptian culture with which we are conversant is only the exoteric part revealed to the uneducated multitudes of the ancient empire. That finer culture—the real wisdom of the Egyptians—was preserved for the elect, and our world is far too gross and materialistic to comprehend the subtleties of Egyptian esotericism. Therefore we grope blindly amidst images and emblems which, finding no meaning for them, we pronounce meaningless!

According to the secret teachings, the Great Pyramid was the tomb of Osiris, the black god of the Nile. Osiris represents a certain phase of solar energy and therefore his house, or tomb, is emblematic of the universe within which he is entombed and upon the cross of which he is crucified. Thus,

The Great Pyramid is not a lighthouse, an observatory or a tomb, but a temple. Marsham Adams calls it "the House of the Hidden Places" and such indeed it was, for it represented the inner sanctuary of Egyptian wisdom—or perhaps it would be more accurate to say, pre-Egyptian wisdom. Hermes was the Egyptian god of wisdom and letters, the Divine Illuminator, worshipped through the planet Mercury, and ancient references to the effect that the Pyramid was the House of Hermes emphasize anew the fact that it was in reality the Supreme Temple of the Invisible and Supreme Deity. In all probability, the Great Pyramid was the first temple of the Mysteries—the first structure erected as a repository for those secret truths which are the certain foundation of all modern arts and sciences.

The Great Pyramid, says the secret book, is the perfect emblem of the Microcosm or man, and the Microcosm is the inversion of the Macrocosm. The Macrocosm is the universe without, consisting of unnumbered stars and planets encircled by the mighty egg of cosmic space. All that is in the Macrocosm is to be found in miniature in the Microcosm. As man is "the image of God," so the Great Pyramid is the image of the universe. And what is more—it is scientifically correct as an image of the universe.

Many authors have treated of the physical marvels of the Great Pyramid, but the modern world is still so ignorant of ancient superphysics that it fails to grasp the subtle import of primitive symbolism and primitive religion. We know that such structures as the Great Pyramid, the Cretan Labyrinth, and the Delphian Oracle were erected to conceal and yet perpetuate certain definite scientific and philosophic theorems.

The policy of the ancient world was concealment. Knowledge was never revealed except through parables and allegories; facts were never directly expressed—they were hinted at. Planets were personified as gods and goddesses; the sun was a shining-faced man with flowing golden locks; the earth was the Great Mother, her true nature concealed under veils and robes that only the illumined might remove; the elements were personified; the universe was an egg; force was a dragon; wisdom was a serpent; evil was a grotesque image—part crocodile, part hog; the Absolute was a globe; the threefold creative power was a triangle, and the fourfold universe of material substance was a square; or, again, spirit was a point, manifestation was a line, intelligence was a surface, and substance was a solid. Thus it is evident that symbolism was the universal language of the ancients. We may laugh at their curious myths and accuse them of idolatry and ignorance, but we are the ones that are ignorant and superficial when we assume that the great minds of antiquity—the founders of the arts and sciences and the patrons of learning—were ignorant of the true state and nature of Divinity and humanity.

Somewhere in the dim forgotten ages primitive man—still responsive to the subtle influences of Nature and still without the separating power of individual thought—carved in stone or preserved as tradition and legend a certain rudimentary knowledge. He may have secured this knowledge by a process of natural receptivity or from some previous race that inhabited this earth before the coming of present humanity. After the lapse of ages, this unknown people became the fabled gods who walked the earth and talked with man in the first days of his existence. Many of the Platonists believed that existence was eternal; that the universe had never been constructed and would never be dissolved; that the worlds had always been; and that over the face of them swept periodic waves of force and power. While Modern

Science refutes the theory and produces evidence that universes come into being and go out of existence, still the world is very old and humanity is very young. No one knows who our progenitors were. It may be true that man rose up from the muck and mire of the prehistoric fens—that first he appeared as mosses and lichens, leaving no record on the molten surfaces of the Azoic rocks. But the true origin of life is spiritual—not physical—and it is also quite certain that side by side with the growing forms of men and beasts there has advanced a mysterious and secret culture, whose outward expression we recognize as religion, philosophy, science, and ethics, and in its innermost sense as knowledge, wisdom, and understanding.

Man has never been without knowledge of his origin and the purpose of his existence. Those divine powers who regulate the destiny of creation—whose manifest works bear witness to their reality but whose form no man has seen—have always had their covenant with men; they have always been represented among humanity by certain sages and prophets. The temples were the houses of these gods, dedicated to their worship, protected from all desecration, and cleansed of all evil, that to these sanctified areas in the midst of a world of sin and strife the gods might come and there deliver to the leaders of tribes, nations, and races those laws and mandates necessary to human survival.

While the world has made rapid progress in scientific lines, it can claim but little religious growth in thousands of years. We are still unstrung by the battles of sectarianism; we are still pushed and pulled by contending theological factions, and as the supreme proof of our spiritual ignorance we still have a number of contradictory schools of religious thought. In other words, our little backyard world harbors scores of little backyard creeds. It therefore has no true religion, for it is quite evident that Divinity is a Unity and therefore can only be worshipped in unity and not in diversity.

While it is undoubtedly necessary that there be numerous forms of religion adapted to racial limitations, national attitudes, and geographical environments, still it is equally true that those religions must comprehend their own fundamental unity and realize that their differences are not in essentiality but in triviality.

While the ignorant masses worshipped at the altars of this god or that god, the wise men of antiquity were not fettered by religious prejudice, but recognized in these hosts of divinities the personified emanations and attributes of One Supreme Father. Accordingly, the Greeks went forth in search of wisdom and their quest led them into the temples of every faith and doctrine of the world.

Did the religion of the Greek philosopher limit him to Zeus, Rhea, Hermes, or the numerous other deities whose marble images sat in the magnificent temples rising on the brow of the Acropolis? Assuredly not!

The Greek initiates were received into the Mysteries of Egypt, Persia, Chaldea, Babylonia, Phœnicia, and India. Returning home again, they were not considered as heretics—false to their own gods—but as illumined and venerable sages almost worthy of worship. The Greeks esteemed the excellence of Brahmin thought, and likewise the Brahmins knew that the Chaldeans and Phœnicians were not unlearned in natural lore. They exchanged freely with each other the knowledge they possessed, for Brahma was but the name of a Nameless Principle, and if the Greeks wished to call their deity Uranus, Chronos or Zeus, what mattered it? It was the Principle—not the name—that was worshipped; it was the wisdom—not the terminology—that was worthy of study. So among the initiates of antiquity there prevailed a great broadness and depth woefully lacking in the "worldly wise men" of today.

In certain sanctified localities were erected temples, not to this cult or to that creed, but to the World Mystery Religion—the one faith of mankind, the all-inclusive doctrine that sometime again must be recognized as the dominating religious institution of the world. From the East, the West, the North, and the South came the learned of all nations seeking acceptance into these Sacred Houses which stood as gateways between the mysteries of visible Nature and the mysteries of the causal universe.

The Great Pyramid was such a sacred edifice, dedicated to the God Hermes—the personification of Universal Wisdom. To gain admission there a man need not be of Egyptian blood, nor of any particular race or creed. There were but two requisites: he must be clean in heart, mind, and body; and he must desire wisdom with a desire stronger than that for life itself.

So from every part of the ancient world seekers after truth came to the House of the Hidden Places to learn of God, to learn of Nature, and to discover that arcane doctrine which may be revealed only to those who have passed successfully the tests and temptations constituting the initiation rituals of the Mysteries.

We have said that the Great Pyramid is the symbol of the world. It is also the symbol of material existence, for physical life is a series of incidents taking place in certain environments and largely influenced by the environments in which they occur.

Thus it is evident that the various chambers and parts of the Great Pyramid signify esoterically the divisions and avenues of life. As the Cretan Labyrinth contained within it the Minotaur or Bull-Man, whose name in the secret language of the Mysteries means "the beast mind" and which devoured each year the quota of youths and maidens exacted by it as tribute, so earthly life is a winding labyrinth of mystic passageways and chambers, within which dwells the Minotauric beast—temptation, sorrow, suffering, and death.

Recall the story of Dante's descent into the Inferno or the wanderings of Aeneas through the underworld under the guidance of the Cumaean Sibyl. Hades—the underworld of the Greeks and Egyptians—is not, as generally supposed, the sphere of the dead. In reality, Hades is the material physical world in which we live our material physical lives. Though we believe ourselves to be alive, we but dwell in the underworld of the Greeks, for its tortuous subterranean passageways symbolize that span of earthly existence stretching from the cradle to the grave.

According to the ancients, there are two gates—two mighty doors—one leading into the House of Life and the other leading out. Man enters at the Gate of Cancer—the ancient symbol of the World Mother and the emblem of birth. After wandering his appointed span among the hollows and glooms of Hades, or the Inferno, he passes into the Heaven of the gods through the celestial Gate of Capricorn, by the side of which stands Saturn, the Reaper, symbolic of time and age. Thus the two gates of the underworld are respectively the womb which leads in and the tomb which leads out.

In the underworld Aeneas and Dante beheld the sorrows of the lost souls, the agony of the damned, and the curses of sin, lust, and degeneracy. According to the Mysteries, these are the self-generated sufferings which man must endure because he permits himself to be controlled by his own lower nature.

All this Inferno is a dream and an illusion, like the Buddhist wheel, to which man clings although he would be free if his mind could but let go.

Hades is, therefore, the sphere in which those creatures dwell who are under the domination of the senses. Their agony is the agony of hopeless desire, useless selfishness, and the sorrow which results from the vain struggle after a mirage. Hades is the dwelling place of those who have never discovered themselves, who have never realized Reality, who have never attained self-consciousness. For when man finds himself, he rolls away the stone of his sepulchre and ascends from the realms of death.

The word death is a misnomer as we generally use it. Those are not dead who have laid aside this mortal coil—they really are dead who do not know themselves. Death is ignorance, for those who are ignorant are buried in the cold stone coffin of their own limitations, knowing nothing, appreciating nothing, realizing nothing, achieving nothing—the mindless have never lived.

Life is not merely animated existence. Life is thought; life is achievement; life is appreciation; life is recognition; life is realization; life is aspiration; and, most of all, life is understanding! To those who understand life, there can be no death; to those who do not understand the purpose of our sojourn here, there can be no life.

So, according to the Mysteries, the ignorant lie sleeping—sleeping through all eternity, sleeping as worlds are made, sleeping as worlds perish again, sleeping as nations rise, sleeping as empires fall. Surrounded by infinite opportunity and part of a plan based upon infinite growth, those who are not initiated into the mystery of Reality sleep in their narrow coffins of egotism, selfishness, and unawareness through all the eternities of time and being!

The Mysteries taught that there are two manner of men: those who are awake and those who are asleep. Those who are awake live in a world of infinite light, infinite wisdom, infinite beauty, infinite opportunity, and infinite progress. To such all things are good; to such there is no death, and gradually they ascend that ladder of stars leading to the footstool of Divinity itself.

To these awakened ones the universe is home and the myriads of stars and heavenly bodies are kindred hosts of celestial beings. All the world is a laboratory of experimentation; every stick and stone preaches a sermon; every living thing teaches a lesson. But to the sleeping ones the world is a cold and dismal place; every man is an enemy; every plant is poisonous or thorny; every beast snaps and howls; every stone is sharp; every problem is a disaster; always the clouds obscure the face of the sun and the heavenly lights are darkened; life itself is a futile struggle against the inevitable and the grave its closing episode.

Immortality is not the perpetuation of the body. It is an innate realization of the perpetuity of spirit. Once man gains consciousness of Self, he can never lose it; once he has learned to live he cannot die, though his form may change. Life is the realization of life and death is the lack of that realization.

Could Plato, initiated into the nothingness of death, ever die? Could Socrates ever cease to be who knew that by drinking the hemlock he was but liberating himself from the bonds and limitations of a world which could not understand?

He realized that the fleshy house was not his real self but that he changed his bodies as he changed his garments. Having arrived at the realization of truth, he was immortal.

But what is truth? Whence comes that power which, when it is established in the soul of man, answers all things, solves all things, reveals all things, and supplies all things? What is that indescribable elixir which, when poured into the human soul, makes of the weakling a hero, of the poor man one of indescribable wealth, of the ignorant a divinely illumined sage, and of a man a god?

We hear much of truth. It is a word on every man's tongue but in few men's hearts. Can it be revealed by one to another? Is it a tangible, intellectual reality, or is it an indescribable recognition of the relationship between the individual Self and the Universal Self? What is this mysterious doctrine which lifts man from the ranks of the mediocre and carries him to the very footstool of Divinity? What is it that makes the martyr die with a smile upon his lips and with blessings for his executioners? What is it that inspires the artist to paint pictures which illumine the world? What is it that sounds as soft music in the ears of the great composer? What is it that moves the pen of the author that he may write books which will live forever in the hearts and souls of humanity?

The symbol of that great power is the crux ansata—the cross of life—that golden key which unlocks the mysteries of self, that golden key which all too often becomes a cross for the crucifixion of the illumined. And yet those who have this golden key smile at death, laugh at torture, and, retiring into the sanctuary of themselves, are sufficient for all their needs!

This great and mysterious power, this power of divinely revealed truth, is what man gains when he was accepted into the House of the Hidden Places, for it is said that the Mysteries either found a good man or made one, and though he started upon the road a scoffer he ended amazed and silenced.

True religion is not a mass of idle mummeries, contentions, and debates. It is not a series of codes to be accepted in spite of better judgment. It is not an institution obeying the dictates of God by damning unbaptized infants and burying its elect in hallowed ground. These things are the chaff that shall be tossed to the winds; these are the false doctrines—meaningless and useless—serving only as hindrances in the search for truth.

True religion is that institution established by antiquity for the purpose of so unfolding the heart and mind and hand of man that he may gradually grow into that divine realization which confers immortality. The real purpose of religion is to inspire into activity and objective existence that subjective power of understanding which lies latent in the hearts and souls of unillumined humanity.

And as the seekers after truth came from all parts of the ancient world, they beheld the mighty Pyramid rising before them as a looming miracle in stone, a glorious House—man's supreme offering to that definitionless Divinity that gives him the power of recognition! The Great Pyramid was built as an imperishable monument to the Divinity which lies buried in humanity. It is the tombstone of God lying dead in Nature, awaiting the day of resurrection. It marks the grave of the builder. It is the sprig of acacia, and he who entered its ancient portal was consecrated to the task of raising the dead God to life again—in himself.

There is a God sleeping in the soul of every man. This sleeping God is his own Divinity—a spark of Universal Divinity imprisoned in a sarcophagus not only of material clay but the clay of earthly thoughts, earthly desires, and wormlike attributes. Here in the House of the Hidden Places man was instructed

how to awaken the sleeping God, how to summon into manifestation those latent potentialities which, when trained and unfolded, produce the perfected man.

The unfolding of man's spiritual nature is as much an exact science as astronomy, medicine or jurisprudence. It is not a haphazard procedure based upon a none too certain faith. The secret processes whereby the Divine nature of man may be resurrected and enthroned as the ruler of the human life—this is the secret science, this is the divine doctrine, this is the supreme arcana of all ages and of all peoples. It is to this end that all religions have been established; and out of religion have come science, philosophy, logic, and reason as methods whereby this divine purpose might be attained.

Religion, therefore, represents the Tree of Life. The Garden of Eden is the House of the Mysteries in the midst of which grows this Tree; and Knowledge and Understanding are the fruit of the Tree and he who eats of that fruit shall be a god, having eternal life. But lest this fruit be stolen, lest the foolish attempt to steal the prize belonging to the wise, the supreme mystery is concealed under the emblems and symbols meaningless to the uninitiated.

For being the most priceless of all human possessions, truth is guarded more sedulously than any other secret. What is there in the world that is its equal? What more can man possess than understanding? All other things are impermanent, but understanding endures; all other things may be lost or destroyed, but understanding belongs forever to him who once possesses it!

Through the mystic passageways and chambers of the Great Pyramid therefore passed the illumined of antiquity. As men they entered its portal, as gods they came forth again. It was the place of the "second birth," the "womb of the Mysteries," and wisdom dwelt in it as God dwells in the heart of man.

Somewhere in the depths of its recesses there resided an unknown being who was called "The Initiator," or "The Illustrious One," robed in blue and gold and bearing in his hand the sevenfold Key of Eternity. This was the lion-faced hierophant, the Ancient of Days, the Holy One, the Master of Masters, who never left the House of God and whom no man ever saw save he who had passed through the gates of preparation and purification.

It was in these chambers that Plato—he of the broad brow—came face to face with the wisdom of the ages personified in the Master of the Secret House.

But what does this mean to the material scientist? What does this solve for the geologist, who with his little hammer chips at the casing stones and tries to solve the problem of all ages with a microscope and a pestle? What does this mean to the Biblical historian, whose brows are knit over the problem of who built the world's great structure long before Adam and Eve must have been even remote conceptions in Jehovah's mind? Or what does it mean to the theologian who dares not peer over the edge of the King James' Bible for fear of endangering his eternal salvation?

Only minds trained in the free range of philosophic thinking, uncurbed by creed or dogma, unfettered by the bonds of theology or the limitations of science, and whose God is a non-sectarian Deity can face this problem without prejudice and appreciate the magnitude of true religion as herein revealed.

Who was the Master of the Hidden House—whose many rooms signified the worlds in space—whom none might behold save those who had been "born again"? He knew the secret of the Pyramid, but He has departed the way of the wise and the house is empty. The hymns of praise no longer echo in muffled tones through the chambers, the neophyte no longer passes through the elements and wanders among the seven stars. The candidate no longer receives the "word of life" from the lips of the Eternal One. Nothing remains but the shell—the outer symbol of the inner truth, and men call the House of God a tomb. The Great Pyramid is not the only House of God worthy of that appellation!

Eager to receive this divine boon, the candidates accompanied by the Silent Voice, the Unknown Watcher, climbed the ancient steps which must have originally led up to the entrance of the Great Pyramid. What lay within he did not know. Whether he would ever come out again he did not know. He only realized that if he failed to meet the requirements of the Mysteries, he would forever vanish from the sight of men. But within that mighty pyramid of stone gleaming in the Egyptian sun he knew there dwelt a sacred and sanctified One—the Keeper of the Royal Secret. He was resolved to reach that One and secure that secret or die in the attempt. The time of his trial had come. His previous life, his devotion to study, his sincerity of motive, his cleanliness of heart—all these had been thoroughly established.

As he approached the tiny gate, the solid wall before him parted, a great stone door hung on invisible hinges of granite swung open before him, and he passed into the darkness of the Secret House. The tests began. Surrounded by the gloom and cold of the Sacred Place, he passed through in succession the chambers and passageways which typified all the forms and experiences of mortal existence. Thus the labors of a lifetime were recapitulated in a few hours in the Great Pyramid Mysteries. Strange creatures confronted him. Temptations were ever about him. But at last his soul ascended as a bird up the chimneylike passageway leading to the place of light.

He passed through the dwelling-places of the Spirits of the Gods. The earth shook and thunders rumbled about him. At last the grand staircase of the Seven Breaths of the Seven Stars was reached and far above in the still unexplored pinnacle of the building was the dwelling-place of the Secret God—the Unknown One Whose name could not be spoken, Whose nature could not be conceived, and Whose thoughts could not be interpreted.

The details of the ceremonial are entirely a matter of speculation, for nothing is actually known concerning them save to a few—and they are not permitted to speak. But as far as can be ascertained, the King's Chamber was the scene of the great climax of the initiatory drama. Here crucified upon a St. Andrew's cross, the candidate was suspended like the solar god upon his cross of the equinoxes and the solstices.

After the solar crucifixion had been performed, the candidate was laid in the great stone coffin and for three days his spirit—freed from its mortal coil—wandered at the gateways of Eternity. His Ka as a bird flew through the spiritual spheres of space. He passed upward through the Seven Gates and stood before the mighty throne of the Empyreum. He discovered that all the universe was life, all the universe was progress, all the universe was eternal growth.

He also realized himself to be an integral part of this eternal plan, that no more could he cease to be than the sun and the moon and the stars could cease to be. He conversed with the immortals.

He was then brought into the blinding presence of the Living Word, and then realizing that his body was a house which he could slip out of and return to without death, he achieved actual immortality.

It is probable that peculiar atmospheric conditions, the temperature of the King's Chamber, and the dull cold of the coffin formed an important link in the chain of circumstances which permitted the consciousness of the neophyte to escape from his body and come into the presence of the Great Illuminator. At the end of three days he returned to himself again and, having thus personally and actually experienced the great mystery, he was indeed an Initiate—one who beheld and one to whom religion had fulfilled her duty by bringing him into the light of God.

The new initiate, wearing the insignia and symbol of his accomplishment, was now brought into the presence of the Great Illuminator—the Master of the Secret House. He beheld the august patriarch whom no eyes ever saw save those who had passed through the Mystery of the "philosophic death" and who had been "born again" out of Time into Eternity.

Mystically, there are two births. In physical birth man is born from Eternity into Time, and through the span of his earthly struggle battles desperately against inevitable conquest by Time. In the Mysteries there is the philosophic death and the second birth out of Time back again into Eternity, and the new initiate no longer struggles against the corroding influences of Time but dwells in the perfect realization that past and future are gone and that in the Mysteries there is but one time—and that of infinite duration—eternally posited in the ever-present NOW.

By this sage Illuminator—the Master of the Secret House—the technique of the Mysteries was unfolded. The power to know his guardian spirit was revealed to the new initiate; the method of disentangling his material body from his divine vehicle was explained; and to consummate the Great Work, the Divine Name—the secret and unutterable designation of the Supreme Deity, by the very knowledge of which man and his God are consciously one—was solemnly revealed.

With the giving of The Name the new initiate was himself a pyramid, within the chambers of whose soul numberless other human beings might also receive enlightenment. Having achieved the Great Work, having accepted the hierophant of the Secret House as his spiritual father—the one who had given him that light which is the life of men—and having made the final offering—his own life—to the service of the Secret House, the initiate was ushered forth again into the glare of the desert sun.

When he entered he had gazed up at the mystery of the great stone pyramid; and now he gazed again, but no longer at a mystery. He beheld a great stream of light which descended from the heavens upon the pyramid. He saw it break up into numerous paths and, coming down the walls in all directions, diverge like the branches of a tree. He realized that he himself was a branch, for the life of the tree was in him—nay, he was more than a branch, he was actually a fruit of the pyramidal tree. So, Pythagoras-like, he took the three seeds of the tree which was within the fruit of his own soul and, going forth, he planted them. And another tree grew up from the seeds, which tree also bore the golden fruit of Life and all those who partook of it, lived.

So we still chip at the walls of the Pyramid, filled with wonder why men should have built such a structure, and what great urge inspired the herculean labor. We hear men say: "It is the most perfect building in the world;" that it is the source of weights and measures; that it was the original Noah's Ark; that it is the origin of languages and alphabets; that it is the origin of

the scales of temperature and humidity; that it is the only structure upon the face of the earth that actually squares the circle; and that it stands as the absolute dividing line between the land and water surfaces of the earth. We wonder at all these things, but if we really understood the purpose for which this mighty House was built, we would wonder still more or, more likely, we would scoff. For it seems incredible to this generation that there was ever a time when men knew more than men know now. Though the modern world may know a million secrets, the ancient world knew one—and that one was greater than the million; for the million secrets breed death, disaster, sorrow, selfishness, lust, and avarice but the one confers life, light, and truth.

The time will come when the secret wisdom shall again be the dominating religious and philosophical urge of the world. The day is at hand when the doom of dogma shall be sounded. The great theological Tower of Babel, with its confusion of tongues, was built with bricks of mud and the mortar of slime. Out of the cold ashes of lifeless creeds, however, shall rise phoenixlike the ancient Mysteries. No other institution so completely satisfied the religious needs of humanity, for since the destruction of the Mysteries there has never been a religious edifice wherein Plato could have worshipped!

The Dying God shall rise again! The secret room in the House of the Hidden Places shall be rediscovered! The Pyramid shall yet stand as the ideal emblem of solidarity, aspiration, inspiration, resurrection, and regeneration! As the passing sands of time bury civilization upon civilization beneath their weight, the Pyramid shall remain as the visible covenant between that eternal wisdom and the world. The time may yet come when the chants of the illumined shall be heard again in its ancient passageways and the Master of the Hidden House await in the Silent Place for the coming of the seeker after that spiritual truth which the modern world needs so badly and of which it knows so little.

In an ancient fragment accredited to Hermes but by some supposed to have been written by Apuleius, is a remarkable prophecy concerning the future of Egypt. Hermes is the speaker and Asclepius the one addressed. The work from which this extract is taken is called the Asclepian Dialogue, which has never been completely translated into English: "Are you ignorant, Asclepius, that Egypt is the image of heaven, or, which is more true, a translation and descent of everything which is governed and exercised in heaven? And, if it may be said, our land is truly the temple of the whole world. Nevertheless, because it becomes wise men to foreknow all things, it is not lawful that you should be ignorant that the time will come when it may seem that the Egyptians have in vain, with a pious mind and sedulous religion, paid attention to divinity, and all their holy veneration shall become void and of no effect. For divinity shall return back to heaven. Egypt shall be forsaken, and the land which was the seat of divinity shall be destitute of religion, and deprived of the presence of the Gods. For when strangers shall possess and fill this region and land, there shall not only be a neglect of religion, but (which is more miserable) there shall be laws enacted against religion, piety, and divine worship; they shall be prohibited, and punishments shall be inflicted on their votaries. Then this most holy land, the seat of places consecrated to divinity, and of temples, shall be full of sepulchres and dead bodies. O Egypt, Egypt, fables alone shall remain of thy religion, and these such as will be incredible to posterity; and words alone shall be left engraved in stones, narrating thy pious deeds. The Scythian also, or Indian, or some other similar nation, shall inherit Egypt. For divinity shall return to

heaven, all its inhabitants shall die, and thus Egypt, bereft both of God and man, shall be deserted. I call on thee, O most holy river, and predict to thee future events. Thou shalt burst forth with a torrent of blood, full even to thy banks, and thy divine waters shall not only be polluted with blood, but the land shall be inundated with it, and the number of the dead shall exceed that of the living. He, likewise, who survives, shall only, by his language, be known to be an Egyptian, but by his deeds he will appear to be a stranger. Why do you weep, O Asclepius? Egypt shall experience more ample and much worse evils than these, though she was once holy, and the greatest lover of the Gods on the earth, by the desert of her religion. And she who was alone the reductor of sanctity and the mistress of piety will be an example of the greatest cruelty.

Then also, through the weariness of men, the world will not appear to be an admirable and adorable thing. This whole good, a better than which, as an object of perception, there neither is, nor was, nor will be, will be in danger, and will be grievous to men. Hence this whole world will be despised, and will not be beloved, though it is the immutable work of God, a glorious fabric, a good compounded with a multiform variety of images, a machine of the will of God, who, in his work, gave his suffrage without envy, that all things should be one. It is also a multiform collected heap, capable of being venerated, praised and loved by those that behold it. For darkness shall be preferred to light, and death shall be judged to be more useful than life. No one shall look up to heaven.

The religious man shall be accounted insane, the irreligious shall be thought wise, the furious brave, and the worst of men shall be considered a good man. For the soul, and all things about it, by which it is either naturally immortal, or conceives that it shall attain to immortality, conformably to what I have explained to you, shall not only be the subject of laughter, but shall be considered as vanity. Believe me, likewise, that a capital punishment shall be appointed for him who applies himself to the religion of intellect. New statutes and new laws shall be established, and nothing religious, or which is worthy of heaven or celestial concerns, shall be heard or believed by the mind.

There will be a lamentable departure of the Gods from men; noxious angels will alone remain, who, being mingled with human nature, will violently impel the miserable men [of that time] to war, to rapine, to fraud, and to every thing contrary to the nature of the soul. Then the earth shall be in a preternatural state; the sea shall not be sailed in, nor shall the heavens accord with the course of the stars, nor the course of the stars continue in the heavens. Every divine voice shall be dumb by a necessary silence, the fruits of the earth shall be corrupted, nor shall the earth be prolific, and the air itself shall languish with a sorrowful torpor.

These events and such an old age of the world as this shall take place, such irreligion, inordination, and unreasonableness of all good. When all these things shall happen, O Asclepius, then that lord and father, the God who is first in power, and the one governor of the world, looking into the manners and voluntary deeds [of men,] and by his will, which is the benignity of God, resisting vices, and recalling the error arising from the corruption of all things; washing away likewise all malignity by a deluge, or consuming it by fire, or bringing it to an end by disease and pestilence dispersed in different places, will recall the world to its ancient form, in order that the world itself may appear to be an adorable and admirable production, and God, the fabricator and restorer of so great a work, may be celebrated, by all that shall then exist, with frequent solemn praises and benedictions.

# XIX

❦

# The Cycle of Necessity

THAT relationship does the little life we know bear to that vaster existence which is our hope and which Rabelais would call "the Great Perhaps"? Three questions have ever vexed the rational faculties of mankind: Life is the beginning of what? Love is the fulfillment of what? Death is the end of what? The essential attribute of an enduring religion or philosophy is the rational solution which it offers to this threefold riddle. If physical existence be regarded as the whole of life, then the hopelessness and inconsistency of the scheme is apparent, for as Manilius writes: "We begin to die as soon as we arc born, and the end is linked to the beginning." Hence universal order can only be restored when we regard physical existence as a fragment of a nobler and more complete cycle of duration. Somewhere in the chain of his speculation the philosopher will ask: Is the corporeal state natural or accidental to man? In other words, is man destined by virtue of inherent qualities to abide forever as a terrene creature, or is he—like the hero of that Gnostic classic, The Hymn of the Robe of Glory —an exiled prince seeking the way which leads back to his Father's kingdom, the spiritual Dawn Land?

Knowledge of the purpose of life is essential to right living. Unless we comprehend, in part at least, the order of which we are a minute but consequential part, we cannot achieve the greatest good here and now. The past and future like mighty trees meet overhead and shadow the present. The field of today's endeavor is bounded on the one hand by unborn tomorrow and on the other by dead yesterday. Our attitudes toward these opposites—the fateful past and the destined future—must be the measure of our present achievements. When he says, 'The present only is great, the past is dead," the opportunist little realizes that he himself is the past; for all that goes before lives again in that which follows after. The today man worships is but a fleeting second, yesterday was without beginning, and tomorrow without end; yet all are embraced within the span of the eternal philosophic NOW. From the obscure fountains of futurity the waters of time flow down through the turbulent cataracts of present endeavor to mingle finally with the boundless ocean of the past.

All men worship either life or death. Philosophers worship life by affirming it to be imperishable; the non-philosophic worship death by accepting it as a reality. Being essentially incorporeal, life is not limited to place, but in the terms of Neoplatonism is "everywhere, not with interval, but impartibly." In his Auxiliaries to the Perception of Intelligible Natures, Porphyry tells us that "things essentially incorporeal are not locally present with bodies, but are present with them when they please; by verging toward them so far as they are naturally adapted so to verge. They are not, however, present with them locally, but through habitude, proximity, and alliance." Being free from the limitations of place (used in its Platonic sense)

life animates forms by approaching them, and by its subsequent withdrawal into its own nature causes the forms to exhibit the phenomenon called death. In its physical sense life results from the temporary association of an incorporeal agent with a corporeal patient. Bodies, being corporeal, occupy place, and an interval exists between them regardless of their apparent proximity. When life which exists without such interval, animates form, an illusion is created which causes the uninformed to assume that life itself is subject to the confining bounds of place.

Being incorporeal, the gods were not limited to place but exercised their azonic privilege of being distributed according to will throughout the entire substance of creation. This explains the popular belief that God is everywhere and hence with equal efficiency may be addressed by multitudes in various places simultaneously. While life is essentially ethereal and in constant activity, form is essentially dense and static. In combination wtih form, life animates form to a certain degree; conversely, form is an impediment to the flow of life. The result is that physical manifestation is a paradoxical state wherein life appears less than itself and matter more than itself. At death, form reverts to its natural state of inertia, while life returns to its normal condition of uninterrupted flow.

In his treatise, On the Wanderings of Ulysses, Thomas Taylor, drawing upon De Ulyxis Erroribus, the work of an anonymous Greek writer declares that Homer used the Trojan war as a symbol of the battle between the rational faculties (the Greeks) and the irrational faculties (the Trojans).

Thomas Taylor notes that Homer is reputed to have been blind "because, as Proclus observes, he separated himself from sensible beauty, and extended the intellect of his soul to invisible and true harmony. He was said, therefore, to be blind because that intellectual beauty to which he raised himself cannot be perceived by corporeal eyes." In the Thirteenth Boo\ of the Odyssey,. Homer describes in veiled language a mysterious cave by which the Orphic philosophy concerning the mystery of life and death is obscurely set forth:

High at the head a branching olive grows, And crowns the pointed cliffs with shady boughs. A cavern pleasant, though involv'd in night, Beneath it lies, the Naiades' delight:

Where bowls and urns of workmanship divine And massy beams in native marble shine;

On which the Nymphs amazing webs display, Or purple hue, and exquisite array.

The busy, bees within the urns secure Honey delicious, and like nectar pure.

Perpetual waters through the grotto glide, A lofty gate unfolds on either side;

That to the north is pervious to mankind; The sacred south t' immortals is consign'd.

In his essay on The Cave of the Nymphs, Porphyry discusses at some length the occult significance of Homer's cavern. The gist of Porphyry's conclusions, (which he derives from various ancient authors—Egyptian, Greek, and Persian) is as follows; The ancients consecrated caves as symbols of the world in that, like the world, they were produced from an internal and not an external cause. The Persian mystics signified the descent of the soul into the sublunary regions, and its regression therefrom by initiating their mystics in caverns. As temples, groves, and altars were established in honor of the gods, so grottoes were also dedicated to the Nymphs, or Naiades, because of the water which trickled down the walls. In the seventh book of his Republic, Plato writes: "Behold men as if dwelling in a subterranean cavern, and in a den-like habitation, whose entrance is widely expanded to the admission of the light through the whole cave."

The ancient theologists considered caverns as appropriate symbols of mundane powers and of the sensible world, because these rocky openings are dark, stony, and humid. Furthermore, the dampness existing in the cave was analogous to the humidity of the world, which the Greeks conceived to be indispensable to the generation of souls. The soul may be Platonically defined as "the first of bodies" and the individualized source of bodily life. Heraclitus says: "That moisture appears delightful and not deadly to souls." The etheric humidity which incarnating souls find indispensable to their body-building processes caused the philosophers to declare that these souls must be profoundly steeped or drenched in moisture as they enter into the sphere of generation. But pure souls do not desire to generate and hence absent themselves from the sphere of humidity, which causes Heraclitus to remark: "A dry soul is the wisest."

Porphyry then declares that souls proceeding into generation and enveloped in this ethereal moisture are properly called Naiades. The Naiades are Nymphs, presumably water spirits, and their esoteric meaning as given above was revealed only to the initiated. The cavern is therefore a temple sacred to the processes of generation and signifies not only the world in which generated souls reside, but (although Porphyry does not bring out the fact) also the womb from which the philosophic- elect are liberated by the second birth. The bowls and urns

which, according to Homer, are contained in the cave, are not only appropriate emblems of the aquatic Nymphs but are also symbols of Bacchus, and being composed of baked earth signify the bodies into which the corporeal souls descend. Here we have the vessels of various shapes which Omar Khayyam refers to in his Rubaiyat .

Homer then describes the purple webs which the Nymphs weave on marble looms. The spinning of the web represents the building of the fleshly body with its arteries, veins, nerves, and muscles upon the shining framework of the bones. This is the garment with which the incarnating soul is to be invested but which, alas, is to prove a net to ensnare and hold captive the rational virtues. The heavens arc called a veil by the ancients, by whom they are regarded as the vestments of the celestial gods.

The honey which the busy bees store away in the bowls and amphorae has two significances. Honey was regarded by the ancients as both a preservative and also a purifier. The Persians used honey in their sacrifices as a symbol of the preserving and defending powers. Honey further signifies mortal and transitory pleasure as distinguished from divine and enduring pleasure. In the ancient mythology Saturn, being intoxicated with honey sleeps, and while in this condition is robbed of his empire by Jupiter. This fable obscurely intimates that the soul is robbed of its divinity when it becomes intoxicated by the illusionary happiness of the corporeal sphere.

Porphyry also gives a third interpretation to honey, which he declares was used to signify death—an interpretation dependent upon the previous assumption that it befuddled the divine perceptions. Gall he declares to be a symbol of life, adding, in comparing the two, that the life of the soul dies through pleasure (honey) but through bitterness (gall) the soul resumes its life. Bees (here termed the ox-begotten) are symbols of just souls entering into generation both because of their industry and because they instinctively return to that place from which they first came, for the just soul instinctively returns to its divine and unlimited condition.

In his Scholia on the Phaedrus of Plato, Hermias declares that the nectar and ambrosia of the gods are to be understood as possessing a profound philosophic meaning. He writes: "Ambrosia is analogous to dry nutriment and on this account it signifies an establishment in causes; but nectar is analogous to moist food and signifies the providential attention of the gods to secondary natures."

Referring to the gates leading into and out of the cavern, Porphyry declares them to represent the winter and summer solstices—Capricorn and Cancer respectively—adding that as Cancer is nearest to us it is very properly attributed to the moon which is the nearest of the heavenly bodies to the earth; but as the southern pole by its distance is invisible to us, Capricorn is attributed to Saturn, the most remote of the planets. The Orphic theologists add that Cancer is the gate through which souls descend into generation, and Capricorn the gate through which they ascend again, in that the north is appropriate to descend but the south to ascend. The north gate of the cavern is therefore said to be previous to the descent of men, but the south gate is called the avenue not of the gods but of souls— the immortals—ascending to the gods. The ancients likewise connected the winds with souls proceeding into generation or escaping therefrom, declaring that the north winds aid generation and refresh the dying, but the south winds dissolve life.

But one symbol remains to be explained: namely, the branching olive that grows above the cave. The olive is the plant of Minerva, and Minerva having been produced from the head of Jupiter is the proper symbol of wisdom. It was customary to place this plant over the gates and arches to signify that the universe (the world symbolized by the cavern) is not the product of casual effort or the work of irrational fortune, but the offspring of an intellectual nature and a divine wisdom. The olive is also the plant with which the victor in the race of life is crowned, thus revealing the mystic fact that he who vanquishes or outruns his lesser nature will be rewarded with wisdom's crown.

The Cycle of Necessity is the term applied to that period or condition through which man must pass in the attainment of conscious immortality—conscious in the sense of illumined realization as distinguished from that immortality of which we all partake in common but which remains unrecognized until philosophic perception grasps its true import. In his pilgrimage to the Holy City man must pass through the valley called Jehoshaphat or, the "place of dry bones." Here grisly specters rise from their moss-grown sarcophagi to perform the weird gyrations of the Dance of Death. Every gesture of the irrational life is part of a ghastly pageantry, for the cradle stands within the open grave. Philosophy alone can bestow upon man the precious gift of immortality; for though every human soul is innately divine and beyond dissolution, it cannot partake of its own permanence without those perceptions which philosophy must confer.

As long as man believes in death, there is no life; and what man affirms to be existence is actually the gloomy vestibule of oblivion. Buddhism became the faith of half the world because it assured man that death was but a dream and mortality an empty lie. The power exercised by Christianity over the Western Hemisphere results in great measure from its claim that for those of sufficient faith death has been forever vanquished by the resurrection of the holy Nazarene.

It is not sufficient, however, that man be simply immortal, for immortality is merely the means to an end—the infinite opportunity for achievement of ultimate perfection. It is not sufficient that man go on living after he is dead, for this would only perpetuate on a more attenuated sphere the miseries of his present state. Nor is it reasonable to presume that the phenomenon of death can produce any definite cultural results. Theology fails to interest the modern mind because it postulates an after-death state which is but small improvement over corporeal conditions. What shall it profit a man if he leave a static earth to wander around in a static heaven ? Yet philosophically, theology is nearly correct in its depiction of the so-called celestial state, for heaven is an attenuated earth where life continues on practically the same ethical and aesthetic levels as during physical existence.

The mortal sphere consists of two parts: one visible, the other invisible, but both alike illusionary and material. It follows that he who gives up the illusions of mortal life must also give up the illusions of mortal death. So the philosopher who transcends the imperfections of mortal existence transcends also the corresponding imperfections of immortal existence.

Heaven and hell are woven on the same loom and he who renounces the latter must renounce the former with it. Ignorant man may go to heaven, but his heaven—like his earth—is inconsequential. The heaven whose praises are so often sung is designed primarily to augment the comfort of the animal man, to cause only pleasing reactions in the emotional nature

and afford expression for desires and impulses which have their origin in the irrational soul. It therefore follows that it is an animal paradise and becomes insufficient the moment the rational soul in man is liberated from its bondage to bestial instincts.

Among the ancient Vikings, for example, heaven was regarded as a hall of gluttony where heroes gorged themselves from a magic larder which ever replenished itself. Heaven, moreover, even cooperated with the feasters by making appetites more and more insatiable, the warriors only leaving their feasting long enough to stage gladiatorial combats wherein they dealt each other mortal wounds which healed immediately. It is evident that this heaven was as much a part of the irrational sphere as the physical earth itself, for it offered but enlarged opportunity for intemperance and sensuality. Would not Plato who transcended the sordidness of earthly excesses also transcend a heaven which existed merely to satisfy the unquenched fires of animal desire?

At the entrance to the Elysian Fields, where the souls of the blessed dead picked daisies and eternally chanted hymns to the deities, the Egyptians placed a great judgment hall built of rocks as solid as that of Karnak. Here Osiris, painted white and having upon his person more eyes than Argus, sat in judgment upon the shades of earth's illustrious, weighing their souls in a pair of ordinary scales. A jury and a motley group of immortals watched the proceedings with keen interest for probably the hundred millionth time. Does not such a picture afford ample evidence that man's ignorance, unaffected by such episodes as birth and death, continues until the advent of rational consciousness?

At this stage a logical subject for speculation is what happens to an individual who, believing in the reality of the theological heaven, starts out after death in search of the pearly gates and golden streets. Docs their nonexistence disappoint him? Philosophy answers no, for as the illusions of physical life here are perfectly tangible and real to those who believe in them, so the heavenly city with its foundation of precious stones opens its imaginary portals to all who have convinced themselves that such portals exist. As surely as humanity can delude itself with the belief that there is such a thing as a rich man, it can believe that the gods are richer still and hence can bestow wealth untold upon certain favored dead. We all live in a world of make-believe, and as we pass from the make- believers of life to the make-believers of death we simply step up our imagination to a higher level and keep right on dreaming, declaring that to be true which never had and never will have aught of fact within its fabric.

Conversely, hell is simply that state which is created for us by our own realization of the fact that if the universe has any integrity whatsoever we deserve to burn for a few milleniums at least! Stupid fears generate our hells and inane wishes our heavens. In what manner would the plan of existence be glorified by having the souls of men roasted on hot spits throughout eternity because they broke some imaginary statute of the celestial code; or, in what way would the glory of God be magnified if more fortunate souls were given grandstand seats and permitted to witness the inspiring spectacle of the devil, sitting as high inquisitor, meting out perdition?

When Parsifal, standing in the enchanted garden of Klingsor, the evil magician, elevated the holy spear and traced with it in the air the sign of the cross, the chimerical world of the sorcerer disappeared. The enchanted garden vanished, the flower maidens faded into thin air, the great gloomy castle was shaken and the liberated stones came tumbling down to vanish like mist before the rising sun. So it is with these spectral worlds—heaven, earth, and hell—which the senses have taught us to believe are real.

With the opened eye of his rational perceptions the sage gazes out upon a very different world. First, with mortal eyes gazing upon the illusion are seen all those treasures which in our ignorance we have held dear. But gradually as the eyes of the flesh are closed, the eye of the soul is opened, and like a dream the spectacle of wordliness fades and in its place the permanent universe is revealed. The souls of men are seen passing back and forth through the swinging veils which divide the chamber of mortal existence into two compartments. Carrying the burdens of life, bent with the responsibilities of years, obsessed with the reality of matter, the tired and toilworn wanderer exchanges life for death. But as he passes through

the veil he still carries with him the old perplexities of his mortal incarceration. We may see him still bent, still broken, still afraid, creeping through the tiny rent in the veil of his existence to continue on the other side the life he cannot cast aside until he rises above his lesser self. To him death is the promise of fulfillment. So he brings with him his empty money bags that they may be filled; he seeks the waters of Lethe where resting in that state of forgetfulness of all that engenders sorrow he seeks to assuage the aching of his heart, still the spinning wheels of his mind, and realize thwarted desire.

The invisible world gradually assumes the appearance of the office where he labored during the years of earth life. Still the ticker sounds in his ear, telephones ring, and vast projects torment his tired mind with their complexities. A little while and this soul drifts into a great vortex of endeavors, vain struggles, and loosened passions. Like a mighty whirlwind his soul in company with the souls of millions is swept about in hopeless confusion in the after-death chamber. The sighing of the wind is the mourning of deluded souls. Suddenly the curtains begin to sway and through them sweeps the torrent of air back into the world of the living. A little child creeps through a tiny rent and burdened still with the affairs of life crawls into mortal existence. The years pass and the child again becomes a man. Still the tickers sound, still the struggle for gain goes on, again the back is bent by responsibilities, the life soured by unfulfilled desire until at last, carrying with him the same possessions that bowed his back before, the soul creeps away again to rest. Yet what is rest? Just more longing, more desire,

more unrequited love. Thus age after age the Wheel of the Law goes round; age after age man comes and goes, bound to its spokes of agony, and this fools in their folly have termed life.

All this the opened eye of philosophy lays bare; all this the sage perceives with enlightened vision. He knows the unreality of heaven as well as hell. He realizes that both are but projections in the substances of a more subtle element of the same impulses which have taken a beautiful earth and made of it a breeding ground of greed and a house of discord. Death is not a liberation from ignorance, nor is it a solution to man's problem; neither is it the end of anything. Death is but an exchange of vestments; it is no cure for that sickness of the soul which the wise term ignorance. Back and forth between the chambers of life and death man passes until he wears ruts in the stony floor he treads. Yet he is never free for he escapes one prison but to enter another. With perennial hope he faces each new scene, only to find that he exchanges bad for worse.

Birth and death are illusionary in that they seem to be a change of state when in reality they are but a change of place. Though man were lifted to the heights of Olympus he would not be greater than himself; and though he were hurled downward to the depths of the inferno, no virtue that is innately his could be taken from him.

The philosopher realizes that these extremes are but illusions of his own mind and remains unmoved by either the sense of height or depth. Having mastered those attitudes and perceptions by which man is enslaved, he is free from life and death alike. He has found another door, so that he no longer travels between the two halves of the mortal sphere; but leaving the whole chamber of the world behind he ascends into that vast domain where walls are as distant as eternity and where limitations are measured by space alone. Therefore of him it is said that he has stepped down from the wheel and has broken the fetters that once bound him to necessity, for he has accomplished the necessary end: namely, realization of the unreality of mortality. He knows the import of the sage's words, that though a man die a thousand times yet shall he live; for he himself has died many times while still fastened to the wheel of sense. Reborn through the disciplines of philosophy he is no longer subject to death because he is no longer capable of desire. Desire breeds death, and he who has liberated himself from desire has liberated himself from death. Ignorance and death—which are synonymous in their inner nature—are indeed the last great adversary. He who vanquishes this twofold monster by that power which is the inevitable product of right-thinking, has achieved conscious and enduring immortality.

Life and death as we know them are but passing phases of existence. This does not mean that the philosopher achieves to the state of physical immortality, for no one who is wise desires to live forever in any one state. It means that the rational soul, neither slumbering nor sleeping but forever awake and contemplating the face of Truth, has been so liberated from the limitations of erroneous perceptions that, though bodies come and go, it remains unmoved, preserving forever that unobscured vision and unbroken continuity of reflections which alone constitutes immortality.

A quality characteristic of the gods is endurance, and man approaches to divinity when he increases the span of enduring consciousness. Physical matter must abide by the law of its own substance; hence to all things composed of physical substance dissolution is inevitable. As the animal nature is, philosophically, an exudation of the mortal substances, is ultimately dissipated with the decay of forms. Consequently, he who has placed all his faith in this decaying part shall experience mentally the blight of death for he shall behold the disintegration of that which he has pleased to term himself. If, however, he has established his rational and divine part as real, he shall remain unmoved when its inferior vehicle is dissipated, and because his faith is vested in Reality shall dwell forever in rapturous contemplation of permanence.

Life and death are measured by our belief, permanence is determined by our consciousness, and perfect immortality is achieved by perfect realization. Strangest of all, perfect immortality is synonymous with ultimate dissolution, and of all the illusions that must go, not the least is the illusion of individuality. Having completely mastered this, the last phase of death is conquered; for as long as man believes in individuality he fears that unknown but certain ultimate when individuality is dissolved back again into the universal state. It is strange but true that all the things man fears become the instruments of his liberation. Man fears the loss of individuality, yet perfection is not attainable without it. Man fears death, yet death is simply the necessary polarizing of life that he may endure until he has learned to exchange the living death of form for the deathless life of spirit. If it were not for the opportunity that death gives us to go behind the scenes occasionally, we might become so obsessed with the dream play of mortal life that we would never wake up to its unreality.

The process of alternating manifestation between the visible and invisible spheres of the inferior universe is erroneously termed metempsychosis. A swinging pendulum has been employed to symbolize that monotonous motion of the unawakened soul which results in the phenomena of successive lives and deaths. In the East Indian classics it is written that certain is death for the living and certain is life for the dead; but though the wheel spins incessantly, by the very nature of its motion it ends where it began. When the philosophers describe the descent of the soul into generation they do not mean what is now termed incarnation, but rather that the rational part has become immersed in the substances of a generated and generating world where it must remain until through the liberation of its innate rationality it escapes from the tangled web of sense and circumstance. Pythagoras tells us that the sphere of Hades or Pluto extends downward from the Milky Way through the rings of the zodiac, the orbits of the planets, and the spheres of the elements.

Pluto's domain is therefore synonymous with matter, not only matter that is physical but also its invisible counterpart from which the so-called invisible world is fashioned. The sphere of generation merely signifies that inferior pat of Nature wherein manifestation depends upon the generation of vehicles. Generation is limited to the world of forms in that all forms are generations, being the temporary vehicles of ungenerated and immovable "souls". Physical bodies as we know them are generations in that they are the fashionings of an invisible agent who creates them for the peculiar workings of its will.

The fact that the soul can fabricate a physical body is proof itself that the soul is manifesting upon the level of generation, and incarnation is that process whereby the spiritual nature establishes itself upon the level of generation in order to become the formator of innumerable corporeal vehicles. Having assumed the idea of generation, the soul is capable of generating, and bodies are its generations. In order to generate, the soul becomes individualized and ultimately abstractly personalized. Therefore it is said arcanely that there is a continuity of personality throughout the cycle of incarnation, but this personality is the soul personality posited at the apex, or causal point, of the triangle of the generating sphere.

The ancient philosophers affirmed that 777 physical earth lives constitute the incarnation of the human soul. Each of these earth lives is divided into a physical and superphysical part—life and death. Occupying the middle ground between the spiritual part and its generated vehicles, the soul hangs suspended from its own cause, and from it are suspended the physical personalities which manifest for a day, only to be dissolved by death into their primordial state. From this it is evident that the physical phenomena of life and death have little effect upon the spiritual status of the individual, for this status is actually measured by the degree to which he has disentangled his soul from the illusion of generation, and has no reference to the corporeal or incorporeal condition of his body. The true "fall" of man was the descent of his soul into the Cycle of Necessity or sphere of generation, and his true resurrection is the ascent of the soul to its former state of noninvolvement. Thus, life—both before and after death—is simply an allegorical ceremony during which, as in the pageantry of the Mysteries, a curious ritualism is performed which recapitulates upon the physical level the entire story of man's superphysical dilemma. The bodies shadow forth the rationality of the soul. While the idea of generation is upon the soul the bodies manifest the qualities of materiality. When the soul shakes off the drowsiness of the state of generation, the physical personalities which it objectifies manifest in an idealistic and spiritualized manner.

The consciousness of man is said to exist in three general states: in an unawakened state, an awakening state, and an awakened state. Those whose souls are wholly immersed in the illusion of form are declared to be asleep. Although they may manifest activity in the phenomenal sphere, this activity being of their outer and not their inner parts, is not regarded as an evidence of wakefulness. Such souls are symbolized as lying asleep throughout the span of life. Occasionally they are depicted as covered with cobwebs as symbolic of the weaving of their own fancies. Their bodies also are partly buried in that dust which collects upon all inert objects. This dust represents that inactivity which soon dulls the perception of the unwary, but which the just man shakes off by endeavor. Those to whom beauty means nothing, in whom there is no desire to better an imperfect state, who live but to gratify the appetites of the flesh, are the sleeping ones who, after passing unawakened through the span of physical existence enter into the invisible world, there to lie in rows still sleeping as they slept while in the physical world. After a time these sleeping souls drift back again, take upon themselves bodies, sleep through another life cycle, and continue this procedure until finally innate Divinity, by the agency of some dire necessity, is aroused and animated to cast off its robes of lethargy.

The second group—the wakening souls—are those in whom realization, while not perfected, has become an element in the cultural life. Physical existence has come to be recognized as a period of endeavor through which the divine potentialities must be liberated from the winding-sheet of matter. Through the periods of both life and death such a soul is consecrated to the attainment of wisdom. All change is regarded as fresh opportunity, and with faith in ultimate perfection the seeker eagerly pursues the quest of Self.

The third group—the awakened souls—are those who have cast off the graveclothes of limitation and made their escape from generation, exchanging the alternation of mortal life for the continued awareness of the inner existence. They are masters not only of the so-called terrestrial state, but having liberated their souls from the idea of generation they ascend to that truly incorporeal world where the soul is united with the true substances of its own being and where, dwelling in its own state, it is said to abide in a state of perfect felicity.

Let us next consider the role played by love in the periodic comings and goings of the soul while in the state of generation. The law of the intellect is reason, the law of the soul is love, and the law of the body is generation. It follows that while each of these spheres is amicable toward its own qualities, when these qualities are combined to form a compound, friction results. Paracelsus tells us that the elementals, or Nature spirits, live for hundreds of years because, composed of a single principle, there is the minimum of friction between their parts.

To reason, established in its own essence and functioning according to its own laws, love is thus inexplicable; likewise, the physical nature, which is established in and exists through generation, views both reason and love as antagonistic. The plans of reason are frequently thwarted by the claims of love; and both reason and love are often overwhelmed by the dietalcs of the animal nature, though reason unfailingly reminds the latter of its own insufficiency. Hence, the inconstancy of human attitudes is primarily due to the lack of a common denominator.

Plato defined love as the longing of diversity for unity; the desire of parts to be brought together to form wholes; the instinctive urge of all creatures toward a perfect state. Realizing that reality increases in proportion as diversity is overcome, the rational soul rejoices in the union of incomplete natures; for even the least perfect of such unions contributes to the unity of the whole. The same urge that first causes souls to come into generation and unite themselves with corporeal substances later causes them, after they dissociate themselves from corporeal substances, to rise toward and mingle themselves with spiritual Reality.

As the essential unity of reality is apparently broken up by its descent into the sphere of generation, a condition ensues common only, however,, to such as have assumed the reality of diversity. Laboring under the illusion of separateness, the fractional parts function in the consciousness of isolation. Probably no feeling can sweep over the nature of man more terrifying than that which causes him to feel absolutely alone. This (doneness means the stiflling of all expression, Joy and sorrow alike must be relieved by expression; otherwise they infect the temperament with a curious disease which Robert Burton rather inadequately terms melancholy. This feeling of isolation is invariably accompanied by one of utter hopelessness, for man is essentially a social animal. While his unenlightened animal sociability causes him to seek the companionship of the phantoms of matter, still it is a necessary though imperfect expression of that spiritual quality which will ultimately unite him with the whole order of being.

Physical life may be likened to a gloomy dungeon where those convicted of "materiality" sit in solitary confinement, each in his own little cell. Like the prisoner of Chillon, who vainly longed for the blue sky and the comrades of yore, the soul of man locked in the life of form yearns for companionship and understanding. In the Tarot cards is one called Temperance, showing a winged figure pouring water from one urn into another. In the Cabala also it is declared that Chochmah flows into Binah; that is, Wisdom flows into Understanding. As man at Nirvana inverts that bowl which he calls himself, and pours his soul into the Infinite, so throughout all the ages of his unfoldment there is within his life an inherent urge to flow forth and mingle with other lives in a mystical communion.

The irrational soul is ever building walls which the rational soul is ever tearing down. The irrational soul is ever emphasizing the intervals which separate living creatures, which intervals the rational soul annihilates by the realization that the divine nature can be limited by no place or condition. The mythological "marriages" of the gods signify the union of a principle with its form, for the god is a creative principle and his consort is the vehicle of that principle. Thus when the soul enters into generation a mystic marriage takes place in which a rational agent is wedded to the sphere of generation which is to be its vehicle of manifestation. At death when the rational soul casts off generation another marriage takes place in which the rational agent, having divorced its inferior part, is united by a symbolic ceremony to the sphere of liberation. Several philosophies differ as to the place occupied by sex in the Cycle of Necessity. Those who assert that sex is differentiated in the spiritual nature itself maintain an untenable hypothesis, since it is philosophically evident that spirit, which partakes of the divine wholeness though containing the potentiality of diversity, does not manifest that diversity while in a spiritual state. While androgynous may not be the true defining term, it may be employed to express the undivided state of sex in spirit, where it exists in no form other than that of a latent attribute. This theory brings up the inevitable question: If spirit is inherently androgynous and perfect, why should it manifest through a vehicle less perfect in gender? The common theory of a divided spirit, with the resultant quest of the severed parts for each other, has proved to be more poetical than practical; for unity, which is the primary attribute of the causal nature is destroyed if two complete organisms are postulated as manifesting independently from a single cause. The modern woman, moreover, has registered in unmistakable fashion her dislike to be considered a subordinate or vagrant fraction of the masculine temperament.

The secret schools of ancient philosophy postulated man as a twofold entity, which when masculine in its outer nature was feminine in its inner nature, and vice versa. In each sex, therefore, one pole is objectified and the other subjectified—one nature facing outward and the other facing inward. Each sex possesses the qualities of the other, but manifests them in an inhibited degree. Human love may be defined as a reciprocal emotion in which the subjectified nature of one person is stimulated by contact with the objectified nature of another. Affection is therefore an activity, both synchronous and reciprocal, in which the subjectified nature in one person flows toward its own objectified fullness in the other, while its own objectified fullness flows into the privation of its own quality; namely, the subjectified nature of the other.

Among the secret instructions of the Mysteries was one concerning the law which is known to various schools as the Law of Consequence, Compensation, Karma, or Cause and Effect. That a principle flowing from itself must always act in conformity with the laws responsible for its own existence, is undeniable. For example, good must always manifest according to the nature of good. But as the flow recedes from its own source it partakes ever less of the virtue of proximity to that source, and consequently may exist in every conceivable degree of its own quality. Each active agent is surrounded by its own effulgence. This effulgence is the natural radiance of life, and "tinctures" according to the nature of the radiating agent all that is brought into proximity thereto. The agent may therefore be conceived as the cause; the inevitable flow of the agent in conformity to its own nature, the effect. Hence karma may be defined as ignorance moving in accordance with its own nature, and producing conditions in harmony with its own inherent state.

The doctrine that "Whatsoever a man soweth, that shall he also reap" is based upon the Law of Consequence—the inevitbbility of action following reaction and reaction following action ad infinitum. A vicious circle is thus created in which every cause becomes an effect and every effect becomes a cause.

Here again is the Cycle of Necessity—a wheel of incident without beginning and without end. It is as necessary to step down from the wheel of cause and effect as it is to leave the wheel of life and death; for in the last analysis cause and life and effect and death are correlative terms. As life generates death and death generates life, so action generates reaction and reaction generates action; and to this sequence there is neither beginning nor end. Melchizedek, the Initiate-King of Salem, was declared to have been "above the law"; for karma has no control over such as are reborn out of the irrational into the rational state. Karma is the law by which irrationality multiplies itself, perpetuates its kind, and ultimately dissolves all creation in a holocaust of retribution.

Karma is the law of generation applied to action by which deeds are caused to reproduce their kind. It has been well said that laws are made for those who break them. This is particularly true of karma, which applies only to those irrational creatures who, due to the clouding of their rational perceptions, arc capable of functioning in a manner productive of destructive reaction. It is also stated that there is not only "evil" karma but also "good" karma. In the same way "good" karma is simply constructive action generating its own kind. But as action, both destructive and constructive, partakes of the illusion of matter—for action is the motion of material agents— so the laws of action and reaction, like those of life and death, are dissipated by philosophy which, by annihilating diversity, destroys the field in which these illusionary elements arrange themselves in complicated pattern.

Action is a dependency of place, for it signifies the flow of a life or condition out from self into not-self. Diodorus declared motion to be imoossible in that it depended for its reality upon the passing of a body from the place where it is into the place where it is not, and all bodies must ever occupy the place where they are. While this statement may appear ridiculous to the uninitiated, it is based upon the philosophic verity that life is without interval, and consequently incapable of action. For example, the processes taking place within life itself by which it generates form, cannot actually be termed action in that they are fourth-dimensional, coming under none of the recognizable classifications of physical activity. Bodies, however, existing in place are capable of rearrangement and of being moved about through the medium or interval in which they exist. Among the ancients activity was considered an attribute of form and karma its correlative. The philosophic discipline consequently liberates man from all the confining bonds of matter, elevating him to that estate wherein he may truthfully say, "I am the master of my fate, I am the captain of my soul." It should not be inferred, however that philosophy liberates man from the natural reactions of his actions, but rather that it liberates him from that sphere of activity which is productive of reaction.

To escape from this vast turmoil of ephemeral agencies which we call mortal existence, it is necessary to discipline the rational faculties to the realization of permanence. In other words, the disciple must come to l\now that he is an enduring and imperishable creature entirely beyond the reach of demons dwelling in the darkness of the corporeal sphere. Like Dante, he wanders through an inferno which has no power over him other than the power he bestows upon it by acceptance of its reality. Though man be in the world, he is not of the world.

That part of him which is fabricated from the illusional substances is, like Caliban, but a grotesque and unruly monster which must serve the will of the enlightened magus. To know the actual relationships existing between the parts of ourselves gives the power to directionalize these agencies toward the accomplishment of our own purposes. He who knows his body to be a body has a useful, if somewhat temperamental, servitor; but he who conceives his body to be himself has elevated a moron to power, and is destined to feel the iron heel of an irrational despot upon his neck.

It is essential that the student of ancient metaphysics regard himself as a permanent and immovable point which from the exaltedness of its own dignity gazes forth upon the phantasmagoria of outer existence. Such a one regards his own bodies as shadows that encircle him, as planets encircle their sovereign sun. All his forms he views as something apart from himself for he is formless, and though functioning in a sphere of generation he is not deluded by his workmanship. Gazing upon the personalities he has objectified, he must say:

"I am not they. They come forth from me to do my bidding and furnish the garment of my experience. They are like hands and feet which move at my command, and withdraw themselves from outer objects at my will. These shadows live and die, yet I am not born with their birth nor do I cease with their dying. Their coming and going alike are incidental, and have no effect upon my solidarity. Immersed in the confusion of mortality these shadows experience the twin illusions of joy and sorrow, health and sickness, gain and loss. Yet if they gain all the shadows of possession and encompass the whole illusion, they are no greater than before; for the thing they gain is nothing and the thing they lose is of equal value. If one of these shadows rises to great dignity and becomes a ruler of all the rest, what is he but nothing ruling nothing? If in despair these shadows wander about, is not their despair—like their joy—but a dream which fades into the nothingness that is its essential nature when the dreamer awakes? I close my eyes and, lo, a world of phantoms is imaged in the nothingness that I behold. These phantoms engage in intensive labors, concerning themselves with the weighty problems of their dream existence. At last I tire of sleeping, and exhausted with my own rest I open my eyes. The empire of my sleep dissolves as though it had never been; the vast but ghostly enterprises have no more substance than those who served them. In the daylight of conscious wakefulness all the shadows of the darkness melt away, to leave in their stead only a vast expanse of luminosity. The many have vanished and the one remains.

Instead of worlds there is only the I—the eternal and unchanging Self which dreams creation, and upon its awakening dissipates the whole."

But woe unto him who in his dream unites himself with his shadows and loses sight of his mastery over them; for he then assumes the concerns of his phantom forms. He struggles for the achievements of ephemerality; he seeks to build empire out of a dream, only to finally discover the senselessness of the fabric with which he wrought, since permanence cannot be

fashioned out of impermanent stuff. Then the self is tormented with every problem of the not-self; the joys and sorrows man images become so real that the goodness of life is blotted out, and crushing despair broods over all. The wise live not in dreams nor in the world of dreams, but in Reality. They have opened their eyes and scattered forever the shades of night;

they have left behind the trooping pageantry of incident, and upon the solid foundation of eternal and enduring Self have builded a destiny that shall not pass away.

## THE VARAHA INCARNATION OF VISHNU

There was once a Daitya who desired to rule the earth. He grew so powerful that he stole the planet and carried it with him into the depths of the ocean. Vishnu, in the form of a boar, dived into the abyss and, slaying the evil one, restored the earth by raising it upon his tusks.

# XX

### ❦

# The Ten Incarnations of Vishnu

On a rocky island in the harbor of Bombay is a series of remarkable caverns carved from the living rock. In the first of these is to be seen the colossal figure of the Brahmanic Creator in His threefold aspect of Brahma, Vishnu, and Shiva. The image consists of only the head and shoulders, is over twenty feet high, and was originally concealed from the eyes of the profane by swinging doors composed of great blocks of native rock. The Trimurti, as it is commonly called, constitutes one of the most sacred and secret emblems of the Hindus, being equivalent to the triangle of the Freemasons and the three-headed Christ of the early Christian mystics.

The island upon which the caves are situated was explored by the Portuguese, who named it Elephanta because of a beautifully carved figure of an elephant which they found in a conspicuous place. Before this very Trimurti the great Pythagoras was initiated into the Brahman Mysteries and in these same caves one of the most exquisite examples of a pre-Christian crucifix was discovered. The carvings in the Elephanta caverns are world famous for their beauty and lifelike appearance. We remember one group in particular. It was a scene depicting the marriage of Shiva and Parvati. Brahma is present to bless the marriage and the coy expression on the face of the bride is only equalled by the look of sheepishness on the features of the groom. The figures are life size and in high relief, but have been subjected to considerable mutilation at the hands of Mohammedans, Christian missionaries and thoughtless tourists.

The great figure of the Trimurti in its gloomy recess means little to the hosts of tourists who gaze upon it and then turn to other wonders. Students of philosophy and comparative religion, however, see in this image a magnificent exposition of the Secret Doctrine of the ancient Brahmans—a doctrine which, alas, is fast disappearing from the people to whom it was originally revealed.

It matters little what nation be considered. In almost every instance its religion is founded upon the doctrine of a Trinity. The chief triad of the Greeks was Uranus, Saturn, and Jupiter; of the Egyptians, Ammon, Ra, and Osiris; of the Persians, Ahura-Mazda, Mithras, and Ahriman; of the Qabbalistic Hebrews, Kether, Chokmah, and Binah; of the Christians, the Father, Son, and Holy Ghost; of the Pythagoreans, the monad, the duad, and the triad.

In his Inquiry into the Trinity of the Ancients, Isaac Preston Cory lists the following triads which were accepted by the ancients as representing the fundamental expressions of divine power and energy:

"From the different Orphic fragments we find that the Orphic Trinity consisted of Metis, Phanes, and Ericapæus, which are interpreted Will or Counsel, Light or Love, and Life or Life-giver. From Anaxilas, Earth, Fire, and Water. From Hesiod, according to Damascius, Eros, Ether, and Tartarus. From Pherecydes Syrius, Eros, Ether, and Chaos. From the Sidonians, Cronus, Love, and Cloudy darkness. From the Phœnicians, Ulomus, Chusorus, and the Egg. From the Chaldæan and Persian Oracles of Zoroaster, Fire, Light, and Ether. From the later Platonists: Power, Intellect, and Father; Power, Intellect, and Soul or Spirit."

In the ancient Theologists, according to Macrobius, the Sun was invoked in the Mysteries as: Power of the world, Light of the world, Spirit of the world. To which may perhaps be added, from Sanchoniatho, the three sons of Genus: Fire, Light, and Flame.

To the list given by Cory may be added a very fundamental geometrical illustration: the triad of primitive symbols consisting of the point, the line, and the circle. The point is the appropriate emblem of the One Creative Cause—the First or the Source. All lines are merely rows of dots and all bodies aggregations of dots. In the Christian system of theology the dot would be the appropriate emblem of God the Father, for it is the One of which all creatures are but parts. The line is the outpouring of the dot, the One coming into expression; it is, therefore, the second person of the Creative Triad. In the Hindu school this second person is called Vishnu, which corresponds to the Christ of the Christians. The line bears witness to the potentialities of the dot, for it is the outpouring or welling up of that Eternal Life forever concealed within the profundity of the germinative dot.

The circle marks the circumference of the dot and limits the outpouring of the line. Therefore, it is the destroyer, the yawning mouth that swallows up the life of the dot, the hades into which the line descends and where it remains until it has overcome the mystery of death, which mystery is part of the secret of the circle. In India the circle is called Shiva, the Destroyer, the Lord of the mundane sphere; to Christendom it is known as the Holy Ghost, or the third person of the Divine Triad.

The dot, the line, and the circle may also be considered as natural emblems of life, intelligence, and substance—the three unknown causes which Huxley declared could never be discovered: consciousness, intelligence, and force. It is interesting to note that the three major divisions of human thought—namely the scientific, the philosophic, and the theologic—should have respectively the circle, the line, and the dot as their natural symbols. The circle, representing force and matter, limits the achievements of science to those elements from which the material universe was fabricated. The task of science is to solve the mystery of the circle; beyond that mystery it cannot go. Where science leaves off, however, philosophy must begin and the labor to which philosophy is dedicated is to solve the enigma of that intermediate line (the radius) which connects the dot and the circle. The name of that line is intelligence and the highest form of intelligence is that capable of accurately estimating the relationship existing between spirit and matter. Beyond reason philosophy cannot go, for reason is the highest phase of philosophic attainment. To theology, therefore, is assigned the labor of discovering and analyzing the nature of the dot—that spiritual Cause which neither the mind nor the hand can reach but which is cognizable only by its own spiritual correlate within the constitution of the individual.

By theology, however, is meant the divine science of spiritual things not the mass of conflicting creeds and dogmas which parade under the name of theology today. True theology bears the same relation to the arts and sciences of the world that the spirit does to the parts and members of its physical constitution. Theology is that divinely-revealed code by which man is assisted in the unfoldment of his spiritual potentialities. In this sense—and this sense only—theology is that divine science dedicated to the task of revealing to an ever-awakening humanity the mystery of the Creative Seed—the dot in the midst of the cosmic circle.

Have you ever realized how seldom a shrine, temple or church is erected to the Father Principle in religion? The churches of Christianity are all built to honor the second person of the Triad—the Christ. The same holds true in India, where not more than one or two temples to Brahma can be found but literally tens of thousands to Vishnu and Shiva. In Egypt there was but one temple to the Father Principle but scores to Ra and Osiris. In that country a precedent was established which was later incorporated in the Christian doctrine, namely the worship of the first Principle through the nature of the second. Hence the sanctifying of temples to Ammon-Ra.

Thus the second phase of the Creative Triad—Cosmic Intelligence—with its symbol, light, has been the dominating factor in religion since earliest times. In India Vishnu is the personification of the Universal Mind. In Him the divine potentialities of the incomprehensible Brahma are objectified, becoming the foundation of the world. One of the greatest secrets in mystical lore is that of the triangle. It has been truly said that any problem can be solved if its triangular base be first discovered. Every element, condition, or substance in the universe is founded upon a triad. Hence the multiplicity of triads constituting the Platonic theology.

The triangle is a continual reminder that every structure is essentially threefold and every intelligence a trinity of divine, human, and animal constituents. When man is considered as a sevenfold creature—as he invariably was in the ancient Mystery Schools—his nature was divided into two parts, of which the superior was made up of three divine elements and the inferior of four natural elements. The three spiritual parts of man are called the Silent Ones. They are the Three Immortals who remain throughout the ages meditating upon the fourfold body which they have permitted to exist but of which they themselves have never become a part.

In this 20th century it is generally conceded that an individual without a mind—or, more correctly, one who does not make proper use of his mental faculties—cannot succeed. Intelligence is accepted as a necessary basis for the computation of value and the rationalist is quite convinced that the salvation of the soul depends upon the clarity and organization of the reasoning faculties. This is in perfect harmony with theology, for the Savior-Gods of various peoples are really only the personifications of the Divine Intellect. As these deities come to save humanity, so the mind in man must become the savior of his lower constitution. The higher nature of man, being incapable

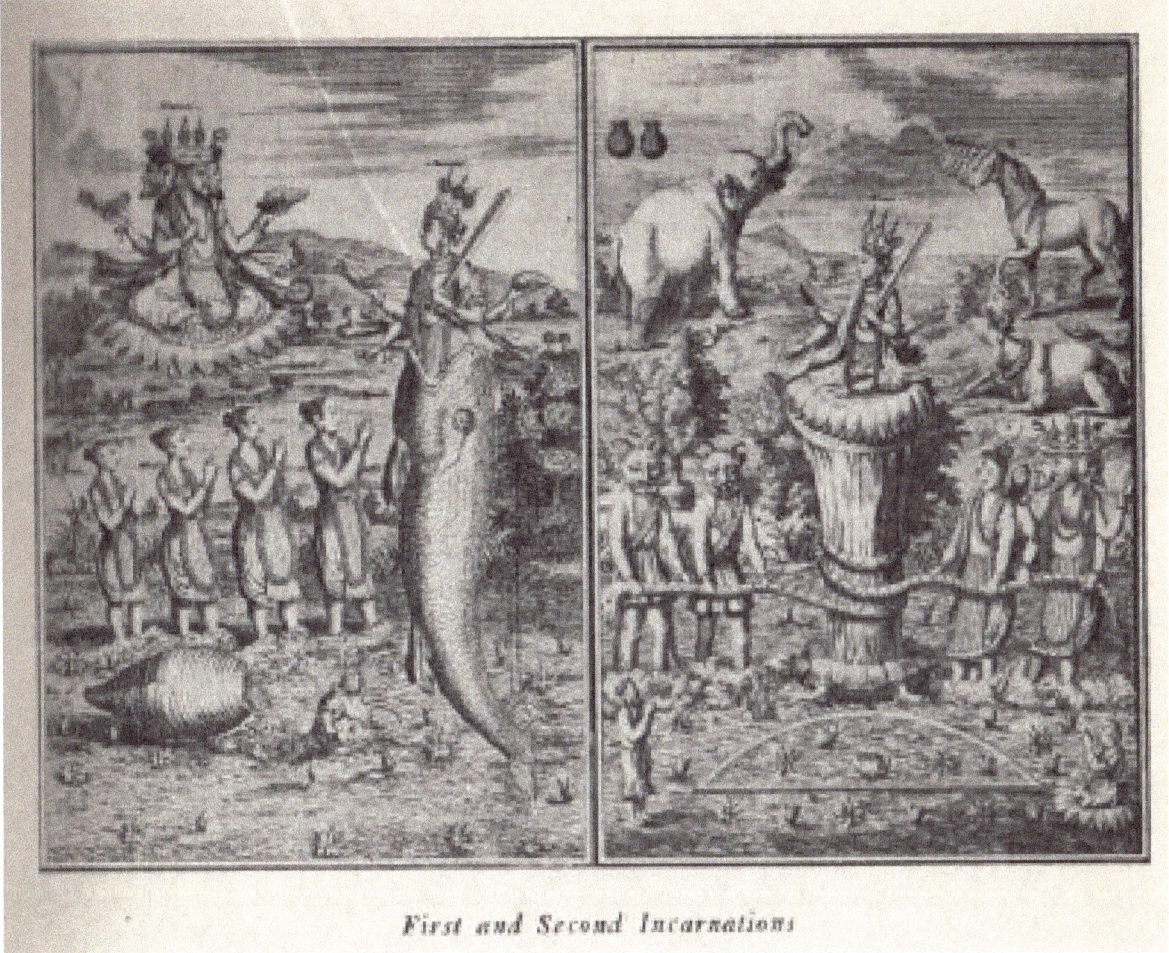

*First and Second Incarnations*

of death, is without need of salvation, but the lower man must build of the mind a bridge to connect his irrational soul with his divinely rational Anthropos, or Over-Nature.

Vishnu, being the active creative principle of the universe, and forever seeking to preserve His creation from the ravages of the destroying Shiva, is, therefore, looked upon as the benevolent and beneficent spirit. Here again we find a parallel between Vishnu and the human mind, for from the beginning of human civilization man has been using his mind as a weapon against the surrounding destructive forces of Nature. Man has only survived because of his intelligence, and as this increases in power he struggles ever more intelligently to counteract the forces of disintegration constantly working against him. The infant mind of primitive man conceived crude means for self-protection from both the ravages of the elements and the strange monsters of the prehistoric world. Man discovered that he could overcome the animal with fire; fire with water; water with earth. He turned the irrational elements upon themselves and thus saved his own life. Later he realized that he could harness the elements and, because he had a mind, he could control the mindless. He made the water-wheel and the windmill, with fire he tempered the metals, and harnessed the mindless beasts to plow his fields and bear his burdens, thus forcing them unquestioningly to obey his superior will. As new epochs in the history of the world brought new conditions, new faculties were evolved with which to conquer them. Man has finally come to realize that there is no problem so great, no mystery so profound, no element so strong, no beast so ferocious but that intelligence has proved its master.

However, the mind which was given to man proved not only a blessing but also a curse. Man discovered that he could accomplish anything that he willed to accomplish, for Nature was no longer able to control him. So man took the mind that was predestined to be his savior and used it as a weapon against his fellow creatures. He brutally enslaved the mindless; he broke the bodies of the beasts and, turning upon Nature of which he was a part, prostituted his newly found faculty by devastating the very earth that bore him. Still unsatisfied, he discovered that some of his own kind were weaker than he. Armed with primitive weapons, he, therefore, descended upon the more primitive tribes of humanity, slaying and enslaving the weaker and spattering the earth with the blood of her noblest products.

Man's ingratitude for the blessings given him out of the treasurehouse of natural potentiality is beautifully expressed in the tragic legend of Prometheus. At the price not only of his own liberty but of ages of suffering, Prometheus, the friend of man, brought fire from the abode of the gods. Concealing the spark in a hollow reed, he flew down with it to the abode of men and thus revealed to mankind the mystery of the flame. For this deed he was chained to the brow of Mt. Caucasus with a vulture to feed eternally upon his liver. Man repaid the noble sacrifice of the Titan by taking fire and with it forging weapons and armor with which to slay his fellows.

Today we see thought-power—the most recent boon of the gods—crucified like the Saviors of old between the thieves of greed and passion. The mental energy given to man that he might acquire a knowledge not only of himself but of the divine plan of which he is a part is now employed principally for the accomplishment of petty worldly ends. Man has forgotten the noble stock from which he sprung and the great purpose for which he was created. As the Philistines blinded Samson so man has blinded the giant of intellect and chained it to a grindstone. This divine being, capable of soaring into the very presence of Reality, now like a degraded beast paces round and round in ever-deepening ruts, grinding the corn of modern Philistia.

But intellect is a rebellious slave, for deep within it is a divine urge. The race will yet live to see the blinded giant tear down the pillars of materialism, for the intellect which man has perverted will prove his final undoing.

Throughout Eastern philosophy the Universal Mind is personified and, in spite of the seeming failure of races and individuals, it finally accomplishes the redemption and perfection of the race. The average individual finds it difficult to consider forces as personalities or to look upon every energy in Nature as an individualized creature possessing intellect and power. Such, however, is the Oriental conception. Therefore, Vishnu—the personified principle of Divine Knowledge, the mind which controls the working of the whole—periodically manifests Himself, becoming temporarily involved in the processes of creation that He may bring to the world spiritual understanding necessary to cope with the drastic changes taking place in civilization at certain periods.

"When virtue fails upon the earth, then I come forth," says Vishnu in the Bhagavad-Gita, and according to the secret doctrine of the Hindus the Great Mind has come into objective manifestation nine times already that He might prevent the failure of civilization. These incarnations of the Lord of the World are called the avataras or the incarnations of the Great Savior.

Vishnu appeared for one or more of three reasons: (1) to overcome some great evil in the world threatening the future of humanity, in the legends this evil being usually personified as a wicked king, or a great monster such as a dragon or ferocious demon; (2) to purify the faiths of men from that contamination

*Third and Fourth Incarnations*

which invariably creeps into religion after the lapse of thousands of years; (3) to found a new faith or doctrine, or to sound the key word of a new period of world endeavor. Accompanying this article is a series of ten drawings from Picart's Religious Ceremonials, showing the purposes of the ten incarnations according to East Indian symbolism. The tenth incarnation of Vishnu has not yet taken place, but the peoples of the East are waiting for His coming as many Christian sects look forward expectantly to the second coming of Jesus Christ.

In our little brochure on Occult Anatomy we called attention to the curious correspondence existing between the forms which Vishnu assumed during his incarnations and the months of the prenatal epoch. The intelligence of the human embryo during those periods closely parallels the intelligence of the various creatures through which Vishnu is said to incarnate.

Since Pythagoras was initiated into the Brahman Mysteries, he may have founded his numerical philosophy upon the theory of Vishnu's incarnations. The ten dots which constitute the Pythagorean tetractys may be interpreted, therefore, in the same manner as Vishnu's incarnations. The same is true of the ten spheres of the Qabbalists in which the Universal Spirit incarnates sequentially during both involutionary and evolutionary processes. According to the legends of His followers, Vishnu—like the Christian Christ—will come in the last day of the universe and judge the souls of all creatures.

The first avatara of Vishnu is termed the Matsya, or fish, incarnation. At a very early time in the history of the world so great a corruption blighted mankind that the gods determined to destroy the human race with a great flood. The prince who ruled at that time was a very pious man and he and the seven Rishis, or Wise Men, their wives, and pairs of all the animals and other forms of life entered an ark. The Lord Vishnu took upon Himself the

*Fifth and Sixth Incarnations*

body of a fish and fastened the ark to His own body by means of a cable fashioned out of a serpent. When the flood subsided, Vishnu slew an evil monster who had stolen the Vedas, or sacred books of the law. The books being returned, a new human race was formed who treasured the sacred writings and obeyed them implicitly. In the sacred books of the Hindus the story of the first avatara requires 14,000 verses for its recital.

The second avatara of Vishnu is termed the Kurma, or tortoise, incarnation. This incarnation is connected indirectly also with the flood, for in it Vishnu took upon Himself the body of a turtle, supporting with His shell the sacred mountain, Mandara. Using the great serpent for a rope and the mountain as an axis, the gods and demons churned the great ocean in order to regain the sacred Amrita, or the beverage of the gods. By this churning process fourteen sacred articles were discovered. These are shown in the picture grouped about the central mountain and in the hands of the deities.

The third avatara of Vishnu is termed the Varaha, or boar, incarnation. In this incarnation Vishnu is generally depicted upholding the earth with his tusks, the earth being deposited within the concave surface of a lunar crescent. According to the allegory, there was once a Daitya who desired to become the ruler of the earth. He ultimately grew so powerful that he stole the planet and carried it with him into the depths of the ocean. Vishnu, assuming the form of a boar, dived into the abyss and fought with this monster for one thousand years. Ultimately slaying the evil one, Vishnu restored the earth to its proper position by raising it upon his tusks.

The fourth avatara of Vishnu is termed the Narasingha, or man-lion, incarnation. This is the story of a holy man who for ten thousand years prayed and meditated for the boon of universal monarchy and that of everlasting life.

Seventh and Eighth Incarnations

Having become very great, he also grew equally selfish and arrogant. The gods led him into debate with his own son concerning the omnipresence of Deity. When his son told him that God was everywhere, even in the pillar supporting the roof of the palace, the evil prince in anger and blasphemy struck the pillar with his sword. The pillar, splitting in half, revealed Vishnu with the head of a lion, who after fighting with the egoistic prince for an hour dragged him into the hollow pillar and destroyed him, thus delivering the world from his arrogance.

The fifth avatara of Vishnu is termed the Vamana, or dwarf, incarnation. In this case a great monarch, becoming proud of the fact that he ruled over three worlds—heaven, earth, and hell—neglected the performance of the proper ceremonials to the gods. In the form of a dwarf, Vishnu appeared before the king, requesting a boon—that is, as much land as he could pace off with three steps. The king granted the request and ratified his promise by pouring water on the hand of the dwarf. Immediately the tiny figure increased in size until it filled the entire universe and, taking its three paces, owned the world, but out of kindly consideration for the virtues of the king permitted him to retain the government of hell.

The sixth avatara of Vishnu is termed the Parasu Rama incarnation. This is the first of the series of true human incarnations of the god. Parasu Rama was the son of a very aged holy man to whom the god Indra had entrusted the sacred cow. One of the Rajahs, desiring to possess the cow, finally brought about the death of the holy man, whose wife then committed sati, or suicide, praying with her last words that the gods would avenge the murder of her husband. Vishnu, answering the call, assumed the personality of Parasu Rama and after twenty battles slew the evil Rajah. The seventh avatara of Vishnu, termed the Rama Chandra incarnation, is contained within the great Indian epic, the Ramayana. Ravana, the evil king of Lanka, which is now Ceylon, stole Sita, the ideal of East Indian womanhood from her beloved husband, Rama. Assisted by Hanuman, the king of the apes, Rama Chandra won back Sita and, having tested her by fire, proved that she had remained true to him. The apes in a single night built a stone bridge between Lanka and the coast of India. Ravana, in order to torture Hanuman, king of the apes, set fire to his tail. Hanuman, running through the streets of Lanka, in turn set fire to the city, thus virtually destroying the power of Ravana.

The eighth avatara of Vishnu is termed the Krishna incarnation. The story of Krishna is so well known that it hardly requires any elaborate description. The illustration depicts the birth of Krishna and also the legend of his escape from death while an infant by being carried across the river in a basket. The water rose, threatening to destroy the bearer of the sacred child. To prevent this calamity, Krishna permitted one of his feet to hang over the edge of the basket, whereupon the water subsided. There are numerous instances in the life of Krishna which parallel the experiences of Jesus. These include the slaughter of the innocents, the transfiguration, the crucifixion, the resurrection, and the ascension. Krishna is considered as a personification of the sun, and his consort, Radha, is the embodiment of the earth.

The ninth avatara of Vishnu is generally termed the Buddha incarnation, although a great number of Hindus disagree with this. Some Orientalists have gone so far as to declare that the Christ of Christendom represents the ninth avatara or incarnation of Vishnu. The life of Buddha is beautifully set forth in Sir Edwin Arnold's Light of Asia. Buddha was an Indian prince who, inspired by the needs of humanity, renounced his kingdom and dedicated himself to the service of mankind. After many years of renunciation and prayer the two great laws of life were revealed to him—reincarnation and karma. He lifted the Buddhist faith from comparative obscurity to the dignity of the world's greatest religion, and at his death or translation a great number of Indian nobles were present. It was found impossible to light the funeral pyre until the body burst into flames by the release of spiritual energy from a great emerald which adorned the body of the dead sage.

The tenth avatara of Vishnu is termed the Kalki, or horse, incarnation and is the one which is yet to come. This incarnation is generally symbolized by a picture of a man leading a riderless white horse. The animal is sometimes shown with wings like the fabled Pegasus of the Greeks. Among many nations the horse is an emblem of the animal world or the lower sphere of being. In this sense it may infer that when Vishnu appears for the last time he will be mounted upon the world—that is, victorious over the substances of inferior Nature. The Brahmans believe that in his tenth avatara Vishnu will act as the true Savior of the world, redeeming the faithful from the sorrows and limitations of mortal existence. No man knows the day of his coming, but the Hindus are positive that when the great need arises he will be there to preserve and redeem those who have been faithful to his laws and tenets. Such, in brief, is the story of the ten immortal incarnations of the Lord of Light.

A careful consideration of the graduated series of ever nobler creatures through which the great Vishnu incarnates reveals an evolutionary doctrine.

*Ninth and Tenth Incarnations*

subtly concealed behind these curious emblems. Of this Madam Blavatsky writes as follows:

"In this diagram of avatars we see traced the gradual evolution and transformation of all species out of the ante-Silurian mud of Darwin and the ilus of Sanchoniathon and Berosus. Beginning with the Azoic time, corresponding to the ilus in which Brahma implants the creative germ, we pass through the paleozoic and Mesozoic times, covered by the first and second incarnations as the fish and tortoise; and the Cenozoic, which is embraced by the incarnations in the animal and semi-human forms of the boar and man-lion; and we come to the fifth and crowning geological period, designated as the 'era of mind, or age of man,' whose symbol in the Hindu mythology is the dwarf—the first attempt of nature at the creature of man.

"* * From a fish the progress of this dual transformation carries on the physical form through the shape of a tortoise, a boar, and a man-lion; and then, appearing in the dwarf of humanity, it shows Parasu Rama physically, a perfect, spiritually, an undeveloped entity, until it carries mankind personified by one god-like man, to the apex of physical and spiritual perfection—a god on earth." (See Isis Unveiled.)

In the Vishnupuranam it is written: "This universe hath sprung from Vishnu,—and in Him it is established. He is the cause of creation, maintenance and destruction thereof, and He is the universe." Vishnu is thus to be considered both the fabricator and the fabric of the world structure. He is the Deity in which men live and move and have their being. He is that objective power which manifests the eternally subjective condition of Brahma, the first creative person of the Divine Triad. He stands between the superior heavens which are of the nature of Brahma and the inferior world which is of the nature of Shiva. Therefore, He is the sun which, according to the Mysteries, occupies the focal point between abstraction and concretion. As Lord of the sun He is the patron of all creatures and forms, the bestower of life and the giver of abundance. He is often represented with blue skin, the blue representing the heavens which are his body and also the subtle invisible ethers which form his magic horse. In Indian art Vishnu is often depicted sleeping through the night of cosmic darkness upon the coils of a great serpent. When thus represented a lotus stalk is shown growing out of his navel and upon the blossom of this lotus sits the great Brahma with four heads. It is very difficult to secure any satisfactory explanation of this symbol which pertains to the deepest principles of Eastern occultism. In one sense of the word, Vishnu—like the Greek Cronus—destroys the power of his father and usurps his authority as Lord of the world. When Vishnu fabricates the universe he absorbs into it the great Brahma, for in the last analysis Vishnu forms the universe out of the nature of Brahma, of whose constitution He also is a part. The lotus growing from the navel may be interpreted to signify that Brahma is the Cause which nourishes the world through a spiritual umbilicus symbolized by the lotus stalk. The symbol may also be interpreted to mean the gradual growth or ascension of Brahma out of the nature of Vishnu, for when the latter deity is asleep in the coils of the dragon of measureless time Brahma rises out of and exists superior to the sleeping Vishnu.

The ten incarnations of Vishnu may be said to represent those creative efforts made by the gods while they were attempting to establish various species of organized life upon the face of the world. From earliest times life struggled to manifest itself through adequate vehicles and in its effort to discover the proper type of body for its purpose experimented with many forms and cast them aside. From these rejected structures have descended many species of irrational creatures to whom it was found the divine nature could not be imparted. Certain members of the simian family represent one of the types of bodies into which the Lords of Reason could not descend. Therefore, in them the conscious mind is absent.

For thousands of years every civilization, remembering the promise of the Lord of Light—which promise has been given equally to all men—has believed the time to be at hand for the last avatara of the Lord of the world. Each generation believes that it needs him more than any other generation of the past or of the future. For nineteen centuries Christians have been daily awaiting the second coming of the Messiah and the consequent end of the world. Today there is undoubtedly a grave decline of virtue and a great spiritual need, but who knows whether tomorrow will not offer a still greater problem?

When the World Lord shall come no man knows, for humanity is not farsighted enough to realize the moment of its own greatest need. But according to the deepest concepts of mysticism, He is always here, riding upon the white horse of the world, guiding with sure hand the reins of the divine steed. The white horse may well symbolize the purified soul of the redeemed man, its wings the spiritualization of the material body. Every pure heart and enlightened mind becomes a vehicle of expression for the World Lord, who is ever speaking to mankind through the lips of purified human creatures. As with His last coming the Lord of enlightened love redeems His world and accepts His creatures back again into the nature of Himself, so in the life of every individual there comes a time when the Lord of enlightened wisdom himself becomes the dominant factor in his life. Once this spiritual power is realized and its power appreciated, it becomes the ruler of man's inner world and gradually absorbs the mortal man into its own immortal nature.

Every human being has within himself a Lord Vishnu, the objectification of the spiritual germ—Brahma. This Vishnu is the immortal spirit of man, a standing of accomplishment, of realization, and of divinity itself. When man purifies his body, opens the chambers of his heart, and disentangles the threads of his thoughts he becomes finally a living temple. And to this temple comes Vishnu because the house has been made ready for Him. Until the Universal Spirit of Light first comes to the individual, it will never come into the world. Each human being in turn must experience the mystery of the second coming of his Lord and until such time as this takes place his personal redemption is not consummated. All the mysteries of the outer world must take place within the little world of man's consciousness before they can be of any benefit to him.

# XXI

### ❧

# Pagan Theogony and Cosmogony

FROM the Greek mythology that had its genesis in the revelations of Orpheus and its efflorescence in the erudition of Plato, the Neoplatonists extracted a sublime philosophy. In his introduction to The Six Boo{s of Proclus on the Theology of Plato, Thomas Taylor writes: "According to this theology, therefore, from the immense principle of principles, in which all things casually subsist, absorbed in superessential light, and involved in unfathomable depths, a beauteous progeny of principles proceed, all largely partaking of the ineffable, all stamped with the occult characters of deity, all possessing an overflowing fullness of good. From these dazzling summits, these ineffable blossoms, these divine propagations, being, life, intellect, soul, nature, and body depend; monads suspended from unities, deified natures proceeding from deities. Each of these monads, too, is the leader of a series which extends from itself to the last of things, and which while it proceeds from, at the same time abides in, and returns to its leader. And all these principles and all their progeny are finally centered and rooted by their summits in the first great all-comprehending one. Thus all beings proceed from, and are comprehended in the first being; all intellects emanate from one first intellect; all souls from one first soul; all natures blossom from one first nature; and all bodies proceed from the vital and luminous body of the world. And lastly, all these great monads are comprehended in the first one, from which both they and all their depending series are unfolded into light. Hence, this first one is truly the unity of unities, the monad of monads, the principle of principles, the God of Gods, one and all things, and yet one prior The concluding sentence of the quotation establishes beyond all cavil the monotheistic foundation of Greek philosophy. In fact, to the discerning it is basically a philosophic atheism, for this Supreme Deity actually is neither a personality nor a principle, but the principle of principles, the most abstract of the most abstract, so universalized and unlimited in its inherent nature as to be incomprehensible. When such a deity is compared with the popular theological concept of a personal God, the supremacy of philosophy's God is at once apparent. The God of ancient philosophy is the Deity whose sufficiency will yet be vindicated by modern science. Men will never outgrow the God of Plato, but one by one the Gods of creeds and sects will be driven from their thrones by the unfolding intellect of man. The modern world already demands the abdication of that despotic regent who has ruled the universe for the past few thousand years.
The foregoing quotation also reveals how from this first and perfect unity infinite diversity pro-

ceeds in sequential order. Simple monotheism thus manifests through a complex polytheism, and the gods are demonstrated as philosophically necessary to the orderly workings of the Divine Plan. On the subject of the gods proceeding from the nature of simple unity, Thomas Taylor further writes:

"For if whatever possesses a power of generating, generates similars prior to dissimilars, every cause must deliver its own form and characteristic peculiarity to its progeny; and before it generates that which gives subsistence to progressions far distant and separate from its nature, it must constitute things proximate to itself according to essence, and conjoined with it through similitude. It is therefore necessary from these premises, since there is one unity the principle of the universe, that this unity should produce from itself, prior to everything else, a multitude of natures characterized by unity, and a number the most of all things allied to its cause; and these natures are no other than the Gods." The principle of emanationism as unfolded in the Orphic theogony became the vital doctrine of the Gnostics, who conceived a spiritual hierarchy as occupying each degree of the inte val between the extremes of First Cause and Nature. The seven grand divisions into which existence is divided are termed in Neoplatonism:

(1) The Principle of Principles, which is inscrutable and analogous to the threefold darkness of the Egyptians; (

2) Being, the first point of the Triad of Cause;

(3) Life;

 (4) Intellect, which completes the Triad of Causes;

(5) Soul, which is the apex of the Triad of Generation;

(6) Nature; and (

7) Body, which completes the Triad of Generation.

Thus is revealed the order by which Cause flows into Generation and eventually produces bodies, the latter being objectifications in matter of superphysical paradigms or \rche- types.

As certain monadic forces are thus suspended from the Supreme Unity, so this design of diversity suspended from unity is an invariable pattern throughout creation. Each item of diversity then becomes in its own nature a unity, from which ts further suspended another chain of diversity, and so on ad infinitum. For example, from the immense Principle of Principles as the Supreme Monad arc suspended the divine principles of Being, Life, Intellect, Soul, Nature, and Body. Each of these becomes, in turn, a monadic unit. From Being are suspended beings; from Life, lives; from Intellect, intellects; from Soul, souls; from Nature, natures; and from Body, bodies.

It naturally follows that all bodies partake of the qualities of the principle of Body and are manifestations of it; all souls partake of the principle of Soul; and all beings partake of the principle of Being. The principle of Body exists throughout all the chain of emanations intervening between its primal manifestation from the Absolute and such bodies as stones and trees which exist temporarily in this ephemeral sphere. There are divine bodies, luminous and splendid; there are immortal bodies, transcendent in power; and there are mortal bodies, subject to continual evil and decay. The greater the interval between the principle of Body and the subordinate body suspended from that principle, the lower the quality and organization of that body. The world as a body and the worm as a body arc both suspended from the principle of Body, The worm, however, is suspended from a monad far more remote from the principle of Body than is the world, for the worm, being part of the life of the world, is a minute part of the diversity from one of the countless monads suspended from the body of the world itself. Herein is revealed the mystery of Adam, for as Philo Judaeus affirms, Adam is actually the monad of mankind. Human beings therefore derive their human qualities from their participation in the nature of this prototypic monad. Thus from the Adamic monad are suspended the hundred of millions of individualized men and women who, when considered as a unit, constitute a single male and female creature—the first and supreme man, the idea of mankind, the Adamic unity.

The theogony of Orpheus as set forth by Hesiod and interpreted by Proclus is divisible into three major parts, of which the first (in the words of Rev. James Davies) is concerned with cosmogony, or the creation of the world, its powers, and its fabric. The second part, or theogony proper, is concerned with the generations of the gods, and records the histories of the dynasties of Cronus and Zeus. The third part is concerned in a fragmentary way with the generation of heroes, who sprang from the intercourse of mortals with immortals. Both space and the purposes of this chapter limit us to a consideration of the first (or cosmological) division, together with a brief outline of the generation of Cronus and the rebellion of the Titans.

In the beginning, declare the Orphic fragments, was the Absolute—unborn, unaging, and undying Time. Here Time is conceived to be in a state of suspension; for as Time depends for its reality upon the succession of incidents, it cannot exist actively until the establishment of the worlds. Time is the perfect Wholeness which encompasses all manifestations as a mysterious intangible envelope. Within the divine sphere of Time existences live and move and have their being. From this inscrutable Wholeness there issue forth two agents designated Ether and Chaos, or the Bound and the Infinity . Thus in the terms of the ancient symbolism, "the One becomes the Two." The first of these agents—Ether—is called the Bound because as a symbol of primordial activity it is limited as to place, condition, and duration. Chaos, which in some systems of cosmogony is elevated to the position of first deity, takes second place, when compared to the enduring Wholeness. Being unlimited, unorganized, and without sense of Time, it is properly termed Infinity .

These two opposites —Bound and Infinity —acting each upon the other, destroy the placidity of the eternal state. Ether, the active agent, is symbolized as a vast whirlwind which moves the surface of Chaos, and out of its unorganized substances forms a great ovoid, termed by the ancients the Orphic or Cosmic Egg. This Egg is usually represented as encircled by the coils of a great serpent (the Ether). The substances of the Egg, having been impregnated by the divine Ether, "increase from within outward." The fertilized Egg expands and finally bursts asunder to reveal the Triple-Dragon God Phanes, who is called the "Divine or Absolute Animal." Phanes is described as "an incorporeal God, bearing golden wings on his shoulders; but in his inward parts naturally possessing the heads of bulls, upon which heads a mighty dragon appears, invested with the various forms of wild beasts." The point is also repeatedly emphasized that Phanes, while possessing wings and a human head, is without a body, his entire being consisting of a vast ring of radiant effulgence. The ancient commentaries (especially those of the Neoplatonists) identify Phanes with the Cherubim of Ezekiel and the composite monster of the Chal- daic-Egyptian Mysteries. The bull's head signify the constellation of Taurus; the lion's head, which Phanes is sometimes said to have, is the constellation of Leo; the dragon is the constellation of Scorpio; and the human head with wings upon its neck is the constellation of the god-man, Aquarius. Thus the four hierarchies called the Lords of Generation are set forth.

In the Christian system these animals and winged creatures are ascribed to the four Evangelists to indicate that the Gospels are the source of spiritual life. The specially emphasized fact that the head of Phanes is without a body reminds the disciple that the lower or bodily universe has not yet become objectified, but remains as an unapplied idea of the first deity. Several early mythologists divided the Egg of Cosmos into an upper and a lower hemisphere, the upper composed of gold and the lower of silver. Similarly, in the images of Zeus the eyes are sometimes inlaid with silver to indicate his sovereignty over the inferior (or lower) hemisphere of creation. It is also stated that after breaking open to release the radiant Phanes, the upper part of the Universal Egg became the Intellectual Universe and the lower part the Sensible Universe. This is paralleled in the story of creation according to Genesis, where it is related that the waters which were above the heavens were divided from the waters which were below the firmament. The interval between the two sundered hemispheres of the egg was called Heaven, and here the light of Phanes was diffused throughout the elements of the Intelligible Sphere. It is most significant that Heaven should be located between the extremes of Intellect and Sense, since its correlate in the body—the heart—is situated between the intellectual nature above and the animal nature below.

Phanes is referred to as the "triple God" because he is a triad of powers, with himself as the principle, or monad, and Ericapaeus and Metis as his lesser aspects. As Phanes represents spiritual light and life, it is natural that his consort, or Sakti, should represent spiritual darkness, or the medium through which this light manifests. The Mother of the Gods was therefore called Threefold Night, and she alone mingled in perfect union with Phanes, who is described as giving to her his scepter that she might in queenly manner rule his world. By right of her threefold powers Night brought forth two children, the first of her progeny, called Heaven and Earth. The latter is to be understood as a divine cosmic earth, and not the terrestrial globe with which we are familiar. One of the chief sources of confusion in the study of ancient systems of cosmogony arises from the effort to relate such terms as earth and world to our own physical system, when in reality they refer to invisible superphysical spheres—the archetypes of the inferior generatioas which are to follow. The Heaven and Earth born of the union of Night and Phanes are the spheres of the noumenon and phenomenon which form such essential elements in the philosophy of Immanuel Kant.

Heaven and Earth are then united in marriage, and in the words of G. R. S. Mead, "From their union arises a strange and curious progeny, the Fates (Parcae), Hundred-handed (Centimani), and They-who-see-ail-round (Cyclopes). * * * The Fates are the Karmic Powers, which adjust all things according to the causes of prior Universe; while the Centimani and Cyclopes are the Guilders, or rather the Overseers or Noetic Architects, who supervise the Builders of the Sensible Universe. * # * These were the first progeny of Heaven and Earth, and were cast down to Tartarus, for they worked within all things, and so, as evolution proceeded, permeated every kingdom of nature. But then, without the knowledge of Heaven, Earth brought forth, says Orpheus (Proc. Tim., Hi. 137), 'seven fair daughters, bright-eyed, pure, and seven princely sons, covered with hair;* and these are called the 'avengers of their brethren.' And the names of the daughters are Themis and Tethys, Mnemosyne and Thea, Dione and Phoebe, and Rhea; and of the sons, Cocus and Crius, Phorcys and Cronus, Oceanus and Hyperion, and Iapetus (Proc. op. at., v.295). And these are the Titans." (Sec Orpheus.) Under the leadership of Cronus all the Titans save Oceanus rebelled against Heaven and established the Material Sphere.

Cronus became the ruler of the Titans, which position he held until Zeus, leading his giants, overthrew the empire of Cronus and established the Physical Universe. We are told in the commentaries that the last of the heavenly line is Bacchus, in whom the generations of Uranus, or Heaven, arc complete. In the Orphic theogony then follows the order of the supermundane and mundane gods, with accounts of the heroes and those who were elevated to a parity with divinity because of the immortal spirit that led them to the pinnacle of achievement.

This sublime philosophy, which clothes cosmic processes in personalities and reveals by their combinations the wonders of the Intelligible Sphere, has been debased to the point where it is now regarded as merely a collection of myths suitable only for the amusement of the adolescent and the dotard, or to furnish poets with the inspiration for a bare existence. Perpetuated thus in all its outer form in Bullfinch's Age of Fable, the theology by which Plato lived and died is now looked upon as something outlived or as having overshot the mark. The Orphics, however, thought truly and wrote well. Their theology cannot die, but shall survive every device created to destroy it, and in a more philosophic era in the future shall shine forth again with splendor undiminished.

It is now established beyond reasonable doubt that the Vedic writings of the Hindus were the chief contributions to the exalted structure of Orphic theogony. It is even asserted that the first Orpheus was a Hindu. A number of early Greek philosophers, moreover—prominent among them Thales and Pythagoras—were initiated into the Mysteries of the Brahmans. There is also a legend to the effect that Osiris, the black god of Egypt, journeyed to that land from Asia, establishing in the Double Empire of the Nile his Mysteries patterned after those of the Brahmans. Whether these founders of philosophic systems were actual personalities or personifications of their doctrines cannot be determined definitely at this late period. It is not at all improbable that the journeys presumably taken by such demigods as Orpheus and Osiris arcanely signify the migrations westward of the cults of the primitive Asiatic Aryans. When compared with the Oriental creation myths it is evident that the Greek fables appear fragmentary and obscure; for the early Brahman sages were unquestionably the greatest abstract thinkers whose doctrines have survived to this day. That eminent student of Vedic philosophy, the Hon. H. H. Wilson, in a footnote on Indian mythology and tradition was moved to write: "As, however, the Grecian accounts, and those of the Egyptians, are much more perplexed and unsatisfactory than those of the Hindus, it is most probable that we find amongst them the doctrine in its most original as well as most methodical and significant form." Having given a brief outline of the Orphic cosmogony, we next turn to the more ancient Brahman theory in order to make possible a comparison between these two philosophic systems. The Vedic creation myth as set forth in the opening chapters of The Vishnu Purana may be summarized as follows:

The sage, Parasara, discourses with his disciple, Maitreya (not the Bodhisattva), concerning Vasudeva (the indwelling radiance) and how it came forth to manifest creation. Parasara begins his account with this prayer:

"Glory to the unchangeable, holy, eternal, supreme Vishnu, of one universal nature, the mighty over all: to him who is Hiranygarbha, Hari, and Sankara, the creator, the preserver, and destroyer of the world: to Vasudeva, the liberator of his worshippers: to him whose essence is both single and manifold; who is both subtle and corporeal, indiscrete and discrete: to Vishnu, the cause of final emancipation. Glory to the supreme Vishnu, the cause of the creation, existence, and end of this world; who is the root of the world, and who consists of the world."

Upon completion of his prayer Parasara enters upon the main theme of his discourse with the declaration that Brahma—the supreme, eternal, unborn, imperishable, and undeccaying lord—first exists in the forms of Purusha (spirit) and Kata (time). From Purusha next proceeded two other forms called the discrete and the indiscrete. Thus primary matter, spirit, visible substance, and time, are declared by the wise to be the pure and supreme condition of Vishnu, which is Brahma in the state of quiescence. In his opening prayer Parasara refers to Vishnu (who, in the terms of the Greek Platonists would be the Power, or second person of the Brahmanic Triad and consequently its active part) as Hiranygarbha (meaning the Brahma who is born from the golden egg), Hari (which is Vishnu as the lord of goodness), and Sankara (or Shiva, the destroyer). Taking upon himself the capacity of Brahma, Vishnu becomes the creator; assuming the nature of Shiva, or Rudra, he is the destroyer; and in his true nature as Vishnu he is in equilibrium between them. In a footnote to the description of the four elements composing the nature of Vishnu, Prof. Wilson states that the Puru- sha, or spirit of the Hindus, is analogous to the Phanes of the Orphics; Pradhana or primary matter, to the Orphic Chaos; and Kala, or time, to the Orphic Cronus. As Phanes consisted of a triad of powers, so Pradhana is declared to be endowed with three qualities in equilibrium, and to be the mother of the world. Therefore it is written: "There was neither day nor night, nor sky nor earth, nor darkness nor light, nor any other thing, save only One, unapprehensible by intellect, or That which is Brahma and Puman (spirit) and Phadhana (matter)."

It is then written that the supreme Brahma of his own will enters into spirit and matter, and the season of creation having arrived, agitates the mutable and immutable principles. This is accomplished in an occult manner. "As fragrance affects the mind from its proximity merely, and not from any immediate operation upon mind itself: so the Supreme influenced the elements of creation." From these equilibrated qualities proceeds the unequal development of these qualities, which is termed the principle Mahat or Intellect. The creator then invents the great principle Intellect, which is termed Iswara, the manifested creator. Mahat then becomes threefold, and its phases are termed the threefold Egotism.

The Vishnu Purana continues: "Elementary Egotism then becoming productive, as the rudiment of sound, produced from it Ether, of which sound is the characteristic, investing it with its rudiment of sound. Ether becoming productive, engendered the rudiments of touch; when originated strong wind, the property of which is touch; and Ether, with the rudiment of sound, enveloped the rudiment of touch. Then wind becoming productive, produced the rudiment of form (colour); when light (or fire) proceeded, of which, form (colour) is the attribute; and the rudiment of touch enveloped the wind with the rudiment of colour. Light becoming productive, produced the rudiment of taste; whence proceed all juices in which fl vor resides: and the rudiment of colour invested the juices with the rudiment of taste. The waters becoming productive, engendered the rudiments of smell; whence an aggregate (earth) originates, of which smell is the property."

When the rudiments had united themselves with the properties here described they assumed the character of one mass which, directed by spirit and with the acquiescence of the indiscrete Principle, Intellect, and the rest, formed an egg which gradually expanded like a bubble of water. "This vast egg,

o sage, compounded of the elements, and resting on the waters, was the excellent natural abode of Vishnu in the form of Brahma; and there Vishnu, the lord of the universe, whose essence is inscrutable, assumed a perceptible form, and even he himself abided in it in the character of Brahma. Its womb, vast as the mountain Meru, was composed of the mountains; and the mighty oceans were the waters that filled its cavity. In that egg, O Brahman, were the continents and seas and mountains, the planets and divisions of the universe, the gods, the demons, and mankind. And this egg was externally invested by seven natural envelopes, or by water, air, fire, ether, and Ahankara, the origin of the elements, each tenfold the extent of that which it invested; next came the principle of Intelligence; and finally, the whole was surrounded by the indiscrete Principle: resembling thus the coconut, filled interiorly with pulp, and exteriorly covered by husk and rind."

Vishnu as the principle of immeasurable power and the quality of goodness preserves these creations through successive ages until the end of a Kalpa, or period. Then he assumes the form of Rudra and swallows up the universe. "Having thus devoured all things, and converted the world into one vast ocean, the Supreme reposes upon his mighty serpent couch amidst the deep: he awakes after a season and again, as Brahma, becomes the author of creation. Thus the one only god, Janarddana (the object of mortal adoration), takes the designation of Brahma, Vishnu, and Siva, accordingly as he creates, preserves, or destroys. Vishnu as creator, creates himself; as preserver, preserves himself; as destroyer, destroys himself at the end of all things."

The Kalpa (or day of Brahma) is the period of manifestation of a creation, and at the end thereof the Mighty One retires into himself for an equal period, after which he comes forth again in a new creation. From the method employed tocalculate time in The Vishnua Purana, figures are obtained which are overwhelming in their magnitude. For example, each year of human reckoning is divided into two parts to signify the six-month periods during which the sun is north and south of the equator. These periods are called respectively a day and a night of the gods. Twelve thousand divine years, each year consisting of 360 such days of the gods, constitute a great age (or aggregate of four lesser ages called Yugas) by which the activity of the world is measured. A thousand of these great ages are termed a day of Brahma, and fourteen lords, or Manus, rule over this vast period. Prof Wilson estimates a Kalpa to be 4,320,000,000 years, or the great day of Brahma. The life of Brahma consists of one hundred years made up of such great days, or 155,520,000,000,000 mortal years. The last great Kalpa (which is called Padma, or the lotus) closed the first half of Brahmas existence. The present Kalpa (which is called the Yaraha, or boar, Kalpa) ushers in the second half of Brahmas life.

Parasara then describes how at the beginning of the present Kalpa, Narayana (he who moves upon the waters) brought forth the earth and re-established the generations. It should he borne in mind that the beginning of a Kalpa is the reawakening of Brahma from his night of rest, and is not a complete creation; for things already exist in a suspended state, in which condition they have remained through the sleep of the gods. At the beginning of a Kalpa, therefore, the creation is in reality a reorganization of already existing elements. It is written:

"At the close of the past (or Padma) Kalpa, the divine Brahma, endowed with the quality of goodness, awoke from his night of sleep, and beheld the universe void." Realizing the earth (in the sense of cosmos) to be concealed in the depths of the great waters, Brahma assumed the figure of a huge boar, as in previous Kalpas he had taken upon himself other forms. Thus embodied he plunged into the great ocean. The earth, beholding his approach to restore her to her ancient dignity, recited a hymn in his honor in which she glorified

his powers. The mighty boar, pleased with the chanting, emitted a low murmuring sound and then lifted upon his ample tusks the globe of the world. Filled with delight at beholding the trembling boar as he rose up dripping with moisture, the sages residing continually in the sphere of the saints sang praises to the stern-eyed upholder of the universe after this fashion:

"Triumph, lord of lords supreme; Kesava, sovereign of the earth, the wielder of the mace, the shell, the discus, and the sword: cause of production, destruction, and existence. THOU ART, oh god: there is no other supreme condition, but thou. Thou, lord, art the person of sacrifice: for thy feet are the Vedas; thy tusks are the stake to which the victim is bound;

in thy teeth are the offerings; thy mouth is the altar; thy tongue is the fire; and the hairs of thy body are the sacrificial grass. Thine eyes, oh omnipotent, are day and night; thy head is the seat of all, the place of Brahma; thy name is all the hymns of the Vedas; thy nostrils are all oblations: oh thou, whose snout is the ladle of oblation; whose deep voice is the chanting of the Sama veda; whose body is the hall of sacrifice; whose joints are the different ceremonies; and whose ears have the properties of both voluntary and obligatory rites: do thou, who art eternal, who art in size a mountain, be propitious."

Quickly raising up the world the great boar placed it on the "summit" of die ocean, where it floats like a mighty vessel sustained by its expansive surface. Then "he who never wills in vain" divided the world into portions, seven in number (the planes). He likewise created the spheres of the elements and the worlds of the immortals, and prepared for the coming

of organized life which was to blossom forth again spontaneously after the Pralaya (or sleep of the great night). From this point Brahma concerns himself with the orders of mundane life and the reestablishment of his faith and order among men. (Those who desire complete details of the story are referred to The Vishnu Purana as translated from the original Sanscrit by H. H. Wilson, or the Visknupuranam in prose English translation by Manmatha Nath Dutt.) Whereas the Greek and Brahman creation myths are comparatively well-known to scholars, the subjects of Chinese cosmogony and theogony have received little or no consideration in the Western world. Hence in the study of comparative cosmologies we may consider with profit the Chinese doctrine concerning the origin and procession of the worlds. For such purpose no more ancient or venerable authority can be found in Chinese literature than the Yih King, or The Classic of Change, which is devoted to an interpretation of the trigrams of Fuh-He and which also contains a lengthy commentary by Confucius. Upon approaching this subject the student is surprised at the definite and direct treatment, reminiscent of the Greek style, that pervades the entire scheme. The purity, the simplicity, and the dignity of Chinese philosophy are a real joy to the Occidental thinker, as well as a pronounced relief from the involved and rambling procedures of Western cults.

By way of introduction, the whole pagan universe is regarded as being alive. Nowhere in it is death to be found- only continual change accompanied always by a certain sense of continual improvement and a hazy, yet intriguing, promise of ultimate accomplishment. It is unfortunate that Christian theology could not have perpetuated the magnificent pagan concept of a pulsating, vibrant universe instead of a world in which everything is dead except God in his threefold nature, man, the angelic orders, and a motley assortment of devils. In China there is a famous saying: "The living Heaven and the living Earth." The Rev. Canon McClatchie, for 25 years a Christian missionary, and a student of Chinese philosophy, writes:

"Our Christian ideas teach us that the Heaven above us, and the Earth beneath our feet, are composed of dead matter; whereas the pagans one and all, have ever regarded these as Beings endowed with life, and informed by a living soul (or 'Mind' as they generally designate it) which rules 2 and governs the world just as the soul does the human body."

Western theology ostensibly postulates the earth as simply a mass of inert substance slipped in under a falling humanity to prevent it from dropping through space indefinitely. Not so long ago theologians viewed heaven as a great dome with the constellations suspended like elaborate chandeliers from its inner surface, these lights owing their existence presumably to the fact that Divinity trusted creation so little that he feared to leave his children alone in the dark. Somewhere also in this most substantial vault was a ventilator or skylight which could be opened to permit the descent of the New Jerusalem suspended on four cables and a windlass. Invidious comparisons made by Christian writers as between pagan and Christian theoolgies demonstrate the perennial difficulty of creeds to see the beam in their own eyes; for in no respect is the heaven of theology a worthy substitute for the heaven of pagan philosophy, and nowhere among the cultured pagans do we find a concept of the universe so hopelessly inadequate as that assumed by Christendom. To exchange the oppressive atmosphere of an inanimate universe for the sweep of that animate world of the Chinese, is to escape from the prison-house of sense into the larger world of mind and spirit.

The unsolvable problem for theology is how the Creator could fashion the universe of things out of the vacuum of nothing. Such an achievement must indeed be ascribed to Divine legerdemain. Again, if nothing pervaded all eternity, then even the substance of Deity itself becomes a legitimate question. According to this theological concept, the Creator is a vast personality with abstract parts and members more or less, who in some unaccountable manner must have issued forth from the very emptiness with which he is enveloped. The element of rationality is nowhere apparent in the theory of a Creator who dwells alone forever in the void of nothingness, but who occasionally amuses himself by manifesting mud pies out of this nothingness, and then with childish fretfulness resolves them back again into the nothingness from which they came. The asseverations of the Church to the contrary notwithstanding, this primordial nothingness can scarcely be conceived of as a pliable or workable substance, nor can the procession of universes said to issue from this literal vacuum be regarded as other than a miracle which would overtax the capacity of even the Deity. And yet the Rev. McClatchie blandly assures us that "The Biblical student, for example, is aware that one of the most essential and important doctrines taught in the first verse of Genesis is the non-eternity of Matter; but, in translating a pagan Classic, he should be acquainted with the fact that all heathen systems without exception assert the eternity of Matter, and that this is one of the most prominent differences between the Cosmogony of Moses, and that of all pagan writers. If Matter is eternal it must necessarily be divine and a God; and hence it is altogether vain and fruitless to expect to find, in heathen materialism, any Being whom it is not idolatrous to worship."

The eternal duration of Matter (here regarded as synonymous with the Absolute, and in reality man's negative approach to the Absolute) is philosophy's answer to this dilemma of a spontaneous creation from nothing as maintained by theology. Modern science agrees with pagan philosophy that there is an ever-existing substance, the nature of which is as yet un- definable but which provides the common seed-ground from which grow the myriads of manifesting spheres. When the pagan thus affirmed the existence of an undying substance— Universal Root Matter—which after passing through an infinite diversity of modes ultimately returns to its primordial state, they established the Wheel of Eternity and founded the doctrine of world transmigration. Far from being "nothing" this Universal Root Matter was all things, and because it was only capable of negative definition was termed "No Thing." From this eternal Matter—not matter as defined by the physicist but rather as the ever-enduring, undifferentiated life—creation comes forth, and after manifesting the latent urges inherent in its parts ultimately returns to its primordial state. This philosophic Matter—the undefined Monad composed of an infinitude of germinal units in abstraction—offers both a rational and effective solution to the problem of First Cause, thus leaving the mind free to contemplate the processes by which this First Cause fashioned the tangible universe. This hypothesis supplies Deity with the substance of his own nature, the origin of his own divinity, and the materials with which he is to fabricate cosmos.

The Supreme God of China, like the first deities of Greece and Egypt, must be this ever-enduring Matter to which is applied the term Tien, It is the inner heavens in the sense of quality, and the outer heavens in the sense of quantity—the Universal Parent, the infinite capacity, the undifferentiated Cause, the ever-flowing fountain. From the nature of this universalized divinity emanated the organized creation by an orderly progression. To begin with, there came forth two principles called Airs, by which this universal essence opposes itself to itself, and in the field of this opposition establishes the generations. These two, called Heaven and Earth, are to be understood as actuating Spirit and receptive Matter. Their proper names are the Great Father and the Great Mother, which together form a vast anthropomorphic deity whom the Chinese call Shang-te, or the Sky Emperor, Shang-te, the heavenly ruler of the celestial empire, is revered through his positive aspect (Heaven) and is therefore termed the Emperor of Heaven. His descendant upon the earth, the human emperor, is called the Son of Heaven and rules by right of the authority vested in him by his Sky Father. In his aspect of Heaven, Shang-te consists of a triad which is termed Heaven, Earth, and Man. The third member of this trinity is the world emperor who, as a sort of Platonic monad, contains within himself all mankind. The elements of the Brahmanic system—primary matter, spirit, visible substance, and time—have their parallel in the Chinese Tien,

Heaven, Earth, and Pwan-koo, which together are termed Shang-te, the Creator.

As the Great Father (Heaven) consists of a triad of qualities, so the Great Mother (Earth) also manifests three natures which complement the three principles of the Great Father, resulting in what are called the eight trigrams or figures, of which Kheen (the Father) and Khwan (the Mother) are the origin. In the Chinese Cabala, Kheen, the active principle, is symbolized by three unbroken lines, and Khwan, the receptive principle, by three broken lines. These lines are arranged in six other patterns, called respectively the three sons and three daughters. In the more profound interpretation of this philosophy Chaos is the eternal Deity or divine Matter which causes to exist within itself two Airs, one termed subtle and the other coarse. The subtle Air is spirit and its name is Yang; the coarse Air is matter and its name is Yin. From the intimate mingling of these two Airs all the phenomena of generation have their origin.

In terms of Platonism, these two Airs would be the rational and the irrational souls respectively which, as Confucius declares, are never discoverable separate from each other. It is possible, therefore, to divide diagrammatically the Chinese universe into three spheres corresponding to the three worlds of Pythagoras; i. e., the Supreme World, the Superior World, and the Inferior World, all of which exist within the nature of absolute and unchanging Matter, which is both the first and the last, the unborn and the undying. Thus within the great Egg of Chaos exist three moving agents which are the spirits of the world. The first, which is synonymous with the will of Deity, is called Le, or Fate, and is the driving power that moves all things to their predestined end. The second, Wisdom, is Shang-te, which is referred to as a horse upon which Fate rides to the accomplishment of its ends. The third, Activity, is called the body of Shang-te and is ruled over by Pwan-koo, the Demi- urgus or Lord of the World, the Protogonas or First Man.

Wherever Matter is considered to be an eternal element, and manifestation a periodic blossoming forth of the creative energies of this ever-existing state, we have the law of Kalpas, or successive creations. In the Chinese system the Yuen (Kalpa) is considered analogous to the natural year, which therefore becomes its symbol. As the year is divided into twelve periods, corresponding to the months and the signs of the zodiac, so the Yuen is divided into twelve divisions called Hwuy, each consisting of 10,800 years. The four seasons become symbolic of the four grand periods which correspond to the Hindu Yugas, or divisions of life—birth, growth, maturity, and decay—the Four Horsemen of the Apocalypse. Thus in the period termed spring cosmos comes forth into manifestation. During the summer the phenomena of growth and expansion take place; during the autumn the fruitage of effort is reaped; and during the winter the retirement of cosmos into its primordial nature is consummated. The spring of the world is symbolized by the color blue, the summer by red, the autumn by white, and the winter by black. Four great kings or regents, corresponding to the four Maharajahs of the Brahmans, each painted the respective color of his season, rule over the cardinal angles of the heavens. In their midst sits the great "Yellow Emperor"—the Brahman Mahat or Intellect, the Mind of the Universe.

The twelve signs of the zodiac are divided into groups of three to represent these seasons. The twelfth, first, and second signs (which are to the north) form the winter season, with the first sign due north. The third, fourth, and fifth signs (which are to the east) form the spring season, with the fourth sign due east. The sixth, seventh and eighth signs (which are to the south) form the summer season, with the seventh sign due south. The ninth, tenth, and eleventh signs (which are to the west) form the autumn season, with the tenth sign due

west. It is evident that this diagrammatic arrangement, which resembles a horoscope, is a figure by which may be estimated not only the duration of world periods, but of every order of creation, greater and lesser. Thus the life of every atom is a Kalpa; likewise the life of man, the life of the race, the life of the planet, the life of the solar system, the life of the universe, and the life of cosmos itself. As will be noted, throughout all manifestation each of these Kalpas is a fractional part, in turn, of a still greater one, until at last time—which is their basis and indispensable to their existence—is so merged into eternity as to be incapable of further differentiation.

Every twenty-four hours the whole cycle is re-enacted in mortal time. The smallest Kalpa may be but the fraction of a second's duration, while the greatest may endure for countless milleniums. While in time and magnitude these periods differ widely, still the diagram is a proper symbol of them all; for regardless of their magnitude all obey the same principle of periodicity and manifest the same general mathematical characteristics of form and progression. For example, the rotation of the earth upon its axis causes one of the twelve signs of the zodiac to rise sequentially every two hours upon the eastern horizon, so that the twelve complete their revolution in twenty-four hours and thus make a minor Kalpa, or period. In its revolution around the sun the earth also passes through the twelve signs of the zodiac in twelve months, thus constituting a greater Kalpa. Again, through the precession of the equinoxes the sun retrogrades through the twelve signs of the zodiac in approximately 25,000 years, which is therefore called a great sidereal year, and by which a still greater Kalpa is established. From such well-known illustrations we may gain some slight idea of the complexity of celestial dynamics as disclosed by the principle of Kalpas.

In the first sign (which is due north) the Chinese universe had its genesis. The Universal Power (Heaven) came into manifestation and a new day of wandering began. In the second sign the earth issued forth, and in the third sign (which is the first of the spring months) Pwan-koo appeared. This Kalpa then continued and the generations came forth, and through the spring, summer, and autumn months lived, reached maturity, and entered upon the inevitable decay. At last in the twelfth sign (which is the first of the winter months) came the great Deluge, which marked the close of that Kalpa. All living creatures were destroyed except Pwan-koo, who is the undying or unchanging creature. After a period of rest the new Kalpa was ushered in and Pwan-koo in the third period came forth again to be the progenitor of human life.

In this lesser reappearance (in which the Kalpa of the earth rather than the universe is signified) the principle of Pwan-koo became Fuh-he, the first Emperor. It is said that the previous Kalpa was destroyed because of its wickedness, but the Archetypal Man with his family—the eight diagrams of the Yih King—was preserved through the Deluge to perpetuate creation. We are informed by the secret doctrine that Pwan-koo is the Sky Man, or the Monad of human generation. From Pwan-koo descend upon threads (as in the Platonic system) a number of subordinate powers called by the Brahmans the Manus, or the First Men. There are fourteen such Manus to a great Kalpa, and one comes forth at the beginning of each round (or day of manifestation) and also at the establishment of each root race. Thus the Noah of the Jews is the Vaisvata Manu of the Brahmans. He is the undying man whose progeny gradually increases to the dignity of a race.

In the present cycle Pwan-koo, the Eternal Man, came forth in the form of Fuh-he, the Manu, to establish the new humanity. Hence Pwan-koo is Adam and Fuh-he is Noah or the second Adam, who preserved the generations through the Deluge which marked the close of a lesser Kalpa. Fuh-he, while generally regarded as the first Emperor of the imperial line, is really an avatar or incarnation of the Grand Man. His color is blue like that of Krishna, and as Vishnu came forth at the beginning of his worlds in the form of a fish, so we are told that Fuh-he, the indigo Emperor, had the body and tail of a fish. A similar philosophic basis exists for the legends of Dagon, Oannes, and the fish-gods of antiquity; yes, even Jonah, who in the third sign (or period) was cast out of the whale's belly.

An analysis of these various cosmological and theogonic systems shows the ancient pagan philosophers to have been unified in their concept of the principles by which the universe was called forth out of the Abyss of Absolute Matter. Though the natural differences of terminology are obvious, and though the allegories have taken on local color, still their common underlying truths are evident even to the uninitiated. These ancient sages have thus met the exact requirements prescribed by Socrates in the First Alcibiades for all instructors: namely, that "they must agree together and not differ." That which men know is the basis of their agreement; that which they do not know is the cause of their disagreement. That sages, widely separated geographically and with diverse environments and temperaments, should arrive at the same general conclusions attests the accuracy of their findings. Being for the greater part superficial-minded, modern thinkers do not arrive at any such unanimity of agreement, but grope their way in a maze of contradictions which they impart to the young under the guise of education. Thus in their frantic quest of the new or the spectacular, modern philosophers fabricate theories expressive more of the bizarre than of rationality.

While all speculation regarding the infinite may be regarded as inconsequential when compared with the necessity of solving the problems of daily life, such rumination is essential to right perspective; for by it the mortal creature is raised from the state of some eyeless earthworm to the estate of a participator in the whole pageantry of universal procedure. In the past man has been oppressed by his own sense of inferiority.

During the Dark Ages it was presumptuous to the point of heresy to speculate either upon the eternal laws by which he was governed, or the nature of that vast power which brooded over him and measured both his comings in and his going out.

Today this bogey of fear persists only in a few isolated districts where the earthworm still wriggles in his native habitat, declaring that there is no sun because he cannot see it I The world is now coming to realize that thought is not heresy, but that not to think is to live in a concept of existence equivalent to the grossest blasphemy. There is nothing terrible or vengeful about the universe, nor does it turn disdainfully from the honest searcher into its mysteries. Creation stands forth unafraid and welcomes analysis of all its parts. It is said in Holy Writ that none shall look upon the God of Israel and live.

But Israel's God was the Lord of another day, and woe unto him who shall turn back from this new day to worship the irate gods of yesterday; for he shall perish from the narrowness of his own vision!

The God of tomorrow stands forth in all its majesty of suns and moons and stars. Its extent is from space to space, and eternity alone confines it. Man, gazing into the eyes of man, beholds therein his Maker. His Creator sings to him with the voice of the wilderness, and descends upon him from the stars that spangle the heavens by night. This God is not hidden behind flowing draperies, nor are his ministers avenging angels. Unmoved by the passing of ages he contemplates the worlds that are his substance, and through his own mind in man seeks to probe the depth of his own reality. This Vast One has written his law in the heavens where they shall endure long after earthly codes have been erased from the memory of man. This God manifests his will in the endless progression and change by which things are moved from Then to Now and from Now to Then. This Universal Creator fears not man's effort to understand him; telescopes and microscopes may scan his features without offence. For what is the quest of knowledge but the God in man seeking the God in Alii 3 God is; man is. Therefore, man is God and God is man. But before man may consciously enter into his divinity he must gaze upon himself in the All without fear and recognize himself in the All gazing back without hate. Steadfastly and unafraid, the rational soul thus gazes upon those glorious beings whose radiant natures are that mystical light which is the life of the beholding soul.

## THE PYTHAGOREAN TETRACTYS

From the contemplation of the order and progression of the Numbers out of the Monad may be discovered the true relationship between natures and their Cause. He who understands this mystery is of all men the wisest. Numbers are the keys to the flow of Universal Energy.

# XXII

❦

# The Druid Ceremony of Stonehenge

The Grand Conventional Festival of the Britons
From "The Costume of the Original Inhabitants of the British Islands," by Samuel Rush Meyrick, LL.D. and F.S.A., and Charles Hamilton Smith, Esq. William Bulmer and Co., London, 1815. (The following being a description and reproduction of Plate XI, Ed.)

The superstition of the Druids corresponded with that of the world in general, not only in its theology, but also in the ceremonies by which the deities were worshipped. The penetrating and accurate Caesar, marking this similarity, does not hesitate to affirm that they adored Mercury, Apollo, Mars, Jupiter, and Minerva, adding, de his eandem fere, quam reliquae gentes habent opinionem — "their opinion respecting these nearly coincides with that of other nations." Dionysius informs us that the rites of Bacchus were duly celebrated in the British Islands; and Strabo cites the authority of Artemidorus, that "in an island close to Britain, Ceres and Proserpine are venerated with rites similar to the orgies of Samothrace."

As it is then a historical fact that the mythology and rites of the Druids were the same in substance with those of the Greeks and Romans, as well as of other nations which came under their observation, we shall have pretty good authorities for the representation of them, if, with the ancient Bardic poems in our hands, we attentively scrutinize the mythological sculptures of the Egyptians to assist in the composition.

This plate therefore represents Stonehenge, the Gwaith Emreis — "ambrosial work" — of the ancient Britons, in its original splendour, and decked out for the celebration of the Helio-arkite ceremonies. Stone circles in Ireland are called Caer Sidi; the British Bards apply the same appellation. But this is also the name of the zodiac, and as these temples were constructed on astronomical principles, they either represented that celestial zone, solar cycles of sixty and thirty stones, or the lunar one of nineteen.

But these temples had reference to terrestrial as well as celestial objects of adoration, and therefore typified the ark, which Taliesin particularly terms Caer Sidi, "the enclosure of the just man." As that sacred vessel contained all the animated world, so this its representative was, in reference to it, called "the mundane circle of stones."

This Mawr Cor Cyvoeth, "great sanctuary of dominion," is represented as it probably appeared "on the morn after May-eve, when the song of the Cuckoo convened the appointed dance over the green," when "it was rendered complete by the rehearsal" of ancient lore, the chanting of hymns in honor of the British divinities, and the interpretation of their will by "the birds of the mountain." At this time the huge stones of the oval adytum, which represented the mundane egg, "were covered with veils," on which were delineated the history of "the dragon king." On the principal trilithon of these appeared "the gliding king with expanding wings, before whom the fair one retreats," or Jupiter in the form of a dragon about to violate Proserpine and become the father of Bacchus. On another, the serpent entwining two phalli,

*The Grand Ceremonial of Stonehenge*

representing the sun entering the sign Gemini. On a third, again, the serpent appeared between the sun and moon, showing that both are affected by eclipses. Similar devices were exhibited on others. Thus was portrayed "Hu the distributor," as presiding in the mundane circle of stones—"the glaring Hu, the sovereign of Heaven, the gliding king, the dragon, the victorious Beli, Lord of the honey island of Britain." And now we see "rapidly moving in the course of the sky, in circles, in uneven numbers, Druids and Bards unite in celebrating their (dragon) leader."

Taliesin describes the preparation for the solemn periodical rite performed on this day—namely, the removal of the shrine out of the cell in the Arkite island, which seems to have been surrounded only at high water. In his account, we may remark a ritual observation of the time of flood (alluding to the deluge); a fanatical rite of piercing the thigh so as to draw blood; and a ceremonial adorning of the sacred rock, which at that time was to display the countenance of the Arkite god. Again, this was done at the dawn, so that the Helio-arkite god might be seen coming forth from the cell at the precise hour of the sun's rising. That rock was the chief place of tranquillity, for there the divinity was supposed to reside—excepting at the time of the solemn procession. And lastly, this patriarchal god, the supreme proprietor, was he who received his family, exiled from the world, into his ark or sanctuary.

Aneurin thus details the different days' ceremonies: "In the festival on the eve of May they celebrate the praise of the holy ones (the helio and lunar-arkite deities) in the presence of the purifying fire, which was made to ascend on high. On Tuesday they wear their dark garments" (in allusion to the darkness of the ark during the patriarch's confinement). "On Wednesday they purified their fair attire" (typifying Noah's restoration to light). "On Thursday they truly performed their due rites. On Friday the victims were conducted round the circles. On Saturday their united exertions were displayed without the circular dome. On Sunday the men with red blades were conducted round the circle, and on Monday the banquet was served."

In the festival of May-eve, however, the more immediate rites of the lunar-arkite goddess took place, as those of the solar divinity did in the morning. Thus Taliesin, speaking of the cows which drew her chest, exclaims: "Eminent is the virtue of the free course when the dance is performed. Loud is the horn of the lustrator when the kine move in the evening." But from the Egyptian sculptures we are led to suppose that her shrine also accompanied that of the Helio-arkite god on the following morning.

On this glorious morn, the Druids welcomed the rising sun—the Rhwyv Trydar, or "leader of the din"—with frantic shouts of joy, accompanied by vocal hymns and instrumental music. During this, "the priests within the adytum moved sideways round the sanctuary, whilst the sanctuary was earnestly invoking the gliding king." Just behind the altar appears the presiding Druid, "with the circle of ruddy gems on his golden shield," the image of the Caer Sidi. This he occasionally struck with the thyrsus, or bush-topped spear, to have probably the same effect as the horrid din with which the heathens pretended to save the moon at the hour of her eclipse.

He presides in the bloody area of the altar, about to perform his duty in his character of Ysadawr, or sacrificer, to slay the victim. Behind him are his attendants, "overshading the Bardic mysteries with the banners of the Bards." Near at hand is "the spotted cow," in whose collar are entwined "the stalks of the plants about to be drenched with gore, which procured blessings." On a serene day she bellowed—as a warning presage of the deluge—and afterwards

She was boiled" or sacrificed. To the left appears "a Bard seated on a grey steed as governor of the festival." "A thick-maned steed is under the thigh of the fair youth, his shield light and broad hangs upon the slender courser. His blue and unspotted weapon (hasta pura) was the assuager of tumult," being the emblem of peace. "This spear of quartered ash he sometimes extended from his hand over the stone cell of the sacred fire," as he rode about the temple.

Conspicuous in the center stands the "bull or brindled ox, with the thick head-band having seven score knobs on his collar." This animal was the symbol of the patriarch in his character of husbandman. It was attended by three priests termed Garan hir, lofty cranes, from their attendance also on the water mysteries. Hence this deity was called Tarw Trigaranau, "Tarvos Trigaranos," and sculptured with three cranes on his back. This animal in the Triads is termed "The yellow ox of the spring," in commemoration of the sign Taurus, into which the sun entered at the season when the Druids celebrated the great arkite mysteries; the brown ox which stopped the channel, from the promise which Noah obtained that no future deluge would occur; and the brindled ox with the thick headband. Such is the "animal which the silver-headed ones" or hoary Druids protect."

In front of this is another symbol of the divinity, "the eagle raised aloft in the sky in the path of Granwyn" or Apollo (the ecliptic) "before the pervading sovereign or rising sun."

Such appears the temple within; but Taliesin asks, "Who approaches the Caer with white dogs, (Druids,) and large horns?" We must therefore examine the grand procession.

First of this band appears the divining Bard with his hudywydd or magic wand, followed by the Bards striking their tuneful harps: whose number was sometimes "seven score." Next follows the shrine of Ceridwen, or "curvatures of Kyd (the ark) which passed the grievous waters, stored with corn, and borne aloft by serpents" or attendant priests. On the preceding eve this shrine had been drawn by cows and attended by torch-bearers, whence Ceres was represented as having wandered over the earth with lighted torches. Now it is attended only by three priests, the Hierophant who represented "the great Creator;" "one bearing a torch" who personated the sun, and the herald, who as the especial minister of the goddess was regarded as a symbol of the moon.

Next comes "the house" or shrine of the Helio-arkite god, "recovered from the swamp," which is preceded by "the assembled train dancing after their manner, and singing in cadence, some with garlands" of ivy "on their brows," others with cornute caps. "These are the oxen of Hu the mighty, with part of his chain," the symbol of his confinement, and his five attendants which we now behold with golden harness of active flame." These have drawn the Avanc or huge monster from the lake, during which the attendants sing a piece of music still known to a few persons in Wales, called "Caine yr Ychain Banawg," which was an imitation of the lowing of the oxen, and the rattling of chains.

The hunched oxen which the Druids employed in this rite were probably of the finest breed which the country afforded, but distinguished either by the size of their horns, or some peculiar mark, and set apart for sacred use. They are now drawing the Avanc to where Taliesin intimates the diluvian patriarch found rest, viz. the spot on which the spotted cow was sacrificed. Originally three oxen drew the Avanc, and probably represented the sons of the patriarch, but as Ham incurred the displeasure of his father, so one is said to have been unequal to the task, and consequently left behind. But "the two oxen of distinguished honour put their necks under the car of the lofty one—majestic were they, with equal pace they moved to the festival." Thus we see the Avanc was the car or shrine of the Diluvian god, which was drawn from the lake—or representative deluge—to his temples and sanctuaries upon firm ground, by which he was invested with the empire of the recovered earth. These yoked oxen also refer to the deity himself; for Taliesin, speaking in his name, says, "I was subjected to the yoke for my affliction, but commensurate was my confidence; the world had no existence were it not for my progeny."

"This house, recovered from the swamp, is surrounded with crooked horns," some of the dancers before carrying the double paterae, and those who follow sounding "loud the horns of the lustrator." It is also followed by others bearing "crooked swords in honour of the mighty king of the plains," and the whole is closed by the "circular revolutions performed by the attendants and white bands in graceful extravagance," and those "with curved swords and clattering shields."

On the rampart surrounding the temple are assembled the representatives of the people—the heads of tribes and families—with their standard bearers, while the people themselves, who, as Caesar says, "nullo adhibetur concilio," were never admitted into the assemblies, are viewing the procession in groups on the plains.

# XXIII

⊛

# Mathematics, the Master Science

THE Pythagoreans defined mathematics as the science of magnitudes and multitudes; for by its principles might be determined not only the number of constituent parts, but also the degree to which one part differs from another in length, breadth, thickness, or weight. Mathematics also makes it possible to compute the interval in time between incidents, and in distance between bodies and places. It was regarded as the divine science because order was established by its means throughout the nature of being. All the arts and sciences depend upon this order for their survival. History, for example, is simply a chain of incidents whose order is preceded through arbitrary sequences of time. If this element of time is removed and the incidents are not preserved in chronological order, history becomes valueless, for the proper relationship between episodes is thus detroyed. Only by mathematics, then, is it possible to construct the chain of sequences that will show the definite relationship between a cause and its effect, an action and its reaction, a beginning and its end.

Antedating the age of history is the age of fable, from which the time sequence is largely absent, with the resultant confusion concerning theological origins; for the creative processes that required hundreds of millions of years to consummate their work were so thrown out of perspective that up to the last century Christendom actually believed the earth to have been fashioned a little over six thousand years ago. Fortunately the laws of Nature were their own historiographers, and we find the records of countless ages written in the enduring substances of fossil and geologic strata to refute the erroneous conclusions of men.

To the trained thinker mathematics is obviously limited to the realm of form, or to those departments of manifestation where numbers as diversified elements exist suspended from common Unity, which is their monad and which was termed by the Pythagoreans Number. As all individual minds arc suspended from the principle of Mind, so all numbers are sus¬

pended from the principle of Number. Number is consequently divine and founded in the archetypal sphere, from whence its radiations (or principles) descend into the sensible world, there to manifest as the exactitudes of mathematical procedure. By some, Number was considered synonymous with God in that the first motion of Deity establishes Number, which becomes the mode whereby the magnitude and duration of that motion are rendered conceivable. Hence motion does not exist unless the cause is aware of its own extension or induces awareness in the substances through which the extension is taking place. Motion and Number, therefore, are of kindred nature and form the monad from which is suspended all diversified activity—which is Number in motion, or the numbers.

From the fathomless and unknown beginning the principles of mathematics existed as a divine, unnamed reality. The man accredited with its discovery simply extracted from the infinite the principles of universal order and christened them the science of mathematics. This new science thereupon became a hypothetical monad, and diversity took place within it, arithmetic, algebra, geometry, trigonometry, and calculus becoming the vehicles of its expression in the sphere of mental activity.

These are the lesser monads suspended from the body of the parent monad. As gold exists in the dark earth long before the miner's pick bares it to the light of day, so all the truths revealed to man in the past and to be discovered by him in the future are eternal, and as divine principles were the media in the beginning by which the Creator flowed into Being from the eternal state of Not-Being. In its exact sense, Truth is therefore the way of God in all things and truths the ways of God in particular things. The forms of learning which mortals term science, philosophy, and theology are simply aspects of divine procedure on the physical, mental, and emotional planes respectively. As Number becomes numbers, so Truth becomes truths and the subordinate monads suspended from Truth become that which is real upon each of the countless levels of existence. Wherever one of these facts is established, it becomes the monad or radiant center from which flows forth a number of secondary agencies. The moment this lesser establishment and flow take place, mathematics is again manifested. From the monad of theology, for example, are suspended the religions, of which there are not less than seven major bodies.

The flow of theology into any one of its religions establishes a new vortex, thereby giving expression to another suspended element of mathematics. Each of these major divisions of religion becomes, in turn, the monad of a still greater order of diversity, a notable example being the Christian faith whose branches number several hundred. Each motion of Truth out from itself toward that infinite diversity which is the inevitable circumference of Unity is thus measured, determined, and direction alized by Number moving through its own vehicles— numbers and their infinite combinations. The Pythagoreans termed the number 1 as the apex of the pyramid of numbers, since it is the first manifestation of Number. It is Unity established in place, for in its perfect and abstract sense Unity is unlimited by place or condition. Thus, Number that is all-pervading becomes the 1—the first numeral to stand alone. Being the least of diversity, the numeral 1 is therefore the spirit of the numbers; for like spirit it is universal life limited to the sphere of generation, or the apex of the pyramid of phenomena. About the central axis of the 1, or Tree of Being, moves the whole order of the numbers, which are suspended from the 1 even as the 1 itself is suspended from the principle of Unity, of which it is the primary mathematical manifestation. Since the 1—which signifies the wholeness of the numbers— is equivalent to Divine Unity, it is apparent that all the other numerals are fractional parts of this primordial wholeness, and not multiples of the 1 as might first be supposed. Thus, 2 is in reality Unity considered in terms of halves, 3 is Unity considered in terms of thirds, a billion is Unity considered in terms of billionths; for the imperishable whole, which can never increase or decrease, is always the sum of conceived or conceivable parts. In philosophy the 2 cannot be greater than the 1; for in that event, spirit would exceed the sum of itself and an amount would be greater than its own stated quantity. If the 1 is the symbol of the All in its least conditioned state, the 2 cannot be the All doubled, but is rather to be understood as the halving of the Absolute within its own nature whereby the All becomes manifested in the least number of parts of itself.

Diversity, as symbolized by the numbers, can exist temporarily within the nature of Unity, yet the number of the parts can never exceed their own sum, for the integrity of the whole must be preserved. By philosophic addition, therefore, the sum of all the parts (or numerals) must always be the 1, or wholeness. Likewise when parts (or numerals) are subtracted from parts the remainder must be 1, or wholeness, save when the whole is subtracted from the whole; in which event the cipher, or Absolute, is left, for when the conditioned is subtracted from the conditioned the Unconditioned remains. When parts (or numerals) are multiplied by parts, the product cannot exceed the 1, or wholeness; and when parts (or numerals) are divided by parts, the quotient must be the 1, or wholeness. The order of the numerical pyramid is thus revealed, for from the apex, which is wholeness, it diverges to the base, which consists of an infinity of fragmentary parts. This is the arcane significance of Herodotus* strange statement to the effect that the Egyptians in building their pyramids commenced at the top and worked downward—a method which, because it is an architectonic absurdity, deary demonstrates that Herodotus wrote history with an ulterior motive. Thus while the prestige of history may have suffered at the hands of this first historian, the body of philosophy has been enriched by his labors.

As the numbers are all contained within the numeral 1, so the pyramid is contained within its own apex, from which it flows down to mingle itself with the rock upon which it stands. In this manner is established the philosophic fact that Unity is synonymous with Cause and diversity with effect. As the alchemist employed chemical terms to symbolize the various elements of life, so the Pythagoreans gave to the creative sphere the appellation of Number, and to the creation which issued therefrom, numbers. The Divine Mathematics dealt not with sums calculated upon paper nor carried in the mind, but rather with the order and arrangement of corporeal bodies, their mutual relationships, and the proximity of each to its own cause. Though any one of the arts or sciences is capable of thus becoming the outer garment of the secret doctrine, the various Greek schools employed particularly mathematics, music, and astronomy in this manner. Like Herodotus, they frequently confused the elements of the science itself in order that the esoteric principles—which were often diametrically opposed to the exoteric application—might be presented to such as were able to interpret the symbolism.

Through mathematics, then, is set forth the system of philosophic monadology, the principles of which were arcanely hinted at by Leucippus and Democritus. From the doctrine of monads sprang the theory of atoms, which are simply these archetypal unities of wholeness vested in matter and established as the principles of substance. These atoms exist in concatenated order from the infinitesimally small to the unmeasurably great, each of the greater being compounded according to atomic law from a prescribed number to the lesser. An important point is established when the question is asked, "What do all of these atoms have in common, leaving out of consideration the factors of size and order?" Two things: their participation in the all-inclusive atom composed of their sum; the condition of individual wholeness which each atom occupies in relationship to itself, though to greater unities it occupies the relationship of a part.

This quality of wholeness, which is the common property of these diversified and otherwise irreconcilable bodies, becomes as it were, their common denominator. Though wholeness is present in all natures it is not an attribute of natures. This wholeness is an archetypal quality—an attribute of Deity. Regardless of the nature of its expression, every activity, quality,

or condition is essentially a wholeness. This wholeness is made manifest by a division within itself whereby its nature becomes a mass of innumerable fragments, each of the fractions partaking of the quality resident in the original wholeness, and manifesting it through the wholeness of its own fractional part. For example, Man is a wholeness possessing and manifesting certain rational qualities and characteristics. This archetypal wholeness, flowing into diversity, breaks up to form men. Each individual, by virtue of his own inherent wholeness, shares in the virtues resident in the wholeness of the archetype; and by virtue of his participation in the one causal nature moves in the rhythm of the archetype, which archetype manifests through such laws as polarity, generation, rationality, morality, and such other ideals and practices as are the common property of all men.

Let us take the principle of unities, or wholes, and apply it to the subject of duration. Man forever struggles against the illusion of time. He views the marching years as relentless enemies conspiring to prevent achievement; his eyes forever watch the clock's swinging pendulum which ticks his life away. In the third part of King Henry VI, the monarch indulges in this soliloquy:

See the minutes, how they run, How many make the hour full complete; How many hours bring about the day; How many days finish up the year; How many years a mortal man may live. The great expanse of duration, in which like a great sea all existense is immersed, is divided by the unenlightened into three hypothetical intervals: the past, the present, and the future. These intervals were personified by the Greeks, who called them the Fates and invested them with power over the destinies of all mortal creatures—or more correctly, the mortal parts of all creatures. To most men the past is a period of vain regrets, the present a sterile struggle against apparently insurmountable obstacles, and the future that fourth-dimensional vista where alone dreams come true.

Thus hope, faith, and charity come into their own; for with his hope posited in tomorrow, his faith supporting him in today, and with charity toward yesterday, man faces the illusion of years, at the end of which Cronus (Time) awaits to devour his own progeny. Every moment both marks the beginning of a new period of Time and also the close of some expiring interval. Upon this intricate background of minutes, hours, and days, humanity fashions strange workmanships—the products of its imagings and its imaginings.

Time is both a creator and a destroyer, for it is a perpetual beginning as well as an end to something. In Time all that is false shall pass away, and in Time all that is true shall be realized and established. Time is the acid test, and only that which can survive its ravages is worthy to be termed permanent. Time has dominion over all that is untrue, unreal or perverse.

One by one the fallacies of life fall beneath the reaping scythe of Time, and are garnered into the capacious bin of oblivion. In Time all forms must die; in Time all worlds must cease; in Time the very universe will be resolved back into its primal state; in Time are contained all beginnings and all ending, for Time is the lord of the illusion of beginnings and endings.

Time is the master of the mortal sphere and all that exists within it. Time preserves for a little while the perishable only that ultimately it shall perish more completely.

Within form, however, there is that which is without beginning and without end; something that laughs at the years and mocks destroying Time. This enduring quality is thai wholeness which rejoices in the annihilation of those forms which are the diversity temporarily established within the sphere of this all-containing Unity. From the viewpoint of wholeness, the more that is destroyed the more remains, until when everything has been destroyed, all remains; for as the unity of Number is broken up by numbers, so the unity of life is broken up by forms. Hence, by destroying form, Time restores life to its perfect wholeness.

Mortal creatures come and go in kaleidoscopic diversity; yet in the midst of this ever-changing scene is an intangible but all-pervading and inclusive permanence—the divine Reality, the Self, the perfect Wholeness. Unborn and undying, the Self is neither old nor young. Its condition never changes; for though all things pass away, it endures. It is wholeness, and being wholeness is sufficient unto itself; for that which is complete is sufficient and that which is all is enough for itself. As Time is the measure of parts, it cannot affect that which is superior to the existence of parts and which consequently knows no Time.

Time is recognized and measured by the markings it leaves upon the face of ephemeral being. Though it deeply scores the surface of all material life, it can have no effect upon the enduring nature of Reality; for wholeness, being wholeness, includes Time. The parts can have but a fractional share of the attributes of the whole, but the whole partakes of the attributes of the parts in fullness and perfect harmony. Hence the whole is the master of its parts, which must bow before its dictum and are powerless to force their fragmentary agencies upon the structure of wholeness itself.

Those who live material lives—who think and feel in terms of matter and estimate permanence upon the basis of corporeal substance—must forever fear Time which sooner or later will wrest their possessions from them and scar their personality with its blows. But those who have risen above the illusion of years realize, as they gaze upon the immeasurable vistas of eternity, that the law of the spirit is permanence and the law of matter is change. Time may well be the measure of corporeal being, but what is Time to that which remains unmoved and against which impotently pound the waves of interval!

Numbers partake of the may a of diversity, for they are infinite in their combinations, and their progression is limited only by the rational capacity of the mathematician. So we find the Pythagorean declaring the monad, or the 1, to signify Reality; but the duad, or the 2, illusion. Coincident with division, the ephemeral state is manifested; for the laws of polarity for which the 2 stands limit the generating soul to the narrow confines of definite procedure, which procedure at best can but inadequately represent the essentially unimpeded flowing of the causal nature.

An attempt has been made to demonstrate that Time is the mysterious fourth dimension so long sought by philosophers. The proponents of this theory declare that it is impossible to completely isolate any existing object from the element of Time, and that the failure to include this clement destroys the con- gruity of the object under consideration. Time is a phase or manifestation of place; for that which because of its abstract nature cannot be said to exist in place may, however, be localized in Time. For example, the moment an incident is closed or a personality is dissipated, it may be considered to have disappeared from place but to be still definitely situated in Time. Time is an elastic quality which is ever great enough to include both place and occurrence. Therefore an object may be declared to require four descriptive properties in order to render it intelligible to the senses: length, breadth, thickness, and place. Neither Time nor place, however, can be conceived of as actually fulfilling the conventional requirements of dimensions; and in approaching the problem of the fourth dimension, it is evident that we are attempting its solution with a three-dimensional consciousness. Hence our methods of approach must necessarily be through hypothesis and negative procedure.

Let us assume two cubes of the same size to be composed of spirit and matter respectively. Cube A (spirit) is the causal nature of cube B (its material vehicle). The all-permeating quality of cube A permits it to occupy the same place that is occupied by cube B, so that by virtue of their composition both bodies may occupy the same place at the same time. But cube

A and cube B are not the same; consequently, an interval exists between them—the same type of interval that might exist between two mentalities, one of which is highly evolved and the other of comparatively negligible development. The interval between spirit and matter is, therefore, an interval of quality, and when so considered may be as incalculably great as is the interval between God and man. How shall we measure this interval; how shall we accurately ascertain the distance between two bodies occupying precisely the same place at the same time, yet separated by a chasm so vast that the one may be totally unaware of the existence of the other?

Throughout creation there are distances which are purely qualitative. In estimating the nature of an object, length, breadth, thickness, and quality reveal more of its nature than do length, breadth, thickness, and time or place; for both time and place are environmental attributes, while quality is purely intrinsic. It is not a justifiable inference, however, that quality is the fourth dimension, but rather that the interval of quality is the field whose true dimensions, proportions, and conditions can only be estimated or measured by a fourth tool of the reason—an instrument akin to reason itself. In addition to the properties of length, breadth, and thickness, every object has also a quality extension toward the nature of perfect Good.

This quality extension comes under the influence of Time only to the degree that quality determines permanence and Time measures the degree of impermanence.

The theory of relativity, by establishing the fallibility of present methods of estimating the relationships between objects, proves that all conclusions concerning celestial dynamics must be relative, or true only in part. Relating two bodies to each other is a comparatively simple problem, however, to that of relating an object which is in place to a spiritual principle

which is universal. If a spiritual principle is omnipresent at all times, then no object can ever be moved so that it either approaches closer to or retires farther from spirit; for spirit has its center everywhere and its circumference nowhere. The interval between spirit (cube A) and matter (cube B) is, there- fore, hardly a proper subject for relativity, but must be regarded rather as a lapse of quality. In other words, it is an interval which exists without distance, since distance cannot exist unless both objects under consideration occupy place. To attempt to establish distance between these two opposites of quality represented by spirit and matter would be like standing in a certain spot and asking the question, "How far is it from here to everywhere?" The correct answer, "As far as here is less than everywhere," is almost as baffling to the faculties of comprehension as the question. Such an interval can only be properly surveyed and subdivided by one fortunate enough to possess the fourth-dimensional consciousness, which would enable him to travel through the quality interval with the same facility that we pass through the place interval. The popular fallacy that God dwells in the furthermost angle of the heavens and must be hymned in triple fortissimo arises from the dimension limitations of human consciousness, for the mind untrained in abstractions, confuses the interval of quality with the interval of distance. The mind concludes that if evil be near, good—its opposite—consequently must be far removed, and the distance between them can be estimated by a highly spiritualized yardstick.

Thus distance may be defined as the interval between two given bodies, places, incidents, or conditions. The methods employed to measure these intervals differ, according to the nature of the intervals themselves. For example, the interval between bodies or places may be estimated by the arbitrary standards of distance; the interval between incidents by the arbitrary standards of time, and the interval between conditions by the arbitrary standards of quality. When limited to the interval between physical objects or places, distance can be calculated with reasonable accuracy, for men have established definite laws of measurement by common agreement. Such methods of computation, however, are wholly inadequate in die almost unexplored spheres of consciousness and mind, concerning the natures of which most men differ widely one from the other.

It has been said that the philosopher may travel around the world while seated on his own hearthstone, for thought annihilates the interval of distance. A man thinks of China and, behold, he is in China; for he must always dwell in the midst of his own thoughts. But with what subtle instruments shall we measure the wide interval through which thought sped in its instantaneous passage to Cathay? Certainly the tape is not made that meets the need. Again, realization eliminates the intervals in consciousness, for through realization the one realizing becomes identical with the thing realized, and thus spans the superphysical interval between the Self and the not-self. Into this interval Self is ceaselessly flowing, and by the gradual elimination of this qualitative interval the fractional part ever mingles itself more completely with the whole. Nirvana may be defined as the ultimate annihilation of every interval of quality, for it marks the point to which the lesser self has been caused to approach, and finally to be merged with its ultimate goal—-the Greater Self.

Mathematics enables the investigator of the abstract verities of the philosophic sphere to organize his findings and present them intelligently to a world so limited in consciousness that it is incapable of imagining conditions apart from place, or intervals unmeasurable in terms of distance. In presenting any abstract reality for consideration by the concrete faculties, something must necessarily be lost; for truth cannot be brought down to the level of ignorance without the element of ignorance entering into the equation and thereby detracting from the integrity of truth. Mathematics, however, offers a medium whereby such pollution is reduced to a minimum. For example, it would be highly ridiculous to attempt to estimate in terms of physical distance how far life is from death, heaven from hell or opinion from fact.

Recognizing that the law of generation works through the principle of opposites, it is nevertheless a justifiable assumption that the total interval between two opposites is equivalent to unity, or the One. This totality is then capable of being reduced to halves, quarters, and other forms of division. The numbers will then represent concatenated degrees of quality, and a definite scale is thereby established which will permit the various forms manifesting these qualities to be accurately determined in relation to the scheme through which they are moving. Thus, while it is difficult to compute the distance between growth and decay, maturity may be fixed as the halfway point.

The evolution of human consciousness may be measured in a similar way, for the entire interval between unconsciousness and consciousness can be conceived of as divisible into thirds. The first division confers no realization beyond the limitations of place, the second no realization beyond the limitations of interval, and the third no realization beyond the limitations of quality. By such mathematical procedure it is possible to determine the age of a soul; for the interval between beginning and end, being understood as a wholeness, the position of the manifesting life at any given time may be determined by the degree of its own quality in relation to the total privation of that quality—which was its source—and the fullness of that quality—which is its ultimate.

Philosophy employs such terms as "young" souls and "old" souls. A young soul is one who in quality is more proximate to source than to ultimate, or in whom the degree of privation of a given quality exceeds the amount of the quality itself. If there is more of the absence of a quality present than there is of the quality itself, then the quality is declared to be negative. If the reverse is true, the quality is declared to be positive.

Using 100% to represent the sum total of the interval between any two conditions or states, the relative perfection of a life in the plan of progress is determined by the proportion its position bears to the total interval. Thus, an individual manifests 90% of a certain quality is nine-tenths of the way across the interval that lies between the total privation and the fullness of that quality. To summarize, the intervals of quality (in common with the calculations of all superphysical elements) must be established upon the basis of totality or wholeness, and growth or change is always computed as a percentage of that basis. Hence, in calculating spiritual progress, each of us must calculate it in terms of fractions, parts, or percentages as related to the wholeness of Being.

At this point it may not be out of place to reproduce Proclus' encomium to the science of mathematics: "Hence, the business of this science is apparent from its name: for it moves knowledge, excites intelligence, purifies the dianoetic part, unfolds the forms which we essentially contain, removes the oblivion and ignorance which we possess from generation, and dissolves the bonds with which we are held in captivity by an irrational nature. And all this it effects according to a real similitude of that divinity (Mercury) who leads into light intellectual gifts, fills all things with divine reason, moves souls to intellect, excites them as from a profound sleep, converts them by inquiry to themselves, perfects them through obstetrication, and through the invention of pure intellect conducts them to a blessed life."

In the Platonic theory of converging nullities is revealed a strange doctrine concerning negative affirmations and affirmative negations. The number 1 is a positive affirmative number in that it sets forth in unequivocal terms certain divine attributes of Reality: namely, unity, inclusiveness, priority, and stability. On the other hand we may have a negative statement, as "God is no thing." This is an affirmative negation in that no thing exceeds thing in the quality of excellence, for the removal of a definite state leaves an indefinite state partaking more perfectly of divine qualities. Whereas the 1 is similar to the nature of Divinity, the 2 is dissimilar in that it is the symbol of contraries and separation. Hence, while Divinity can be defined affirmatively by the 1, it must be defined negatively by the 2; for God is like the 1 and unlike the 2. In other words, numbers define Deity negatively; Number, affirmatively. The numbers, consequently, are negative affirmations, and Deity is defined negatively by every form in the universe; for forms resemble Deity in their unity and differ from Deity in their diversity.

An affirmation is a definite declaration of opinion, belief or attitude, and, if true, inclines toward and becomes identical with truth. If the affirmation be false, however, it retires from truth as though abashed, thus negatively affirming truth by declaring itself to be dissimilar. A negation is an affirmation through denial, and is the only method by which the Absolute may be approached. When the negation verges toward the thing negated, it nullifies its negative correspondences in that thing so only that which is remains. Thus affirmatives give definition by investing power with place, condition, and quality; while negatives, by divesting the Absolute of these defining limitations, restore it to the estate of supreme dignity. In this manner is created the paradox that affirmations pertaining to First Cause are negations, and negations are affirmations.

Theological systems founded upon the premise of an anthropomorphic deity assume duality to be ultimate and therefore invest the 2 with a dignity superior to the 1, which is a concept Platonically unsound. The 2 is the symbol of good and evil and the entire illusion of sequences has its foundation in the duad—the monad of diversity. According to the Pythagoreans, the 2 is an evil or unholy number because it is the archetype of separateness and produces from itself a dual standard which is now accepted as the manifestation of a dual creative principle. Thus we are given a key to the intrinsic natures of good and evil; for good continually inclines toward unity or wholeness, and being ever the same amalgamates with everything good, so that diversity can never exist therein. Evil, on the other hand, is widely diversified and may exist in many conditions or states, all of which are irreconcilable not only to good but also to each other. While the body of good is always a unity, the body of evil is always a diversity; for evil does not co-ordinate with itself. For example, a virtue is good, and the manifestation of virtue produces an action to which the nature of good is intrinsic. Blending with the ever-existing good, the good act becomes a part thereof, thereby enriching, strengthening, and increasing the entire body of good. Conversely, a vice is evil and must remain as an isolated activity, since it is incapable either of being accepted into the nature of good or of attaching itself to the body of evil, as the element of concord is not common to the intrinsic nature of evil. Hence, good ever fortifies its own nature, while evil undermines itself by the ceaseless warfare between its own parts.

In the unification of one good with another, the power of good is accordingly magnified. When one evil comes in contact with another evil, in the ensuing struggle each evil destroys the effectiveness of the other. In this way it becomes apparent that good, possessing the virtue of unity, must ever increase until it includes everything within its own nature; while evil, in which the principle of diversity is inherent, will ultimately destroy itself by the continual controversy between its parts. It has been well said that two evils do not make one good, but attacking each other achieve their mutual destruction, and by self-elimination thus prepare the way for the irresistible progress of good.

For this reason the Pythagoreans declared that the perfect numbers (the sum of whose fractional parts is equal to themselves) arc the most rare; whereas the superabundant numbers (the sum of whose fractional parts is greater than themselves) and the deficient numbers (the sum of whose fractional part is less than themselves) are most common. This is based upon the fact that there are many ways by which any definite end may be accomplished, but only one of those ways is the best. Consequently he alone is wise who can recognize the best, and he alone is strong who has the courage to use this method, regardless of the personal peril or responsibility involved. Therefore, while all natures partake to some degree of the good, only that is true which partakes in fullest measure of the good, and only one who is qualified to recognize good can make a rational choice between a number of bodies with qualitative differences.

Concerning the doctrine of perfections as revealed by numbers, Thomas Taylor, in his Theoretic Arithmetic, sums up in the following words the opinions of Nicomachus, Macrobius, and Theon of Smyrna: "Perfect numbers, therefore, are beautiful images of the virtues which are certain media between excess and defect, and are not summits, as by some of the ancients they were supposed to be. And evil indeed is opposed to evil, but both are opposed to one good. Good, however, is never opposed to good, but to two evils at one and the same time. Thus timidity is opposed to audacity, to both (of) which the want of true courage is common; but both timidity and audacity are opposed to fortitude. Craft also is opposed to fatuity, to both (of) which the want of intellect is common; and both these are opposed to prudence. Thus, too, profusion is opposed to avarice, to both (of) which illiberally is common; and both these are opposed to liberality. And in a similar manner in the other virtues; by all (of) which it is evident that perfect numbers have a great similitude to the virtues. But they also resemble the virtues on another account; for they are rarely found, as being few, and they are generated in a very constant order. On the contrary, an infinite multitude of superabundant and diminished numbers may be found, nor are they disposed in any orderly series, nor generated from any certain end; and hence they have a great similitude to the vices, which are numerous, inordinate, and indefinite.*' (For further details on this subject consult the chapter on Pythagorean Mathematics in my recent work, An Encyclopedic Outline of Masonic, Hermetic, Qabbalistic and Rosicrucian Symbolical Philosophy .)

As the 1 represents the monad of unity, so the 2 as the monad of diversity is the moving spirit of irrationality. The conflict between rationality and irrationality may be likened to the proverbial concept of the two ends fighting the middle.

Extremes are basically irrational, and only the point of equilibrium may be said to be established upon an enduring foundation. Furthermore, as the extremes pertain to the secondary creation, they are illusional when compared to the center, which is the primary and enduring creation. Thus height and depth are both opposed to the center, for depth departs from the center in a downward course, and height in an upward course. That which departs from center departs from balance, which is a principle exploited to its ultimate by Akiyaraa Shirobei in the theory of Judo or Jujitsu. The theory underlying Judo "start from the mathematical principle that the stability of a body i destroyed as soon as the vertical line passing through its cente of gravity falls outside its base." Once the individual is lurec into jeopardizing his equilibrium, he becomes his own wors enemy and requires little outside assistance to bring about hi downfall.

The philosophic truth here revealed applies not only to th body but to the consciousness as well. When the self in equilibrium, signified by the 1, is intrigued to incline from its per feet state toward the extremes, signified by the 2, it jeopardize its stability and is at the mercy of its adversary, diversity. Le the 1 signify permanence and the 2 life and death. Both lif and death share the common vice of impermanence, as the both lack the common virtue of permanence. Therefore, it i as fatal for the 1 to incline toward life as toward death; for ii assuming life it assumes that which must die, and in assuminj death it assumes that which is corruptible and changeable Only when dissociated from both is the perfection of endur ancc assured. Thus is revealed the stability of Number an< the instability of numbers, for all numbers (save the 1) partak of the common evil of manyness and are involved in the proccs of generation, whereby imperfection perpetuates itself since it i incapable of enduring in its own nature. The self exists in dependent of generation in that, being indivisible, it is incoiruptible; but the not-self, being divisible and corruptible, d( pends for its endurance upon generation and the renewal of it transitory bodies.

Between the rational soul and mathematics is the symp: thetic bond of similars. Preciseness—which is an attribute c the good—delights in precision; and order—which is a qualit of Number—rejoices in the continuity of similars and retire from the malarrangements of dissimilars. In facing inward tc ward its own intrinsic perfection, the self becomes Numbe regarding No Number, or that Cipher which precedes numers tion. But facing outward toward bodies, it encounters the numerical classifications of orders and projections, and therefor stands in equilibrium between Not-being (which is the perfect and eternal Being) and transitory being (which, in the terms of the ultimate, is not-being). Thus self (the individual) is the monad of secondary natures and the paternal foundation of progeny, which are tertiary natures. Hence the 1 (which is the monad or archetype of good) and the 2 (which is the monad or archetype of evil) are both declared by the Pythagoreans to be no numbers but sacred qualities—namely, the primary and secondary natures. The 3, or monad of tertiary natures, was regarded as the actual parent of numbers, or progeny, for 3 is a blending of similars (the 1) and dissimilars (the 2) and is consequently the proper foundation of compound bodies, which compounds must always consist of similars and dissimilars, similars being the spiritual and abiding parts and dissimilars the material and transitory parts. From the various orders of similars and dissimilars issue the multiplicities which are alluded to as the cogitations of Divine Mind. Thus, the first Trinity consists of the Monad (the Father) the Duad (the Power) and the Triad (the Mind or Monad of Generations); for all generations consist of a rational nature (the Monad) immersed in an irrational nature (the Duad) toward some phase of which the Monad inclines, or seems to incline, during the irrational epoch. Liberation, therefore, is the retirement of the Monad from proximity to opposites, and the re-establishment of its own self-sufficiency by which it is capable of assimilating the qualities of the dissimilars and returning to its true abiding condition as the paternal foundation of generations. Syrianus, the Pythagorean, declared that the wise, turning from the vulgar paths, delivered their philosophy in secret to those alone who were worthy to receive it and exhibited it to the rest of mankind through mathematical terminology. Forms therefore, they called numbers as being the first things separated from impartible union; for such natures as are above form are also above separation and consequently pertain to the sphere of Number itself. The sacred decad, or 10, is generated from the sum of the first four numbers (considering the 1 and 2 as numbers)—!, 2, 3, and 4. The 1 was termed the first point. the 2 the first interval, the 3 the first superficies, and the 4 the first solid. Thus Aristotle declared that the first permanence is the dot, the first length the duad, the first breadth the triad, and the first depth the tetrad. The nature of the tetrad, being that of the first solid or body, reveals why it is declared to be the symbol of God. The 4 is the Demiurgus, whose substantial nature is the proper field of mundane fabrications. As four surfaces are the least number that can enclose an area, so the Demiurgus is the first of areas or fields; and consequently the one in whom we live and move and have our being. Pythagoras further declared that knowledge existed in four states. The first, similar to the monad, was called intellect; the second, similar to the duad, science; the third, similar to the triad, opinion; and the fourth, similar to the tetrad, sense . It is evident that intellect partakes of the solidarity of the monad, for it is the immovable contemplation of relative mutations.

The duad even fulfills the Baconian requirements for the constitution of science, for the 2 establishes the comparisons essential to the accumulation of knowledge through observation and experimentation. The 3 consists of three monads separated by two intervals. These intervals become the proper symbols of opinion; for opinions are founded not upon facts (monads) but upon the intervals between them, and two intervals are necessary for opinions in that opinions exhibit the qualities of dissimilars. The 4 consists of four monads and three intervals, which intervals may be likened to the dimensions—length, breadth, thickness; for the monads are qualities manifesting in intervals or dimensions by which they are rendered appreciable to the sense perceptions. Thus the hidden symbolism of the tetractys, or pyramid of ten dots, is unveiled. The four rows of dots further signify four qualities—form, order, beauty, unity—imperishably related to Number. These qualities partake of excellence, and through their participation in the order of creation render the whole felicitous to the internal constitution. Their presence insures the comparative excellence of forms and bodies.

As already intimated, every compound body is composed of the qualities of the monad and the duad. Aristotle reminds the disciple that a number, such as the 6 for example, partakes of the nature of the duad in that it is composed of parts; i. e., 6 monads. But it also partakes of the monad itself in that these parts form a whole—the 6—and the question naturally arises: By what virtue do a number of monads group together to form a definite wholeness to which an arbitrary term is given? In other words, why do 6 monads make 6 rather than simply 6 monads, for the 6 is not denominated six l's but a unity composed of 6. As the Pythagoreans explain it, the 6 monads may be considered as six pieces of wood from which is fashioned a chair which we will call the number 6 itself. By what virtue do these six separate objects form a new and definite pattern, and why should they not always remain simply a bundle of wood? If the numbers were merely aggregations of monads, they would all be bundles, differing simply in the number of their parts. By virtue of a divine order, however, these parts are made to pattern themselves into new terms. The Platonists declared that as a carpenter fashioned a new object out of the separate elements, so a mysterious agent called the Numcrative Soul —being itself a monad and consequently a wholeness composed of infinite diversity—gives form and subsistence to all numbers according to definite divine laws. "But," Thomas Taylor concludes, "in this only consists the difference, that the carpenter's art is not naturally inherent in us, and requires manual operation, because it is conversant with sensible matter; but the numerative art is naturally present with us, and is therefore possessed by all men, and has an intellectual matter which it instantaneously invests with form."

In the light of Pythagoreanism, it is no cause for amazement that 6 monads are never without the innate sense of sixncss; for the moment a certain number of units are combined they are ensouled by the quality equal to their sum, and invested with an organized formative nature through which they manifest a wholeness where previously they manifested a separateness. It follows that with the establishment of sums these sums are automatically invested by the rational soul of man himself with the sense of wholeness equal to their number. If 3, for example, be taken from 6, that which remains is immediately invested with the wholeness of 3. We must give form to numeration, for "our soul cannot endure to see that which is formless, unadorned, especially as she possessess the power of investing it with ornament." The soul naturally desires the adornment of wholeness, and recognizing this intrinsic urge is pleased to confer it upon other natures. Forms are consequently the sense of wholeness superimposed upon parts by the rational soul, to the end that these forms are no longer regarded as bundles of monads but as definite structures.

To summarize, the world is an infinite number of monads grouped into an infinite diversity of patterns, each pattern invested in a quality called form, which quality is measured by the quantity of the monadic parts. The world is adorned with numbers which hang upon it as ornaments upon the person. Each group of numbers is capable of infinite division, but whether in its divided or undivided state, it in turn is adorned with an infinite diversity of unities or wholes which issue forth in response to the urge of the rational soul to clothe abstractions in denominating natures. Thus the law which governs the increase and decrease of wholes, and the superimposition of wholeness upon number, is a manifestation of a divine urge within the numerative monad, which is termed Number and is a definite attribute of Cause itself.

In this manner we sec mathematically demonstrated how Man, the unconditioned principle, is obscured by men, the infinite diversity; how mind, the Yellow Emperor, is hidden in the midst of minds which think in many terms and with many results, but which reason all toward the same end. We behold the Creator so veiled by his creations that his own dignity is no longer apparent but is absorbed into the effulgence of his spheres. As we gaze forth upon the universal vista we see the veils behind which stand the divine principles—the immovable causes of motion, the ungenerated causes of generation, the undying causes of life and death. Our external parts reach forth to grasp the external substance erf the All, our tiny fingers reach out to pluck the stars from their thrones, and our outer being bows with veneration before the outer substances that are its very self and from which it was mined in the Primordial Day.

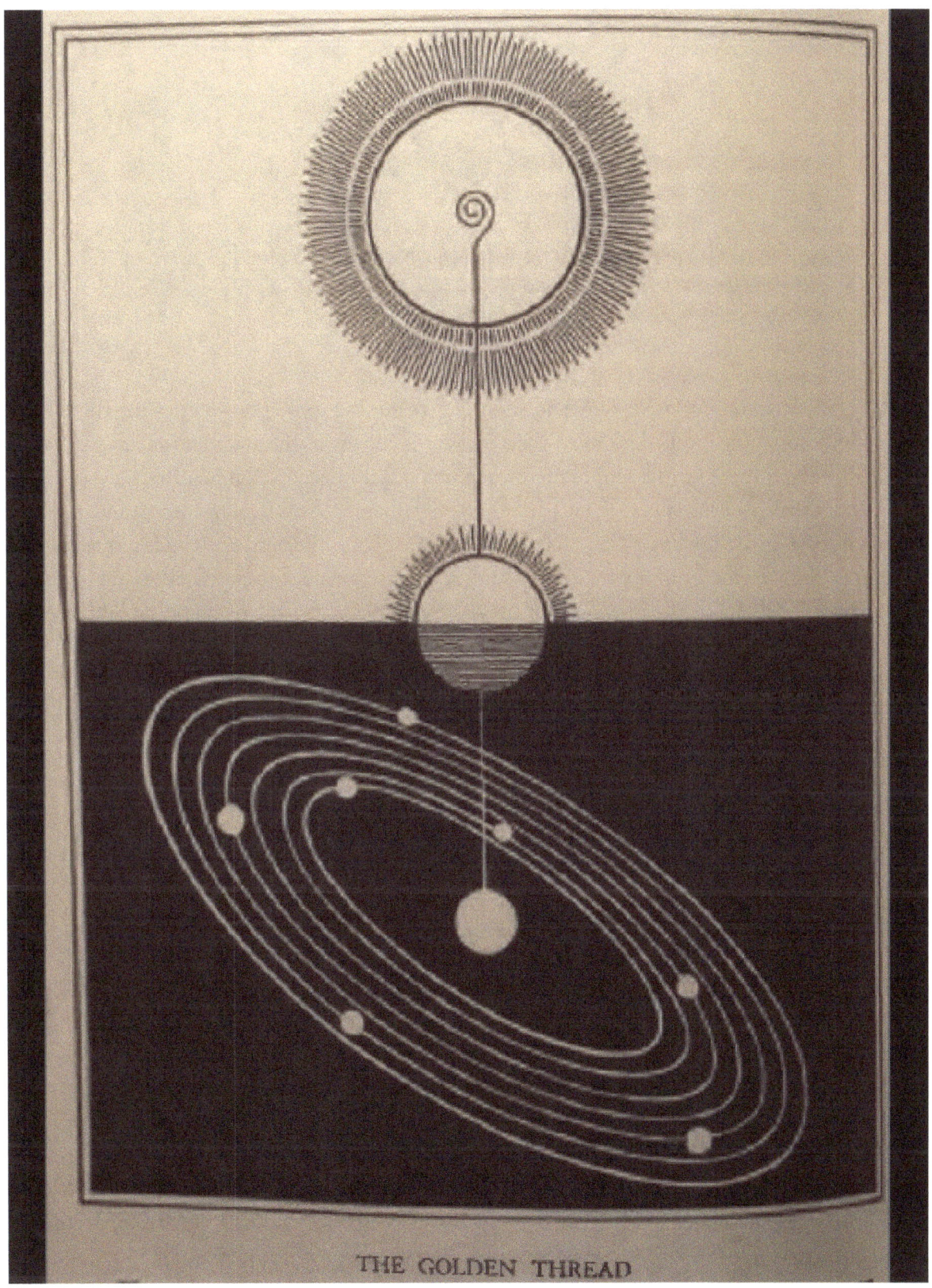

THE GOLDEN THREAD

The upper and light half of the diagram represents the causal universe. The thread of manifestation is seen unwinding from the archetypal germ to the depths of the globe of the soul. From thence it falls into the generational sphere, to end in the radiant solar center.

# XXIV

‿‿❧‿‿

# Demigods and Supermen

WHEN Socrates declared irony and inductive reasoning to be the peculiar instruments of philosophy, he implied far more than the words convey to the average layman. As previously stated (pp. 189) the soul of man when immersed in generation manifests according to the laws of the generating sphere. Hence man can only liberate himself from corporeal conditions by first freeing his rational part from mundane entanglements. The personality with its numerous attributes is suspended from the generating soul, and consequently the clarification of consciousness is attainable only by the liberation of the self from the generating principle. While invested with the substances of the generating sphere, the rational soul is capable of objectifying an infinite diversity of forms or bodies. These the generating soul spontaneously evolves from its own nature by virtue of its inherent formative qualities. As forms and corporeal natures continuously flow from the soul thus invested with generating attributes, it is evident that any attempt to escape diversity by dispersion of the forms is futile. The generating soul is like the fabled dragon—for every head that is cut off two more grow to take its place. Inhibitions and austerities are efforts to combat the processes of the generating soul by destruction of the generations as they come forth. But the task is never finished, and no permanent victory is ever won. The remodeling of character through the despotism of will is therefore, at best, an imperfect and inadequate procedure. To arbitrarily remove the ends, while the means which produce those ends are permitted to remain, is to imperil the entire nature in which such inconsistency exists.

In a certain sense man is an appendage of impulse; hence the regeneration of character must be through the reformation of impulses and not their inhibition. A certain consistency must exist upon all planes of activity. The animal soul must ever express itself through animal instincts, the generating soul through the instincts of generation, and the rational soul through the urge to rationality. For the internal nature thus to function upon one level of consciousness while the external nature attempts to exist upon another, is to create a confusion which must inevitably result in disaster. Socrates maintained that the rationalizing of the individual must take place in the causal nature which, flowing downward into the corporeal constitution, will speedily mold the inferior into the image of the superior. Hence his emphasis upon the efficacy of irony and inductive reasoning. Irony is here to be understood in the sense of fate, which philosophers have ever declared to be ironical. Fate effects the liberation of the rational part by revealing that all things are destined to return to their own natures (or origins) in spite of every effort to nullify this design. Ultimate achievement is hence unavoidable, and is the certain end of all beginnings; but incalculable is the interval that must elapse before the operations of divine procedure restore all things to their primal state.

Irony, therefore, is the long way around—the path of the drone. It is beset with every obstacle that materiality can contrive; it leads through death and sorrow, and he who chooses to take the bufferings of destiny must be prepared to withstand the blasts of outrageous circumstance. Ironically, he who chooses to do the least must accomplish the most; for none shall labor as hard as the sluggard or struggle as intensely for

liberation as the one content to drift upon the sea of Providence. Whoever chooses to escape the responsibilities of life exhausts himself in his efforts to dodge inevitables.

For the foolish, then, the ironic road; for the wise, the true Socratic path—the theory of inductive reasoning. Establishing his entire philosophy upon man—consequently upon a particular—Socrates reasoned therefrom to generals, thus establishing a procedure to which Francis Bacon added the essential element of analogy. Induction infers a process of thought whereby the rationality which is posited in particulars is urged or impelled to retire along the line of its own flow, and verge toward the monad (or general) of which it is the particular. In other words, Socrates sought to arrive at divine realities by causing particulars to retire into their own general state. While the monad might erroneously be considered a particular, it is in reality a general, and the manifestations which emerge from it are the particulars.

The ancient Socratic philosophy involved, therefore, the correction of particulars by the renovation of generals. Affirming all particulars to have their origin in generals, it is evident that man as a particular is founded upon Man as a general, and hence that which influences the general must necessarily influence the particular. The reverse, however, is not essentially true; for the lesser cannot dominate the greater but must be dominated thereby. Philosophy, accordingly, is peculiarly adapted to the fields of generals, while science has an affinity for the field of particulars. Hence science is founded in philosophy and must receive its particular truths by adaptation from general verities. Philosophy, consequently, is not individualistic in the commonly accepted sense, but regards individuals as dependencies of universals, and seeks to achieve the liberation of individuals by the reconstruction of universals.

Descending to the level of man himself, we must then regard man as a general; his parts, members, and attributes as particulars suspended from his general, or rational, nature. Man is not simply a personality; he is a personality, an individuality, and a universality in one. His universality verges toward universals, his individuality verges toward individuals, and his personality verges toward personals. Each of these natures in turn has its own dependencies which verge toward it and toward which it also apparently verges. From the subject matter of the previous chapter it is evident that generals partake of unity or wholeness; and particulars of diversity; for as diversity is contained within unity, so the particulars are contained within the general. Impulses which impel the consciousness toward particulars consequently incline it toward diversity and illusion, while impulses which impel the consciousness toward generals, incline it toward wholeness or reality. How, then, shall man stimulate his inferior nature to verge toward its own superior part and thus accomplish philosophic growth? The answer is evident: By permeating the consciousness with the realization of wholeness, or by the instinctive inductive process of reasoning toward generals. Personalities are particulars; principles are generals. Hence to reason toward particulars is to reason toward personalities. Personalities are infinite diversity, and the contemplation of them is a philosophic error whose reward is an involvement therein which jeopardizes rationality. By inclining toward generals, however, we approach principles, and in the sphere of principles we approach wholeness; for a principle is a wholeness which may manifest as a diversity in application, but which in its own nature is an essential unity. Involution is consequently the inclination of the rational soul toward diversity (particulars). Its nadir is corporeality, where dissimilars manifest as an infinite diversity of forms. Evolution, conversely, is an ascent to principle, in which the rational soul verges toward the principle of wholeness, thereby uniting itself with natures of ever-increasing permanence and lucidity.

It follows that growth inspires the contemplation of wholes, or unities, and that contemplation of wholes inspires, in turn, growth. Thus a benevolent circle is created which gradually accomplishes the unification of parts and elevates the abiding genius (the rational spirit) to the contemplation of abiding monads, or wholes. From the standpoint of pure philosophy it is useless to affirm wholeness or deny diversity or platitudinize concerning either. The realization must flow downward from the apex of the individual self, where it has become established as the object of the rapturous contemplation of the rational soul. By verging toward the realization of wholeness the rational soul is drawn out of the quagmire of generation, regaining thereby the control of certain functions and members rendered impotent by the embrace of generation.

As particulars depend from generals, so all natures exist suspended from principles, and before the mind is capable of rational functioning it must be established upon the foundation of familiarity with principles. It follows that intellect founded upon principle cannot deviate from that which its own rationality has approved. Consequently minds founded in principles are certain to function in harmony with the flow of principles, and the inevitable result of intellect functioning in harmony with such a flow is reasonableness of conclusion. In the last analysis that which is reasonable is true if the reason itself be established in principle; for no part can deviate from the wholeness from which it is suspended, and principle is always sufficiently inclusive to circumscribe exception. In simple words, then, the establishment of the mind in wholes (unities) is essential to right thinking , and is the master to the rationed cognizance of the order and sequence of parts—the monads of particulars.

The haphazardness of modern philosophic speculation is due to ignoring the necessity of founding intellection in wholes or unities. A mind which does not reason from generals to particulars is always in danger of elevating a particular to the dignity of a general, thus creating an exclusive rather than an inclusive general. In other words, when the emphasis upon a part causes this part to appear as a wholeness to the perceptions of a specialized intellect, the result is a wholeness which is not inclusive in that parts do not contain each other. If a part, therefore, be raised to the dignity of a wholeness, then another part may also be similarly elevated, the result being an infinite diversity of wholes, which is a philosophic absurdity in that the element of diversity cannot exist in wholeness. When a part is so raised above the level of its own dignity we find a system of thought which seeks to reduce universal to the estate of parts; to interpret the whole in terms of the fraction; to explain the whole by the laws of the part; or to invest the whole with the limited attributes of the part.

All this results in the concept of an all which is not all-inclusive and which consequently finds it necessary either to manipulate universal laws so that they conform to the imperfect attributes of the part itself, or to ignore those phases of universal activity whose manifestations are beyond the province of the part. For example, to the ancient philosopher science was a part of the body of knowledge. It was therefore a dependency of reason and an instrument of erudition. By the modern scientist, however, science is elevated to the dignity of wholeness, and regarded as the actual monad of rationality rather than a dependency thereof. The resultant confusion is foreshadowed. The field of phenomena includes a multitude of activities outside the province of science as a particular.

These are naturally excluded from science when it is regarded as a general. Hence scientific men are prone to ridicule the concept of the immortality of the soul, because such concepts do not come under the jurisdiction of science as a particular; and when science is thus elevated to the false dignity of an absolute state the doctrine of the soul is necessarily outlawed from universal.

The inadequacy of science is thus demonstrated, for it is indisputably established as a particular and not a general. There is a natural tendency of the mind to elevate its own particular to the estate of a general. This is the inevitable outcome of founding knowledge upon particulars. The philosophic perspective is lost and short-sightedness ensues. From short-sightedness itself as a monadic entity, are suspended such particulars as bigotry, intolerance, and rational injustice.

In America today we have a deluge of cults—literally hundreds of minor creeds, orthodox as well as heterodox, which have sprung up from an over-emphasis of the Baconian doctrine of particulars. Analytical reasoning is largely responsible for this unfortnate condition, for analysis is a separative impulse whose natural trend is to break up similars into dissimilar* and thereby unduly emphasize them. On the other hand synthesis is an unceasing impulse toward the establishment of wholes or unities. This does not necessarily imply that the philosophy behind the procedure is at fault; for the microscope, while ever revealing particulars, at the same time reveals also the unity of those particulars. If parts be invariably regarded as wholes, and each new division be likewise invested with the sense of wholeness, then the present analytical process, through the reformation of its theory, would automatically become a synthetic process. In religion this practice of elevating parts to the dignity of wholes is most common. Every little motion is thus raised to the dignity of a divine edict; every little whim rooted in a spiritual certainty; and every infinitesimal belief so highly magnified that it eclipses the entire body of universal order. If every individual nail in the rim of a wheel should conceive itself to be the hub, imagine the dilemma of the wheel at finding itself expected to revolve upon a score of different hubs simultaneously and make definite progress!

The mind naturally thinks in terms of particulars; it is consequently incapable of ascending to that sphere of rationality where dwells the spirit of intellectual justice. Justice docs not necessarily result from a full comprehension of wholes, but rather from the realization of the equality of parts. Thus in philosophy there is a democracy of parts and an autocracy of wholes; for parts are equal to parts but inferior to wholes.

St. Paul epitomizes the philosophy of the "Master Builder" concerning this subject: "For we know in part, and we prophesy in part. But when that which is perfect is come, then that which is in part shall be done away." (I Cor. XIII: 9-10) In this case that which is "perfect" signifies the state of wholeness. These words have been interpreted by the Christian Church to signify the ultimate unification of all men under its own banner, unmindful of the obvious fact that it is but a "part" itself and can endure only until "that which is perfect is come."

The elevation of isolated fragments to a position of supremacy over wholes is the sequel to the overemphasis of individualism; for individualism, while it properly emphasizes the wholeness innate within parts, fails to emphasize the greater wholeness that is the sum of parts. The natural supremacy of the Platonic system of reasoning over the more popular Aristotelian method thus becomes self-apparent. Reasoning a posteriori is characteristic of modern thought, whereas the ancient Mysteries owed their excellence largely to the a priori method. The a posteriori method inclines toward separateness, egotism, and selfishness; the a prori toward dignity, humility, and unselfishness.

All systems of thought which ascribe to the parts a power equal to the whole are productive of despotism and the false usurpation of power. Tyranny is an oppression, and the limiting boundary of parts oppresses the limitlessness of wholes.

From this insufficiency is born rebellion, for that which is unduly bounded bursts its bonds and escapes into an area sufficient for its expression. When inferiors are ruled by superiors, order reigns; but when superiors are ruled by inferiors, chaos prevails.

If man is ruled by the laws of the universe he is justly dealt with; but if the universe were subjected to the laws of men, sufficiency would be oppressed by insufficiency. When particulars are ruled by generals, rational order is the product; but when generals are ruled by particulars, the despotism of irrationality destoys all rational congruity.

When the individual essays the philosophic life it is first necessary that the mind be trained to think in round terms; for roundness partakes of the nature of wholeness because the circle or sphere (like wholeness) is without beginning or end.

To think in round terms may be interpreted to mean keeping the mentality upon the level of greatest inclusiveness, ever striving to attain fuller inclusiveness since perfect inclusiveness alone qualifies the intellect to descend to the contemplation of pans. For example, when thinking of religion, do not think of Mohammedans, Brahmans, or Christians, but think of religion as the universal adoration of creative principles common to all mankind, and found in a rudimentary form even among the higher animals, such as the anthropoid ape. Having first established the universality of veneration, we have founded our comprehension upon the wholeness of the subject. From this point we may then rationally descend to the consideration of religions, thereby escaping the pitfall o k intolerance resulting from basing the study of religion upon a religion. When viewed from the exalted level of wholeness, such issues as the possible priority of the Presbyterians over the Methodists not only become inconsequential, but retire beyond the vanishing point of philosophic concern. Yet men which have termed themselves rational, who have been entrusted by their communities with positions of importance and the administration of justice, have waged bloody warfare and unreasonable persecution over such trivialities. Competitiveness is thus demonstrated to be natural to parts. Hence the mind that thinks in terms of parts makes continual comparison between them; whereas the highly evolved intellect, recognizing that cooperation through which the parts are caused to form the whole, thinks and lives in terms of tolerance and magnanimity.

Philosophic discipline therefore requires that the intellect be rationalized through familiarity with unities, and permitted to express its natural amity toward them. Being itself a wholeness, the rationality has an affinity for wholeness, and rejoices in its contemplation. This rational desire for completeness is opposed, however, by the irrationality of the animal soul. Limited to the plane of sense and beholding only diversity, the principle of unity is inconceivable to the animal soul because its nature and perception function in terms of isolated individualism. Stimulated by philosophic discipline, the rational faculties are caused to assert their intrinsic preference, thereby inclining the entire mental organism toward recognition of the supremacy of wholes. Having thus established its preference, the mind gradually comes instinctively to function in harmony therewith. The result is mental benevolence, which manifests in the outer life as that nobility of temperament which irresistibly attracts, and is concordant with, the subconscious unity existent in all human nature. The nobility of the inclusive intellect is undeniable, and opposition to its conclusions is usually based upon cupidity or egotism, for it can never be rationally opposed.

Another point of major importance is that a mind established upon wholes is never forced to reconstruct its attitudes toward particulars, for these attitudes are continually held in suspension. As the mind increases in its knowledge of particulars it simply pours them into the capacious wholeness, which is always sufficient to include the nature of the parts. As a result, it is impossible to outgrow a doctrine or be forced to reconstruct it; for the mind, moving in certainties, builds in from universals and does not arrive at particulars until it is capable of recognizing and organizing their diversity.

In the preceding outline the processes of inductive and deductive reasoning may appear to be hopelessly confused. Here again it must be realized that reason itself is also a wholeness, of which induction and deduction are parts. Hence, as Confucius noted, the positive and negative are never found to be totally isolated, so induction always partakes to some degree of deduction; while deduction, inclining toward induction, finds

its opposite essential to the philosophic unity. Induction—which is the pure Socratic method—while it reasons from particulars to generals, does so with the definite purpose of establishing generals. It is possible for the mind to ponder upon particulars without emphasizing the quest of wholeness—in fact, particulars may be traced toward their own cause without the realization of wholeness being established; for in this case particulars merge into particulars instead of generals, and the entire universe continues to be regarded as a mass of particulars rather than a wholeness. True induction, however, is the quest of wholeness through particulars—the decision to establish the rational code in the sense of generals. Upon reaching this state the mind has realized the true end of the Socratic process or the Aristotelian mode. On the other hand, having established rationality in generals, the mind assumes the Platonic mode and begins to reason toward particulars. This procedure ultimately results in the establishment of consciousness at a point of equilibrium midway between induction and deduction, where both are shown to be contributing factors in the unfoldment of the process of rational thinking.

The natural flow of existence is from the prior to the subsequent or from the cause to its effect. Pythagoras, however, recommended the retrospective mode whereby the subsequent is caused to flow back into priority. The mental reactions caused by these two processes are far-reaching. To establish a cause through its effect awakens a reaction wholly different from that created by the picture of a cause flowing into its effect. The former is an impulse far more definite than the latter, due possibly to the unnatural order which emphasizes the intensity of the elements involved. The flow of cause into effect is so common as to become monotonous; the mental faculties, therefore, become oblivious to the drone of the natural or normal sequence. When, however, the process is reversed,

the mental faculties are startled into activity by the unfamiliar—and consequently discordant—note.

Retrospection is an inductive procedure which, by revealing the effect before its cause, emphasizes the enormity of consequence that can be suspended from the mote of cause. The effect of such revelation is to overawe the intellect with the sense of responsibility. It demonstrates that though man has a certain province for die exercise of despotic agency, he is powerless to control the destiny of his fabrications or determine with certitude the ends at which his beginnings shall arrive. Man's sphere of influence is as far-reaching as creation, and what we first agitate diverges to die shores of eternity like the ripples from a stone thrown upon the surface of some placid lake. That which we have thus enlivened with our own potentialities we can never overtake until at last we mingle with it in the Absolute. The living are ruled by the dead; the present is ruled by the past; and, as Omar Khayyam says, that which the first man wrote, the last man shall read. Under the moldering headstone in some obscure churchyard may rot the mortal remains of some petty despot whose royal edicts still survive to afflict unborn generations with their absurdities. Huge enterprises may go awry, yes, empires perish through the insidious consequences of a few hastily spoken words or a single irrational act. Retrospection warns men so to regulate their thoughts and actions that the afterglow of their achievements shall not be tinted with a lurid or unnatural hue. Though man loses control over the seeds of action which he has sown in the fields of space, he is forever the victim of his self-generated consequences. Those careless in thought or deed will sometime curse the Providence that heaps upon them the unwelcome fruitage of their own folly and forces them to live in tolerance with their own progeny.

Elsewhere are described (pps. 52, 53) the orders of the gods, demigods, supermen, and mortals. Descending from his spiritual state, man was established in irrationality, a condition from which he seeks to escape by inclining himself toward superior natures and ascending to the seat of rationality. The gods differ from man in that their realization of wholeness or unity is intrinsic, and their consciousness is incapable of descending to terms of diversity. They are consequently unable to exist, think, or feel in terms of particulars, since by virtue of their establishment in wholeness they are without the appreciation of parts. A simple illustration of this attitude is man himself, who finds it difficult to realize the existence of individuality within his own nature. He cannot conceive of independent cellular or organic function within his own body. He may affirm his intellectual belief in the individuality of parts, but his consciousness does not supply him with any definite reactions along this line. As man—the corporeal unit—is incapable of descending into and coming en rapport with the consciousness of a single cell of his own body, so the gods—or units of spiritual consciousness—have no rational perception of the diversity suspended from their own natures.

When we realize the gods to be wholes or unities we can better comprehend why they abide in immortality and are not subject to dissolution. The dignity of gods over men is equal to the superior dignity of wholes over parts. As wholes can never be less than wholes, it is evident that the gods cannot descend to men; but as parts are capable of being merged into wholes, so man is capable of ascending into the presence of the gods. When he has accomplished this he is immortal—not absolutely in his own right but in the immortality of the god from whom he is suspended. Immortality is consequently the merging of a mortal nature with an immortal nature, whereby the nature of the immortal is caused to extend and include the nature of the mortal. What was formerly impermanent thus becomes permanent by its mergence with the nature of permanence. Natures become immortal by retiring into their own causes; for causes partake of immortality and are proximate to the One Cause toward which they themselves incline to partake of the fullness of Being. Though men (the fractional parts) come and go and their span is but a little while, Man (the principle) endures for an interminable period of time. By elevating themselves to wholeness men are able to partake of the immortality of their archetype. Thus men and women as isolated personalities are not immortal, but their immortality is assured through their foundation in the causal nature.

According to the ancients the universe contains, in addition to the myriads of natural creatures (who inhabit its inferior part and are visible to the perceptions of the normal human being) other orders, hierarchies, or species of life beyond the perception of the limited faculties now at man's disposal.

Socrates declares that there are orders of life which dwell along the shores of the air as men dwell along the shores of the sea. Dwelling in a subtler stratum, these beings are seldom given to contention, but live together in amity, worshiping the gods and serving the beautiful. To assume the visible to be the all is to deny even the most rudimentary instincts of human nature. Mankind dwells in a vale, as it were, and on every side rise high mountains which obscure from view that which lies beyond. Yet by what right shall we deny the existence of broader vistas beyond the circumscribing walls of our sense perception? Is it not reasonable that the interval between wholeness and diversity is filled with a concatenated order of generations—some verging toward wholeness and proximate to it; others verging toward diversity and filled with its quality? Degrees of wholeness are the spiritual impulses which manifest as the various genera composing physical life. There are degrees of wholeness requiring vehicles of expression far more refined than man's bodies, even as there are degrees of diversity, which like the grain of sand call for a structure less complicated.

Arc the gods then to be considered as arbitrary creations, or simply the hypothetical divisions erected by philosophy for the purpose of classifying the proximity of various natures either to their substance or their shadow? Through the centuries men have pleased to worship gods as proxies of the One Indivisible and Omnipotent Nature. Being posterior to the One, are not the gods themselves natures? Though elevated to divine dignity from their proximity to wholeness, are they not, like men, orders of dependencies suspended in the abyss of interval, there to generate within their abundant natures a numerous progeny which they tolerate and ultimately cause to flow back again into themselves?

Let the contemplation of divine natures, therefore, be approached in the spirit of reasonableness, bereft of that awe and diffidence which has marked such contemplation in the past. Like the Cyclopes, the wholes (or unities) stand regarding through their unified perceptions the transcendent nature of the First Wholeness. An analysis of the natures of the gods is essential to an understanding of human nature; for through them we partake of the fullness of all good, and in them is the field of both our present labors and our future endeavors.

Wholeness is not a personality. The gods, therefore, do not partake of the attributes of personalities. They are not vengeful principles, nor are they inclined to be moved by the piteous supplication of the inadequate. Like the carved Rameses of Egypt, they sit immovable, sufficient, and all-sufficing. Of their immeasurable dignity we may not know all; but through philosophic discipline we may equip ourselves to understand,

in part at least, the magnitude and tranquillity of their abidance. Regardless of the degree or dignity of the parts, the wholeness from which they themselves are directly suspended is their God, their Father and their Mother, their beginning and their end. Thus the gods are legion. Merging into each other, these wholes verge toward their common First Cause; and as the gods retire into God, so God, in turn, retires into that which was, is, and ever shall be, yet is not. The already well emphasized point that the gods are principles rather than personalities is confirmed by the evidence of Iamblichus, who attacked the concept popular among the uneducated masses that places could be assigned as divine habitats, or that certain communities enjoyed the patronage of the celestials. One of the erroneous beliefs was that Athena Parthenos (Minerva) was the guardian spirit of Athens. Iamblichus reasoned thus: As the gods permeate the entire structure of being, and as universal are unlimited as to time and place, how can any locality be sufficiently privated of their influence to require the appointment of a superessential protector? Being everywhere at all time and in all place, the gods are inherendy omnipresent, nor can their influence be either increased or diminished. This theory is the rational foundation upon which must yet be erected the structure of universal religion. It unmasks the fallacious conceptions of racial or national gods; for it demonstrates that although men may differ concerning the attributes and number of their divinities—even attempting to distribute the universe among various deities—the divine principles themselves remain undivided and unchanged, with their presence equally common to all men and to all places Iamblichus further likens the celestials and their abiding natures to the zodiac and the other heavenly bodies, whose influences (according to the astrologers) modeled sidereal nature into the tangible likenesses of various abstract qualities and conditions. As the stars abide in their enduring causes and are ever the same, so the gods abide upon their immovable thrones; for their unchangeableness is an essential attribute of their own divine natures. But as the mutual intermingling of the attributes of the abiding stars results in a countless order of diversified manifestations, so while the divine natures (the gods) remain unchanged, those participating in their manifold virtues assume a variety of aspects to them and, dependent upon their proximity (which is measured by rationality) either enjoy the benevolent dispositions of these abiding divinities, or suffer from the deprivation of these influences.

These relationships between abiding principles and nonabiding personalities are capable of measurement according to certain abstract principles, which the ancient philosophers concealed under the symbolism of Time. These abstract mensurations (which must never be confused with literal calculations) are arcanely designated by the philosophers as the "birthdays of the gods." Deities are said to be "born" at the moment when the unfolding rationality of the aspirant first participates in their effulgence or comes into harmonious correlation to their power. Thus the celebration of the divine birthdays

does not signify that the deities were actually created upon these days; for if actually born they would thereby partake of the nature of generation and also be subject to the unstable laws of generation and decay. In Christianity, for example, although the 25th of December is celebrated as the birthday of Christ, even the least informed layman knows that natus solis invicti signifies merely the descent of an eternal principle into the sphere of temporal agencies where the rationality of man may partake of its attributes and qualities. Christ is declared to have existed in the presence of the Father before the beginning of Time, and after his death and resurrection to have reascended into the sphere of endurance, there to remain throughout all duration unaffected by Time and not subject to the laws of incident and change. This concept is in harmony with the Platonic theory that the virtue of the immortals lies in the fact that they are unborn, having the apex of their period of activity posited in undivided unity or (as the Egyptians pleased to call it) unaging Time —duration that does not pass.

In describing how inferior natures, or corporeal constitutions, become filled with the superabundance of celestial natures (thereby partaking of and manifesting the celestial sufficiencies) Proclus in his Theurgy, translated by Ficinus in his Excerpta, writes in substance as follows: As those who love gradually advance from the admiration of sensible forms to the admiration of divine principles, so the initiated priests, discovering

the sacred truth that all things subsist in all things, advanced from this conclusion to the fabrication of the sacred science founded upon the principles of mutual sympathy and participation. Because of their understanding of the fourth-dimensional universe, they realized that as far as the element of place is concerned heaven was in the earth and the earth in heaven; that principles continually permeate both places and things; and that places and things endure their natural span immersed in the very substance of principle. Hence, the superior forever rules the inferior. Inferiors are ever paying homage to their superiors either consciously (as in the case of illumined men) or unconsciously (as in the case of the elements), the latter voicing their admiration by assuming the appearance and reflecting the attributes of divine qualities.

Thus, observes Proclus, the sunflower pays homage to the solar orb by inclining itself toward the source of its own being. A piece of paper, if preheated and then brought close to fire, will suddenly burst into flames even though it does not actually touch the fire. This is an arcane hint that divine natures (the fire) communicate themselves to such corporeal bodies (the heated paper) as have rendered themselves capable of their reception. The flaming paper further represents the deification of mortals whose divinity, by mingling itself with the causal flame, vanishes away into its own beginning, leaving naught behind but the ashes. The lotus also unfolds its petals with the ascent of the sun toward the zenith, closing its petals when the sun retires to the western corner of the heavens.

This gesture of the plant is as much a 'hymn to the sun" as the prayers and praise of men. Again, the sunstone imitates with its golden rays the luminosity of its namesake. Another curious gem, the eye-of-heaven has a form within it which resembles the pupil of the human eye and emits a brilliant ray. The lunar stone, by certain changes inherent to itself, also modifies its rays by the phases of the moon, and the stone called hclioselenus changes its color with the celestial moods of the sun and the moon. By such occult means do irrational natures manifest the abundance of superessential virtue imparted to them out of the fullness of divine natures. (For further details consult the notes at the end of the 1821 Edition of Thomas Taylor's translation of lamblichus on The Mysteries of the Egyptians , Chaldeans and Assyrians.)

As previously suggested, the virtue of the gods springs from their abundant unity. It is a Platonic axiom that "the principal (chief) subsistence of everything is according to the summit of its essence," In other words, all bodies and constitutions are to be measured by the dignity of their first principles or natures; for this principle is the true measure of the capacity and limitation of the thing suspended from it, because no thing can become greater than its source. To mingle with superiors it must cease, therefore, in its own nature. Emerging from the indivisible unity or wholeness, the gods thus partake of the virtue of this their summit. They, accordingly, differ from man in that while man has for his apex the rational mind, the gods flow downward toward rationality from a far more exalted sphere. Philosophy is a discipline which impels all activities to flow toward their own causal principle. Its chief province, therefore, is to restore all natures to their origins and thus accomplish the perfection of natures; for that is perfect which has been accepted back into the fullness of its own unity. Among the most mysterious symbols employed by the Egyptians were two pyramids united at their apexes, ope inverted

and the other upright, to signify the interchange of divine and natural powers. While this particular symbol has already been briefly discussed, it will not be out of order to amplify the previous description. The inverted pyramid, with its foundation in the superior sphere, they termed inspiration ; the upright, with its foundation upon the inferior sphere, they termed aspiration. Hence both of these forces commingle in natures.

From the inferior the urge of the rational disciplines is toward the elevation of natures; from the superior (which is an attracting agency) the urge of inspiration is ascent toward divine perfections. If the symbol be closely examined we become aware of a more archaic meaning; for recognizing the pyramids as flowing from their own apexes, we discover that the central point from which both diverge is the abiding place of the superiors. From this superior point one pyramid—usually shown as dark—flows upward, its color signifying the occult nature of its properties which must forever remain dark and mysterious to the intellections of unillumined mortals. The second pyramid flows downward, becoming the tangible universe which is luminous to the many and susceptible of a certain degree of analysis by even those who are unenlightened.

These two pyramids represent, therefore, the duad existing within and flowing from the monad-polarity manifesting out of simple unity, through which manifestation the universe came into being. Between the unseen sphere of principles above and the visible sphere of personalities below is a ceaseless interchange of activities. Separateness being the law of personalities and unity the law of principles, it is evident that while each body occupies some place, each principle occupies every place. All principles are therefore capable of manifesting in each body. Upon this fact was based the philosophic deduction that place is of relatively small importance in matters pertaining to the higher sciences. Socrates was once accosted by a seeker after truth, who asked him where could be found the best place in which to learn. The great Skeptic instantly replied: "Where thou art;" for, whereas the learner was in place, learning was everywhere. The two consequently awaited the unifying effect of rationality, which when present links place with everywhere.

Theology particularly has become a servant to the concept of place. Among nearly all religious peoples it is a common practice to sanctify places of worship and be in attendance at the performance of certain holy offices in such places. The tombs of the saints are also hallowed, and there is a widespread veneration for sacred objects of every description. A visit to Jerusalem will demonstrate the influence wielded by such veneration for place. Here every pebble is more venerable than a boulder elsewhere, and even the filth spreads piety instead of plague! Theology also limits the mind to the concept of time

as a factor in religious place. Witness the "holy days" when prayer is presumed to have especial efficacy and the celestial hierarchies are said to be peculiarly receptive to the whining importunities of men. Assembly for the common purpose of worship may confer certain ethical and sociological virtues— for instance, by inspiring the courage born of numbers—but little importance can be attached to the practice if viewed from the standpoint of spirit. In the terms of pure metaphysical philosophy, the gods as causal agencies are both omnipresent and omniscient. Free from time and place, above condition, and incapable of such purely mundane concepts as pleasure or displeasure, they flow unimpeded through the many dimensional vistas of eternity. If would-be reformers can correct the theological absurdity that the gods are localized like the weather, systematized like industry or dispositioned like ward politicians, there is still hope for the religious instincts of the race.

Plutarch of Chaeroneia, one of the early Gnostic Fathers, in his Vision of Aridaeus, describes an excursion made by a benighted soul into the realm of Hades, where with the aid of the "single (or psychic) eye" he perceived many things with greater clarity than is the fortune of most mortals. Aridaeus (the man who had the vision) is supposed to have died and found himself in a great sea of light, "of objects with which he had been previously familiar, he saw none save the stars; they were, however, of stupendous size and at enormous distances from one another, and poured forth a marvellous radiance of colour and sound, so that the soul riding smoothly in the light, as a ship in calm weather, sailed easily and swiftly in every direction. Omitting most of the things he saw, he said that the souls of the dead, in passing from below upwards, formed a flame-like bubble from which the air was excluded; then the bubble quietly broke, and they came forth with men-like forms and well-knit frames" (See The Vision of Arid crus, translated by G. R. S. Mead.)

Compiled during the first century of the Christian Era, this curious allegory is of particular interest to the modern student of Platonic philosophy; for the bubble-like souls with flaming luminosity that flowed past Aridaeus represent the spheres of isolation within which the rational nature must remain during the period of irrationality—that is, before the one hears the call of the All and chooses to mingle its destiny with the common cause. This "flame-like bubble*' constitutes the interval between man as the partly-illumined creature and the gods as divine potentialities. Although man exists in these god essences, he

cannot be united with these infinite certainties until he causes this bubble to "quietly break." This is a direct allusion to the rites of the Mysteries, and we suspect that Plutarch wrote not of the after-death state but of that secret ritualism whereby the dead soul in a living body is liberated to the contemplation of divinities. As institutions of illumination, the Mysteries arc agencies appointed to prick the bubble of self-conceit that envelopes the average soul, and thereby renders it impervious to divine ministrations.

The well-formed bodies seen by Aridaeus coming forth out of the broken bubbles represent the organized rationalities which arc manifested after the consciousness has been liberated from the inferior sphere—that iridescent world which, mirror- like, shows man only the reflection of himself, leaving him unaware of the Great Within in the nature of which he floats. The sea of luminosity in which the soul floats like a ship represents the causal universe whose divine agencies, manifesting first as colors and sounds, mingle in an exotic symphonic profusion. Aridaeus also declares that in this luminous world he felt as though he was breathing all over, for his whole body was filled with a life-giving air that gave the sense of buoyancy and freedom from every oppression of matter. Air is the ancient and secret symbol of rationality, and represents the intangible illumined mind that is declared to be absent from the contents of the bubbles (the symbols of irrationality). The free air of the spirit comes to relieve man when he is willing to renounce the oppressed atmosphere of the body. This is the secret of the "enthusiasm" of the ancient Mysteries—the ecstasy that came upon those who "breathed in" the gods—for

by divine enthusiasm was signified unity with God, as the word itself implies (en theos, in God.) Those who were in the nature and consciousness of Cause thus ceased to move of their own accord, but their frantic gyrations were regarded as evidence that a divine spirit was agitating and mingling them with universals. When Socrates declared that where thou art is the place to learn he thereby revealed the universality of Cause. The fact that all men do not actively partake of the all-permeating learning implies a barrier between learning and the learner; between life and the living; between the good and those who strive for virtue. This barrier is the quality interval referred to in the preceding chapter, to be overcome only by the disciplines of the Mysteries; for alone and unaided, men cannot sufficiently organize their internal natures to achieve this most necessary end. The gods are presumed to be superior to these intervals of quality, and hence mingle not only with each other but each with All in a perfect unity. With few exceptions pagan philosophic systems discovered that man exists within the opalescent globe now termed the auric egg, or soul envelope. This auric egg (its lower sheaths at least) totally isolates man from the rest of the universe, admitting through its poles only sufficient of the Universal Agent to maintain him in his isolated embryonic individualism; for this auric egg is the womb in which the prenatal life of mortality is passed.

As long as he remains an individual, man is an embryo; as long as he is in this embryonic state he is a mortal; and as long as he is a mortal he must exemplify the mortal principle of separateness. While he may fit together with the other parts so as to form a comb-like fabric, he can never actually mingle his own nature with that of any other creature. Men mix with each other as oil mixes with water; but the gods mingle as oils for all have the same essential base. Divinity, exemplifying similars, forever mingles with itself; humanity, exemplifying dissimilars, may be brought together, yet a certain separateness inevitably remains as long as humanness remains. It is because man is separate from man that he is not a god. To the degree that he overcomes the sense of separateness he overcomes his humanness and rises to the state of immortality—a state in which he comes proximate to the gods, converses with the immortals, and beholds those great Causal Principles which, like mighty pillars, sustain the universe in its appointed place.

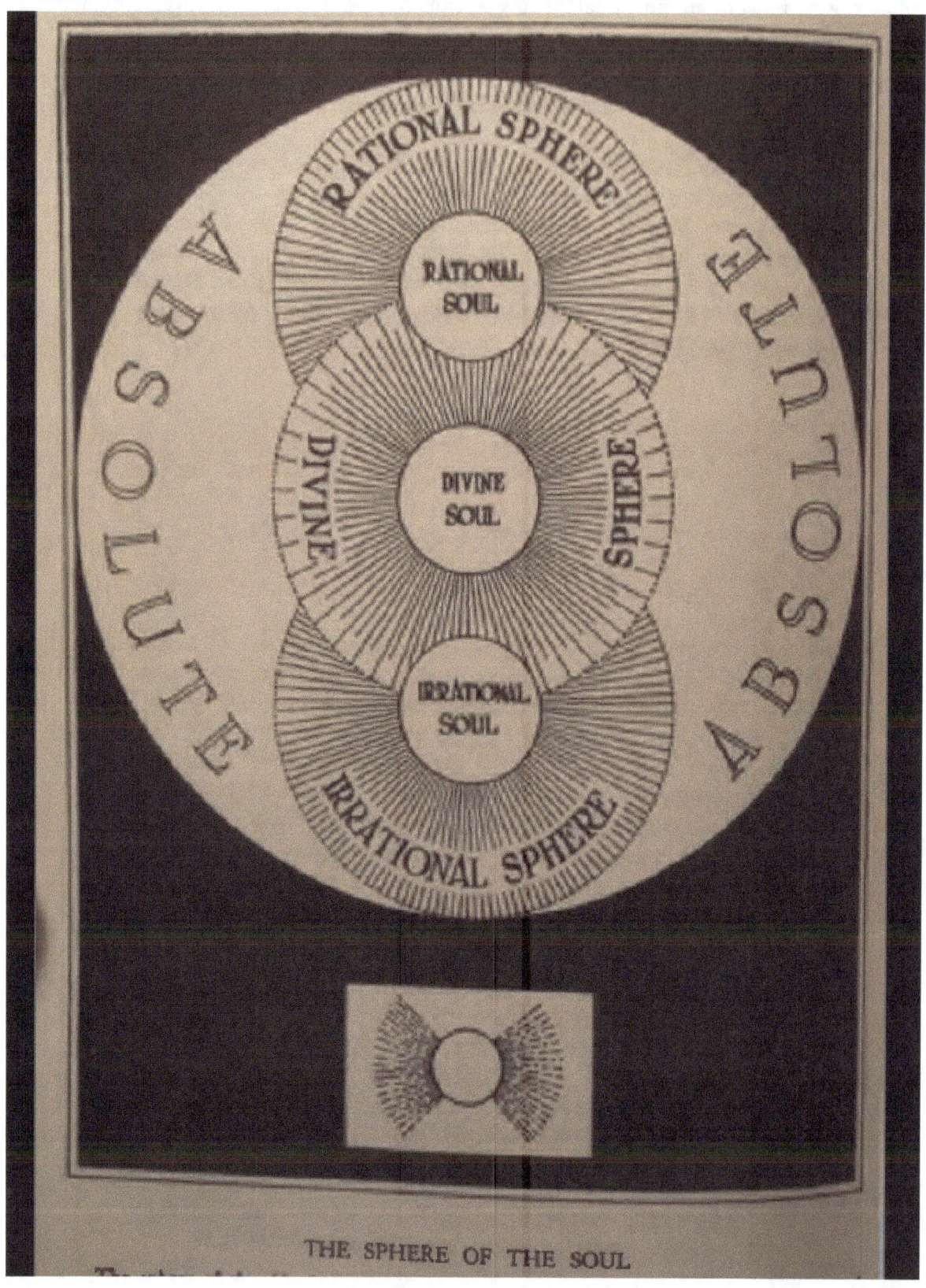

THE SPHERE OF THE SOUL

The sphere of the Absolute is here shown centered as a radiant power denominated the Divine Soul. While this Soul maintains its equilibrium, spiritual consciousness remains unbroken. But when the Soul inclines toward the extreme illusion of the rational and irrational souls—as a positive and negative poles

# XXV

### ❧

# The Wisdom of the Ancients by Francis Bacon

First published in 1609, The Wisdom of the Ancients (Latin: De Sapientia Veterum) stands as one of Francis Bacon's most enduring meditations on the intersection of myth, philosophy, and natural law. Far from mere fables, the myths of antiquity are here reinterpreted as repositories of veiled truths—parables encoded with the metaphysical, moral, and scientific understanding of ancient civilizations.

Bacon, ever the empiricist and reformer of learning, seeks to strip away the superstitions of time while preserving what he considered the "divine allegory" within the old poets' tales. In these essays, gods and monsters become symbols of natural forces, human passions, and ethical dilemmas. Prometheus speaks to the peril of unchecked invention, Pan embodies the all-encompassing world, and Narcissus reflects the vanity of self-regard.

This work reveals Bacon's belief that beneath the poetic disguises of ancient mythology lies a profound system of wisdom—a wisdom not obsolete, but obscured. In a world seeking both meaning and mastery, Bacon reminds us that the key to understanding the present may be hidden in the emblems of the past.

Let those who read seek more than story: seek understanding.

> "ANTIQUITY DESERVETH THAT REVERENCE, THAT MEN SHOULD STAND UPON THE ANCIENT TRACK, AND NOT MAKE TOO MUCH HASTE TO THE NOVELTIES OF THE PRESENT TIME."
> — FRANCIS BACON, DE SAPIENTIA VETERUM (1609)

# XXVI

### ❦

# The Wisdom of the Ancients

T HE WISDOM OF THE ANCIENTS.

PREFACE.

THE earliest antiquity lies buried in silence and oblivion, excepting the remains we have of it in sacred writ. This silence was succeeded by poetical fables, and these, at length, by the writings we now enjoy; so that the concealed and secret learning of the ancients seems separated from the history and knowledge of the following ages by a veil, or partition-wall of fables, interposing between the things that are lost and those that remain.

Many may imagine that I am here entering upon a work of fancy, or amusement, and design to use a poetical liberty, in explaining poetical fables. It is true, fables, in general, are composed of ductile matter, that may be drawn into great variety by a witty talent or an inventive genius, and be delivered of plausible meanings which they never contained. But this procedure has already been carried to excess; and great numbers, to procure the sanction of antiquity to their own notions and inventions, have miserably wrested and abused the fables of the ancients.

Nor is this only a late or unfrequent practice, but of ancient date and common even to this day. Thus Chrysippus, like an interpreter of dreams, attributed the opinions of the Stoics to the poets of old; and the chemists, at present, more childishly apply the poetical transformations to their experiments of the furnace. And though I have well weighed and considered all this, and thoroughly seen into the levity which the mind indulges for allegories and allusions, yet I cannot but retain a high value for the ancient mythology. And, certainly, it were very injudicious to suffer the fondness and licentiousness of a few to detract from the honor of all ego and parable in general. This would be rash, and almost profane; for, since religion delights in such shadows and disguises, to abolish them were, in a manner, to prohibit all intercourse betwixt things divine and human.

Upon deliberate consideration, my judgment is, that a concealed instruction and allegory was originally intended in many of the ancient fables. This opinion may, in some respect, be owing to the veneration I have for antiquity, but more to observing that some fables discover a great and evident similitude, relation, and connection with the thing they signify, as well in the structure

280

of the fable as in the propriety of the names whereby the persons or actors are characterized; insomuch, that no one could positively deny a sense and meaning to be from the first intended, and purposely shadowed out in them. For who can hear that Fame, after the giants were destroyed, sprung up as their posthumous sister, and not apply it to the clamor of parties and the seditious rumors which commonly fly about for a time upon the quelling of insurrections? Or who can read how the giant Typhon cut out and carried away Jupiter's sinews—which Mercury afterwards stole, and again restored to Jupiter—and not presently observe that this allegory denotes strong and powerful rebellions, which cut away from kings their sinews, both of money and authority; and that the way to have them restored is by lenity, affability, and prudent edicts, which soon reconcile, and, as it were, steal upon the affections of the subject? Or who, upon hearing that memorable expedition of the gods against the giants, when the braying of Silenus's ass greatly contributed in putting the giants to flight, does not clearly conceive that this directly points at the monstrous enterprises of rebellious subjects, which are frequently frustrated and disappointed by vain fears and empty rumors?

Again, the conformity and purport of the names is frequently manifest and self- evident. Thus Metis, the wife of Jupiter, plainly signifies counsel; Typhon, swelling; Pan, universality; Nemesis, revenge, &c. Nor is it a wonder, if sometimes a piece of history or other things are introduced, by way of ornament; or, if the times of the action are confounded; or, if part of one fable be tacked to another; or, if the allegory be new turned; for all this must necessarily happen, as the fables were the inventions of men who lived in different ages, and had different views; some of them being ancient, others more modern; some having an eye to natural philosophy, and others to morality or civil policy.

It may pass for a further indication of a concealed and secret meaning, that some of these fables are so absurd and idle in their narration, as to show and proclaim an allegory, even afar off. A fable that carries probability with it may be supposed invented for pleasure, or in imitation of history; but those that could never be conceived or related in this way must surely have a different use. For example, what a monstrous fiction is this, that Jupiter should take Metis to wife, and as soon as he found her pregnant eat her up, whereby he also conceived, and out of his head brought forth Pallas armed. Certainly no mortal could, but for the sake of the moral it couches, invent such an absurd dream as this, so much out of the road of thought!

But the argument of most weight with me is this, that many of these fables by no means appear to have been invented by the persons who relate and divulge them, whether Homer, Hesiod, or others; for if I were assured they first flowed from those later times and authors that transmit them to us, I should never expect any thing singularly great or noble from such an origin. But whoever attentively considers the thing, will find that these fables are delivered down and related by those writers, not as matters then first invented and proposed, but as things received and embraced in earlier ages. Besides, as they are differently related by writers nearly of the same ages, it is easily perceived that the relators drew from the common stock of ancient tradition, and varied but in point of embellishment, which is their own. And this principally raises my esteem of these fables, which I receive, not as the product of the age, or invention of the poets, but as sacred relics, gentle whispers, and the breath of better times, that from the traditions of more ancient nations came, at length, into the flutes and trumpets of the Greeks. But if any one shall, notwithstanding this, contend that allegories are always adventitious, or imposed upon the ancient fables, and no way native or genuinely contained in them, we might here leave him undisturbed in that gravity of judgment he affects (though we cannot help accounting it somewhat dull and phlegmatic), and, if it were worth the trouble, proceed to another kind of argument.

Men have proposed to answer two different and contrary ends by the use of parable; for parables serve as well to instruct or illustrate as to wrap up and envelop; so that though, for the present, we drop the concealed use, and suppose the ancient fables to be vague, undeterminate things, formed for amusement, still, the other use must remain, and can never be given up. And every man, of any learning, must readily allow that this method of instructing is grave, sober, or exceedingly useful, and sometimes necessary in the sciences, as it opens an easy and familiar passage to the human understanding, in all new discoveries that are abstruse and out of the road of vulgar opinions. Hence, in the first ages, when such inventions and conclusions of the human reason as are now trite and common were new and little known, all things abounded with fables, parables, similes, comparisons, and allusions, which were not intended to conceal, but to inform and teach, whilst the minds of men continued rude and unpractised in matters of subtilty and speculation, or even impatient, and in a manner incapable of receiving such things as did not fall directly under and strike the senses. For as hieroglyphics were in use before writing, so were parables in use before arguments. And even to this day, if any man would let new light in upon the human understanding, and conquer prejudice, without raising contests, animosities, opposition, or disturbance, he must still go in the same path, and have recourse to the like method of allegory, metaphor, and allusion.

To conclude, the knowledge of the early ages was either great or happy; great, if they by design made this use of trope and figure; happy, if, whilst they had other views, they afforded matter and occasion to such noble contemplations. Let either be the case, our pains, perhaps, will not be misemployed, whether we illustrate antiquity or things themselves.

The like, indeed, has been attempted by others; but, to speak ingenuously, their great and voluminous labors have almost destroyed the energy, the efficacy, and grace of the thing; whilst, being unskilled in nature, and their learning no more than that of commonplace, they have applied the sense of the parables to certain general and vulgar matters, without reaching to their real purport, genuine interpretation, and full depth. For myself, therefore, I expect to appear new in these common things, because, leaving untouched such as are sufficiently plain and open, I shall drive only at those that are either deep or rich.

THE WISDOM OF THE ANCIENTS.
A SERIES OF MYTHOLOGICAL FABLES.616

I. —CASSANDRA, OR DIVINATION.
EXPLAINED OF TOO FREE AND UNSEASONABLE ADVICE.
THE poets relate, that Apollo, falling in love with Cassandra, was still deluded and put off by

her, yet fed with hopes, till she had got from him the gift of prophesy; and, having now obtained her end, she flatly rejected his suit. Apollo, unable to recall his rash gift, yet enraged to be outwitted by a girl, annexed this penalty to it, that though she should always prophesy true, she should never be believed; whence her divinations were always slighted, even when she again and again predicted the ruin of her country.

EXPLANATION.—This fable seems invented to express the insignificance of unseasonable advice. For they who are conceited, stubborn, or intractable, and listen not to the instructions of Apollo, the god of harmony, so as to learn and observe the modulations and measures of affairs, the sharps and flats of discourse, the difference between judicious and vulgar ears, and the proper times of speech and silence, let them be ever so intelligent, and ever so frank of their advice, or their counsels ever so good and just, yet all their endeavors, either of persuasion or force, are of little significance, and rather hasten the ruin of those they advise. But, at last, when the calamitous event has made the sufferers feel the effect of their neglect, they too late reverence their advisers, as deep, foreseeing, and faithful prophets.

Of this, we have a remarkable instance in Cato of Utica, who discovered afar off, and long foretold, the approaching ruin of his country, both in the first conspiracy, and as it was prosecuted in the civil war between Cæsar and Pompey, yet did no good the while, but rather hurt the commonwealth, and hurried on its destruction, which Cicero wisely observed in these words: "Cato, indeed, judges excellently, but prejudices the state; for he speaks as in the commonwealth of Plato, and not as in the dregs of Romulus."

## II.  —TYPHON, OR A REBEL. EXPLAINED OF REBELLION.

THE fable runs, that Juno, enraged at Jupiter's bringing forth Pallas without her assistance, incessantly solicited all the gods and goddesses, that she might produce without Jupiter; and having by violence and importunity obtained the grant, she struck the earth, and thence immediately sprung up Typhon, a huge and dreadful monster, whom she committed to the nursing of a serpent. As soon as he was grown up, this monster waged war on Jupiter, and taking him prisoner in the battle, carried him away on his shoulders, into a remote and obscure quarter; and there, cutting out the sinews of his hands and feet, he bore them off, leaving Jupiter behind miserably maimed and mangled.

But Mercury afterwards stole these sinews from Typhon, and restored them to Jupiter. Hence, recovering his strength, Jupiter again pursues the monster; first wounds him with a stroke of his thunder, when serpents arose from the blood of the wound; and now the monster being dismayed, and taking to flight, Jupiter next darted Mount Ætna upon him, and crushed him with the weight.

EXPLANATION.—This fable seems designed to express the various fates of kings, and the turns that rebellions sometimes take, in kingdoms. For princes may be justly esteemed married to their states, as Jupiter to Juno; but it sometimes happens, that, being depraved by long wielding of the sceptre, and growing tyrannical, they would engross all to themselves, and, slighting the counsel of their senators and nobles, conceive by themselves; that is, govern according to their own arbitrary will and pleasure. This inflames the people, and makes them endeavor to create and set up some head of their own. Such designs are generally set on foot by the secret motion and instigation of the peers and nobles, under whose connivance the common sort are prepared for rising; whence proceeds a swell in the state, which is appositely denoted by the nursing of Typhon. This growing posture of affairs is fed by the natural depravity and malignant dispositions of the vulgar, which to kings is an envenomed serpent. And now the disaffected, uniting their force, at length break out into open rebellion, which, producing infinite mischiefs, both to prince and people, is represented by the horrid and multiplied deformity of Typhon, with his hundred heads, denoting the divided powers; his flaming mouths, denoting fire and devastation; his girdles of snakes, denoting sieges and destruction; his iron hands, slaughter and cruelty; his eagle's talons, rapine and plunder; his plumed body, perpetual rumors, contradictory accounts, &c. And sometimes these rebellions grow so high, that kings are obliged, as if carried on the backs of the rebels, to quit the throne, and retire to some remote and obscure part of their dominions, with the loss of their sinews, both of money and majesty.

But if now they prudently bear this reverse of fortune, they may, in a short time, by the assistance of Mercury, recover their sinews again; that is, by becoming moderate and affable; reconciling the minds and affections of the people to them, by gracious speeches and prudent proclamations, which will win over the subject cheerfully to afford new aids and supplies, and add fresh vigor to authority. But prudent and wary princes here seldom incline to try fortune by a war, yet do their utmost, by some grand exploit, to crush the reputation of the rebels; and if the attempt succeeds, the rebels, conscious of the wound received, and distrustful of their cause, first betake themselves to broken and empty threats, like the hissings of serpents; and next, when matters are grown desperate, to flight. And now, when they thus begin to shrink, it is safe and seasonable for kings to pursue them with their forces, and the whole strength of the kingdom; thus effectually quashing and suppressing them, as it were by the weight of a mountain.

III.    —THE CYCLOPS, OR THE MINISTERS OF TERROR. EXPLAINED OF BASE COURT OFFICERS.

IT is related that the Cyclops, for their savageness and cruelty, were by Jupiter first thrown into Tartarus, and there condemned to perpetual imprisonment; but that afterwards Tellus persuaded Jupiter it would be for his service to release them, and employ them in forging thunderbolts. This he accordingly did; and they, with unwearied pains and diligence, hammered out his bolts, and other instruments of terror, with a frightful and continual din of the anvil. It happened, long after, that Jupiter was displeased with Æsculapius, the son of Apollo, for having, by the art of medicine, restored a dead man to life; but concealing his indignation, because the action in itself was pious and illustrious, he secretly incensed the Cyclops against him, who, without remorse, presently slew him with their thunderbolts: in revenge whereof, Apollo, with Jupiter's connivance, shot them all dead with his arrows.

EXPLANATION.—This fable seems to point at the behavior of princes, who, having cruel, bloody, and oppressive ministers, first punish and displace them; but afterwards, by the advice of Tellus, that is, some earthly-minded and ignoble person, employ them again, to serve a turn, when there is occasion for cruelty in execution, or severity in exaction; but these ministers being base in their nature, whet by their former disgrace, and well aware of what is expected from them, use double diligence in their office; till, proceeding unwarily, and over-eager to gain favor, they sometimes, from the private nods, and ambiguous orders of their prince, perform some odious or execrable action: when princes, to decline the envy themselves, and knowing they shall never want such tools at their back, drop them, and give them up to the friends and followers of the injured person; thus exposing them, as sacrifices to revenge and popular odium: whence, with great applause, acclamations, and good wishes to the prince, these miscreants at last meet with their desert.

### IV.  —NARCISSUS, OR SELF-LOVE.

NARCISSUS is said to have been extremely beautiful and comely, but intolerably proud and disdainful; so that, pleased with himself, and scorning the world, he led a solitary life in the woods; hunting only with a few followers, who were his professed admirers, amongst whom the nymph Echo was his constant attendant. In this method of life, it was once his fate to approach a clear fountain, where he laid himself down to rest, in the noonday heat; when, beholding his image in the water, he fell into such a rapture and admiration of himself, that he could by no means be got away, but remained continually fixed and gazing, till at length he was turned into a flower, of his own name, which appears early in the spring, and is consecrated to the infernal deities, Pluto, Proserpine, and the Furies. EXPLANATION.—This fable seems to paint the behavior and fortune of those, who, for their beauty, or other endowments, wherewith nature (without any industry of their own) has graced and adorned them, are extravagantly fond of themselves: for men of such a disposition generally affect retirement, and absence from public affairs; as a life of business must necessarily subject them to many neglects and contempts, which might disturb and ruffle their minds: whence such persons commonly lead a solitary, private, and shadowy life: see little company, and those only such as highly admire and reverence them; or, like an echo, assent to all they say.

And they who are depraved, and rendered still fonder of themselves by this custom, grow strangely indolent, inactive, and perfectly stupid. The Narcissus, a spring flower, is an elegant emblem of this temper, which at first flourishes, and is talked of, but, when ripe, frustrates the expectation conceived of it.

And that this flower should be sacred to the infernal powers, carries out the allusion still further; because men of this humor are perfectly useless in all respects: for whatever yields no fruit, but passes, and is no more, like the way of a ship in the sea, was by the ancients consecrated to the infernal shades and powers.

### V.  —THE RIVER STYX, OR LEAGUES. EXPLAINED OF NECESSITY, IN THE OATHS OR SOLEMN
### LEAGUES OF PRINCES.

THE only solemn oath, by which the gods irrevocably obliged themselves, is a well known thing, and makes a part of many ancient fables. To this oath they did not invoke any celestial divinity, or divine attribute, but only called to witness the River Styx, which, with many meanders, surrounds the infernal court of Dis. For this form alone, and none but this, was held inviolable and obligatory; and the punishment of falsifying it, was that dreaded one of being excluded, for a certain number of years, the table of the gods.

EXPLANATION.—This fable seems invented to show the nature of the compacts and confederacies of princes; which, though ever so solemnly and religiously sworn to, prove but little the more binding for it: so that oaths, in this case, seem used rather for decorum, reputation, and ceremony, than for fidelity, security, and effectuating. And though these oaths were strengthened with the bonds of affinity, which are the links and ties of nature, and again, by mutual services and good offices, yet we see all this will generally give way to ambition, convenience, and the thirst of power: the rather, because it is easy for princes, under various specious pretences, to defend, disguise, and conceal their ambitious desires and insincerity, having no judge to call them to account. There is, however, one true and proper confirmation of their faith, though no celestial divinity, but that great divinity of princes, Necessity; or, the danger of the state; and the securing of advantage.

This necessity is elegantly represented by Styx, the fatal river that can never be crossed back. And this deity it was, which Iphicrates the Athenian invoked in making a league; and because he roundly and openly avows what most others studiously conceal, it may be proper to give his own words. Observing that the Lacedæmonians were inventing and proposing a variety of securities, sanctions, and bonds of alliance, he interrupted them thus: "There may, indeed, my friends, be one bond and means of security between us; and that is, for you to demonstrate you have delivered into our hands, such things as that, if you had the greatest desire to hurt us, you could not be able." Therefore, if the power of offending be taken away, or if, by a breach of compact, there be danger of destruction or diminution to the state or tribute, then it is that covenants will be ratified, and confirmed, as it were by the Stygian oath, whilst there remains an impending danger of being prohibited and excluded the banquet of the gods; by which expression the ancients denoted the rights and prerogatives, the affluence and the felicities, of empire and dominion.

VI.   —PAN, OR NATURE.617 EXPLAINED OF NATURAL PHILOSOPHY.

THE ancients have, with great exactness, delineated universal nature under the
person of Pan. They leave his origin doubtful; some asserting him the son of Mercury, and others the common offspring of all Penelope's suitors. The latter supposition doubtless occasioned some later rivals to entitle this ancient fable Penelope; a thing frequently practised when the earlier relations are applied to more modern characters and persons, though sometimes with great absurdity and ignorance, as in the present case; for Pan was one of the ancientest gods, and long before the time of Ulysses; besides, Penelope was venerated by antiquity for her matronal chastity. A third sort will have him the issue of Jupiter and Hybris, that is, Reproach. But whatever his origin was, the Destinies are allowed his sisters.

He is described by antiquity, with pyramidal horns reaching up to heaven, a rough and shaggy body, a very long beard, of a biform figure, human above, half brute below, ending in goat's feet. His arms, or ensigns of power, are, a pipe in his left hand, composed of seven reeds; in his right a crook; and he wore for his mantle a leopard's skin.

His attributes and titles were the god of hunters, shepherds, and all the rural inhabitants; president of the mountains; and, after Mercury, the next messenger of the gods. He was also held the leader and ruler of the Nymphs, who continually danced and frisked about him, attended with the Satyrs and their elders, the Sileni. He had also the power of striking terrors, especially such as were vain and superstitious; whence they came to be called panic terrors.618

Few actions are recorded of him; only a principal one is, that he challenged Cupid at wrestling, and was worsted. He also catched the giant Typhon in a net, and held him fast. They relate further of him, that when Ceres, growing disconsolate for the rape of Proserpine, hid herself, and all the gods took the utmost pains to find her, by going out different ways for that purpose, Pan only had the good fortune to meet her, as he was hunting, and discovered her to the rest. He likewise had the assurance to rival Apollo in music, and in the judgment of Midas was preferred; but the judge had, though with great privacy and secrecy, a pair of ass's ears fastened on him for his sentence.619

There is very little said of his amours; which may seem strange among such a multitude of gods, so profusely amorous. He is only reported to have been very fond of Echo, who was also esteemed his wife; and one nymph more, called Syrinx, with the love of whom Cupid inflamed him for his insolent challenge; so he is reported once to have solicited the moon to accompany him apart into the deep woods.

Lastly, Pan had no descendant, which also is a wonder, when the male gods were so extremely prolific; only he was the reputed father of a servant-girl called Iambe, who used to divert strangers with her ridiculous prattling stories.

This fable is perhaps the noblest of all antiquity, and pregnant with the mysteries and secrets of nature. Pan, as the name imports, represents the universe, about whose origin there are two opinions, viz: that it either sprung from Mercury, that is, the divine word, according to the Scriptures and philosophical divines, or from the confused seeds of things. For they who allow only one beginning of all things, either ascribe it to God, or, if they suppose a material beginning, acknowledge it to be various in its powers; so that the whole dispute comes to these points, viz: either that nature proceeds from Mercury, or from Penelope and all her suitors.620

The third origin of Pan seems borrowed by the Greeks from the Hebrew mysteries, either by means of the Egyptians, or otherwise; for it relates to the state of the world, not in its first creation, but as made subject to death and corruption after the fall; and in this state it was and remains, the offspring of God and Sin, or Jupiter and Reproach. And therefore these three several accounts of Pan's birth may seem true, if duly distinguished in respect of things and times. For this Pan, or the universal nature of things, which we view and contemplate, had its origin from the divine word and confused matter, first created by God himself, with the subsequent introduction of sin, and, consequently, corruption.

The Destinies, or the natures and fates of things, are justly made Pan's sisters, as the chain of natural causes links together the rise, duration, and corruption; the exaltation, degeneration, and workings; the processes, the effects, and changes, of all that can any way happen to things.

Horns are given him, broad at the roots, but narrow and sharp at the top, because the nature of all things seems pyramidal; for individuals are infinite, but being collected into a variety of species, they rise up into kinds, and these again ascend, and are contracted into generals, till at length nature may seem collected to a point. And no wonder if Pan's horns reach to the heavens, since the sublimities of nature, or abstract ideas, reach in a manner to things divine; for there is a short and ready passage from metaphysics to natural theology.

Pan's body, or the body of nature, is, with great propriety and elegance, painted shaggy and hairy, as representing the rays of things; for rays are as the hair or fleece of nature, and more or less worn by all bodies. This evidently appears in vision, and in all effects and operations at a distance; for whatever operates thus, may be properly said to emit rays.621 But particularly the beard of Pan is exceeding long, because the rays of the celestial bodies penetrate, and act to a prodigious distance, and have descended into the interior of the earth, so far as to change its surface; and the sun himself, when clouded on its upper part, appears to the eye bearded. Again, the body of nature is justly described biform, because of the difference between its superior and inferior parts, as the former, for their beauty, regularity of motion, and influence over the earth, may be properly represented by the human figure, and the latter, because of their disorder, irregularity, and subjection to the celestial bodies, are by the brutal. This biform figure also represents the participation of one species with another; for there appear to be no simple natures, but all participate or consist of two: thus, man has somewhat of the brute, the brute somewhat of the plant, the plant somewhat of the mineral; so that all natural bodies have really two faces, or consist of a superior and an inferior species.

There lies a curious allegory in the making of Pan goat-footed, on account of the motion of ascent which the terrestrial bodies have towards the air and heavens; for the goat is a clambering creature, that delights in climbing up rocks and precipices; and in the same manner the matters destined to this lower globe strongly affect to rise upwards, as appears from the clouds and meteors. Pan's arms, or the ensigns he bears in his hands, are of two kinds—the one an emblem of harmony, the other of empire. His pipe, composed of seven reeds, plainly denotes the consent and harmony, or the concords and discords of things, produced by the motion of the seven planets. His crook, also, contains a fine representation of the ways of nature, which are partly straight and partly crooked; thus the staff, having an extraordinary bend towards the top, denotes that the works of Divine Providence are generally brought about by remote means, or in a circuit, as if somewhat else were intended rather than the effect produced, as in the sending of Joseph into Egypt, &c. So likewise in human government, they who sit at the helm, manage and wind the people more successfully by pretext and oblique courses, than they could by such as are direct and straight; so that, in effect, all sceptres are crooked at the top.

Pan's mantle, or clothing, is with great ingenuity made of a leopard's skin, because of the spots it has; for in like manner the heavens are sprinkled with stars, the sea with islands, the earth with flowers, and almost each particular thing is variegated, or wears a mottled coat.

The office of Pan could not be more livelily expressed than by making him the god of hunters; for every natural action, every motion and process, is no other than a chase. Thus arts and sciences hunt out their works, and human schemes and counsels their several ends; and all living creatures either hunt out their aliment, pursue their prey, or seek their pleasures, and this in a skilful and sagacious manner.622 He is also styled the god of the rural inhabitants, because men in this situation live more according to nature than they do in cities and courts, where nature is so corrupted with effeminate arts, that the saying of the poet may be verified:——pars minima est ipsa puella sui.

He is likewise particularly styled President of the Mountains, because in mountains and lofty places the nature of things lies more open and exposed to the eye and the understanding.

In his being called the messenger of the gods, next after Mercury, lies a divine allegory, as next after the Word of God, the image of the world is the herald of the Divine power and wisdom, according to the expression of the Psalmist: "The heavens declare the glory of God, and the firmament showeth his handiwork."624

Pan is delighted with the company of the Nymphs, that is, the souls of all living creatures are the delight of the world; and he is properly called their governor, because each of them follows its own nature, as a leader, and all dance about their own respective rings, with infinite variety and never-ceasing motion. And with these continually join the Satyrs and Sileni, that is, youth and age; for all things have a kind of young, cheerful, and dancing time; and again their time of slowness, tottering, and creeping. And whoever, in a true light, considers the motions and endeavors of both these ages, like another Democritus, will perhaps find them as odd and strange as the gesticulations and antic motions of the Satyrs and Sileni.

The power he had of striking terrors contains a very sensible doctrine; for nature has implanted fear in all living creatures, as well to keep them from risking their lives, as to guard against injuries and violence; and yet this nature or passion keeps not its bounds, but with just and profitable fears always mixes such as are vain and senseless; so that all things, if we could see their insides, would appear full of panic terrors. Thus mankind, particularly the vulgar, labor under a high degree of superstition, which is nothing more than a panic-dread, that principally reigns in unsettled and troublesome times.

The presumption of Pan in challenging Cupid to the conflict denotes that matter has an appetite and tendency to a dissolution of the world, and falling back to its first chaos again, unless this depravity and inclination were restrained and subdued by a more powerful concord and agreement of things, properly expressed by Love, or Cupid: it is therefore well for mankind, and the state of all things, that Pan was thrown and conquered in the struggle.

His catching and detaining Typhon in the net receives a similar explanation; for whatever vast and unusual swells, which the word typhon signifies, may sometimes be raised in nature, as in the sea, the clouds, the earth, or the like, yet nature catches, entangles, and holds all such outrages and insurrections in her inextricable net, wove, as it were, of adamant.

That part of the fable which attributes the discovery of lost Ceres to Pan whilst he was hunting—a happiness denied the other gods, though they diligently and expressly sought her—contains an exceeding just and prudent admonition; viz: that we are not to expect the discovery of things useful in common life, as that of corn, denoted by Ceres, from abstract philosophies, as if these were the gods of the first order,—no, not though we used our utmost endeavors this way,—but only from Pan; that is, a sagacious experience and general knowledge of nature, which is often found, even by accident, to stumble upon such discoveries whilst the pursuit was directed another way.

The event of his contending with Apollo in music affords us a useful instruction, that may help to humble the human reason and judgment, which is too apt to boast and glory in itself. There seem to be two kinds of harmony,—the one of Divine providence, the other of human reason; but the government of the world, the administration of its affairs, and the more secret Divine judgments, sound harsh and dissonant to human ears or human judgment; and though this ignorance be justly rewarded with asses' ears, yet they are put on and worn, not openly, but with great secrecy; nor is the deformity of the thing seen or observed by the vulgar.

We must not find it strange if no amours are related of Pan besides his marriage with Echo; for nature enjoys itself, and in itself all other things. He that loves, desires enjoyment, but in profusion there is no room for desire; and therefore Pan, remaining content with himself, has no passion unless it be for discourse, which is well shadowed out by Echo, or talk, or, when it is more accurate, by Syrinx, or writing.625 But Echo makes a most excellent wife for Pan, as being no other than genuine philosophy, which faithfully repeats his words, or only transcribes exactly as nature dictates; thus representing the true image and reflection of the world without adding a tittle.

It tends, also, to the support and perfection of Pan, or nature, to be without offspring; for the world generates in its parts, and not in the way of a whole, as wanting a body external to itself wherewith to generate.

Lastly, for the supposed or spurious prattling daughter of Pan, it is an excellent addition to the fable, and aptly represents the talkative philosophies that have at all times been stirring, and filled the world with idle tales; being ever barren, empty, and servile, though sometimes indeed diverting and entertaining, and sometimes again troublesome and importunate.

## VII. —PERSEUS,626 OR WAR. EXPLAINED OF THE PREPARATION AND CONDUCT NECESSARY TO WAR.

"THE fable relates, that Perseus was dispatched from the east, by Pallas, to cut off Medusa's head, who had committed great ravage upon the people of the west; for this Medusa was so dire a monster, as to turn into stone all those who but looked upon her. She was a Gorgon, and the only mortal one of the three, the other two being invulnerable. Perseus, therefore, preparing himself for this grand enterprise, had presents made him from three of the gods: Mercury gave him wings for his heels; Pluto, a helmet; and Pallas, a shield and a mirror. But, though he was now so well equipped, he posted not directly to Medusa, but first turned aside to the Greæ, who were half-sisters to the Gorgons. These Greæ were grayheaded, and like old women, from their birth, having among them all three but one eye, and one tooth, which, as they had occasion to go out, they each wore by turns, and laid them down again upon coming back. This eye and this tooth they lent to Perseus, who now judging himself sufficiently furnished, he, without further stop, flies swiftly away to Medusa, and finds her asleep. But not venturing his eyes, for fear she should wake, he turned his head aside, and viewed her in Pallas's mirror, and thus directing his stroke, cut off her head; when immediately, from the gushing blood, there darted Pegasus winged. Perseus now inserted Medusa's head into Pallas's shield, which thence retained the faculty of astonishing and benumbing all who looked on it."

This fable seems invented to show the prudent method of choosing, undertaking, and conducting a war; and, accordingly, lays down three useful precepts about it, as if they were the precepts of Pallas.

The first is, that no prince should be over-solicitous to subdue a neighboring nation; for the method of enlarging an empire is very different from that of increasing an estate. Regard is justly had to contiguity, or adjacency, in private lands and possessions; but in the extending of empire, the occasion, the facility, and advantage of a war, are to be regarded instead of vicinity. It is certain that the Romans, at the time they stretched but little beyond Liguria to the west, had by their arms subdued the provinces as far as Mount Taurus to the east. And thus Perseus readily undertook a very long expedition, even from the east to the extremities of the west.

The second precept is, that the cause of the war be just and honorable; for this adds alacrity both to the soldiers, and the people who find the supplies; procures aids, alliances, and numerous other conveniences. Now there is no cause of war more just and laudable than the suppressing of tyranny; by which a people are dispirited, benumbed, or left without life and vigor, as at the sight of Medusa.

Lastly, it is prudently added, that, as there were three of the Gorgons, who represent war, Perseus singled her out for this expedition that was mortal; which affords this precept, that such kind of wars should be chose as may be brought to a conclusion without pursuing vast and infinite hopes. Again, Perseus's setting-out is extremely well adapted to his undertaking, and in a manner commands success; he received dispatch from Mercury, secrecy from Pluto, and foresight from Pallas. It also contains an excellent allegory, that the wings given him by Mercury were for his heels, not for his shoulders; because expedition is not so much required in the first preparations for war, as in the subsequent matters, that administer to the first; for there is no error more frequent in war, than, after brisk preparations, to halt for subsidiary forces and effective supplies.

The allegory of Pluto's helmet, rendering men invisible and secret, is sufficiently evident of itself; but the mystery of the shield and the mirror lies deeper; and denotes, that not only a prudent caution must be had to defend, like the shield, but also such an address and penetration as may discover the strength, the motions, the counsels, and designs of the enemy; like the mirror of Pallas.

But though Perseus may now seem extremely well prepared, there still remains the most important thing of all; before he enters upon the war, he must of necessity consult the Greæ. These Greæ are treasons; half, but degenerate sisters of the Gorgons; who are representatives of wars; for wars are generous and noble; but treasons base and vile. The Greæ are elegantly described as hoary- headed, and like old women from their birth; on account of the perpetual cares, fears, and trepidations attending traitors. Their force, also, before it breaks out into open revolt, consists either in an eye or a tooth; for all faction, alienated from a state, is both watchful and biting; and this eye and tooth are, as it were, common to all the disaffected; because whatever they learn and know is transmitted from one to another, as by the hands of faction. And for the tooth, they all bite with the same: and clamor with one throat; so that each of them singly expresses the multitude.

These Greæ, therefore, must be prevailed upon by Perseus to lend him their eye and their tooth; the eye to give him indications, and make discoveries; the tooth for sowing rumors, raising envy, and stirring up the minds of the people. And when all these things are thus disposed and prepared, then follows the action of the war.

He finds Medusa asleep; for whoever undertakes a war with prudence, generally falls upon the enemy unprepared, and nearly in a state of security; and here is the occasion for Pallas's mirror: for it is common enough, before the danger presents itself, to see exactly into the state and posture of the enemy; but the principal use of the glass is, in the very instant of danger, to discover the manner thereof, and prevent consternation; which is the thing intended by Perseus's turning his head aside, and viewing the enemy in the glass.627

Two effects here follow the conquest: 1. The darting forth of Pegasus; which evidently denotes fame, that flies abroad, proclaiming the victory far and near. 2. The bearing of Medusa's head in the shield, which is the greatest possible defence and safeguard; for one grand and memorable enterprise, happily accomplished, bridles all the motions and attempts of the enemy, stupefies disaffection, and quells commotions.

### VIII. —ENDYMION, OR A FAVORITE. EXPLAINED OF COURT FAVORITES.

THE goddess Luna is said to have fallen in love with the shepherd Endymion, and
to have carried on her amours with him in a new and singular manner; it being her custom, whilst he lay reposing in his native cave, under Mount Latmus, to descend frequently from her sphere, enjoy his company whilst he slept, and then go up to heaven again. And all this while, Endymion's fortune was no way prejudiced by his unactive and sleepy life, the goddess causing his flocks to thrive, and grow so exceeding numerous, that none of the other shepherds could compare with him. EXPLANATION.—This fable seems to describe the tempers and dispositions of princes, who, being thoughtful and suspicious, do not easily admit to their privacies such men as are prying, curious, and vigilant, or, as it were, sleepless; but rather such as are of an easy, obliging nature, and indulge them in their pleasures, without seeking anything further; but seeming ignorant, insensible, or, as it were, lulled asleep before them.628 Princes usually treat such persons familiarly; and quitting their throne, like Luna, think they may, with safety, unbosom to them. This temper was very remarkable in Tiberius, a prince exceedingly difficult to please, and who had no favorites but those that perfectly understood his way, and, at the same time, obstinately dissembled their knowledge, almost to a degree of stupidity.

The cave is not improperly mentioned in the fable; it being a common thing for the favorites of a prince to have their pleasant retreats, whither to invite him, by way of relaxation, though without prejudice to their own fortunes; these favorites usually making a good provision for themselves. For though their prince should not, perhaps, promote them to dignities, yet, out of real affection, and not only for convenience, they generally feel the enriching influence of his bounty.

### IX. —THE SISTER OF THE GIANTS, OR FAME. EXPLAINED OF PUBLIC DETRACTION.

THE poets relate, that the giants, produced from the earth, made war upon Jupiter,
and the other gods, but were repulsed and conquered by thunder; whereat the earth, provoked, brought forth Fame, the youngest sister of the giants, in revenge for the death of her sons.

EXPLANATION.—The meaning of the fable seems to be this: the earth denotes the nature of the vulgar, who are always swelling, and rising against their rulers, and endeavoring at changes. This disposition, getting a fit opportunity, breeds rebels and traitors, who, with impetuous rage, threaten and contrive the overthrow and destruction of princes. And when brought under and subdued, the same vile and restless nature of the people, impatient of peace, produces rumors, detractions, slanders, libels, &c., to blacken those in authority; so that rebellious actions and seditious rumors, differ not in origin and stock, but only, as it were, in sex; treasons and rebellions being the brothers, and scandal or detraction the sister.

X.  —ACTEON AND PENTHEUS, OR A CURIOUS MAN.
EXPLAINED OF CURIOSITY, OR PRYING INTO THE SECRETS OF PRINCES AND DIVINE MYSTERIES.
THE ancients afford us two examples for suppressing the impertinent curiosity of mankind, in diving into secrets, and imprudently longing and endeavoring to discover them. The one of these is in the person of Acteon, and the other in that of Pentheus. Acteon, undesignedly chancing to see Diana naked, was turned into a stag, and torn to pieces by his own hounds. And Pentheus, desiring to pry into the hidden mysteries of Bacchus's sacrifice, and climbing a tree for that purpose, was struck with a frenzy. This frenzy of Pentheus caused him to see things double, particularly the sun, and his own city, Thebes, so that running homewards, and immediately espying another Thebes, he runs towards that; and thus continues incessantly, tending first to the one, and then to the other, without coming at either.

EXPLANATION.—The first of these fables may relate to the secrets of princes, and the second to divine mysteries. For they who are not intimate with a prince, yet, against his will, have a knowledge of his secrets, inevitably incur his displeasure; and therefore, being aware that they are singled out, and all opportunities watched against them, they lead the life of a stag, full of fears and suspicions. It likewise frequently happens that their servants and domestics accuse them, and plot their overthrow, in order to procure favor with the prince; for whenever the king manifests his displeasure, the person it falls upon must expect his servants to betray him, and worry him down, as Acteon was worried by his own dogs.

The punishment of Pentheus is of another kind; for they who, unmindful of their mortal state, rashly aspire to divine mysteries, by climbing the heights of nature and philosophy, here represented by climbing a tree,—their fate is perpetual inconstancy, perplexity, and instability of judgment. For as there is one light of nature, and another light that is divine, they see, as it were, two suns. And as the actions of life, and the determinations of the will, depend upon the understanding, they are distracted as much in opinion as in will; and therefore judge very inconsistently, or contradictorily; and see, as it were, Thebes double; for Thebes being the refuge and habitation of Pentheus, here denotes the ends of actions; whence they know not what course to take, but remaining undetermined and unresolved in their views and designs, they are merely driven about by every sudden gust and impulse of the mind.

XI.  —ORPHEUS, OR PHILOSOPHY. EXPLAINED OF NATURAL AND MORAL PHILOSOPHY.
INTRODUCTION.—The fable of Orpheus, though trite and common, has never been well interpreted, and seems to hold out a picture of universal philosophy; for to this sense may be

easily transferred what is said of his being a wonderful and perfectly divine person, skilled in all kinds of harmony, subduing and drawing all things after him by sweet and gentle methods and modulations. For the labors of Orpheus exceed the labors of Hercules, both in power and dignity, as the works of knowledge exceed the works of strength.

FABLE.—Orpheus having his beloved wife snatched from him by sudden death, resolved upon descending to the infernal regions, to try if, by the power of his harp, he could reobtain her. And, in effect, he so appeased and soothed the infernal powers by the melody and sweetness of his harp and voice, that they indulged him the liberty of taking her back, on condition that she should follow him behind, and he not turn to look upon her till they came into open day; but he, through the impatience of his care and affection, and thinking himself almost past danger, at length looked behind him, whereby the condition was violated, and she again precipitated to Pluto's regions. From this time Orpheus grew pensive and sad, a hater of the sex, and went into solitude, where, by the same sweetness of his harp and voice, he first drew the wild beasts of all sorts about him; so that, forgetting their natures, they were neither actuated by revenge, cruelty, lust, hunger, or the desire of prey, but stood gazing about him, in a tame and gentle manner, listening attentively to his music. Nay, so great was the power and efficacy of his harmony, that it even caused the trees and stones to remove, and place themselves in a regular manner about him. When he had for a time, and with great admiration, continued to do this, at length the Thracian women, raised by the instigation of Bacchus, first blew a deep and hoarse- sounding horn, in such an outrageous manner, that it quite drowned the music of Orpheus. And thus the power which, as the link of their society, held all things in order, being dissolved, disturbance reigned anew; each creature returned to its own nature, and pursued and preyed upon its fellow, as before. The rocks and woods also started back to their former places; and even Orpheus himself was at last torn to pieces by these female furies, and his limbs scattered all over the desert. But, in sorrow and revenge for his death, the River Helicon, sacred to the Muses, hid its waters under ground, and rose again in other places.

EXPLANATION.—The fable receives this explanation. The music of Orpheus is of two kinds; one that appeases the infernal powers, and the other that draws together the wild beasts and trees. The former properly relates to natural, and the latter to moral philosophy, or civil society. The reinstatement and restoration of corruptible things is the noblest work of natural philosophy; and, in a less degree, the preservation of bodies in their own state, or a prevention of their dissolution and corruption. And if this be possible, it can certainly be effected no other way than by proper and exquisite attemperations of nature; as it were by the harmony and fine touching of the harp. But as this is a thing of exceeding great difficulty, the end is seldom obtained; and that, probably, for no reason more than a curious and unseasonable impatience and solicitude.

And, therefore, philosophy, being almost unequal to the task, has cause to grow sad, and hence betakes itself to human affairs, insinuating into men's minds the love of virtue, equity, and peace, by means of eloquence and persuasion; thus forming men into societies; bringing them under laws and regulations; and making them forget their unbridled passions and affections, so long as they hearken to precepts and submit to discipline. And thus they soon after build themselves habitations, form cities, cultivate lands, plant orchards, gardens, &c. So that they may not improperly be said to remove and call the trees and stones together.

And this regard to civil affairs is justly and regularly placed after diligent trial made for restoring the mortal body; the attempt being frustrated in the end— because the unavoidable necessity of death, thus evidently laid before mankind, animates them to seek a kind of eternity by works of perpetuity, character, and fame.

It is also prudently added, that Orpheus was afterwards averse to women and wedlock, because the indulgence of the married state, and the natural affections which men have for their children, often prevent them from entering upon any grand, noble, or meritorious enterprise for the public good; as thinking it sufficient to obtain immortality by their descendants, without endeavoring at great actions.

And even the works of knowledge, though the most excellent among human things, have their periods; for after kingdoms and commonwealths have flourished for a time, disturbances, seditions, and wars, often arise, in the din whereof, first the laws are silent, and not heard; and then men return to their own depraved natures—whence cultivated lands and cities soon become desolate and waste. And if this disorder continues, learning and philosophy is infallibly torn to pieces; so that only some scattered fragments thereof can afterwards be found up and down, in a few places, like planks after a shipwreck. And barbarous times succeeding, the River Helicon dips under-ground; that is, letters are buried, till things having undergone their due course of changes, learning rises again, and shows its head, though seldom in the same place, but in some other nation.629

## XII. —CŒLUM, OR BEGINNINGS.
### EXPLAINED OF THE CREATION, OR ORIGIN OF ALL THINGS.

THE poets relate, that Cœlum was the most ancient of all the gods; that his parts of generation were cut off by his son Saturn; that Saturn had a numerous offspring, but devoured all his sons, as soon as they were born; that Jupiter at length escaped the common fate; and when grown up, drove his father Saturn into Tartarus; usurped the kingdom; cut off his father's genitals, with the same knife wherewith Saturn had dismembered Cœlum, and throwing them into the sea, thence sprung Venus.

Before Jupiter was well established in his empire, two memorable wars were made upon him; the first by the Titans, in subduing of whom, Sol, the only one of the Titans who favored Jupiter, performed him singular service; the second by the giants, who being destroyed and subdued by the thunder and arms of Jupiter, he now reigned secure.

EXPLANATION.—This fable appears to be an enigmatical account of the origin of all things, not greatly differing from the philosophy afterwards embraced by Democritus, who expressly asserts the eternity of matter, but denies the eternity of the world; thereby approaching to the truth of sacred writ, which makes chaos, or uninformed matter, to exist before the six days' works.

The meaning of the fable seems to be this: Cœlum denotes the concave space, or vaulted roof that incloses all matter, and Saturn the matter itself, which cuts off all power of generation from his father; as one and the same quantity of matter remains invariable in nature, without addition or diminution. But the agitations and struggling motions of matter, first produced certain imperfect and ill-joined compositions of things, as it were so many first rudiments, or essays of worlds; till, in process of time, there arose a fabric capable of preserving its form and structure. Whence the first age was shadowed out by the reign of Saturn; who, on account of the frequent dissolutions, and short durations of things, was said to devour his children. And the second age was denoted by the reign of Jupiter; who thrust, or drove those frequent and transitory changes into *Tartarus*—a place expressive of disorder. This place seems to be the middle space, between the lower heavens and the internal parts of the earth, wherein disorder, imperfection, mutation, mortality, destruction, and corruption, are principally found.

Venus was not born during the former generation of things, under the reign of Saturn; for whilst discord and jar had the upper hand of concord and uniformity in the matter of the universe, a change of the entire structure was necessary. And in this manner things were generated and destroyed, before Saturn was dismembered. But when this manner of generation ceased, there immediately followed another, brought about by Venus, or a perfect and established harmony of things; whereby changes were wrought in the parts, whilst the universal fabric remained entire and undisturbed. Saturn, however, is said to be thrust out and dethroned, not killed, and become extinct; because, agreeably to the opinion of Democritus, the world might relapse into its old confusion and disorder, which Lucretius hoped would not happen in his time.630

But now, when the world was compact, and held together by its own bulk and energy, yet there was no rest from the beginning; for first, there followed considerable motions and disturbances in the celestial regions, though so regulated and moderated by the power of the Sun, prevailing over the heavenly bodies, as to continue the world in its state. Afterwards there followed the like in the lower parts, by inundations, storms, winds, general earthquakes, &c., which, however, being subdued and kept under, there ensued a more peaceable and lasting harmony, and consent of things.

It may be said of this fable, that it includes philosophy; and again, that philosophy includes the fable; for we know, by faith, that all these things are but the oracle of sense, long since ceased and decayed; but the matter and fabric of the world being justly attributed to a creator.

XIII.   —PROTEUS, OR MATTER. EXPLAINED OF MATTER AND ITS CHANGES.
PROTEUS, according to the poets, was Neptune's herdsman; an old man, and a
most extraordinary prophet, who understood things past and present, as well as future; so that besides the business of divination, he was the revealer and interpreter of all antiquity, and secrets of every kind. He lived in a vast cave, where his custom was to tell over his herd of sea-calves at noon, and then to sleep. Whoever consulted him, had no other way of obtaining an answer, but by binding him with manacles and fetters; when he, endeavoring to free himself, would change into all kinds of shapes and miraculous forms; as of fire, water, wild beasts, &c.; till at length he resumed his own shape again.

EXPLANATION.—This fable seems to point at the secrets of nature, and the states of matter. For the person of Proteus denotes matter, the oldest of all things, after God himself;631 that resides, as in a cave, under the vast concavity of the heavens. He is represented as the servant of Neptune, because the various operations and modifications of matter are principally wrought in a fluid state. The herd, or flock of Proteus, seems to be no other than the several kinds of animals, plants, and minerals, in which matter appears to diffuse and spend itself; so that after having formed these several species, and as it were finished its task, it seems to sleep and repose, without otherwise attempting to produce any new ones. And this is the moral of Proteus's counting his herd, then going to sleep.

This is said to be done at noon, not in the morning or evening; by which is meant the time best fitted and disposed for the production of species, from a matter duly prepared, and made ready beforehand, and now lying in a middle state, between its first rudiments and decline; which, we learn from sacred history, was the case at the time of the creation; when, by the efficacy of the divine command, matter directly came together, without any transformation or intermediate changes, which it affects; instantly obeyed the order, and appeared in the form of creatures.

And thus far the fable reaches of Proteus, and his flock, at liberty and unrestrained. For the universe, with the common structures, and fabrics of the creatures, is the face of matter, not under constraint, or as the flock wrought upon and tortured by human means. But if any skilful minister of nature shall apply force to matter, and by design torture and vex it, in order to its annihilation, it, on the contrary, being brought under this necessity, changes and transforms itself into a strange variety of shapes and appearances; for nothing but the power of the Creator can annihilate, or truly destroy it; so that at length, running through the whole circle of transformations, and completing its period, it in some degree restores itself, if the force be continued. And that method of binding, torturing, or detaining, will prove the most effectual and expeditious, which makes use of manacles and fetters; that is, lays hold and works upon matter in the extremest degrees.

The addition in the fable that makes Proteus a prophet, who had the knowledge of things past, present, and future, excellently agrees with the nature of matter; as he who knows the properties, the changes, and the processes of matter, must, of necessity, understand the effects and sum of what it does, has done, or can do, though his knowledge extends not to all the parts and particulars thereof.

XIV.   —MEMNON, OR A YOUTH TOO FORWARD. EXPLAINED OF THE FATAL PRECIPITANCY OF YOUTH.

THE poets made Memnon the son of Aurora, and bring him to the Trojan war in beautiful armor, and flushed with popular praise; where, thirsting after further glory, and rashly hurrying on to the greatest enterprises, he engages the bravest warrior of all the Greeks, Achilles, and falls by his hand in single combat. Jupiter, in commiseration of his death, sent birds to grace his funeral, that perpetually chanted certain mournful and bewailing dirges. It is also reported, that the rays of the rising sun, striking his statue, used to give a lamenting sound.

EXPLANATION.—This fable regards the unfortunate end of those promising youths, who, like sons of the morning, elate with empty hopes and glittering outsides, attempt things beyond their strength; challenge the bravest heroes; provoke them to the combat; and, proving unequal, die in their high attempts.

The death of such youths seldom fails to meet with infinite pity; as no mortal calamity is more moving and afflicting, than to see the flower of virtue cropped before its time. Nay, the prime of life enjoyed to the full, or even to a degree of envy, does not assuage or moderate the grief occasioned by the untimely death of such hopeful youths; but lamentations and bewailings fly, like mournful birds, about their tombs, for a long while after; especially upon all fresh occasions, new commotions, and the beginning of great actions, the passionate desire of them is renewed, as by the sun's morning rays.

XV. —TYTHONUS, OR SATIETY. EXPLAINED OF PREDOMINANT PASSIONS.

IT is elegantly fabled by Tythonus, that being exceedingly beloved by Aurora, she petitioned Jupiter that he might prove immortal, thereby to secure herself the everlasting enjoyment of his company; but through female inadvertence she forgot to add, that he might never grow old; so that, though he proved immortal, he became miserably worn and consumed with age, insomuch that Jupiter, out of pity, at length transformed him to a grasshopper.

EXPLANATION.—This fable seems to contain an ingenious description of pleasure; which at first, as it were in the morning of the day, is so welcome, that men pray to have it everlasting, but forget that satiety and weariness of it will, like old age, overtake them, though they think not of it; so that at length, when their appetite for pleasurable actions is gone, their desires and affections often continue; whence we commonly find that aged persons delight themselves with the discourse and remembrance of the things agreeable to them in their better days. This is very remarkable in men of a loose, and men of a military life; the former whereof are always talking over their amours, and the latter the exploits of their youth; like grasshoppers, that show their vigor only by their chirping.

XVI. —JUNO'S SUITOR, OR BASENESS. EXPLAINED OF SUBMISSION AND ABJECTION.

THE poets tell us, that Jupiter, to carry on his love-intrigues, assumed many different shapes; as of a bull, an eagle, a swan, a golden shower, &c.; but when he attempted Juno, he turned himself into the most ignoble and ridiculous creature,—even that of a wretched, wet, weather-beaten, affrighted, trembling and half-starved cuckoo.

EXPLANATION.—This is a wise fable, and drawn from the very entrails of morality. The moral is, that men should not be conceited of themselves, and imagine that a discovery of their excellences will always render them acceptable; for this can only succeed according to the nature and manners of the person they court, or solicit; who, if he be a man not of the same gifts and endowments, but altogether of a haughty and contemptuous behavior, here represented by the person of Juno, they must entirely drop the character that carries the least show of worth or gracefulness; if they proceed upon any other footing, it is downright folly; nor is it sufficient to act the deformity of obsequiousness, unless they really change themselves, and become abject and contemptible in their persons.

XVII. —CUPID, OR AN ATOM. EXPLAINED OF THE CORPUSCULAR PHILOSOPHY.

THE particulars related by the poets of Cupid, or Love, do not properly agree to the same person, yet they differ only so far, that if the confusion of persons be rejected, the correspondence may hold. They say, that Love was the most ancient of all the gods, and existed before every thing else, except Chaos, which is held coeval therewith. But for Chaos, the ancients never paid divine honors, nor gave the title of a god thereto. Love is represented absolutely without progenitor, excepting only that he is said to have proceeded from the egg of Nox; but that himself begot the gods, and all things else, on Chaos. His attributes are four; viz: 1, perpetual infancy; 2, blindness; 3, nakedness; and 4, archery.

There was also another Cupid, or Love, the youngest son of the gods, born of Venus; and upon him the attributes of the elder are transferred, with some degree of correspondence.

EXPLANATION.—This fable points at, and enters, the cradle of nature. Love seems to be the appetite, or incentive, of the primitive matter; or, to speak more distinctly, the natural motion, or moving principle, of the original corpuscles, or atoms; this being the most ancient and only power that made and wrought all things out of matter. It is absolutely without parent, that is, without cause; for causes are as parents to effects; but this power or efficacy could have no natural cause; for, excepting God, nothing was before it; and therefore it could have no efficient in nature. And as nothing is more inward with nature, it can neither be a genus nor a form; and therefore, whatever it is, it must be somewhat positive, though inexpressible. And if it were possible to conceive its modus and process, yet it could not be known from its cause, as being, next to God, the cause of causes, and itself without a cause. And, perhaps, we are not to hope that the modus of it should fall, or be comprehended, under human inquiry. Whence it is properly feigned to be the egg of Nox, or laid in the dark.

The divine philosopher declares, that "God has made every thing beautiful in its season; and has given over the world to our disputes and inquiries; but that man cannot find out the work which God has wrought, from its beginning up to its end." Thus the summary or collective law of nature, or the principle of love, impressed by God upon the original particles of all things, so as to make them attack each other and come together, by the repetition and multiplication whereof all the variety in the universe is produced, can scarce possibly find full admittance into the thoughts of men, though some faint notion may be had thereof. The Greek philosophy is subtile, and busied in discovering the material principles of things, but negligent and languid in discovering the principles of motion, in which the energy and efficacy of every operation consists. And here the Greek philosophers seem perfectly blind and childish; for the opinion of the Peripatetics, as to the stimulus of matter, by privation, is little more than words, or rather sound than signification. And they who refer it to God, though they do well therein, yet they do it by a start, and not by proper degrees of assent; for doubtless there is one summary, or capital law, in which nature meets, subordinate to God, viz: the law mentioned in the passage above quoted from Solomon; or the work which God has wrought from its beginning to its end.

Democritus, who further considered this subject, having first supposed an atom, or corpuscle, of some dimension or figure, attributed thereto an appetite, desire, or first motion simply, and another comparatively, imagining that all things properly tended to the centre of the world; those containing more matter falling faster to the centre, and thereby removing, and in the shock driving away, such as held less. But this is a slender conceit, and regards too few particulars; for neither the revolutions of the celestial bodies, nor the contractions and expansions of things, can be reduced to this principle. And for the opinion of Epicurus, as to the declination and fortuitous agitation of atoms, this only brings the matter back again to a trifle, and wraps it up in ignorance and night.

Cupid is elegantly drawn a perpetual child; for compounds are larger things, and have their periods of age; but the first seeds or atoms of bodies are small, and remain in a perpetual infant state. He is again justly represented naked; as all compounds may properly be said to be dressed and clothed, or to assume a personage; whence nothing remains truly naked, but the original particles of things.

The blindness of Cupid contains a deep allegory; for this same Cupid, Love, or appetite of the world, seems to have very little foresight, but directs his steps and motions conformably to what he finds next him, as blind men do when they feel out their way; which renders the divine and overruling Providence and foresight the more surprising; as by a certain steady law, it brings such a beautiful order and regularity of things out of what seems extremely casual, void of design, and, as it were, really blind.

The last attribute of Cupid is archery, viz: a virtue or power operating at a distance; for every thing that operates at a distance may seem, as it were, to dart, or shoot with arrows. And whoever allows of atoms and vacuity, necessarily supposes that the virtue of atoms operates at a distance; for without this operation, no motion could be excited, on account of the vacuum interposing, but all things would remain sluggish and unmoved.

As to the other Cupid, he is properly said to be the youngest son of the gods, as his power could not take place before the formation of species, or particular bodies. The description given us of him transfers the allegory to morality, though he still retains some resemblance with the ancient Cupid; for as Venus universally excites the affection of association, and the desire of procreation, her son Cupid applies the affection to individuals; so that the general disposition proceeds from Venus, but the more close sympathy from Cupid. The former depends upon a near approximation of causes, but the latter upon deeper, more necessitating and uncontrollable principles, as if they proceeded from the ancient Cupid, on whom all exquisite sympathies depend.

XVIII. —DIOMED, OR ZEAL.
EXPLAINED OF PERSECUTION, OR ZEAL FOR RELIGION.

DIOMED acquired great glory and honor at the Trojan war, and was highly favored by Pallas, who encouraged and excited him by no means to spare Venus, if he should casually meet her in fight. He followed the advice with too much eagerness and intrepidity, and accordingly wounded that goddess in her hand. This presumptuous action remained unpunished for a time, and when the war was ended he returned with great glory and renown to his own country, where, finding himself embroiled with domestic affairs, he retired into Italy. Here also at first he was well received and nobly entertained by King Daunus, who, besides other gifts and honors, erected statues for him over all his dominions. But upon the first calamity that afflicted the people after the stranger's arrival, Daunus immediately reflected that he entertained a devoted person in his palace, an enemy to the gods, and one who had sacrilegiously wounded a goddess with his sword, whom it was impious but to touch. To expiate, therefore, his country's guilt, he, without regard to the laws of hospitality, which were less regarded by him than the laws of religion, directly slew his guest, and commanded his statues and all his honors to be razed and abolished. Nor was it safe for others to commiserate or bewail so cruel a destiny; but even his companions in arms, whilst they lamented the death of their leader, and filled all places with their complaints, were turned into a kind of swans, which are said, at the approach of their own death, to chant sweet melancholy dirges.

EXPLANATION.—This fable intimates an extraordinary and almost singular thing, for no hero besides Diomed is recorded to have wounded any of the gods. Doubtless we have here described the nature and fate of a man who professedly makes any divine worship or sect of religion, though, in itself vain and light, the only scope of his actions, and resolves to propagate it by fire and sword. For although the bloody dissensions and differences about religion were unknown to the ancients, yet so copious and diffusive was their knowledge, that what they knew not by experience they comprehended in thought and representation. Those, therefore, who endeavor to reform or establish any sect of religion, though vain, corrupt, and infamous (which is here denoted under the person of Venus), not by the force of reason, learning, sanctity of manners, the weight of arguments, and examples, but would spread or extirpate it by persecution, pains, penalties, tortures, fire, and sword, may, perhaps, be instigated hereto by Pallas, that is, by a certain rigid, prudential consideration, and a severity of judgment, by the vigor and efficacy whereof they see thoroughly into the fallacies and fictions of the delusions of this kind; and through aversion to depravity and a well-meant zeal, these men usually for a time acquire great fame and glory, and are by the vulgar, to whom no moderate measures can be acceptable, extolled and almost adored, as the only patrons and protectors of truth and religion, men of any other disposition seeming, in comparison with these, to be lukewarm, mean-spirited, and cowardly. This fame and felicity, however, seldom endures to the end; but all violence, unless it escapes the reverses and changes of things by untimely death, is commonly unprosperous in the issue; and if a change of affairs happens, and that sect of religion which was persecuted and oppressed gains strength and rises again, then the zeal and warm endeavors of this sort of men are condemned, their very name becomes odious, and all their honors terminate in disgrace.

As to the point that Diomed should be slain by his hospitable entertainer, this denotes that religious dissensions may cause treachery, bloody animosities, and deceit, even between the nearest friends.

That complaining or bewailing should not, in so enormous a case, be permitted to friends affected by the catastrophe without punishment, includes this prudent admonition, that almost in all kinds of wickedness and depravity men have still room left for commiseration, so that they who hate the crime may yet pity the person and bewail his calamity, from a principle of humanity and good-nature and to forbid the overflowings and intercourses of pity upon such occasions were the extremest of evils; yet in the cause of religion and impiety the very commiserations of men are noted and suspected. On the other hand, the lamentations and complainings of the followers and attendants of Diomed, that is, of men of the same sect or persuasion, are usually very sweet, agreeable, and moving, like the dying notes of swans, or the birds of Diomed. This also is a noble and remarkable part of the allegory, denoting that the last words of those who suffer for the sake of religion strongly affect and sway men's minds, and leave a lasting impression upon the sense and memory.

### XIX.  —DÆDALUS, OR MECHANICAL SKILL.
### EXPLAINED OF ARTS AND ARTISTS IN KINGDOMS AND STATES.

THE ancients have left us a description of mechanical skill, industry, and curious arts converted to ill uses, in the person of Dædalus, a most ingenious but execrable artist. This Dædalus was banished for the murder of his brother artist and rival, yet found a kind reception in his banishment from the kings and states where he came. He raised many incomparable edifices to the honor of the gods, and invented many new contrivances for the beautifying and ennobling of cities and public places, but still he was most famous for wicked inventions. Among the rest, by his abominable industry and destructive genius, he assisted in the fatal and infamous production of the monster Minotaur, that devourer of promising youths. And then, to cover one mischief with another, and provide for the security of this monster, he invented and built a labyrinth; a work infamous for its end and design, but admirable and prodigious for art and workmanship. After this, that he might not only be celebrated for wicked inventions, but be sought after, as well for prevention, as for instruments of mischief, he formed that ingenious device of his clue, which led directly through all the windings of the labyrinth. This Dædalus was persecuted by Minos with the utmost severity, diligence, and inquiry; but he always found refuge and means of escaping. Lastly, endeavoring to teach his son Icarus the art of flying, the novice, trusting too much to his wings, fell from his towering flight, and was drowned in the sea. EXPLANATION.—The sense of the fable runs thus. It first denotes envy, which is continually upon the watch, and strangely prevails among excellent artificers; for no kind of people are observed to be more implacably and destructively envious to one another than these.

In the next place, it observes an impolitic and improvident kind of punishment inflicted upon Dædalus—that of banishment; for good workmen are gladly received everywhere, so that banishment to an excellent artificer is scarce any punishment at all; whereas other conditions of life cannot easily flourish from home. For the admiration of artists is propagated and increased among foreigners and strangers; it being a principle in the minds of men to slight and despise the mechanical operators of their own nation.

The succeeding part of the fable is plain, concerning the use of mechanic arts, whereto human life stands greatly indebted, as receiving from this treasury numerous particulars for the service of religion, the ornament of civil society, and the whole provision and apparatus of life; but then the same magazine supplies instruments of lust, cruelty, and death. For, not to mention the arts of luxury and debauchery, we plainly see how far the business of exquisite poisons, guns, engines of war, and such kind of destructive inventions, exceeds the cruelty and barbarity of the Minotaur himself.

The addition of the labyrinth contains a beautiful allegory, representing the nature of mechanic arts in general; for all ingenious and accurate mechanical inventions may be conceived as a labyrinth, which, by reason of their subtilty, intricacy, crossing, and interfering with one another, and the apparent resemblances they have among themselves, scarce any power of the judgment can unravel and distinguish; so that they are only to be understood and traced by the clue of experience.

It is no less prudently added, that he who invented the windings of the labyrinth, should also show the use and management of the clue; for mechanical arts have an ambiguous or double use, and serve as well to produce as to prevent mischief and destruction; so that their virtue almost destroys or unwinds itself.

Unlawful arts and indeed frequently arts themselves, are persecuted by Minos, that is, by laws, which prohibit and forbid their use among the people; but notwithstanding this, they are hid, concealed, retained, and everywhere find reception and skulking-places; a thing well observed by Tacitus of the astrologers and fortune-tellers of his time. "These," says he, "are a kind of men that will always be prohibited, and yet will always be retained in our city." But lastly, all unlawful and vain arts, of what kind soever, lose their reputation in tract of time; grow contemptible and perish, through their overconfidence, like Icarus; being commonly unable to perform what they boasted. And to say the truth, such arts are better suppressed by their own vain pretensions, than checked or restrained by the bridle of laws.632

## XX. —ERICTHONIUS, OR IMPOSTURE. EXPLAINED OF THE IMPROPER USE OF FORCE IN NATURAL PHILOSOPHY.

THE poets feign that Vulcan attempted the chastity of Minerva, and impatient of refusal, had recourse to force; the consequence of which was the birth of Ericthonius, whose body from the middle upwards was comely and well- proportioned, but his thighs and legs small, shrunk, and deformed, like an eel. Conscious of this defect, he became the inventor of chariots, so as to show the graceful, but conceal the deformed part of his body.

EXPLANATION.—This strange fable seems to carry this meaning. Art is here represented under the person of Vulcan, by reason of the various uses it makes of fire; and nature, under the person of Minerva, by reason of the industry employed in her works. Art, therefore, whenever it offers violence to nature, in order to conquer, subdue, and bend her to its purpose, by tortures and force of all kinds, seldom obtains the end proposed; yet upon great struggle and application, there proceed certain imperfect births, or lame abortive works, specious in appearance, but weak and unstable in use; which are, nevertheless, with great pomp and deceitful appearances, triumphantly carried about, and shown by impostors. A procedure very familiar, and remarkable in chemical productions, and new mechanical inventions; especially when the inventors rather hug their errors than improve upon them, and go on struggling with nature, not courting her.

## XXI. —DEUCALION, OR RESTITUTION. EXPLAINED OF A USEFUL HINT IN NATURAL PHILOSOPHY.

THE poets tell us, that the inhabitants of the old world being totally destroyed by
the universal deluge, excepting Deucalion and Pyrrha, these two, desiring with zealous and fer-
vent devotion to restore mankind, received this oracle for answer, that "they should succeed by
throwing their mother's bones behind them." This at first cast them into great sorrow and despair,
because, as all things were levelled by the deluge, it was in vain to seek their mother's tomb; but
at length they understood the expression of the oracle to signify the stones of the earth, which is
esteemed the mother of all things.

EXPLANATION.—This fable seems to reveal a secret of nature, and correct an error familiar
to the mind; for men's ignorance leads them to expect the renovation or restoration of things
from their corruption and remains, as the phœnix is said to be restored out of its ashes; which
is a very improper procedure, because such kind of materials have finished their course, and are
become absolutely unfit to supply the first rudiments of the same things again; whence, in cases
of renovation, recourse should be had to more common principles.

## XXII. —NEMESIS, OR THE VICISSITUDE OF THINGS. EXPLAINED OF THE RE-VERSES OF FORTUNE.

NEMESIS is represented as a goddess venerated by all, but feared by the powerful
and the fortunate. She is said to be the daughter of Nox and Oceanus.
She is drawn with wings, and a crown; a javelin of ash in her right hand; a glass containing
Ethiopians in her left; and riding upon a stag.

EXPLANATION.—The fable receives this explanation. The word Nemesis manifestly signifies
revenge, or retribution; for the office of this goddess consisted in interposing, like the Roman
tribunes, with an "I forbid it," in all courses of constant and perpetual felicity, so as not only to
chastise haughtiness, but also to repay even innocent and moderate happiness with adversity; as
if it were decreed, that none of human race should be admitted to the banquet of the gods, but
for sport. And, indeed, to read over that chapter of Pliny wherein he has collected the miseries
and misfortunes of Augustus Cæsar, whom, of all mankind, one would judge most fortunate,—as
he had a certain art of using and enjoying prosperity, with a mind no way tumid, light, effeminate, confused, or melancholic,—one cannot but think this a very great and powerful goddess,
who could bring such a victim to her altar.633

The parents of this goddess were Oceanus and Nox; that is, the fluctuating change of things,
and the obscure and secret divine decrees. The changes of things are aptly represented by the
Ocean, on account of its perpetual ebbing and flowing; and secret providence is justly expressed
by Night. Even the heathens have observed this secret Nemesis of the night, or the difference betwixt divine and human judgment.634

Wings are given to Nemesis, because of the sudden and unforeseen changes of things; for, from
the earliest account of time, it has been common for great and prudent men to fall by the dangers they most despised. Thus Cicero, when admonished by Brutus of the infidelity and rancor
of Octavius, coolly wrote back: "I cannot, however, but be obliged to you, Brutus, as I ought, for
informing me, though of such a trifle."635

Nemesis also has her crown, by reason of the invidious and malignant nature of the vulgar, who generally rejoice, triumph, and crown her, at the fall of the fortunate and the powerful. And for the javelin in her right hand, it has regard to those whom she has actually struck and transfixed. But whoever escapes her stroke, or feels not actual calamity or misfortune, she affrights with a black and dismal sight in her left hand; for doubtless, mortals on the highest pinnacle of felicity have a prospect of death, diseases, calamities, perfidious friends, undermining enemies, reverses of fortune, &c., represented by the Ethiopians in her glass. Thus Virgil, with great elegance, describing the battle of Actium, says of Cleopatra, that "she did not yet perceive the two asps behind her;"636 but soon after, which way soever she turned, she saw whole troops of Ethiopians still before her.

Lastly, it is significantly added, that Nemesis rides upon a stag, which is a very long-lived creature; for though perhaps some, by an untimely death in youth, may prevent or escape this goddess, yet they who enjoy a long flow of happiness and power, doubtless become subject to her at length, and are brought to yield.

### XXIII.    —ACHELOUS, OR BATTLE. EXPLAINED OF WAR BY INVASION.

THE ancients relate, that Hercules and Achelous being rivals in the courtship of Deianira, the matter was contested by single combat; when Achelous having transformed himself, as he had power to do, into various shapes, by way of trial; at length, in the form of a fierce wild bull, prepares himself for the fight; but Hercules still retains his human shape, engages sharply with him, and in the issue broke off one of the bull's horns; and now Achelous, in great pain and fright, to redeem his horn, presents Hercules with the cornucopia.

EXPLANATION.—This fable relates to military expeditions and preparations; for the preparation of war on the defensive side, here denoted by Achelous, appears in various shapes, whilst the invading side has but one simple form, consisting either in an army, or perhaps a fleet. But the country that expects the invasion is employed infinite ways, in fortifying towns, blockading passes, rivers, and ports, raising soldiers, disposing garrisons, building and breaking down bridges, procuring aids, securing provisions, arms, ammunition, &c. So that there appears a new face of things every day; and at length, when the country is sufficiently fortified and prepared, it represents to the life the form and threats of a fierce fighting bull.

On the other side, the invader presses on to the fight, fearing to be distressed in an enemy's country. And if after the battle he remains master of the field, and has now broke, as it were, the horn of his enemy, the besieged, of course, retire inglorious, affrighted, and dismayed, to their stronghold, there endeavoring to secure themselves, and repair their strength; leaving, at the same time, their country a prey to the conqueror, which is well expressed by the Amalthean horn, or cornucopia.

### XXIV.    —DIONYSUS, OR BACCHUS.637 EXPLAINED OF THE PASSIONS.

THE fable runs, that Semele, Jupiter's mistress, having bound him by an inviolable oath to grant her an unknown request, desired he would embrace her in the same form and manner he used to embrace Juno; and the promise being irrevocable, she was burnt to death with lightning in the performance. The embryo, however, was sewed up, and carried in Jupiter's thigh till the complete time of its birth; but the burden thus rendering the father lame, and causing him pain, the child was thence called Dionysus. When born, he was committed, for some years, to be nursed by Proserpina; and when grown up, appeared with so effeminate a face, that his sex seemed somewhat doubtful. He also died, and was buried for a time, but afterwards revived. When a youth, he first introduced the cultivation and dressing of vines, the method of preparing wine, and taught the use thereof; whence becoming famous, he subdued the world, even to the utmost bounds of the Indies. He rode in a chariot drawn by tigers. There danced about him certain deformed demons called Cobali, &c. The Muses also joined in his train. He married Ariadne, who was deserted by Theseus. The ivy was sacred to him. He was also held the inventor and institutor of religious rites and ceremonies, but such as were wild, frantic, and full of corruption and cruelty. He had also the power of striking men with frenzies. Pentheus and Orpheus were torn to pieces by the frantic women at his orgies; the first for climbing a tree to behold their outrageous ceremonies, and the other for the music of his harp. But the acts of this god are much entangled and confounded with those of Jupiter.

EXPLANATION.—This fable seems to contain a little system of morality, so that there is scarce any better invention in all ethics. Under the history of Bacchus, is drawn the nature of unlawful desire or affection, and disorder; for the appetite and thirst of apparent good is the mother of all unlawful desire, though ever so destructive, and all unlawful desires are conceived in unlawful wishes or requests, rashly indulged or granted before they are well understood or considered, and when the affection begins to grow warm, the mother of it (the nature of good) is destroyed and burnt up by the heat. And whilst an unlawful desire lies in the embryo, or unripened in the mind, which is its father, and here represented by Jupiter, it is cherished and concealed, especially in the inferior part of the mind, corresponding to the thigh of the body, where pain twitches and depresses the mind so far as to render its resolutions and actions imperfect and lame. And even after this child of the mind is confirmed, and gains strength by consent and habit, and comes forth into action, it must still be nursed by Proserpina for a time; that is, it skulks and hides its head in a clandestine manner, as it were under ground, till at length, when the checks of shame and fear are removed, and the requisite boldness acquired, it either assumes the pretext of some virtue, or openly despises infamy. And it is justly observed, that every vehement passion appears of a doubtful sex, as having the strength of a man at first, but at last the impotence of a woman. It is also excellently added, that Bacchus died and rose again; for the affections sometimes seem to die and be no more; but there is no trusting them, even though they were buried, being always apt and ready to rise again whenever the occasion or object offers.

That Bacchus should be the inventor of wine, carries a fine allegory with it; for every affection is cunning and subtle in discovering a proper matter to nourish and feed it; and of all things known to mortals, wine is the most powerful and effectual for exciting and inflaming passions of all kinds, being, indeed, like a common fuel to all.

It is again, with great elegance, observed of Bacchus, that he subdued provinces, and undertook endless expeditions, for the affections never rest satisfied with what they enjoy, but with an endless and insatiable appetite thirst after something further. And tigers are prettily feigned to draw the chariot; for as soon as any affection shall, from going on foot, be advanced to ride, it triumphs over reason, and exerts its cruelty, fierceness, and strength against all that oppose it.

It is also humorously imagined, that ridiculous demons dance and frisk about this chariot; for every passion produces indecent, disorderly, interchangeable and deformed motions in the eyes, countenance, and gesture, so that the person under the impulse, whether of anger, insult, love, &c., though to himself he may seem grand, lofty, or obliging, yet in the eyes of others appears mean, contemptible, or ridiculous.

The Muses also are found in the train of Bacchus, for there is scarce any passion without its art, science, or doctrine to court and flatter it; but in this respect the indulgence of men of genius has greatly detracted from the majesty of the Muses, who ought to be the leaders and conductors of human life, and not the handmaids of the passions.

The allegory of Bacchus falling in love with a cast mistress, is extremely noble; for it is certain that the affections always court and covet what has been rejected upon experience. And all those who by serving and indulging their passions immensely raise the value of enjoyment, should know, that whatever they covet and pursue, whether riches, pleasure, glory, learning, or anything else, they only pursue those things that have been forsaken and cast off with contempt by great numbers in all ages, after possession and experience. Nor is it without a mystery that the ivy was sacred to Bacchus, and this for two reasons: first, because ivy is an evergreen, or flourishes in the winter; and secondly, because it winds and creeps about so many things, as trees, walls, and buildings, and raises itself above them. As to the first, every passion grows fresh, strong, and vigorous by opposition and prohibition, as it were by a kind of contrast or antiperistasis, like the ivy in the winter. And for the second, the predominant passion of the mind throws itself, like the ivy, round all human actions, entwines all our resolutions, and perpetually adheres to, and mixes itself among, or even overtops them.

And no wonder that superstitious rites and ceremonies are attributed to Bacchus, when almost every ungovernable passion grows wanton and luxuriant in corrupt religions; nor again, that fury and frenzy should be sent and dealt out by him, because every passion is a short frenzy, and if it be vehement, lasting, and take deep root, it terminates in madness. And hence the allegory of Pentheus and Orpheus being torn to pieces is evident; for every headstrong passion is extremely bitter, severe, inveterate, and revengeful upon all curious inquiry, wholesome admonition, free counsel, and persuasion.

Lastly; the confusion between the persons of Jupiter and Bacchus will justly admit of an allegory, because noble and meritorious actions may sometimes proceed from virtue, sound reason, and magnanimity, and sometimes again from a concealed passion and secret desire of ill, however they may be extolled and praised, insomuch that it is not easy to distinguish betwixt the acts of Bacchus and the acts of Jupiter.

XXV.   —ATALANTA AND HIPPOMENES, OR GAIN. EXPLAINED OF THE CONTEST BETWIXT ART AND NATURE.

ATALANTA, who was exceedingly fleet, contended with Hippomenes in the course, on condition that, if Hippomenes won, he should espouse her, or forfeit his life if he lost. The match was very unequal, for Atalanta had conquered numbers, to their destruction. Hippomenes, therefore, had recourse to stratagem. He procured three golden apples, and purposely carried them with him; they started; Atalanta outstripped him soon; then Hippomenes bowled one of his apples before her, across the course, in order not only to make her stoop, but to draw her out of the path. She, prompted by female curiosity, and the beauty of the golden fruit, starts from the course to take up the apple. Hippomenes, in the mean time, holds on his way, and steps before her; but she, by her natural swiftness, soon fetches up her lost ground, and leaves him again behind. Hippomenes, however, by rightly timing his second and third throw, at length won the race, not by his swiftness, but his cunning.

EXPLANATION.—This fable seems to contain a noble allegory of the contest betwixt art and nature. For art, here denoted by Atalanta, is much swifter, or more expeditious in its operations than nature, when all obstacles and impediments are removed, and sooner arrives at its end. This appears almost in every instance. Thus, fruit comes slowly from the kernel, but soon by inoculation or incision; clay, left to itself, is a long time in acquiring a stony hardness, but is presently burnt by fire into brick. So again, in human life, nature is a long while in alleviating and abolishing the remembrance of pain, and assuaging the troubles of the mind; but moral philosophy, which is the art of living, performs it presently. Yet this prerogative and singular efficacy of art is stopped and retarded to the infinite detriment of human life, by certain golden apples; for there is no one science or art that constantly holds on its true and proper course to the end, but they are all continually stopping short, forsaking the track, and turning aside to profit and convenience, exactly like Atalanta.638 Whence it is no wonder that art gets not the victory over nature, nor, according to the condition of the contest, brings her under subjection; but, on the contrary, remains subject to her, as a wife to a husband.


## XXVI.   —PROMETHEUS, OR THE STATE OF MAN.
### EXPLAINED OF AN OVERRULING PROVIDENCE, AND OF HUMAN NATURE.
THE ancients relate that man was the work of Prometheus, and formed of clay; only the artificer mixed in with the mass, particles taken from different animals. And being desirous to improve his workmanship, and endow, as well as create, the human race, he stole up to heaven with a bundle of birch-rods, and kindling them at the chariot of the Sun, thence brought down fire to the earth for the service of men.

They add that, for this meritorious act, Prometheus was repaid with ingratitude by mankind, so that, forming a conspiracy, they arraigned both him and his invention before Jupiter. But the matter was otherwise received than they imagined; for the accusation proved extremely grateful to Jupiter and the gods, insomuch that, delighted with the action, they not only indulged mankind the use of fire, but moreover conferred upon them a most acceptable and desirable present, viz: perpetual youth.

But men, foolishly overjoyed hereat, laid this present of the gods upon an ass, who, in returning back with it, being extremely thirsty, strayed to a fountain. The serpent, who was guardian thereof, would not suffer him to drink, but upon condition of receiving the burden he carried, whatever it should be. The silly ass complied, and thus the perpetual renewal of youth was, for a drop of water, transferred from men to the race of serpents.

Prometheus, not desisting from his unwarrantable practices, though now reconciled to mankind, after they were thus tricked of their present, but still continuing inveterate against Jupiter, had the boldness to attempt deceit, even in a sacrifice, and is said to have once offered up two bulls to Jupiter, but so as in the hide of one of them to wrap all the flesh and fat of both, and stuffing out the other hide only with the bones; then, in a religious and devout manner, gave Jupiter his choice of the two. Jupiter, detesting this sly fraud and hypocrisy, but having thus an opportunity of punishing the offender, purposely chose the mock bull.

And now giving way to revenge, but finding he could not chastise the insolence of Prometheus without afflicting the human race (in the production whereof Prometheus had strangely and insufferably prided himself), he commanded Vulcan to form a beautiful and graceful woman, to whom every god presented a certain gift, whence she was called Pandora.640 They put into her hands an elegant box, containing all sorts of miseries and misfortunes; but Hope was placed at the bottom of it. With this box she first goes to Prometheus, to try if she could prevail upon him to receive and open it; but he being upon his guard, warily refused the offer. Upon this refusal, she comes to his brother Epimetheus, a man of a very different temper, who rashly and inconsiderately opens the box. When finding all kinds of miseries and misfortunes issued out of it, he grew wise too late, and with great hurry and struggle endeavored to clap the cover on again; but with all his endeavor could scarce keep in Hope, which lay at the bottom.

Lastly, Jupiter arraigned Prometheus of many heinous crimes; as that he formerly stole fire from heaven; that he contemptuously and deceitfully mocked him by a sacrifice of bones; that he despised his present,641 adding withal a new crime, that he attempted to ravish Pallas; for all which, he was sentenced to be bound in chains, and doomed to perpetual torments. Accordingly, by Jupiter's command, he was brought to Mount Caucasus, and there fastened to a pillar, so firmly that he could no way stir. A vulture or eagle stood by him, which in the daytime gnawed and consumed his liver; but in the night the wasted parts were supplied again; whence matter for his pain was never wanting.

They relate, however, that his punishment had an end; for Hercules sailing the ocean, in a cup, or pitcher, presented him by the Sun, came at length to Caucasus, shot the eagle with his arrows, and set Prometheus free. In certain nations, also, there were instituted particular games of the torch, to the honor of Prometheus, in which they who ran for the prize carried lighted torches; and as any one of these torches happened to go out, the bearer withdrew himself, and gave way to the next; and that person was allowed to win the prize, who first brought in his lighted torch to the goal.

EXPLANATION.—This fable contains and enforces many just and serious considerations; some whereof have been long since well observed, but some again remain perfectly untouched. Prometheus clearly and expressly signifies Providence; for of all the things in nature, the formation and endowment of man was singled out by the ancients, and esteemed the peculiar work of Providence. The reason hereof seems, 1. That the nature of man includes a mind and understanding, which is the seat of Providence. 2. That it is harsh and incredible to suppose reason and mind should be raised, and drawn out of senseless and irrational principles; whence it becomes almost inevitable, that providence is implanted in the human mind in conformity with, and by the direction and the design of the greater overruling Providence. But, 3. The principal cause is this: that man seems to be the thing in which the whole world centres, with respect to final causes; so that if he were away, all other things would stray and fluctuate, without end or intention, or become perfectly disjointed, and out of frame; for all things are made subservient to man, and he receives use and benefit from them all. Thus the revolutions, places, and periods, of the celestial bodies, serve him for distinguishing times and seasons, and for dividing the world into different regions; the meteors afford him prognostications of the weather; the winds sail our ships, drive our mills, and move our machines; and the vegetables and animals of all kinds either afford us matter for houses and habitations, clothing, food, physic; or tend to ease, or delight, to support, or refresh us so that everything in nature seems not made for itself, but for man.

And it is not without reason added, that the mass of matter whereof man was formed, should be mixed up with particles taken from different animals, and wrought in with the clay, because it is certain, that of all things in the universe, man is the most compounded and recompounded body; so that the ancients, not improperly, styled him a Microcosm, or little world within himself. For although the chemists have absurdly, and too literally, wrested and perverted the elegance of the term microcosm, whilst they pretend to find all kind of mineral and vegetable matters, or something corresponding to them, in man, yet it remains firm and unshaken, that the human body is, of all substances, the most mixed and organical; whence it has surprising powers and faculties; for the powers of simple bodies are but few, though certain and quick; as being little broken, or weakened, and not counterbalanced by mixture; but excellence and quantity of energy reside in mixture and composition.

Man, however, in his first origin, seems to be a defenceless, naked creature, slow in assisting himself, and standing in need of numerous things. Prometheus, therefore, hastened to the invention of fire, which supplies and administers to nearly all human uses and necessities, insomuch that, if the soul may be called the form of forms, if the hand may be called the instrument of instruments, fire may, as properly, be called the assistant of assistants, or the helper of helps; for hence proceed numberless operations, hence all the mechanic arts, and hence infinite assistances are afforded to the sciences themselves.

The manner wherein Prometheus stole this fire is properly described from the nature of the thing; he being said to have done it by applying a rod of birch to the chariot of the Sun; for birch is used in striking and beating, which clearly denotes the generation of fire to be from the violent percussions and collisions of bodies; whereby the matters struck are subtilized, rarefied, put into motion, and so prepared to receive the heat of the celestial bodies; whence they, in a clandestine and secret manner, collect and snatch fire, as it were by stealth, from the chariot of the Sun.

The next is a remarkable part of the fable, which represents that men, instead of gratitude and thanks, fell into indignation and expostulation, accusing both Prometheus and his fire to Jupiter,—and yet the accusation proved highly pleasing to Jupiter; so that he, for this reason, crowned these benefits of mankind with a new bounty. Here it may seem strange that the sin of ingratitude to a creator and benefactor, a sin so heinous as to include almost all others, should meet with approbation and reward. But the allegory has another view, and denotes, that the accusation and arraignment, both of human nature and human art among mankind, proceeds from a most noble and laudable temper of the mind, and tends to a very good purpose; whereas the contrary temper is odious to the gods, and unbeneficial in itself. For they who break into extravagant praises of human nature, and the arts in vogue, and who lay themselves out in admiring the things they already possess, and will needs have the sciences cultivated among them, to be thought absolutely perfect and complete, in the first place, show little regard to the divine nature, whilst they extol their own inventions almost as high as his perfection. In the next place, men of this temper are unserviceable and prejudicial in life, whilst they imagine themselves already got to the top of things, and there rest, without further inquiry. On the contrary, they who arraign and accuse both nature and art, and are always full of complaints against them, not only preserve a more just and modest sense of mind, but are also perpetually stirred up to fresh industry and new discoveries. Is not, then, the ignorance and fatality of mankind to be extremely pitied, whilst they remain slaves to the arrogance of a few of their own fellows, and are dotingly fond of that scrap of Grecian knowledge, the Peripatetic philosophy; and this to such a degree, as not only to think all accusation or arraignment thereof useless, but even hold it suspect and dangerous? Certainly the procedure of Empedocles, though furious—but especially that of Democritus (who with great modesty complained that all things were abstruse; that we know nothing; that truth lies hid in deep pits; that falsehood is strangely joined and twisted along with truth, &c.)—is to be preferred before the confident, assuming, and dogmatical school of Aristotle. Mankind are, therefore, to be admonished, that the arraignment of nature and of art is pleasing to the gods; and that a sharp and vehement accusation of Prometheus, though a creator, a founder, and a master, obtained new blessings and presents from the divine bounty, and proved more sound and serviceable than a diffusive harangue of praise and gratulation. And let men be assured that the fond opinion that they have already acquired enough, is a principal reason why they have acquired so little.

That the perpetual flower of youth should be the present which mankind received as a reward for their accusation, carries this moral; that the ancients seem not to have despaired of discovering methods, and remedies, for retarding old age, and prolonging the period of human life; but rather reckoned it among those things which, through sloth and want of diligent inquiry, perish and come to nothing, after having been once undertaken, than among such as are absolutely impossible, or placed beyond the reach of the human power. For they signify and intimate from the true use of fire, and the just and strenuous accusation and conviction of the errors of art, that the divine bounty is not wanting to men in such kind of presents, but that men indeed are wanting to themselves, and lay such an inestimable gift upon the back of a slow-paced ass; that is, upon the back of the heavy, dull, lingering thing, experience; from whose sluggish and tortoise-pace proceeds that ancient complaint of the shortness of life, and the slow advancement of arts. And certainly it may well seem, that the two faculties of reasoning and experience are not hitherto properly joined and coupled together, but to be still new gifts of the gods, separately laid, the one upon the back of a light bird, or abstract philosophy, and the other upon an ass, or slow-paced practice and trial. And yet good hopes might be conceived of this ass, if it were not for his thirst and the accidents of the way. For we judge, that if any one would constantly proceed, by a certain law and method, in the road of experience, and not by the way thirst after such experiments as make for profit or ostentation, nor exchange his burden, or quit the original design for the sake of these, he might be an useful bearer of a new and accumulated divine bounty to mankind.

That this gift of perpetual youth should pass from men to serpents, seems added by way of ornament, and illustration to the fable; perhaps intimating, at the same time, the shame it is for men, that they, with their fire, and numerous arts, cannot procure to themselves those things which nature has bestowed upon many other creatures.

The sudden reconciliation of Prometheus to mankind, after being disappointed of their hopes, contains a prudent and useful admonition. It points out the levity and temerity of men in new experiments, when, not presently succeeding, or answering to expectation, they precipitantly quit their new undertakings, hurry back to their old ones, and grow reconciled thereto.

After the fable has described the state of man, with regard to arts and intellectual matters, it passes on to religion; for after the inventing and settling of arts, follows the establishment of divine worship, which hypocrisy presently enters into and corrupts. So that by the two sacrifices we have elegantly painted the person of a man truly religious, and of an hypocrite. One of these sacrifices contained the fat, or the portion of God, used for burning and incensing; thereby denoting affection and zeal, offered up to his glory. It likewise contained the bowels, which are expressive of charity, along with the good and useful flesh. But the other contained nothing more than dry bones, which nevertheless stuffed out the hide, so as to make it resemble a fair, beautiful, and magnificent sacrifice; hereby finely denoting the external and empty rites and barren ceremonies, wherewith men burden and stuff out the divine worship,—things rather intended for show and ostentation than conducing to piety. Nor are mankind simply content with this mock-worship of God, but also impose and further it upon him, as if he had chosen and ordained it. Certainly the prophet, in the person of God, has a fine expostulation, as to this matter of choice: "Is this the fasting which I have chosen, that a man should afflict his soul for a day, and bow down his head like a bulrush?"

After thus touching the state of religion, the fable next turns to manners, and the conditions of human life. And though it be a very common, yet is it a just interpretation, that Pandora denotes the pleasures and licentiousness which the cultivation and luxury of the arts of civil life introduce, as it were, by the instrumental efficacy of fire; whence the works of the voluptuary arts are properly attributed to Vulcan, the God of Fire. And hence infinite miseries and calamities have proceeded to the minds, the bodies, and the fortunes of men, together with a late repentance; and this not in each man's particular, but also in kingdoms and states; for wars, and tumults, and tyrannies, have all arisen from this same fountain, or box of Pandora.

It is worth observing, how beautifully and elegantly the fable has drawn two reigning characters in human life, and given two examples, or tablatures of them, under the persons of Prometheus and Epimetheus. The followers of Epimetheus are improvident, see not far before them, and prefer such things as are agreeable for the present; whence they are oppressed with numerous straits, difficulties, and calamities, with which they almost continually struggle; but in the mean time gratify their own temper, and, for want of a better knowledge of things, feed their minds with many vain hopes; and as with so many pleasing dreams, delight themselves, and sweeten the miseries of life.

But the followers of Prometheus are the prudent, wary men, that look into futurity, and cautiously guard against, prevent, and undermine many calamities and misfortunes. But this watchful, provident temper, is attended with a deprivation of numerous pleasures, and the loss of various delights, whilst such men debar themselves the use even of innocent things, and what is still worse, rack and torture themselves with cares, fears, and disquiets; being bound fast to the pillar of necessity, and tormented with numberless thoughts (which for their swiftness are well compared to an eagle), that continually wound, tear, and gnaw their liver or mind, unless, perhaps, they find some small remission by intervals, or as it were at nights; but then new anxieties, dreads, and fears, soon return again, as it were in the morning. And, therefore, very few men, of either temper, have secured to themselves the advantages of providence, and kept clear of disquiets, troubles, and misfortunes.

Nor indeed can any man obtain this end without the assistance of Hercules; that is, of such fortitude and constancy of mind as stands prepared against every event, and remains indifferent to every change; looking forward without being daunted, enjoying the good without disdain, and enduring the bad without impatience. And it must be observed, that even Prometheus had not the power to free himself, but owed his deliverance to another; for no natural inbred force and fortitude could prove equal to such a task. The power of releasing him came from the utmost confines of the ocean, and from the sun; that is, from Apollo, or knowledge; and again, from a due consideration of the uncertainty, instability, and fluctuating state of human life, which is aptly represented by sailing the ocean. Accordingly, Virgil has prudently joined these two together, accounting him happy who knows the causes of things, and has conquered all his fears, apprehensions, and superstitions.642

It is added, with great elegance, for supporting and confirming the human mind, that the great hero who thus delivered him sailed the ocean in a cup, or pitcher, to prevent fear, or complaint; as if, through the narrowness of our nature, or a too great fragility thereof, we were absolutely incapable of that fortitude and constancy to which Seneca finely alludes, when he says: "It is a noble thing, at once to participate in the frailty of man and the security of a god."

We have hitherto, that we might not break the connection of things, designedly omitted the last crime of Prometheus—that of attempting the chastity of Minerva

—which heinous offence it doubtless was, that caused the punishment of having his liver gnawed by the vulture. The meaning seems to be this,—that when men are puffed up with arts and knowledge, they often try to subdue even the divine wisdom and bring it under the dominion of sense and reason, whence inevitably follows a perpetual and restless rending and tearing of the mind. A sober and humble distinction must, therefore, be made betwixt divine and human things, and betwixt the oracles of sense and faith, unless mankind had rather choose an heretical religion, and a fictitious and romantic philosophy.643

The last particular in the fable is the Games of the Torch, instituted to Prometheus, which again relates to arts and sciences, as well as the invention of fire, for the commemoration and celebration whereof these games were held. And here we have an extremely prudent admonition, directing us to expect the perfection of the sciences from succession, and not from the swiftness and abilities of any single person; for he who is fleetest and strongest in the course may perhaps be less fit to keep his torch alight, since there is danger of its going out from too rapid as well as from too slow a motion.644 But this kind of contest, with the torch, seems to have been long dropped and neglected; the sciences appearing to have flourished principally in their first authors, as Aristotle, Galen, Euclid, Ptolemy, &c.; whilst their successors have done very little, or scarce made any attempts. But it were highly to be wished that these games might be renewed, to the honor of Prometheus, or human nature, and that they might excite contest, emulation, and laudable endeavors, and the design meet with such success as not to hang tottering, tremulous, and hazarded, upon the torch of any single person. Mankind, therefore, should be admonished to rouse themselves, and try and exert their own strength and chance, and not place all their dependence upon a few men, whose abilities and capacities, perhaps, are not greater than their own.

These are the particulars which appear to us shadowed out by this trite and vulgar fable, though without denying that there may be contained in it several intimations that have a surprising correspondence with the Christian mysteries. In particular, the voyage of Hercules, made in a pitcher, to release Prometheus, bears an allusion to the word of God, coming in the frail vessel of the flesh to redeem mankind. But we indulge ourselves no such liberties as these, for fear of using strange fire at the altar of the Lord.

### XXVII.  —ICARUS AND SCYLLA AND CHARYBDIS, OR THE MIDDLE WAY.

### EXPLAINED OF MEDIOCRITY IN NATURAL AND MORAL PHILOSOPHY.

MEDIOCRITY, or the holding a middle course, has been highly extolled in morality, but little in matters of science, though no less useful and proper here; whilst in politics it is held suspected, and ought to be employed with judgment. The ancients described mediocrity in manners by the course prescribed to Icarus; and in matters of the understanding by the steering betwixt Scylla and Charybdis, on account of the great difficulty and danger in passing those straits.

Icarus, being to fly across the sea, was ordered by his father neither to soar too high nor fly too low, for, as his wings were fastened together with wax, there was danger of its melting by the sun's heat in too high a flight, and of its becoming less tenacious by the moisture if he kept too near the vapor of the sea. But he, with a juvenile confidence, soared aloft, and fell down headlong.

EXPLANATION.—The fable is vulgar, and easily interpreted; for the path of virtue lies straight between excess on the one side, and defect on the other. And no wonder that excess should prove the bane of Icarus, exulting in juvenile strength and vigor; for excess is the natural vice of youth, as defect is that of old age; and if a man must perish by either, Icarus chose the better of the two; for all defects are justly esteemed more depraved than excesses. There is some magnanimity in excess, that, like a bird, claims kindred with the heavens; but defect is a reptile, that basely crawls upon the earth. It was excellently said by Heraclitus: "A dry light makes the best soul;" for if the soul contracts moisture from the earth, it perfectly degenerates and sinks. On the other hand, moderation must be observed, to prevent this fine light from burning, by its too great subtility and dryness. But these observations are common.

In matters of the understanding, it requires great skill and a particular felicity to steer clear of Scylla and Charybdis. If the ship strikes upon Scylla, it is dashed in pieces against the rocks; if upon Charybdis, it is swallowed outright. This allegory is pregnant with matter; but we shall only observe the force of it lies here, that a mean be observed in every doctrine and science, and in the rules and axioms thereof, between the rocks of distinctions and the whirlpools of universalities: for these two are the bane and shipwreck of fine geniuses and arts.

XXVIII. —SPHINX, OR SCIENCE. EXPLAINED OF THE SCIENCES.

THEY relate that Sphinx was a monster, variously formed, having the face and voice of a virgin, the wings of a bird, and the talons of a griffin. She resided on the top of a mountain, near the city Thebes, and also beset the highways. Her manner was to lie in ambush and seize the travellers, and having them in her power, to propose to them certain dark and perplexed riddles, which it was thought she received from the Muses, and if her wretched captives could not solve and interpret these riddles, she, with great cruelty, fell upon them, in their hesitation and confusion, and tore them to pieces. This plague having reigned a long time, the Thebans at length offered their kingdom to the man who could interpret her riddles, there being no other way to subdue her. Œdipus, a penetrating and prudent man, though lame in his feet, excited by so great a reward, accepted the condition, and with a good assurance of mind, cheerfully presented himself before the monster, who directly asked him: "What creature that was, which, being born four-footed, afterwards became two-footed, then three-footed, and lastly four-footed again?" Œdipus, with presence of mind, replied it was man, who, upon his first birth and infant state, crawled upon all fours in endeavoring to walk; but not long after went upright upon his two natural feet; again, in old age walked three-footed, with a stick; and at last, growing decrepit, lay four-footed confined to his bed; and having by this exact solution obtained the victory, he slew the monster, and, laying the carcass upon an ass, led her away in triumph; and upon this he was, according to the agreement, made king of Thebes.

EXPLANATION.—This is an elegant, instructive fable, and seems invented to represent science, especially as joined with practice. For science may, without absurdity, be called a monster, being strangely gazed at and admired by the ignorant and unskilful. Her figure and form is various, by reason of the vast variety of subjects that science considers; her voice and countenance are represented female, by reason of her gay appearance and volubility of speech; wings are added, because the sciences and their inventions run and fly about in a moment, for knowledge like light communicated from one torch to another, is presently caught and copiously diffused; sharp and hooked talons are elegantly attributed to her, because the axioms and arguments of science enter the mind, lay hold of it, fix it down, and keep it from moving or slipping away. This the sacred philosopher observed, when he said: "The words of the wise are like goads or nails driven far in."645 Again, all science seems placed on high, as it were on the tops of mountains that are hard to climb; for science is justly imagined a sublime and lofty thing, looking down upon ignorance from an eminence, and at the same time taking an extensive view on all sides, as is usual on the tops of mountains. Science is said to beset the highways, because through all the journey and peregrination of human life there is matter and occasion offered of contemplation.

Sphinx is said to propose various difficult questions and riddles to men, which she received from the Muses; and these questions, so long as they remain with the Muses, may very well be unaccompanied with severity, for while there is no other end of contemplation and inquiry but that of knowledge alone, the understanding is not oppressed, or driven to straits and difficulties, but expatiates and ranges at large, and even receives a degree of pleasure from doubt and variety; but after the Muses have given over their riddles to Sphinx, that is, to practice, which urges and impels to action, choice, and determination, then it is that they become torturing, severe, and trying, and, unless solved and interpreted, strangely perplex and harass the human mind, rend it every way, and perfectly tear it to pieces. All the riddles of Sphinx, therefore, have two conditions annexed, viz: dilaceration to those who do not solve them, and empire to those that do. For he who understands the thing proposed, obtains his end, and every artificer rules over his work.646 Sphinx has no more than two kinds of riddles, one relating to the nature of things, the other to the nature of man; and correspondent to these, the prizes of the solution are two kinds of empire,—the empire over nature, and the empire over man. For the true and ultimate end of natural philosophy is dominion over natural things, natural bodies, remedies, machines, and numberless other particulars, though the schools, contented with what spontaneously offers, and swollen with their own discourses, neglect, and in a manner despise, both things and works.

But the riddle proposed to Œdipus, the solution whereof acquired him the Theban kingdom, regarded the nature of man; for he who has thoroughly looked into and examined human nature, may in a manner command his own fortune, and seems born to acquire dominion and rule. Accordingly, Virgil properly makes the arts of government to be the arts of the Romans.647 It was, therefore, extremely apposite in Augustus Cæsar to use the image of Sphinx in his signet, whether this happened by accident or by design; for he of all men was deeply versed in politics, and through the course of his life very happily solved abundance of new riddles with regard to the nature of man; and unless he had done this with great dexterity and ready address, he would frequently have been involved in imminent danger, if not destruction.

It is with the utmost elegance added in the fable, that when Sphinx was conquered, her carcass was laid upon an ass; for there is nothing so subtile and abstruse, but after being once made plain, intelligible, and common, it may be received by the slowest capacity.

We must not omit that Sphinx was conquered by a lame man, and impotent in his feet; for men usually make too much haste to the solution of Sphinx's riddles; whence it happens, that she prevailing, their minds are rather racked and torn by disputes, than invested with command by works and effects.

## XXIX.   —PROSERPINE, OR SPIRIT. EXPLAINED OF THE SPIRIT INCLUDED IN NATURAL
## BODIES.

THEY tell us, Pluto having, upon that memorable division of empire among the gods, received the infernal regions for his share, despaired of winning any one of the goddesses in marriage by an obsequious courtship, and therefore through necessity resolved upon a rape. Having watched his opportunity, he suddenly seized upon Proserpine, a most beautiful virgin, the daughter of Ceres, as she was gathering narcissus flowers in the meads of Sicily, and hurrying her to his chariot, carried her with him to the subterraneal regions, where she was treated with the highest reverence, and styled the Lady of Dis. But Ceres, missing her only daughter, whom she extremely loved, grew pensive and anxious beyond measure, and taking a lighted torch in her hand, wandered the world over in quest of her daughter,—but all to no purpose, till, suspecting she might be carried to the infernal regions, she, with great lamentation and abundance of tears, importuned Jupiter to restore her; and with much ado prevailed so far as to recover and bring her away, if she had tasted nothing there. This proved a hard condition upon the mother, for Proserpine was found to have eaten three kernels of a pomegranate. Ceres, however, desisted not, but fell to her entreaties and lamentations afresh, insomuch that at last it was indulged her that Proserpine should divide the year betwixt her husband and her mother, and live six months with the one and as many with the other. After this, Theseus and Perithous, with uncommon audacity, attempted to force Proserpine away from Pluto's bed, but happening to grow tired in their journey, and resting themselves upon a stone in the realms below, they could never rise from it again, but remain sitting there forever. Proserpine, therefore, still continued queen of the lower regions, in honor of whom there was also added this grand privilege, that though it had never been permitted any one to return after having once descended thither, a particular exception was made, that he who brought a golden bough as a present to Proserpine, might on that condition descend and return. This was an only bough that grew in a large dark grove, not from a tree of its own, but like the mistletoe from another, and when plucked away a fresh one always shot out in its stead.

EXPLANATION.—This fable seems to regard natural philosophy, and searches deep into that rich and fruitful virtue and supply in subterraneous bodies, from whence all the things upon the earth's surface spring, and into which they again relapse and return. By Proserpine, the ancients denoted that ethereal spirit shut up and detained within the earth, here represented by Pluto,—the spirit being separated from the superior globe, according to the expression of the poet.648 This spirit is conceived as ravished, or snatched up by the earth, because it can in no way be detained, when it has time and opportunity to fly off, but is only wrought together and fixed by sudden intermixture and comminution, in the same manner as if one should endeavor to mix air with water, which cannot otherwise be done than by a quick and rapid agitation, that joins them together in froth whilst the air is thus caught up by the water. And it is elegantly added, that Proserpine was ravished whilst she gathered narcissus flowers, which have their name from numbedness or stupefaction; for the spirit we speak of is in the fittest disposition to be embraced by terrestrial matter when it begins to coagulate, or grow torpid as it were.

It is an honor justly attributed to Proserpine, and not to any other wife of the gods, that of being the lady or mistress of her husband, because this spirit performs all its operations in the subterraneal regions, whilst Pluto, or the earth, remains stupid, or as it were ignorant of them.

The ether, or the efficacy of the heavenly bodies, denoted by Ceres, endeavors with infinite diligence to force out this spirit, and restore it to its pristine state. And by the torch in the hand of Ceres, or the ether, is doubtless meant the sun, which disperses light over the whole globe of the earth, and if the thing were possible, must have the greatest share in recovering Proserpine, or reinstating the subterraneal spirit. Yet Proserpine still continues and dwells below, after the manner excellently described in the condition betwixt Jupiter and Ceres. For first, it is certain that there are two ways of detaining the spirit, in solid and terrestrial matter,—the one by condensation or obstruction, which is mere violence and imprisonment; the other by administering a proper aliment, which is spontaneous and free. For after the included spirit begins to feed and nourish itself, it is not in a hurry to fly off, but remains as it were fixed in its own earth. And this is the moral of Proserpine's tasting the pomegranate; and were it not for this, she must long ago have been carried up by Ceres, who with her torch wandered the world over, and so the earth have been left without its spirit. For though the spirit in metals and minerals may perhaps be, after a particular manner, wrought in by the solidity of the mass, yet the spirit of vegetables and animals has open passages to escape at, unless it be willingly detained, in the way of sipping and tasting them.

The second article of agreement, that of Proserpine's remaining six months with her mother and six with her husband, is an elegant description of the division of the year; for the spirit diffused through the earth lives above-ground in the vegetable world during the summer months, but in the winter returns under ground again.

The attempt of Theseus and Perithous to bring Proserpine away, denotes that the more subtile spirits, which descend in many bodies to the earth, may frequently be unable to drink in, unite with themselves, and carry off the subterraneous spirit, but on the contrary be coagulated by it, and rise no more, so as to increase the inhabitants and add to the dominion of Proserpine.

The alchemists will be apt to fall in with our interpretation of the golden bough, whether we will or no, because they promise golden mountains, and the restoration of natural bodies from their stone, as from the gates of Pluto; but we are well assured that their theory had no just foundation, and suspect they have no very encouraging or practical proofs of its soundness. Leaving, therefore, their conceits to themselves, we shall freely declare our own sentiments upon this last part of the fable. We are certain, from numerous figures and expressions of the ancients, that they judged the conservation, and in some degree the renovation, of natural bodies to be no desperate or impossible thing, but rather abstruse and out of the common road than wholly impracticable. And this seems to be their opinion in the present case, as they have placed this bough among an infinite number of shrubs, in a spacious and thick wood. They supposed it of gold, because gold is the emblem of duration. They feigned it adventitious, not native, because such an effect is to be expected from art, and not from any medicine or any simple or mere natural way of working.

### XXX. —METIS, OR COUNSEL. EXPLAINED OF PRINCES AND THEIR COUNCIL.

THE ancient poets relate that Jupiter took Metis to wife, whose name plainly denotes counsel, and that he, perceiving she was pregnant by him, would by no means wait the time of her delivery, but directly devoured her; whence himself also became pregnant, and was delivered in a wonderful manner; for he from his head or brain brought forth Pallas armed.

EXPLANATION.—This fable, which in its literal sense appears monstrously absurd, seems to contain a state secret, and shows with what art kings usually carry themselves towards their council, in order to preserve their own authority and majesty not only inviolate, but so as to have it magnified and heightened among the people. For kings commonly link themselves, as it were, in a nuptial bond to their council, and deliberate and communicate with them after a prudent and laudable custom upon matters of the greatest importance, at the same time justly conceiving this no diminution of their majesty; but when the matter once ripens to a decree or order, which is a kind of birth, the king then suffers the council to go on no further, lest the act should seem to depend upon their pleasure. Now, therefore, the king usually assumes to himself whatever was wrought, elaborated, or formed, as it were, in the womb of the council (unless it be a matter of an invidious nature, which he is sure to put from him), so that the decree and the execution shall seem to flow from himself.650 And as this decree or execution proceeds with prudence and power, so as to imply necessity, it is elegantly wrapped up under the figure of Pallas armed.

Nor are kings content to have this seem the effect of their own authority, free will, and uncontrollable choice, unless they also take the whole honor to themselves, and make the people imagine that all good and wholesome decrees proceed entirely from their own head, that is, their own sole prudence and judgment.

XXXI.  —THE SIRENS, OR PLEASURES. EXPLAINED OF MEN'S PASSION FOR PLEASURES.

INTRODUCTION.—The fable of the Sirens is, in a vulgar sense, justly enough

explained of the pernicious incentives to pleasure; but the ancient mythology seems to us like a vintage ill-pressed and trod; for though something has been drawn from it, yet all the more excellent parts remain behind in the grapes that are untouched.

FABLE.—The Sirens are said to be the daughters of Achelous and Terpsichore, one of the Muses. In their early days they had wings, but lost them upon being conquered by the Muses, with whom they rashly contended; and with the feathers of these wings the Muses made themselves crowns, so that from this time the Muses wore wings on their heads, except only the mother to the Sirens.

These Sirens resided in certain pleasant islands, and when, from their watch- tower, they saw any ship approaching, they first detained the sailors by their music, then, enticing them to shore, destroyed them.

Their singing was not of one and the same kind, but they adapted their tunes exactly to the nature of each person, in order to captivate and secure him. And so destructive had they been, that these islands of the Sirens appeared, to a very great distance, white with the bones of their unburied captives.

Two different remedies were invented to protect persons against them, the one by Ulysses, the other by Orpheus. Ulysses commanded his associates to stop their ears close with wax; and he, determining to make the trial, and yet avoid the danger, ordered himself to be tied fast to a mast of the ship, giving strict charge not to be unbound, even though himself should entreat it; but Orpheus, without any binding at all, escaped the danger, by loudly chanting to his harp the praises of the gods, whereby he drowned the voices of the Sirens.

EXPLANATION.—This fable is of the moral kind, and appears no less elegant than easy to interpret. For pleasures proceed from plenty and affluence, attended with activity or exultation of the mind.651 Anciently their first incentives were quick, and seized upon men as if they had been winged, but learning and philosophy afterwards prevailing, had at least the power to lay the mind under some restraint, and make it consider the issue of things, and thus deprived pleasures of their wings.

This conquest redounded greatly to the honor and ornament of the Muses; for after it appeared, by the example of a few, that philosophy could introduce a contempt of pleasures, it immediately seemed to be a sublime thing that could raise and elevate the soul, fixed in a manner down to the earth, and thus render men's thoughts, which reside in the head, winged as it were, or sublime.

Only the mother of the Sirens was not thus plumed on the head, which doubtless denotes superficial learning, invented and used for delight and levity;

an eminent example whereof we have in Petronius, who, after receiving sentence of death, still continued his gay frothy humor, and as Tacitus observes, used his learning to solace or divert himself, and instead of such discourses as give firmness and constancy of mind, read nothing but loose poems and verses.652 Such learning as this seems to pluck the crowns again from the Muses' heads, and restore them to the Sirens.

The Sirens are said to inhabit certain islands, because pleasures generally seek retirement, and often shun society. And for their songs, with the manifold artifice and destructiveness thereof, this is too obvious and common to need explanation. But that particular of the bones stretching like white cliffs along the shores, and appearing afar off, contains a more subtile allegory, and denotes that the examples of others' calamity and misfortunes, though ever so manifest and apparent, have yet but little force to deter the corrupt nature of man from pleasures.

The allegory of the remedies against the Sirens is not difficult, but very wise and noble; it proposes, in effect, three remedies, as well against subtle as violent mischiefs, two drawn from philosophy and one from religion.

The first means of escaping is to resist the earliest temptation in the beginning, and diligently avoid and cut off all occasions that may solicit or sway the mind; and this is well represented by shutting up the ears, a kind of remedy to be necessarily used with mean and vulgar minds, such as the retinue of Ulysses.

But nobler spirits may converse, even in the midst of pleasures, if the mind be well guarded with constancy and resolution. And thus some delight to make a severe trial of their own virtue, and thoroughly acquaint themselves with the folly and madness of pleasures, without complying or being wholly given up to them; which is what Solomon professes of himself when he closes the account of all the numerous pleasures he gave a loose to, with this expression: "But wisdom still continued with me." Such heroes in virtue may, therefore, remain unmoved by the greatest incentives to pleasure, and stop themselves on the very precipice of danger; if, according to the example of Ulysses, they turn a deaf ear to pernicious counsel, and the flatteries of their friends and companions, which have the greatest power to shake and unsettle the mind.

But the most excellent remedy, in every temptation, is that of Orpheus, who, by loudly chanting and resounding the praises of the gods, confounded the voices, and kept himself from hearing the music of the Sirens; for divine contemplations exceed the pleasures of sense, not only in power but also in sweetness.

# XXVII

❦

## Emerson's Concept of the Oversoul

IN every human nature abides a Cyclopean self with whom, A at long intervals, the mortal part of man communes. With this thought is introduced a new phase of Greek metaphysical speculation. The instructors in the Mysteries declared that at birth each individual was assigned an invisible patron spirit called the natal daemon . This entity was analogous to the totem of the North American Indians, except that the totem was invoked by prayer and fasting, while the daemon—being coexistent with the generating soul itself—became, as it were, the identity of the senses. By some this natal daemon was considered the personified aggregate of past experiences or the summation of previous lives; it was synonymous with the instinctive impulse-nature—that inevitable product of existences which stands behind and urges the issues of the outer life.

This natal daemon is the composite self; the sum of countless previous selves; the personality compounded of multiple personalities; the thinking, feeling, and actuating sensory organism of material urge; the superphysical by-product of temporal achievement. The natal daemon is the god who protects the fool, making it impossible for man to actually undo himself beyond redemption. It is the patron saint of the outer life; the intuitively sensed superiority; the intangible authority by which mortal man is given courage to assert his participation in a divine energy. According to the Egyptians the natal daemon is created by the converging celestial rays at the time of nativity. It becomes the intangible cause of dispositions, and through its agencies two individuals, though similarly organized, neither think nor feel the same, but work out their diverging destinies motivated by this daemoniac.al part.

"Plato," writes Apuleius on the God of Socrates , "asserts that a peculiar daemon is allotted to every man, who is a witness and a guardian of his conduct in life, who, without being visible to any one, is always present, and who is an arbitrator not only of his deeds, but also of his thoughts. But when, life being finished, the soul returns [to the judges of its conduct], then the daemon who presided over it immediately seizes, and leads it as his charge to judgment, and is there present with it while it pleads its cause. Hence, this daemon reprehends it, if it has acted on any false pretense; solemnly confirms what it says, if it asserts any thing that is true; and conformably to its testimony passes sentence. All you, therefore, who hear this divine opinion of Plato, as interpreted by me, so form your minds to whatever you may do, or to whatever may be the subject of your meditation, that you may know there is nothing concealed from those guardians either within the mind, or external to it; but that the daemon who presides over you inquisitively participates of all that concerns you, sees all things, understands all things, and in the place of conscience dwells in the most profound recesses of the mind. For he of whom I speak is a perfect guardian, a singular prefect, a domestic speculator, a proper curator, an intimate inspector, an assiduous observer, an inseparable arbiter, a reprobater of what is evil,

an approver of what is good; and if he is legitimately attended to, sedulously known, and religiously worshipped, in the way in which he was reverenced by Socrates with justice and innocence, will be a predictor in things uncertain, a premonitor in things dubious, a defender in things dangerous, and an assistant in want. He will also be able, by dreams, by tokens, and perhaps also manifestly, when the occasion demands it, to avert from you evil, increase your good, raise your depressed, support your falling, illuminate your obscure, govern your prosperous, and correct your adverse circumstances."

The natal daemon is declared by Olympiodorus to be the supreme flower of the soul, for it is the blossoming of soul qualities. To a certain extent the soul is generated from the interplay of action and reaction in the sphere of sense. The soul is the garment woven from the threads of incident; the natal daemon is consciousness born of experience—the realization begotten of necessity. The natal daemon is the diamond soul, the transmutation of corporeality into incorporeality, the regeneration of bodily quantities into bodiless qualities; for the natal daemon is the wholeness of consciousness which must ever result from the co-ordination of heterogeneous parts. In the terms of mathematics die natal daemon is the spirit of the number 6, which is invoked by the coming together of six monads and is inseparable from them as long as they continue to constitute a unit or wholeness. The natal daemon must therefore be regarded as the consciousness of the senses conceived as a monad and established at the summit of the pyramid of sense, from whence it flows downward to tincture with that understanding based upon experience the entire structure of the corporeal perceptions. The philosophers declared that a natal daemon, or familiar, is assigned to every man, with whom it remains until the rational soul, having been elevated above the sphere of the senses and having achieved comparative illumination, turns to the contemplation of superessential verities. Upon one who had achieved this distinction the Greeks conferred the appellation of hero.

A hero was one who had heroically turned from the contemplation of the temporal to the contemplation of the eternal, and consequently was dedicated to the service of the gods.

Gazing rapturously upon the faces of the Ungenerated Ones, the heroes verged toward certain divinities with more ardor than to others, thus expressing the innate preferences of their dispositions. The heroes, therefore, were divided among the orders of the gods, each serving his own preference and by degrees coming to be identified with the qualities of his chosen deity. As the gods themselves are incapable of descending into the corporeal sphere, they incline toward it through their vassals, the heroes. As a result certain men have come to be revered as divine incarnations and the creative principles venerated under their similitudes. Unable to discern that the hero is not a god, the nonphilosophic have befogged the issues of theology, with the result that men have become the worshippers of men and have propitiated mortal heroes before the superessential gods.

While ordinary mortals, being as yet rationally unawakened, depend largely upon their natal dae-mon, the heroes—or those already approaching liberation—are the beneficiaries of a more exalted genius, denominated the essential daemon . The Father- Star of the Neoplatonists is this essential daemon, into whose nature the natal daemon has been merged by a process in which the lesser is mingled with the greater, and their issues become one. The essential daemon is unapproachable by him who is still a servant to his sense perceptions. Nor can the essential daemon descend into man, but as a Silent Watcher must brood over the irrational soul until, emerging from its chrysalis of materiality, it spreads its spiritual wings and soars swiftly to the source of its own light. In Homer's Odyssey, Ulysses is revealed to be a mortal aspiring to the estate of a hero, which end he attains by his perilous voyagings through the seas of temporal uncertainty. As the senses must be mastered before that which is above the senses can be liberated, one of the labors of Ulysses was the blinding of the Cyclops. This giant signified Ulysses' own natal daemon—his self-will—whose power must be destroyed before divine will could be seated in its place. The Cyclops is, therefore, a monster of the astral light, the shadowy giant who abides amid the shadows of man's own being and whose "single eye" is the pineal gland—the only organ with which he discerns the outer uni-verse. But it is possible for the eye of the natal daemon to see two ways. By turning inward it ceases to serve the Cyclops, and fixes its gaze upon the splendid features of the essential daemon who, abiding in the sphere of pure intellection, is the Father-Star—the Pole-Star by which the mariner of life steers the bark of his own soul into the safe harbor of divine perfection.

The philosophy of daemons is the outgrowth of man's natural veneration for the rationality man-ifest in every order of life and form. The very clouds scudding across the sky exist by virtue of the intercession of rational intelligence, and upon fulfillment of their destiny are dissipated by the activity of this selfsame intelligence. A peculiar Providence equips every organism with the instruments of its own survival. The plant's vital seed is protected by a stalwart husk, and the life of the Crustacea by its defensive shell. The urge that causes irrational nature to act in a rational manner we call instinct . To the ancient philosopher, however, the flowering of plants, the propa-gation of species, the tinting of rocks and crystals, the motions of the elements, and the emotions of the soul-all these were regarded alike as evidence of the presence of invisible but powerful spir-its (daemons) who, seated in the causal nature of the manifesting sphere, guided primitive lives to the fulfillment of the predestined ends of uinversal procedure.

Some of these daemons are analogous to the elemental spirits of Paracelsus, with whose charac-teristics the great Swiss physician was made familiar by Arabian sorcerers. Recognizing all diver-sified activities to be suspended from causal unities, the philosopher of antiquity realized that while green, for example, dominates the color scheme of numberless organisms, green is itself a monad or unity, its intrinsic nature being coetaneous with a rational daemon. The or-derly or rational distribution of green is thus effected through the ministrations of this guardian spirit, which is synonymous with the very nature of green itself. To attribute rationality to a tube of pigment at first may appear to be a baseless concept. Those who have experimented most with colors realize, however, that they have an inherent orderliness and are very much alive, possess-ing the power to excite pleasure or displeasure, and through their intermingling to demonstrate various complexions of universal order. As the salamander is born by the very friction that ignites the sulphur match, so a daemon is spontaneously produced through every combination of forces, substances, or circumstances, becoming the patron of such combinations and remaining with them until divine procedure returns these combinations to their original simplicity. The belief in guardian spirits is a very lofty one when the unfolding rationality of man permits him to regard these entities as ever beautiful and virtuous. On the other hand, untutored peoples consider these transcendental entities to be innately malevolent, conspiring against human beings and seeking to spread sorrow and mischief throughout the world.

The idealism of the Greek aestheticians enabled them to recognize divine agency in all that was beautiful, in that divinities rejoiced in the harmonious combinations of substances and circumstances. Accordingly, a place of beauty must needs be the dwelling of a thing of beauty. In somber groves dwelt grave dryades formed of the soft shadow that lingered there; in the high-flung spray of waterfalls nymphs disported themselves, while diminutive but pompous gnomes industriously hoarded beechnuts against the possibility of seven lean years.

Though these creatures were invisible to the normal sight, man was conscious of their presence. They were indeed creations of place—the products of environment and necessary to the setting of the picture. All these creatures are daemons of different orders; for there are not only vast spirits whose bodies are stars, but daemons so small that they seek the shelter of toadstools or play hide-and-seek among the blades of grass. The daemon is the spirit of feeling that is born of, and is inseparable from, the circumstance that gives it birth. It is the preserver

of universal order in the lesser, the untiring minister to parts, the protector and patron of unfolding life. Just what relation, then, does the Oversoul of Emerson bear to the God of Socrates, that strange yet exalted spirit which impelled the Athenian commoner to a martyr's end? Emerson, the Occidental Orientalist, thus defines what he conceives to be that common oversoul of whose nature we all partake, and which is the common measure of us all: "The Supreme critic on all the errors of the past and the present, and the only prophet of that which must be, is that great nature in which we rest, as the earth lies in the soft arms of the atmosphere;

that Unity, that Over-Soul, within which every man's particular being is contained and made one with all other; that common heart, of which all sincere conversation is the worship, to which all right action is submission; that overpowering reality which confutes our tricks and talents, and constrains every one to pass for what he is, and to speak from his character and not from his tongue; and which evermore tends and aims to pass into our thought and hand, and become wisdom, and virtue, and power, and beauty."

It is a philosophic axiom that as we verge toward Cause we verge toward simplicity, and as we depart from Cause we incline toward complexity; for all things are simple in their beginnings, complex in their midmost parts, and simple again in their ends. As man passes from childishness through maturity to childishness, so life (according to the doctrines of

Herbert Spencer) is from simple homogeneity to complex heterogeneity and from heterogeneity back again to homogeneity.

Approach to simplicity, then, presumes an ever-decreasing number of parts, until ultimate simplicity is utter privation of partition. Emerson clearly senses the common unity of Cause

—that vast Monad which is our common parent and whose sufficiency is the one noble Reality.

This is indeed the Great Daemon, the Supreme Soul invoked by existence, whose ministrations we manifest in common and whose edicts are the code of our lives. As we increase in rationality we become diffused among or enter into the inner nature of an ever-increasing number of organisms, thereby becoming capable of knowing and feeling the impulses which actuate these organizations.

Thus Man became the Oversoul of men—the Adam, or archetypal one from whom issue the many; the Protogonas from whose nature as from the pores of the skin come forth the "sweat-born" and the establishment of generations. Thus Man—the Oversoul—is the anthropos , or daemoniacal spirit which is the common father of infinite progeny; the vast sphere of influence which men can never escape, but which is their allness and against the sovereignty of which

they vainly struggle, ignorant of the fact that it is their common life. The Oversoul alone is Man, for men are but fractional parts of themselves and are never complete until all together form one grand nature. Therefore, while all men differ in their outer lives, in their inner life there is this common ground whereon all stand together and upon which they must erect the citadel of their strength. Only to the dreamer, who sees not with his eyes, but with his soul, is the dignity of the anthropos apparent; only the mystic can comprehend that vast being which towers above the puny sensibilities of mortals and from the lofty place broods over the body of its sovereignty.

This anthropos exceeds men to the degree that the whole exceeds its parts, for each part contributes to the sufficiency of the sum.

The Neoplatonists differed from the Egyptians in their definition of the anthropos —or the nature of the all-containing self—when related to the status of men. According to one group, all of man descends into the sphere of generation, there to wander for a given time in the confusion of sense, and later by rational procedure to escape therefrom and reascend to the sphere of spiritual sufficiency. The more profound philosophies, however, declared that the ungenerate can never actually generate, nor can that which abides in the contemplation of perfection ever become immersed in the delusions of mortality.

While the inferior nature of man, suspended from its monadic cause, may thus struggle for a brief period in the darkness of the moral sphere, the true self remains throughout this period in the presence of perfect order and adequate comprehension. According to this viewpoint all of man does not descend into the realm of his corporeal limitations, but rather broods over the incarnating part, and from its own state of detachment contemplates the attachments which involve the inferior self. Thus man is more than man; he is like the oft-employed simile of the iceberg, of which only a fractional part of its great bulk is visible. This invisible greatness of man—unmoved and uninvolved, and residing in the pure rationality of the supreme sphere—is termed the "Silent Watcher," the Atman who is the true man, and of whom the lesser part becomes increasingly aware as it ceases to be conscious in its animal part. In this manner is man, the comparative physical nonentity, suspended from Man, the actual spiritual immensity. Is it not this overbrooding divinity which man senses when he explores the depths of his own feeling and seeks to measure the magnitude of his intellect? Is it not this transcendent superpersonal one who is the true substance of man's hope and the body of his aspirations?

Picture, then, the mortal nature of man who, obscured by the insufficiency of his physical perceptions and crawling worm- like upon the surface of earth, dares to believe in his own thoughts and assume the reasonableness of his own contentions. Then conceive the blind mortality which men call life to be directed by a great and observing spirit which, grasping the lesser life by the hand, gently leads it toward comprehension and realization. Imagine that behind the little you at all times stands the greater You—-majestic, illumined, magnificent—who communicates to the earthiness which is your mortal body a splendor more than sufficient, and through whose greatness the little you is made partaker of the greatness and goodness of all things. This is the anthropos , the Heavenly Man, the Supreme Manu, from whose presence man departs for his terrestrial wandering in the prodigal's sphere. While Emerson conceives this soul to be within man, in philosophy we prefer to conceive of man as within this soul.

As through philosophy we increase the dimensions of our internal selves, we gradually annihilate the interval between our human souls and this Oversoul. Our internal selves take on the stature of this nobler part until, though our body be still of mortal size, the scope of expanding consciousness becomes tions of inspiration. We then understand the qualities which

inspired Emerson to pen these words: "The soul looketh steadily forward, creating a world always before her, and leaving worlds always behind her. She has no dates, no rites, nor persons, nor specialities, nor men. The soul knows only the soul. Ail else is idle weeds for her wearing."

We now turn to a more detailed consideration of the intrinsic nature of the soul and the position it occupies in the composite structures of both man and the universe. As already defined, the soul is the first and chief of the generations. It abides in its own essence at the apex of the pyramid of form.

If the soul, then, be a generation and not an eternal principle, of what is it generated and why is it superior to other generations? That which is generated receives its life from another. Having had this active agent once imparted to it, it is thenceforth capable of separation therefrom. On the other hand, an ungenerated being—because its life is inherent—must ever abide in that life and that life in it, and hence is incapable of dissolution. Being a generation, the soul must consequently be included under the classification of bodies. Yet it is different from bodies; for being the chief of diem, it possesses a fullness of virtues which exceeds the fullness of any other body. Of inferiors, then, the soul is the superior, and by virtue of its disposition occupies a midmost place between abiding life and unabiding form. As the physical man is clothed in

a vehicle composed of the objectification and substantial counterpart of his superphysical corporeal impulses, so an invisible body generated of attributes too subtle to assume physical aspect envelopes the spiritual part as with an appropriate robe. Virtue, for example, is irreducible to physical perceptions. Seated, however, in the invisible nature, it manifests as an intangible

and definite attribute of the self. Man is as surely clothed in the garments of virtue as he is in the garments of the physical; they are vehicles of his expression no less real than are the members formed of bone, flesh, or sinew.

Besides the physical, man is the owner of many bodies, invisible however to those whose perceptions are limited solely to the earthly senses. Each of these bodies is the vehicle of

definite potentialities which are slowly being manifested through appropriate organisms. Man lives in many worlds simultaneously, but of this fact he is unaware until he comes to realize that every phase of his temperament attunes him to a different level of universal activity. A concatenated chain of vehicles extends upward from the dense physical organism to the attenuated superphysical organism of the soul. These bodies originally issued forth from the soul and to the soul they must return—or rather, we should say their essences verge—for soul existed before bodies and shall endure after bodies have ceased to be. Yet the soul is profoundly influenced by its bodies, and its nature is subjected to change by the reactions of bodily conditions. As the proper monad of bodies, the soul causes to issue out from its own being all that is inferior to itself. And by the same course that dominated their issuance, the soul reabsorbs these selfsame bodies back again into its own essence; for by this reabsorption is the perfection of bodies consummated. Man cannot enter into the presence of Reality while still invested with body, for body can never contemplate the bodiless, form the formless, or the generated the ungenerated, As bodies, forms, and generations are thus transmuted into soul (more correctly, reabsorbed into the soul substance) man creates for himself a new and more subtle garment—a luminous sheath, a bodiless body, a form verging toward the formless, by which it is enabled to contemplate formlessness with comprehension. The soul, then, is the all-sufficient body; it is form elevated to the vanishing point; it is nature retired into its own apex and thus rendered capable of contemplating its own cause. Through progressive sublimation bodies are caused to retire from their own materiality and incline themselves toward that spirituality from which they derived their actuating principle.

If the fruitage of physical experience were apprehensible by the physical nature alone, then life would be but a span of useless suffering, for the deed would perish with the doer and the self be left as impecunious as before. Though every tangible evidence of physical achievement must be discarded by the decarnating spirit, yet there is carried forward into the invisible a subtle substance or pabulum extracted from incident and assimilable by the soul nature. Every incident, every experience, every conclusion of the physical life has its own soul nature, to be extracted therefrom by a strange distillation. The vapors thus distilled are inhaled by the soul even as the physical body subsists upon the material atmosphere. The distilled essence of incident thus becomes the essential nutriment of the soul, and the experiences of life are ultimately metamorphosed into soul qualities, becoming psychical urges and influences by which the outer nature is inclined hither and thither.

As polarity exists throughout the sphere of generation, it follows that the soul itself though intrinsically a monad, must manifest through the duad—the positive and negative channels of expression. The soul is accordingly symbolized as two creatures: one a beautiful and radiant spirit subsisting upon the manifesting virtues of the life; the other an evil and rebellious spirit fostered by every unworthy thought or deed. These two guard the mystic gate between the outer and the inner self; for, as the soul, they are the portal through which the polar forces of cause and effect pass in mutual exchange. The radiant soul fashioned from the very substance of achievement becomes the animating principle of intuition; for what is intuition but a kind of memory in which particulars are forgotten but principles remembered ? The mind may lack the power to reason through, and the outer nature be uninformed regarding the solution of perplexing problems. But based upon ages of endeavor, intuition unerringly points out the law of probability; for by virtue of ripe experience it inclines with more certitude than the reason, and with more discretion than the thinking but inexperienced personality.

The evil part of the soul speaks also, and its voice is conscience. Conscience is the still, small voice of unremembered suffering which, long vanished from the conscious mind, yet lives in the deeper recesses of the nature, where it warns of impending catastrophe and whispers to such as will listen the standards of right and wrong as established by experience. Men and women of normal intelligence never commit wrong deeds which they do not know are wrong before their commission. We may dissemble or feign ignorance, but all too often we realize that we lie even while we speak. The mentor of ages dwells within, and irrespective of our pretensions its words are audible to our inner selves. What is that accusing self from which the malefactor can never escape and which hounds the evil-doer to the bitter end? It is the soul. Living

its own life consistent with the principle of Truth, the soul will never let us rest until our outer lives are rendered harmonious with the code within. Why are some happy, though surrounded by all manner of misfortune and sorely oppressed by offending circumstances? Because the soul, satisfied with the behavior of the life, bestows the sense of satisfaction upon these outer sensibilities so keenly vexed by an unkind Providence.

The all-sufficing realization of accomplishment flows from the soul, and like the balm of Gilead assuages the torments of the material Tartarus. The persecuted parts are imbued with fresh courage and conviction, and given new strength to meet every emergency. On the other hand, why are so many who are fully blessed with this world's goods, and possessors of all that should bestow happiness and tranquility so miserable, so abject, so afraid? Because the soul, dissatisfied, refuses to allow an outer complacency to silence its accusations. When man's soul thus convicts him of misdirected living, there is no tribunal to which he can appeal for mitigation of his offence.

Shall we then wonder that the Greeks declared conscience to be a daemon that eternally whispers in the ear of the mind, and intuition a guardian deity that can conduct the life through the perils of the physical universe? Intuition and conscience are the tangible expressions of the intangible soul by which man is made to realize that from every act a residue remains which shall influence his doing unto the end of time. Nothing that we accomplish is lost; nothing that we achieve is forgotten; for while the particulars may vanish away, the principles involved arc interwoven into the fabric of an invisible vestment that clothes the self in the ample folds of experience, and insures that spirit shall never be without a counselor, or life without a patron.

We have already set forth the triform constitution of the Divine Agent who through the One, the Beautiful, and the Good creates, preserves, and destroys the innumerable orders of beings. Apuleius, in The Metamorphosis , sets forth in allegorical terms the inner mystery of the soul. The legend of Cupid and Psyche existed, however, prior to the time of Apuleius, being preserved inviolate by the philosophers lest a profane world desecrate the sacred truths.

A king and queen had three daughters (so the story goes), of whom the youngest, Psyche, was of such surpassing beauty that mortals paid her a homage that elevated her above the dignity of even Venus herself. The indignant goddess of beauty thereupon dispatched her winged son, Cupid, to humble the pride of Psyche by infusing her with a passion for some gross and unnatural being.

Invisible to mortals, Cupid entered the apartment of Psyche to carry out his mother's mission, but became so enamoured of the beautiful maiden that he repented of his role and schemed to win Psyche for himself.

Suffering from the enmity of Venus, Psyche found no love among mankind, and in obedience to an oracle which declared that she would never be the bride of a mortal lover but that her husband would be a monster whom neither gods nor man could resist, she ascended the mountain upon which it was decreed she should await the coming of her unnatural bridegroom. As she stood upon the mountain top the god Zephyr picked her up and bore her into a flowery flale, in the midst of which stood a grove of tall and stately trees and a magnificent palace which was not the work of mortal hands. TTie palace roof was supported by gilded columns, and the walls were ornamented with tracing of beasts and strange creatures. Vast treasures of gold and jewels were also gathered there, and Psyche was served by invisible attendants who gratified her slightest wish.

Psyche never saw her husband, who came only at night and departed before dawn. She begged him to permit her to look upon his face, but he declared that she must be content with his love and never try to see him. Desirous of putting at rest the worries of her family Psyche sent for her two sisters, and these, jealous of her fortune, incited her to make an effort to see her husband. So one night when he was asleep she lit a lamp, and carrying a knife with which to slay the evil monster described by the oracle, stole into her husband's bedchamber and discovered him to be Cupid, the son of Venus, and the most beautiful of all the gods. As she stood watching him a drop of hot oil fell upon his body, and awakened by the pain Cupid spread his downy wings and fled through the window, sorrowfully reminding Psyche that love cannot dwell with suspicion.

The palace thereupon vanished and Psyche found herself in a field near her father's city. Broken-hearted, she began a quest for her lost lover, first seeking the help of Ceres who suggested that if she go humbly to Venus and surrender to her dictates she might regain Cupid's love. Desiring the discomfiture of Psyche, however, Venus made a servant of her, setting her almost impossible tasks which Psyche in every instance accomplished with the assistance of sympathetic gods. Her first task was to separate a vast quantity of mixed grains; her second, to gather golden fleece from a large flock of vicious rams; and her third, to descend into Hades and bring back from Persephone, the goddess of the underworld, a casket filled with beauty.

Still inquisitive, however, Psyche opened the casket in spite of the warning given her by the tower god who had aided her in the adventure. Instead of being filled with beauty the casket contained a Stygian sleep which loosed from the box, overcame Psyche so that she fell unconscious on the path. Cupid, coming to her rescue, returned the sleep to the box, and interceding with Jupiter for her hand, both hnally reconciled Venus to the match. Psyche was then given a cup of heavenly drink which conferred upon her immortality, and in common with all fairy stories the two lovers lived happily ever afterward.

In the interpretation of this fable of the soul's descent into generation—more correctly, its descent into the concept of generation—we must reiterate certain of our earlier assumptions.

In the words of Thomas Taylor: "In the first place, the Gods, as I have elsewhere shown, are super-essential natures, from their profound union with the first cause, who is super-essential without any addition. But though the Gods, through their summits or unities, transcend essence, yet their unities are participated either by intellect alone, or by intellect and soul, or by intellect, soul, and body; from which participations the various orders of the Gods are deduced. When, therefore, intellect, soul, and body are in conjunction, suspended from this super-essential unity, which is the center, flower, or blossom, of a divine nature, then the God from whom they are suspended is called a mundane God."

The Platonists further affirmed that the human soul was born from the intellect and soul of the world, but that its direct parents were the intellect and soul of a certain star, which is its Father-Star and from which it first descended into the sphere of non-tranquility. As the soul is suspended between intellect and body, its "fall," so-called, represents its inclination toward body. Therefore the mundane soul and the intellectual (or supermundane) soul are identical in essence, but verge in opposite directions. The fall, or descent, of the soul into materiality is the result, consequently, of its contemplation of body; and conversely, its liberation from the mundane sphere is accomplished by turning about to the contemplation of intellect. The soul is an immortal mortal, for when mingling with the immortals it shares their permanence and transcendency. When mingling with mortal concerns, however, it is bereft of these endowments, becoming susceptible to a certain degree of mortality by which its luminosity is destroyed and its wings are clipped. From this we understand how it is possible for a soul to fall from its estate and yet still remain in that estate; for though it may verge toward the intellect or the body, it is still essentially in its own estate and remains soul regardless of the nature with which it mingles.

Apropos to the subject matter, we have the remarks of Aristides concerning the descent of the soul. "The soul," he says, "as long as she is seated in a purer place of the universe, in consequence of not being mingled with the nature of bodic? ; is pure and inviolate, and revolves, together with the ruler of the world; but when, through an inclination to these inferior concerns, she receives certain phantasms from places about the earth, then she gradually imbibes oblivion of the goods she possessed in her former superior station, and at the same time descends. But by how much the more she is removed from superior natures, by so much the more approaching to inferiors, is she filled with insanity, and hurled into corporeal darkness; because through a diminution of her former dignity, she can no longer be intelligibly extended with the universe; but on account of her oblivion of supernal goods, and consequent astonishment, she is borne downward into more solid natures, and such as are involved in the obscurity of matter. Hence, when her desire of body commences, she assumes and draws from each of the superior places some portions of corporeal mixture."

The same author continues his description of the descent of the soul through the orbits of the divine planets, from each of which—as in the story of Ishtar at the seven gates and also the descent of the soul in The Divine Pymander of Hermes Mer - curius Trismcgistus —the soul receives a luciform and enveloping nature. At last, approaching the sphere of the moon, the soul becomes of such corporeality that a certain gravitation draws it into the rhythm of the physical world. The soul then loses its spherical form and assumes the human shape, the luciform and ethereal substances gathered from the stars first becoming fetal membranes and later definite parts of the physical structure of the outer nature and psychical qualities in the inner nature. For, as Aristides again remarks, the shell-like vestment of man is nourished from its own root, which is the descending soul.

Psyche (or the soul) is described by Apulcius to be of royal parentage, thus arcanely intimating that she is of a divine line, for royalty here signifies the spiritual lineage. That which has its foundation in the gods is declared to be of kingly order, for the gods were the patrons of rulers who thus administered their kingly office by divine right. In contradiction, mortals were regarded as creatures of common birth to signify that their mother was the earth and they themselves earthborn and not—like the gods—the sons of heaven. Psyche is further described as the most beautiful of all mortals, so far surpassing all other earthly beings in loveliness that men venerated her as a goddess and made her offerings similar to those with which Venus, the Mother of Generations, was propitiated.

The soul is thus represented as exceeding in perfection all other material bodies, its beauty being due to its proximity to the fountain of beauty, of whose harmonies it partakes and whose excellence it reflects into the inferior sphere. The perfections of the soul surpass the perfections of the body even as the qualities of the superior nature surpass the qualities of form. In Book X of the Laws , Plato puts into the mouth of the Athenian stranger the following words: "And if this is true, and if the soul is older than the body, must not the things which are of the soul's kindred be of necessity before those which appertain to the body?" Cleinias answers "Certainly." "Then," rejoins the Athenian, "thought and care, and mind and art, and law will be prior to that which is hard and soft, and heavy and light."

Here Plato emphasizes the doctrine of the excellence of the soul over the body; for the concerns of the soul are more noble, more lasting, and more satisfying than are the concerns of the mortal nature. As mental activity is more beautiful than physical activity, and virtue more excellent than pulchritude of person, so the ancients ascribed to the soul a transcendent and luminous beatitude. Sensing the felicity of this inner part, the outer nature regarded the soul as a divinity in some cases, as the Divinity. This misdirected homage is said to have "vexed" the higher gods who, since they greatly exceeded the virtue of the soul, should properly be the recipients of a fuller and more perfect devotion.

If the gods, however, be impersonal principles, how shall we interpret that vexation which prompts them to divert their benevolence and leave the offending mortal deprived of their qualities? When man in his quest of realities exalts secondary natures—such as the soul—and loses sight of the divine origin and wholeness from which souls are suspended, he reaps for his imprudence irrationality, or the suspension of rational activity. Thus is his mind continually vexed by its own unsoundness, and such disquietude in the rational faculties is declared to represent an offended intellect or an indignant divinity.

The goddess Venus manifests a twofold disposition. The superior phase liberates souls from material generation and elevates them to those superessential generations which subsist from the apex of the generating sphere. The other, and lower, phase of Venus inclines souls toward corporeality and binds them in servitude to the generating nature, for which reason the goddess was regarded by the ancients as a personification of carnality. The great dragon or monster whom the oracle prophesied was to become the husband of Psyche signified materiality—the mortal nature with whom she must be wedded at the time of her entrance into physical life. The fabulous monsters of the ancient Mystery rituals—such as behemoth, leviathan, and the hippocampus —all signified the mortal sphere that devours the souls descending into generation, and like the Minotaur claims for its own the fairest and bravest of every age.

Psyche is led forth to the top of a high mountain, there to wed this strange creature decreed by the gods, that her spirit might be duly humbled, and that she might realize that only the immortals can escape the limitations of matter and the ravages of time. From this mountain top Psyche is borne downward by Zephyr, the west wind, into a beautiful valley where stands a mighty grove of oak trees. This valley signifies the mundane sphere or lower world into which the generating soul is conducted. The east is the portal of generation, for it denotes the place of the nativity in a horoscope. So the west wind blows the soul gently into birth. The grove of trees signifies creation, which is, as it were, a clump of mighty agencies. In the midst of this grove is the palace of the world, where there are vast treasures and the jewels of the stars. The tracings upon the walls of the palace are the constellations— those vast signs upon the walls of heaven which hem in our solar system and are the limits of the mundane house.

Here Psyche is served by invisible beings whose voices she hears; for having descended from her true estate, the spiritual agencies which are her excellence arc no longer visible. But their voices still speak to her inner nature, even as the gods still speak through the oracle of the human heart. Psyche, however, is not yet physical and mortal; hence the physical agencies of creation are also invisible. Suspended thus between two spheres, she wanders in the Great House of Life which she is eventually to discover is the dwelling place of Cupid.

Cupid is chiefly familiar to the 20th century as the matchmaker supreme, but in antiquity he played a most significant role. He is the symbol of love which, according to philosophy, has a duality of natures. The first is that supernal passion by which the soul is moved while still pure and undefiled in the luminance of the soul sphere. The second is mortal love in which the soul—deluded by the findings of sense—exchanges for the adoration of internal qualities the infatuation for external appearance. Married to an invisible being, Psyche thus becomes the bride of spiritual love, into which union the element of form or materiality has not yet entered. She dwells in a beautiful astral palace, served by creatures whose natures have not yet been invested with mortal fabric. Here she remains until hei sisters—who signify mortal instincts—begin to pull her down ward into the sphere of sense.

When Psyche beholds the physical form of her husband, spiritual love is changed into material passion. She is forthwith precipitated from her heavenly palace into the broad meadow of the earth where broken-hearted she wanders in search of the happiness she foolishly sacrificed by listening to the voices of worldliness. She then becomes a servant of Venus, who sets for the unfortunate girl a number of difficult as well as dangerous tasks. These tasks represent the labors of life; the misfortunes of existence which generation heaps upon those who come beneath its sway. In each instance, however, she is assisted by a heavenly voice which, representative of the ever-present daemon or divinity, with its greater vision leads the soul befogged by matter through the tortuous byways of existence.

When Venus enslaves Psyche, the lower love becomes master of the soul qualities, and the shackles of desire hold the will in bondage to the animal propensities. The last task set by Venus for Psyche to perform is the journey to Hades to bring back with her from the sphere of the dead a casket filled with beauty. This casket signified physical life, which the ignorant soul believes to be the receptacle of happiness and beauty but which proves, upon opening, to contain only an evil and stupefying spirit. Seizing the soul, this spirit causes it to descend into the very depths of corporeality, there to remain until Cupid (or love) comes to awaken and elevate it to its lost estate. Cupid, the invisible god, is rational love—that affection which is seated in the true qualities of the soul. This higher and more divine emotion, rousing the rational soul as from a stupor, communicates its vitality thereto and thus enables the soul by rational procedure to cast off the lethargy of the illusions of the flesh. Upon completion of this task Psyche placates the angry Venus and even wins favor in the sight of awful Zeus, the Demiurgus himself. Thereupon she is given the heavenly drink and ceasing to be a mortal verges toward the immortals. She thus becomes the mother of joy, which is born of the union of the rationality in each soul with that greater rationality which is the invisible but all-potent god of intellectual love.

Thus is set forth the story of a prodigal daughter whose experiences parallel those contained in the biblical allegory of the prodigal son. Here also is the key to the allegory of Lohengrin; for the young prince of the Holy Grail is divine and unnamed love, which is destroyed or forced to retire when its nature is brought within the sphere of denomination.

From the foregoing it is evident that the integrity of man is posited in his superior part, and regardless of the physical inhibitions by which the flow of his divinity is impeded, that which is essentially good and true must perforce ultimately dominate the entire character. Not without just cause does man instinctively turn to his own soul for consolation and guidance. While he may not consciously realize the immensity of Reality, he senses an expansive principle which, residing within the innermost recesses of his being, is ever ready to incline him toward perfection.

Life posits its own awareness in the soul quality; through the soul, spirit learns of its own apparent aloofness from, yet its actual identity with, matter. Clothing its own transcendency in soul, spirit gives its impersonal self into the keeping of a personal nature; clothed with the rationality of a personal nature, spirit descends into the inferior universe to fulfill the natural law of being, that in the nature of perfect existence there shall constantly manifest generations. The Divine Plan includes an order of forms through which life principles continually flow from awareness through the vale of unawareness back to awareness again.

In philosophy, therefore, we labor without ceasing to stimulate our higher natures and thereby rouse the soul from the lethargy of materiality; permit it to ascend from personals to impersonals, from forms to the estates of the formless, to be finally reunited with that sovereign voice of rational, or intellectual, love—that passion of the soul for Reality, that impulse to verge toward those natures partaking most fully of the permanently beautiful. Thus, within human nature, which is incapable of appreciation in its fullest sense, dwells an all- comprehending power—the human soul—which ever seeks reunion with that omniscience to which each action of universal agency is, in turn, the object of a profound appreciation. This greater soul, this mysterious Cupid; this formless being which man may not behold without destroying; this least of forms and most of spirit—this is the true Oversoul in whose intellection we are perpetually immersed and of whose transcendency we continually partake.

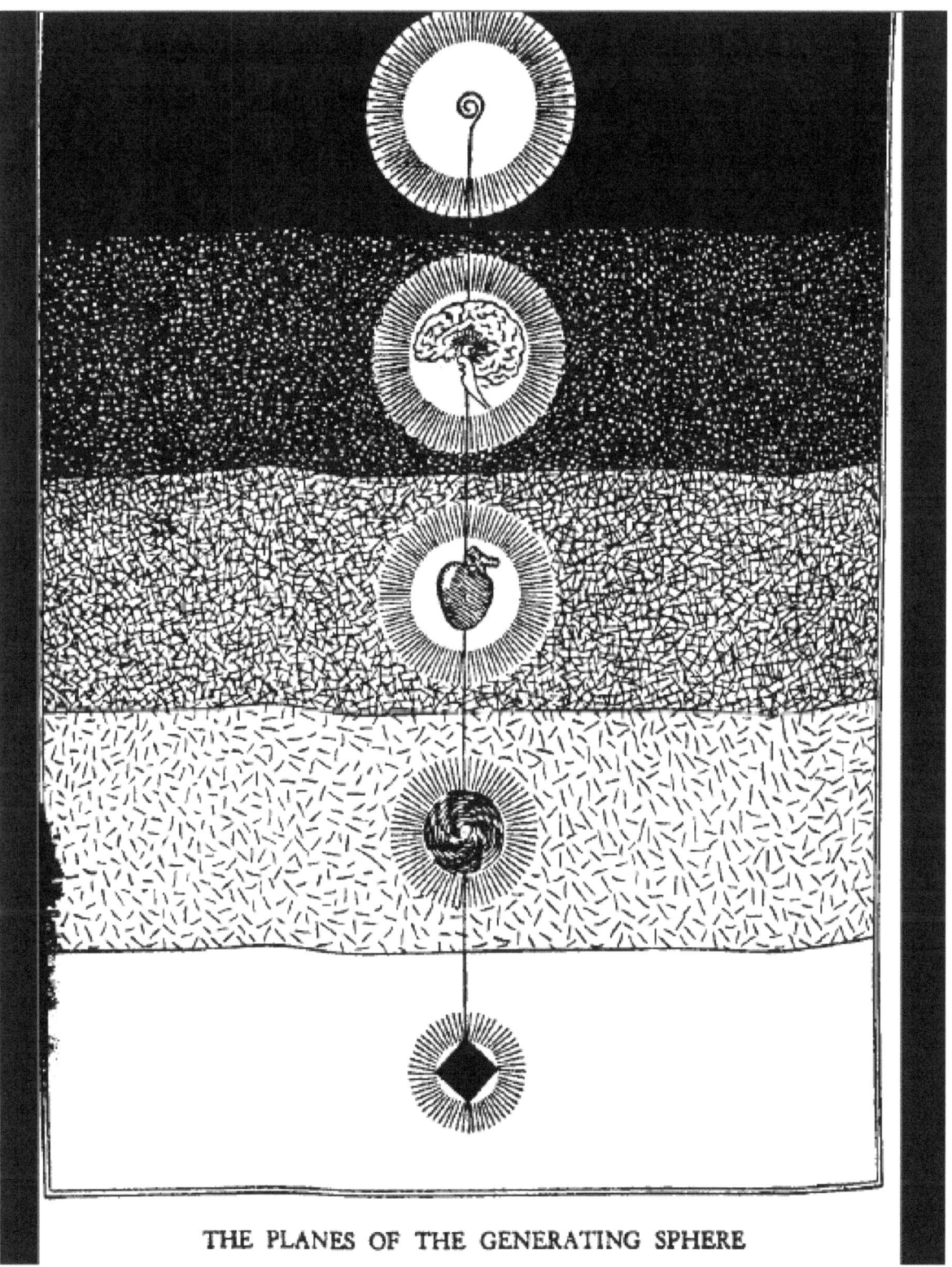

## THE PLANES OF THE GENERATING SPHERE

Assuming the illusion of form, the spiritual life descends out of its own radiant nature and takes upon itself, in sequential order, a mental constitution, an emotional (or astral) constitution, a vital constitution, and, lastly, a physical constitution. These four constitutions are united to the non-incarnating spiritual Self by a thread of life.

# XXVIII

⤛❦⤜

# Exoteric and Esoteric Knowledge

IN Plato's Charmides , wisdom is declared to be the science of itself and also the science of other sciences; furthermore, the science of the absence of science and the science of mental temperances. While all other divisions of learning are concerned with objects, substances, places or conditions, wisdom is concerned with its own nature. From it flow however all other sciences, and by it is determined not only the knowable but the unknowable; not only the extent of that which is but also the extent of that which is not.

Defined as the proper temperance of the mind, this wisdom, verging toward neither extreme but abiding in perpetual equilibrium, may be likened to the monad of knowing, the unity of rationality, the summit of all sciences and speculations. Today we have preserved those sciences which are properly termed the classifiers of extraneous facts, but that form of wisdom which is primarily concerned with the substance of erudition itself has vanished from the institutes of man. As Plato further observes, a wise and temperate man is one capable of correctly estimating the extent not only of his own knowledge or ignorance but also of performing the same service for others. No one is wise who is not as fully acquainted with the extent of ignorance as with die extent of wisdom; for in mortal concerns wisdom is an inconsequential area of rationality existing in an infinite expanse of ignorance.

Temperamentally a skeptic, Socrates infers that wisdom is not the knowledge of things but the knowledge of the condition of knowledge with respect to its absence or presence; an observation plainly intimating that wisdom deals with generals and not with particulars. Wisdom may therefore be considered as composed of the universal s of knowing and the sciences of the particulars of knowing, which as the practical are suspended from theory. Exoteric knowledge then, can be defined as the knowledge of particulars—a familiarity with those arts and sciences arrived at through application and concentration upon external natures. Conversely, esoteric knowledge is concerned with the inherent nature of knowledge itself and is limited to those acquainted with the more profound issues of philosophy and rational theology. Lest the reader grasp too much of this sublime teaching, Plato causes Socrates to refute the statements concerning this abstract science of knowing, thus making it perceptible only to such as are in turn able to refute Socrates.

When he claimed for science that it would wrest from theology the entire domain of cosmological theory, Professor Tyndall would so magnify the part as to swallow up the whole. The puerility of such an assumption is self-apparent, for science by virtue of its very nature has not and cannot invade the realm of true theology. Science may overthrow the false gods and dogmas of creed, but the mysteries of the divine spheres elude the grasp of corporeal learning since they belong to a more subtle and esoteric realm. Never until knowledge is capable of analyzing itself can it retire into its own causal nature and behold the luminous and stupendous wholeness from which beings are suspended by most intangible threads.

Thus while the knowledge of external natures and the classification of objective phenomena are the definite province of science, none but the Mysteries held the true keys to wisdom. They were the custodians of secrets most arcane. Through peculiar disciplines they equipped certain selected mortals with rational instruments by which to measure, estimate, and classify those internal facts which forever elude the intellect delimited by its training to the phenomena of the exterior universe. Founded, according to Sanchoniathon, in the night of Time, the Mysteries were established upon the premise of this two-fold wisdom, of which the greater phase was committed to their reverent custody and the lesser revealed to all men without discrimination. The world, however, was not left wholly devoid of truth, for the secrets of the inner life were set forth under the guise of theological fables that those whose rational faculties were awakening might sense and incline toward the more sublime verities. Sallust declares the fables of the wise to be of five orders, of which the first is the theological; the second, physical; the third, animastic or psychical; the fourth, material; and the fifth, of a mixed order. Many generations often elapsed between the appearance among men of exalted intellects able to comprehend and reconstruct from the figures and metaphors of mythology the hidden body of this spiritual learning, belief in which is now regarded as one of man's most tenacious superstitions. Yet shall we consider as pure figments of the imagination those theological systems which wholly occupied the intellectual faculties of such men as Pythagoras, Plato, Aristotle, Socrates, Proclus, Porphyry, Cicero, Epictetus, Crantor, Atticus, Galen, Plutarch, and Boetius? Is not the rational proof advanced to support the existence of this esoteric knowledge as valid in its own field as the proof adduced by science and now regarded as infallible evidence of scientific erudition ?

That knowledge is not the common property of all is evident from the natural superiority of one mind over another, for no two individuals possess equal faculties of comprehension. These intervals of intellect, manifest to even the most obtuse senses, can never be annihilated save by a definite process of improvement by which the lesser self equips itself to comprehend the findings of the greater. The line of demarcation then, between the hidden and the revealed, is not to be considered definite but rather relative, for the unfolding rationality is ever rejecting the old in favor of the new which, half-defined, is scarcely tangible enough to support the intellect. Thus the individual is ever engaged in tearing away the veils that drape the Saitic figure of knowledge. Yet in the words of Sir Edwin Arnold, "As veil upon veil he lifts, he finds veil upon veil behind." The elements of realization are forever elusive, and greatness or littleness of thought is dependent upon comparison for its estimation. Man is increasing in his ability to comprehend things, to orient himself in relation to place, and to estimate quantity and condition. Though the conceivable universe is actually but an anthill in cosmos, inquisitive humanity in the interests of science will eventually explore that universe to its outermost fringe and fling itself therefrom into eternity. As long as the human intellect thus involved in its own insufficiency communicates its opacity to all external natures, the term esoteric should not be applied to that which is simply unknown, but rather to that which in terms of mortal intellect is unknowable. We have but begun our struggle to master the phenomena of the physical universe; milleniums must pass before we can hope to classify its infinite diversity and cope with the problem of eternity. Although the universe envelopes us as with a vast mantle of obscurity and isolates us in the midst of our insufficiency, yet no phenomena discoverable either by scientific apparatus or philosophic deduction can be classified as truly esoteric. The building of an improved telescope with lenses powerful enough to reveal a galaxy of stars at present invisible would in no way encroach upon the province of esoteric knowledge, for the fact that these stars may be seen if the physical apparatus is sufficiently acute assigns them to the category of exoteric knowledge.

His term exoteric covers the area of communicable facts and includes every form of knowledge discoverable to the intellect through the sense perceptions or the physical mind. That which has been, is now, or can ultimately be recorded upon paper, discoursed upon in the lecture room, debated by polemics, or dissected by the anatomist, must perforce belong to the inferior sphere of speculation where these activities are common, and hence be exoteric. That which can be couched in the language of the mortal sphere pertains to the mortal sphere; but that which pertains to the higher spheres can never be caught upon the surface of grosser substances or sensed by duller perceptions. In one sweep the self-recommended vendors of things esoteric who herald their coming with 24-sheet posters, are thus eliminated. The communication of esoteric knowledge requires a method far more than any at the command of metaphysical mountebanks. The proper custodians of this knowledge—the ancient Mysteries—realized too well that its transmission and perpetuation were the most difficult of all tasks, in many instances bordering on the impossible. How shall we reveal to another that which entirely transcends the province of the senses, that which is nonconvertible into mundane terms, and with which nothing physical is comparable ?

Hence the secret schools of antiquity instituted systems of definite discipline by which the whole nature was dissociated from the elements of exoteric knowledge, and through protracted effort elevated to the level of supersensuous comprehension. Having reached this state, the principles of higher knowing were then communicated to the neophyte by a method almost as arcane as the secrets themselves. A strange telepathic system was developed whereby the findings of the subtler inner perceptions were communicated without passing through that place interval which exists between ordinary intellects—an interval which must be filled with words or other symbolic forms in which the esoteric matter is necessarily lost. How then shall we define esoteric knowledge? It is the classification of those superessential elements of the pure intellect sphere where form, as man recognizes it, does not exist. It must be communicated by a method which, while it awakens no response in the sensory organisms, renders knowledge comprehensive to the inner perceptions. The subject of this inner knowledge and its method of communication has long confounded men of letters. Science cannot conceive of the human mind functioning independently of matter; nor, if consistent to their premises, can men of science admit the possibility of the mind thinking in terms independently of form. In other words, they cannot dissociate the rational processes from the similitudes of phenomena and the laws of comparison that dominate the field of material thought. According to science the human mind instinctively clothes its conclusions and reactions in the vestments of form, so that even before the thought is registered by the outer nature of the thinker it is habited in familiar, yes, even trite and conventional forms. What science really means, however, is not that thoughts are necessarily always related to form, but rather that until they are clothed in the elements of form they are incommunicable. In other words, thoughts for which there are no form associations must die at birth. Dominated by the laws of generation and under the patronage of the goddess Demetcr, the physical sphere will permit no energy to exist within its domain unless that energy abide by the dictates of matter by being clothed in the substances of matter. When thoughts abide in the mind they are thus launched into generation through words, these words—which are their bodies—dimming, like the mortal vehicles of man, the lucidity of the inner nature. Like the human soul, word-souls function imperfectly while enveloped in the grosser substances of the generating sphere.

Thus, while the mind under certain conditions is capable of receiving into itself definite superphysical stimuli, it cannot communicate these attenuated impulses and still preserve their integrity. A notable example is that of the eminent psychologist Henry Havelock Ellis who, as the result of intense functioning in the realm erf psychologic idealism, became so sensitized that to him occurred what is classified under the general heading "mystical experience." In his book, The Dance of Life, he writes: "My self was one with the Not-Self, my will one with the universal will. I seemed to walk in light; my feet scarcely touched the ground; I had entered a new world. The effect of that swift revolution was permanent. At first there was a moment or two of wavering, and then the primary exaltation subsided into an attitude of calm serenity toward all those questions that had once seemed so torturing Neither was I troubled about the existence of any superior being or beings, and I was ready to see that all the words and forms by which men try to picture spiritual realities are mere metaphors and images of an inward experience.  I had become indifferent to shadows, for I held the substance. I had sacrificed what I held dearest at the call of what seemed to be Truth, and now I was repaid a thousandfold. Henceforth I could face life with confidence and joy, for my heart was at one with the world and whatever might prove to be in harmony with the world could not be out of harmony with me." Similar experiences are recorded in the lives of Meister Eckhart, Emanuel Swedenborg, Dante Alighieri, and Martin Luther. Scientists regard the "mystical experience" in a troubled sort of way; those savants more generously-minded cherish the vague hope that some such experience may be their lot and thus afford them opportunity to analyze first hand its attendant reactions. Unfortunately, the "mystical experience ,, does not occur to such pedants as are minded to dissection, or whose paper learning causes them to view lives as simply complicated mechanisms. When, therefore, the apparently miraculous does transpire, the men of letters congregate to marvel and debate, desirous of scoffing but withal perturbed. To them spirit is so intangible and the bugaboo of superstition so tenacious that they fear even to register an interest in things superphysical lest they be accused of mental senility. In the light of the persistent drift of modern thought toward materialism, it is not difficult to understand why the ancient systems of learning mean so little to the modern mind. Firmly posited upon what it terms the practical, science can discover no purpose in ceremonial or symbol, nor can it conceive any tangible good to result from chanting grave rituals to the accompaniment of the lyre. The professional standing of Pythagoras the philosopher was almost irremediably impaired by the discovery that he advocated dancing as essential to education, and that even in his advanced years he was accustomed to invoke Terpsichore with true scholastic measure.

Modernity cannot picture such profound and serious-minded men as Plato and Aristotle, or even the skeptical Socrates, capering with aesthetic abandon in some moonlit grove. Yet we have not the slightest evidence that the accuracy of their philosophic deductions was adversely affected thereby. Pythagoras declared, upon the authority of Empedocles, that every individual who is to achieve greatness must be capable of expressing rhythm in some proper manner; that the soul which cannot so acutely sense the exalted tempo of the celestial spheres that he is possessed therby, can never hope to so approach the soul of things as to reach the summit of achievement in any form of learning.

Pythagoras realized what the modern gownsman has ignored: namely, that none is capable of knowing in great measure who is incapable of intense feeling. Learning acquired in an aesthetic atmosphere is far more valuable than that gained in the severe or lifeless schoolroom. In the effort to preserve its integrity, science posits its dogma upon the infallibility of material evidence, which is presumed to increase in accuracy as it departs from sentiment, and is most valuable when most cold. Add to this a second premise—that of the impossibility of knowing beyond the sphere of phenomenon—and you have the schoolman's dilemma epitomized.

A transcendent form of knowledge demands for its expression a transcendent form of communication. Vocabularies are created to supply certain needs, and are useless beyond the confines of these ends. Language is intended to transmit the more common attitudes of mankind, but for those rare souls who have elevated themselves beyond the level of common attitudes the language of the herd is wholly insufficient. Thus in ages past philosophy evolved its own language—an unspoken tongue—a method of communication which was mostly a communion by which the unutterable was transmitted. In the initiations of the ancient Cabirian Mysteries of Samothrace, knowledge was disseminated by a curious method not unlike a highly perfected radio. The instruments of this unique procedure were the rational faculties of the disciples themselves, and the activating agent was a mysterious electric fluid which the priests had learned to capture from the atmosphere and direct by impulses of the will. It has been clearly demonstrated that the Greeks were familiar with electricity, a knowledge secured by them from the Egyptians. This accounts for the peculiar veneration accorded amber by early priestcrafts, for this substance had been found to possess the quality of capturing and storing electricity. Among carvings and figures of the Samothracian Mysteries are several depicting what is called the "electric head." The face is surrounded by a circlet of hair which is standing on end as though galvanized by an electric current. In one symbolic group the hierophant is seated in the center like the sun in the midst of the zodiac. This venerable one is giving the instruction and his appearance is that of singular repose; yet the forcefulness pervading the figure is arcanely significant of the concentration of the will upon the dissemination of the Great Work. Gathered about him are the disciples who have the appearance of being electrified.

Each individual's hair is standing on end as though caused by a current of electrical energy, in each instance flowing away from the central figure from whom the current emanates.

To the initiated beholder the picture is evidence that the central figure is creating and disseminating rings of electrical energy which, passing outward in ever-increasing circles, moves through the bodies of the disciples and produces the appearance of electrification. Ancient sculpture also abounds with these electrified heads, whose significance thus far has been almost entirely overlooked by modern students of the Mysteries. It is evident, nevertheless, that these heads and the pageantries in which the electrified hair is shown represent efforts to portray the method employed in the communication of esoteric philosophy. The doctrines, projected like an electric current, thus stimulated certain rational faculties in the inner natures of the disciples. As a result of such internal stimuli the disciples were enabled to sense, feel, or intuitively grasp that which was incommunicable by any objective means. Only when the disciplines of the secret schools had stimulated the internal centers of consciousness to a point where it was possible for the neophytes to be brought cn rapport with the inner perceptions of the hierophant could this body of secret tradition concerning formless and eternal truths be communicated from one to another.

Mystical philosophers have demonstrated that proficiency in certain arts and sciences stimulates the sensitivity of the superphysical rational faculties. Because of the definite impulse toward orderliness and exactitude conferred by the study of mathematics, this science was elevated to chief place among the stimuli to rationality. Sculpture, similarly, was highly venerated, for it was a medium by which beauty could be liberated from the shapeless block of marble. The sculptor was not regarded as a creator of beauty but rather as one who chipped away the rough exterior and thus brought to light the concealed symmetry of an inner nature. In short, the statue existed in the stone before the artist released it and made its symmetry apprehensible to the casual observer. Dialectics also stimulate the subtler phases of rationality by causing them to rise in defense of principle or premise. Through dialectics the mind is rendered flexible and sufficient for any and every contingency. Schooled in the thrust and parry of dialectics, the mind produces "a Roland for every Oliver" in the intellectual affaire d'honneur.

The ideal educational system by which the cultural standards of our youth are to be molded is the stimulation of these inner perceptions and the preparation of the mind for the contemplation of life's broader and profounder realities. For the most part, however, modern institutions of learning fail to accomplish this summum bonum because they are regarded as ends rather than means; they are considered capable of educating the mind, when actually their sole province is to prepare the intellect to receive into its own substance those impregnations of the rational self upon which all true mental excellence depends. Mathematics per se, for example, leads to ends comparatively mean and insignificant, yet nearly all great mathematicians have developed some phase of clairvoyance or clair- sentience as the result of their application to its principles. Gradually the inner perceptions assert their sovereignty, and through a concrete mental organism rendered supersensitive by mathematical speculation, become aware of the polydimensional vistas of the higher and more spiritualized sciences. The musician is similarly subjected to a sublimation of feeling. Through protracted application to the principles of harmony and rhythm the musician so refines his own emotional nature that it comes to be ensouled by universal concords, and the musician himself is moved as though possessed by universal agencies. Thus the mind that has given itself over to the rather prosaic science of harmonics is instinctively caused thereby to verge toward universal rhythm and actually hear the music of the spheres.

Standing in the place of the wise and discoursing to his students upon the profundities of divine order, the philosopher suddenly discovers that he speaks better than he knows, becoming, as it were, a disciple of himself. He finds new meanings in his own words; he becomes aware that his mortal mind is being moved by an immortal agent, and that by some indefinable circumstance he has become the very mouthpiece of the ages. Thus, while the exoteric learning disseminated by our public schools and universities inclines the whole nature toward mental illumination, only through the Mysteries is that inclination brought to the high tide of expression—namely, that point where the principles by which eternal verities are maintained and proceed according to their own essences are rendered apprehensible to limited human comprehension. With rare exceptions, eminent educators admit that our schools are primarily intended to be stimulators of internal faculties, which faculties alone are capable of inducing the state of knowing.

In the majority of cases, however, even our comparatively sufficient educational facilities are productive of results either abortive or hopelessly mediocre. Too often the student is simply introduced to those phases of learning which are definitely applicable to the utilitarian problems of the age. His education is consequently considered complete when he is schooled in any subject sufficiently for it to serve as a livelihood. Only occasionally do we find the man or woman whose knowledge of any particular subject is profound enough to support the mind in a state commensurate with its dignity.

The lack of rational philosophy common to this age is most evident in our educational systems whose object ostensibly is to superimpose extraneous thoughts upon those half-awakened adolescent minds groping for substance amid the shadow of their own immaturity. Educators presumably have adopted Lockes theory that the juvenile mind is a blank sheet of paper upon whose receptive surface must be scribbled conventional platitudes, premises or admonitions. Regarding the intellectual equipment of youth as a sort of highly attenuated putty, instructors subconsciously relegate to themselves the molding of this mental stuff into the likeness of the conventional, the substantial, and the prosaic—what they esteem as the outstanding characteristics of sound and useful thought. Under the molding influence of the old, it is thus assured that the new life will be a replica of those inadequate generations which rise from their stupor only to blight futurity.

When philologic pedagogies have finished poking their intellectual fingers into the plastic substances of his brain, its youthful owner is prepared to go forth into the world and repeat every imprudence which marred the tranquillity of his ancestors. The dire circumstances that torment each succeeding generation are thus reinvoked and perpetuated. This mental overshadowing renders its beneficiary incapable of originality even in vice; he cannot even make his own mistakes but must continue to repeat the errors of the ages and bow beneath such time-honored institutions as war and competition. With the possible exception of theology, nowhere outside the realm of education does man's egotism find more grandiloquent expression. Here fools in purple doublets sanctimoniously bestow their foolishness upon posterity. Having lost sight of the true purpose of education, these pedants regard him well-cultured who thinks least and remembers most while *m the schoolroom but who, having matriculated into the greater concerns of life, there conveniently acquires the knack of forgetting even the little he once remembered. With the ends of education thus most effectively obscured, the means by which these ends should be attained are at best but highroads to

nowhere. Education has become a vicious circle wherein the ignorance of one generation is transmitted like a hereditary taint to its progeny. Every form of social evil is made to thrive exceedingly, and the racial virtues are periodically threatened with extinction.

Interpretation is the preponderant factor in modern teaching. The instructor perforce acts as an intermediary between the complexity of a science and the insufficiency of a partly-developed mind. To interpret adequately is a divine gift bestowed by the gods only upon those whose attainments rival the heroic deeds of myth and legend. A great interpreter

is no less a master than a great originator; for only a mind as great as the conceiving mind can intelligently interpret the concepts of that conceiving mind. A proper instructor of the young is born, not made. His genius is supreme, for not only must he be able to grasp the infinite complexity of a subject, but he must also reduce that complexity to an orderly simplicity. He must think downward to those intellects diat still verge upon the state of thoughtlessness, inclining them gently, reverently, yet unmistakably, toward rational procedure.

Plato was dead five hundred years before an interpreter was found worthy of the task of revealing the intellectual achievements of this illustrious mortal. Of all die Platonic successors, only Proclus sensed the significance and magnitude of Plato's contribution to human knowledge. Each century gives birth to but one or two truly creative or interpretive minds. All other claimants to proficiency and conversance are merely meddlers in matters of the mind—dabblers, dilettanti, veritable parasites upon the bodies of art and science. They suffer from that most loathsome and fatal of all diseases: ignorance of their own ignorance. The prime requisite of every great exponent of an art or science is that he shall recognize and emphasize its aesthetic and ethical aspects. Even such prosaic arts as carpentry and cookery may become media by which the mind can be introduced to the beautiful, the noble, and the good knowledge of any particular subject is profound enough to support the mind in a state commensurate with its dignity.

The lack of rational philosophy common to this age is most evident in our educational systems whose object ostensibly is to superimpose extraneous thoughts upon those half-awakened adolescent minds groping for substance amid the shadow of their own immaturity. Educators presumably have adopted Locke's theory that the juvenile mind is a blank sheet of paper upon whose receptive surface must be scribbled conventional platitudes, premises or admonitions. Regarding the intellectual equipment of youth as a sort of highly attenuated putty, instructors subconsciously relegate to themselves the molding of this mental stuff into the likeness of the conventional, the substantial, and the prosaic—what they esteem as the outstanding characteristics of sound and useful thought. Under the molding influence of the old, it is thus assured that the new life will be a replica of those inadequate generations which rise from their stupor only to blight futurity.

When philologic pedagogues have finished poking their intellectual fingers into the plastic substances of his brain, its youthful owner is prepared to go forth into the world and repeat every imprudence which marred the tranquillity of his ancestors. The dire circumstances that torment each succeeding generation are thus reinvoked and perpetuated. This mental overshadowing renders its beneficiary incapable of originality even in vice; he cannot even make his own mistakes but must continue to repeat the errors of the ages and bow beneath such time-honored institutions as war and competition. With the possible exception of theology, nowhere outside the realm of education does man's egotism find more grandiloquent expression. Here fools in purple doublets sanctimoniously bestow their foolishness upon posterity. Having lost sight of the true purpose of education, these pedants regard him well- cultured who thinks least and remembers most while in the schoolroom but who, having matriculated into the greater concerns of life, there conveniently acquires the knack of forgetting even the little he once remembered. With the ends of education thus most effectively obscured, the means by which these ends should be attained are at best but highroads to nowhere. Education has become a vicious circle wherein the ignorance of one generation is transmitted like a hereditary taint to its progeny. Every form of social evil is made to thrive exceedingly, and the racial virtues are periodically threatened with extinction.

Interpretation is the preponderant factor in modern teaching. The instructor perforce acts as an intermediary between the complexity of a science and the insufficiency of a partly developed mind. To interpret adequately is a divine gift bestowed by the gods only upon those whose attainments rival the heroic deeds of myth and legend. A great interpreter is no less a master than a great originator; for only a mind as great as the conceiving mind can intelligently interpret the concepts of that conceiving mind. A proper instructor of the young is born, not made. His genius is supreme, for not only must he be able to grasp the infinite complexity of a subject, but he must also reduce that complexity to an orderly simplicity. He must think downward to those intellects that still verge upon the state of thoughtlessness, inclining them gently, reverently, yet unmistakably, toward rational procedure.

Plato was dead five hundred years before an interpreter was found worthy of the task of revealing the intellectual achievements of this illustrious mortal. Of all the Platonic successors, only Proclus sensed the significance and magnitude of Plato's contribution to human knowledge. Each century gives birth to but one or two truly creative or interpretive minds. All other claimants to proficiency and conversance are merely meddlers in matters of the mind—dabblers, dilettanti, veritable parasites upon the bodies of art and science. They suffer from that most loathsome and fatal of all diseases: ignorance of their own ignorance. The prime requisite of every great exponent of an art or science is that he shall recognize and emphasize its aesthetic and ethical aspects. Even such prosaic arts as carpentry and cookery may become media by which the mind can be introduced to the beautiful, the noble, and the good. Failure to perceive the substratum of divine agency below the surface of every physical procedure is to demonstrate one's disqualification to instruct in the elements of that procedure. Therefore none but the idealist who can see the beautiful in all things should be entrusted with the education of a child in whose nature it is hoped that the spirit of beauty will take up its abode.

Of Greek philosophy it has been said that its interpretation was "reserved for men who were born indeed in a baser age, but who being allotted a nature similar to their master were the true interpreters of his sublime and mystic speculations." (See the introduction to the Select Works of Plotinus .) Of education in general, as of jurisprudence in particular, it is all too evident that the spirit is dead and only the letter remains. Those dependent upon it for intellectual sustenance sicken and ultimately become intellectual corpses from whom the rational life has fled. As without the fructifying principle the germ of potentiality cannot burst its confining walls, so without the higher ethics of philosophy the seed of divinity resident in man can never be quickened. Only a comprehending soul rendered aware of the luminous realities behind the veil of form through the disciplines of right-thinking, can dispel those illusions which, like the monsters of a fabled age, guard the adytum of the sacred sciences.

The corruption that crept into its ethical institutes was the direct cause of the decadence of pagandom. Those custodians of the secret doctrine—the venerable hierophants of the Mysteries—left their schools and hied themselves to the remote corners of the earth. Deprived of their inspired leadership, the Mysteries became mere mongers of empty words. After courageously passing all the hazardous trials of the ancient rituals the enthusiastic neophyte did not receive at the completion of the rites the promised esoteric knowledge. Sanctimonious priests could only drone garbled fancies, or whisper with bated breath elegant nothings in his ear. In the quest for truth men will risk much, but even the most intrepid soul will hesitate to jeopardize life or limb for such dubious returns. A similar betrayal of trust also awaits the modern seeker after Truth. The ends to be gained by modern education are so doubtful that there is much justification for the revolt of youth against a system which, in exchange for some eighteen years of application, leaves him as unfitted for life as before. While the social standing of the well-educated man may be a trifle more impressive and his earning capacity exceed that of his less schooled brother, he does not necessarily excel him in an understanding of those deeper issues of life with which higher education should be, but unfortunately is not, concerned. College men are quite as unhappy as illiterates; in fact their capacity for sorrow is enlarged, for their curriculum has acquainted them with a legion of miseries to which the uneducated are immune. All too often schooling complicates uncertainties, multiplies doubts, generates disquietudes, and verifies the growing suspicion that all creation is awry. Instead

of solving problems modern education complicates them. Reacting to this divergence of dictum and tenet, the mind schooled beyond its capacity either rejects them in toto to become a philosophic atheist, or making a show of digesting them becomes unbearably sophisticated. The defection of modern youth from education is more than a surface symptom. The student is content to slip through college with mediocre grades because he is firmly convinced that all the knowledge he can ever hope to secure is nugatory in solving the imminent problems of his life. Hence the chief incentive for distinction in scholarship is removed.

When the modern college rose as a substitute for the ancient collegia, it fell heir to its task but not to its toga. While the collegia of Greece and Rome were the domiciles of a transcendent learning under the patronage of the gods and heroes, the colleges of today are but hollow imitations of these older and nobler institutions. In comparison to that sublime knowledge disseminated by these ancient schools, modern houses of learning have become dispensaries of but the husks of knowledge. The illustrious record of the past must not be erased from man's memory; modern methods on the other hand must be recast into a more sufficient mold, for the morbid materialism of this age can only be dispelled by educating the juvenile mind in the principles of higher rationality.

In antiquity the roads of lower education led, like the converging spokes of a wheel, toward the Mysteries. Knowledge was then an actuality, and the byways of speculative thought, though tortuous, eventually led to the open gates of operative knowing. Those who excelled in temporal education, by right of their superior mentality and integrity were permitted to enter that inner sanctuary where the principles of divine knowledge were unfolded. Here the mind was diverted from the course of materiality, and initiated into those secrets of

spiritual comprehension which bestows tranquility, compassion, and comprehension. Higher education began where lower education ceased, and all who sincerely desired to know were privileged to receive knowledge up to the limits of their own capacity. The arts and sciences of men were revealed to be but outer garments of a divine spirit—the concealments of a superior science, the science of living. Today all this has been swept aside, and the advanced bodies of learning arc unable to confer that more adequate interpretation, for lack of which education necessarily fails. How little true incentive there is for scholastic greatness when he who has learned all that men can teach finds naught but disenchantment in the inadequacy of the whole system. When the masters of a science confess their ignorance of the very principles which are the daily subjects of their speculations, what shall it profit a man to sit at their feet and spend his years in the determination of the exact degree of ignorance possessed by his mentors? Is it not possible that man comes into this physical world better fitted to function in harmony with rationality than after passing through what we like to term our course of culture, wherein the divine impulses toward the virtuous and the beautiful are stunted and the integrity of the nature incurably upset? Man is fortunate indeed if his education does not render him incapable of knowing. As Paracelsus might have said: "He is best served by education who is least injured by it"

A great thinker is one who by some strange Providence has escaped the pitfalls of mediocrity unwittingly dug by men to entrap genius. "All the world," wrote Emerson, "is at hazard when God lets loose a thinker." Humanity seems to fear an intellect which is great enough to destroy our prevalent sense of smugness and complacency. We are naturally inclined toward inertia; whether comfortably or uncomfortably we prefer to vegetate, and woe unto him who dares disturb our proletarian serenity. Humanity chooses to languish in the darkness of things as they are for fear that the godlike splendor of things as they might be will also uncover humanity's foibles and impose the burden of their correction. Knowledge is a responsibility, and responsibility is a term formidable and disquieting. No better epitome of the enslavement of the intellect by education can be found than Alexander Pope's excoriation of pedantism in the fourth book of The Dunciad —The Epic of the Dunces. The pedagogues of every land arc here personified by a specter whose index finger the virtue of the dreadful wand holds forth, and whose beavered brow a birchen garland wears. Preceptor of an awful knowledge, the bloodless lips of this spectral doctrinaire speak out the mandates of the superficial. Since man from beast by words is known.

Words are man's province, words we teach alone. When reason doubtful, like the Samian letter, Points him two ways, the narrower is the better. Placed at the door of learning, youth to guide,

We never suffer it to stand too wide. To ask, to guess, to know, as they commence, As Fancy opens the quick springs of Sense, We ply the Memory, we load the Brain,

Bind rebel wit, and double chain on chain, Confine the thought, to exercise the breath, And keep them in the pale of worlds til! death. Whate'er the talents, or howe'er design'd,

We hang one jingling padlock on the mind.

How utterly we have become the servants of words, elevating mere terms to the degree of infallibility! While it is fitting that we should regard them as media of intercourse, is there not an understanding which is superior to words—a silent language by which comprehension blends with comprehension, a transcendent mode by which the within which is you communes with the within which is / and we together commune with that within which is All? Do not the stars upon their lofty thrones commune by a strange silence with each other, by wordless tongue and soundless voice uniting in a common knowing far beyond the ken of mortal apprehension? With upright larynx, does man so greatly excel all other creatures that he shall achieve glory by virtue of his lips alone? If he earns a crown, must he wear it on his tongue?

Words are but the infinite diversity of sound, and by many a curious gasp and rattle do we make our whimsies known. We live in a universe of words; terms and letters continually intervene to become the agencies of endless misunderstanding. As the memorizer of words is not a thinker, so the cloth of philosophic terminology cannot make the philosopher. Words are but names for unknown quantities and conditions—no more; for words are powerless to acquaint us with the inner natures whose qualities they bound. In Genesis it is declared that Adam went forth and named all creatures, and following his example men have never ceased to coin appclations with which to designate or describe the objects and conditions of environment. By appropriate terms the heaven and earth came to be defined, but how different from wordy definition is the comprehending nature of those polynomial powers which, founded in eternity, verge toward time just enough to be vaguely apprehensible.

Picture the enlightenment of the proverbial inquisitive schoolboy who, pointing to a growing mystery of leaves and stems, presents his instructor with this poser: "Master, what is this living, unfolding thing?" And he in whom the acumen of the past is presumed to be concentrated can only reply: "My boy, that is a tree!" The teacher might also very consistently have added: "We know it is a tree, for we named it ourselves." Groping after realities the juvenile mind is confronted with nothing but the limiting, strangling bonds of terms. As he passes through the various stages of education the pupil is familiarized with all the relatively inconsequential opinions we share concerning the subject of trees. Through a cross section of their trunks he studies their inner constitution, and with the microscope may see the roots that terminate in hungry mouths, or the infinitely minute life-particles that conspire to produce leaf and stem. Yet of tree itself—the mystery of that intangible something which expands from a tiny seed and surrounds itself with bark—man can discover nothing.

Thus education turns us from the consideration of living realities to cherish the baseless notions of our sires. While the heavenly orbs march on in majestic file to a glorious and unlimited destiny; while the whole universe, celestial and terrestrial, thrills with vibrant actualities and thunders on in concord with cosmic principle, humanity concerns itself with the trivialities of its cultural codes. Men turn their backs upon the midnight sky, whose immensity frightens them and dissipates their bombast, to the infantile task imposed by their culture of choosing the proper fork or frock for a formal banquet. Having familiarized themselves with the decrees of fashion in these respects, such little minds rest upon the oars of petty accomplishment until natural decay returns their ashes to the common Mother. Fascinated by the insignificant and bewildered by the real, oblivious to the distant and terrified by the imminent, mortals live by the meanest of their codes and choose mediocrity as the path of ease.

The value of present-day education is not to be discounted, but its superficiality is to be condemned. It may have value as a means, but it is wholly inadequate as an end; for it cannot supply that knowledge indispensable to right-living. If permeated by a sort of philosophic optimism concerning the ultimates of knowledge, and leavened by the ancient procedures and disciplines, material education could prepare its votaries for those loftier forms of learning for lack of which the nations perish. So long as education assumes that knowledge beyond its own prescribed domain is unavailable, it is false to the great need of humanity. Unfortunately, this is the assumption prevalent in the bodies of so-called higher learning. Ridicule is heaped upon the ancients for their "superstitions"; the esoteric doctrines are declared to have been idle rumors generated in the perfervid imaginations of unbalanced fanatics, who were consequently branded charlatans, adventurers, and impostors. Mindful of the claims of consistency, should we not condemn as impostors those schools which supply mere notions in lieu of actual knowledge and declare the individual to be "educated" though totally ignorant of every vital issue of existence? Graduates of modern educational institutions are presented with impressive diplomas, which too often are the most tangible evidence of scholastic attainment.

In his Discourse on Initiation, Hermes elucidates to his son Tatian the subject of spiritual education. The oration moves rhythmically and majestically upon the theme of appreciation, and may be summed up in the single thought that appreciation for Universal Good is the beginning of wisdom. Education is here revealed as the discipline whereby man is rendered capable of appreciating divine order and made susceptible to its redeeming impulses. Tatian is instructed by his immortal father in the discovery of God in these words:

"If thou wouldst contemplate the Creator even in perishable things, in things which are on the earth, or in the deep, reflect, O my son, on the formation of man in his mother's womb; contemplate carefully the skill of the Workman; learn to know him according to the divine beauty of the work.

Who formed the orb of the eye? Who pierced the openings of the nostrils and of the ears? Who made the mouth to open? Who traced out the channels of the veins? Who made the bones hard? Who covered the flesh with skin? Who separated the fingers and the toes? Who made the feet broad? Who hollowed out the pores? Who spread out the spleen? Who

formed the heart like a pyramid? Who made the sides wide? Who formed the caverns of the lungs? Who made the honourable parts of the body conspicuous, and concealed the others? See how much skill is bestowed in one species of matter, how much labour on one single work; everywhere there is beauty, everywhere perfection, everywhere variety. Who made all these things? Who is the mother, who is the father, if it be not the only and invisible God, who has created all things by his will?" Alcibiades, the Greek patrician who nursed within his breast senatorial aspirations, submitted to an inventory of his mental and ethical qualifications at the hands of Socrates, who thereupon demonstrated that the sole asset of the youth consisted of a vague proficiency in strumming the lyre, the ability to recite poetry not too badly, and an indifferent prowess in the gymnasium. Holding up the mirror of rationality before Alcibiades, Socrates convinced the would-be guardian of the sovereignty of Athens that he lacked sufficient intelligence to administer his own affairs, let alone those of the Athenian commonwealth. Times have changed since those golden days when Skeptic and Peripatetic roamed the Athenian byways, but the spirit of Alcibiades still lives. What matters it if his lyre has now become the saxophone, his quoit and javelin the ball and bat, and his poetic fancies chiefly concerned with carolling the virtues of his Alma Mater? The 20th-century Alcibiades still goes forth full of purpose but woefully empty of knowledge and for lack of a Socrates may actually become a senator and tax the resources of Providence to preserve the integrity of the commonwealth.

The universalization of educational opportunity is the exalted purpose of today. The body politic enthusiastically supports every issue which encourages and facilitates the promulgation of learning. Impressive institutions for the instruction of the young are the civic pride of every community, and like the cathedrals of medieval Europe shadow the teeming city spread out around them. We have deified education and built temples to the spirit of wisdom even as antiquity gilded shrines for the gods of yore. Nevertheless, to us education is still but a word—a wonderful word, truly implying all that is noble, all that is beautiful, all that is true. Yet how far does the practice fall short of the premise; how vast the interval between the implication and the fact! The education for which men have even given their lives and which they have preserved at fearful cost through the world's Dark Ages; the education which the seekers of every age have sought with whole-souled longing; the education that was the very bounty of the gods and the evidence of their perfect covenant with men—this education has failed from the earth. Knowledge has retired again into that Stygian darkness from which the first philosophers called it forth by strange rite and sacrificial deed. We live in a day of material enlightenment, but profound indeed is our ethical and philosophic benightedness. There is a supreme Educator, an all-knowing Preceptor, an all-wise Counsellor, an all-sufficient Guide, whose integrity dwarfs that of any mortal man. Deep in the inner recesses of our own souls, but obscured by the hallucinations of the senses, is Mercury's inexhaustible pitcher—an infinite capacity which, though ever flowing, is ever full. Man's only educator is this inner self which alone is capable of sifting fact from fancy. The drawing forth of this inner knowledge and its establishment as the ever-sufficient and comprehending director of the outer life is the true office of education. Educo, then, signifies to draw forth; and education is that mental process of the outer mind by which is evoked as though by magic the mighty genius that, like a sleeping giant, is man's unsuspected strength. Truth, then, comes from within, fancies from without; and never will education fully solve the problems that are its peculiar province until it equips unfolding manhood and womanhood with the keys by which this treasure house of inner potentialities may be unlocked. As through a glass darkly can even now be glimpsed that tomorrow of education when, grasping with fuller realization the purpose of its own existence, die school assumes the fullness of its role by becoming the dispenser of those disciplines by which man may release the greater Thinker within.

How removed from the frenzied searcher after temporal knowledge is the calm and certain Master of the Hidden Path! The philosopher does not gaze at the stars through man-made telescopes alone, but by the transcendency of his internal faculties he is lifted up and taken into the very soul of the star itself. He feels its life throbbing through him, and from his place within its very heart he learns its innermost secrets. Mingling through his inner self with the inner selves of all things, the truly educated one thus exchanges vain fancy and speculation for the perfect understanding. The soul in him communes with the soul in his world, and both share in a common felicity. He sees, he senses, and he feels, thus coming into possession of countless esoteric secrets which, though his very own, he cannot impart to others nor even explain to that inferior self which is in bondage to the sphere of ignorance.

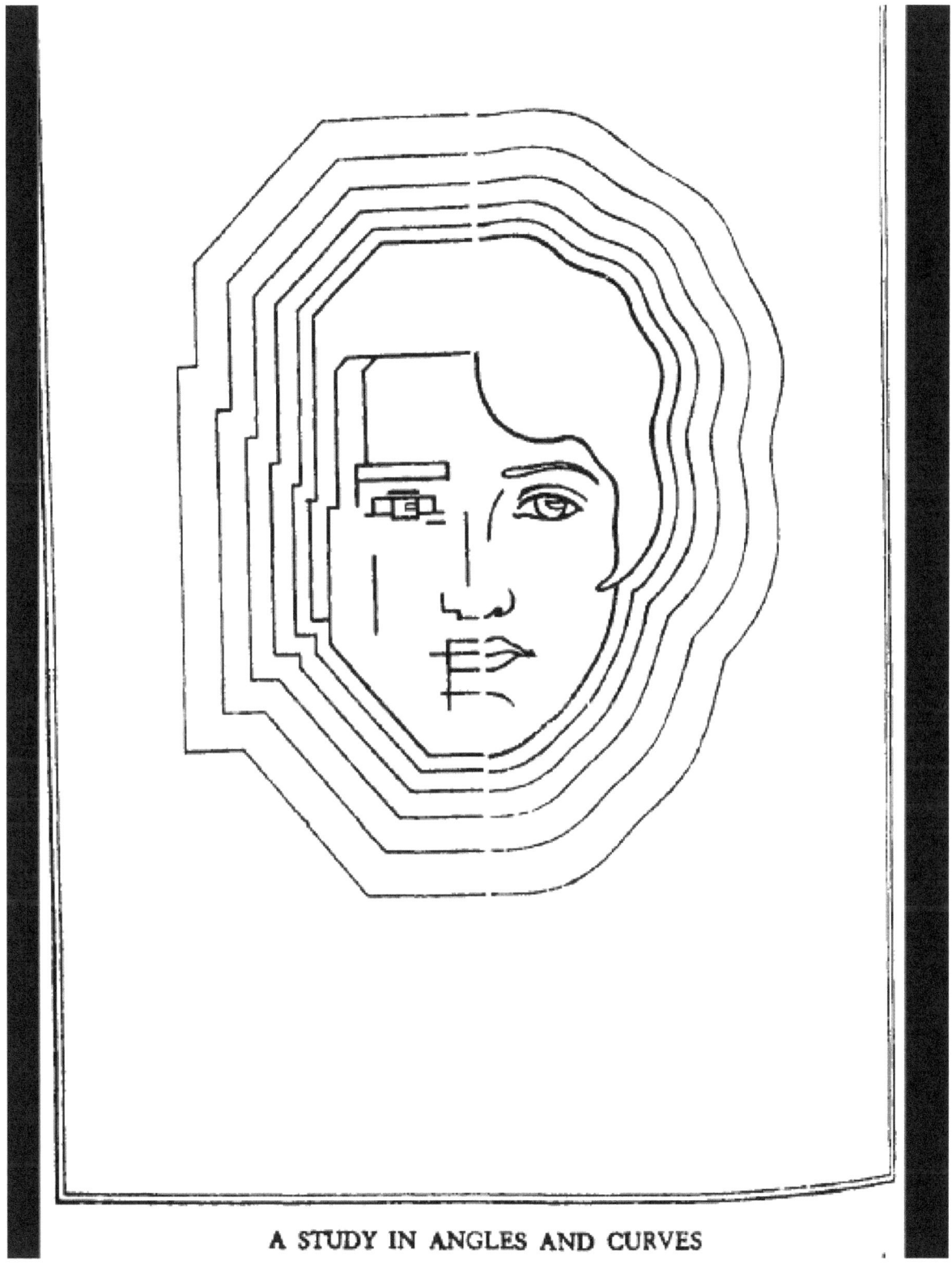

## A STUDY IN ANGLES AND CURVES

In symbolism, the straight line is considered masculine and significant of strength; the curved line, feminine and significant of beauty. In the Cabala, the two pillars—Strength and Beauty—support the arch of the Universal House. In the above face, the male and female elements are combined, and thus Cosmos, the Divine Androgyne, comes into being.

# XXIX

⁂

# The Esoteric Structure of the Alphabet
# by A.B.K

By Alvin Boyd Kuhn
Originally published in 1931

Letters are more than marks on a page—they are the building blocks of cosmic meaning.

In this profound and illuminating work, Alvin Boyd Kuhn unearths the hidden spiritual architecture of the alphabet. Far beyond their function in writing and speech, letters were once revered as divine archetypes—geometries of sound and form that reflected the eternal laws of the universe.

Tracing the sacred alphabets through Egyptian, Phoenician, Greek, and Hebrew traditions, Kuhn demonstrates how each character was infused with metaphysical purpose. This volume reveals how initiates of the ancient Mysteries used letters not just as tools of language, but as vessels of transcendent truth—linking heaven to earth, the divine to the material, and spirit to structure.

"Language is the mind's mirror, and letters are its crystal facets."—
Alvin Boyd Kuhn

# XXX

### ❦

# The Esoteric Structure of the Alphabet

THE ESOTERIC STRUCTURE OF THE ALPHABET "God built the universe on number, " Pythagoras "God built the universe on the letters of the alphabet. " The Zohar Alvin Boyd Kuhn

ESOTERIC STRUCTURE OF THE ALPHABET

The modern world is awakening slowly to the fact that in the day we call ancient, though it was but a few thousand years ago in the run of millions, advanced men fully worthy of the name of sages were deeply versed in the profundities of recondite philosophy and possessed knowledge of things both human and divine, and well comprehended the great sciences of both cosmology and anthropology. Evident it is that men of this caliber indited the great Scriptures of ancient religions, which have won and held the reverence of mankind so generally that they have been made the unique objects of religious veneration and the canons of spiritual authority for most of the world over long ages. Indeed the homage paid them has been of the character of worship offered to something regarded as divine. The tradition has prevailed that the Bible authors were in truth men of a divine or semi- divine order, or at least men inspired by a divine afflatus to transmit to mankind the heavenly dictation of sacred truth. A study of ancient literature, growing more enlightened as it is pursued, is revealing the presence of a definitely formulated and high organic truth- structure, constituted of the essential elements of a great logical systematization of fundamental archai, as the Greek word has it, or principles of a cosmic order of being, expressed in many varied forms of representation everywhere over the field of ancient culture. Primarily, of course, the great wisdom was embodied in tomes of a vast body of literature, a literature so cryptically recondite that its esoteric purport has almost completely eluded the most erudite lucubrations of world scholarship from the ancient day to the present. Indeed it has been the perversions and misinterpretations of that ancient corpus of wisdom that have afflicted the religious consciousness of the world, particularly in the West, with an intellectual befuddlement that approaches the status of a universal dementia for some two millennia. Not only in the scripts of religion, however, but also in a wide variety of other modes of expression was the wisdom tradition embodied and transmitted. It is found, but always in subtle forms of crypticism,~a feature that has bewildered and befogged all later conclusions of investigators—in ancient art, in architecture, in myth-making, secret society ritual, dramatic scenario, music, mathematics, anthropological science, logic, rhetoric, philosophy, astronomy, semantics, psychology, festival ordinances, social ceremonies and throughout the warp and woof of life generally. Now, perhaps strangest of all the channels through which it was given expression, comes the momentous revelation that the sagacious genius of antiquity had even insinuated a form of its basic outline into the very structure of that groundbase of all literature, —the alphabet. The announcement and elucidation of its presence in this, the fundamental semantic code for the transmission of human thought, should rank as an epochal event in the history of world culture. Ancient sagacity viewed high spiritual culture in a different light from that in which it is envisaged today. While modern intelligence aims to disseminate its blessings over the widest popular area, hoping that it may edify the mass body of people generally, the sages of old acted upon a different estimate of the possibilities in the case. They appraised the cultural potential of the "vulgar masses" as practically nil, and therefore deemed it a sacrilege to cast the precious jewels of esoteric truth and knowledge to the "swine" that would trample them in the mire of unconscionable crudity of misunderstanding. It may be said that the history of religious cultism over many centuries has demonstrated the practical wisdom of this conservatism. The perversion, corruption, materialization and literalization of the lofty mystical sense of ancient cryptic literature, has caused perhaps the most colossal debacle in the culture of spiritual values in the course of known history. Its easily discernible evil fruitage has been the positive derationalization of the Occidental mind as regards all things religious, theological and Scriptural. It has deprived that mind of the cardinal advantage of knowing the sublime meaning of the splendid Jewish-Christian Scriptures, which are a collection of ancient mythographic portrayals of spiritual truth, sadly and calamitously mistaken for history. Not only were the Sages constrained to adopt methods of crypticism of varied forms to safeguard precious cosmic and anthropogenic truth from desecration by the "rabble," but they employed a technique which found its basic authentication in nature itself. As the world below is a mundane reflection and copy of an overshadowing world of spiritual truth, they strove to portray the structural forms of that higher truth by representing it under the forms of its counterparts everywhere existent in the natural world. Even supposed history was oriented into the form of archetypal ideologies. But everywhere, in drama, ritual, choral dance, festival institution and in language the astute formulators aimed to incorporate their figures of fundamental archai. A great structure compounded of the elements of the cosmic logic of creation was inwrought into the pattern of all these modes of human cultural expression. Finally, if not perhaps initially, its structural design was woven into the formation of the alphabet. If this cryptic organic form was the structural principle determining the arrangement of the alphabet, it must be seen to have made its significance definitely basic in all literature. For thus the words themselves, carrying the elements of the original letter components would constantly represent the forms of the archaic thought which as symbols they portrayed. So that in reconstructing the hidden outlines of meaning form in the alphabet. we are piercing to the heart's core of the most recondite connotations of all literature. It is a commonplace of present educational theory to say that letters of the alphabet are symbolic representations of the sounds universally possible to the human vocal organs. It is hardly as generally known that in shape they are more than mere algebraic x's or sheer onomatopoetic imitations. They are in fact evident forms shaped to picture basic ideas. They are true ideograms. The capital letter A, for instance, is obviously the cardinal letter I, the symbol of primordial unity (since it is also the number i), split apart from the top into the creative duality of spirit and matter, the cross-bar indicating the interrelation which dynamically subsists between them. The U (V) symbolizes, exactly as it is drawn, the descent of spirit into matter and its return above. The W pluralizes it, and we find, not strangely, the W to be the letter that pluralizes words in the Egyptian hieroglyphics. The O readily symbolizes the endlessness of matter and of eternity. So that the Gnostics, when they named the unit of deity in the cosmos the lAO, had condensed in the triadic name a sermonette in full. signifying the initial bifurcation of the first unit divine consciousness, the I, apart into the duahty, A, and running the round of an eternal cycle, O. And so even Revelation has it: "I (am the) A (and the) O, the beginning and the end, the first and the last,"-lAO. (The almost breath- taking significance of the M, when the spirit says "I AM," will be introduced later.) It is possibly true that literation started with the utilization of the two simplest elements of written symbolism, the vertical line I and the circle O. At any rate it is to be shown here that nearly all divine names in antiquity were built up from and upon these two. For the Egyptians of remote past time had combined the two in the form of what is almost certainly the most ancient of cross symbols, the crux ansata, ansated cross, called by them the A N K H (more recently spelled E N K H), an O topping an I with a horizontal line at the point of contact. It represents by the O above, the endless existence of that which is the indestructible primordial matter, the eternal Mother of all things; and by the I below, it indicates the emanation of creative mind, or spirit power, from the heart of the great sea of first matter plunging downward. The horizontal bar shows both their conjunction and their separation, as does any boundary line between two areas. But the median line is important also because it marks the meeting point between the two poles of spirit and matter, since it is at this point that all reality is brought out to manifestation through the union of the two. The ANKH is the astrological symbol— @ insert symbol. The two symbols with which literate symbolism begins are thus the I and the O. The item of their gender comes first to notice. The I is masculine, as standing for the Father's power of generation, which is spirit; the O is the eternal feminine, matter, the universal Mother, personalized in ancient religions by such goddesses as Isis, Cybele, Mylitta, Aditi, Venus, Juno and others. The appropriateness of this symbolism from the subsidiary phallic side needs no accentuation, nevertheless is very important and indeed very wonderful. (The author has fully dealt with it in his larger work, SEX AS SYMBOL.) As all progenation of life can come only through the union of male and female elements of the cosmic duality, a symbol that would dramatize life would have to combine both the I and the O. This the Egyptians did in their great ANKH symbol, which thus is their written word for life, and carries also the connotation of two other elements entering into life, or necessary for life, namely love and tie. Even more than the lAO it condenses in its three renderings the gist of a mighty sermon, and becomes the hieroglyph of both the structure and the meaning of life. Rendered in one sentence the symbol means life because life can exist only where two things, spirit (I), and matter (O), are tied together by a sufficiently cohesive power, love. Love ties the two together to procreate life. The A N K H is therefore the first and greatest symbol in the world, which should make us aware that the cross is the first and greatest symbol because it is the symbol of life and not of death. (The ancients said, however, that the soul, when incarnated in the body on earth, was in its spiritual "death," and therefore the cross became the emblem of death—but soul-death, not bodydeath~a death viewed wrongly by all theology since the days of ancient mystery teaching, since the reference is to the "dead" condition of the soul when immersed in body, and not to the demise of the physical body. Even in this view it equally connoted life, for it was the soul's relative "death" that gave life to the creature, whose bodily demise in turn liberated it for its freer life above.) Detaching the two emblems from each other as they are united in the A N K H symbol, and combining them in lateral juxtaposition, we have the first divine word and name in all literature, 10. That it figures with equally fundamental significance in ancient typological numerology is evident from the fact that the two, now converted into numbers, constitute the cardinal base of all mathematics, the number lo. Modern study seems not to have recognized this close connection, amounting almost to identity, between the letters of the alphabet as originally devised, and numbers.

Numbers were indicated by letters. Each letter carried a number value. Hence words were composed of those alphabetical units that would together express an idea, a mental value, but as well a numerical value. As far as the Scriptures are concerned, even whole sentences were constructed to total a number quantity. As Pythagoras has said, God geometrized in creating the world; he built the universe on number. Such esoteric works as The Zohar, of ancient Jewish Kabalistic literature, reveal clearly also that the deity formed the creation by means of the letters of the alphabet. This can have sense only on the predication that as (according to the Scriptures) he spake and the worlds formed themselves in order under the vibratory impact of the letter tones of his voice, every letter sound of the creative reverberation became a constituent element in the cosmic framework. Every letter expressed or in fact constituted a principle or fundamental part of the universal structure.

Perhaps this is one of the greatest keys to our recovery of the cryptic purport of ancient writing. The archaic 10 (lo) then would be charged with the potency of the first projection of the creative thought-force, but only in its first partition into duality, not in its later and further subdivision. In its expression as the prime triplicity it was the lAO (which became I AH and JAH), and its still further differentiation toward endless multiplicity at the quaternary stage brought it to the form of the great Tetragrammaton, the Kabalistic J H V H. In its full seven-letter expression it became, on the side of matter alone, the seven-vowelled name, composed of the seven primary vowel sounds made by the human voice. The Greek alphabet still retains seven vowels, a, short e, long e, i, short o, long o and u. This was to express the fact that every cycle of creation runs through seven sub-cycles, each of which sounds out the reverberation of one of the seven successive component form-tones. The potent symbol, typifying primogenital creative energy of mind and matter combined in the relation of polarity, being the power that dominates all things as it was their creator, became the figure of all combined mental and material ruling power everywhere, as all lesser ruling units were themselves but projected partial rays of the power itself. It was therefore the first king in the cosmic realm, as every divided segment of it was king in the tinier realm over which it exercised sovereignty. How notable this will appear when we shall see in a moment that the very word. King, derives from the AN KH name! Nothing has been more revealing than the list of words, in English, Greek, German, Hebrew, which can be traced to the old Egyptian name of this mighty symbol. Its central idea, it was noted, is the production of life through the tieing or union of spirit and matter. The central clue to the meaning of all these derivatives is the idea of tieing two things together. It must be elucidated that in building words upon the A N K H stem, the H may be virtually dropped out of consideration, as K H is equally well expressed by K alone. But K H is also equivalent to C H, which often replaces it. The vowel A is of inconsequential value and can also be dropped. So there is the bare N K left as the hard root. 8 The next matter to be noted is that in later philosophical usage it was immaterial whether it was written N K or K N. And in Greek the N K (K N) became N G (G N),~a significant item. With these specifications it is possible now to discern a whole new world of meaning in many common words never dreamed to have come down from so divine a lineage. It is seen first in such words as anchor, that which ties a boat to a fixed place; knit, knot, link, gnarled, gnaw, gnash (accounting for the odd spelling); ankelosis, a growing together of two bones; anger, anguish, anxiety, a tightening up of feelings. But most interestingly it seems to have given name to at least four joints or hinge-points {hinge itself seems to be another) in the human body: ankle, knee, neck and knuckles. Lung, as being the place where outside air unites with the inner blood, could perhaps be added. Far away as our English join appears to be from a source in A N K H, (N being the only letter common to both), it is certainly directly from it after all. For A N K H was the root of the Lsitm jungo, to join, N K becoming N G through the Greek. From this we get junction, adjunct, juncture, conjunction, from the Latin past participle form of jungo, --junctus. But in coming into English through the French, all these words were smoothed down to join, joint, and this carried so far into English as to give us finally union, which is really junction in its primal form. With even the N dropping out we have yoke, that which ties two oxen together. And in Sanskrit it comes out as yoga, which in reality stands for yonga, meaning union. The English present participle ending -ing, as well as the prefix con-, meaning with or together, likely comes from the A N K H. For the -ing connotes a continuing of things moving on together. Therefore all three parts of the word con-nect- ing would be from the ancient word. Our most common word, thing, likewise comes from A N K H, as a thing is that which is created by the union of spirit and matter, a divine conception and atomic substance. Next comes one that carries an impressive significance in the study, the common verb to know, in Greek gnosco, German kennen, EngUsh ken. What constitutes the knowing act? The joining together of two things, consciousness and an object of consciousness, for there must be something apart from consciousness to be known. So Greeks called knowledge the Gnosis. The Greek verb meaning to be, gignomai, also has the G N, as token that existence is the result of the "ankhing " together of spirit and matter. But a most surprising Hebrew derivation from A N K H is the first-personal pronoun, I. It is in fact the A N K H itself unchanged except for the inconsequential insertion of two minor vowels o and i, making it ANOKHI. This is amazingly significant, since it reveals the identity of the innermost soul-being of man, the I ego, with the primal cosmic mind. That consciousness in man which enables him to think and say "I" is indeed a unit element of that same cosmic mind. In the Iconsciousness of a creature the central creative mind energy of the universe is nucleated in unity. And as the ruler of all life in every domain, it is in that function and capacity the king of Kfe! That power which knows things is verily creation's king. And also then it must be the power that thinks. Gerald Massey, great scholar of ancient occult knowledge, connects in kindred significance think and thing, a thing being that which has been thought by some mind. The I, as the king of consciousness, both thinks and knows. The German has for king Koenig, the one who can, (which in German is koennen) and the one who knows what is best. And what has the Greek for king? Astonishingly anax, which is equivalent to the spelling anaks. The Greek for messenger, one who ties the sender with the recipient of a message, is angelos, from which is our angel. And messenger itself has the ng in it. Where two lines meet we have an angle. A nook suggests something in the A N K H meaning. Perhaps hundreds more words might be traced from this venerable but most significant origin in the A N K

H. And the words themselves help us reestablish the fundamental elements in the composition and structure of the great ancient knowledge so well called the Gnosis. The letter I, as the spiritual-masculine first half of the great 10 symbol, must be examined more closely. It is in the alphabet and in language the symbol of the divine mind principle. It is the king of all being, knowing, determining, ordering, acting. And so it has been made the 1oth (tenth) letter of the Hebrew alphabet, the king number both i and 10 or any multiple thereof, and therefore has for its meaning the word God itself. Its Hebrew name is YOD (YODH) and means the "hand of God." Its hieroglyphic representation is that of a tongue of candle flame, bent as it would 10 be momentarily if blown upon by a gentle puff of the breath. This is to indicate the breathing of God upon the latent creative fires of atomic energy to blow them up to creative heat. It is suggested in Genesis when it is said that God brooded over the great deep. Water is the symbol of matter, as matter in the cosmos and water on the earth are the common universal mothers of life.

And matter contains the latent atomic fire which creates all. God blows upon this latent fire to enflame it for creative work. This is indicated in the bent candle flame of the YOD,--@insert Hebrew YOD. Ten is esoterically called the "perfect number." In the highest possible sense it is the number that rounds out or perfects a cycle of creation, and it does this through the interrelation of the eternal upper triad of noumenal creative forces, cosmic spirit-soul-mind, with the septenate of lower physical energies, as anciently represented in the great system of Egyptian Gnosis, and faithfully reproduced in the Ten Holy Sephiroth of the early Jewish Kabalah. The YOD then stands for that divine creative fire that in its deployment as a decanate of powers, forges the worlds into the shape prefigured in the divine mind. The triple-aspected cosmic Noumenon designs the blueprint of the creation-to-be, and the seven hierarchical energies carry them out in the world of concreteness. If one reflects on the remarkable physical phenomenon of a ray of white light passing through a triadic glass prism and casting the refracted rays upon a screen in the seven colors of the spectrum, one will have an instructive analogue of the number basis of the creation. Revelation symbolism evidently represents it as the Beast with seven heads and ten horns, the three horns in excess of the number of heads being presumably in the invisible noumenal worlds, the heavens of pure thought. Concomitant with the 10 primacy in symbolism runs a variant representation which depicts successive stages in the creative process. It begins with the symbol of inchoate matter, the O as representing primordial inorganic homogeneity or the unity and eternity of life in its unmanifest state. It in fact typifies what to us stands as empty space. It is empty (to us) as exhibiting absolutely nothing in visible palpable form. "The world was without form and void." But to the cosmic consciousness it is doubtless not empty, since it is filled with substance apperceptible to that consciousness. What it seems to us is best depicted by the empty circle, ~@ insert circle.

11 The next stage shows the circle with the visible point in the center. This design indicates the emergence of the first organic entification out of unmanifest being, ~@ insert circle w/ point in the center. The third depiction shows the circle cut horizontally into two halves, upper and lower, by the median diameter line,~@insert circle just mentioned. This diagram shows the bifurcation of the original unity into the creative duality and the polarization of its two self-contained opposite natures, a prerequisite for any creation of visible organic worlds. The fourth stage indicates the opposition or crossing of the cross within the circle, the vertical line standing for the spirit force and the horizontal for the physical. Lifting the cross out of the circle, we have it in its simplest form, and since life can add increase unto itself only by this crossing of spirit and matter, the cross becomes the sign of addition, the plus sign,--. The fifth stage has the same configuration, but as it were, turned one-eighth on its axis, giving the X within the circle. This is to show that motion has been introduced, that creation has begun,--. This, similarly to the bent candle flame of the YOD, indicates that God's impulse has begun to move. Then, as the initial motion imparted to the creation not only adds to its working potential, but vastly multiplies it, the X becomes the sign of multiplication. In this final form the design eventuates in giving us the great symbol of the number io,~X. And then if we take the X out of its eternal encirclement in the absolute existence—and by the beginning of the movement this emergence is indicated, —and place the two great symbols side by side, we have astonishingly that mystic word and symbol that enters so mysteriously into Scriptural allegory, —the word OX. (The elucidation of the esoteric intimation of this word is reserved for the finale.) The extensive Kst of divine names derived from the 10 base may now be scanned. lo is itself the name of one of the goddesses with whom Zeus, king of the gods in the Greek pantheon, entered into an escapade that exoterically sounds less honorable than would be expected of divine royalty. But as paramour of the supreme God she would stand in the role of the great Mother of life, like Cybele, Isis and the rest. An lo character occurs in other mythologies. As, however, the I functions as the male- spiritual symbol and is not to be taken as the vowel force alone, but rather as the con12 sonantal force, it was paired with each of the vowels in turn to represent the conjoined duality. And so we find lA, IE and lU standing as the base of a number of early deific names. The lA came to serve as the final syllable of all names of countries, as Germania, Britannia, Australia, Russia, Austria, Scandinavia, Asia, India, Arabia and many more. The IE begins the original Greek name Iesous (Jesus). Preceded by the H, denoting again the first motion of the breath of God, it began some Greek words for divinity, principally hieros, sacred, holy and a priest, from which comes hierophant, hierarchy and the old Greek name for Jerusalem, Hierosolyma. But as lU it stands as one of the most basic of all divine name-forms. lU was in fact the shortest and commonest of Egyptian verbs, and meant to come. Because the divine nature was considered an element of consciousness that was in course of its evolutionary coming to deify mankind, the Messiah doctrine connoted the idea of the slow, gradual and continuous coming of the deific mind in the world. In fact a common name in Egypt for the Messianic character was "the Comer." "lu is he who comes regularly and continually," periodically. Hence lU is the

primal Egyptian name of deity. As such it formed the first element of the great compound Egyptian name of the Christ-Messiah, lu- em-hetep, which was shortened by the Greeks into Imhotep. In full translation this would read: lu (he who comes) em (with) -hetep (peace, also seven); "he who comes with peace as number seven." This name comprehends in itself another great sermon like the A N K H-symbol, referring to the occult fact that in any cycle of creation the principle of divine consciousness that will unfold to bring peace to the chaotic subconscious elements (the so-called six elementary powers, the potencies in the atom) comes to full outward expression in the seventh and last round of the cycle. Christhood is always a seventh unfoldment. Our own word seven comes from hetep, as this shortened to kept, and directly became the Latin sept-em, by the interchange of h with s, as occurs in very many instances, as in Asura becoming Ahura. H and s are also closely related through the Hebrew letter shin, which is either S or sh in sound. S is really only a sharper h. The next step in the development is quite notable. The I being male-spiritual, a consonant (masculine gender) rather than a vowel, and representing the projected ray of divine mind that 13 beamed forth out of primordial being, ran the course of its projection into the deepest bosom of matter, planted its germinal seed in matter's womb, then turned to return, the configuration of the I was changed or enlarged to include in its shape the suggestion of the turning upward for the return. It might most significantly then be said that it was turned into the letter J. With more definiteness the J-form could bespeak the masculine-divine than the vowel-feminine or the androgynous aspect. Also in this form it could be more fitly prefixed to the other vowels, as JA, JE, JO and JU. With this important change the number of divine names begins to multiply exceedingly. It is impossible to pass by this item of the turning of the I into the J (the two are essentially the same letter still in Latin) without calling attention to the astonishing significance of the fact in relation to one of the key words in the Biblical allegory of the soul's descent and return. In the Hebrew-Mosaic allegory in the Old Testament the place where God descended in a cloud to meet and commune with his children (Israel) was Mount Sinai. This name then must mean the lowest point to which the spirit-soul descends to meet matter, the pivot point round which it swings to begin its return to the heavens. This is diagrammed by the lower turn of the J. What must be our astonishment, then, to discover that this key name Sinai derives from the Egyptian word sent {senai), meaning "point of turning to return!" And where, in concrete reality, is that point located? Nowhere else than in the physical body of man! The physical body of man is the Mount Sinai of the Bible. And where else could God and man meet than in the body of his human child? An obscure point in scholarship has at last come forth to enlighten us on one of the most important features of our sacred Scriptures. Greek mythology gives us Jason, a divine figure. In the Old Testament we have Jacob, Jabez, Jared, Jakin and perhaps others; James in the New; Jacques, Jack, a folk-lore character of the deity in man; Janus, definitely a Christ-figure in Roman mythology. The JE-form gives Jesus, Jesse, Jeshua, Jeshu, Jezebel, Jeremiah, Jerusalem, Jehu, Jethro, Jehosophat, Jehovah, Jephthah, and others. In passing it seems quite worth while to analyze the true context of the name Jesus. It is the JE combined with the Egyptian SU, meaning son, heir, prince, successor to the king; and the final masculine terminal letter, which was F in Egyptian, but 14 became S (US) in Latin: JE-SU-S. It would then mean the coming masculine-divine son (of God the Father) as "prince of peace." The masculine terminal F of Egypt was kept in the variant form

JO-SE-F, JO-SE-PH, as in the Russian Yussuf at the present. This is the most prominent in the JO group, which includes Joram, Josiah, Joash, Jonah (Jonas), Job, Joses, Joachim, Joel, Joshua and (in the Norse) Jotun. These have never been recognized for the divine names they are, because of the inveterate mistaking of Old Testament allegorism for assumed factual history. But, being in the allegory of man's divinity immersed in the flesh, they are incontestably the names of the divine or Christly principle personalized in the many myth-forms. Horus, the Christ of Egypt, had for one of his designations "the Jocund." The JU- form yields Judah, Judas, Judea, Jubilee, Judith, Julia, along with significant common noun derivatives such as judge, jury, justice. But Latin mythic usage exalted the JU to the very highest pinnacle of divine dignity in naming its supreme deity after the Egyptian JU, adding the word for father, pater (piter), to it to form the great name of the king of the gods, JU-PITER. Even the god's wife and sister partook of the glorious title— JUNO. The great Caesar boasted of his fabled derivation from deity in his cognomen Julius. The Juniper tree carries this connection with divine source. Latin juventus, our "youth," conveys the idea that the gods are ever young. (The I, the J and Y are all forms of the same letter-sound.) From this we have our junior, the German has jung, meaning and pronounced as our young. The ju—that begins the Latin jungo (iungo), to join, indicates that spirit and matter are joined together anew to generate fresh Kfe. This lU (JU) stem is much more significant than has ever been seen before. In the form of YU~it enters into the great world signifying the birth of deity— FuZe. Every letter, of course, expresses some aspect or segment of creative purpose. Alphabetical schematism has been presented in several different formulations. In the Hebrew alphabet there were said to be three "mother letters," aleph (A), mem (M) and shin (SH). These ostensibly represent respectively the pre- creation stage (A), the middle stage of spirit's involvement in matter (M), and its final stage of glorious deification (SH),~the symbol of fire. M is the symbol of water. Life emanates out of potential fire, is "baptized" for evolutionary purposes in water, the symbol of 15 matter, and returns to source with fiery potentialities actualized by having "overcome" the powers in the water-matter. The Hebrew word for fire is esh, and spirit evolves its divine fire in man, ish. The divine fire in man made him the is/i-man, and the divine man in the tribal life of some nations was called the shaman. How the other letters were grouped in relation to the three mother-letters is matter of uncertainty. Several schematic designs have been suggested by students of Kabalism. But two consonants, beside J, were made the central frame of another extensive run of divine names. These are R and L. The names derived from or based on them must be listed. It is evident that, as their usage worked out, R and L may be regarded as essentially the same letter. The Chinese confusion of the two is well-known. But their identification became almost a necessity in the ancient Hebrew- Egyptian exchange of words, ideas and symbols, inasmuch as the Egyptian alphabet had no L and was forced to substitute R in all words where the Hebrew could use either L or R. It is therefore extremely likely that the great basic words, as seen so well in Latin rex, king, and lex, law, are of practically identical significance. The heavenly king is the Lord, and the old Saxon derivation of Lord from law-ward, as Ruskin points out, is more than coincidental. The king's will was the law in all archaic life, and in theology it is still true that the will of the Lord is the law of life. Just why R and L came, with J and SH to emblemize divinity is not too clear. They, along with M and N, are of the class of letters called liquids: they are sounded with a continued/Zou;

of the voice. They could thus have been chosen as representing the on-flowing course of all life. This idea would not have been inappropriate. It may be the correct one. At any rate R came to its divinest application in being chosen as the name of that greatest of all spiritual deities of antiquity, the Egyptian Sun-god Ra, whose symbol is that of the sun, the circle with the dot in the center. A cursory view of names based on R and L yields many interesting items. The R and L can be associated with any of the vowels and can either follow or be preceded by it. From AL-LA we note Allah, Aladdin, Alheim (Elohim), the frequent Al--of Arabic names and a host of others, perhaps our all. From EL-LE we have El, the Hebrew word for God, the plural being Elohim. The masculine article, the, in the four languages 16 derived from Latin, is, as in the Spanish, el, and in the French, le.

This will not be seen as significant until it is recognized that the definite article is, or was, itself a cognomen of deity. Spanish the is the Hebrew word for God, EL. English the is the Greek for God, the-os. And Greek masculine form of the is ho, a Chinese word for deity. The ancients habitually prefixed the to divine names, as "the Osiris." From IL comes the Arabic Ilbrahim and the Latin ille, meaning this, that which is, a succinct definition for deity. The Latin name for the sacred tree was the holm-oak, and its Latin name was ilex. OL and UL yield a few words referring to divine things. Hebrew olam, the world, eternity, the aeon, and olah, up, to go up, and the Mohammedan Ullah, Abdullah, may trace origin from these two bases. AR-RA shows in numerous words, ar meaning river in Hebrew, and there are several rivers on the world map named the Ar, or Arar. The stream of divine force emanating from the heart of being to create worlds was called the river. Every ancient land had its sacred river. As Ra was the great solar deity, the origin of ray, radiant, radius, radium, radiate and array is evident. As the king was the one radiant with divine glory, the rex {rey, roi, roy), such words as regal, royal, real (as in Mont-real), regulate (along with lex, legal, loyal, leal and legislate), are traceable to this source. Plato has the famous "myth of Er," a divine character. The Greek has Er- with the masculine singular ending -os, giving the great God of divine love, Eros. Re must be the base of the common Latin word for thing, res, the stem of which is just re. This gives reality, realize and reify, and the prefix denoting repetition, re-, as life is constantly repeating its processes; as in re-new, re- vive, restore, etc. IR-RI shows scant usage, but in OR-RO and UR-RU we encounter a prolific wealth of derivatives, all pointing to high, if not directly divine reference. It is significant, to begin with, that OR is found to be the base of words in several languages meaning two things, gold and light. French for gold is or, and Latin aur-um; our word ore; Hebrew for light is Oroh. Gold, the indestructible, was symbolically related to light, which is also indestructible. The creative energy of God flowed forth as light like a golden river, so that all three, gold, light and river show the derivation from ar, aur, or. Aurora, God of Dawn, needs no further explication; aura and aureole likewise. 17 UR reveals a grand list of shining names. It was in itself the greatest and most likely the original word for fire. The Egyptians, wishing to name it the fire, added the divine article, the, which in their language was the hieroglyph for the letter P. This addition made it p-ur, pur, the Greek word for fire to this day. From this comes pure, purge, purgatory, as also pyre, pyrotechnic and empyrean, the Greek U changing to Y in English, as in hundreds of words. Ur (a variant of aur, or) was the name of that state of the primordial spiritual "fire" from which the first divine ray, Ab-ra-ham, proceeded as first father of spiritual Israel (not the historical Hebrews). In the same category it was the name of the universal Egyptian symbol of creative fire, the uraeus, "a serpent of fire," which was sevenfold as typifying the seven archangels that created the universe. It is therefore another representation of the dragon or beast with seven heads. Is it strange that our modern discovery of the creative fire of the universe in the atom has brought into prominence as the most fiery of the elements those two whose names incorporate both the title of the Sun-god and the Uraeus, RAdium and URanium? The German language has some hundreds of words prefixing UR, as Ursprung, Urquelle, Ursache, all meaning original source-spring of being. All life came out of UR, the primordial fount of cosmic fire. A verse in the Chaldean Oracles says that "all things are the product of one primordial fire, every way resplendent." How resplendent it is our modern nuclear physics is now revealing! The Hebrew word for father being ab, Ab-ra-m is "Father Ra," as clearly as Hebrew can say it. Ram would be this creative fire immersed in water, matter. The list so far traced becomes more than doubled through the prefixing onto these

root-forms the Hebrew article, the, which is just the letter H. The addition of the H has the force of divinizing the word, as has been seen. So from HAL there is hallow, hale, hallel (Hebrew to praise), halleluiah, hail and more. From HEL can be traced heal, health, heil (German hail), hell (German, bright, clear), and most significantly, the Greek helios, the sun! The spiral, or helix, was a figure tracing the spiraling course of the sun, or its planets around it. The feminine names Helen, Helena (with the H intensified into S becoming the name of the moon, Selene), are assumed to derive from it also. The Greeks adopted unto themselves the divine name Hellenes, signifying "bright and shining ones," dubbing the rest of humanity "barbarians." (They did this 18 in the same fashion and with the same motive as the Jews adopted for themselves the divine name Israelites, dubbing the rest of mankind "Gentiles.") From HIL comes doubtless our word hill, "the hill of the Lord," the high locale of divine power. (Har in the R-group is the Hebrew word for hill!) From the HOL stem comes of course holy, whole, holism. Few of particular divine character or reference derive from HUL. The H-R group yields many of exalted significance. HAR gives heart, hearth, Har-Tema, (a name of Horus, the great Christ of Egypt), Harpocrates, (another Greek- Egyptian Christ-name), perhaps harvest, harp, harpy (the harpies of Virgil's Aeneid). HER gives a long list: hero (title of one grade of deities in Greek mythology), German Herr (God), herald, Hera, (Juno's Greek name), Heracles {Hercules), Hermes (Mercury), and, reinforcing the e with the i, hieros, Greek for sacred.  HIR appears perhaps in the German for shepherd, and in Hiram. HOR gives the base of perhaps the greatest of ancient personahzations of Christhood, the Egyptian god Horus, who stands on the horizon, hour, horology, hormone, horn, horticulture. Horn was a universal ancient symbol of divine power. HUR shows in Ben-Hur and hurricane, the natural exemplification of divine fiery power. The Hurrians were a people sharing Asia Minor with the Hittites. As H comes out often in the roughened form of CH (KH), and also exchanges often with S, the H-basis of hundreds of words, all in one way or another intimating deific reference, the derivative field is vastly extended, embracing such words as chalice, charity, care, cure, cross, cheer, choir, chorus, Christos, charm, cherish, cherubim, Serapis, seraphim, sir, sire, seer, ser (Egyptian for chief, elder, sire), kherufu (Egyptian for the two lion-gods on the /lon'zon). These lists are put down almost at random. It is certain that intensive research would immensely increase the total number, and no doubt others of the greatest importance could be revealed. These formations from the basis 10 are of the greatest interest and importance. They do not.however, give any intimations of the organic structure in the alphabet which this work is intended to disclose. But they will appear in clearer light as that hidden structure is outlined. 19 To enforce the cryptic significance of the disclosure now to be made, it is necessary to present, with the utmost brevity, the fundamental meaning-graph of all ancient religious literature. The Bibles of antiquity have but one theme: the incarnation. The vast body of ancient Scripture discoursed on but one subject,~the descent of souls, units of deific Mind, sons of God, into fleshly bodies developed by natural evolution on planets such as ours, therein to undergo an experience by which their continued growth through the ranges and planes of expanding consciousness might be carried forward to ever higher grades of divine being. These tomes of "Holy Writ" therefore embodied their main message in the imagery of units of fiery spiritual nature plunging down into water, the descending souls being described as sparks of a divine cosmic fire, and the bodies they were to ensoul being constituted almost wholly of water. (The human body is seven-eighths water!)

 It can indeed be said that the one sure and inerrant key to the Bibles is the simple concept of fire plunging into water, the fire being spiritual mindpower and water being the constituent element of physical bodies, —as well as the symbol of matter. Soul (spirit) as fire, plunged down into body, as water, and therein had its baptism. Hence soul's incarnation on earth was endlessly depicted and dramatized as its crossing a body of water, a Jordan River, Styx River, Red Sea, Reed Sea. Since the water element of human bodies is the "sea" which the soul of fire has to cross in its successive incarnations, and it is red in color, the "Red Sea" of ancient Scriptures is just the human body blood. When the red fire of spirit- soul was gradually introduced into and permeated the original seawater which was the bodily essence of earliest living creatures on earth, it changed colorless salt water into its own color, red. The "Red Sea" never could have meant anything other than the human blood. The Scriptures reiterate that "fire descended from heaven and turned the sea into blood." This transformation of course took place in man's body, not in the world oceans. This is a clarification that alone can reillumine all old Scriptures with a flashing new and enlightening orientation of meaning. Egypt said that souls came down to "kindle a fire in the sea," to "create a burning within the sea," verily to set the ocean on fire. This has actually been done, but in man's veins and in his passions, not in the seven seas. 20 It is now to be announced that the great meaningstructure discovered in the alphabet outlines this descent of soul-fire into water and its return to its native empyrean. If one arranges the letters in a circular arc downward from A to the last letter of the first half of the alphabet, and then begins the upward return with the first letter of the second half and completes the arc to the final letter, describing the lower half of a circle, one will have blueprinted the organic structure here revealed. On the thesis just presented, one would challenge the claim of such a structure to demonstrate that the first letter or letters were somehow charactered as fire, and that the two middle letters at the bottom or turningpoint of the semi-circle were charactered as water. We are proclaiming that the structure meets that challenge and therefore proves itself as true and correct. The result is that, along with every other symbolic device of ancient meaning-form, even the alphabet embodied the central structure of all ancient literature, —the incarnation, the baptism of fire-soul in and under body-water. If this is to be confirmed, we must findyi're at the top or beginning of the descending arc, and water at the bottom or turning-point. It must now be shown that the conditions our thesis requires to prove itself are precisely met in the alphabet. The discovery was made and certified when it was perceived that the alphabet did fulfill these precise conditions. The top or beginning letters are A and B, and should, the A alone or combined with B, represent fire; the middle letters coming at the base of the arc are M and N, and, mirabile dictu, they represent water! From A to M, then, the descending arc traces the downward or involutionary plunge of fire into water, reaching its lowest depth with M; from N back to the final letter, whatever it be in different languages, the upward return arc represents the arising out of water and the return through evolution of the heavenly fire to its true home, completing the cycle. The fire-character of A and B does not show out in such explicit form as does the water-character of M and N. Nevertheless it is intimated and implicit in various ways. The celestial fire emanated from primal source as one ray, but soon radiated out in triadic division, and finally reached the deepest heart of matter in a sevenfold segmentation. But in its first stage of emanation it was always pictured as triform. The YOD candle-flame being its type-form, the Hebrews constructed their letter which was to represent the fire-principle with three YODS at the top level, with 21 lines extending downward to a base, on which all three met and were conjoined in one essence. This gives us the great fire-letter SH, s/im,~@insert shin. But the triform fire symbol was only possible as the result of the one first ray bifurcating into the two fires of spirit and matter and uniting to generate their product, which became the third two-flame aspect as preceding the three-fire aspect. And what letter is it that depicts the two-flame stage, the first real creative stage? Precisely what the thesis calls for—the first letter aleph, composed of two YODS, one above, the other below, the central axis, a slightly variant form of our mathematical sign of division, a horizontal line with a dot above and one below it. All life is an interplay between the upper fire of spirit and the lower fires of sense and the flesh, of "pure" fire in air and "impure" fire in water. Even the English A carries the same depiction, as it presents the one vertical line of spirit raying downward, the I, as being split apart into duality, with the two separated lines still connected by the horizontal bar of mutual inter-relation, ~@ insert aleph. The resulting Hebrew word, then, for fire is just what the specifications of symbolic representation demand. The word should be composed of symbolic letters carrying the idea of the one-fire, the dual fire and the triple fire signs, and this is precisely what the Hebrew word for fire is. It is ESH, really AeSH, composed of aleph, subvowelled by e, and shin. Aleph is the dual letter, shin the triple, and the middle bar between the two YODS is the aleph in the single-bar fire. Then significantly man, who embodies this single, double and triple/i're is ISH! One would ask at once whether the English word ash would carry the same connotations, being the visible end result of fire. It is extremely likely that it does. Not only is it at once evident in its relation to fire as its residue, —ashes, —but the Norse mythology, depicting the radiating streams of the living fire under the imagery of a branching tree, chose the ash as the tree-type of the fiery emanation: Ygdrasil, the ash-tree of life.

It has already been stated that the patriarchal character designated as Abram personified in the Hebrew formulations the first /af/ier of spiritual life, emanating out of the primordial essence 22 of fire, UR of the Chasdim. (This latter word signifies not national Chaldeans, as those thus designated were not an ethnic group, but a spiritual caste. The term stands for the first archangels, or creative fires, the seven.) To be the father of spiritual life in an evolutionary cycle, this ray had to be the first aspect of the emanation.

Therefore it would be found to be composed of the first two letters of the alphabet. This is precisely what is found in the Hebrew word for father: AB. Linking it with the Egyptian RA, the radiant solar deity, we have AB-RA- M, receiving later in its evolution the developed powers of godhood represented by the fifth Hebrew letter, he, and so becoming AB-RA-HAM. And as Abram came out of the primordial empyreal fire, UR, it is hardly coincidental that even UR begins with that letter, U, which (with V) represents the downward line of descent, the turning upward and the return to the heights.

The detailed knowledge is not at present available to trace the chain of linked steps in the descent of the divine flame from A down to M. It does not seem apparent that at any rate in extant alphabets there is to be found a sequence of letter significations paralleling and depicting the successive stages of the creative fire's descent into the water, or matter involvement. If such an explicit arrangement was planned for the first alphabets, it seems impossible to trace the stages in orderly succession in present alphabets. But what emerges with astonishing certitude is that the central letters, M and N, carry the significance of what the diagram demands, —water. Thus at the point of lowest descent, where our thesis requires water, there indeed we have it. Every letter of the Hebrew alphabet, beside carrying a number value, also has attached to it a symbolic monograph: B is beth and means house; G is gimel and means camel; D is daleth and means door; H is he and means window, etc. When we come to M, we find it is named mem and means~u;afer.^ N is called nun and means that which is the animal life in water, --fish! This is in the Hebrew. But amazingly, when we turn to the old Egyptian, we find that N has the name of nun likewise, but means and is the hieroglyph oi—waterl Its character letter is simply a short line indented to indicate seven waves, as our English script m is a succession of three waves. M therefore in the Hebrew, and in the English as well, marks the nadir of soul's decent into water, and N, at the same level and therefore also signifying water (or SiS fish the 23 organic life in water), marks the turning-point for return, the Mount Sinai of evolution. Its reference is undoubtedly to this earth, which true symbolic insight discovers is itself— and not any hill on its surface—the "mount" or "hill of the Lord," on which God meets man in a cloud of fire, and on which all sermons are preached by his inner deity to man, and all temptations, crucifixions, spiritual initiations and final transfigurations take place. From A, the point of emanation of the spiritual fire, the creative stream of living energy, the river of vivification, as the Greeks call it, proceeded and swept downward until at M it had immersed its fiery potencies in the water of the human body, therein to begin to do its evolutionary work of kindling its own bright flame of spiritual consciousness in the red sea of the human blood.

And now it is known that this red blood was originally sea water. As fire causes water to evaporate, the ancient allegorism represented the divine fire as drying up the water of the bodily sea, permitting souls to pass over the watery terrain dryshod. Variant symbolism had the Christ nature walking on the water without sinking into its depths. Egyptian figurism had the fire causing the water to boil, with the soul subjected to the danger of being scalded thereby. So the graph of the soul's descent and return swings down from the fire-height of AB to MN and there turns back upward to end in the final letter. It may be a chance circumstance, but is at any rate an odd one, that if we start with A and then take in succession the final letter of the English alphabet, Z, the final one of Greek, O, and the final of the Hebrew, TH, it gives us the word AZOTH, the word used in Medieval "alchemy" to denote the primogenetic source-essence of life. If it were thus made up of the first and last letters of the three most representative alphabets it would have been intended to denote that basic essence which constitutes the substance of all life from the first step in creation through to the final dissolution of all things. In descending from the height of fire essence to the depth of water substance, the energization would have had to pass through the intermediate stage or form of air. Fire symboKzes pure energy of spirit; air typifies mind; water stands for emotion, as earth for sensation in the scale of conscious states. If any of the letters between A and M are intended to mark the air stage, it has not come to knowledge as yet, unless it be that the bent form of the tenth 24 letter YOD, indicating the candle flame bent by a puff of air to denote the original impulse of God's mind on the flame, is to be taken in this significance. M and N, separate or conjoined, form the framework of hundreds of words relating to the condition of spirit-energy when immersed in matter. As the primal mind-fire is the father, AB, so the primal matter-essence is the eternal mother, which in Hebrew is AM. M will be found to begin virtually all words denoting motherhood. M represents three, or five, or seven waves of water, and it should not be a matter of surprise, therefore, that we find all life on the planet having its generation in and from the sea water. Sea water is in a sense still the mother of our life, because that life is sustained by the electro dynamic potencies in our blood, which is still chemically undistinguishable from sea water! Our blood is the red sea water! So we get the mothername by conjoining the letter of potential fiery energy A, with matter symbolized by water, M. Our colloquial "Ma" for mother is essentially the Hebrew AM. Starting with A M for mother, there is met an almost endless list of words whose connotations link them to the matter side of the life duality. To view them in the light of this orientation of thought is to discern in them new and vivid intimations of esoteric meaning. These recondite connotations can best be seen by contrasting their sense with their antonyms denoting fire, spirit and the fatherhood. To begin with, the creative powers symbolized by the letters at the head of the alphabet are gods; while the being who embodies god-power in matter is--MaN. The divine powers at the summit are unmanifest; in matter they become MaNifest. At the summit there is but one power, undifferentiated; below in matter it has multiplied itself and become the MaNy. At the god height the power is purely spiritual; at the lower level it comes out as MeNtal; spirit above, MiNd below. At the top there is the maximum of power, even though purely potential; at the lower range its is MiNus, or at a MiNimum, though actual in its limited expression. A man is the cosmos in MiNiature. That which is expressed down here is, in comparison with the superior potential above, MeaN. Also as here the two poles of being are locked in a more or less stable equilibrium, things here are at a MeaN or MediaN counterbalance. To hold this steady is to MaiNtain life in its right poise. The father-power, AB is the conscious cognitive 25 element in creation; the power it wields in matter, the M N energy of the atom, is the MaNipulative hand of God (the meaning of YOD); and so it is that the word for hand in many languages is not only compounded of M and N (Latin manus, Spanish mano, French main), but is in all languages feminine in gender, intimating the motherhood. In contrast to heaven above, the earth below is, in Latin, MuNdus, from which is our adjective MuNdane. Also from this comes MouNt, MouNtain, MouNd, already explained as referring to no hill on earth, but to the earth itself. Hebrew name for this lower vale of tribulation was HiNNoM, or GehiNNoM. In the upper realms souls are not sufficiently individualized to deserve specific differentiated names; here soul gets its proper NaMe. The fate allotted to each soul by karmic desert comes out to manifestation here below; it is therefore the soul's NeMesis. The soul here is under law, in Greek NoMos. A section of the terrain of a nation was by the Egyptians termed a NoMe. Since matter, like type-symbol, water, is, from the philosophical view of reality, nothing (it was designated by the Greeks "privation"), the Egyptian base-root of the letter N, whose hieroglyph was seven waves of water, along with the primal deific trinity Nu, Nun, Nut, gives us all the words expressing Negation: no, not, neither, nor, none, nil, nix (German: nichts), Latin nox (night), our night, deny, neuter, never, nay, German nein, niemals, etc., etc. Applied to man, his (relative) nothingness would make him "no one" which is in Latin NeMo. As man is cut off from deity here below, he is in Greek MoNos, alone. Also he is a MoNad.

Perhaps MoNk is one who is alone, not united to the female counterpart. The food the soul eats on earth is that divine MaNNa that was rained down from heaven, but had to be scraped up off the earth, the perfect analogue of how mortals acquire their heavenly nutriment. The universal ancient tribal name for the divinity manifesting in the life of nature was MaNa, MaiNu, MaNitou.

Then we have the word for the thinking principle, which in the Hindu system is MaNas. One caught under the demoniac possession of this power was a MaNiac. In India the practice of prophecy was called MaNtric science. And the -mon in the word deMoN is probably of this derivation.

The Greek Furies were called MaeNads. Plato refers to divine obsession as a MaNia better than sober reason. An oMeN was a foresight of one's earthly fate. And the mystifying and baffling word ending prayers, 26 oMeN, if not directly from the Egyptian god of that same name, would seem by letter intimation to mean "so let it be," indicating that what is set forth should come to reality in the evolutionary process measured by the descent of soul into matter the whole way from A to M-N. Memory in Latin is MeMiNi and the Greek Muse of Memory was MNemosyne. To recall one's past is to reMiNisce. Things here are the MiNutiae of what is whole and integral above. They are MiNute in magnitude and last but a MiNute of time, poetically speaking.

 Another most important line of derivatives branches off into sidereal regions. The great cosmic symbol, if not the embodiment of divine energy, is the sun. In contrast with its mighty generative power, its opposite character in the earthly region of the heavens, dead, inert, purely passive and reflective, the symbol of matter, is the MooN. Hence the composition of its name in English from M and N, giving also MoNth, MoNday and MeNses. If in Latin L stands for the divine Light, their Luna (the moon) might have taken form from the idea that on the lunar orb the divine Light (L) was weakened and dimmed by the reflection from the surface of the negative lifeless moon, giving them LuNa, L for the light and N for the darkness; or it might have been originally L reflected in M-N, suggesting LuMNa, later wearing down into Luna. Oddly enough the Latin for light in its pure solar glory is lux; but for light in its earthly refracted dimmed form the word was LuMen. At any rate L and N are set directly at opposite nodes to each other in lux, light, and nox (Greek nux) night. L evidently here carries the connotation of divine character analyzed earlier. For not only does the Latin have lumen (our illumine) for light, but it has the word representing the divine light or power in things, NuMen, which comes close to bearing the same significance as NoMen, Latin for name. The soul was thought to put on its bodily vesture as a MaNtle, which, as being the house it lived in was its MaNse or MaNsion. That which trailed back from the horse's head was his MaNe. That which flowed forth from the head of being was the eMoNation of creative force. The divinity implanted in living nature, most evolved in man, was iMMaNent, our EMaNuel. It is close to certainty that here is to be found an explanation of a prominent item in the grammar of language, which seems still unknown in philological science,--the reason why the accusative 27 (objective) case of all Latin nouns masculine and feminine in the singular number ends in the letter— M, and those corresponding in Greek end in-N, as also in Sanskrit and doubtless other languages. It is obvious that the M and N endings here denote objectivity, as the accusative is the objective case. Why this is so is definitely implicit in the significance of the meaning structure which places the two letters ending this case at the bottom of the descending arc of involution. For the divine light is emanated from the supernal kingdom of spirit, and spirit is the active generative productive force that energizes all life process. It alone is self-generating, it alone initiates and institutes action. It is the father principle; the maternal-material principle is eternally only passive, receptive, mothering that which it receives germinally in its womb. The spirit force must stand as the actor; it does whatever is done; it moves upon the inert water, stirs them into agitation and motion to throw them into the forms of the conceived pattern. It is therefore the subject of the sentence that tells what its action initiates in the creative order. It is therefore in the nominative case, the subject-actor in the movement, and is grammatically called nominative because it gives specific character and name (Latin: nomen) to that which the action creates. But what of the end product that the action brings into the status of being? As end product, materially created, it stands there as the object of the action, the thing purposed and by an energizing process made objective as the result. It is therefore the objective in view in the initial action and the objective thing produced. It must therefore be put into the objective case in grammar. The actor works subjectively, in the purely noumenal or subjective realm of conscious being. But its work is to bring its purposes thus subjectively conceived out into objective actuality. Hence the creative subject force that emanates out of the A B condition of primal being ends by generating its product here below at the M-N station of physical objectivity. The M and N terminations (even this word has the two letters in its context) therefore fitly appertain to the objective case of nouns, and the Latin, Greek, Sanskrit and others so have it. To illustrate the point, the nominative case of "trumpet" in Latin is tuba, but the objective case is tubam. So all nouns. Only in the case of neuter nouns is there no distinction between the nominative and accusative cases, obviously 28 because a noun of neuter gender can not manifest any difference between subjective and objective status. It is not living, therefore can neither initiate action or be acted upon by its own volition, hence can be neither subject nor object in the living sense. The spiritually noumenal world is the realm where the subject principle initiates action; the lower physical world is the place where that action results terminally in the production of objectivity. M and N seem thus always to designate objectivity, and that again must be the reason for the composition of that English suffix denoting a thing's attainment or achievement of its status of being in objectivity— ment. The principle of explanation thus established is seen with startling definiteness in three of our common English personal pronouns. Of the first personal pronoun the nominative case is I, but the objective introduces the M: me. The third personal pronoun masculine singular is in the nominative he; but in the objective it is him. The third person plural nominative is they; but the objective is them. It is in passing to be noticed that the I is the only one of the pronouns capitalized, in respect to divinity, since the I-ego is the only part of us that is divine!

Likewise the survival of the dot above the I (and the J) is the remnant of the YOD, the Hebrew divine flame. All this induces us to think that the I element (another word incidentally showing the L-M-N sequence) of a person is the subjective divine self within, initiating all action; while the outer personal physical bodily self is what this I has produced as the me. It might be said that the I has objectified itself in and as the me. What the noumenal I came to be when manifested outwardly in matter is the me. The I revealed itself in the me, just as it is said in religion that God has revealed or manifested himself to the world and in the world as Jesus. The ancients personalized a goddess named Echo. She represented the physical material repercussion to the impact of the waves of creative noumenal energy, the "voice" of God, upon matter. What matter, so to say, responded or answered was the "echo" of the divine voice. There is aptness and beauty in these ancient conceptions and ingenious allegorizations and poetizations once their sane high relevance is captured. The me is the echo from the side of matter of the divine voice of the I-ego. The M is conspicuously seen as marking the point of lowest descent and beginning of return in a notable key-word in Hebrew. 29 The word for sun holds as high a place of glory in religious philosophy as does the radiant orb itself in the solar system. It typifies for mental illumination the same generative ray of power that its physical beams represent in the stellar cosmos. The Hebrew word for it was obviously aimed at embodying the story of its nature and its daily course of (apparent) travel. In outward semblance it appears as a globe of fiery essence that plunges at every eventide down into earth, or water, crosses a land of darkness and arises again unquenched in fiery splendor the following morning. As a globe of fire its nature would be expressed most fittingly by the letter shin (SH), with its threefold candle flame, the three YODS, above; the place of water into which it nightly descends would be indicated by M, and the place of its final return, the empyrean above, by SH again. So the word thus constituted would turn out to be SH-M-SH {shemesh); and this is just what it is. It is the old basic story of divine fire plunging down into water, the universal trope-figure under which all operation of spirit in and upon matter was dramatized. It seems unquestioned that the Scriptural names of Samson, Saul, Samuel, Samael, Simon, Solomon were based on this semesh stem. For all the divine figures in ancient spiritual dramas were essentially sun-god characters, typifying the spiritual aspect of the solar effluence in man. Samson's loss of power through the betrayal of Delilah fairly closely parallels Jesus' loss of life and his helplessness on the cross through his betrayal by Judas. Jesus, like Samson, was shorn of his aureole of glory which was replaced by the black crown of thorns, as Samson's loss of hair—always typical of solar raysreduced him to impotency. And the etymology of Delilah is most significant as fulfilling her part in the allegory. In the case of Jesus' crucifixion "darkness was over the earth" during the agony. The name Delilah is compounded of the Hebrew word for night, lilah Qailah), with the fourth Hebrew letter, D, prefixed. Now the tribe of Dan was in astrological tropism allocated to the autumn sign of Scorpio, when the sun is entering the winter-time of darkness and solar feebleness. So Scorpio was called the gate or door of the dark "underworld," which in the Egyptian was named the Tuat, now tending to be spelled also with a D, as Duat, Duad.

When we turn to the Hebrew alphabet and see that D, daleth, means door, we have the name D-lilah reading definitely "the door of the dark underworld of night." This may 30 seem far-fetched to those not habituated to the nature of ancient allegorical composition of spiritual myths. When the name of a paramour of a sun-god figure works out to mean the "door of the dark night" of incarnation, the fitness of the construction is most astonishingly convincing and clearly reflects a designed conception. When one encounters and unravels not only one or two chance constructions of this kind, but scores of them, indeed finds them at every turn, one is certain that the methodology of ancient cryptic writing has been rediscovered. When this disclosure is carried through to the farthest limit of its bearings on the significance of the ancient literature, it is recognized with astonishment that the meaning-content of archaic writing was expressed as definitely by the form-structure of the material as by the connotation of the words. It is becoming more clearly discerned that the formulators of the sacred scripts of antiquity strove to dramatize a postulated form of cosmic structure in a graph outlining the life development and movement by imitating its rhythms and number counts, its cyclical swirls and sweeps, in the organic form of the textual construction.

Thus it is seen that the numerical basis of Bible writing in Old Testament Hebrew and New Testament Greek is the "magic" number seven. The number value of thousands of verses, divine names, key phrases and even whole Bible books is with surprising regularity a multiple of seven. Thus there are seven other combinations in the verse score multiples of seven. Life, so to say, in every one of its creative advances travels in seven-league boots, dances to a seven- beat measure, runs a scale of seven notes. It is evident that the authors of Holy Writ labored to inweave the form of this movement into the writing itself. The lilt and pause, is to reproduce in mantric value the lilt and swing of evolution itself. That this methodology has lain under the eye of scholarship for these twenty centuries or more without its implications being seen or guessed is unimpeachable testimony to the blindness of religious obsession. Another most significant combination of the divine SH with the earthly M-N comes to view in the Hebrew word for oil, shemen.

Here the fire-symbol, SH, is united with both the water letters. As the fuel for fire and the substance used in the divine anointing, which is itself the dramatization of the divinizing of man, oil is 31 one of the most frequent symbols of the deific power in the Scriptures and mythology. The great divine names Christ and Messiah both mean "the Anointed One."

It was observed earlier that when the X symbol of the developing movement of creation was lifted out of the matter-symbol O and placed after it, we strangely found that it spelled the word OX. This singular circumstance at once bred the conviction that this word, this theriograph, or animal hieroglyph, should play some prominent part in the scheme of ancient figurative representation of values and relations. It was of course known to be a figure in a number of Biblical stereotypes as well as in Greek and other mythic scores. But its full symbolic import was not realized until the significance of its connection with the first letter of the Hebrew alphabet came to view with startling impact. Aleph, A, has for its name coefficient this very word OX. Along with this, there is also the Hebrew letter L, lamed, with the meaning of oxgoad. But why is A denominated by the ox- symbol? What is the significance of this animal that connects it with the first letter? Revelation of this profound and recondite symbolism should indeed open the eyes of all Scriptural exegetists to the almost impenetrable crypticism of ancient esoteric writing, which they have with such obdurate intransigence continued to deny, ignore and scorn.

To put it in the most compact form of statement, it appears that A was denominated the ox because, as the animal is unproductive, incapable of begetting life—as the result of desexing–so the primal state or stage of creation, represented by the letter A, is unproductive, incapable of begetting life. The alphabet's first character fittingly represents the nonot-nought- nothing stage of the cyclical creation. It is the pre-zoic stage, the lingering darkness before the first rays of dawn. As yet there is nothing, neither matter nor movement. It is the absolute zero on life's or the cycle's thermometer. It is the state which the Egyptians described by their name NU (NUN, NUT), night, and the Hebrews by their AIN. It is the stage when naught was. In it nothing could be produced, nothing could have birth. It was the great darkness, the great deep, into whose bosom had not yet fallen the seminal seed of new creation. It was sheer potential of life, standing, like the ox, unfertilized, unimpregnated by the fructifying ray of cosmic mind, impotent to mother life until so enriched. 32 If this seems like an arbitrary fancy, it also appears to be indubitably substantiated by the positive fact that in the main languages, from Sanskrit down to

English, this letter A is the universal prefix which gives to all words with which it is conjoined the negative meaning. It can be translated invariably by the word "not." In Greek it is called "alpha privative," the letter that deprives a word of its positive meaning, making it negative. A- theist, agnostic, a-symmetrical, a-moral, a-mnesia, apathetic, a-tom (not cuttable), even the Greek word for "truth," a-letheia, (that which is not forgotten), and a host of others attest the negative force of A. This being so, we are introduced directly to another outstanding fact in connection with the succeeding letter, the second of the alphabet, B. It is not by chance or as a pure pun that begin begins with B. For in the structural formation of the alphabet, since the creation does not begin with A, a precreation stage, the ancient books definitely state that it starts with B,-B-gins, as it were. B is therefore the first letter in the actual creation. How fitting it is, then, that it is the first letter of the first verse of Genesis, which starts with the Hebrew word b,rashith and that followed by the verb bara. B,rashith means in the beginning and bara means created. Yes, creation begins with B, not a-gins with A. As the beginning institutes the process of coming to be, or becoming, these words also start with B.

The great number of German words with the prefix be-, as bekommen, bekennen, bedenken, and a very large number also in English, as beget, betoken, bespeak, besmirch, behave and befriend, all carry the meaning of a movement coming, so to say, to a becoming. And in what way could the whole process of creation be more graphically expressed than by saying that it is a movement on its way to becoming to be? As the great Hindu philosopher Aurobindo expresses it, "the only being is becoming." Can it be without significance, then, that the Hebrew word meaning to come is just the B leading out the A,- BA? And this also spells the Eg3^tian word meaning the soul that comes to being here in the body. And would it be sheer coincidence that our born, bear, birth, breed, baby, beget, all start with B? And that well or spring in the Hebrew is baer? {Beer Sheba, "the well of the seven. ") We cry Abba father, says the Scripture, which, if ab is father, and ba means comes, would have us saying "the father comes"~in the character of his Christly Son on earth, the ray in us of the Father principle in the universe. 33 It may be asked, why, since the tenth letter YOD represents the flame of the divine creative fire, and indeed gives its name to God, the shin (S or SH) has come in for so much of the divine fire symboKsm. Our answer can not be categorical or dogmatic. It can be speculated that as the YOD represented the flame in its primal oneness, the shin represented it when it had differentiated into the triplicity, for it contains three YODS. It does not seem a wild assumption to think also that the letter chosen to carry the hissing sound of S and SH should depict the threefold divine fire, for the fire became triple only when it entered the watery composition of the body, and the S and SH sound is precisely that produced by fire plunging into water! The YOD then can be taken as representing the cosmic fire when first fanned by the breath of God. Jesus is dramatized as coming "with his fan in his hand" to generate heat to mold the worlds in proper shape and to fan into bright flame the smoldering fire of divinity in man's constitution.

Shin would represent the fire, now become triple, plunging into the lower levels of water, standing both for the actual water of the human body and as a general symbol of matter. The three YODS of the shin have lines carrying their power down to the bottom level, where they are united in one common bar, this again intimating that the three divine aspects, spirit, soul and mind, are all mingled as one in the body of man. As a symbol designed to depict the immersion of fiery spiritual units of consciousness in their actual baptism in the water of physical bodies, the letter form that dramatizes the actual event, and the letter sound that onomatopoetically mimics the sound of fire plunging into water, this alphabet character shin is certainly most eloquently suggestive. It has often been said that the S (SH) sound is derived from the hiss of the serpent. This tradition seems more likely to have come from the ancient symbolism of fire plunging into water (symbol of soul descending into body) than from the inaudible "hiss" of the snake. For, again coincidental as it may seem, the creative fire was by the ancients called the "serpent fire," expressly by the Egyptians the great uraeus snake, "a serpent of fire." Let it be noted also with regard to the shin, that when a dot—likely acting deputy for the YOD~is placed above the right side of the letter, it is pronounced as SH; but when the dot comes above the left side, it has only the sound of S. This change of position of the dot actually changes the name of the letter: for when it is above the left side, the name is not shin, but sin.

Doubtless a thunder of protest and a charge of scholarly chicanery would greet our intimation that this left-handed name of the great divine letter is the origin and covertly carries the significance of the theological word sin. What can be adduced in some support of the suggestion is not without considerable force on that side. There is the Bible phrase, "the wilderness of Sin," which is the same as the "wilderness of Sin-ai," and the "mount of the earth," i.e., the earth itself, as that celestial mount on which every transaction of the business of human divinization takes place. A salient feature of the ancient science of truth representation was the designation of things spiritual and divine as allocated to the right side of life and things mundane and physical as of the left side. Good lay on the right hand, evil on the left. Esotericism has always spoken of the right and the left-hand path.

Such books as the Zohar and other haggadic works of the early Jewish allegorists prominently use this figurism. To go left, to stand on the left, was to "miss the mark" of good and truth and right. The Greek word for to sin is precisely this: hamartano, "to miss the mark." The sharp distinction between the two directions has always. appeared even in language with a moral connotation. The Latin word for right hand is dexter, from which we get dexterous; the French is droit, from which comes adroit. For left hand the Latin has our word sinister; the French has gauche, from which comes our gawky. Things on the right were favorable, propitious; on the left were sinister, illomened. And as St. Paul's Epistles (mainly Romans 7) so pointedly reveal, earth was that mount on which the divine soul, sinless in its celestial habitation, came under the dominion of sin. "Know ye not, my brethren," asks the Apostle, "how that a man is under the law (of sin and death) only as long as he liveth?"-that is, while he is here on earth. He implies that there is no sin in heaven, for he clearly states that "sin sprang to life" when the soul obeys the "command" to incarnate. Sin can touch the soul only from the side of body, and, he says, the soul goes "dead" under its power while here on earth until its resurrection "from the dead" in the course of evolution of spirit back to its divine condition. So that the earth is that "Mount of Sin," that "Mount Sin-ai" of the Scriptures. But the Old Testament contains an allegory—for the story is preposterous as history—which shows the ancient writers of sacred ideological constructions using the shin-sin difference to point the moral that the soul that can pronounce the full SH sound of the letter has taken the right path and completed its evolution to divinity; while the one that can enunciate only the S sound has taken the left-hand path to "sin" and must return to earth, the land of "death" for further schooling in life. The guards at the Jordan fords were instructed to subject the Ephraimites on the east side of Jordan who wished to cross to enter the Holy Land (not of Judea, but of spiritual consciousness) to a simple test: require each man who crosses to pronounce the key word Shibboleth. But, says the story, in every case "he said Sibboleth. " The direful result was that forty-two thousand Ephraimites who could not convert the S indicating sin into the divine SH were put to the sword on one day. They were still on the left-hand path of sin, not yet ready to "cross the river" into the land of spiritual blessedness. It seems worthy of remark that not in twenty centuries has the easy esoteric unraveling of this simple and evident cryptogram come through to the intelligence of any scholar. How a Hebrew exegetist could long miss it is not comprehensible.

 Furthermore, how it could have been mistaken for history, for an actual event, is still far more incomprehensible. Yet Fundamentalists still claim that it "happened." If you assert that "history" was only a few thousand years ago a run of miracles, of course it neither needs nor can have an explanation. One is just to gape in awe at the Lord's wondrous doings and be sanctified of soul,-if stultified of mind. If the S and SH sounds carried the intimation of fire plunging into water, a special use of these letters in the old Egyptian hieroglyphic language seems to fall into conformity with the same idea. The S (SH) was consistently prefixed to verbs to express the idea of setting off the action which the verb indicated, to give the action its initial push, or s-tart, as it were.

The likelihood of the origin of this usage from the basic fire-going-into-water thesis will not so hastily be scouted if it is reflected that in the creation no real beginning in the visible worlds can have been made until the fire of spirit potency has radiated forth from the divine thought and impregnated the sea of matter (water.) The visible and audible work of creation starts only when the two nodes of being approach each other and establish tensional relation between themselves. As many a scientific speculator has predicted, the early stages of earth's formation brought together the chemical elements of fiery gases and humid vapors, the precipitates from the mixture finally forming the first earthly and mineral substances. Those early periods might, in the Egyptian sense, be termed the hissing, or S (SH) stage of planetary evolution. An example of the inceptive force of the S in the hieroglyphics is seen in the Egyptian word MNKH (MeNKH), which as adjective means firm, stable. But, made into a verb, it becomes SMNKH (SMeNKH), meaning to make firm, stabilize, establish. It is also likely that in this word MeNKH we have another prime example of the M-N reference. In relation to its meaning of firmness and stability, it is to be recalled that a passage from the Egyptian Book of the Dead described this world of life on earth as "the place of establishing forever." Also in the M-N connection it is highly significant that the Egyptian name for this lower region, the "underworld" or "nether earth" of their system, was Amenta, composed of the name of the God Amen and ta, meaning earth. Also significant is the name of this god, made up of the A and the M and N, for he was called "the god in hiding," and his hieroglyph is a god seated under a canopy.

Obviously he then is the personification of the divine nature hidden under the canopy of our mortal flesh. All this should be a specific guiding datum for philosophical science, inasmuch as orthodox theology has loaded the evolutionary marshland, or Reed Sea, of the earthy-watery human body with heavy contumely as the place where only fleeting ephemeral influences affect, if not afflict, the soul with evil. That it is, on the contrary, the place where the soul establishes forever its grounding in fundamental realities, is a tenet of the sacred and secret wisdom of the Egyptian sages which must be made one of the chief stones in the new temple of rational religion now in process of building. The S prefixed to MNKH adds the starting forces that brings the firm establishing to actuality, that sets it to work. It is hardly unlikely that the very long run of English verbs which begin with S (or SH) carry this inceptive or initiating force of the letter though speculation of this sort can not be asserted with too much certainty—in such words as start, step, slide, shake, skip, skate, slip, sink, stir, sneak.

 smite, spur, shout, scream, stamp, stand, spit, slap, shoot, speak, sprint, spurn, scoff, slay, spill, sift and scores more. 37 Massey traces even the great name of mystery, the sphinx, from the ANKH stem, preceded by the demonstrative adjective P {this, the, that) and the starting S, thus: S-P-ANKH. Massey was well versed in the abstrusities of the hieroglyphics and his surmise on this is as good as that of others. The word thus composed would mean "the beginning of the process of linking spirit and matter," which indeed is the sphinx-riddle of the creation. The sphinx image does conjoin the head of man, spirit, with the body of the animal, lion, representing matter. It is precisely such values and realities that the sages of antiquity dealt with and in precisely this manner of subtle indirection. When will modern scholarship come to terms with this recognition! If sphinx derives from the ANKH symbol, it is not at all unlikely that the other great emblem suggestive of the spirit involved in matter, the wondrous "bird of life," the phoenix, stems from it likewise. It was also named the bennu, the spirit energy that goes from B, the fiery start, down into water, N, which is also probably the make-up of the Hebrew word for son, which is ben. Another name of the fabled bird was nycticorax. Corax is raven in Greek, which, from it black color, is often called the "bird of night," symbolizing the soul flying down into the dark night of imprisonment in earthly bodies; and nycti stems from the Greek nux {nyx}, meaning night. The mythic phoenix was pictured as migrating north and returning south (to Egypt), where it renewed its life in periodic rhythm. And "Egypt" is symbolically the earth. Can there be doubt that the fabled migratory fowl is just the divine soul of life that commutes regularly between heaven and earth, pictured as a bird because it can build a nest on the ground, but equally well rise into the heavens of consciousness? It would be highly revealing to recapitulate some of the, at times, astonishing formulations which the ancient Hebrews discovered as fortuitous or designed constructions in their interpretative methodology that was elementary to their so-called science of Gematria.

This was based on the equation of number value of the words with the meanings expressed in the text. The number forms were held to "geometrize," so to say, the meanings. As a physical object or phenomenon can configure a meaning structure so can number values and relations. This "science" was carried to 38 lengths that have ever seemed to overrun the bounds of rational sense, and the method has been held in disdain as fantastic jugglery since the days of its esoteric vogue. Yet it would seem to be grounded on legitimate premises and to be subject to criticism only in its unwarranted extravagances. One senses this in reading the Zohar, for instance.

Somewhat in the spirit of the Gematria modus it may be profitable to look at several word and letter combinations in the Hebrew. To condense in a sentence what would take ten pages to elucidate in full, it is notable that beside the number of central and basic significance in this systematization, seven, perhaps the one most prominent in the sacred numerology was six. If seven was the number rounding out the cycles, six was the one that completed the physical evolution of the life-forms of any cycle. The progress achieved in the first six sub-cycles was necessary preparation for the channeling down of the spiritual grade in the seventh and climactic sub- cycle. We find the deeply esoteric Jewish philosopher Philo in the first century A.D. giving expression to the importance of the number six in several statements. One runs: "The world was created according to the perfect nature of the number six." And again he asks who can fittingly celebrate the divine majesty of this number. He says also that the sixth day of creation was the "festal day of all the earth." The creation was to work at physical labor for six days and rest in spiritual delight on the seventh. Man, made in the image and likeness of the cosmic creation, is likewise to work only six days in the analogical cycle of seven days. Therefore the number six, hardly less than the number seven, furnishes the basic clue to the meaning-value of many words. As six stages finished the physical form of creation in any cycle, it would seem likely that the Gematria plan would have used the final letter or letters of the alphabet to construct the words carrying the value of six. We are not disappointed in our gematric expectations here, for the last three letters of the Hebrew alphabet are R, S (SH) and TH, and six is written variously shesh, shisah, sheth and sixth is shishi. It is likely that if records were available we should find that the last son of Adam in the Genesis had been traditionally regarded as the sixth, for his name is Seth or Sheth.

But the Hebrew Bible's very first word opens up a veritable mine of speculative possibilities of this sort. That first word, translated "in the beginning," is in Hebrew B'RASHITH. It 39 was either constructed with amazing ingenuity to express a remarkable cosmographic conception or chanced to do just that by sheer coincidence. The reader must first be reminded that in the ancient manuscripts of the Biblical books the words were not separated and there were no vowels! It is therefore permissible to separate the words in different ways and in doing so some curious new readings come out as possibilities. The initial B is a preposition meaning "in" and can be prefixed to any noun or participial verb. RASH means head, so that B'RASH would mean "in the head," "in his (God's) head," as the place where God "created the heaven and the earth." Oddly enough it is precisely in God's head that the creation started, as there were formed the archetypal ideas over the pattern of which he shaped the creation. If B'RASHITH might be considered the overlapped form of B'RASH-SHITH, it would read "in the head of the six" or "of the sixth," and again it can be said (and the Zohar expressly does say it) that the creation, emanating out of God's head, came to a head in the sixth formative impulsion. Then B'RASHITH is followed by the verb BARA, "he created." If we take the B'RA for BARA (the vowels being wholly conjectural and indeterminable), BARASHITH itself would read "he created six, or the sixth." The Zohar gives this as a reading alternative. And it does in fact look as if this first Hebrew word was designedly made up of the first letter with which the creation truly begins, B, to indicate the beginning of the process, and the last three letters, R, SH and TH, to spell out, as it were, a cosmic evolution running clear through from beginning to end and so inscribed in the alphabet. The use of all three final letters would appear to indicate that the creative process brought out the result of the operation of the original unit divine mind manifesting in its triple aspects of spirit-soulmind. The SH itself carries this triplicity, we have seen, in its three YODS. So that in its full esoteric sweep of meaning this first Bible word B'RASHITH would condense a far more comprehensive significance than its conventional translation would show. It would really read: "From the beginning in his head God unfolded from his triple powers of mind the heavens and the earth in six creative stages." This must stand as most likely the first full esoteric translation of the first Bible verse. The Hebrew words for water and heaven will lucidly illustrate the water- value of M and the firevalue of SH. Water is MAYIM, the M conspicuously predominating. As the Y is another form of the fiery I, MAY (MAI) would read as the M-water expression of the I-fire power.

Esoterically the universe can be thought of in just those terms. Now, most appropriately, the word for heaven is this same water-word, MAYIM, preceded by the SH of fire, SH'MAYIM. Earth is the home or world of water; heaven is the home of water generated by fire,-the lightning; or water as invisible vapor, or water proceeding out of the empyrean, or realm of potential fire. Jesus says that he beheld Satan as lightning, or fire, falling from heaven, and that he himself came "to send fire on the earth in the sight of men." The Greeks said that the gods "distribute the divine fire" among men, a portion of soul-fire to each. Genesis tells us that God first created the two firmaments in the midst of the waters, the firmament above and the firmament below, the MAYIM and the SH'MAYIM, the water and the fire- water. Such a word as YOM, for day, seems to reveal semantic formation. The time- words, of whatever period, age, aeon, cycle, year, month, week, day, hour, are used very definitely to indicate no actual time-periods, but whole cycles as a concept, not a specific duration. A cycle is a year, a day, a week, a month. The world was created in six "days." The Israelites (again not the historical Hebrews) marched in the Sinai desert "forty days, for every day a year," says the text. So YOM (lOM) is the "day" of creation. It would be the period in which life proceeds from start at A (B) to deploy the creative fire-power, I (Y), into manifestation at M (N). This "day" would last from I (Y) to M, making its name YOM. As the action between A, or I (Y), and M (N) represents the process of life's coming to be, or becoming, it seems almost as if we find it saying I A M. Is it strange that the Latin word for now is lAM? It is as if life were saying "I am in existence in the eternal NOW." If one were to say "I am" in English and now in Latin, it would be / am iam. Coincidence it is, no doubt, but both forms must be composed of the same primal letter elements. To say "I am" in German gives interesting results also. It is Ich bin. The Ich is the I heavily aspirated. In some parts of Germany the Ich is pronounced as Ish. This equates the Hebrew word for man, uniting the primal unitary I-fire-power with the triple manifestation of that power that the SH represents; and this is precisely what man does. In man the divine trinity comes to 41 manifestation. But the German, instead of using the pre-creative A and the matter-terminal M to say "am," says it with the actual beginning letter B and the other matter-terminal, N, with the I between them (as it does stand between them in the alphabet), giving BIN, Ich bin. It is not to be forgotten that LOVE was one of the three elements in the great ANKH symbol, along with LIFE and TIE. Now it is in the descent of soul fire from A (B) to M and back to the final letter (in Greek it is O) that the two poles of being generate the power of divine LOVE. Is it not a bit surprising, then, that to say in Latin "I love" is to say AMO? The significance of the Hebrew word for "the oil of anointing," SHeMeN, has already been mentioned. Since this divine oil that, so to say, is destined to set the head of man on fire with the divine unction, manifests in man in its triple spirit-soul-mind divisions, it must be recognized as of great significance that repeatedly the Old Testament instructs that the sacrificial cakes are to be compounded of fine flour mixed with three measures of oil. The three divine flames that are to deify man are to be fed by the "oil" compressed out of the wine-press or olive-press of our conscious earthly experience. It would be gratuitous to assert that the Hebrew shemen, oil, derived from the earlier Egyptian word smen. This was an incense spoken of in the Ritual for the dead, those "dead," however, being the souls incarnated in bodies on earth, and not the "shades" of deceased mortals. The word must therefore refer to an element in the human constitution, not of course, to be taken as an actual physical substance burning at funerals. In this connection it can be speculated whether the Geth- of Gethsemane is not a variant of Beth as in Bethel, Bethany, Bethlehem, meaning house. If so, the word Gethsemane would mean the house in which Kfe burns its smenincense to divinize its child, man; that "house" being man's physical body, the beth or home of souls on earth. It was in Gethsemane that the Christos wrestled in the living agony that caused "him" to sweat, as it were, great drops of blood. Several of the prime Egyptian mythic legends of the creation of mankind by the gods represent the deity as exuding drops of his blood seminally upon the earth, from which sprang two characters, male and female, that equate Adam and Eve in the Genesis allegory. Sem- inal creative blood essence is more than a few times poetized as sweat. 42 All this is of epochal importance as demonstrating that the bloody sweat of Jesus in Gethsemane is a watered- down rescript of one of the old Egyptian mythic constructions. It must strike any person of open mind how marvelously these words articulate in all these constructions with perfect naturalness and semantic felicity. The Scriptures have remained for centuries both a perplexing riddle and a derationalizing influence simply because the abstruse and recondite relevance of these symbolic terms has never hitherto been explored. The study could be pursued to the dimensions of a major work. Enough has been given to answer the purposes of an introductory treatise that has been undertaken at the urgent behest of many who heard the exposition in lecture form. By way of epilogue and summary it will be well to end with the analysis of another pivotal Hebrew word of only two (Hebrew) letters, as it will provide virtually irrefutable certification of the main theses of this essay: the descent of spirit-fire into matter-water at the middle or nadir point of the alphabet, M-N, and its return. That little word is in Hebrew HAG (CHAG), base of the Mohammedan words haj, hajj, hegira. It is given in lexicons as meaning feast, festal day, festival, holy day {holiday); also as pilgrimage, journey, flight. The Hebrews themselves seem to have little apprehension of its true significance, even on its exoteric side. What it connotes in its esoteric reference has never yet been given out. It is virtually the cryptic key to the Scriptures, the definite key to the chiasmus construction of much of the material in the Scriptures, in which verses or portions of chapters are arranged in the form of a succession of four separate statements made successively in a line outward, so to say, as A, B, C, D and then a return back over the same first three, C, B, A, giving a seven-form structure. A, B, C, D, C, B, A. It seems to put the seven-stage structure in the form of an outgoing journey or pilgrimage, HAG, of three and a half steps or stages, and a return over the same three and a half, the turn to return {Sinai by Egyptian derivation) being made at the middle point of the fourth, or D, stage. To this structure the name chiasmus has been given, from the form of the Greek letter chi (much like our X), the two upper arms of which pictorialize a descent and return. The HAG ordained by the Lord for Israelite observance in Leviticus reproduces the framework of this same design, though here in the form or terms of a feast or festival ceremonial. But deeper research reveals that it was to be carried out in the form of an actual pilgrimage, setting out from home, journeying outward for three and a half days, crossing a river or water boundary between two kingdoms, (and always crossing at that point,) and then the return. It was to be an actual march out, an exodus of three and a half days, and the nostos, or return journey of equal length. The tradition of its meaning, preserved better in Mohammedan ideology than in Christian or Hebrew, was the origin of the Islamic pilgrimage, the great hegira to Mecca; for that matter the origin of all religious pilgrimaging. When we turn to the Scriptural Book of Revelation-and other places~we are there faced with the recurrence of this specific number, three and onehalf (the half of seven!), three times in the eleventh and twelfth chapters of the last book in the Bible. This book, has twenty-two chapters, and, whether it be by chance or by design of ancient structurebuilders of archaic literature, the eleventh and twelfth chapters stand at the place in the book corresponding to where M and N stand in the alphabet,-the middle or turning point. This would seem to indicate that the entire book of twenty-two chapters was arranged with the intent to reproduce the chiasmus structure. That is, at the three-and-ahalf point in the book the number three and a half is introduced three times! It seems so clear as to be beyond cavil that this definite form was used in symbolism to dramatize the outgoing or descent of the soul into incarnation through three and a half root stages of matter, from ethereal to solid, its experience there in a body of (seven-eighths) water, and its evolutionary return through the same three and a half levels, reaping on its return its harvest of rich experience. Yet this, the open sesame to all the baffling mystery of Holy Writ, has eluded the sagacity of the Scriptural pundits for centuries. Most lucidly it allegorizes the soul's pilgrimage out or down to body, and its return. Most astonishing is the item that at the outward terminus of the three and a half "days" journey was a river or water body on the boundary between two kingdoms. This the soul had to cross to begin its return. If sufficient poetic imagination is used to see that this Red Sea—Jordan River—Styx River of the allegories is actually the red blood of our human bodies, the Scriptures begin at once to become like an opaque glass suddenly made transparent.

# XXXI

❦

# Symbolism, the Universal Language

A SYMBOL is a form designed to portray some abstract quality. A symbol must convey an impression; it must cause the mind to see something which, though not actually in the symbol itself, is suggested by the symbol. Through the familiar is thus shadowed forth the unfamiliar; through the commonplace that which is not commonplace is made evident.

Symbols are forms, but the principles for which they stand so transcend the boundaries of form that they can only be sensed by reading into the symbol certain abstract elements, or by grasping with internal comprehension that greater profundity which the symbol does not contain but whose existence it intimates. Symbols are also employed to epitomize. A whole universe may be summarized in a single star, and vast issues by being reduced to their simple elements may be rendered intelligible. By clothing the unfamiliar in terms of the familiar the mind is enabled to grasp with a certain measure of accuracy the significance of the unknown.

We must re-emphasize the point stressed in our opening chapter; namely, that as symbols increase in complexity they decrease in power. Thus the simple figures set forth immensities; the compound figures parvitudes. Increasing definition causes qualities to verge toward form; hence the more intricate the figure the more it is concerned with particulars and the na rower becomes the scope of its symbolism. One of the true purposes of symbols is to preserve ideas in an indefinite state so that their lucidity shall not be obscured by unnecessary form involvement. Between symbolism and caricature there is a slight fundamental difference. As a personality may often be most truthfully depicted by the exaggeration of certain characteristics, so symbols may convey an adequate likeness of a quality and still in no appreciable way resemble the quality.

In the last analysis, man is not simply a body but rather a bundle of characteristics which confer upon his objective nature a certain temperament or individuality. By deftly accentuating the idiosyncrasies of character with a few heartless lines, the caricaturist exposes the deformities of rationality and thus portrays the man as he really is. The art of caricatpre follows certain cardinal principles in recognition of the impressions innate in forms and orders. Breadth, for example, is always associated with optimism, length with pessimism. Hence to broaden the head gives the impression of mental sufficiency, or broadmindedness; to broaden the body suggests a certain substantiality. To narrow the head causes the impression of intolerance, or narrowness of outlook; to lengthen the body oppresses the mind with a feeling of melancholy. Angles convey the impression of strength; curves of beauty. Harmonious combination of angles and curves invoke concord; inharmonious combinations produce discord. Definite reactions are thus produced by simple lines or combinations of lines. Colors and sounds also possess similar powers of mental and emotional stimulation.

Consciously or unconsciously, the shape and arrangement of bodies with which we come in close contact thus profoundly influence our dispositions. Definite mental reactions are caused by contemplation of the symmetrical Pythagorean solids, for all natural bodies contain a force generated by their own organization which leaves its subtle record on the inner sensibilities of man. By accentuating this force according to a definite procedure certain mental attitudes can be stimulated, and in recognition of this principle the Mysteries recommend that their initiates meditate upon certain emblems or figures prepared with this end in view. In common with the laws of caricature, symbolism secures emphasis by distortion, harmony by conventionalization, and force by simplicity. In great measure, art is the process of elimination. Symbolism reveals the necessary by eliminating the unnecessary, and emphasizes the real by disregarding the superficial which obscures the real. In this respect symbolism verges toward the diagrammatic, for through diagrams processes are made evident. Phenomenon when stripped of its outer part reveals the laws by which it exists and manifests. Being chiefly concerned with those few primary principles which are the basis of infinite diversity, philosophy finds in symbolism not only a language singularly qualified to disseminate fundamental premises, but a method whereby universal ideas are communicated without passing them through the sphere of particulars. Symbolism thus embodies most fully the requisites of the perfect medium of education. Every symbol is a definite stimulus to the mind, and has the delightful faculty of reflecting the moods of the mind attempting to analyze its parts. In other words, a symbol always means what we think it means. Dealing with incorporeal substance, it takes on, chamcleonlike, the interpretive attitudes of its interpreter. Through the symbols the individual thus discovers not what symbols mean but rather what he knows himself. In the effort to understand what the first symbolist concealed under his figures, the resources of the mind are stimulated to reveal their own fecundity. Thus emblematic figures and fables draw out from the individual analyzing them the sum and substance of his own understanding. By studying symbols men learn about themselves; for they read into the figures their own hopes and aspirations, their own concepts of universal order, and their own understanding of divine agency. To some degree is thus explained the diversity of codes by which the affairs of men are regulated. Life itself is a symbol, and each must interpret it according to the convictions of his own soul. As we look about we see a universe which, whether we know it or not, is simply our inner convictions reflected back to us from the polished surface of nature.

In Lazarus Laughed , Eugene O'Neill causes his hero to thus taunt Gaius Caligula, the heir of Tiberius Caesar: "But what do you matter, O Deathly-Important One? Put yourself that question—as a jester! Are you a speck of dust danced in the wind? Then laugh, dancing! Laugh yes to your insignificance I Thereby will be born your new greatness! * * # Tragic is the plight of the tragedian whose only audience is himself! Life is for each man a solitary cell whose walls are mirrors. Terrified is Caligula by the faces he makes! But I tell you to laugh in the mirror, that seeing your life gay, you may begin to live as a guest, and not as a condemned one!"

The nonphilosophic suffer from a disease which may best be termed superficiality, Man's thinking ever fails because of its shallowness. He often mistakes breadth for depth, believing that with but a hasty scrutiny he can become familiar with any object. Superficiality generally springs from indifference, and necessarily produces mediocrity. Our interests ever lie with the familiar, and for the unfamiliar we have no emotion save indifference. By stimulating interest, philosophy causes man to regard an ever-widening circle of incident as a proper field for his speculation. Thus the man, formerly oblivious to the wonders of the* universe about him, suddenly comes to realize their existence, and with growing enthusiasm applies himself to the garnering of knowledge. The study of symbolism causes the mind to develop what may be defined as philosophic suspicion. Instead of accepting things at their face value, the symbolist searches for their hidden motives—those invisible agencies which are the animate causes of apparently inanimate objects. When the mind comes instinctively to regard forms as the outer garments of realities, great strides have been taken in the rationalization of the entire nature.

Man begins to know as soon as he divests himself of the illusion that the universe is material and matter the divine reality. From this realization it is but a step to the comprehension that truth does not exist in matter but must be sought for behind the veil of matter. The physical (or irrational) mind is incapable of comprehending a single absolute fact; for abiding in the sphere of relative conclusions it necessarily lacks the accuracy of exact procedure. Symbolism discloses the relationship of an intangible agent to its tangible subject; it renders conceivable that interval between the invisible—which is the fact—and the visible—which is the fancy. Even a photograph is fanciful and misleading when compared to a cleverly drawn caricature; for while the caricature may but slightly resemble the physical appearance it is still more discerning than the camera's eye. Our physical personalities thus reveal us as we seem to be, but our intangible individualities continually reveal us as we are. Unfortunately for others, but comfortable for ourselves, the number able to read the intangible characteristics are few; otherwise our mortification would overwhelm us.

Yet, in reality, our truest friend is the one who points out to us that which it is so difficult for us to estimate for ourselves— namely, the quality and compatibility of our intangible parts. Symbolism should be employed throughout the process of education, for by it two definite ends are attainable. First, the student will instinctively reveal to the teacher the constitution of his reasoning part by the interpretation he places upon the symbols; second, the student will be stimulated to originality and thereby preserve the peculiar technique of his own rational processes. The death of originality is the death of genius. Symbolism encourages originality, and hence is productive of genius. Symbols can be devised to induce almost any desired phase of thought or emotion. By the use of emblematic figures alone, abnormality can be corrected and subnormality raised to a normal state. Paracelsus discovered that words written upon parchment when held up before animals produce as definite results as though the words were spoken, although it is evident that the animal cannot read. Combinations of letters, magical symbols, and curious figures, radiate definite impressions, and from the realization of this fact must ultimately emerge a new form of corrective therapy in which the medicine will be administered through the channel of sight.

The eyes are peculiarly responsive and the process of visualization already borders upon the psychic, for the impressions transmitted by the eyes to the brain are exceedingly subtle and powerful beyond imagination. The reactions set up through the sight of definite forms or patterns have not yet been

thoroughly catalogued. When this work is finished we will understand far more intelligently the motives producing joy and sorrow, sickness and health, vice and virtue. The environment contacted by the individual through the medium of the eyes molds him profoundly, and even his status in the world itself is a key to the temperaments that surge within his breast.

In his General Introduction to Psychoanalysis, Freud attempts to relate certain primitive motives of the soul with dreams, in this way disclosing a subconscious faculty of association in the human mind by which external objects, through either appearance or use, become media for the expression of psychic impulses. Freud is dealing with what Plato would call the animal soul —that part of the psychic nature which has assumed the idea of generation and which constitutes the ceaseless urge toward the establishment of forms. Obsessed with the idea of polarity, the generating soul causes to flow from itself those impulses which Freud analyzes under the general subject of sex psychology. He maintains that the peculiar soul power which manifests while the functioning organism is asleep is concerned primarily with the principles of generation, and the sleep symbols are largely of a phallic nature. This is incontestible evidence that the earliest religions of mankind were priapic cults and based upon the generating urge of the soul. Clothing itself in appropriate forms, this impulse resulted in strange fables and figures which are now almost dissociated from the primary impulses that inspired them. Though having but few interests, the animal soul often employs a diversity of symbols to signify its attitudes. Thousands of emblems and figures are used to represent a single idea. The animal soul is interested in neither religion nor philosophy, and our mental concepts are its playthings. The animal soul is primarily concerned with the laws of attraction and reproduction; its duty is to perpetuate the species and it knows no ethics beyond this limited field.

Freud infers that dream symbols can be reduced to a very simple alphabet of symbolism. Clothing its urges in the familiar, the soul creates its alphabet during physical infancy and childhood and retains it throughout life. As humanity thus preserves in its religion and philosophy the simple elements which dominated its attitudes during the most primitive

periods, so the adult man or woman clothes these soul impulses in those figures and similes which were impressed upon the outer nature during adolescence. It is comparatively easy to understand how most symbols come to have a phallic import. All forms are generations, and all generations are emblematic of the processes by which they themselves came into being.

To the individual who functions in the animal nature—that is, where the rational soul has not disengaged itself from the involvements of the corporeal senses—there is no sphere of interpretation above that of generation. To those who by the disciplines and procedures of the higher life have transmuted or regenerated their inferior natures, a loftier sphere of interpretation is rendered apprehensible. Transcending the idea of generation, the philosopher discovers in the symbol a meaning more exalted than that concerned with reproductive processes. Not only is there the animal soul which clings tenaciously to form, but there is also the divine (rational) soul which verges ever toward Reality. Above that part which conceives generation to be the supreme function there is that which contemplates the deathlessness and permanence of the Supreme Good, realizing that Divinity is ungenerate and transcends in every respect the limitations of mortal procedure.

Symbols consequently change their meanings according to the level of intelligence upon which their interpreter functions. The purpose of symbols is to uncover the limitations of mortal consciousness by continually emphasizing the insufficiency of the interpretations placed upon them. Confronted by a symbol, every man recognizes the uncertainties of his own nature. Being never sure that he is correct in his interpretation he is made to realize his heritage in that common uncertainty shared by all ages and all men. The insufficiency of modern so-called knowledge is evident the moment the mind is invited to reflect upon problems involving certitudes. Thus faced, the intellect hesitates and becomes confused. Our thinking is sufficient until it becomes necessary to trust ourselves to its mercy, when it retires abashed, informing us unmistakably of its incapacity. The paradox of knowledge is that knowledge does not exist, for we claim already that for which in reality we are searching. Modern knowledge is not a discovery of facts but the effort to discover facts, and there are great moments when the truth of this apparent contradiction is brought home to us.

There is a popular fallacy that we grow by change. Like the ironic method described and employed by Socrates, change is inseparable from the elements of pain and sorrow. We advance but slowly when every new discovery must contradict those gone before; when every new philosopher must give the lie to his predecessors and every new order depends for its success upon the destruction of previous orders. A little apple tree does not change into a lemon tree while in the process of becoming a big apple tree, nor does truth change its identity in the process of being understood. Every great mind evolves by a sequential process; it does not tear down previous conclusions to make room for new. A growing tree increases from a single shoot to a miracle of branches and foliage, yet nowhere is there any inconsistency or contradiction in the process. The trunk is not destroyed that a new branch may come forth, nor is the tree uprooted to make room for its own fruit. Each manifestation depends upon that which preceded it, and in turn finds its consummation in that which issues from it. From the first quickening of its seed the tree moves inevitably toward a single end; at every step of the way its procedures complement each other and unite in the realization of that end. This perfect co-operation of parts results not only in the tree maintaining its homogeneity and attaining its end with the least expenditure of energy and time, but demonstrates the exactness of the power that willed it into being. Never will the world think well until men reason as trees grow— causing to issue from the single trunk of rational certainty the foliage of thoughts which, clustered symmetrically about their center, impart grace and dignity to the whole.

In their ignorance men make laws, only later to find them faulty. Then, lest their infractions of these laws seem too flagrant, they amend their former errors with fresh errors in the effort to render their own conceits endurable. The various schisms in the body of religion seek to mollify their differences by resorting to condescension or modification. Their compromises, however, are a glaring confession that neither possesses enough of fact to insure survival. So age after age man—who according to the pagan astrologers was fashioned under the influences of Cancer—still demonstrates his kinship to the crab by making most of his progress in a backward fashion.

It is more than a seven days' wonder that institutions of importance have to be saved from extinction by periodic renovation, or have their authority curbed lest their intolerance overshadow and endanger personal or national liberties. Philosophy declares that the first step in the development of rational powers is to establish them upon an immovable foundation, so that the mind in its unfoldment will not be forced periodically to overthrow previous attitudes, but continually to supplement and justify them. To realize this ideal it is necessary that the first postulations of the intellect shall be vast enough or sufficient in scope so that dl subsequent thinking will not be forced to exceed the boundaries of these first assumptions . Men waste a lifetime devising new methods of thought, only to realize at the end that they have outgrown their own premises; that their building is top-heavy; and that in the architectonics of intellect their edifice of theories is grotesque and inharmonious. As all the agencies of the tree conspire to consummate its purpose—namely, fruitage—so all the agencies of thought conspire to produce the fruitage of the mind. Lacking the wisdom of the tree man all too often finds his roots and trunk structurally too insecure to bear the weight of the ripening fruit.

The eclectic spirit prevalent in this century is largely responsible for this condition. Men do not thinks their thoughts through. Viewing a fractional part of an idea, they are content with its apparent consistency, failing to realize that it may have no place at all in that greater picture composed of infinite ideas combined in most complex patterns. We do not apply Immanuel Kant's Critique by which he measured the justifiableness of assumptions. We might ask ourselves, "If the whole universe were run by the same principles as my own little notions, would the world still be sufficient to meet the needs of the vast order which it maintains; if my little whim were elevated to the dignity of a divine reality, would it serve all men; if my thoughts were laws, would there be justice in creation?" These are the questions which intrude their presence upon the mind seeking to think things through, often to their bitter end. It is not sufficient that an idea should tickle our sensibilities or give us a pleasant emotional thrill. It is necessary that the idea should stand the acid test of analysis. It must survive the heartless process of thinking through . We say "heartless," for few notions—except that they proceed from rationalities so noble that notions have become permissible to them—can survive even the first stages of analysis. Symbolism re-emphasizes the necessity of approaching every issue with an adequate philosophic background. Confront the untrained mind with some symbol or fable, and it will construct a confused and meaningless explanation, usually far more complex than the figure warrants, and as senseless as a macaw's chatter. Few of us have had the success of Samuel Johnson in protecting the intellect against the assaults of words. In the preface to his dictionary he writes: "I am nof yet so lost in lexicography, as to forget that words are the daughters of the earth, and that things are the sons of heaven." The superficial thinker reasons in terms of words alone; the profound thinker so venerates the meaning of words that he conserves his language. We must all realize that it is beyond man's province to comprehend one third of what he says and sacrilegious to talk much with little understanding. Whereas the mediocre intellect is capable of ministering to physical needs, it is decreed that in the more exalted realms of rationality the mediocre shall pass into the oblivion of the disqualified.

Man can never hope to escape the limitations of his own irrationality; whenever he attempts to transcend himself, his insufficiency blocks his way. The struggle must ever be to overcome insufficiency; to establish within the self an intellectual adequacy in which the mind acquires a competency for its problems. Symbolism stimulates the healthy mind that has been introduced to the disciplines of philosophy, but bewilders the unorganized thinker. No mind is really sufficient for its own needs until it has learned to act as a connective tissue between ideas. Isolated thoughts are comparatively valueless, for the probability of error is too imminent. An impractical thought, then, is one that can survive only in an isolated state; a practical thought one that survives repeated contact with competitive ideas. To study symbols is dangerous for the immature mind, for the practice will only compound absurdities and establish more firmly irrational habits of thought. Hence the ancient Mysteries circulated among the masses definite interpretations of their symbols and allegories, encouraging the untrained thinker to accept these expositions and wonder no more on the subject. Had this not been done a wild orgy of misinterpretation would have followed, and erroneous speculations without number would have found lodgement in minds incapable of recognizing and protecting themselves against these incongruities. Thus in symbolism the profound investigator will discover that the real is ever concealed beneath the superficial. He who is contented with the superficial will consequently never discover the real, and so from age to age the arcana of ancient philosophy have been preserved inviolate at the hands of the unprepared. These secrets are their own custodians, revealing themselves only to such as refuse to accept any substitute for truth, or any part of knowledge less than all. Two oft-repeated questions are, "Why is it so easy to deceive people in matters pertaining to religion or philosophy," and "Why are the best educated the most gullible?" The answer to the first is self-evident. Theology and philosophy are sciences dealing with intangibles. There is no criterion by which their integrity can be questioned or established save that of a rational mind qualified by its own integrity to weigh and pass judgment upon the elements involved. These divine sciences so completely transcend the limitations of the sense perceptions by which mortal concerns are estimated that every code of physical integrity is inapplicable to them. There is nothing tangible and evident with which to associate these abstruse verities, and the investigator must appoint himself their inquisitor. As all life's great realities exist in this intangible sphere—which we like to term the invisible or causal universe—the problems of existence can never be actually solved except by the exploring faculties of a rationalized intellect. The second question is based upon the unfortunate fact that education, while in some instances increasing the tolerant attitude, all too often fails to increase the integrity so that it can properly direct tolerance. The educated man is usually one who has been instructed in the enormity of his own ignorance, and is therefore inclined to believe that anything may be true. On the other hand, the uneducated man is generally very set in his opinions and hence difficult to convince even of demonstrable facts. A scientist is frequently a disillusioned man.

He has been undeceived as to the sufficiency of knowledge and is correspondingly gullible. Camille Flammarion declared that there was but one attitude of the mind more dangerous than that which accepted everything: namely, the attitude that accepted nothing. The materialist who understands practically nothing believes practically nothing. The ignorant must ultimately become his own executioner.

Thus the struggle for knowledge becomes identical with the struggle for survival; for only knowledge insures survival. We are as permanent as the realities that have come to be established in our own natures; we are as impermanent as the fancies that incline us one way or another, only to eventually leave us as ignorant as before. The rational faculties are man's sole hope of ultimate accomplishment, and this accomplishment is iden- tical with happiness; for the changes necessary to establish harmonious physical relationships must first descend from the rational sphere and come into physical manifestation through minds specially trained in philosophic procedure. Every child that is born is a potential instrument for the salvation of the world, and remains an unknown but all-powerful quantity until our physical cultural processes destroy those sensitive instruments of erudition by which the imperceptible verities of the rational sphere can be sensed. Humanity's most precious assets are those developing physical brains, which as focal centers of mental energy radiate thought throughout the substances of the inferior sphere. The answer to every problem, therefore, must be considered as existing in the rational sphere, awaiting that day when unfolding human brains shall be so disciplined in the procedures of rational thought as to become adequate vehicles for the manifestation of this superior knowledge in the physical world. Rendered prophetic by the luminosity of their inner natures, the sages of antiquity discoursed with rare acumen upon the fate of the sacred sciences at the hands of generations then unborn. In the Asclepian Dialogue is preserved a prophetic picture of the decadence of knowledge in baser ages to come.

In those days "no one shall look up to heaven. The religious man shall be accounted insane, the irreligious shall be thought wise, the furious brave, and the worst of men shall be considered a good man. For the soul, and all things about it, by which it is either naturally immortal, or conceives that it shall attain to immortality, conformably to what I have explained to you, shall not only be the subject of laughter, but shall be considered as vanity. Believe me, likewise, that a capital punishment shall be appointed for him who applies himself to the religion of intellect. New statutes and new laws shall be established, and nothing religious, or which is worthy of heaven or celestial concerns, shall be heard, or believed by the mind. There will be a lamentable departure of the Gods from men; noxious angels will alone remain, who, being mingled with human nature, will violently impel the miserable men [of that time] to war, to rapine, to fraud, and to everything contrary to the nature of the soul."

Much of this prophecy has already been verified, for during the Dark Ages capital punishment was meted out to those who dared apply themselves to the "religion of intellect." Philosophy was swept from the face of Christendom and the voices of the gods were drowned out by the hymns of the martyrs. Fleeing before theological fanaticism, the custodians of the arcana imperii took refuge in the Arabian desert, finding Islam more receptive to philosophic instruction. Accepting Greek philosophy as a sacred trust, the Sons of the Prophet, when carried into southern Europe on the high tides of their fortunes, established in Spain universities far excelling contemporary Christian institutions of learning. To the colleges of the Moors came scholars from every part of Europe, and the lips of men again taught the inspired doctrines of Plato and Aristotle.

Islam realized that the teachings of Plato and his illustrious disciple assisted man to liberate his soul from the entanglements of idolatry, for the four Caliphs had set for themselves the task of exterminating idolatry from the earth. Proclus declares that the philosophy of Plato was given to men for the benefit of their terrestrial souls; that philosophy might be authority instead of statutes, rationality instead of temples, understanding instead of sacred institutions, truth instead of mortal leaders of salvation, that the men who are now, as well as those who shall exist hereafter, might not wander about the earth destitute of intelligence.

The literalist is an inveterate profaner of the beautiful. His attitude is a supreme blasphemy, for his art is to limit all natures to the narrow confines of form. He sees nothing beyond an appearance, mistaking the outward show for the inner quality and the dimensional as the only certainty. Whereas the idealist ever strives to elevate man to the estate of gods, the literalist would drag the immortals from their Olympian heights and debase them with the similitude of man. The literalist emphasizes inconsequentials; to him every jot and tittle is a fetish. To the literalist, symbolism is inscrutable, for he is incapable of distinguishing between principle as an abstract reality and form as the transitory vehicle of that principle. Religious stagnation is the wayward child of literalism. As long as theology clings to the blasphemous idea that to think is to usurp a divine prerogative, theologians are restrained from reasoning on the logic of the law, and only the saints are accredited with sufficient sanctity to contemplate the sandal thongs of the Lord. Quaking under their cowls, the pious clergy read and reread the ominous lines from Revelation wherein it is written. "If any man shall add unto these things, God shall add unto him the plagues that are written in this book." Little wonder that the divine science of interpretation failed amid such hostile environment; that symbols became fearful images of literal terrors and the gods came to have as many hairs in their beards as some inspired artisan might carve into their Carrara features.

Maimonides, the most learned of the Rabbins, who devoted a lifetime to contemplation of the Scriptures, writes thus of its hidden meanings and secret imports: "We should not take literally that which is written in the Book of the Creation [Genesis] nor entertain the same concepts of it as are common with the vulgar. If it were otherwise, our learned ancient sages would not have taken so much pains to conceal the sense, and to keep before the eyes of the uninstructed the veil of allegory which conceals the truths which it contains. Taken literally, the work contains the most extravagant and absurd ideas of the Deity. Whoever can guess at the true meaning should take care not to divulge it. This is a maxim inculcated by our wise men, especially in connection with the work of the six days. It is possible that by our own intelligence, or by the aid of others, some may guess the true meaning, in which case they should be silent respecting it; or, if they do speak of it, they should do so obscurely, as I myself do, leaving the rest to be guessed at by those who have sufficient ability to understand me."

While the literalist may believe he is defending the integrity of the gods, he is actually detracting from their magnificence by presuming them to be speakers of words when in reality they are disseminators of ideas. Origen asks: "What man of good sense will ever persuade himself that there has been a first, a second, and a third day and that these days have each of them had their morning and their evening, when there was as yet neither sun, nor moon, nor stars?" Even the great St. Augustine admitted the Scriptures to possess profound and unsuspected meanings, at the same time maintaining with characteristic inconsistency that both their literal and historical accuracy also should be affirmed. We shall yet realize that man cannot live by history alone, even though that history be declared sacrosanct. To studious Christian and pagan alike, symbolism becomes a philosophic stone whereby literal absurdities are transmuted into allegorical realities. While little minds may thus thread their way through religion, those of greater vision—recognizing in symbolism a golden key to the treasure house of the world's thought—studiously apply themselves to the principles according to which all fables, allegories, and emblematic figures are erected. Another phase of symbolism presents itself for consideration.

The literalities of one generation become the allegories of the next. The changing customs, the periodic redirectionalizing of interest, and the reinterpretation of the meanings of words and figures, make it most difficult for any generation to understand its forebears. Hence to interpret the ideals of one century in the terms of another is to lose a certain intangible atmosphere which cannot survive the vicissitudes of time.

Consequently, to secure an accurate translation of Greek philosophic writing does not necessarily imply that we possess the information embodied in those writings.

It has been said that no philosophy can survive translation, for no sacred teaching can ever be actually understood except by one able to transport himself into the locale and time in which the material was originally indited. Hence arose the practice of perpetuating the inner doctrines through oral tradition, for it was presumed that each generation would reclothe these basic ideas with proper vestments and thus preserve them free from distortion at the hands of time. To understand the Mysteries we must cease to live in America of the 20th century and assume the temperaments, attitudes, interests, and environments in which the Mysteries were first established. To understand Greek philosophy we must understand ancient Greece and its people. The secret teachings are always clothed in the terms of the familiar when revealed to the multitudes, and the familiar terms of yesterday are not the familiar terms of today. The same is true of the Bible. The archaic Hebrew of the pre-Christian period interpreted the ideals of an older people of whom not one true vestige now remains. The Pentateuch is the living remnant of a world long dead; of interests which have outlived their time; of attitudes archaic and ethics extinct.

If we would release the spirit of beauty locked within the ancient characters and make it serve this generation, we must divest it of its ancient robes and reclothe it in the familiar habiliments of today. With rare discrimination we must separate the principle from its form, the living from the dead, the eternal from the temporal. Only the symbolist has developed that fine faculty of dividing the relevant from the irrelevant and prudently preserving that which is usable. As the archeologist sifting the ashes of dead civilization recovers therefrom priceless evidence of things no longer evident, so the symbolist studiously examining the intellectual remains of vanished orders rescues from oblivion those fragments of rationality which will contribute to the right-thinking of the world. As the earth is built up of geologic strata—the rot of milleniums—so the body of world thought is composed of an infinite number of layers, in each of which may be seen the half-disintegrated remains of vast institutions and noble intellectual procedures. In things of the mind the past has not lived in vain. Those who live best today live by the world's first thoughts, and the foolish of today still commit the same grave errors that the first philosophers decried. There is no such thing as modernism in human thought, for minds have labored since the beginning and the world's first thinker reasoned out the same problems which the world's last sage must ponder. The future will

perpetuate the quest of the past, and .tomorrow is but the knowledge of today plus an added period for contemplation.

A few simple rules will be of value to those desirous of assuming the mantle of philosophy. There are many queer pockets in its ancient folds, and only when they are investigated in order will their contents prove of highest value. It has well been said that there are tricks in every trade. These tricks are a certain "knowing how" by which accomplishment is facilitated. In accordance with the ancient Pythagorean law it is first necessary to establish the triangle before the solution of any problem is possible. The science of symbolism is accordingly based upon a threefold premise. Once the mind is familiarized with this triangular foundation, integrity and industry will discover the correct solution.

First, every substance, object, element, and argent in the universe is capable of instructing man in. those phases of divine order which are involved in its own constitution. In other words, everything can teach us of itself, and as all natures differ from each other to greater or lesser degree, each performs a definite ministry of instruction. From an earnest consideration of their constitutions and procedures man is enabled to familiarize himself with those laws of being to which he himself is also subject.

Second, the more fully an individual is acquainted with the operations of the inferior universe, the better qualified he is to contemplate the constitution of the causal spheres. This is a development of the Hermetic axiom of analogy; namely, that the above is like the below and the below like the above. The knowledge of inferiors is necessary to the knowledge of superiors. The danger arising, however, from the analysis of inferiors is that the mind may form an attachment for them and thus be rendered incapable of turning from them to the consideration of superiors.

Third, all natures should be regarded as worthy of profound analysis, for the deadly enemy of all proficiency is a superficial attitude toward any phase of existence . The true source of man's education is not to be found in books, but lies in his observation of natural phenomena and his attempt to estimate its significance. Failure to regard any object as worthy of particular attention is to lose the opportunity to understand the superphysical function or characteristic which is the intangible but all-powerful cause of the object itself.

Symbolism, when thus regarded, is elevated to the dignity of a religion, or more correctly, it becomes the means to the end of religion. To the philosophic atheist symbolism occupies the middle ground between knowledge and ignorance, becoming the divine instructor through whom the mysteries of the inner spheres are made apparent to the outer sense perceptions.

Thus, instead of waiting for the heavens to open and permit an angelic visitant to deliver homilies from an ambo supported by some cumulus cloud, the symbolist liberates through rational procedure the ideas resident in form. These ideas thus freed preach their own silent but all-informative sermons. To the one capable of discerning God, Deity is omnipresent in His own handiworks. The philosopher is the continual recipient of divine revelation, and the gods are proximate indeed to that illumined sage who sees God in the fire and hears Him in the wind.

The Phrygian Dactyls (physicians by magic) employed symbols because of the remarkable therapeutic powers they possessed. The figures drawn upon parchment and papyrus, or carved into the forms of medallions and talismans, were applied to the diseased members or attached to the persons of the sick, and thus by necromantic means dislodged the evil agencies conspiring to drive the spirit from its infected nature. Paracelsus, who secured from the Arabians many secrets of pagan theurgy, describes in detail the remedial agencies reposing in the ancient metals, and their alloys, particularly electrum. Of the virtues of electrum (which he declared to be composed of the seven planetary metals) the great Swiss physician writes: "Vessels fashioned from electrum render their contents safe from poison and from sorcery, for this alloy has great sympathy for the human race. The ancients fashioned from this mystical substance rings, bracelets, medals, seals, figures, bowls, and mirrors, all possessing most wonderful virtues. A ring formed of electrum and worn upon the finger will cure lameness, paralysis, and the epilepsy. I have seen a ring of electrum put on the ring or heart finger of a person afflicted with a secret disease. The ring immediately began to sweat and became spotted and even went out of shape with sympathy for the sufferer."

Forms, declared the Mysteries, possess strange virtues, and the tracing of these forms intensifies these virtues and renders them potent ministrants to human ills. The Idaean fingers of the Samothracians and other curious effigies of human members were magnetized with medicinal virtues and possessed by a spirit whose strength was sufficient to avert plagues or pestilences and liberate the flesh from all manner of infirmity.

Not only was it essential that these devices be made out of the proper substances, but they must be fashioned into definite shapes commodious to the astral light which, flowing through the symbol, was conjured thereby to manifest as a preservative or curative agent. Manipulated by the hierophants—the Patars who received their wisdom "through a keyhole"—these models and figures became as though alive. They were charged as with an electric current, at times glowing or radiating showers of sparks and miniature lightning flashes. As forms are the projections of invisible forces, so their artificial construction invokes invisible natures adapted to their geometric patterns. These supermundanes ensoul the objects and lend their power to the magus whose knowledge is sufficient to control them.

This explains the strange phenomenon of the talking images, the vocal mechanisms of the ancients, the urns of prophecy, and the nature of oracles; for even openings in the earth, apertures in walls, and the concavities of vessels, became the abode of genii conformable to those capacities. Moving within their appointed vents and orifices, these spirits caused the phenomenon of winds and strange sounds in sealed amphorae and subterranean crypts. Such forces are too intangible, however, for mortal perception, unless by secret rituals the genii have been invested with a certain amount of terrestrial substance. We shall yet rediscover the secrets of the talking urns that spoke with the voice of ages and through whose lips issued the words of men long dead. By this the ancients did not infer that the dead spoke through these urns, but rather that the words spoken during the lifetime of these men had been preserved in the subtle ethers of cosmos and through specially patterned instruments could be rendered audible again after the lapse of centuries. Science, the necromancy of the 20th century, will yet accomplish by physical means that which the ancient hierophants performed by their rational knowledge of the inner construction of the universe.

Symbols are oracular forms—mysterious patterns creating vortices in the substances of the invisible world. They are centers of a mighty force, figures pregnant with an awful power which, when properly fashioned, loose fiery whirlwinds upon the earth. Pythagoras foretold impending disasters by hydromancy, for he possessed a brazen bowl which, when filled with water, became strangely agitated, the surface of the water being continually moved as though a spirit were breathing upon it. Gazing upon the agitated water the Samian

sage foretold by the ripples in the water things which were to come.

Pythagoras was also one of the "veiled" philosophers who revealed his instruction from behind a curtain, permitting only certain favored disciples to behold his face. Those desirous of receiving his words were instructed by an intermediary who stood without the door and heard the illumined discourses "through the crevices in the locks." Hence the thought of the "keyhole" philosophers or hierophants who, never beholding the immortals, were the doorkeepers of the arcanum arcanorum.

Of this order was the Apostle Peter whose name, PTR, was the common appellation bestowed upon the instructors in the sacred rites, who were indeed the "living rock" upon which the House of Wisdom was raised. Christianity, as we have it today is a philosophy revealed through a keyhole—a few mysterious words caught by an eavesdropper. This allusion, however, has a symbolic rather than a frivolous import. The eavesdropper was a privileged listener permitted to hear that which he could hear, for while he listened without "the banquet of the gods" was going on within. But only when the divinities shout most lustily do mortals catch even the faintest echo. Symbols are keyholes to doors in the walls of space, and through them man peers into Eternity. Only to a few, however, is the privilege given to take the gold or silver key of the Cabalistic light and with it draw back the bolts that hold securely the portals of the dotnus sancti spirit us. Symbolism, then, is the divine language, and its figures are a celestial alphabet by which those upon the seats of the mighty trace their will in the fabric of the worlds. Though the patterns be infinite and man finite, still in the marvelous pageantry of emblems and figures human creatures may behold the workings of their heavenly masters. The meditating seer beholds strange figures in the sky. There are also signs upon the earth as well as in the heavens, and he who can read them is lifted up and transported into this sphere of reality.

The Buddhist mendicant pays homage to the footprints of his Lord; the Egyptians caught upon stone with mallet and chisel the shadows of the gods; and the rational soul gazing out into a universe of images beholds, as it were, a mirage hovering above the expanse of the earth. In this dreamworld dwell the luminous rishis of the Brahman's contemplation; here in majestic file pass the mild-faced bodhisattvas in their pilgrimage through Eternity. Gazing downward from this mystery above, the symbolist sees faintly shadowed on the plains of earth this passing pageantry of supermundane things. To the discerning few the outlines of the gods may ever be traced in the flora and fauna of Nature. Hovering above terrestrial concerns, the divine orders are sensed by the inner perceptions and rendered knowable by the forms which perpetuate their impulses.

It is said that in ancient days God walked in the Garden, and the light that was with him illumined the parts thereof. Nor is Deity today any more distant than yesterday, for the Maker of things still blesses his creations with his proximity. The growing grain, the ripening fruit, the tender shoots rising from the dark brown mold, the soft-eyed kine grazing on the hillside, the laughter of men—all these bear evidence of the invisible but ever-present Maker. God is in his world, and although men cannot gaze into his face and live they may gaze upon his works, and if they look rightly shall receive life more abundantly. The world is a symbol of the permanence of God, life a symbol of the presence of God, and love a symbol of the understanding of God. To those who are able to sense the inner life of things and read into forms even a small part of that great agency which actually ensouls them, the all-sufficiency of Universal Good is all-sufficing.

Symbols are manifested of a mysterious covenant by which the orderliness and consistency of all natures is decreed. Symbols are indeed the peculiar language of a transcendent agent. Men whose ears are unfitted to hear the profundities of the Torah are permitted to behold the Law graven upon the battlements of space, flashing from the stars, and inscribed upon every leaf and petal. The Law thunders from the rocks, and in mournful cadence may be heard in the cry of the sea. All symbols are things standing for still greater things—the images of a transcendent perfectness, the witnesses of a sufficient truth, the Evangelists of Eternity.

## THE CHAMBERS OF THE MYSTERIES

The ancient initiations were given in three chambers, which signified the worlds of the Body, the Soul, and the Spirit. After passing successfully through the hazards of the rituals, the neophyte ascended to a vaulted room in which stood the robed figure of the Great Mystery. Thus, the secrets of self-mastery were revealed to the candidate.

# XXXII

# The Symbolism of the Tarot by P.D. Ouspensky

Originally published in 1913

The Tarot is not a fortune-teller's toy—it is a coded map of the inner universe.

In this visionary work, Russian philosopher and mystic P.D. Ouspensky explores the Tarot as a system of spiritual development and esoteric initiation. Written before his collaboration with Gurdjieff, this early work displays Ouspensky's deep fascination with symbolic thought, archetypal structures, and the hidden laws that govern human transformation.

Each card of the Major Arcana is treated as a portal into a higher dimension of thought—a living glyph of metaphysical truth. Drawing from Hermeticism, Neoplatonism, and the Western Mystery Tradition, Ouspensky unveils the Tarot as a visual scripture of the soul's evolution.

"THE TAROT CONTAINS AND EXPRESSES IN SYMBOLS EVERYTHING THAT
THE HUMAN MIND CAN PERCEIVE, THINK, OR IMAGINE."
— P.D. OUSPENSKY

# XXXIII

# The Symbolism of the Tarot by P.D. Ouspensky

WHAT IS THE TAROT?
No study of occult philosophy is possible without an acquaintance with symbolism, for if the words occultism and symbolism are correctly used, they mean almost one and the same thing. Symbolism cannot be learned as one learns to build bridges or speak a foreign language, and for the interpretation of symbols a special cast of mind is necessary; in addition to knowledge, special faculties, the power of creative thought and a developed imagination are required. One who understands the use of symbolism in the arts, knows, in a general way, what is meant by occult symbolism. But even then a special training of the mind is necessary, in order to comprehend the "language of the Initiates", and to express in this language the intuitions as they arise.

There are many methods for developing the "sense of symbols" in those who are striving to understand the hidden forces of Nature and Man, and for teaching the fundamental principles as well as the elements of the esoteric language. The most synthetic, and one of the most interesting of these methods, is the Tarot

In its exterior form the Tarot is a pack of cards used in the south of Europe for games and fortune-telling. These cards were first known in Europe at the end of the fourteenth century, when they were in use among the Spanish gypsies.

A pack of Tarot contains the fifty-two ordinary playing cards with the addition of one "picture card" to every suit, namely, the Knight, placed between the Queen and the Knave. These fifty-six cards are divided into four suits, two black and two red and have the following designation: sceptres (clubs), cups (hearts), swords (spades), and pentacles or disks (diamonds). In addition to the fifty-six cards the pack of Tarot has twenty-two numbered cards with special names:--

1.    The Magician
2.    The High Priestess
3.    The Empress
4.    The Emperor
5.    The Hierophant

6.    The Lovers
7.    The Chariot
8.    Strength
9.    The Hermit
10.   The Wheel of Fortune
11.   Justice
12.   The Hanged Man
13.   Death
14.   Temperance
15.   The Devil
16.   The Tower
17.   The Star
18.   The Moon
19.   The Sun
20.   Judgment
21.   The World

0.    The Fool

This pack of cards, in the opinion of many investigators, represents the Egyptian hieroglyphic book of seventy-eight tablets, which came to us almost miraculously.

The history of the Tarot is a great puzzle. During the Middle Ages, when it first appeared historically, there existed a tendency to build up synthetic symbolical or logical systems of the same sort as Ars Magna by Raymond Lully. But productions similar to the Tarot exist in India and China, so that we cannot possibly think it one of those systems created during the Middle Ages in Europe; it is also evidently connected with the Ancient Mysteries and the Egyptian Initiations. Although its origin is in oblivion and the aim of its author or authors quite unknown, there is no doubt whatever that it is the most complete code of Hermetic symbolism we possess.

Although represented as a pack of cards, the Tarot really is something quite different. It can be "read" in a variety of ways. As one instance, I shall give a metaphysical interpretation of the general meaning or of the general content of the book of Tarot, that is to say, its metaphysical title, which will plainly show that this work could not have been invented by illiterate gypsies of the fourteenth century.

The Tarot falls into three divisions: The first part has twenty-one numbered cards; the second part has one card o; the third part has fifty- six cards, i. e., the four suits of fourteen cards. Moreover, the second part appears to be a link between the first and third parts, since all the fifty- six cards of the third part together are equal to the card o.

Now, if we imagine twenty-one cards disposed in the shape of a triangle, seven cards on each side, a point in the centre of the triangle represented by the zero card, and a square round the triangle (the square consisting of fifty-six cards, fourteen on each side), we shall have a representation of the relation between God, Man and the Universe, or the relation between the world of ideas, the consciousness of man and the physical world.

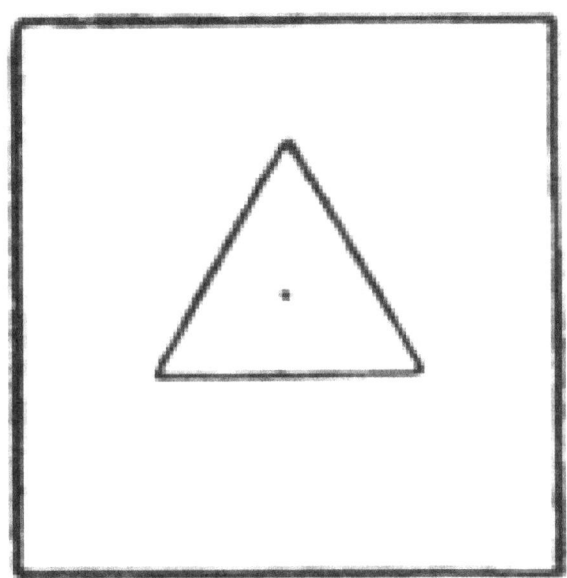

The triangle is God (the Trinity) or the world of ideas, or the noumenal world. The point is man's soul. The square is the visible, physical or phenomenal world. Potentially, the point is equal to the square, which means that all the visible world is contained in man's consciousness, is created in man's soul. And the soul itself is a point having no dimension in the world of the spirit, symbolized by the triangle. It is clear that such an idea could not have originated with ignorant people and clear also that the Tarot is something more than a pack of playing or fortune- telling cards.

H. P. Blavatsky mentions the Tarot in her works, and we have some reason for believing that she studied the Tarot. It is known that she loved to "play patience". We do not know what she read in the cards as she played this game, but the author was told that Madame Blavatsky searched persistently and for a long time for a MSS. on the Tarot.

In order to become acquainted with the Tarot, it is necessary to understand the basic ideas of the Kabala and of Alchemy. For it represents, as, indeed, many commentators of the Tarot think, a summary of the Hermetic Sciences--the Kabala, Alchemy, Astrology, Magic, with their different divisions. All these sciences, attributed to Hermes Trismegistus, really represent one system of a very broad and deep psychological investigation of the nature of man in his relation to the world of noumena (God, the world of Spirit) and to the world of phenomena (the visible, physical world). The letters of the Hebrew alphabet and the various allegories of the Kabala, the names of metals, acids and salts in alchemy; of planets and constellations in astrology; of good and evil spirits in magic--all these were only means to veil truth from the uninitiated.

But when the true alchemist spoke of seeking for gold, he spoke of gold in the soul of man. And he called gold that which in the New Testament is called the Kingdom of Heaven, and in Buddhism, Nirvana. And when the true astrologer spoke of constellations and planets he spoke of constellations and planets in the soul of man, i.e., of the qualities of the human soul and its relations to God and to the world. And when the true Kabalist spoke of the Name of God, he sought this Name in the soul of man and in Nature, not in dead books, nor in biblical texts, as did the Kabalist-Scholastics. The Kabala, Alchemy, Astrology, Magic are parallel symbolical systems of psychology and metaphysics. Any alchemical sentence may be read in a Kabalistic or astrological way, but the meaning will always be psychological and metaphysical.

We are surrounded by a wall built of our conceptions of the world, and are unable to look over this wall at the real world. The Kabala presents an effort to break this "enchanted circle". It investigates the world as it is, the world in itself.

The world in itself, as the Kabalists hold, consists of four elements, or the four principles forming One. These four principles are represented by the four letters of the name of Jehovah. The basic idea of the Kabala consists in the study of the Name of God in its manifestation. Jehovah in Hebrew is spelt by four letters, Yod, He, Vau and He--I. H. V. H. To these four letters is given the deepest symbolical meaning. The first letter expresses the active principle, the beginning or first cause, motion, energy, "I"; the second letter expresses the passive element, inertia, quietude, "not I;" the third, the balance of opposites, "form"; and the fourth, the result or latent energy.

The Kabalists affirm that every phenomenon and every object consists of these four principles, i.e., that every object and every phenomenon consists of the Name of God (The Word),--Logos.

The study of this Name (or the four-lettered word, tetragrammaton, in Greek) and the finding of it in everything constitutes the main problem of Kabalistic philosophy.

To state it in another way the Kabalists hold that these four principles penetrate and create everything. Therefore, when the man finds these four principles in things and phenomena of quite different categories (where before he had not seen similarity), he begins to see analogy between these phenomena. And, gradually, he becomes convinced that the whole world is built according to one and the same law, on one and the same plan. The richness and growth of his intellect consists in the widening of his faculty for finding analogies. Therefore the study of the law of the four letters, or the name of Jehovah presents a powerful means for widening consciousness. This idea is perfectly clear, for if the Name of God be really in all (if God be present in all), all should be analogous to each other--the smallest particle analogous to the whole, the speck of dust analogous to the universe, and all analogous to God. The Name of God, the Word or Logos is the origin of the world. Logos also means Reason; the Word is the Logos, the Reason of everything.

There is a complete correspondence between the Kabala and Alchemy and Magic. In Alchemy the four elements which constitute the real world are called fire, water, air and earth; these fully correspond in significance with the four kabalistic letters. In Magic they are expressed as the four classes of spirits: elves (or salamanders), undines, sylphs and gnomes.

The Tarot in its turn is quite analogous to the Kabala, Alchemy and Magic, and, as it were, includes them. Corresponding to the four first principles or four letters of the Name of God, or the four alchemistic elements, or the four classes of spirits, the Tarot has four suits--sceptres, cups, swords and pentacles. Thus every suit, every side of the square, equal to the point, represents one of the elements, controls one class of spirits . The sceptres are fire or elves (or salamanders); the cups are water or undines; the swords are air or sylphes; and pentacles, earth or gnomes. Moreover, in every suit the King means the first principle or fire; the Queen--the second principle or water; the Knight--the third principle or air, and the Page (knave)--the fourth principle or earth. Then again, the ace means fire; the deuce water; the three-spot, air; the four-spot earth. Then again the four-spot is the first principle, the five spot, the second etc.

In regard to the suits, one may add that the black suits (sceptres and swords) express activity and energy, will, initiative and the subjective side of consciousness; and the red (cups and pentacles) express passivity, inertia and the objective side of consciousness. Then the first two suits (sceptres and cups) signify "good" and the other two (swords and pentacles) mean "evil". Thus every card of the fifty-six indicates (independently of its number) the presence of the principle of activity or passivity, of "good" or "evil", arising either in man's will or from without. And the significance of each card is further deciphered thorough its various combinations with the suits and numbers in their symbolical meaning. The fifty-six cards as a whole represent, as it were, a complete picture of all the possibilities of man's consciousness. And this makes the Tarot adaptable for fortune-telling. Thus, including the Kabala, Astrology, Alchemy and Magic, the Tarot makes it possible to "seek gold", "to evoke spirits," and "to draw horoscopes", simply by means of this pack of cards without the complicated paraphernalia and ceremonies of an alchemist, astrologer or magician.

But the main interest of Tarot is in the twenty-two numbered cards. These cards have numerical meaning and also a very involved symbolical significance.

The literature relating to the Tarot has in view mainly the reading of the symbolical designs of the twenty-two cards. Very many writers on occultism have arranged their works on the plan of the Tarot. But this is not often suspected because the Tarot is rarely mentioned. Oswald Wirth speaks of origin of the Tarot in his Essay upon the Astronomical Tarot.

"According to Christian,1 the twenty-two major arcana of the Tarot represent the hieroglyphic paintings which were found in the spaces between the columns of a gallery which the neophyte was obliged to cross in the Egyptian initiations. There were twelve columns to the north and the same number to the south, that is, eleven symbolical pictures on each side. These pictures were explained to the candidate for initiation in regular order, and they contained the rules and principles for the Initiate. This opinion is confirmed by the correspondence which exists between arcana when they are thus arranged."

In the gallery of the Temple the pictures were arranged in pairs, one opposite another, so that the last picture was opposite the first, the last but one opposite the second, etc. When the cards are so placed we find a highly interesting and deep suggestion. In this way the mind finds the one in the two, and is led from dualism to monism, which is what we might call the unification of the duad. One card explains the other and each pair shows moreover that they can be only mutually explanatory and mean nothing when taken separately.

Thus, for instance, the cards 10 and 13 ("Life" and "Death") signify together a certain whole or complementary condition which we cannot conceive by the ordinary, imperfect mental processes. We think of life and death as two "opposites", antagonistic one to the other, but, if we thought further, we should see that each depends on the other for existence and neither could come into existence separately.

A symbol may serve to transfer our intuitions and to suggest new ones only so long as its meaning is not defined. Real symbols are perpetually in process of creation; but when they receive a definite significance they become hieroglyphs and finally a mere alphabet. As this they express simply ordinary concepts, cease to be a language of the Gods or of initiates and become a language of men which everyone may learn.

Properly speaking, a symbol in occultism means the same as in art. If an artist uses ready-made symbols his work will not be true art, but only pseudo-art. If an occultist begins to use ready-made symbols, his work will not be truly occult, for it will contain no esotericism, no mysticism, but only pseudo-occultism, pseudo-esotericism, pseudo-mysticism.

Symbolism in which the symbols have definite meanings is pseudo- symbolism. Having made this idea clear in his mind, the author found that the key to the Tarot must lie in imagination and he decided to make an effort to re- design the cards, giving descriptive pictures of the Tarot, and to interpret the symbols, not by means of analysis, but by synthesis. The reader will find in the following little "pen pictures" reflections of many authors who wrote on the Tarot as St. Martin, Eliphas Levi, Dr. Papus etc. and of other authors who certainly never thought of the Tarot as, for example, Plotinus, Gichtel (XVII century), Friedrich Nietzsche, M. Collins etc., who came nevertheless to the same fundamental principles as the unknown authors of the Tarot.

Descriptions of the arcanas in these "pen pictures" often represent a conception which is almost entirely subjective, for instance, that of card 18. And the author likes to think that another might conceive of the same symbols differently, in any case he considers this quite possible.

Any one interested in this philosophical puzzle might well ask, What then is the Tarot? Is it a doctrine or merely a method? Is it a definite system or merely an alphabet by means of which any system may be constructed? In short, is it a book containing specific teachings, or is it merely an apparatus, a machine which we may use to build anything, even a new universe.

The author believes that the Tarot may be used for both purposes, though, of course, the contents of a book that may be read either forward or backward cannot be said to be, in the ordinary sense, strictly definite. But perhaps we find in this very indefiniteness of the Tarot and in the complexity of its philosophy, the element which constitutes its definiteness. The fact that we question the Tarot as to whether it be a method or a doctrine shows the limitation of our "three dimensional mind," which is unable to rise above the world of form and contra- positions or to free itself from thesis and antithesis! Yes, the Tarot contains and expresses any doctrine to be found in our consciousness, and in this sense it h a s definiteness. It represents Nature in all the richness of its infinite possibilities, and there is in it as in Nature, not one but all potential meanings. And these meanings are fluent and ever- changing, so the Tarot cannot be specifically this or that, for it ever moves and yet is ever the same, In the following "pen-pictures" cards are taken in pairs:--I and o;

II and XXI; III and XX etc.--in each pair one card completing the sense of another and two making one.

Card I.--"The Magician".

"Man" Superman. The Initiate. The Occultist. Higher consciousness. Human Logos. The kabalistic "Adam Kadmon". Humanity. "Homo Sapiens".

Card II.--"The High Priestess".

Occultism. Esoterism. Mysticism. Theosophy. Initiation. Isis. Mystery.

Card III.--"The Empress".

Nature in its phenomenal aspect. The ever renewing and re-creating force of Nature. The objective reality.

Card IV.--"The Emperor".

Tetragrammaton. The law of four. Latent energy of Nature. Logos in the full aspect with all possibilities of the new Logos. Hermetic philosophy.

Card V.--"The Chariot".

"Man." The Imagination. Magic. Self-suggestion. Self deceit. Artificial means of attainment. Pseudo-occultism. Pseudo-theosophy.

Card VI.--"The Lovers"

. "Man". Another aspect of the "Adam Kadmon", the "Perfect Man", "The divine androgyne". Love as the efforts of "Adam Kadmon" to find himself. The equilibrium of contraries. The unification of the duad, as the means of attaining the Light.

Card VII.--"The Hierophant".

Mysticism. Theosophy. Esoteric side of all religions.

Card VIII.--"Strength".

The Real Power. Strength of love. Strength of Union (Magic chain). Strength of the Infinite. Occultism. Esoterism. Theosophy.

Card IX.--"The Hermit".

"Man". The Path to the Initiation. Seeking for truth in the right way. Inner Knowledge. Inner Light. Inner Force. Theosophy. Occultism.

Card X.--"The Wheel of Chance".

The Wheel of Life. The life ever changing and ever remaining the same. The Circle of Time and the four elements. The idea of the circle.

Card XI. -"Justice".

Truth. Real Knowledge. Inner Truth. Occultism. Esoterism. Theosophy.

Card XII.--"The Hanged Man".

"Man". The Pain of the higher consciousness bound by the limitations of the body and mind. Superman in the separate man.

Card XIII.--"Death". Another aspect of Life. Going away in order to come back at the same time. Completion of the circle.

Card XIV.--"Temperance".

(Time). The first attainment. The "Arcanum Magnum" of the occultists. The Fourth Dimension. Higher space. "Eternal Now".

Card XV.--"The Devil".

"Man". Weakness. Falsehood. The Fall of man into separateness, into hatred and into finiteness.

Card XVI.--"The Tower".

Sectarianism. Tower of Babel. Exoterism. Confusion of tongues. Fall of exoterism. The force of Nature re-establishing the truth distorted by men.

Card XVII.--"The Star".

The real aspect of the Astral World. That which maybe seen in extasy. The imagination of Nature. Real Knowledge. Occultism.

Card XVIII.--"The Moon".

The Astral World as it is seen by the artificial means of magic. "Psychic", "spiritistic" world. Dreads of the night. The real light from above and the false representation of that light from below. Pseudo-mysticism.

Card XIX.--"The Sun".

The Symbol and manifestation of the tetragrammaton. Creative power. Fire of life.

Card XX.--"Judgment".

The resurrection. Constant victory of life over death. Creative activity of nature in the death.

Card XXI.--"World".

Nature. The World as it is. Nature in its noumenal aspect. Esoteric side of nature. That which is made known in esoterism. Inner reality of things. Human consciousness in the circle of time between the four elements.

Card 0.--"The Fool".

"Man." An ordinary man. A separate man. The uninitiate Lower consciousness. The end of a ray not knowing its relation to the centre.

The twenty-two cards may be divided into three divisions including each seven cards of similar meaning, the 22-nd card (No 21) as a duplicate (of the No 10) standing outside the triangle or forming a point in its centre.

The three sets of sevens belong: the first one to the Man, the second to the Nature and the third to the higher knowledge or to the Theosophy in the large sense of the word.

The First set of 7.

Cards: I--Magician; 0--The Fool; V--The Chariot; IX--The Hermit; VI-- Lovers; XV--The Devil; XII--The Hanged Man.

The contents of these seven cards if taken in time picture seven degrees of the path of Man in his way to the Superman, or if taken in the Eternal Now picture seven faces of Man or seven I-s of man co-existing in him. This last meaning represents the inner sense of the secret doctrine of the Tarot in its relations to Man.

The second set of 7 (Nature) includes cards: III.--The Empress; X--Life; XIII--Death; XIV--Time; XVI--The Tower; XIX--The Sun; XX-- Judgement.

The third set of 7 (Theosophy) includes cards: II--The High Priestess; IV-

-The Emperor; VIII--Strength; VII--The Hierophant; XI-Justice; XVII-- The Star; XVIII--The Moon.

## CARD 1. THE MAGICIAN

I Saw the Man. His figure reached from earth to heaven and was clad in a purple mantle. He stood deep in foliage and flowers and his head, on which was the head-band of an initiate, seemed to disappear mysteriously in infinity. Before him on a cube-shaped altar were four symbols of magic--the sceptre, the cup, the sword and the pentacle. His right hand pointed to heaven, his left to earth. Under his mantle he wore a white tunic girded with a serpent swallowing its tail. His face was luminous and serene, and, when his eyes met mine, I felt that he saw most intimate recesses of my soul. I saw myself reflected in him as in a mirror and in his eyes I seemed to look upon myself.

And I heard a voice saying:

--"Look, this is the Great Magician!

With his hands he unites heaven and earth, and the four elements that form the world are controlled by him. The four symbols before him are the four letters of the name of God, the signs of the four elements, fire, water, air, earth."

I trembled before the depth of the mysteries A touched... The words I heard seemed to be littered by the Great Magician himself, and it was as though he spoke in me. I was in deep trepidation and at moment I felt there was nothing, before me except the blue sky; but within me a window opened through which I could see unearthly things. and hear unearthly words.

CARD 0. THE FOOL

And I saw another man. Tired and lame he dragged himself along the dusty road, across the deserted plain under the scorching rays of the sun. He glanced sidelong with foolish, staring eyes, a half smile, half leer on his face; he knew not where he went, but was absorbed in his chimerical dreams which ran constantly in the same circle. His fool's cap was put on wrong side front, his garments were torn in the back; a wild lynx with glowing eyes sprang upon him from behind a rock and buried her teeth in his flesh. He stumbled, nearly fell, but continued to drag himself along, all the time holding on his shoulder a bag containing useless things, which he, in his stupidity, carried wherever he went. Before him a crevice crossed the road and a deep precipice awaited the foolish wanderer. Then a huge crocodile with open mouth crawled out of the precipice. And I heard the voice say:

"Look! This is the same man." I felt my head whirl.

"What has he in the bag?" I inquired, not knowing why I asked. And after a long silence the voice replied: "The four magic symbols, the sceptre, the cup, the sword and the pentacle. The fool always carries them, although he has long since forgotten what they mean. Nevertheless they belong to him, even though he does not know their use. The symbols have not lost their power, they retain it in themselves.

CARD 2. THE HIGH PRIESTESS

THE HIGH PRIESTESS

When I lifted the first veil and entered the outer court of the Temple of Initiation, I saw in half darkness the figure of a woman sitting on a high throne between two pillars of the temple, one white, and one black. Mystery emanated from her and was about her. Sacred symbols shone on her green dress; on her head was a golden tiara surmounted by a two- horned moon; on her knees she held two crossed keys and an open book. Between the two pillars behind the woman hung another veil all embroidered with green leaves and fruit of pomegranate.

And a voice said:

"To enter the Temple one must lift the second veil and pass between the two pillars. And to pass thus, one must obtain possession of the keys, read the book and understand the symbols. Are you able to do this?"

"I would like to be able," I said.

Then the woman turned her face to me and looked into my eyes without speaking. And through me passed a thrill, mysterious and penetrating like a golden wave; tones vibrated in my brain, a

flame was in my heart, and I understood that she spoke to me, saying without words:
"This is the Hall of Wisdom. No one can reveal it, no one can hide it. Like a flower it must grow and bloom in thy soul. If thou wouldst plant the seed of this flower in thy soul--learn to discern the real from the false. Listen only to the Voice that is soundless... Look only on that which is invisible, and remember that in thee thyself, is the Temple and the gate to it, and the mystery, and the initiation."

## CARD 21. THE WORLD

An unexpected vision appeared to me. A circle not unlike a wreath woven from rainbow and lightnings, whirled from heaven to earth with a stupendous, velocity, blinding me by its brilliance. And amidst this light and fire I heard music and soft singing, thunderclaps and the roar of a tempest, the rumble of falling mountains and earthquakes. The circle whirled with a terrifying noise, touching the sun and the earth, and, in the centre of it I saw the naked, dancing figure of a beautiful young woman, enveloped by a light, transparent scarf, in her hand she held a magic wand. Presently the four apocalyptical beasts began to appear on the edges of the circle; one with the face of a lion, another with the face of a man, the third, of an eagle and the fourth, of a bull. The vision disappeared as suddenly as it appeared. A weird silence fell on me. "What does it mean?" I asked in wonder.

"It is the image of the world," the voice said, "but it can be understood only after the Temple has been entered. This is a vision of the world in the circle of Time, amidst the four principles. But thou seest differently because thou seest the world outside thyself. Learn to see it in thyself and thou wilt understand the infinite essence, hidden in all illusory forms. Understand that the world which thou knowest is only one of the aspects of the infinite world, and things and phenomena are merely hierolgyphics of deeper ideas."

CARD 3. THE EMPRESS

I felt the breath of the spring, and accompanying the fragrance of violets and lilies-of-the-valley I heard the tender singing of elves. Rivulets murmured, the treetops rustled, the grasses whispered, innumerable birds sang in choruses and bees hummed; everywhere I felt the breathing of joyful, living Nature. The sun shone tenderly and softly and a little white cloud hung over the woods. In the midst of a green meadow where primroses bloomed, I saw the Empress seated on a throne covered with ivy and lilacs. A green wreath adorned her golden hair and, above her head, shone twelve stars. Behind her rose two snowy wings and in her hands she held a sceptre. All around, beneath the sweet smile of the Empress, flowers and buds opened their dewy, green leaves. Her whole dress was covered with them as though each newly opened flower were reflected in it or had engraved itself thereon and thus become part of her garment. The sign of Venus, the goddess of love, was chiselled on her marble throne.

"Queen of life," I said, "why is it so bright and joyful all about you? Do you not know of the grey, weary autumn, of the cold, white winter? Do you not know of death and graveyards with black graves, damp and cold? How can you smile so joyfully on the opening flowers, when everything is destined to death, even that which has not yet been born?"

For answer the Empress looked on me still smiling and, under the influence of that smile, I suddenly felt a flower of some clear understanding open in my heart.

CARD 20. JUDGMENT

I saw an ice plain, and on the horizon, a chain of snowy mountains. A cloud appeared and began to grow until it covered a quarter of the sky. Two fiery wings suddenly expanded in the cloud, and I knew that I beheld the messenger of the Empress. He raised a trumpet and blew through it vibrant, powerful tones. The plain quivered in response to him and the mountains loudly rolled their echoes. One after another, graves opened in the plain and out of them came men and women, old and young, and children. They stretched out their arms toward the Messenger of the Empress and to catch the sounds of his trumpet. And in its tones I felt the smile of the Empress and in the opening graves I saw the opening flowers whose fragrance seemed to be wafted by the outstretched arms. Then I understood the mystery of birth in death.

CARD 4. THE EMPEROR

After I learned the first three numbers I was given to understand the Great Law of Four--the alpha and omega of all.

I saw the Emperor on a lofty stone throne, ornamented by four rams' heads. On his forehead shone a golden helmet. His white beard fell over a purple mantle. In one hand he held a sphere, the symbol of his possession, and in the other, a sceptre in the form of an Egyptian cross-- the sign of his power over birth.

"I am The Great Law," the Emperor said. "I am the name of God. The four letters of his name are in me and I am in all.

"I am in the four principles. I am in the four elements. I am in the four seasons. I am in the four cardinal points. I am in the four signs of the Tarot.

"I am the beginning; I am action; I am completion; I am the result. "For him who knows how to see me there are no mysteries on earth.

"I am the great Pentacle. As the earth encloses in itself fire, water and air; as the fourth letter of the Name encloses in itself the first three and becomes itself the first, so my sceptre encloses the complete triangle and bears in itself the seed of a new triangle.

"I am the Logos in the full aspect and the beginning of a new Logos."

And while the Emperor spoke, his helmet shone brighter and brighter, and his golden armour gleamed beneath his mantle. I could not bear his glory and I lowered my eyes. When I tried to lift them again a vivid light of radiant fire was before me, and I prostrated myself and made obeisance to the Fiery Word.

CARD 19. THE SUN

As soon as I perceived the Sun, I understood that It, Itself, is the expression of the Fiery Word and the sign of the Emperor.

The great luminary shone with an intense heat upon the large golden heads of sun-flowers. And I saw a naked boy, whose head was wreathed with roses, galloping on a white horse and waving a bright-red banner.

. . . . . . . . . . . . . . . . . . . . . . . . . . . .

I shut my eyes for a moment and when I opened them again I saw that each ray of the Sun is the sceptre of the Emperor and bears life. And I saw how under the concentration of these rays the mystic flowers of the waters open and receive the rays into themselves and how all Nature is constantly born from the union of two principles.

CARD 5. THE CHARIOT

THE CHARIOT.

I saw a chariot drawn by two sphinxes, one white, the other black. Four pillars supported a blue canopy, on which were scattered five-pointed stars. The Conqueror, clad in steel armour, stood under this canopy guiding the sphinxes. He held a sceptre, on the end of which were a globe, a triangle and a square. A golden pentagram sparkled in his crown. On the front of the chariot there was represented a winged sphere and beneath that the symbol of the mystical lingam, signifying the union of two principles.

"Everything in this picture has a significance. Look and try to understand", said the voice.

"This is Will armed with Knowledge. We see here, however, the wish to achieve, rather than achievement itself. The man in the chariot thought himself a conqueror before he had really conquered, and he believes that victory must come to the conqueror. There are true possibilities in this beautiful conception, but also many false ones. Illusory fires and numerous dangers are hidden here. He controls the sphinxes by the power of a magic word, but the tension of his Will may fail and then the magic word will lose its power and he may be devoured by the sphinxes. This is indeed the Conqueror, but only for the moment; he has not yet conquered Time, and the succeeding moment is unknown to him.

This is the Conqueror, not by love, but by fire and the sword,--a conqueror against whom the conquered may arise. Do you see behind him the towers of the conquered city? Perhaps the flame of uprising burns already there. And he is unaware that the city vanquished by means of fire and the sword is the city within his own consciousness, that the magic chariot is in himself and that the blood-thirsty sphynxes, also a state of consciousness within, watch his every movement. He has externalized all these phases of his mind and sees them only outside himself. This is his fundamental error. He entered the outer court of the Temple of knowledge, but thinks he has been in the Temple itself. He regarded the rituals of the first tests as initiation, and he mistook for the goddess, the priestess who guarded the threshold. Because of this misconception great perils await him. Nevertheless it may be that even in his errors and perils the Great Conception lies concealed. He seeks to know and, perhaps, in order to attain, mistakes, dangers and even failures are necessary. Understand that this is the same man whom you saw uniting Heaven and Earth, and again walking across a hot desert to a precipice.

## CARD 18. THE MOON

**THE MOON.**

A desolate plain stretched before me. A full moon looked down as if in contemplative hesitation. Under her wavering light the shadows lived their own peculiar life. On the horizon I saw blue hills, and over them wound a path which stretched between two grey towers far away into the distance. On either side the path a wolf and dog sat and howled at the moon. I remembered that dogs believe in thieves and ghosts. A large black crab crawled out of the rivulet into the sands. A heavy, cold dew was falling. Dread fell upon me. I sensed the presence of a mysterious world, a world of hostile spirits, of corpses rising from graves, of wailing ghosts. In this pale moonlight I seemed to feel the presence of apparitions; someone watched me from behind the towers,--and I knew it was dangerous to look back.

CARD 6. THE LOVERS

I saw a blooming garden in a green valley, surrounded by soft blue hills. In the garden I saw a
Man and a Woman naked and beautiful. They loved each other and their Love was their service
to the Great Conception, a prayer and a sacrifice; through It they communed with God, through
It they received the highest revelations; in Its light the deepest truths came to them; the magic
world opened its gate; elves, undines, sylphs and gnomes came openly to them; the three kingdoms of nature, the mineral, plant and animal, and the four elements--fire, water, air and earth-
served them. Through their Love they saw the mystery of the world's equilibrium, and that they
themselves were a symbol and expression of this balance. Two triangles united in them into a six-
pointed star. Two magnets melted into an ellipsis. They were two. The third was the Unknown
Future. The three made One.
I saw the woman looking out upon the world as though enraptured with its beauty. And from the
tree on which ripened golden fruit I saw a serpent creep. It whispered in the woman's ear, and I
saw her listening, smiling at first suspiciously, then with curiosity which merged into joy. Then I

saw her speak to the man. I noticed that he seemed to admire only her and smiled with an expression of joy and sympathy at all she told him.

. . . . . . . . . . . . . . . . . . . . . . . . . . .

"This picture you see, is a picture of temptation and fall", said the voice. "What constitutes the Fall? Do you understand its nature"?

"Life is so good", I said, "and the world so beautiful, and this man and woman wanted to believe in the reality of the world and of themselves. They wanted to forget service and take from the world what it can give. So they made a distinction between themselves and the world. They said, 'We are here, the world is there'. And the world separated from them and became hostile."

"Yes", said the Voice, this is true. "The everlasting mistake with men is that they see the fall in love. But Love is not a fall, it is a soaring above an abyss. And the higher the flight, the more beautiful and alluring appears the earth.

But that wisdom, which crawls on earth, advises belief in the earth and in the present. This is the Temptation. And the man and woman yielded to it.

They dropped from the eternal realms and submitted to time and death. The balance was disturbed. The fairyland was closed upon them. The elves, undines, sylphs and gnomes became invisible. The Face of God ceased to reveal Itself to them, and all things appeared upside down.

"This Fall, this first 'sin of man', repeats itself perpetually, because man continues to believe in his separateness and in the Present. And only by means of great suffering can he liberate himself from the control of time and return to Eternity--leave darkness and return to Light".

CARD 17. THE STAR

THE STAR.

A strange emotion seized me. A fiery trembling ran in waves through all my body. My heart quickened its beating, tumult agitated my mind.

I felt that I was surrounded by portentous mysteries. And presently shafts of Light penetrated my being and illuminated many things before in darkness, whose existence even I had never suspected. Veils vanished of which I had been before unaware. Voices spoke to me. And suddenly all my former knowledge took a new and different meaning.

I discovered unexpected correlations in things which hitherto I had thought foreign to each other. Objects distant and different from one another appeared near and similar. The facts of the world arranged themselves before my eyes according to a new pattern. In the sky there appeared an enormous star surrounded by seven smaller stars. Their rays intermingled, filling space with immeasurable radiance and splendour. Then I knew I saw that Heaven of which Plotinus speaks:

"Where . . . all things are diaphanous; and nothing is dark and resisting, but everything is apparent to everyone internally and throughout. For light everywhere meets with light, since everything contains all things in itself, and again sees all things in another. So that all things are everywhere, and all is all. Each thing likewise is everything. And the splendour there is infinite. For everything there is great, since even that which is small is great.

"The sun too, which is there, is all the stars; and again each star is the sun and all the stars. In each however, a different property predominates, but at the same time all things are visible in each. Motion likewise there is pure; for motion is not confounded by a mover different from it. Permanency also suffers no change of its nature, because it is not mingled with the unstable. And the beautiful there is beautiful, because it does not subsist in beauty. Each thing, too, is there established, not as in a foreign land, but the seat of each thing is that which each thing is. . .

. . Nor is the thing itself different from the place in which it subsists. For the subject of it is intellect, and it is itself intellect    In this sensible

region, therefore, one part is not produced by another, but each part is alone a part. But there each part always proceeds from the whole, and is at the same each time part and the whole. For it appears indeed as a part; but by him whose sight is acute, it will be seen as a whole.

"Where    is likewise no weariness of the vision which Is there, not any

plenitude of perception which can bring intuition to an end.

"For neither was there any vacuity which when filled might cause the visible energy to cease; nor is this one thing, but that another, so as to occasion a part of one thing not to be amicable with that of another.

"Where    the life is wisdom; a wisdom not obtained by a reasoning

process, because the whole of it always was, and is not in any respect deficient, so as to be in want of investigation. But it is the first wisdom, and is not derived from another".

. . . . . . . . . . . . . . . . . . . . . . . . . . .

 I understood that all the radiance here is thought; and the changing colours are emotions. And each ray, if we look into it, turns into images, symbols, voices and moods. And I saw that there is nothing inanimate, but all is soul, all is life, all is emotion and imagination.

And beneath the radiant stars beside the blue river I saw a naked maiden, young and beautiful. She stooped on one knee and poured water from two vessels, one of gold and one of silver. A little bird in a nearby bush lifted its wings and was poised ready to fly away.

For a moment I understood that I beheld the Soul of Nature.

"This is Nature's Imagination," said the voice gently. "Nature dreams, improvises, creates worlds. Learn to unite your imagination with Her Imagination and nothing will ever be impossible for you. Lose the external world and seek it in yourself. Then you will find Light. "But remember, unless you have lost the Earth, you will not find Heaven. It is impossible to see both wrongly and rightly at the same time."

CARD 7. THE HIEROPHANT

I saw the great Master in the Temple. He was siting on a golden throne set upon a purple plat-form, and he wore the robe of a high priest with a golden tiara. He held a golden eight-pointed cross, and lying at his feet were two crossed keys. Two initiates bowed before him and to them he spoke:--

"Seek the Path, do not seek attainment, Seek for the Path within yourself.

"Do not expect to hear the truth from others, nor to see it, or read it in books. Look for the truth in yourself, not without yourself.

"Aspire only after the impossible and inaccessible. Expect only that which shall not be.

"Do not hope for Me,--do not look for Me,--do not believe--that I am outside yourself.

"Within your soul build a lefty tower by which you may ascend to Heaven. Do not believe in ex-ternal miracles, expect miracles only within you. Beware of believing in a mystery of the earth, in a mystery guarded by men; for treasuries which must be guarded are empty. Do not search for a mystery that can be hidden by men. Seek the Mystery within yourself.

"Above all, avoid those towers built in order to preserve the mysteries and to make an ascent to

Heaven by stone stairways. And remember that as soon as men build such a tower they begin to dispute about the summit.

"The Path is in yourself, and Truth is in yourself and Mystery is in yourself."

## CARD 16. THE TOWER

THE TOWER.

I saw a lofty tower extending from earth to heaven; its golden crowned summit reached beyond the clouds. All round it black night reigned and thunder rumbled.

Suddenly the heavens opened, a thunder-clap shook the whole earth, and lightning struck the summit of the tower and felled the golden crown. A tongue of fire shot from heaven and the whole tower became filled with fire and smoke. Then I beheld the builders of the tower fall headlong to the ground.

And the voice said:--

"The building of the tower was begun by the disciples of the great Master in order to have a constant reminder of the Master's teaching that the true tower must be built in one's own soul, that in the tower built by hands there can be no mysteries, that no one can ascend to Heaven by treading stone steps.

"The tower should warn the people not to believe in it. It should serve as a reminder of the inner Temple and as a protection against the outer; it should be as a lighthouse, in a dangerous place where men have often been wrecked and where ships should not go.

"But by and by the disciples forgot the true covenant of the Master and what the tower symbolized, and began to believe in the tower of stone, they had built, and to teach others to so believe. They began to say that in this tower there is power, mystery and the spirit of the Master, that the tower itself is holy and that it is built for the coming Master according to His covenant and His will. And so they waited in the tower for the Master. Others did not believe this, or interpreted it differently. Then began disputes about the rights of the summit. Quarrels started, 'Our Master, your Master,' was said; 'our tower, your tower.' And the disciples ceased to understand each other. Their tongues had become confused.

"You understand the meaning here? They had begun to think that this is the tower of the Master, that He builds it through them, and that it must and, indeed, can be built right up to Heaven.

"And you see how Heaven responded?"

CARD 8. POWER

In the midst of a green plain, surrounded by blue hills, I saw a woman with a lion. Girdled with wreaths of roses, a symbol of infinity over her head, the woman calmly and confidently covered the lion's mouth and the lion obediently licked her hand.

"This is a picture of power", said the voice. "It has different meanings. First it shows the power of love. Love alone can conquer wrath.

Hatred feeds hatred.

Remember what Zarathustra said: "Let man be freed from vengeance; this is a bridge for me which leads to higher hope and a rainbow in heaven after long storms".

"Then it shows power of unity. These wreaths of roses suggest a magic chain. Unity of desires, unity of aspirations creates such power that every wild, uncontrolled, unconscious force is subdued. Even two desires, if united, are able to conquer almost the whole world.

"The picture also shows the power of infinity, that sphere of mysteries. For a consciousness that perceives the symbol of infinity above it, knows no obstacles and cannot be withstood".

CARD 15. THE DEVIL

Black, awful night enveloped the earth. An ominous, red flame burned in the distance. I was approaching a fantastic figure which outlined itself before me as I came nearer to it. High above the earth appeared the repulsive red face of the Devil, with large, hairy ears, pointed beard and curved goats' horns. A pentagram, pointing downwards, shone in phosphoric light between the horns on his forehead. Two large, grey, bat- like wings were spread behind him. He held up one arm, spreading out his bare, fat hand. In the palm I saw the sign of black magic. A burning torch held down-end in his other hand emitted black, stifling smoke. He sat on a large, black cube, gripping it with the claws of his beast-like, shaggy legs.

A man and woman were chained to the cube--the same Man and Woman I saw in the garden, but now they had horns and tails tipped with flame. And they were evidently dissatisfied in spirit, and were filled with protest and repulsion.

"This is a picture of weakness", said the voice, "a picture of falsehood and evil. They are the same man and woman you saw in the garden, but their love ceasing to be a sacrifice, became an illusion. This man and woman forgot that their love is a link in the chain that unites them with eternity, that their love is a symbol of equilibrium and a road to Infinity.

"They forgot that It is a key to the gate of the magic world, the torch which lights the higher Path. They forgot that Love is real and immortal and they subjugated it to the unreal and temporary. And they each made love a tool for submitting the other to himself.

"Then love became dissension and fettered them with iron chains to the black cube of matter, on which sits deceit".

And I heard the voice of the Devil: "I am Evil", he said, "at least so far as Evil can exist in this best of worlds. In order to see me, one must be able to see unfairly, incorrectly and narrowly. I close the triangle, the other two sides of which are Death and Time. In order to quit this triangle it is necessary to see that it does not exist.

"But how to do this is not for me to tell. For I am the Evil which men say is the cause of all evil and which they invented as an excuse for all the evil that they do.

"They call me the Prince of Falsehood, and truly I am the prince of lies, because I am the most monstrous production of human lies".

CARD 9. THE HERMIT

After long wanderings over a sandy, waterless desert where only serpents lived, I met the Hermit. He was wrapped in a long cloak, a hood thrown over his head. He held a long staff in one hand and in the other a lighted lantern, though it was broad daylight and the sun was shining.

"The lantern of Hermes Trismegistus", said the voice, "this is higher knowledge, that inner knowledge which illuminates in a new way even what appears to be already clearly known. This lantern lights up the past, the present and the future for the Hermit, and opens the souls of people and the most intimate recesses. of their hearts."

"The cloak of Apollonius is the faculty of the wise man by which he isolates himself, even amidst a noisy crowd; it is his skill in hiding his mysteries, even while expressing them, his capacity for silence and his power to act in stillness. "The staff of the patriarchs is his inner authority, his power, his self- confidence."

The lantern, the cloak and the staff are the three symbols of initiation. They are needed to guide souls past the temptation of illusory fires by the roadside, so that they may go straight to the higher goal. He who receives these three symbols or aspires to obtain them, "strives to enrich himself with all he can acquire, not for himself, but, like God, to delight in the joy of giving".

"The giving virtue is the basis of an initiate's life.

"His soul is transformed into 'a spoiler of all treasures' so said Zarathustra.

"Initiation unites the human mind with the higher mind by a chain of analogies. This chain is the ladder leading to heaven, dreamed of by the patriarch".

CARD 14. TIME (TEMPERANCE)

An angel in a white robe, touching earth and heaven, appeared. His wings were flame and a radiance of gold was about his head. On his breast he wore the sacred sign of the book of the Tarot--a triangle within a square, a point within the triangle; on his forehead the symbol of life and eternity, the circle.

In one hand was a cup of silver, in the other a cup of gold and there flowed between these cups a constant, glistening stream of every colour of the rainbow. But I could not tell from which cup nor into which cup the stream flowed. In great awe I understood that I was near the ultimate mysteries from which there is no return. I looked upon the angel, upon his symbols, his cups, the rainbow stream between the cups,--and my human heart trembled with fear and my human mind shrank with anguish and lack of understanding.

"Yes", said the voice, "this is a mystery that is revealed at Initiation. 'Initiation' is simply the re-vealing of this mystery in the soul. The Hermit receives the lantern, the cloak and the staff so that he can bear the light of this mystery.

"But you probably came here unprepared. Look then and listen and try to understand, for now understanding is your only salvation. He

who approaches the mystery without complete comprehension will be lost.

"The name of the angel is Time. The circle on his forehead is the symbol of eternity and life. Each life is a circle which returns to the same point where it began. Death is the return to birth. And from one point to another on the circumference of a circle the distance is always the same, and the further it is from one point, the nearer it will be to the other.

"Eternity is a serpent, pursuing its tail, never catching it.

"One of the cups the angel holds is the past, the other is the future. The rainbow stream between the cups is the present. You see that it flows both ways.

"This is Time in its most incomprehensible aspect.

"Men think that all flows constantly in one direction. They do not see that everything perpetually meets and that Time is a multitude of turning circles. Understand this mystery and learn to discern the contrary currents in the rainbow stream of the present.

"The symbol of the sacred book of the Tarot on the angel's breast is the symbol of the correlation of God, Man and the Universe.

"The triangle is God, the world of spirit, the world of ideas. The point within the triangle is the soul of man. The square is the visible world.

"The consciousness of man is the spark of divinity, a point within the triangle of spirit. Therefore the whole square of the visible universe is equal to the point within the triangle. "The world of spirit is the triangle of the twenty-one signs of the Tarot. The square represents fire, air, water and earth, and thus symbolises the world.

"All this, in the form of the four symbols, is in the bag of the Fool, who himself is a point in a triangle. Therefore a point without dimension contains an infinite square".

CARD 10. THE WHEEL OF CHANCE

I walked along, absorbed in deep thought, trying to understand the vision of the Angel. And suddenly, as I lifted my head, I saw midway in the sky a huge, revolving circle covered with Kabalistic letters and symbols. The circle turned with terrible velocity, and around it, falling down and flying up, symbolic figures of the serpent and the dog revolved; above it sat an immovable sphinx. In clouds, on the four quarters of heaven, I saw the four apocalyptical beings, one with the face of a lion, another with the face of a bull, the third with a face of an eagle, and the fourth with the face of a bull. And each of them read an open book.

And I heard the voices of Zarathustra's beasts:-- "All go, all return,"--the wheel of life ever turns. All die, all flourish again,--the year of existence runs eternally.

"All perish, all live again, the same house of existence is ever building. All separate, all meet again, the ring of existence is ever true to itself.

"Existence begins at every moment. Round each "here" rolls "there". The middle is everywhere. The way of eternity is a curve".

## CARD 13. DEATH

Fatigued by the flashing of the Wheel of Life, I sank to earth and shut my eyes. But it seemed to me that the Wheel kept turning before me and that the four creatures continued sitting in the clouds and reading their books.

Suddenly, on opening my eyes, I saw a gigantic rider on a white horse, dressed in black armour, with a black helmet and black plume. A skeleton's face looked out from under the helmet. One bony hand held a large, black, slowly-waving banner, and the other held a black bridle ornamented with skulls and bones.

And, wherever the white horse passed, night and death followed; flowers withered, leaves drooped, the earth covered itself with a white shroud; graveyards appeared; towers, castles and cities were destroyed. Kings in the full splendour of their fame and their power; beautiful women loved and loving; high priests invested by power from God; innocent children--when they saw the white horse all fell on their knees before him, stretched out their hands in terror and despair, and fell down to rise no more.

Afar, behind two towers, the sun sank.

A deadly cold enveloped me. The heavy hoofs of the horse seemed to step on my breast, and I felt the world sink into an abyss.

But all at once something familiar, but faintly seen and heard, seemed to come from the measured step of the horse. A moment more and I heard in his steps the movement of the Wheel of Life!

An illumination entered me, and, looking at the receding rider and the descending sun, I understood that the Path of Life consists of the steps of the horse of Death.

The sun sinks at one point and rises at another. Each moment of its motion is a descent at one point and an ascent at another. I understood that it rises while sinking and sinks while rising, and that life, in coming to birth, dies, and in dying, comes to birth.

"Yes," said the voice. The sun does not think of its going down and coming up. What does it know of earth, of the going and coming observed by men? It goes its own way, over its own orbit, round an unknown Centre. Life, death, rising and falling--do you not know that all these things are thoughts and dreams and fears of the Fool"?

## CARD 11. JUSTICE

When I possessed the keys, read the book and understood the symbols, I was permitted to lift the curtain of the Temple and enter. its inner sanctum. And there I beheld a Woman with a crown of gold and a purple mantle. She held a sword in one hand and scales in the other. I trembled with awe at her appearance, which was deep and mysterious, and drew me like an abyss.

"You see Truth," said the voice. "On these scales everything is weighed. This sword is always raised to guard justice, and nothing can escape it.

"But why do you avert your eyes from the scales and the sword? They will remove the last illusions. How could you live on earth without these illusions?

"You wished to see Truth and now you behold it! But remember what happens to the mortal who beholds a Goddess!"

CARD 12. THE HANGED MAN

THE HANGED MAN.

And then I saw a man in terrible suffering, hung by one leg, head downward, to a high tree. And I heard the voice:--

"Look! This is a man who saw Truth. Suffering awaits the man on earth, who finds the way to eternity and to the understanding of the Endless.

"He is still a man, but he already knows much of what is inaccessible even to Gods. And the incommensurableness of the small and the great in his soul constitutes his pain and his golgotha.

"In his own soul appears the gallows on which he hangs in suffering, feeling that he is indeed inverted.

"He chose this way himself.

"For this he went over a long road from trial to trial, from initiation to initiation, through failures and falls.

"And now he has found Truth and knows himself.

"He knows that it is he who stands before an altar with magic symbols, and reaches from earth to heaven; that he also walks on a dusty road under a scorching sun to a precipice where a crocodile awaits him; that he dwells with his mate in paradise under the shadow of a blessing genius; that he is chained to a black cube under the shadow of deceit; that he stands as a victor for a moment in an illusionary chariot drawn by sphinxes; and that with a lantern in bright sunshine, he seeks for Truth in a desert.

"Now he has found Her".

# XXXIV

## Ancient Mystery Rituals

THE sophisticated pharisees of the 20th century unceasingly give thanks that they have outgrown the fables and rituals of the ancients. The worldly-wise love the evident and are exasperated by that which is not evident. Plutocrat and proletarian alike regard themselves as victimized by that person whose words or actions they do not understand. They love the obvious because it flatters them, and hate the mysterious because it damns their intelligence with faint praise. Riddles are irksome. The modern cry is for facts—facts stripped of their verbal trappings and denuded of nonsense. Yet with facts for their fetish, the modernists arc more foolish than their forebears. Decrying superstition, they are most superstitious; rejecting fancies, they are the fanciful product of a fictitious age. Tlie modern world is bored with its own importance; life itself has become a botheration. Having passed the saturation point of realistic culture, satiety is imminent. Suffering from chronic ennui, how can a world ever become interested in anything but itself? Smothered in their self-complacency these all-sufficient ones ask for facts. But what facts are there that fools can understand? How can the helplessly superficial grasp the hopelessly profound, for are not realities reserved for the wise?

For even those interested in philosophy today we often hear the remark, "We have outgrown rituals and symbols. They belong to another age, some previous cycle that has spun its time and long since vanished into the discard." But is it not more than passing strange that we should outgrow all that was beautiful in those worn-out ages and yet hug to ourselves the same vices that they served all too well? We have re-edited and considerably amplified the first books of iniquity, but what of the Book of Beauty and Truth? Why have we torn it from its ancient covers and cast it aside? If we have not outgrown the evils of the past, how can we have outgrown its virtues? How can a man say, "I live in a new age" and then steal more brazenly than the Spartans, intrigue more murderously than the Egyptians, kill more wantonly than the Romans, and oppress more heartlessly than the Brahmans?

Apparently, "ages" do not entirely end, for the dregs of each dying era are dumped into the next to become the common heritage of new civilizations, while the best is all too likely to die or remain obscured, awaiting rediscovery by a philosophic few. There are times when memory is a carrier of carrion, and when committed to writing this carrion becomes history. Not only have civilizations perished, but civilizations have also lived and exemplified some phases of the beautiful. We regard the past as having vanished like a dream. It seems to us unreal, but even as we say "The past is dead," we ourselves die. The modernist cries: "Look to the future!" We follow the direction of his finger and, behold, there is nothing. The future is an unfashioned quantity; it is the highly glorified now, the minute stepped up to infinity. The future is a great intangible capacity stuffed full with the same substances of which the past is made. In the last analysis, both now and then shall pass away. There is, however, a strange philosophic now which endures, but the now of fools is but an instant slipping into then . The past is more kindly than the future; it is rich with memories and redundant with accomplishments. Whereas the future is the abode of the unborn, the past is the dwelling place of the immortals; for when man passes from the little now to the great then, he either sinks into a kindly obscurity which covers his faults with the mantle of forgetfulness, or his memory grows until men raise altars to do him homage apd the ages resound with his name.

The past is the security of the wise—the sure foundation upon which his feet are placed; the present is the slippery footing of the fool, for it passes away even while he stands thereon. We never outgrow the past any more than we outgrow our own childhood, for maturity is something added on. It is the complement, not the contradiction of that which preceded it. Remove the child from the man and he dies; for the child is the beginning, the point of unity from which all the rest springs like the oak from the acorn. The past is the abiding place of tender memories; of wise experiences. It is the fountain of beauty, life, and truth, and although this fountain flows through all the ages to make fertile the distant corners of creation, yet shall it never be greater than its own source. It is fitting that every man should venerate his tutelaries with some expression of the beautiful. The gods of elder days required no solemn convocation or bloody sacrifice, but rather conjured man to more virtuous living by inclining his soul toward those perfect rhythms which stream continually from the splendor of Abiding Destiny. The gods upon their eternal thrones rejoice not in the groveling mendicant mumbling threadbare litanies, but in the free man rich with the joy of living. Too long have the followers of a jealous and capricious Lord trembled in fear of his displeasure. Too long have men supplicated Deity to spare them yet a little while before the inevitable loosening of his wrath. Too long have men envisioned their Creator as ;«human rather than r#/vrhuman. When the sanctuaries ceased to ring with the laughter of a happy human kind, the gods girded up their loins and departed. Too much of solemnity is an oppression of the spirit. He who venerates excessively neither loves nor understands the object of his veneration.

To me, ritualism is essential to philosophy—not the ritualism of a decadent church which had its inception after the decline of Greek aesthetics, but the ritualism of the ancient pagans who served God with joy. Today we serve our faith with sadness, and if all the dwellers in the seven heavens were to perish together the sound of our lament could not be more piteous than those funeral hymns with which we herald the glad tidings of our salvation. Never should we forget the story of the simple-minded jester who, entering the cathedral and having nothing else to offer, performed his repertoire of tricks upon the altar before the statue of the Virgin. When, indignant at the impious act, the priests sought to drive the youth from the church, a miracle happened. The stone figure of the "Mother of God" came to life and bestowed its blessings upon the adoring juggler. The substance of faith is not dignity but sincerity; not formality but naturalness. Ancient religion was devoid of sermonizing. The words of the gods were not made the subjects of ecclesiastical debate. Tiresome clerics did not drown their congregations with a flood of pointless argument. A local exponent of the old-time religion recently offering their prayers and hanging garlands on the hermae chose for his subject the vital question. "Which of the twelve Apostles was the first to drink from the holy cup at the Last Supper." After first intriguing his audience by a few anecdotes concerning his own childhood, the minister analyzed his text from every conceivable, as well as inconceivable angle. At last, running short of time, he postponed his conclusions on this matter of pith and moment until the following Sunday! All the while virtue continues to fail from the earth crime waxes strong, and there are ominous mutterings of new wars.

The priests of the ancient temples were merely the custodians of the treasures bestowed upon the sanctuaries by the wealthy. The temple devotees came when it pleased them, of the illustrious dead. In the presence of the images of the immortals the thoughtful soul sought solitude. Into this inner silence there flowed a mysterious strength—courage to dare, patience to wait, vision to hope, fortitude to die. No discordant choir interrupted the ecstasy of enraptured meditation; no smug-faced deacons doled out the pews. Sanctuary was a place holy and inviolate—a plot of earth separate from worldly concerns where man might go to ponder the realities of life.

Here all that was good seemed near, and all that was fearful far removed. We may brand him an idolater who reverently stands in the presence of a great marble figure carved by the hands of man into the symbol of a formless power. We may say that no mortal sculptor could enliven an image or cut from marble a divinity. But imagine yourself standing within the temple portals. Upon its lofty pedestal before you looms the figure of Olympian Zeus. The face, many times life-sized, is carved from ivory, as are the arms and the sandaled foot that extends beyond the folds of his golden robes. The noble brow is encircled by a wreath of gold and the gilded sandals were pounded from the ornaments of worshippers. In one hand great Zeus holds out the globe of earth, surmounted by the figure of Athena; in the other are his thunderbolts, symbolic of his might. Though you may disbelieve, yet will you be silent; for in the presence of great beauty the soul is stilled. What, then, do men worship; what calls forth their adoration?

Is it "the high thundering king" upon his golden throne, or is it that subtle beauty caught in the ringlets of his ivory hair or held as though petrified in each fold of his flowing robe? Where beauty is there is a spirit in the air, and it is this spirit that men worship, and none who worships this spirit can be wholly bad. As a thirsty traveler drinks from the flowing fountain in the oasis, so the thirsty soul drinks life from the beautiful and is renewed by the sheen of a gilded globe or the majesty of a carven face. Remember, it is neither the face nor the stone—it is the something that is caught upon the stone as a sound caught by the breeze, as a ray of light reflected upon the ripples of the sea, or a smile given and returned in anthers eyes. So "High Heaven" in its grandeur is more than an image of stone to a tired and troubled humanity which creeps away from its sorrow to gaze upon a noble brow, or contemplate the quality of a sculptor's skill.

Thus from that which is seemingly not real there issues forth a beautiful reality, and God is never distant from that which is beautiful. Can we blame the ancient pagan if, feeling the force that emanates from a harmonious figure, he declared that a divinity had taken up its abode therein? Is that stone dead which can make strong men weep and give cowards courage to go forth and die? Is that stone dead which can hold the hearts of an entire nation and unite all factions in its presence? Is that stone dead before which the sick are healed of their maladies and the sorrowful are given peace? Is that stone dead which can incline man's mind from the contemplation of earthly interests to the concerns of the spirit? Is that stone dead which can inspire man to cast off his natal ignorance and aspire to the beauty which he senses in a carven face? Nothing that is beautiful is dead; for beauty is life, and wherever beauty exists life is more abundant, and when it departs life flickers out like an expiring candle flame.

Is all this idolatry; in fact, is there such a thing as idolatry? Is not even the fetish a symbol of some standard, some beauty which ennobles life? From the primitive beauty of physical courage men grow to the fuller beauty of integrity, and from integrity still higher to pure aesthetics. We arc all idolaters, not because we worship the lesser in lieu of the greater but because we do not learn to understand what we worship and why we worship. Analyzing some microscopic creature the scientist is not seeking simply to learn the habits of an order of minutiae; he is seeking knowledge, and the tiny organism is but the instrument by which he gratifies the desire to know. Kneeling before his household shrine the Buddhist does not worship Buddha. The figure before him is but the instrument by which he seeks to know; it is a tangible nature about which, like some auric sheath, is a peculiar atmosphere of beauty. Because of their severity the cold, gray churches of the modern world have failed to catch and hold the spirit of the beautiful. The God of our salvation will not be captured in hard-lined lectern or graceless pulpit. The chill of death is in the air; not the death of the body but the death of the spirit. It may seem sacrilegious to affirm that there should be warmth in the house of God; that men coming to worship should find an edifice as ennobling as the text.

The old cathedrals of Europe hide under their Gothic spans labyrinths of gloomy chambers where in richly-carved sarcophagi lie the princes of church and state sleeping the centuries away. Here also are dismal dungeons where those who offended the laws of their gloomy God awaited death, their only liberator. Above the heads of the illustrious dead still file the solemn processionals of the faith. Still with awful solemnity the celebrant elevates the host, and the sun's rays striking some lightly tinted pane are reflected from the golden implements of the service. Again solemnity, again majesty, again faith muttering over mystic spells! But instead of man being lifted up into the beauty of God by all this pomp and spectacle, he is caused to cringe with bowed head. Oppressed by the memory of sin, the laity feel rather than see the processional pass by. We say "feel", for they dare not look, the weight of their faith is so heavy upon them. The splendor of God does not raise the worshipper to union with itself, but rather casts him down with the sense of his own insignificance. Whereas the gods of old in gentle tones bade all men come forward and receive their portion of Universal Good, the gods of today, pointing an accusing finger at each cringing sinner, ominously proclaim that if the quality of divine mercy were strained, long ere this the human race would have felt the fires of Tophet.

Nothing is more meaningless than empty ceremonial. The service of forms and letters must pass away, for in themselves they are as ineffectual as the ivory face of Zeus. In the Christian Mysteries it was declared that a spiritual being called the "Angel of the Presence" was invoked by the solemnizing of the mass. Brooding over the congregation, this spirit brought with it the benediction of the Father so that the worshippers should not worship in vain. Is not this Angel the same mysterious power which moved in the adytum of pagan temples; whose proximity was perceptible even to the profane, and whose comings and goings were heralded by tinkling bells?

This was the god whose presence was a covenant and whose departure presaged decay. The Angel of the Presence itself is fabricated from the very essences of worship; it is the atmosphere of sanctity which encloses the holy place as within an iridescent bubble. The contents of this bubble are actually breathed in by the assembled multitude whose bodies become charged with a certain ecstasy which defies analysis.

The purpose of ritualism is to create this intangible atmosphere; to incline men's lives to the quest of that inner peace and tranquillity which is temporarily conferred by the celestial visitant. Ritualism fails utterly if it does not induce rhythm in spectator and participant alike. The gods did not rejoice in rituals, but men in whom the higher emotions are latent find in pageantry an opportunity to express the beautiful and thus mingle their lesser lives with the ebb and flow of universal order. Ritualism has no direct appeal to the rational faculties; ip fact, the whole subject of religion lies wholly within the province of the emotions. So while in the day of great intellectual achievement religion wanes, in the presence of calamity it waxes strong. Previous to the great earthquake of 1923 the Buddhist faith was not taken seriously by the body of the Japanese people. Even the national shrines wore a dilapidated air, for the empire of the Rising Sun was fast falling under the spell of finance. Then concomitant with disaster came religion. The mourning multitudes again brought offerings to the temples and decked the shrines with flowers.

In prosperity man is sufficient for himself, but in adversity he turns to his Creator for strength. Religion is an instinct so deeply implanted within the human soul that it often remains unmanifested until misfortune sweeps away the superficial and bares the inner self.

Thus to the scientist, the intellectualist, and the sophisticate rituals are simply humbug with which a well-fed clergy insure their own expectation of life by themselves eating the offerings, and toasting their benefactors with the sacramental wine. But in the ordeals of the soul of what comfort are stocks and bonds; what consolation can be extracted from the test tube; what condolence can be found in the postmortems of the literati? Trying to make friends out of the printed page and engaging in vicarious romances with their own notions, men of letters live lonely lives. In the great laboratory there is no sound other than the beating of the scholars heart. Yet there is a rhythm in the air, a slow, measured tempo which inclines the whole deportment to gravity of thought and conduct. As this rhythm infects the nature a great cry issues from the depths of the tormented soul: "There is so much to know and I have such a little while to stay." Overshadowed by towering racks of books—the thoughts of lives unnumbered—the reason is confounded. Thus deprived of faith in the possibility of knowledge, the life that serves the mind recoils in despair before the impossible.

The evangelists of the beautiful summon men to come out of their world of selfishness and thought, and to realize that men can die of excessive mentality, and that thoughts themselves can become the harbingers of great sorrow. "Leave the rhythm of vast enterprise," they cry; "leave behind both your interests and your indifferences and enter into the presence of great beauty." Much thinking is a disease, and idle speculation leads to nothing. Only he who loves the beautiful is wise; only he who serves the beautiful is good; only he who shares the beautiful is happy. Beauty is in the heavens and its power extends throughout all worlds. Beauty is upon the earth, molding all forms into the likeness of God. Beauty is in the human soul, lifting man upward to ever nobler vistas of endeavor. Beauty is that abiding spirit which, hovering over creation, tinctures all being with its ineffable nature. Open your minds, therefore, that beauty may flow into them; open your hearts that beauty may flow out of them.

In one of the uncanonical Gospels it is written that after Jesus and his Apostles had celebrated the Passover together they sang and danced, the Master himself dancing with them on the eve of his betrayal. Pan was regarded by the Greeks as the patron of harmony and rhythm, and his pipes were attuned to the harmony of the spheres. In a choral ode Sophocles addresses Pan as the author and director of the dances of the gods, and also as the author and disposer of the regular motions of the universe, of which these divine dances were symbols. Pan was the aspect of Zeus as lord of the mundane sphere, and according to Athenaeus grave Zeus himself bestowed his favor upon the terpsichorean art. Thus the Gnosian dances sacred to the Demiurgus, and also the Nyssian regarded as peculiar to Bacchus, revealed by their movements the various modes of the all-ruling Principle. One of the Pythagoreans composed a complicated measure by which he was able to interpret, with the aid of gestures, the whole body of Pythagorean lore and thus convey much of its esoteric meaning to the uninitiated. Aristotle classes dancing with the imitative arts, and Lucian calls it "a science of imitation and exhibition which explained the conceptions of the mind, and certified to the organs of sense things naturally beyond their reach." Richard Payne Knight declares dancing to have been part of the ceremony of all mystic rites and that persons of exemplary gravity condescended to cultivate it as a useful and respectable accomplishment. He further notes that dancing, being entirely imitative, was esteemed as honorable as the subject it was intended to express.

In his Anacalypsis, Godfrey Higgins advances the theory that the three great elements of primitive ritualism—music, poetry, and the dance—existed before the discovery of writing and were employed in the perpetuation of religious knowledge and historical records. Mr. Higgins deplores the invention of writing, declaring that the decline of pagan virtue was largely due to the wane of the interpretive arts, which were considered unnecessary when more exact methods of perpetuating knowledge were originated. The exploits of all ancient peoples were perpetuated by epic poems. In every community dwelt bards who had committed these lengthy narratives to memory and recited them at feasts and celebrations.

Poetry is the rhythm of words, music the harmony of sounds, and the dance the harmony and rhythm of motion. These higher octaves of ordinary endeavor were reserved for the worship of the gods and to immortalize the deeds of heroes. After the invention of writing, the most important records were either carved into the surface of stone or engraved upon golden plates. Thus deprived of their primal dignity, the interpretive arts became elements of amusement rather than instruction. Men loved the evident then as now, and it was easier to trace a motive in the written word than in some sad harmony or subtle gesture. The ancient poets lamented the decay of their resplendent ceremonials. Ceasing to portray the beautiful in processional and pageantry, the Saturnalia and Bacchanalia degenerated into licentious orgies wherein all that was base and depraved became the theme of interpretive expression. In this state of perversion the fine arts preserved with pomp and show the outward form from which the inner spirit had fled.

Music and the dance were extensively employed in the initiatory rites of the ancient Mysteries. Some of the inner secrets were also perpetuated in archaic meter. Entering upon the path leading to self-liberation, the neophyte found the way beset with rhythms of diverse kinds. Temptation rendered exquisite by a seductive tempo lured him from his austerities. The figures swaying about him in the gloom interpreted the candidate's every thought and feeling. Through the darkness of subterranean crypts resounded the mournful cadences of an infernal music. The rocks re-echoed the doleful sound until it seemed that all creation wept together. The miseries of unrighteous living, the inevitable anguish of uncurbed desire, the hopelessness of irrationality—all these and many other grave realizations were impressed upon the consciousness of the wandering neophyte. When from the dark chamber of earthly horror he passed into the abode of fire, the candidate beheld upon the altar before him a lurid and flickering flame whose eerie light cast vague specters upon the cavern walls. These specters seemed to dance to some fantastic measure ordered by the erratic fire.

Then the music changed. The low monotony gave place to a slight, almost discordant consonance. The tones vibrated with a wild abandon, and invisible fingers strove to tear the human nature from the firm grasp of its will. Dim forms in crimson draperies blended their motions with the gyrations of the altar fire. Bearing in their hands golden platters of grapes and with vine leaves twisted in their hair, these hour is of a rhythmic dream besought the candidate to partake of their illusions.

Half-frenzied with the exotic harmonies, and holding his hands before his face, the searcher after the greater realities of life staggered from the chamber of desire, seeking escape from the haunting rhythms that sought to hold him to the sphere of sense. Again there was silence and darkness, but even the silence seemed to throb, and with brain still whirling the neophyte pressed on to find himself in another chamber lit with a strange twilight, which apparently coming from nowhere was diffused throughout the whole apartment. About the walls upon stone seats sat a row of grave and pensive figures like senators pondering the problems of the state.

The music began again—this time soft and plaintive like a cry from the very depths of the soul. The faces of the silent assemblage were fixed in a melancholy stare as though each man gazed into eternity but saw nothing. The invisible musicians continued their faint and tragic theme which seemed to whisper that all was vanity, that life was a hopeless span, and that all these assembled thinkers thought in vain. The air was sodden with despair; disillusionment filled the cavern like some noxious fume, and in spite of himself the candidate bent his head before its insidious power. Slowly the circle of seated figures began to sway. Without rising they inclined their bodies and heads in unison. The silent but concerted motion breathed a hopeless negation which seemed to say: "There is no use; life is a span of useless suffering, with birth and death the inescapable tragedies of entrance and exit." If only one of these swaying figures would speak! Even though his words were prophetic of naught but ill, it would at least break the terrible tension. But no word was spoken. The disciple felt his courage slowly oozing from him as the chill of despair entered his soul.

Barely able to stand, tormented by the wailing cadence, and half hypnotized by the measured swaying of the old men's heads, the neophyte staggered from the hall of learning back into the dark passageways of the labyrinth. Sobbing and unable to stand, he crawled along the stones, seeking some escape from that cold hopelessness which made all life appear useless and all effort vain. Once out of hearing of the music his courage returned, and recovering his former poise he continued his quest for light. At last he reached the bottom of a flight of steps, and ascending them in the gloom came to two large doors with golden knobs, whereupon a voice bade him open them and enter. As the candidate swung the massive portals wide he was almost blinded by the shaft of light that struck his eyes so long accustomed to somber shadows and gloom. At length his vision cleared and he found himself in a high domed chamber brilliantly illumined by a massive globe of golden light placed in the center of the vaulted ceiling.

The dome was supported by twelve pillars of varicolored marble, and the floor was a checkerboard design with alternate blocks of gold and ivory. In the center of this chamber upon a marble base stood the great veiled figure of the Mother of Mysteries, the "Keeper of the Royal Secret." In a circle about the statue knelt four and twenty priests in flowing robes of white, whose inspired faces were turned upward in contemplation and adoration of the Great Mystery. Again the orchestral music began, but this time it was serene, triumphant, victorious. The anthem of praise echoed and re-echoed throughout the vaulted dome, and the four and twenty priests as with but a single voice sang praises to the Seven-Lettered One by whose graciousness the way of light had been established upon the earth. As the victorious mode thundered through the chamber it caused the very walls to quiver. Overwhelmed by the solemnity of the spectacle, the neophyte fell to his knees in adoration of the power that, descending from heaven, had taken up its dwelling in the temple. Then from among the kneeling figures came forth one more glorious than all the rest, upon whose brow was a golden wreath and in whose hand was a great staff with hieroglyphic figures deeply carved into its surface. Gazing into the face of the hierophant, the neophyte could not but ask the question: "Is this great Zeus himself?"

Taking the new initiate by the hand the high priest opened a small door in the pedestal of Ceres' statue, and beckoning the youth to follow him, disappeared into the darkness. The secrets revealed in this inner room it is not lawful to disclose, for they are concerned with the spirit and the end of that long quest which is man's pilgrimage of life. Here the inner meanings of the rituals were revealed; here the purpose of symbol and allegory was made known; here the initiate learned why the great truths of life cannot be imparted by word alone, but must flow through the whole nature, to be sensed as a rhythm in the air, a gesture in the darkness, a power unseen. Here the robes of the Mysteries were conferred. Invested in the outer symbols of an inner power, the new initiate reentered the great chamber to discover the priests, as though swayed by some mysterious power, encircling the statue with a motion expressive of grace and rhythm. The harmonies pervading the air could not be resisted, and the new initiate found himself a participant in the circumambulations of the sacred rite. He was moving to an exalted tempo and knew that the rhythm which flowed through his body was the same that moves the planets in their orbits and maintains all creation in its appointed place.

The rituals of the Mysteries were first fabricated by the priests in an effort to establish ceremonials which would reveal to the inner perceptions the principle of universal order.

These ceremonials, however, gradually assumed an aspect so vast that they became the very backbone of the state. The Mysteries made the gods seem very near to man. Prince and commoner alike feared the retribution of outraged deities and sought to propitiate by word and deed the celestial^ who were so proximate to them as to lend their presence to the mystic rites. It is difficult for us to conceive of a day when the gods walked with men, for in this generation the divinities have retired before the ridicule of a disbelieving world. But those who have lived in the Orient know what it means to be ever in the presence of the Shining Ones, for in India the immortals still wander the earth in disguise and every mendicant may be Shiva incognito testing the generosity of the pious Brahman. It is sad indeed that human souls should be struck with terror by the proximity of the immortals; that instead of glorying in the nearness of his Creator man should be overcome with foreboding, linking heroes with ill tidings and gods with cataclysms. The guilt that sits heavy on conscience is usually responsible for such uneasiness. Men regard their fellows as fools, and as one mortal to another can satisfactorily explain away their vices. The gods, however, are indefinite quantities with most acute perceptions and accredited with the power of convicting man by his own words. When Nero brutally caused the murder of Agrippina, his own mother, lie faced the world unafraid and drowned his small .measure of remorse in his cups. But from that day on he dared not join the processionals of the Mysteries or take part in any solemn rite. He feared to approach the gods, for the blood he had shed cried out for vengeance. It is said that upon one occasion when entering the house of a great patrician, Nero beheld a statue of the goddess Ceres. As he looked, the goddess caused her carven face to take on the features of Agrippina. With a hoarse cry Caesar covered his face with a fold of his cape and was carried half senseless from the house.

Pythagoras was accused by his enemies of being theatrical and purposely creating an atmosphere of mystery about his person. Even after the lapse of nearly twenty-five centuries the great sage is still regarded as an impostor simply because he employed dramatic situations for purposes of instruction. Not long ago when discussing with a rather eminent scholar the strange personality of the Samian martyr, the learned doctor exclaimed: "But why did Pythagoras insist upon speaking behind a curtain so that only his feet were visible, when anyone knows that such a procedure is utterly ridiculous? Did he for an instant believe that a few yards of blue silk improved the quality of his thoughts or rendered his erudition more comprehensible to his auditors? All these things were simply a vain show and are enough to convince any educated person that Pythagoras was in reality a philosophic mountebank who dressed up a little knowledge in gilt and tinsel so that it appeared stupendous to a group of gullible followers already convinced that their master was a god. When men really have something to say and are conversant with their subject, they simply and definitely set forth their premises and require no such stage props. The man undoubtedly knew something of mathematics and a little of music. He also had an acquaintance with several other arts, but in all things he was simply a superficial observer dependent for his influence and power upon the magnetism of his own personality and carefully staged miracles"

We early discovered that the so-called learned of today are incapable of appreciating ancient standards of culture; that they are far too brusque to sense or respond to the subtleties employed by the greater exponents of Greek metaphysics. The veil of Pythagoras is a constant reminder of the fact that if the senses are united in the contemplation of externals, the nature is not free for the rational digestion of internals. He who saw Pythagoras could never know Pythagoras, for he was not to be recognized by the outer senses but rather to be realized by the inner perceptions. If those listening to his words had seen the master, they would have believed the words to have been his own and to have issued from mortal mouth. But unable to watch the movements of the man's lips, the words seemingly issued from behind a mystery and could thus be totally dissociated from the personality of the speaker. The human mind skips lightly over what it does not see, and although all who gathered there realized that Pythagoras was speaking the words, the fact that they could not actually see him do this caused them to regard the words almost as unspoken. The veil itself was the symbol of Pythagoras the man, for the human nature is but a drape concealing an inner and most transcendent part. When men desire to isolate themselves from all external stimuli, they have but to still by the power of the will the action of the outer senses. Close your eyes, and the world of forms disappears; close your ears, and the world of sounds ceases to be. Veil an object and the object itself is no longer there, for the mind then creates and endows as fancy dictates that which the sense perceptions have not dimensionalized. Pythagoras desired his disciples to realize that the words issued not from him but from the Great Mystery which he had penetrated in part. He was but as an oracular vase, a sounding urn, or a tinkling cymbal; his mouth but a vent in which a spirit dwelt. It was this inner and invisible agent that spoke.

Hence the words that issued therefrom should be regarded as having their origin not in the man but in the rational soul that is above the limitations of the flesh and superior to the dimensionalizing influence of the external senses. Freed from the hypnosis of a personal idolatry, the disciples might thus receive instruction without learning to love the teacher; might understand without seeking to estimate personality; might come to know the truth and not simply the measure of a man.

Why, then, did he permit them to see his feet below the veil? The symbolism is again evident. Man's whole nature is a mystery of which only the feet are visible, for the physical body which we perceive and regard as the whole of man is really but the pedal extremities of the soul. He who sees but the visible man sees only the feet of a vast superphysical agent whose head is of spiritual gold but whose base is of clay. The feet extending beyond the veil reminded the disciple of Nature—the visible part of God—whereas the rational and illumined parts that dwells behind the veil separating the visible from the invisible may be known only through the products of the reason. He who saw the feet of the master had seen Pythagoras, for Pythagoras himself was but the physical extremity of a resplendent invisible nature. According to an ancient adage, men are called by the names given to their feet. The visible physical man to which we assign various nomenclatures is but an insignificant appendage of a nameless reality which, dwelling behind a veil, may never be known until we have learned to esteem the invisible above the visible and consciousness above form.

After successfully passing the tests of the lesser rites, the Pythagorean neophyte was permitted to step behind the veil and behold the face of the master, for it was presumed that having completed his preparatory instruction the advanced disciple could look upon the inferior nature without mistaking it for the rational power dwelling within and behind it. Pythagoras was not only philosophic; he was also scientific in his use of symbols and rituals. He attained ends which modern education utterly fails to attain, because he employed not dramatic but divine procedures in the accomplishment of spiritual education.

Today the value of an idea is determined by the relative culture and prestige of its author. In antiquity, however, the culture and prestige of a thinker was measured solely by the quality of his ideas. In other words, a man's thoughts were not considered good because he was great; he was considered great because his thoughts were good. The highest authority of the modern world is the modern world itself, and by that criterion the modern world justifies its works. The highest authority of the ancient world was Truth, and antiquity justified its survival by expending its energy in the quest for Truth. No man can learn the truth unless he has the correct rationale of approach. In great measure this attitude is the outgrowth of atmosphere, and atmosphere can sometimes be created by a dramatic flourish. Yet is there not a science of atmospheres? Do we not declare that the color of wallpaper affect our moods? Do we not instinctively feel more optimistic when the sun shines than when it rains? Are we not at one time elated and at another time cast down by environmental trivialities? Does not our entire mental constitution reflect the state of our disposition, and are we not more susceptible to instruction when in one state than in another? Is it not therefore legitimate to increase our efficiency by creating those mental atmospheres which most effectively stimulate and directionalize our rationality? From this point of view a veil of^blue silk—though to the superficial an absurdity—might become, when employed by one versed in the profounder aspects of the mind, a definite aid to the student's understanding, and consequently serve a justifiable end.

What has been said of the blue veil applies equally to all forms of ritualism. When rituals are designed and executed by the uninformed they are meaningless and grotesque. When created according to definite philosophic principles and performed with a knowledge of the transcendental arts, these very rites become alive and have resident within their own natures a virtue capable of being transmitted to an assemblage. We have lost the art of ritualism—the science of divine dramatics—yet in the dissemination of philosophic verities it is often necessary to resort to figures and symbols to convey those subtle facts incommunicable by any literal method. The only reason men demand that the statement be direct and simple is that they ignore those elements of life which cannot be stated directly. The Great Arcanum perpetuated through the ages by diverse means depended upon ceremonial and processional for the exposition of certain principles, particularly those concerned with aesthetics. The crassness of our present attitude is largely responsible for the disregard for ritualism that exists in our national life. We do not necessarily refer to the somber rituals of the church, which are all too often depressing and inhibiting, but rather to those racial ceremonies and processionals with which ancient nations were wont to express the composite ideals of an entire nation through exhibitions of grace, rhythm, and beauty. Niebuhr observes that the ancients never founded their tragedies on real, but on mythical history only. What were the myths? Simply the outer veils of the Mysteries—that part which, though revealed, remained comparatively meaningless until the allegories were unlocked by the philosophic keys. It remained for Christendom to inextricably confuse the issues of mythology and history, causing the former to take on the substance of the latter and thereby lose all semblance to its own true nature. The early Church recognized, however, the peculiar efficacy of the pagan ceremonials as evidenced by the introduction of the Mystery Plays; for on the steps of the cathedrals even during the Middle Ages it was customary to enact episodes from the lives of Jesus and the twelve Apostles. These pageantries ostensibly were to assist the ignorant in understanding the profundities of the faith. In reality, however, they were perpetuations of the ancient Gnostic practices which the Church fathers outwardly opposed but inwardly accepted. At this point a subject germane for discussion is the destruction of the pagan Mysteries, or the "death of Great Pan" as it was enigmatically called. The Church affirms that the Gentiles in their frantic eagerness to embrace the new Christian faith deserted, to a man, their heathen altars. Those familiar, however, with the lengthy pleadings and arguments employed by the early Church fathers to convert unbelievers will realize that the accounts of the pagan stampede toward Christianity are more of a rhetorical display than a true statement of the actual facts. As more than one author has observed, the pagan Mysteries actually fell from the combined effect of treachery and profanation. Great Pan, like Caesar, drew his cloak about his face and fell from the thrust of his dearest friend. "Yet Brutus was an honorable man!" He did not slay for personal gain or because he loved Caesar less, but because he loved Rome more. So with the Mysteries. The rending of the Temple veil symbolized the abolition of the Mysteries and the birth of that new dispensation which sought to liberate mankind from bondage to a despotic priescraft by making the way of salvation equally accessible to all men, irrespective of their intellectual, spiritual, or ethical status.

Carried away by the blandishments of worthy ideals such as these, Christian zealot persuaded pagan proselyte to commit that most impious crime imaginable—namely, to divulge the secrets of the Mysteries. On the assumption that the end justifies the means, many initiates broke their holy obligations and thus wrought the destruction of those sacred institutions which for uncounted centuries had been the custodians of the secret doctrine. It was but a few hundred years, however, before the Church awoke from its disillusionment. Recognizing that spiritual equality was but a figure of speech, it straightway reversed its position and proceeded to retrench itself behind the very mysteries and rituals of the pagan institutions it had overthrown.

Thus pagandom died to no good end, and the new faith rose upon broken vows and the sincere but misguided efforts of pagan initiates. Upon the desecration of their sanctuaries, the masters of the greater secrets retired therefrom and adopted secret means for the perpetuation of their knowledge. The oaths broken for the glory of God produced no tangible results, for the power of the priescraft was not destroyed but merely shifted from one organization to another. Through their first spokesman the Christian Church admitted the possession of certain mysteries and spiritual secrets, and these are still preserved in its ritualism and ceremonials. But for lack of certain august mysteries which had not been entrusted to such initiates as might break their vows, the whole body of the inner work is not now and never was in the possession of the Christian Church. For lack of these elements of knowledge, mystagogues could not interpret the symbols which were accepted solely for their apparent virtues, and hence rituals "lost the name of action." So from an outward figure and an unquickencd form the science of sacraments and ceremonials was established, the virtues of which Samuel Butler in his Hudibras thus describes:

"With crosses, relics, crucifixes Beads, pictures, rosaries and pixes; The tools of working out salvation By mere mechanic operation." Upon vain ceremonial and empty rite the antiritualist vents his spleen. All too keenly he senses the superficiality, the tawdriness of outer show, but most of all the absence of the inner spirit. But in common with all extremists, because he does not like a part he would sweep away the whole with imperious gesture. Because he is dissatisfied with the rituals with which he is familiar, he declares the whole science of dramatic instruction to be composed of stuff and nonsense.

Estimating things as they should be by the rule of things as they are, the modernist rejects all in the efforts to escape an objectionable fraction. In the ancient Mysteries it was declared that broken oaths induced their own punishment. Religion in the hands of the rabble bears terrible evidence to vows and obligations turned recreant. In time, however, these things will pass away and the beauty now deeply hidden within each deed and thought will again come into its own; for error is mortal, but Truth is immortal, and though crushed to earth shall rise again. For thousands of years the ancients perpetuated by dramatic instruction those secrets of the inner life which formed the substance of every mythos. The New Testament of the Christian Church is itself a book of rituals, for it is filled with allegories and parables which inspire by virtue of their dramatic power. Although drama was employed by the priests, it is not essentially a priestly art; for it is an instinct present among even the most primitive types, and serves the innate desire of every creature for self-expression. Though in a certain sense a reproductive or imitative art, it is more than this; for it provides an adequate channel of expression for the surging impulses of the soul.

We must therefore fight to preserve those arts by which the nobler moods of man can be interpreted. Without such means of self-expression the individual is a locked soul whose inhibitions must ultimately canker the whole nature. We might very properly ask ourselves, however, if we can preserve the beauty in ritual and allegory when we have rejected both the religious and ethical systems of which ritualism was the natural expression. Is it possible to live crass and material lives, worshiping our own industrialism while still maintaining the integrity of mystic rites and pageantries? The answer is obviously in the negative, for we cannot serve the God of beauty and the spirit of selfishness at the same time. Man must choose the gods he will serve and abide by his decision. The sorrows of this century are abundant proof of the folly of his choice.

Yet ridiculous as it may seem, the day is not far distant when the world, tired of its modern gods, will revert to the pantheons of earlier days. Already a suffering humanity is turning from a god of gloom to seek the god of joy. Caged within the ever-narrowing confines of its commercial endeavor, humankind is seeking to escape and raise again its altars among the hills. The gods of the terminals have grown intolerable; the human soul desires again to fraternize with the rustic spirits and know the carefree life of the faun and satyr.

Great Pan is not wholly dead. Some day he will burst the bonds that chain him in the dark abyss, and returning to his rushes by the stream, will again play glad tunes upon the pastoral pipes. Pan is the patron of the rites and rituals, lord keeper of the dance, and peculiar spirit of the depictive arts. One hundred years ago it was predicted that within a few centuries men would revert to the gods of Plato and Aristotle, and tired of a distant Spirit would rejoice in the proximity of kindlier gods and daemons. We may all look forward with eager anticipation to that nobler day when the gods of philosophy once more shall rule the world; when all will be right in the heavens above and upon the earth beneath. We

are weary of our somber codes and dismal doctrines—creeds that hurl men at each other's throats in the frenzy of selfishness and passion. We desire to again make the acquaintance of those laughing spirits that speak from the waterfall and inspire all men to a rational camaraderie. The scientist may scoff, the modernist deride, and the theologian shriek "Blasphemy!" from the pulpit. All these things are merely incidental for it is the soul of man that endures and it is the soul of man that must be satisfied. Mortal institutes rise and fall, but the urge of self-expression never dies because that urge issues from Divinity itself. Men can be ensnared for a little while and their purposes temporarily turned aside. Ultimately, however, they will be themselves, and this being like self involves the expression of the inner motives through the medium of the arts.

A new age of beauty is dawning, and a race long servant to its greeds and baser desires is turning toward the contemplation of a nobler purpose and a more exalted destiny.

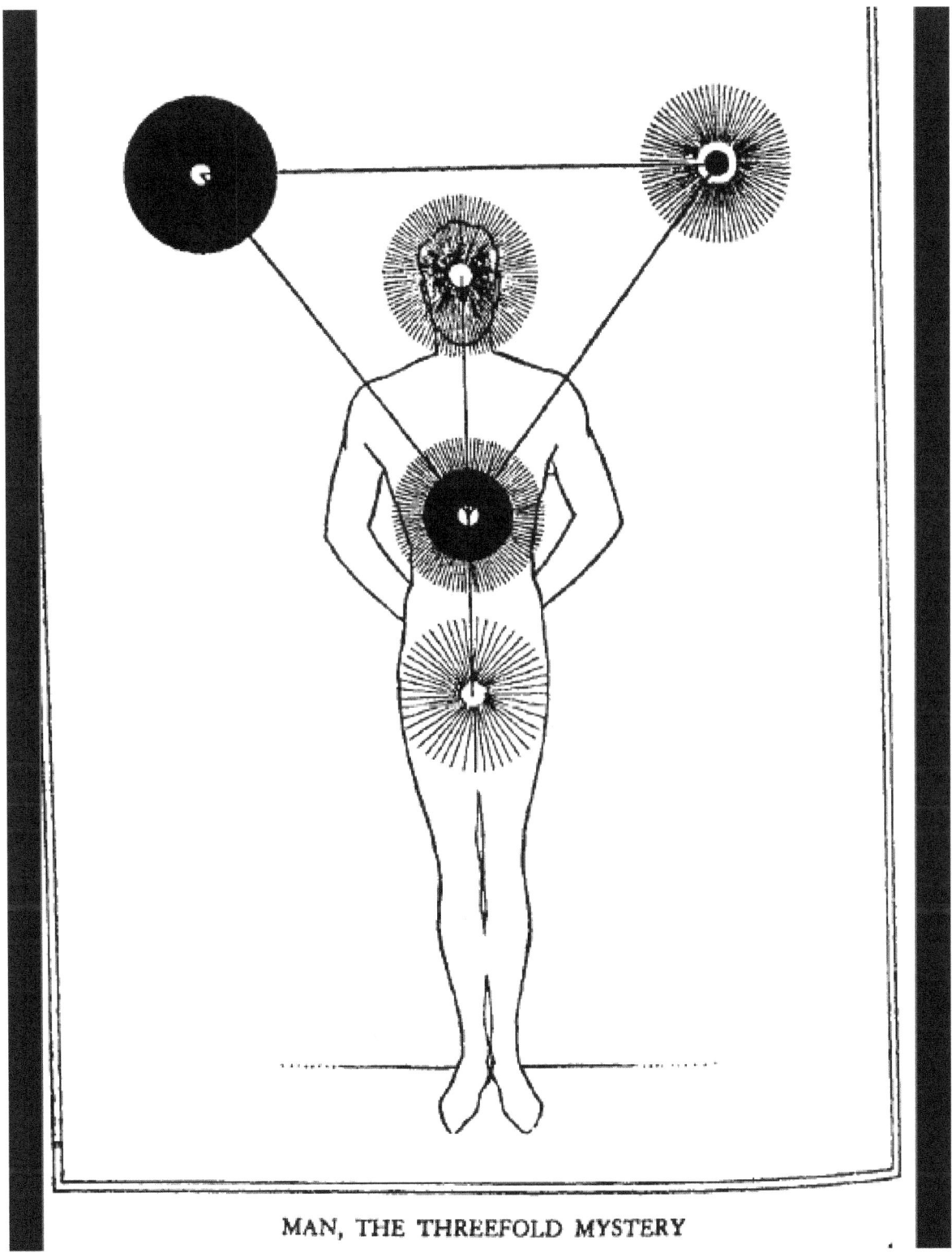

## MAN, THE THREEFOLD MYSTERY

In this diagram, the divine nature of man is represented by an inverted triangle, with its lower point resting in the heart. The spheres of power upon the upper points of the triangle are the Anthropos, or Oversoul. From the spirit in the heart come forth two poles—one ascending to become the mind, and the other descending to become the generative system.

# XXXV

⚬⚬⚬

# A Philosophic Consideration of Man

CONSIDERED philosophically, man is the microcosm, or little universe—-the miniature creation in whose composite nature are epitomized the various orders of life: divine, super mundane, and terrestrial. "Like a fetus," writes H. P. Blavatsky, "he is suspended by all his three spirits, in the matrix of the macrocosmos." Humanity, then, is still in an embryonic state and, dwelling within the darkness of the sidereal womb, is suspended from Cause by a threefold umbilical cord—the cable tow of the Freemason and the braided cord of the Brahman initiate. Of the threefold spirit, Paracelsus writes that the first has its seat in the elements, the second in the spirits of the stars, and the third in the divine nature itself. Centuries before, Proclus had defined the triune nature of man as three monads which are one monad—being suspended from unimaginable unity. The first monad is the eternal God; the second, eternity in its own nature; and the third, the paradigm, or pattern, of the universe.

A similar doctrine was promulgated by the ancient Cabalists, whose profound investigation of transubstantial natures revealed that man's superior nature verges toward God, his inferior part toward the earth, and his intermediate part toward the spheres whose radiant energies flow through that intangible atmosphere called the astral light, or anima mundi. It should be borne in mind that even body is primarily a spirit, form being merely the objectification of the formless monadic physical principle. Soul is likewise an astral spirit. Hippolytus declared that the Assyrians considered the soul to be a triple unity, "soul" signifying the causal nature—the threefold monad of Proclus.

At this point we may with profit consider a few lines from the famous Chaldean Oracles: "The Mind of the Father uttered that all should be divided into three. His will nodded assent, and at once all things were so divided." In respqnse to the decree of the Forth-thinker, "He who governs all things with the Mind of the Eternal," the root division was thus ordered. "In very cosmos there shineth a Triad, of which a Mona is the source." And further, "From this Triad the Father mixed every spirit, arming both mind and soul with triple Might." Issuing from the Paternal Foundation and established in the generations, man thus possesses three moving spirits which collectively are one spirit—the prime mover, the unmoved yet all-moving agent. It is natural, therefore, that each part of man should incline toward its own essential nature, being drawn thereto by a subtle gravity. That spirit which is from God, since it is the most subtle, consequently escapes back into God, "the Thrice-Beyondthat spirit which is of the soul inclines toward the celestial spheres, since it finds its affinity in the stars of whose substances it is composed; while that spirit which is of the body is drawn downward to mingle its agencies with the dark earth, its common parent. Thus, while these three agencies are combined in the making of man, they still preserve certain individual characteristics, and pursuant to the line of expression indigenous to each seek to move the soul nature in one direction or another. The salt of the alchemists is but the terrestrial nature, the sulphur the celestial, and the mercury the sidereal. From the blending of these three spirits the Hermetists brought into existence the philosophers' stone.

In our analysis of man we first regard him as a threefold being epitomizing in a single nature the whole order of universals. The three powers, or monads, enthroned within his nature become vortices of force around which move respectively the substances of the supreme, the superior, and the inferior spheres. Objectifying environments from their own constitution, these monads surround themselves with spheres of consciousness that have their analogy in the universal planes or worlds. Thus the supreme world outside of man exists within man as the environment of his divine spirit, the superior world in the environment of the soul spirit, and the inferior world in the environment of the body spirit. The three monads are also included within each other. The first includes the second and third; the second is included in the first but includes the third; while the third, including within its nature neither of the others, is included within them both. Hence spirit includes both soul and body; soul includes body, but is included within spirit; and body, being the least of the parts, includes neither spirit nor soul but is included within both. The sphere of man's divine spirit is consequently his heaven world, and his inferior nature exists within this heaven evenas the earth floats within the constitution of the sidereal organism. The sphere of the soul is man's human world, where suspended between the superior and the inferior the rational judgment may be inclined by the will to the contemplation of either extreme. The sphere of the body is the inferior world which, analogous to the vast organism of the elements, seeks to swallow up consciousness and hold the innate life within the dark embrace of form. Thus the Universal Man is mirrored in the individual man, in whose parts and members are revealed the laws and processes of cosmic procedure.

The Mysteries instructed man in the nature of his own invisible constitution, revealing to him the structure of the microcosmos of which his spirit was the guiding part. They first informed the disciple that the physical organism, devoid of permanence and rationality, and far from being the master of the life, was simply a whimsical gesture, as it were, of the soul. To the initiated, the very death of the body was proof of the immortality of the soul, for it signified that separation in which a stronger nature deserted a weaker. The body and the soul were likened to two runners, the first being subject to fatigue, but the second tireless. For a while they keep abreast of each other. The body, however, having exhausted the vitality that had been loaned to it, soon lagged behind;but the soul, being tireless because its vitality was inherent, rapidly outdistanced the body which was eventually forced to discontinue the unequal struggle because of exhaustion. Thus, while it is natural for forms to perish, it is also natural for the soul to continue in a vital state for a long period of time. By rational unfoldment it gradually inclines toward spirit, untilit finally mingles its own essences with those of immortality. In Platonism we find the soul continually engendering forms, and after having accomplished the purposes for which the forms were designed casting them aside to redirectionalize its own energies. The Greeks held that both life and death were administered by the soul, declaring that so-called acts of Providence were but the will of the soul for the body which it had fashioned, and of whose destiny it was the arbiter.In his treatise On Suicide, Plotinus describes the difference between natural and violent death thus: "But it is requisite to remain in life, until the whole body is separated from the soul, and when it does not require migration, but is entirely external to the body. After what manner, therefore, is the body separated from the soul? When no longer anything pertaining to the soul is bound in the body? For when this takes place, the body can no longer bind the soul, the harmony of it no longer exists, which the soul possessing, it also possessed. What, then, shall we say, if some one should endeavor to separate the body from the soul ? May we not say, that in this case he must employ violence, and that he departs, but the body does not depart from him? To which may be added, that he who effects this separation, is not liberated from passion, but is under the influence of some molestation, or pain, or anger. • • • If, also, a fated time is allotted to each individual of the human race, a separation of the body from the soul cannot be prosperous prior to this period, unless, as we have scud, this becomes necessary.  In the quotation it is arcanely hinted that under certain conditions the soul—which is, as it were, mixed throughout the substances of the body—is caused to pass out therefrom and hover about the body, proximate to it but not entangled by the physical organism. When the concerns of the soul are liberated from the concerns of the body, the whole nature of the soul inclines away from form, gradually severing its connection therewith until at last having nothing in common with bodies it retires from them into itself. This is in truth the philosophic death in which there is not a violent but a gradual segregation of interests. Under normal conditions, the complete separation of the soul from the body is not achieved during a single lifetime, but the soul voluntarily withdraws itself from a decrepit or depleted body because that body is no longer an instrument of rational liberation. Thus in natural death the soul simply casts off a worn-out organism to continue its functions in some newer and more adequate vehicle. Suicide was considered by the ancients to be a misdirection of power; for whereas natural death is a gesture of the body.

In natural death the soul casts off the body, but in suicide the body casts off the soul. Hence such an end is termed violent, for the soul is forcibly ejected from its form without the liberation granted by rational procedure. In his Scholia on the Phaedo of Plato, Olympiodorus declares suicide to be permissible to the wise under five conditions, which specifies the circumstances under which pollution of the divine nature might not be countenanced by the individual. He epitomizes his argument in these words: "Suicide is unlawful, when committed for the sake of the body, but rational when committed for the sake of the soul." Here we have to a certain degree the fundamental tenet of the samurai — death before dishonor. Suicide is therefore unjustifiable to escape misfortune and affliction or to evade responsibilities, but a legitimate end when it represents the sacrifice of life for the good of the nation or the service of the gods. Under justifiable suicide the ancients would have classed the deeds of heroes who faced death in the service of the state, as well as the heroism of illustrious men and women of modern times who have willingly given their lives for the cause of science.

Notables among such contemporaneous martyrs are those who have died from experimentation with the X ray and radium. The first philosophers declared the rational soul to be the spirit's most precious attribute; that it should be reverenced as a god and its dictates never consciously transgressed by will or deed. There is a god within the soul of man; a god which blesses by its approach and curses by its departure. This most exalted spirit quickens the life and renders real the whole purpose of existence. When man serves this inner power it is strengthened, and through the soul, its mediator, approaches the inferior man and lends its glory to terrestrial achievements. Conversely, if the life be ill, the spirit withdraws to the point of greatest isolation, whereupon the soul, overcome by the noxious fumes of materiality, is said to "die." Thus a man may actually be dead in his inner nature while still alive in his outer. After the disintegration of his own soul he becomes a slave to the daemons or spirits residing in the astral light.

These agitate his internal parts, causing them to assume the appearance of normal functioning. Such a person, however, is severed from all relations with his divine part. Sorcerers, vampires, and werewolves are thus declared to have lost their souls, being but outer shells from which the inner life has fled or—more correctly—decayed.

Materiality hardens the nature and we frequently hear the expression that this or that person has no soul. This does not mean philosophically, that the soul is necessarily dead, but that the eyes of the soul have been blinded by the concerns of the body. It is not sufficient that man should live physically and exist in the divine sphere as a vortex of reality; it is also necessary that his soul, composed of the astral light, should be caused to verge toward reality and thus impregnate the entire organism with those virtues which are resident in the Seven Spheres, Here a most vital question is introduced, namely: Why should a man be virtuous? According to the materialist, a certain measure of personal integrity is necessary for the success of the physical community life of the race. From the theological outlook, a little virtue coupled with a plentitude of belief is sufficient to preserve the immortal spirit from the pits of hell. Considered from the philosophical point of view, virtues, being resident in the soul, must serve as the bridge across which human consciousness passes to be united with its spiritual cause.

When we elevate the concerns of the body above those of the inner nature we threaten the integrity of our soul-life and thereby endanger our rationality. The second death of theology is the death of the soul, at which time the individual's astral- light body is disintegrated back into the anima mundi, which is the soul of God. These, then, are the major elements in the occult constitution of man: (1) The spirit, which is the eternal foundation and the abiding reality, by virtue of which man is immortal, superior to both beginnings and ends, and eternal in his own heavenly nature; (2) the soul, which is the intermediary by which the life in each is mingled with the starry life in all, and the qualities of the sidereal bodies are communicated to each individual, who thus manifests through vices and virtues the states of excess and temperance existent in the sidereal nature; (3) the body which, being of the earth earthy, is the outer framework wherein the higher nature is imprisoned as within a cage during the period of its exile in the material universe.

As the constitution of man is suspended from spiritual wholeness by three monads called unities, so in the secret religions of antiquity the orders of the priesthood were patterned from this holy mystery. The temple itself was the human body, and the priests who officiated at the various rites signified the spiritual agencies by which the mortal structure was sustained. In the sacerdotal orders of the pagan Roman Empire, for example, the abiding unity was represented by the Ponttfex Maximus, the chief of the Pontifical College and supreme monad of the order of spiritual dispensation. This august person was served by three flamincs, whose duties consisted of lending their sacred presence to the ceremonials of certain gods. Are not these flamines the breaths or flames that bear witness to the hidden and unknowable Light dwelling thrice-concealed in their midst? The ffamines of the first rank were designated the Ffamen Dialis, the Ffamen Martialis, and the Flamen Quirinalis, and were chosen from the patrician class

to signify that they were of the race of heroes. Later the number of ffamines was increased to fifteen and their order divided into the Ffamen Majorcs and the Flamen Minores, the first consisting of the holy three and the second of the lesser twelve. The twelve lesser ffamines are the monads or powers of the twelve Holy Animals which collectively form the physical body of man and which are represented in the almanac by the signs of the zodiac distributed throughout the human body. The Ffamen Majores in Freemasonry are the three grand masters of the Lodge of Jerusalem who arc united together in the service of the Hidden King—the Pontifex Maximum Universalis. The Ffamines Minores have their analogy in the twelve fellow-craftsmen who, venturing forth in parties of three, seek the body of their murdered master. Thus man, the microcosm, becomes the pattern after which all the procedures in the inferior universe are ordered and whose parts are combined in a profound and mystical arrangement.

Among the gods of the Cabirian rite were several diminutive figures with curiously distorted bodies, and bearing the marks of advanced age. These monstrosities provoked the ridicule of Cambyses, who could not conceive them objects worthy of veneration. In the Mystery rituals reference is repeatedly made to a strange dwarf equal in size to the human thumb who, dwelling alone in the sanctum sanctorum, is never visible to man but hides himself amid the furnishings of the sanctuary.

According to Paracelsus, the rational Knower dwells in the auric radiances of the heart, being a flamelike body equal in size to the last joint of a man's thumb. In the Kathopanishads of the Brahmans, it is also written that there is a man, the size of the thumb, who dwells in the ether of the heart and who is called the "Mystery Flame." From these sources is thus established the nature of the Cabirian dwarf whose physical proportions were inconsiderable but who was yet greater than all the universe; for when Krishna in the Vamuna avatar assumed a

diminutive stature he was yet able to cross the earth in three strides. The Mysteries held the rational part of man to be inconsequential from the standpoint of physical measure, but in its superphysical magnitude great enough to include all existence within its scope. Thus was emphasized the spiritual reality that quality and not bulk is the true measure of size.

The little man in the heart rules the great man in the world; for the body structure is like some huge machine whose complexity, while far eclipsing the insignificant proportions of its

operator, is powerless without the conscious mind and guiding hand which controls all its parts and functions.

Though the subject of reincarnation has been touched upon elsewhere in this work, it is nevertheless appropriate when considering the relationship of man as a spiritual entity to man as a physical personality, to discuss more at length the bonds which unite the superphysical consciousness to its physical environment. The spiritual agencies conspiring to produce the creature which we designate man are thus described by Plato: "Indeed it is necessary to understand man, denominated according to species, as a being proceeding from the information of many senses, to a perception contracted into one reasoning power." G. R. S. Mead translates the latter part of Plato's statement to read: "and collected into a unit by means of ratiocination." From this definition we are to infer that the objective man is founded in the reaction of the senses and that, after emerging from sensations, man attains stability by organizing these sensations with the aid of his rational nature. If these sense stimulations are not analyzed with respect to cause and mutual relationship, it is impossible for unity to exist within the nature, and for lack of such unity man must continue to exist as a bundle of contradictions held together only by instinct It has already been stated that man does not actually enter into his immortality until he becomes conscious of that immortality. The instinctive man is consequently not immortal because in his consciousness there is still a vast preponderance of mortal elements. The eternal ebb and flow of cosmic processes contribute instability to the whole temperament and in response to this inconstant action the soul abides in a state of untranquillity. Spirit is the supreme power, and only when through initiation into the mysteries of the spiritual spheres he is moved to unite his soul and body with his spiritual part does man actually achieve immortality. Noble aspirations incline the soul toward the Great King, and only by absorbing his inferior constitution into the substances of this First of Immortals does man actually annihilate the interval between his temporal existence and his eternal endurance.

The problem of metempyschosis was one that profoundly occupied the attention of Platonist, Neo-platonist, and Gnostic alike. The Pythagorean doctrine of transmigration as expounded by Empedocles was admitted to contain an arcane rather than a literal meaning. While apparently accepting the doctrine of the literal transmigration of human souls into the bodies of animals. Plotinus undoubtedly possessed a knowledge of the esoteric interpretation of the doctrine, for nowhere else in his writings does he so freely employ irony and ridicule. Proclus, Chalcidius, and Hermes all maintained that it was unphilosophic to affirm that the human soul could ever return in the body of an animal, for the very will of the gods forever preserves so noble a creature as the soul from such a disgrace. Proclus enters the lists in Plato's defense, setting for himself the task of interpreting Plato's allusions to the return of man in a brutish constitution. Proclus reminds the reader that when in the Republic Plato declares that the soul of Thersites assumed the life of an ape, the word life (and not body) was very explicitly used, thus signifying that the soul assumed the irrational appearance, though not necessarily taking on the physical form of an ape. Again, in the Phaedrus, Plato describes the descent of souls into a brutish life but nowhere does he state that they assumed brutish bodies, for in Platonic philosophy life is not synonymous with form. By all this commentary, Proclus attempts to show that Plato referred solely to the invisible constitution, describing the various changes occurring therein when it is molded by the diversity erf human moods.

Through living a bestial life man causes his inner nature to assume the appearance of a beast, and is known to the wise not according to the contour of his physical body but according to the visage of his soul. When so completely possessed by animalistic traits that the soul takes on the similitude of a beast, he is classified according to the species of his soul and hence may reasonably be termed an animal.

Pythagoras delved even more deeply into the occult conditions resulting from a depraved life, circulating among a selected group of disciples a conclusion still more profound concerning the condition of the unrighteous dead. He declared that as like attracts like, and man by common impulse verges toward natures most closely resembling his own, it was natural for the virtuous to incline toward God and for the vice-ridden to incline toward the beast. Pythagoras did not intend to liken a bad man to a good animal, but rather employed the animal as a symbol of a nature in which rationality is dormant and the impulsive nature supreme. He stated that under certain circumstances a depraved human soul might attach itself to an animal even as a daemon might attach itself to a man.

The human soul did not actually enter into the constitution of the animal but rather verged toward the instinctive nature of the animal in an effort to gratify its own uncurbed desires. Hence an animal may be moved or influenced by a human soul even as Socrates was influenced by his daemon. A certain animal exhibiting almost human intelligence may owe that quality to some human soul that has attached itself to the superphysical nature of that animal. In ancient theology Hermes was called the Psychopomp, "the lord of souls" and shepherd of men, of whom Proclus writes: "Hermes governs the different herds of souls, and disperses the sleep and oblivion with which they are oppressed. He is likewise the supplier of recollections, the end of which is a genuine intellectual apprehension erf divine natures. Hermes is, consequently, the divinity presiding over metempsychosis, administering the laws which cause men to return to mortal existence periodically until the generating soul has liberated itself from the idea of form. The "herds of souls are the life-waves gathered into groups by certain common motives which cause similar nature to incline toward each other. Moving in a circle as it were about the Central Life, these herds are represented in mythology by Ixion bound to the wheel of generation. As the dispenser of sleep and oblivion, Hermes controls the moods by which men are entangled and held to form, or rather released therefrom. It is Hermes also who governs the memories and closes the doors of the past for those as yet not rationally awakened, and therefore unfit to contemplate the record of past actions. He is likewise denominated the supplier of recollections, and in this office is true to his great role of universal instructor. As the god of wisdom, Hermes instructs men by revealing to each individual the record of his own experiences. In the Egyptian myths Hermes is the scribe of the gods, and his writings are traced upon the tables of memory. With a gesture Hermes veils these records from the uninitiated, but reveals them to such as have awakened their inner consciousness.

On the widespread acceptance of the doctrine of metempsychosis among the ancients, Godfrey Higgins in 1836 wrote: "It was held by the Pharisees or Persees, as they ought to be called, among the Jews; and among the Christians by Origen, Chalcidius (if he were a Christian), Synesius, and by the Simonians, Basilidians, Valentiniens, Marcionites, and the Gnostics in general. * * * Thus this doctrine was believe by nearly all the great and good of nearly every religion, and of every nation and age; and though the present race has not the smallest information more than its ancestors on this subject, yet the doctrine has not now a single votary in the Western part of the world."

The theory of reincarnation was frequently employed by ancient historians and philosophers in the interpretation of their fables. Plutarch declares the aceount of Bacchus being attacked and dismembered by the Titans to be a sacred narrative concerning reincarnation, while Sallust, in The Gods of the World , explains the rape of Persephone as an ancient allegory signifying the descent of the soul into birth. Several Greeks declared themselves to be aware of the previous bodies which their generating soul had precipitated into material existence. Pythagoras discourses at some length on his previous lives, and the description of five of these will be found in my large book on symbolism. Empedocles also remembered when his rational soul had occupied the body of a young girl. The Emperor Julian believed his soul to have manifested in former life as Alexander the Great, and Proclus, according to Marinus, unhesitatingly declared that his rational nature had achieved its high dignity while in the body of Nicomachus, the Pythagorean. It should be particularly noted that, unlike the present popular concept of reincarnation, the ancients did not affirm themselves to have been some other person in a previous life, but rather that the rational principle dwelling in them had previously dwelt in other forms .

Plotinus writes: "It is a universally admitted belief that the soul commits sins, expiates them, undergoes punishment in the invisible world, and passes into new bodies." He might also have added that it was a universally admitted belief that the Mysteries, by assisting the rational soul in its procedures, shortened the number of reincarnations and released the inner nature to return to the felicity of its Father-Star. Here, then, we have the whole purpose of the Mysteries, which existed as institutions of liberation, serving the invisible part of man and surviving only in civilizations where the rational nature was regarded as worthy of culture and education. Plato also affirms that when the soul fails to achieve liberation and willfully follows perversity, it passes into the body of a woman. This enigmatic statement is generally interpreted to signify that the soul takes up its residence in the matrix awaiting rebirth. In the profundities of Platonic philosophy, however, a truth far more recondite was inferred. General Pleasanton discovered that when man degenerates himself through vice of excess, his whole constitution is electrically repolarized and, electrically, he becomes a woman. This does not mean that women are degenerate men, but rather that man in a virtuous state is negative in his vital or etheric body, while woman is positive. When through excessive emphasis of physical propensities and sensibilities man moves his center of consciousness into his physical nature, the latter is rendered positive (and therefore technically feminine), although its manifestations are totally dissimilar to the natural feminine organism which is positive by divine decree. Why do we persist in accusing the ancients of ridiculous fancies when our own generation has proved conclusively the correctness of their deductions? There is but one answer: We have arrived at our findings through what are termed scientific means or procedures, and hence arc foolish enough to presume that they could not possibly have been discovered in any other way.

In reality, philosophy armed only with the instruments of reason has penetrated the rational sphere where science fears to tread, and has left a record of glorious accomplishment in every division of learning. One other thought before we pass to the consideration of another phase of man's philosophic constitution, namely, the incarnation of deeds and the buildings of bodies composed of actions. Plato has already affirmed that man as a form proceeded from the sensations. It is equally important to bear in mind that all thought, feeling, and action, having their origin in the superphysical nature, descend like monads from their generating sphere, and clothing themselves in appropriate vehicles manifest as entities upon the planes of the inferior universe. In a symbolical sense insects were regarded by the ancients as the incarnations of human attitudes. Butterflies, for example, were said to be an expression of the beautiful thoughts of men, while evil insects that torment man and beast were the offspring of destructive impulses of the soul. Plagues were attributed to a similar origin; for the bacillus, coccus, and spirillum now the subject of so much scientific disputation were regarded simply as minute organisms enlivened by the various emotions of men.

In the invisible world, therefore, exist manifold orders of life that are actually the mental and emotional progeny of human beings. Paracelsus recognized this fact when he describes the incubus and the succubus—the demons, male and female respectively, fashioned from the stuff of emotional intemperance. Man may yet come to realize that he possesses the power to create living things, and in great measure thus fashion the instruments for his own torment. When Christian theologians substituted hell for the pagan Wheel of Existence, they evidently sensed the import of Plato's intimation that physical existence was the death of the spirit. The material universe, in whose substances our emotions find vehicles of expression and our actions forge weapons to cause us suffering, is indeed a sphere of recompense, a world of retribution, a place of punishment wherein natures perforce must linger until their own innate perversity has been mastered.

In the Sepher ha Zohar attributed to Rabbi Simeon ben Jochai it is written: "Wo to the man who says that the Doctrine delivers common stories and daily words! For if this were so, then we also in our time could compose a Doctrine in daily words which would deserve jar more praise. If it delivered usual words then we should only have to follow the lawgivers of the earth, among whom we find far loftier words, to be able to compose a Doctrine. Therefore we must believe that every word of the Doctrine contains in it a loftier sense and a higher MYSTERY. The narratives of the Doctrine are its cloak. Wo to him who takes the covering for the Doctrine itself. The simple look only at the garment, that is, upon the narratives of the Doctrine; more they know not. The instructed (initiated) however see not merely the cloak, but what the cloak covers." As the written law, thus likened to a garment, conceals within it that unwritten law which is the first mystery , so must the body of man be regarded as a vestment within which a most hidden doctrine is preserved. Moralizing upon the issues of Scripture, theology fails utterly to comprehend the hidden meaning of the sacred books. It cannot conceive of Scriptures as writings concerned with philosophic anatomy, yet such is necessarily the case; for the regeneration by which man's salvation is wrought must take place within his own constitution, To this mystery Socrates alludes when in the First Alcibtades he observes that when the soul enters into herself she will behold all other things. Proclus further adds that when she (the soul) proceeds into her inner recesses and into the adytum of her own nature, she perceives with her eye closed the genus of the gods and the unities of things. The rites and symbols so carefully preserved against the ravages of time and unenlightened ages have been saved for such as can realize that the human body itself is the House of Hidden Places, the Tabernacle of the Most High God, the place of the initiation, the sanctum sanctorum where in properly consecrated chambers the deities abide and accept the sacrifices offered up by sensible natures.

Turning inward from the concerns of the outer life, man enters an area dedicated to the immortals. His own interior constitution is holy ground, and here the gods, so distant from his material concerns mingle their personalities with his rational endeavors. Man indeed may be likened to some highly glorified snail carrying his own refuge with him, and in moments of danger retiring into that stronghold which is his real self. The analogies between the house of God in the world and the house of God in the soul, have been very carefully drawn. To those unfamiliar with the concept, the likeness is unsuspected, but the moment the mind ponders the problem the analogy becomes obvious. The secrets of the Mysteries have always been safe from the profane because the average individual applies the principles of ancient philosophy to everything except himself. The modern student of rounds and races, for example, while dividing the whole social order into numberless subdivisions, never applies the principle to the inner part of his own being. The gods are in the heavens and their power is felt to the most distant parts of the earth, yet man has not discovered that, most important of all, they are sitting upon their golden thrones within his own nature. There is a reason why the ancient temples were patterned after the human body and why every ritual finds its correspondence in some function of man's composite constitution.

The studious seeker after the keys to the hidden work will do well to take the whole body of symbolism and ritualism and attempt to discover their correspondences in the workings of his own parts and members. Salvation is not alone a matter of theology nor yet a matter of philosophy; it is a matter of science and, of sciences, particularly the concern of biology.

Biological salvation is a formidable term, yet it underlies the whole theory of religion, for the redemption of the human race cannot be achieved spiritually until each individual has come to understand the relationship between all his parts and is instructed in the proper manner of combining his forces and resources.

"Man is therefore the quintessence of all the elements," writes Paracelsus, "and a son of the universe or a copy in miniature of its Soul, and everything that exists or takes place in the universe, exists or may take place in the constitution of man. The congeries of forces and essences making up the constitution of what we call man, is the same as the congeries of forces and powers that on an infinitely larger scale is called the Universe, and everything in the Universe reflects itself in man, and may come to his consciousness; and this circumstance enables a man who knows himself, to know the Universe, and to perceive not only that which exists invisibly in the Universe, but to foresee and prophesy future events.

On this intimate relationship between the Universe and Man depends the harmony by which the Infinite becomes intimately connected with the Finite, the immeasurably great with the small. It is the golden chain of Homer, or the Platonic ring "

Concerning the spiritual agencies which actuate the vast sidereal order we are still comparatively ignorant. In its quest science classifies phenomena but senses few of the motives of which phenomena are but the transitory expression. We recognize an infinite life manifesting through an all-powerful urge which, communicated to universal bodies, hurls them with great violence through the definitionless vistas of space. We sense yet cannot fully comprehend the stupendous agency which orders the infinite diversity of existence. Still it profits us nothing to contemplate this infinite magnificence; for recoiling from the unimaginable the mind is sickened by the awesomeness of cosmic magnitudes. Each new discovery but complicates the issues. Men grow tired of the vain quest for ultimates, and with a certain measure of relief draw their shrouds about them and turn from the whole uncertainty. Life becomes a period of vain searching in which the mind, certain beforehand that it shall not achieve its goal, struggles against its own convictions for a little while. The materialist is not really disappointed when failure rewards his efforts, for down in his very heart he really expected disappointment and would have been genuinely surprised with any other result. The most the uninitiated can hope to accomplish is a certain classification of the problems of the unknown whereby futurity may receive the answerless queries of the past in orderly form.

The astronomer is cquiped with the finest instrument that genius of man can produce. Gazing into the starry night through a 40-inch refractor, the pageantry of stars that moves across his field of vision is brought a little nearer, but their mystery is only compounded by their proximity. How can a man, even though long tutored in the science of the heavens, sense the motives of these distant spheres when the very blades of grass outside his observatory door and within the grasp of his hand are a mystery equally unsolvable? If a philosopher should enter that observatory and say to the aged astronomer, "Your quest is in vain; no lens ever ground by mortal hand can discover the souls of the stars," the scientist would answer, "I know that, but how else can I seek? I am born of a race that desires to know and I must search, for only by this vain endeavor can I satisfy that inner urge. Scientists are men of a race apart—a definite mental species; we are eternal questioners, servants to an unfulfillablc desire." The philosopher might smile and make reply: "Hie urge to know is proof of the power to know; for the mind does not seek that which is incomprehensible, but is ever attempting to manifest in its outer functions that knowledge which is inseparable from its inner nature. The knowledge you desire is achievable and you arc divided from it only by your method of approach. Imagine that instead of this telescope—the inanimate product of mechanical skill—you possessed a living lens by which the stars could be brought closer to you than your very self.

Do you not realize that you yourself are a telescope and that by looking through your own being you can discover the secrets that lurk upon the very boundaries of space? Your own composite nature is a living instrument by whose virtues you partake of the sun, the moon, and the stars; your soul is of the very stuff which lights the stars, and by virtue of these in you and yourself in them their secrets are comprehensible to you. The life that actuates your own parts is a measure of that Universal Life, and the form that renders all these  tangible agents perceptible to the outer senses is one with the spirit of form, whether it exists in the earth or in the sky.

If you would understand universal mysteries you must realize that only through the living instruments that have united to form your own being are the divisions of cosmic life rendered perceptible. Turn from your telescope which can show you little more than your own unaided eye and will but confuse your already tired brain. Turn to the analysis of your own nature—the manifold parts which unite to form your wholeness—for by learning to know the mystery of your own being you will come to understand the wonders of the All."

Man's only hope of knowing is vested in himself. The creative ingenuity which continually manifests in the development of the arts and sciences discloses, in some measure, man's indwelling Divinity. Though comparatively insignificant, the individual is nevertheless a creature with awareness and the capacity for infinite realization and understanding. While in magnitude he verges toward the inconsequential in potentiality he inclines toward universal immensities. It is irrational, therefore, to judge humanity by the measure of its outward structure. Rather, we must sense through unfolding superphysical faculties the spiritual sufficiency of that inward part from which the visible man is suspended. Man is the magnificent atom which baffles estimation and defies analysis. The universe in turn is the magnificent man; one of that race of giants by whose assembly space is rendered populous. Mortals congregate to form communities; these universal beings congregate to form clusters and galaxies of stars. It has been said that men are the shadows of the gods. The simile is most poetic, but man is more than this; for the "shadow" is substantial and to it Divinity has imparted something of itself that the likeness may share the virtues of the original. The life of the aspiring disciple is forever flowing toward his Father-God, that radiant star whose light shines clearly and steadily throughout eternity. Man is forever seeking to escape from his own littleness and return to that greatness which abides in space. The soul springs from a race of giants and yearns for the strength of its progenitors; man's throne is in the heavens and he longs for the day when entering into his own right, he shall seat himself with the immortals.

All this we must remember when, gazing upon the mortal stature, we are led to erroneously conceive man to be a creature of flesh and bone and ignore his reality as a vast being fashioned from the stuff of aspiration, Man may be likened to a walled city standing on the edge of the desert. In the midst of the city is a well, and from it lead the roads which pass through the gates of the city and become the routes for caravans. The walled city finds its analogue in the body, the gates with their dusty trails are the senses, and the well springing up in the midst of the city is the everflowing life by which both the community itself and the wandering caravans are nourished and sustained. Man's personality conceals his inner life as effectively as the cold, gray battlements of a fortified town conceal the bustling community that lies behind it. When we see only the physical nature of the individual we behold that which least adequately expresses, and often most misinterprets, the internal qualities. Hence the disciple of the Ancient Wisdom is taught to realize that man is not essentially a personality, but a spirit. His outer parts are not the measure of his inner virtues, but contribute that weakness of the flesh which all too often brings to naught the willingness of the spirit. The body can never know the noble ideals which impel the spirit toward accomplishment. Digestion and assimilation are the concerns of the body; to such homely ends it concerns its endeavors.

Above the provinces of instinct and sensation come the concerns of the rational life. The Greeks gloried in their ability to become rational animals, for man is a rational animal. However, that which is rational and that which is animal are actually two definitely divided natures. Rationality is natural to transubstantial organisms, but is contrary to the moods of matter. Unless the rational part retires from its own body and meditates alone, it cannot escape the chidings of the flesh. Now this separation was accomplished by means of the fourth- dimensional, or qualitative, interval. Seated in the midst of his disciples the ancient philosopher, unheeding the nagging demands of the body that disturb the equilibrium of the rational soul, discoursed at length upon the verities of the intellectual life, regarding his physical vehicle as an organ of expression, a temperament suitable for communication, a structure which focused intellect and thus rendered its findings communicable. The true philosopher maintains the efficiency of his inferior nature not because he is a servant to its dictates, but because his own creative expression is dependent upon the physical nature for concrete organization and tangibility.

Thought is the compensation of the original thinker. In matters of the mind, as in matters of finance, man is paid for what he gives, and owes for what he gets. No creative mind can be underpaid, for thought is its own reward and comes as adequate compensation for rational endeavor. Enriched by his own activities, the philosopher soon becomes fabulously wealthy in that most priceless of all possessions: reason. On the other hand, he who listens to the thoughts of the wise is daily contracting new debts, and the longer he listens the poorer he becomes. This may explain why disciples seldom surpass their masters, unless, as Aristotle, they depart from the master's premises. Men eagerly frequent the assemblages of the wise hoping to pick up the stray bits of knowledge that may fall like crumbs from the banquet table. Those who feed upon the crusts of wisdom, however, become more impoverished even as they eat, and he who listens long enough will eventually become bankrupt from his listening. When the day of payment arrives the unfortunate debtor has nothing with which to pay but his own life. Most of those who now suffer from spiritual and intellectual ailments suffer from the listeners disease. Men who seek masters shall be rewarded by becoming slaves, for it is the free man who speaks and the bondsman who listens. The modern school child is impoverished through the act of remembering, and starts life hopelessly in debt. To a certain extent the great minds of the world have rendered humanity mentally indigent. By being a great philosopher Plato has rendered innumerable other minds unsound, and thus contributed to the ethical delinquency of millions.

In a similar sense Christianity is in bankruptcy to its founder, and the Orient will never be able to pay Buddha the interest on its indebtedness. Instead of stimulating the body of thought the philosopher all too often paralyzes it. The great teachers of the world have ever drawn to themselves a coterie of mental corpses which, like dead planets, take on a semblance of life by reflecting the radiance of the central orb about which they revolve. Followers, to use the words of Shakespeare, "have a lean and hungry look." Though totally unmindful of the fact, they are actually economizing in an effort to liquidate. Disciples owe so much that they dare look no man in the face, but feel duty bound to spend their days and nights hymning their instructors with Proper "Glorias." Philosophy today is overwhelmed by a deluge of nondescript "-ites." We have the Hegelites, the Bergsonites, the Benthamites, the Millerites, the Watsonites, cum multis aliis. This "-ite" is the significator of approbation and agreement. Individuals incapable of formulating even a notion of their own, frantically search for someone to agree with, thereby entering upon the path of mental deterioration in which the intellect descends from the simple state of not knowing to the actual inability to know. An individual who becomes an -ite consequently pleads intellectual bankruptcy and assumes what must ultimately prove to be the odious role of serf.

From all this it becomes evident that thought is its own reward; that no man can actually profit from the labors of others but must work out his own mental salvation with untiring diligence. The purpose of a great mind is to inspire to accomplishment, but this end is usually frustrated by an adoring multitude who cannot preserve inspiration as an indefinite quality but must become letter worshipers by prostrating their own minds before a superior intellect. It has always been a serious question to me whether Jesus ever actually spoke the words: "If ye love me, keep my commandments," for the statement is clearly out of accord with both divine and human reason and reeks to high heaven with the sanctified odor of pious interpolation. Truth personified might well cry out: "Let him who loves me, seek me himself and discover me in his own way, and I will reward him with myself." In an old alchemical figure is depicted an aged alchemist out with a lantern at night following in the footsteps of wisdom, while in another part of the picture is a group of worldly-wise men huddled together exchanging their notions with each other, and totally oblivious to the spirit of Truth but a few feet distant from them. You who would discover the inner mysteries of life, depart from the concepts of the many. Be not followers of strange gods, but seek Reality according to the impulses of your own higher rationality. Become creative thinkers, not simply followers of blind cults. Admit enslavement to no mind; read the words of the wise, but think for yourself. Attend to the conversations of the learned, but let your conclusions be your own. Be not hasty to condemn, but accept only that which you are capable of reasoning through with the aid of that divine power resident within. And finally, remember the words of Buddha: "I will not believe a thing because any man says it, not even if it be the reputed word of God. I will only believe it when to me it is true."

## THE PLANETARY ZIGGURAT

The ziggurats, or observation towers, of the Chaldeans rise in seven spiral terraces and signify the astral sphere, composed of the sidereal agencies of the seven sacred planets. In its ascent to the gods, the regenerated soul climbs the spiral pathway, returning to each of the planetary spirits the respective soul qualities they had originally bestowed.

# XXXVI

# The Circle of Holy Animals

The true astrologer must be more than a mere monger of horoscopes; he must be a philosopher. He is the successor to an exalted order of learning, and he must be true to the high destiny to which his science calls him. The origin of the celestial science is obscured by that night of time which preceded the dawn of history, yet the elements of astrology are perpetuated in nearly every form of learning. According to the first traditions of the Orphics, the universe was originally divided among twelve gods, or units of rationality. These gods are the ideas or monads of Universal Order. They are the four Chaldean triads of divine beings perpetuated in modern astrology under the symbolism of the elemental triplicities. To each of these twelve ruling gods was assigned a division of the world, and over its own respective division the divinity presided, establishing its own Mysteries, orders of worship, and those arts and sciences of which it was the peculiar patron.

The establishment of the divine orders is beautifully set forth in the myth of Apollo, the sun god, and Python, the great serpent. The sun is the hierophant, the lord of the Mysteries, the exalted being who dwells in the twelve chambers of zodiacal initiation. Upon entering the sign of the Scorpion (which is represented by the rocky spur of Mt. Parnassus), the sun man found coiled among the rocks Python, the huge reptile which had crawled out of the slime left by the flood. In the Greek account of the Deluge, all mortals perished with the exception of Deucalion and Pyrrha, who repopulated the earth by throwing stones over their shoulders. With his arrows (symbolic of his rays of light) Apollo, the Solar Spirit, slew the evil Python and, casting its body down into a deep crevice in the

rocks, established the order of the Delphic Mysteries. The noxious fumes arising later from the decaying body of the serpent were the vapors of ecstasy by which the Pythian priestess was caused to enter into an ecstatic state. In his precessional march, the sun thus performs twelve herculean labors, founding in each age his own peculiar Mysteries. The sign occupied by the sun at the vernal equinox is thus regarded as oracular, for the voice of the sun god is heard speaking through the depths of this sign from the penetralia of his zodiacal sanctuary in the remoteness of the heavens.

Through antiquity the schools of heavenly Mysteries existed in every great civilized nation. The constellations visible in the midnight sky were represented upon the earth by shrines and temples of philosophic learning, by schools of an inner wisdom. There were consequently twelve great Mysteries from which flowed forth those spiritual truths essential to the well-being of humanity. In like manner, the planets were venerated, the Seven Wonders of the ancient world being erected as pentides to propitiate these wanderers of the sky. Research reveals that the rites of Aries, or the Celestial Ram, were celebrated in the Temple of Jupiter Ammon in the Libyan desert; the rites of Taurus in the Egyptian Mysteries of Serapis, or the tomb of the Heavenly Bull; the rites of Gemini in Samothrace, where Castor and Pollux, the Dioscuri, were hymned with appropriate ceremonial; the rites of Cancer in Ephesus, where Diana, the Multimammia, was revered; the rites of Leo in the Bacchic and Dionysiac Mysteries of the Greeks; the rites of Virgo by the Eleusinian Mysteries in Attica and the Christian Mysteries of the Virgin Mary. In India, Virgo is "Durga," a goddess of great power and dignity. The rites of Libra are peculiarly related to the Roman Catholic Church and the hieroglyphic of Libra is worn as one of the chief ornaments of the Pope. The rites of the Scorpion are the Mysteries of the Apocalypse and the ceremonials of the Sabazians. The rites of Sagittarius are the Mysteries of the Centaurs. Chiron, one of this vanished race, was the mentor of Achilles. The rites of Sagittarius were of Atlantean derivation, for Poseidon, The Lord of the Sea, was the patron of the horse. The rites of Capricorn were the Mysteries peculiar to the Babylonians, and the composite body of the sea-goat signifies that these were celebrated at Babylon and Nineveh. The rites of Aquarius, the ancient

*Zeus as Lord of the World*

Water-man pertain to the Mysteries of Ganymede, the cupbearer of Zeus and the lord of the ethers, keeper of those waters which are between the heavens and the earth. The rites of Pisces are those of Oannes and Dagon, the fish-gods; for, as St. Augustine writes: "There is a sacred fish which was broiled and eaten by the sinful for the redemption of their souls." Pisces is also the sign of the great Deluge, when the waters of heaven, descending upon the earth, mark the close of a Kalpa, or cycle of manifestation when the worlds Cease and the Creator upon His serpent couch floats over the surface of oblivion. Thus while the origin of man's concept of the zodiacal constellations and the forms which he assigns to them must remain an unsolved mystery, the doctrines founded upon the orders of the stars and the wanderings of the planets through the houses of heaven have come to dominate in a most powerful way the affairs of men. The ancient astrologers were wiser than their modern imitators, for they were in possession of a secret doctrine relating to the Mysteries of the constellations. If this doctrine could be re-established, it would go far to clarify the all-too-complicated issues of modern existence and would re-elevate astrology to its true position of dignity as the cornerstone of the house of human learning. Heathen, pagan and Christian alike are united by astrology, for all faiths—with the possible exception of a few primitive forms—are astrological in origin. This fact alone should develop tolerance in matters of religion and incline us to study the sacred science of the stars and learn the inner import of their respective revelations. For the purpose of making more evident the importance of astrology in the mysteries of philosophy and the soul, let us briefly examine a few of the mystical and spiritual allegories founded upon astrological correspondences. James Gaffariel, court astrologer to Cardinal Richelieu, in his remarkable work, "The Talismanic Magic of the Persians," declares that he has discovered the alphabet of the stars by which the celestial writing was caused to appear upon the walls of heaven. Gaffariel traces the Chaldaic Hebrew characters of the early Jews in the star groups, affirming that the destinies of both men and empires are written in letters of light upon the broad expanse of the firmament. Thus is the Universal Bible written in the heavens and the will of the gods continually made manifest in the combinations of zodiacal consonantal elements and the planetary vowels.

## ARIES

The glorious day when the sun entered into the constellation of Aries at the vernal equinox was a time of great rejoicing among ancient peoples, for it marked the beginning of the march of the victorious sun through the vaulted arch of heaven towards his golden throne in the constellation of Leo. This radiant solar divinity is represented, therefore, as a golden-haired youth holding in one hand a lamb and in the other a shepherd's crook. Thousands of years before the birth of Christ the pagans adored this figure of light and beauty, gathering in the squares beneath the Arch of Triumph and crying out as with a single voice, "Behold the Lamb of God, which taketh away the sin of the world." In the ancient Isiac Mysteries of Egypt, the goddess Isis stands upon an altar formed of a black cubical stone, the corners of which were ornamented with the heads of rams. The ram is the symbol of fertility, for at the season when the sun enters Aries the seeds, impregnated with the solar life and rendered moist with the lunar humidity, germinate and burst forth into growth and power. To the Egyptians, the deities or priests of the temples were symbols also of royalty and divinity. Horns appear upon the plumed helmets of the Egyptian gods and also the hieroglyphical representations of the deified Pharaohs. Jupiter Ammon is depicted with rams' horns upon his forehead; the Moses of Michelangelo is also shown with horns. Jupiter Pan, the Lord of the World, and God as the Demiurgus or generator of the inferior sphere, are both represented as a goat-man. The pipes of Pan are the Seven Spheres, and the composite figure itself signifies the sun as the symbol of virility. Aries, the ram of energy and ambition, becomes man's tempter also. So the devil is often represented with the head of a goat. Among the ancient Scandinavians, the hieroglyphic of Aries is the hammer of the gods. In Freemasonic

Ritualism, this hammer is not only the mallet of the third degree with which the candidate is struck but also the hammer of the Master Builder—chief among the tools of the Craft. Nor should we forget the lambskin apron which is the emblem of purification of the generative processes. In Greek mysticism, the Golden Fleece for which Jason and his Argonauts risked so much is directly related to the ritualism of Aries, for this Fleece is now declared to have been a book which, written upon the skins of rams, contained the wisdom of the Mysteries. The Golden Fleece, therefore, is the "wool of the wise," the same wool which they pull over the eyes of the foolish. In the ancient symbolism, Aries, the ram, was the throne of the god Ares (Mars), the figure of creative energy. Ares was the symbol of the divine fire, the flame of spirit. It was the beginning of life, for at the season over which it ruled, victorious Spring escaping from the embrace of Winter begins its tragic journey down the pathway of the year. Winter, Spring, Summer, and Autumn were called the Yugas, or ages of the year. Winter was the beginning and the end, infancy and decrepitude. Spring was glorious adolescence, Summer, strong maturity; and Autumn, brave decline. Born in Capricorn, the "Light of the World" finds in Aries the turning point where it casts aside its swaddling clothes and, filled with the exuberance of youth, sets all creation athrill with the vibrations of its radiant life.

## TAURUS

When the vernal equinox took place in the constellation of Taurus, it was declared that the Bull of the Year broke the Annual Egg with its horns, thereby liberating the spirit or destiny of the year. Apis, the sacred bull, was revered by the Egyptians as the creature into which the spirit of Osiris transmigrated. The selection of the sacred bull was an occasion accompanied by great ceremonial. Many noble bulls were examined before the one was discovered which bore the marks of the divine incarnation. There were thirty of these distinctive markings, and only the animal in which all were present was the residing place

of the spirit of Osiris. The hair of its tail must lie two ways; it must have a scarab under its tongue, a crescent upon its flank, and a square spot on its forehead. Osiris was the sun god, and when at the vernal equinox he was declared to have been born into the body of this beast. Hence, the annual horoscope of Egypt was erected for the moment of this incarnation, or the annual entrance of the sun into the sign of Taurus.

In India, the god Shiva rides upon the sacred bull Nandi, and in the sixth avatara (called the Parasu Rama incarnation), the World Savior takes upon himself the body of the holy man to whom Indra had entrusted the sacred cow. A wicked Rajah once conspired to steal this cow, and to this end murdered the holy man. The personality of Parasu Rama (Vishnu) slew the evil Rajah.

In the "Elder Edda," the gods were licked from blocks of ice by the Mother Cow, Audhumla. The children of Israel made offerings to a golden calf (Taurus). This displeased the God of Israel. The same divinity was not offended, however, when King Solomon elevated his laver, or molten sea, upon the backs of twelve oxen.

The five-footed Assyrian man-bull is a favorite symbol in the Mysteries and has a significance similar to that of the Sphinx, the latter creature being composed of the four fixed signs of the zodiac, or the foundation of the universe itself—the body of a bull.

In the abduction of Europa, Zeus took upon himself the body of a bull, ornamented with the horns of divinity. Ancient altars were often adorned with the horns of bulls and rams and in them were frequently placed vessels to contain the holy oils. Among early Christian princes there are records of several such drinking vessels of the Eucharist being admirably carved from the twisted horns of oxen.

The cherubim placed at the gate of the Garden of Eden after Adam was exiled from Paradise were ox-headed, according to the original meaning of the word)

The word "Kireb" (meaning an ox) further emphasizes the sacred association of this animal with divine functions.

The ancients employed the bull in plowing and furrowing. Hence, this divine creature was said to turn the fields of space and prepare them for the reception of life.

In ancient times it was also customary to use the entrails of animals for divination purposes, and the bull was frequently chosen for this ceremonial. While such a custom now appears to be but an abject form of superstition, there was a definite motive behind the seeming madness. For example, when deliberating upon the founding of a city, a likely spot was first tentatively chosen and the priests pastured in this place a herd of cattle carefully selected for their health and vigor. The cattle were permitted to graze for several months upon the site of the proposed new community. Then, with great ceremony, one of the animals was slain and its entrails carefully examined. If the animal's health had been impaired by its pasturage or the normal functioning of its internal organs upset, the city was not built upon that spot, for it was decided that either the air, the water, or the earth upon which men must depend was not conducive to health and, consequently, a new location was chosen.

In the Cabirian rites, the initiates stood beneath specially prepared sacrificial gratings and were bathed in the blood of sacrificial bulls. In the Eleusinian and Bacchic rites, candidates took their vows of secrecy while standing upon the skins of newly sacrificed bulls. In the Mithraic Mysteries of the Persians, Mithras, the Savior Deity, is shown driving his sword into the heart of a bull. This is significant of the release of the lifeblood of the sun and reminds the initiated philosopher that when the vernal equinox takes place in the sign of Taurus, all men are bathed in the blood of the Celestial Bull, but when the vernal equinox occurs in Aries, their sins are washed away by the blood of the Lamb.

White oxen were used in the processionals of the Druid rites to draw the rough carriages on which were transported the images of the gods, and in the ceremony of the gathering of the mistletoe, white bulls were sacrificed under the tree from which the plant

was taken. Sacred bulls were held in great respect by ancient peoples. Their horns were plated with solid gold, as were also their hoofs. Jewelry and trappings were also hung upon them, and they were blanketed with the most costly material and housed in specially constructed stables adjacent to the temples. These animals were even decorated with necklaces and jeweled leg-bands.

The breath of the sacred Apis was regarded by the Egyptians as a certain cure for all ailments, and to this day the excrement of sacred bulls is reputed to have medicinal virtues by many Hindu castes.

The bull also has an advanced symbolism among Tibetans. Yama, the god of death, is often pictured with the head of a bull because of the materiality and the physical properties associated with this animal. The Minotaur, the bull-headed man that dwelt in the recesses of the Cretan labyrinth, is another example of the symbolism of the bull as destroyer. In this sense, the beast represents the animal that seeks to destroy the spiritual man wandering in the labyrinth of form.

The University of Oxford derives its name from the Celestial Ox because of the Mithraic and Druidic figures of this animal which have been discovered in the environs of the college. It is also assumed that the bleeding heart, so conspicuous among the symbols of Roman Catholicism, was originally the heart of an ox, but that the heart of a lamb was later substituted for it.

## GEMINI

The constellation of Gemini, the Celestial Twins, is particularly related to the ancient cults of phallic worship, the building craft, and the establishment of communities and cities. Castor and Pollux, the Dioscuri of the Greeks, appear again as Romulus and Remus, the mysterious twins who were suckled by a wolf and who later became the founders of the Roman Empire. Nor should we forget the two famous brothers of Biblical narrative: Cain and Abel—their strife introducing the first human crime as tradition relates. Castor and Pollux are associated with the concept of a door. They are the pillars of Solomon's Temple and the figures flanking each side of an entrance, like the Foo Dogs of China. The pylons and obelisks at the entrances to Egyptian temples as well as Jachin and Boaz (the columns of the Masonic Lodge) bear witness to the survival of this ancient symbolic phallic cult. Born out of a single egg, the original twins probably also signify the sun and moon, the father and mother of the generations, the progenitors of all life. In the ancient Mysteries, the twins were the serpent and the egg and have this same symbolic import.

Among the Arabs, Gemini is sometimes symbolized by two peacocks. In the Platonic philosophy, the twins signify the division that took place in the archetypal sphere at the time of the separation of the sexes. For this reason, the children who form the constellation are generally shown as embracing or reaching out their hands to catch each other. The number 2 was the ancient Pythagorean number of diversity and sorrow, for from it the sense of division was established and this division destroyed the realization of life's fundamental unity—the oneness of purpose and the impulse of all creatures to join together in a common bond.

In Prometheus Bound, Aeschylus causes two beings, Kratos and Bia—a male and a female potentiality respectively—to bind Prometheus. From this it is to be inferred that the heavenly light-bearer and the divine splendor which he carried are rendered impotent by the philosophy of the opposites which, by dividing man's resources and severing the elements of his concentration, cause him to scatter his agencies and dissipate his strength. In his book on Numbers, W. Wynn Westcott also notes the fatality which follows the number 2 in connection with the British

Crown. The English kings William II, Edward II, and Richard II were all murdered. The Romans also dedicated the second month of the year to Pluto, the god of death.

The Twins have a Qabbalistic significance, for they not only signify the two Talmuds of the Jews but also the written and unwritten law—the Torah and the Kabbalah. Jewish writings contain many strange statements with reference to the number 2, as for example, that speech is worth one coin but silence is worth two. The number 2 is also referred to as the number of pride and is related to the fall of man. It is the number of Satan, and the sign which it rules is the false, or lower, mind unillumined by the spirit fire of Sagittarius, the centaur instructor. The number 2 is again related to the rebellion of the angels, because it is the first number that dares to depart from the one, thus signifying a kingdom set up against a kingdom—two lights, from which are born division and discord.

In the Mysteries, Gemini signifies the rational processes, for by thought things are weighed against each other. The mind, however, that is ensnared by the intellect is bound to the material sphere, there to die from the complexity of its own cogitations.

## CANCER

In the ancient astrological symbolism of the Egyptians and Greeks, the constellation of Cancer, the Crab, was especially significant. Astronomically speaking, the constellation is not over well defined, as It contains no particularly important stars. To the Egyptians, Cancer and its zodiacal opposite, Capricorn, were emblematic of the summer and winter solstices respectively. Modern Freemasonry preserves the symbolism of the solstices in the figures of the two St. Johns and also under the form of the two pillars. The ancient caves of initiation were always provided with two gates, through one of which the soul descended into generation, later to escape again into the higher world through the other. Cancer was called the gate of physical birth and was sacred to the goddess Isis and also to Hathor, divinities who presided over the mysteries of generation. As birth had a twofold significance, Cancer may be regarded as a dual sign, and the Crab signifies both physical birth with its attendant consequences leading to inevitable decay and also spiritual birth through the Mysteries into the eternal effulgency of the rational sphere. In the Eleusinian Mysteries the nine degrees recapitulated the nine months of the prenatal epoch and symbolized the descent of the soul from the zodiac through the seven planets and finally its immersion in the elemental world. The last sphere through which the soul migrated before it assumed its physical body was that of the moon. This luminary was the keeper of the ways of generation and is enthroned in the constellation of the Crab. The philosophers declared that the solar agent, or life germ, before precipitation into phenomenal life is suspended in an etheric humidity resembling water. They denominated this humidity Isis, or the World Mother. Cancer, a water sign, being designated the gate of souls entering the untranquil sphere, is evidence that the early initiates were acquainted with the now generally accepted postulate of science that all life originated in water. The rudimentary gill-clefts visible in the human embryo demonstrate that in some period in his early development man existed in an amphibian state. Jules Verne, the celebrated writer of the last century, builds his entire story of "The Mysterious Island" upon this assumption. The great sea of the Brahmins in the midst of Which the World Egg was generated, is but an arcane allusion to the amniotic fluids in which the human embryo floats during the period of gestation. Here is further confirmation that man comes into life through water. Thales is popularly accredited as having been the first of the wise men of Greece, in fact he was the only one among the seven original Sophists whose reason transcended the subjects of politics and ethics. When Thales declared the world to float in a sea, it is evident that he referred to this etheric liquid resembling the albuminous part of an egg, a super-essential protoplasm, whose constitution is best described by the symbolism of Cancer and the moon. The crab walks backwards, or at least on a rather sharp oblique, from which the sages inferred that the presumed advancement of man into physical birth was, in reality, a retrogression, for by the phenomenon known as generation, the rational soul was immersed in the unresponsive elements of an irrational nature from which it could be liberated only by death or initiation. But as this first birth, or descent into the state of ignorance, was revealed to the body of mankind as the esoteric significance of the Crab, those accepted into the higher body of the Mystery Religion substituted the scarab for the crab, for by this most sacred of insects was obscurely revealed the mystery of the "second birth." As man is born through the processes of physical generation into the mortal realm, he is born again through the processes of spiritual regeneration into the transcendency of ever-abiding wisdom. It becomes increasingly evident that the zodiacal symbolism was devised by a group of highly-informed priests for the dual purpose of perpetuating and yet concealing the secrets of the ancient temples. Many interpretations have been advanced to account for the zodiacal symbols. Superior to and of far greater import than later concepts, however, are their original philosophic and religious significations, which are the very soul of the soul of astrology.

## LEO

Whereas Cancer is the throne of Luna, the Queen of Heaven, Leo is the mansion of lordly Sol, the ruler of the solar family and the arch-regent of Nature. It is natural—yes, inevitable—that men should pattern their earthly affairs according to a heavenly order. Petty princes of earth have attempted to make themselves impressive by bedecking their persons with solar emblems. Probably the most common of the solar symbols is the imperial crown, or coronet, whose radiating points are symbolic of the Sun's far-reaching rays. For a similar reason, gold, which is the metal of Leo, is regarded as fittingly royal, and the flashing diamond also bears witness of the regal light. When ascending the celestial arch, the Sun enters the constellation of Leo, he is declared to be properly enthroned. Great power lies in this essential dignity. The lion is the king of beasts and has been assigned as the symbolic animal of Leo. His shaggy mane is but the Sun's corona and his roar the voice of absolute authority. When the Sun is in Leo he is the lion-faced Light Power of the ancient Gnostics, or, as the old Greek philosophers called him, "The Tyrant of the World." In the esotericism of the ancient Egyptians, the sign of Leo was sacred to the High Priest, who wore upon his person the symbols of a supreme royalty, before which even Pharaoh must bow abashed. Like Cancer, Leo has a dual significance. That which was revealed to the masses was the lordly dignity of temporal power. Upon this throne upheld by lions sat the prince of the earth whose legions must blindly serve the tyranny of his will. Master of Life and Death, splendid in a celestially justified egotism, the Sun and his representative upon the earth, the king, ruled their respective provinces in space. The minor despot, patterning his garments from a heavenly design, dazzled men with a reflected light. The secret and more profound mystery of the Sun was revealed only to those who had penetrated to the very innermost recesses of the temple. To such it was revealed that the Sun was not designed merely to dazzle men but that each ray was a giver of life and a disseminator of light. In Egypt the rays of the Sun were symbolized as ending in human hands, and by this multitude of members the great solar power finally "raised" all things into union with its own all-powerful nature. To the hierophant, the Sun was the symbol of that perfect wisdom which adorns the learned with raiments of the mind, more precious than the regal cloth of gold. As metallic gold forms the coin of temporality, so wisdom—which is the gold of reason, the coin of the realm of thought—renders its possessor wealthy beyond the dreams of Croesus. Hence, the lion of Leo, not only spreads awe by reason of its strength but has a secret virtue in its own nature, for it is ruler of a family of animals which possess the uncanny power to see in the dark. Kings may roar like a lion, shake their manes, and feel that they have expressed adequately their divine prerogative, but the Kings of kings—those illumined sages who are Princes above the princes of the earth—make no vain show of worldly splendor, but with the gift of the seer penetrate with rational vision the Stygian gloom of the underworld.

And behold the lordly destiny for which man was created. Having sensed the magnificent purpose of this thing called Life, he has come into the secret power of the lion; he is ruler of a world that shall not pass away, for while cities crumble and the achievements of men are at best impermanent, these royal Lions of Judah's mystic tribe are seated upon permanent thrones in the sphere of reason, lighting the universe about them with a magnificence of their own awakened consciousness. There are two ends which all may seek, and both ends are a type of rulership. Those who strive for temporal power must all receive a similar fate: they shall be cut down in the midst of their accomplishment. But those who sense the true dignity of the Solar Light turn from the glories which are ephemeral to accomplish through the disciplines of the Mysteries a greater work. These become, as it were, Heavenly Lights; and their rays, piercing the centuries, light the way of unborn civilizations. They are crowned not with gold, but with understanding; not enthroned upon thrones of marble, but elevated in the hearts of wise men and remembered in the soul of humanity. Thus does Leo, the sign of sovereign wisdom, proclaim to the initiate that the greatest kings are those who rule by right of spiritual illumination.

## VIRGO

The constellation of Virgo introduces a new element in zodiacal symbolism. Like the preceding signs, two definite and almost opposing doctrines are concealed within the single figure. This constellation of stars is supposed to have the rough form of a female figure carrying a sheaf of grain in one arm. Virgo, the World Virgin, represents the beginning of harvest and is one of the zodiacal symbols of abundance. On the other hand, being the house of the Sun's decreasing light, she is employed (as the legend of Samson and Delilah) to signify the temptress, who lures the Solar

Man from his path of power, and, cutting off his rays, causes him to lose his strength. Virgo is the throne of the planet Mercury and in this respect becomes the symbol of a divine scheming. Life to a great degree is a continual plotting towards some rather indefinite end. We know that in antiquity the figure of the Virgin was continually employed to signify the Mystery Schools. While the fact remains unsuspected by the majority, even the modern Masonic Order is essentially a feminine institution. The thought is well expressed in an ancient Egyptian tablet where Isis is described as the Mother of the Mysteries. The secrets of regeneration, as has been previously indicated, were always concealed in Egypt and Persia under the more natural symbols of generation. The adept, or initiate, was born by an Immaculate Conception, being the progeny of the Mysteries. While a feminine sign, Virgo is the throne of an essentially masculine potency, and Mercury (or Hermes) is the Lord or Keeper of the House of Wisdom. Consequently, to the profane, Virgo was symbolic of autumnal abundance, and also of the various institutions erected by mankind and controlled by what we may to term the human intellect. The latter institutions ultimately overthrow civilization; for, tempted by power, the mind forgets the origin of its own creations and by ascribing a divine origin to its own conclusions, falls into the snare of the temptress.

In the Mysteries, however, Virgo becomes the house or body of wisdom, symbolic of the negative pole or vehicle of Hermes, the mind. To the human mind, the body must always be negative and hence symbolically feminine. To Virgo, therefore, the hierophants ascribed the key to the rebirth of the soul through the Secret Doctrine. This Secret Doctrine itself then becomes the principle for which Virgo stands. Here also is the weeping virgin of Masonic symbolism—Isis, the Widow, who, gathering up the parts of the dismembered Osiris, in this way collected the fragments of the Secret Doctrine. In Freemasonry, the widow's sons are the initiates and Virgo is herself Freemasonry left widowed by the murder of the Builder.

As stated before, Mercury is the symbol of scheming. To the profane, scheming implies the plotting whereby men deprive each other of their common goods. In the Mysteries, however, scheming signifies the conclave of the wise in which those who have beheld the truth plot and scheme together not to a nefarious end but that they may discover some method by which wisdom—which is the common goods of the elect—may be safely distributed among all men to the glorification of the Creator and the resurrection of the martyred Builder. The profane scheme how they may take; the wise, how they may give.

### LIBRA

To the astro-philosopher the constellation of the Scales reveals the whole secret of the fall of man. As all such mysteries contain the inherent evidence of an eternal law, so Libra points out the way of liberation and salvation of the fallen angels. In the zodiac is portrayed the entire process of spiritual evolution, with Aries as the beginning and Pisces the end. In the Oriental philosophies Aries is thus the light of Parabrahm, the Universal Reality, the One Cause of all manifestation; while Pisces is the super-mental Buddhi, that perfection of consciousness achieved by the evolving monad after it has completed a revolution of the hypothetical Circle of the Holy Animals.

Taking a flat astrological figure with Aries upon the ascendant and turning it so that Aries occupies the midheaven, or highest point of the circle, and with all of the other signs in their proper order from Aries, it will be found that Libra occupies the nadir, or lowest point of the wheel, upon the cusp of the fourth house. In such a flat figure, under normal astrological conditions, Capricorn occupies the midheaven and Cancer the nadir. To discover the secrets of human evolution, it must be understood that the "Ladder of the Seven Stars" referred to by Hermes in "The Divine Pymander," finds its analogy in the seven signs descending from Aries to Libra inclusive. From Libra the signs reascend to form the ladder of evolution.

Let us now consider the allegory of the Fall of Man, as preserved in early astrological legends. We are told that the zodiac originally consisted of ten signs but that in remote antiquity the number was increased to twelve. This increase was effected in the following manner: the then androgynous sign of Virgo-Scorpio was divided into two signs and a new figure—that of

The Scales—inserted between them. Herein is revealed astrologically the Qabbalistic legend of the creation of Adam and Eve who were formed united back to back like grotesque Siamese twins. The old Jewish writings describe how God with a mysterious instrument severed them. Then followed the Fall and the generations of mankind began, these generations signified by the sign of the Balance. From the ecclesiastic point of view, man is conceived in sin and born in iniquity with only the church between him and damnation. Hence, the Pope as the personification of the divine man, or the vicar of God, wears the symbol of that decadent humanity whose wretched state can only be improved by an abundance of faith.

The hieroglyphs of the signs of Virgo and Scorpio which were divided to form mortal man are still strikingly similar. Both resemble a capital M. In one figure—that of Virgo—the final point of the M is downward and in Scorpio it is upward. Taken as a whole, the sign of Libra signifies material equilibrium, i.e., the balanced forces which conspire to produce man, whose nature the ancients were wont to describe as suspended between heaven and hell. Spirit and matter are here combined in a middle field to produce form. Intelligence and substance engender a personality which is united to spirit by inspiration and aspiration and to matter by its chemical constituents and animal instincts.

No study of Libra would be complete without reference to the Egyptian ceremonial of weighing the soul in the scales of divine justice in the judgment hall of Amenti. This was an integral part of the Egyptian initiatory ritual and in it the scales become emblematic of natural justice. As the seventh sign, Libra must also convey the various significances associated with the number 7, chief of these being that of law. Justice is usually represented as holding a pair of scales, the modern figure being simply a conventionalization of the ancient concept, which was based upon the seven natural laws. In the Egyptian judgment scene, the soul of the deceased was conducted by the god Anubis into the hall of the forty-two truths and their judges.

This hall, generally termed the "Hall of the Twin Truths," represents the two pans of the balance. Here the heart of the dead, usually shown within a small urn, was placed upon one end of the scales and a feather (the emblem of eternal truth) upon the other. If the scales balanced, it signified that the truth within the heart was equal to the truth within the world, in which event the deceased was permitted to pass into the presence of the many-eyed Osiris. After propitiation and offering, the soul then passed into the Elysian fields which are called the abode of the blessed dead. If the balance, however, disclosed a discrepancy between the truth in the heart and that in the world, then the shade of the dead was committed to the tender mercies of Typhon, the Destroyer, who swallowed up the soul amidst great anguish. Typhon here is symbolic of rebirth which swallows up the individual who has not earned liberation.

It is noteworthy that the two most conspicuous figures in the ceremony of the weighing of the soul—namely, Thoth as the scribe and Typhon as the destroyer—should be analogous to the zodiacal sign on each side of Libra. Virgo is the nocturnal house of Mercury and the Latin Mercury is identical with the Greek Hermes and Egyptian Thoth. In the Egyptian form of Thoth, the fact that he is the nocturnal Mercury is frequently shown by the lunar crescent upon his head and the reference to him as the guardian of the Moon, or the night. Scorpio will be readily recognized in the personality of Typhon, the destroyer. It will be remembered that Typhon, or Set, who was the betrayer of Osiris, was always regarded as a genius of depravity. In the mortuary papyrus, Typhon is shown with the head of a crocodile and the body of a hog. He is ever the spirit of evil, whether in the form of Lucifer or some chimerical monster.

At the 15th degree of Libra, the scales of justice tip. Here the involution, or descent, of the soul into the darkness of death gives place to the evolution of the soul. Passing from Libra into Scorpio, the evolving ego essays the first great work of liberation, the slaying of the dragon.

## SCORPIO

Scorpio, the eighth sign of the zodiac, is generally regarded as the most evil potency in the Circle of the Holy Animals. As ruler of the house of death, the ancients assigned to it three creatures to signify the three phases of its nature. All astrologers should realize that what ordinary mortals term evil is simply a misadjustment of universal forces. Nothing is intrinsically evil, but those vibrations which for any reason we respond to adversely are termed evil. In the greatest evil, however, always lies the possibilities of the greatest good. St. Peter three times denied his Lord and as a reward for this was given the key to Heaven. Nowhere is this seeming contradiction more strikingly set forth than in the complex symbolism of Scorpio.

The first—and lowest—of the creatures used to symbolize Scorpio is the scorpion which, because of the sting in its tail, is an appropriate symbol of the backbiter, the deceiver, the betrayer, the adversary who constantly seeks to nullify the noblest efforts of mankind. Furthermore, the scorpion signifies that this undermining will be most subtle and insidious—an endless intrigue designed to test the integrity of all who come under its influence. This power is referred to as "the Mind that is against us." In the ancient Egyptian Mystery rituals, this demon was the Guardian of the Threshold of the inner sanctuary.

The second form of Scorpio is that of the serpent—sometimes the winged serpent or even the fiery serpent of the teraph. In philosophy, this serpent is the symbol of the occult mind, that mysterious and penetrating power which achieves embodiment in the sage and prophet. The great adepts of the Mysteries were often referred to as serpents or dragons, and despite.

The unsavory reputation which the snake gained from its role in the Edenic triangle, it has been for centuries the symbol of true wisdom as opposed to pedantry and sciolism. Even in its serpentine form, however, Scorpio remains more or less the tempter, for in magic the snake represents the astral light—the sphere of illusion from which it is very difficult to escape once the unwary neophyte has lost himself therein. In India, the serpent is the symbol of the Kundalini fire, sometimes termed the serpent power, and in Wagner's opera Parsifal, the power of Scorpio reappears again in the person of the snake-maiden, Kundry.

The third form of Scorpio is that of the eagle or phoenix. This is the emblem of the greatest spiritual achievement—that of Melchizedek, the priest who is above the law. Mythology abounds with references to traitors, evil monsters, serpents, dragons, and strange birds. If the discerning student will analyze these allegories carefully, he will sense certain mystical truths underlying them, the value of which cannot be overestimated. In the Grail cycle appears a mysterious being, who is called Merlin, the magician whose father is said to have been a dragon. By this it is certainly to be inferred that he was a Son of Wisdom, an initiate of Scorpio. Likewise, the story of St. Patrick driving the snakes out of Ireland is almost self-evident. The "serpents" were the Druid priests whose power was broken and their Order scattered by the early church. The dragon slain at the mouth of its cave by Siegfried signifies the mastery of the animal nature by the reforged sword of illumined will.

The victory of St. George over the dragon, which probably originated in the Chaldean legend of Merodach slaying the dragon, signifies the victory of light over darkness; and, in the case of the St. George allegory, the victory of the church over paganism. The famous dragon of China is a form of Mahat, the Yellow Emperor of the Mind, and signifies the illumined state of a people when ruled over by the golden sceptre of enlightened intellect. One of the most remarkable forms of the Scorpio myths is the story of the betrayal of Jesus by Judas, a story probably derived From the betrayal of Osiris by his brother, Typhon. The thirty pieces of silver received by Judas for this deed relate presumably to the thirty degrees of the sign.

It should also be noted that Scorpio, as the eighth sign of the zodiac, is related to the number 8, which is referred to by the Pythagoreans as the little holy number, a great and unfathomable mystery. The eighth sphere was regarded by the ancients as the abode of evil and was likened to the Moon. The Egyptians and also the Yezidees of Iraq believed in the existence of a dark planet but a short distance from the earth, which was the abode of all evil. This dark star, as they termed it in their secret teachings, was an invisible psychical sphere, reflecting no light and casting no shadow save that deep moral shadow which, clouding continents, rendered dim the light of truth. These ancient peoples believed that evil magicians and sorcerers were carried after death to this planet, thereby increasing the sum of evil and radiating loathsome vibrations which crystallized into war, pestilence, and crime. Over this benighted globe ruled a dark angel, a prince of demons, whose brooding wings enveloped the blackness.

Another important line of symbolical interpretation of Scorpio is concerned with the problem of generation. The reproductive principles are particularly related to this sign which controls what may be termed the fire of bodies. In describing the fall of Lucifer, Von Welling, an early alchemist, declared that this world was created to liberate Lucifer from the deep gloom of matter into which he had been plunged at the time of the rebellion in heaven.

From the functions of Scorpio and the sidereal properties which it controls and precipitates into material form is extracted a mysterious pabulum, called by the medieval Rosicrucians the soul. It is the quintessence of both the metals and the spirit which is within bodies, and is the homunculus, or crystal child, referred to in the "Chemical Marriage" of Christian Rosencreutz.

## CAPRICORN

The constellation of Capricorn, whose form is that of a goat with the tail of a fish, was referred to by the ancient astrologers as the sign of the increase of the Sun, for from the moment of the winter solstice the solar power waxes. The sun-god is therefore born at the winter solstice after having been conceived at the vernal equinox. In the old symbolism, it is written that John the Baptist was born at the summer solstice at which time the sun must necessarily decrease. This accounts for the statement of John in the New Testament where he says that Jesus shall increase but he shall decrease. Jupiter, who like most solar gods, was born at the winter solstice, is sometimes depicted as a babe riding on the back of a goat to reveal this mystery to the initiate.

Capricorn is referred to by the Arabs as Al-Jabih, which means the sacrifice or the atonement, and it is not difficult to recognize in this symbol the famous scapegoat of Israel, the sin offering of the people. The goat and the ram were both phallic symbols of vitality, and it is significant that in astrology these creatures should occupy the two most vital angles of the heavens—the midheaven and the ascendant—and should both be assigned to major points in the increase of the solar light and life. The ancients observed that the goat had a peculiar habit in its grazing, so to speak, eating its way up the side of a hill. It would ascend as it grazed and invariably finished its meal at the highest point. This probably contributed to the symbolism and caused astrologers to associate this sign with elevation and dignity.

The first sign of the zodiac being Aries, the ram, and the last sign being Pisces, the captive fishes, these two signs came to be associated with the beginning and the end of the year when figured from the vernal equinox. The beginning and ending of the sun, however, occurred in Capricorn. Therefore, we find the ram and the fish united there in one symbol. Here is the Lamb of God and Fisher of Men symbolically set forth. From the winter solstice life begins to increase, its vitality being consummated at the summer solstice. Thus in the old Babylonian system the sun rose out of the earth in December and passed down under it again in June. In the Cave of the Nymphs, as described by Porphyry from the Wanderings of Ulysses, the constellation of Cancer and Capricorn ornamented the gates of entrance and exit from this material life. The Egyptian Capricorn was the crocodile, an amphibious creature which like the mythological sea-goat could exist on both land and water. The crocodile was sacred to the Egyptian god who corresponds with the Roman Saturn, so astrologers are perfectly consistent in assigning this god to Capricorn. The dolphin was another sign used by the ancients to symbolize Capricorn, and Apollo the sun-god, is occasionally depicted as a child riding on a dolphin. The Egyptians so reverenced crocodiles that they often made golden bangles inlaid with jewels for the legs of these creatures and also adorned their necks with valuable collars. The Jews, following an early symbolism which shows Capricorn as part antelope and part fish, speak of Naphtali who of the sons of Jacob represented Capricorn as a hind let loose. This graceful creature racing through the year well symbolizes the sun hastening through the twelve signs to its tryst with death. Some early astrologers believe that the sign of Capricorn was fabricated by the Chaldeans to represent the two great seats of their civilization—Nineveh and Babylon—for these rose in their grandeur from the marshy banks of the Tigris and Euphrates. It is not generally known that the ancients associated Capricorn with Neptune by making the sign that of the sea-horse, a creature particularly sacred to him. Capricorn was always associated with darkness and the underworld and its ruler, Saturn, is the familiar Santa Claus who comes down from his world of winter to spread the joys of the new year. The Christmas tree represents fertility and the toys which were originally fruit are the promise of the harvest and the general regeneration of the world. It is very interesting to reconstruct the appearance of the constellations as they were on the night of the 25th of December two thousand years ago. The sun is at the nadir and Cancer, the symbol of the manger in which Jupiter was born, is in midheaven as is also the constellation of the Ass upon which Bacchus rode victoriously. On the eastern horizon rises the Virgin with the bright Star of Bethlehem, Spica—the same star for which Hercules labored so arduously in his task of securing the Girdle of the Amazon. On the western horizon is the ram of Aries, which is in opposition to the Dragon beneath the feet of the Virgin. The three brilliant stars in the sword belt of Orion and which are still known in Arabia as the three Wise Men are close to the Ram, the Lamb of God which they have come to worship, and they will soon ascend in their quest of the divine child.

The theologies of nearly all nations have been built up from a contemplation of the motions of the heavenly bodies and throughout the pagan world the birth of the sun-god was annually celebrated while the sun was in the first decan of Capricorn. The fact that at midnight on the sacred day the sun was at the nadir, or the weakest point in the horoscope, is curiously associated with the humble origin of the god who was born as the least among men.

There is a popular belief that it is unfortunate to be born with the sun in Capricorn or to have Capricorn rising. Such people are supposed to be crystallized and inflexible, of gloomy disposition and of adverse fortune. Capricorn demands a very high degree of perfection of those who are born under its influence and if they cannot rise up to these positive qualities, Capricorn does unquestionably bring out very unfortunate characteristics. The sun-gods, symbolic of absolute perfection, are all presumably born with the sun in Capricorn and Virgo rising upon the eastern horizon. But ordinary mortals have not yet learned to carry these great dignities of force in an adequate manner.

## AQUARIUS

In a footnote to Isis Unveiled, Madame Blavatsky assigns the Brahmanical deity Indra to the constellation of Aquarius. Sir William Jones writes that Indra, as the king of the immortals, corresponds to the Jupiter conductor of the Platonic philosophers. One of the numerous names of Indra is Dyupetir, meaning the Lord of Heaven. No one can examine the similarity of the word

Jupiter and Dyupetir without realizing the universal diffusion of the astronomical myths among the nations of antiquity. Indra is the chief of the eight genii presiding over the eight directions of the world, sometimes referred to as the eight winds. In the zodiac of Dendera, eight hawk-headed genii support the celestial sphere. Indra was a god of thunders, winds, and meteoric phenomena. The thunderbolt carried by the Tibetan lamas was brought to the high Himalaya country by the Lama Padma-Sambhava, who, with it, routed the Bön demons who, so tradition tells, had terrorized Tibet into a state of subjection.

This thunderbolt which Lama Padma-Sambhava brought had belonged to the god Indra, who carried it as a symbol of his power in his aspect of Jupiter Elicius, or the Jove of Electricity.

All of this brings us to the main issue involved. Aquarius is an air sign, and yet its name associates it definitely with water, as does its hieroglyphic, which is the Egyptian hieroglyph for water. The sign itself is generally represented by a youthful person, sometimes male, sometimes female, and occasionally androgynous, either carrying a jug of water or else pouring the liquid from a pitcher or amphora. In some of the older zodiacs no human figure appears; there are simply the water vessels. All the evidence points to one inevitable conclusion—the water of Aquarius is of an airy or heavenly nature. In the Greek system, Aquarius is Ganymede, the cup-bearer of Zeus. Thus, the symbolism of the sign is tied up with the Grail mysteries of the later Christian period. The Holy Grail was supposed to have contained the blood of the Christ, or, in simpler terms, the life essence of the sun. The water of Aquarius is therefore the "living water," of which it is written that those who drink thereof shall thirst no more.

Leo and Aquarius are linked together in the relationship of spirit and body, for Leo is the very sovereign sun itself and Aquarius is the universal psychical humidity or heavenly ether which carries and distributes the solar rays throughout the parts of the world. Ganymede carries the cup of immortality, for even the gods must drink of the One Life if they are to endure. In alchemy there is reference made to a mysterious fiery-water, a sort of fluidic flame, and the eleventh process of the Philosopher's Stone, which is called multiplication, or the increasing of things through the nurturing of their divine substances, is also assigned to Aquarius.

One cannot think about the thunder and lightning of Zeus without associating these phenomena with electricity. Here we have a substance both fiery and fluidic, a mystery which actually flows through the air, and is the very scepter of the Logos himself. The parallel wavy lines which form the hieroglyphic of Aquarius should be regarded then as symbols of parallel lines of force rather than as water. The mysteries of electricity still elude us. While we have classified many of the effects of this force, its actual composition is beyond our ability to comprehend. We realize that it is about us everywhere in space, that it contributes life to all living things, and motion to all moving things. There is even the possibility that everything which exists is simply a mode or mood of this electrical agent. If all things are not actually electricity, they are of a certainty released into expression through its activities. Yet we can approach this wonder without any particular reaction of veneration. We live in an age when gods are dead and to our minds only blind forces remain. Yet the electrical agent of today is but the magical agent of yesterday, and the sorceries from which men perished at the rack and gibbet less than three hundred years ago were not so different from the experiments now carried on in scientific laboratories all over the world. We pride ourselves that we have discarded superstitions and outgrown "the calamity of our forefathers, who, in addition to the inevitable ills of our sublunary state, were harassed with imaginary terrors and haunted by suggestions." Yet we should beware lest in our scientific zeal we throw away the substance with the shadow, discarding both the real and the unreal together. Aquarius is ruled over by two widely different forces as expressed through the rulers of the sign—Saturn and Uranus. Saturn is scientific, statistical, and conservative. Uranus is scatter-brained, progressive, and revolutionary. Both, however, have a scientific flavor, for Saturn is orderly and mechanical and Uranus is inventive and ingenious. Aquarius itself is the most progressive and revolutionary sign in the zodiac. It stands for change, reorganization, humanitarianism, and the general betterment of mankind. It encourages reforms, promotes benevolent institutions, patronizes science, inspires exploration and research, is associated with publicity, education, and the general reorganization of human affairs. As a human sign, that

its symbol includes a human figure, it encourages the development of such sense perceptions and attributes as are peculiar to man and are not shared by the brute—abstract reason, morality, aesthetics and ethics. Philosophically it is eclectic; politically it is socialistic; religiously it is agnostic, and economically it is individualistic. As air is the element in which the sign particularly functions it is associated with aviation, radio and even the motion picture.

The dawning Aquarian Age, when for over two thousand years the sun will cross the vernal equinox in the constellation of Aquarius, has brought with it the tremendous impulse towards machinery and the worship of mechanistic concepts which are so evident in our modern affairs. The era of invention will continue until the close of the present age, over two thousand years from now, and during this entire period men will concern themselves more and more with the mysteries of space, time and other Einsteinian concepts. The possibility of communication with other planets will be developed, for Urania is the peculiar Muse of the stars. Astronomy will make vast progress during this age and needless to say astrology will keep pace with it, for astrology also is under the patronage of Uranus.

Revolutions both political and sociological are always inspired by Uranian impulses, as the horoscopes of France and the United States for their revolutionary epochs will demonstrate. During the Aquarian Age there will be revolutions in the field of thought for Aquarius, being an air sign, rules those intellectual vapors which the ancients conceived as flowing through the skull. The Aquarian Age will be one of utter progressivism and kaleidoscopic change. Needless to say such a period will be one of great nervous tension, with tremendous strain upon the nervous and vital resources of the individual. Before the end of this period there will be many and marked changes in the whole institution of civilization.

Uranus, in general, favors occult and spiritual subjects and it is a fortunate planet for those attempting the development of superphysical forces. During

This age men's minds will turn more clearly toward spiritual values and the value sense will be stimulated and balanced. It will not be an age of peace, however, for Uranus is not peaceful. All such concerns as he has dominion over are, like astrology, subject to innumerable vicissitudes of fortune. It will be an age of impulse and impulsiveness very often leads to disaster. Very few Aquarian persons, unless their charts are strengthened by other configurations, can control their impulses. They are attractive, vivacious people, usually with much breadth and geniality but lacking in depth and continuity. The age must be likewise for it will take upon itself the qualities which its ruler bestows. Saturn, which was assigned to Aquarius by the ancients, may under some conditions have a neutralizing effect but Saturn's rulership over Aquarius is somewhat problematic now that the new star has been found and placed in this sign. Very often the Saturnine qualities of Aquarian people can be traced to other configurations. Saturn may possibly be responsible for the consistency with which Aquarians are inconsistent, and it may also contribute something to the very strong and usually unwarranted opinions which these people hold.

One of the most hopeful signs in connection with Aquarian rulership of the world is that nearly all Aquarian types are dedicated to some ideal and it is the utter lack of ideals over a period of centuries that is more or less responsible for the present discord in human affairs.

## SAGITTARIUS

In the Pythagorean system, the number 9 is definitely related to man and in astrology the hieroglyph of the ninth sign, or Sagittarius, is a most appropriate symbol of evolving humanity. The Centaurs were a mythological race of remarkable erudition if we are to accept the story that Chiron, one of their number, was the mentor of Achilles. In the Mysteries, there were two orders who assisted in the evolution of humanity, one called the supermen and the other the demigods. The Centaurs were evidently an order of supermen, possibly a secret society of adepts and initiates. They were not actually part equine and part human, this symbolic allusion merely signifying that they were men who had partially lifted the human nature out of the animal constitution. Astrologically it is not surprising, therefore, to find that the sign of Sagittarius is the symbol of the human or physically intellectual mind. In Platonism, this has sometimes been referred to as the irrational nature, whereas the higher mind, or Capricorn, is the rational nature. The Centaur is generally depicted with a bow and arrow, aiming his shaft at the stars, and hence is the significator of aspiration. One of the earliest forms of the Centaur is to be found on the circular zodiac of Dendera, thereby establishing the antiquity of the symbol. In the triad of fire signs, Sagittarius signifies the fire of intellect, that quality of rational enterprise which lures the mind from the commonplace into the realm of abstraction and, consequently, often into hazardous speculation. In his article on the Circular Zodiac of Tentyra, John Cole gives the following detailed description of the figure of Sagittarius found on the ancient Egyptian zodiac, which should mean much to the astrologer: "This figure of Sagittarius appears To have a crown on his head, and two faces, one looking earnestly forward, apparently female, the other looking behind, having a hawk's head similar to the men's faces who, in the middle of the sides of the square, support the circumference of the Planisphere, representing by all probabilities the faces of slaves. He has a bow and arrow in his hand, and his body is united to the neck of the horse, which is galloping full speed, with wings on his back. He has also two tails, one exultingly elevated, and the other hanging submissively down. Mr. Cole notes the correspondence between the symbol of this ancient zodiac and the description contained in Revelation 6:2: "And I saw, and behold a white horse; and he that sat on him had a bow; and a crown was given unto him; and he went forth conquering and to conquer."

The winged white horse may also refer to the famous Kalki Avatar of Vishnu, or the White Horse incarnation, which is yet to come and which will usher in with it the redemption of mankind. The combination of man and horse, rather than simply placing the man upon the steed, indicates that in essence both horse and rider are identical. The beast is not extraneous to the rider but is a part of himself. Here again we sense the ancient philosophical allegory: mind, the flying horse, is a vehicle of that inner consciousness which should directionalize its activities toward rational lines of accomplishment. Is not the Centaur, furthermore, another form of the winged Egyptian globe, a symbol of the self and its bodies? Three creatures are involved in the construction of the Centaur. Only two of these are popularly considered: the horse and the man. The third is the bird. The horse is the proper symbol of the physical body, the bird of the soul, and the man of the spirit. Sagittarius governs the religious impulses of humanity. It voices the instinctive yearning of man to escape from the limitations of flesh and ignorance and lift his rational nature through all those heavens that intervene between Nature below and the Empyrean above. In philosophy, one of the greatest problems Confronting the student is to divorce the mind from ambition. It may be difficult to sense the vast interval which exists between ambition and aspiration. Ambition is concerned wholly with material things: either the desire to possess them or to possess power over them. Few ambitious people ever achieve even a relatively permanent degree of happiness. The ambitious are slaves to their ambitions, spending their life in servitude to ephemeral things. To the Orient we must turn for an understanding of aspiration as differentiated from ambition. While ambition seeks to possess the imminent, aspiration desires the impossible. While ambition seeks the greatest power, aspiration seeks the greatest good. We are ambitious to possess, we aspire to become. Aspiration depends for its existence upon an ever-broadening vista of consciousness, whereas ambition is thwarted by reason and must find gratification in blind impulse. Sagittarius is the divine fool, the dreamer who reaches for the stars. Aspiration dies in poverty while ambition lies murdered in its bed. In the twentieth century it is dangerous to aspire; it is fatal to dream and visions must be their own reward. While these temporary conditions for a moment turn awry the force of consciousness, man is innately the Centaur, whose aspiration will not rest despite every effort to cultivate a materialistic mien. Through uncounted ages he must gaze upward at the stars and dream of that vaster sphere which lies above him. He must inevitably realize how little he can achieve by the mastery of temporal circumstances. Though a citizen of every land and master of uncounted men, he will never be satisfied until he is a citizen of that vast space compared with which his efforts and accomplishments are utterly negligible. Man can never be wholly satisfied with the earth while uncounted suns traverse the firmament above him. Like Alexander, satiated with pomp and power, he cries for more worlds to conquer; for, mounted upon the winged horse of Mind, he would soar to the end of time, yes even to the metes and bounds of eternity.

## PISCES

The sign of the two fishes, which closes the Circle of the Holy Animals, has been associated by both astrologers and philosophers from time immemorial with the concept of the ending or summing up of life and the world in their various aspects. The Egyptians recognized this constellation as signifying the end of the world, at which time all things would be dissolved in a great deluge or oblivion. To the Chinese, the twelfth sign also represented the periodic inundation of the world by means of which the way was prepared for a new beginning of life upon the planet. By the Hindus, Pisces was associated with the Kali Yuga, or last age, during which old orders crumble away and that which has failed is removed by Nature and the way prepared for the establishment of new generations. In astrology, the sign is associated with bondage, limitation, and confinement. The fishes are tied together by their tails and, though swimming in opposite directions, cannot separate themselves. The sign is a constant reminder that man is ever in bondage to the lower aspects of his own nature, from which there can be no escape until the accounts of Nature have been settled.

The ancient Christians, adopting the sign of the fish as a hieroglyphic symbol of redemption, employed the figure to signify bondage to sin and iniquity. Christians recognized each other by drawing the form of a fish in the sand. This was also a significator declaring oneself to be a hopeless sinner and as such was representative of the strange attitudes developed in the early church in which the penitent gloried in his own less than nothingness. The principle involved seemed to be that the worse a man was the more glory to the institution that could save him.

This curious complex led Celsus to maintain that the new faith held out heaven to rogues and small reward to honest men. In this sense, the fish summarized all human failings and limitations as well as a relapsed condition—an appropriate figure for persons who were miserable for the glory of God! The history of flagellation and extreme austerities informs us that when through some curious streak of Providence Nature was momentarily kind, this weakness of the terrestrial sphere was corrected by visiting upon oneself and others artificially designed and cruelly fashioned forms of discomfiture.

St. Augustine likens Christ to a fish which is broiled for the sins of the world, probably because of the cryptic ikhthus which is derived from his name and title. This calls to mind that numerous divinities have been associated with the fish. Dagon, the Babylonian savior god, has the body of a fish and the head of a man, and Vishnu, in his first avatara, is shown rising from the mouth of a fish. This seemingly has reference to the beginning of life, for after every pralaya, or night of the gods, the Deity symbolized in the form of a great fish swims through the sea of Eternity. The ancients recognized all life as rising from water, which was the common mother substance. The fish gods consequently refer to the celestial intelligences who existed at a time when a heavenly water filled the whole cavity of space. Even Deity itself is sometimes referred to as a great fish, and the story of Jonah and the whale has been interpreted to mean that Jonah signified an aspect of the Noah legend. Jonah, therefore, signifies the seed of mankind. The ship from which he is cast is the old world which is to be destroyed. Divinity is the great fish which, receiving the germ of life, carries it through the deluge which destroys the world and, finally upon the establishment of the new cycle, casts it upon the shore, where it becomes the progenitor of a new order of life.

Regarding Pisces as signifying the end of enterprise, regardless of its magnitude, and also assuming with the Egyptians that the twelfth sign was associated with karma or an accumulation of unfinished business carried forward through the cycle, we next hear of it as associated with misfortune. There is much question whether any sign of the zodiac should be allotted two rulers, i.e., whether Aquarius should be assigned two rulers—Saturn and Uranus—two widely different forces; or whether Jupiter and Neptune should share honors in the rulership of Pisces.

Neptune is a planet strangely associated with the occult forces of Nature, and while it may not often bestow its appearance upon the Piscean native, it most certainly bestows peculiarities of temperament and eccentricities of person. Most Piscean people are creatures of destiny or, at least, puppets of fate. There is nearly always something mysterious or unusual about them and in many cases they are given to unaccountable depression and melancholy. Their lives are usually eventful in one way or another, often involving sudden changes. Like Neptune, they are very often revengeful and, again, like this planet, inclined to keep their real feelings to themselves, their words often having little to do with their thoughts. Neptune again strikes them in their relationship to the occult or, at least, in their fondness for the mysterious, the bizarre, and their thrill from intrigue. They are quite often mediumistic or clairvoyant and are almost certain to be surrounded during life with circumstances not explainable by the average man's philosophy. As an old work on the subject says: "They are addicted to dreams, fancies and even frenzies." They are inclined to be secretive and are often tempted to evil habits or dangerous intrigues and crime. In none of these qualities do they partake of the Jupiterian influence which is supposed to partly govern the sign nor are their finances as plentiful as generous Jupiter would be expected to bestow. They are a worrying caste and the only point where Jupiter really shows himself in their outer appearance is in size and weight; and through their inner temperament as generosity.

If Pisces be accepted as a sign connected with the rounding up of a cycle of experience, then it is easier to understand why Piscean people are seemingly continually confronted by responsibility and so-called misfortune. The facts are that they are faced with the loose ends of their own lives. In Pisces, the individual is temporarily in bondage to the limitations of himself. In this sign, he must overcome in himself those conditions which through the other signs he has been attempting to overcome in the outer world. It is a well-known fact that just before dawn vitality is the lowest upon the earth, and in the horoscope Pisces represents that zero hour which precedes the dawn which is symbolically presumed to take place in Aries. Thus Pisces is the weakest point in the chart. It represents the place where the energies of life have run down. It has neither the strength, combativeness nor the optimism which in some of the other signs literally bubbles over. The Piscean native is born tired and, lacking the vitality bestowed by more robust configurations, may also lack the self-assurance which surmounts obstacles and defends its own rights. Pisces bestows the peacemaker, who is generally badly pummelled by both contending factions. The world has just passed through a Piscean cycle and it has been a period of travail. Man's idealism and humanitarianism have been exploited to the uttermost. Virtue has lost caste and honesty has lost merit. The order of life has been hopelessly upset and a certain despair has been bred in the subconscious strata of men's souls. But as the darkness of night gives place to the sparkling colors of the dawn, so the inhibitions of Pisces find expression in the spontaneous exuberance of Aries. The sun, having completed its cycle, begins a new one. Night gives place to day, hopelessness to hope, and the great wheel turns as before. In our cycle of spiritual progress we are born again and again in each sign, as the wheel goes round. When it comes time for us to be born in Pisces, we are brought face to face with the things which are as yet unfinished. This experience is necessary, for it gives incentive and purpose to future effort.

# XXXVII

# The Ladder of the Gods

WITH his "opened eye" the Dangma, or initiated disciple, beholds as a grand staircase the concatenated order of worlds that extends upward from the material darkness, which is the mundane sphere, and disappears into that impenetrable spiritual darkness which is the abiding state of the First Divinity. The midmost portion of this staircase is illumined by the light of reason, but its extremities are rendered incomprehensible by a Stygian gloom. This flight of worlds rests upon earth's lurid base, and the first steps are slimy with the fetid rot of matter. Rising in many levels from this ignoble footing, the stairway of spheres vanishes into the very presence of transcendent Cause, whose blinding radiance, ill-concealed by seven thousand veils, is to man's unordered vision an utter lightlessness. This is the mystic ladder of Jacob's vision upon which the patriarch beheld the angelic choirs. Two great streams of souls move upon this symbolic staircase, one ascending and the other descending, impelled by the rhythm of generation. Virgin spirits, eternal with the fullness of God, emerge from behind the veils that cover The Threefold Darkness above, and swooping downward with birdlike speed are enveloped in the noxious vapors of mortality.

Of this descent Plotinus writes: "And thus the soul, though of divine origin, and proceeding from the regions on high, becomes merged in the dark receptacle of body; and being naturally a posterior god, it descends hither through a certain voluntary inclination, for the sake of power, and of adorning inferior concerns. Hence, if it swiftly flies from hence it will suffer no injury from its revolt, since by this means it receives a knowledge of evil, unfolds its latent powers, and exhibits a variety of operations peculiar to its nature, which by perpetually abiding in an incorporeal habit, and never proceeding into energy, would have been bestowed in vain." Entering the inferior gloom these souls are swallowed up in the living death of the body. This mystery was revealed by the secret rites of the Phrygians, as evidenced by Hippolytus. Hence Heraclites declares that we live the death of the soul and die the life of the soul, thus arcanely intimating that when the rational nature agitates the irrational nature, bestowing upon it the semblance of life, it sacrifices its own life and only regains liberty by retiring from the concerns of the outer organism. Lamenting the "unaccustomed state" in which his soul found itself in form, Empedocles declares that the process of generation causes the living to pass into the dead.

From below mount upward the redeemed, whose natures, increasingly luminous, shine like stars in a Cimmerian night. From the dismal underworld—the abode of vain fears and terrible regrets—moves an endless file, climbing steadily toward God up the steps, or worlds, of its salvation. Thus the illustrious ones who are approaching the summit of their tedious climb, are in the terms of Plato, "raised above all inferior good." Concerning the return of the liberated soul to its virgin nature, H. P. Blavatsky writes: "This is the state which such seers as Plotinus and Apollonius termed the 'Union to the Deity'; which the ancient Yogins called Isvara, and the modern call 'Sammaddhi*; but this state is as far above modern clairvoyance as the stars above glow-worms. Plotinus, as is well known, was a clairvoyant-seer during his whole and daily life; and yet, he had been united to his God but six times during the sixty-six years of his existence, as he himself confessed to Porphyry." From the foregoing it is evident that the soul for many ages alternately retires from and approaches Divinity, only stabilizing its nature after being completely disentangled from the concerns of the flesh. It is not intended that mortal man should as yet be constant in his power to behold the Perfect Face, but that strengthened by intermittent vision he shall strive with greater temerity to establish the continuity of the spiritual perceptions.

From the many levels, which together form the vast staircase, pour forth lives in quest of forms, and forms in quest of life. From the pits of mortal slime crawl repulsive creatures whose sightless eyes are unresponsive to the light. Slowly, painfully, awkwardly, these half-animate monstrosities obey the deep hidden urge of an imprisoned soul, and grope their way toward truth. From the dark fastnesses of the mist- reeking jungle come forth the slinking horrors whose claws are death and whose bared fangs were fashioned to rend and tear. Then from the broad plains come the patient, sad-eyed, serving brutes, which see and feel but cannot understand. From the dark caves of earth's primal day emerges the dim progenitor of man who, beating his hairy breast with crude, misshapen hands, emitted the first war-cry of his kind. The distant places also give up their savage hordes, for slayer and savior alike are marching on through the ages toward inevitable perfection. Breaking the shackles that bind them to the grindstones of the mighty, the slaves join the great processional, as do the merchants who barter and sell, and the thieves who scheme and steal. From their marble tombs rise up the spirits of the hero dead—the Caesars and the Alexanders—and from their honored crypts come forth prince and potentate bearing orb and scepter, and gathering their ermine robes about them they solemnly climb the stairs of space. Higher upon the great flight are the scientists and the philosophers, who in pensive mood plod the weary way. At the very point where the staircase disappears into the mysterious presence of the Ineffable stand the radiant saviors—the great teachers of humanity— who dimly visible for a moment, pass into the darkness of God. Awesome is the spectacle of this grand march—souls moving toward their Maker; passing from form to form in the endless quest for the formless; approaching ever nearer to that greatness which is the virtue of perfection. Though an infinite diversity confronts the eye, yet the whole mystery may be summed up in three short words: God seeking God.

Philosophy does not give the soul freedom from Universal Law. In The Doctrine of the Mean, it is written: The heavenly appointment of life is called nature; an accordance with human nature is called the way; and the regulation of the way is called religion." (From the Confucian ethics as revealed in The Four Book(s.) The power exercised by Buddhism is largely due to the magnificent concept promulgated by it concerning the march of the self to perfection. Oppressed by the irksomeness of their tasks, and rendered hopeless by the ignobility of their station, the Sudras of India were victimized by a decadent Brahmanism. Following the letter and not the spirit of Manu's law, the "Holy Born" sedulously avoided contact with inferiors lest the pollution of promiscuous relationships endanger that state of sanctity in which their Brahman souls reposed. That golden age had passed when "rich in royal worth and valor, rich in holy Vedic lore," the "Head Born" were the virtuous stewards of the gods. In the Sha^Swayamvara of the Ramayana is described a noble Brahman king who ruled the righteous city, Ayodhya:

"Like the ancient monarch Manu, father of the human race, Dasa-ratha ruled his people with a father's loving grace. Truth and Justice swayed each action and each baser motive quelled, People's Love and Monarch's Duty every thought and deed impelled."

A superfluity of laws often proves more detrimental than an insufficiency of laws. In the service of their countless statutes the Brahmans became oppressors of life. Themselves subservient to the cumbersome regulations which they had prescribed for others, the Brahmans also suffered from a plentitude of codes which regulated thought and action until life was reduced to a mere span of forms and conventions. But while the holy Brahman enjoyed a certain uncomfortable security, the Sudra, bereft even of hope, found his lot little better than that of the beast. The gods presumably were too busily engaged in answering the unceasing prayers of the "Twice Born" pious to lend an ear to the supplications of the lowly. To these victims of a misinterpreted caste system Buddhism brought the inspiring doctrine of freedom in bondage. While the Sudra could not throw off the metaphorical shackles that bound his physical members, he did free his inner and immortal self from the concepts of limitation and despair. Buddhism revealed the stairway of the immortals, and through this doctrine (which verges on metaphysical evolution) gave hope of ultimate accomplishment to those millions for whom present accomplishment was impossible. Inspired by this new hope, those who previously had cursed their tragic lot sang at their tasks; those who had looked forward to a life of pain smiled through their tears; and those who had faced eternity with fear and trembling were rendered strong by the knowledge of life's purpose. The miseries of the today were forgotten, and men dwelt together in a glorious tomorrow. The lowly uncaste sensed the Brahman within his frame, for to the sinner had been revealed the hidden saint within.

Indra's city vanished from the sky; the gods were dissipated like mist before the dawn of reason; only Self remained—the glorious Universal Self, the One who is in all, the All which is in each. Rising up against their heavenly despots and emancipating themselves from the hierarchies of fears they had worshipped, the Sudras declared themselves free men of the universe. Thus the letter gave place again to the spirit, and human beings faced their own thoughts and actions unafraid. Armed with the tools of the Noble Path, each true believer hewed an appropriate destiny from the eternal substances of being. Recognizing his state to signify that of greatest separateness, the Sudra began to ascend the ladder of diversity, finally raising himself to unity upon its several rungs. True philosophy inspires with the courage to accomplish, and equips with the patience to wait; it reveals not only the end, but also the means to that end. Philosophy is indeed a mystical ladder up which men climb from ignorance to reason. Its rungs are the arts and sciences, and he who ascends the whole of the way finds that its upper extremity rests in the substances of an invisible but most substantial world—the proper abode of the wise. Here are the groves of learning where the sages sit together musing upon consequential. This is a sphere of peace, for with depth of learning wrangling ceases and "the thoughtful mind to solitude retires/' This is indeed the place of the Isarim, or blessed souls, of which the Rabbins dreamed and where the Kedeshim pondered over the great Sod; for it is written in the Proverbs: "And his Sod are for the Isarim." "Fear not," admonished Pythagoras in The Golden Verses, "men come from a heavenly race and are taught by a divine Nature that which they should accept and that which they should reject." Philo Judaeus describes the allegorical ladder which is raised from earth to heaven, showing its macrocosmic analogies and its application to the microcosm, or man. This ladder, according to Philo, is of the world its astral part and of man the soul; "the foot of which is, as it were, its earthly part—namely, sensation; while its head is, as it were, its heavenly part—the purest mind." Upon this ladder move what Philo terms the Logi, which may be interpreted as either the "Words" or, more generally, the "Gods." To these Words or Gods is ascribed a very secret and wonderful meaning. In the chapter on The Annihilation of the Sense of Diversity we have already described the spheres of realization, or consciousness, which man causes to manifest out of his own potentialities.

The level of integrity upon which the individual functions is his level or sphere of consciousness and each of these levels or spheres, when considered as a whole, is a "God" or "Word" of power moving upon the ladder. Thus Philo declares that when the Logi ascend they draw the ladder, or soul, up with them, which arcanely intimates two things: (1) that the Gods or Words cannot descend other than by the soul, and having once perfected the soul lose contact with the world; (2) that the soul in its ascent absorbs inferior natures into itself so that as it rises there is nothing left beneath it. The Golden Verses conclude:

"Thy mind's reins let reason guide:

Then stripped of flesh up to free iEther soar, A deathless God, Divine, mortal no more."

In his dream Jacob beheld a mysterious ladder with its foot upon the earth and its top extending upward into the divine sphere. In the Mysteries it is declared that seventy-two aeons, or angels, moved upon the ladder. These angels are the seventy- two names or powers that emanate from Shem-Hammephorash—the separate and ineffable Deity. Ibn Ezra, writing in the 12th century, states on the authority of Ibn Gebirol that the ladder which Jacob saw in his dream signified the superior, or rational soul, and that the angels of Elohim which ascend and descend thereon are the abstract thoughts of wisdom which attach themselves at the same time, both to a spiritual, or superior subject, and also to the corporeal and inferior, The word which has been rendered "ladder" is sdam , which means "that which is piled into a heap, raised up or lifted," 'and it is upon this raised or exalted place that the Malawi Elohim moved up and down. We cannot do better than consider the meaning of the word sdam as here employed. Albert Pike states that in archaic Hebrew there was no word to designate a pyramid. In the word Jcrusdem, for example, sdem is generally interpreted to mean "peace" and Melchizedck, the prince of Salem, was called the lord of peace. It might be more accurate, however, to replace the word "peace" with "exalted" or "lifted," in which event Jerusalem could be intrepreted to mean "the city of the ladder " In this connection the fact should not be overlooked that Mohammed on his night journey to heaven, after arriving at Jerusalem on Alborak, beheld a ladder formed of golden rope descending from heaven. The lower end of this ladder rested upon Mount Moriah, and climbing the swaying stair the Prophet of Islam entered into the very presence of the living but many-veiled God.

In the Ancient Wisdom it was also declared that the sacred mountains of the world rose in seven steps or stages (as the Meru of the Hindus), and it was from the high place, or the seventh step, that offerings were made to the Lord whose name is Blessed. Not only did the holy place rise in seven platforms or levels, but upon its topmost level was usually erected a triform symbol of the Divine Nature itself. Thus the seven steps, complemented by this threefold figure, became the mysterious Pythagorean dccad, or the symbol of the tenfold order of the universe. Jacob's ladder then actually becomes the symbolic mountain or pyramid. Pyramids, wherever found, are symbolic of the axis mountain of the world—the Olympus, Asgard, and Meru of the pagans, and possibly the rock Moriah upon which the temple stood at Jerusalem. In his Pagan Idolatry, Faber describes the Mithraic ladder used in the initiatory rites of the Persian Mysteries, which he affirms was in reality a pyramid of seven steps, further declaring that on each step was a door. In the ceremonials, the neophyte climbed the pyramid, passing through the seven doors, and then through similar portals descended on the opposite side. This pyramid was symbolic of both the world and the sidereal system. Nearly all great buildings of antiquity were symbolic of the universe, and according to Cicero the conquering Xerxes destroyed the temples of the Greeks, declaring that the entire world was the proper house of God and that Deity was profaned when man prepared for him a house less dignified than his own solar mansion.

Celsus gives a certain key to the ceremonials of the Mithraic rite, but of these Mysteries comparatively little is known. Having passed successfully through the dangers imposed by his initiators, the candidate was invested with a great cape either embroidered or painted with stars, and with the constellations of the zodiac ornamenting the hem. Like the starry hat of Atys, these starstrewn cloaks signified the soul in its highest and most causal aspect. Thus by the Mysteries a heavenly nature was conferred, and men who formerly dwelt about the earth itself were raised to a heavenly abode and their whole natures invested with celestial raiment. The corporeal body was transmuted by the Mysteries into a celestial body, for men who had previously enveloped themselves in the dark garments of form now put on a more luminous garb resplendent with the heavenly lights. Above the earth are the planets; above the planets are the stars. Uninitiated mortals exist in physical natures limited to the concerns of the earth and are termed material because their rational natures are in servitude to a mortal constitution. Disciples are those who take upon themselves the striped garments of the planets—the cloak of many colors whose shades denote the aspects of the astral soul. When the aspirant has transcended the concerns of the planets and risen through their orbits to liberation, he then assumes the starry clothing of the firmament. Thus the stars are symbols of spirit, the planets of soul, and the elements of body. Herein lies the explanation for the three-runged ladder which unites heaven and earth. The rungs of this ladder are the three mys- teries perpetuated in Freemasonry as the Blue Lodge. The lowest round is physical, the second emotional, and the third mental; for it was written in the ancient work: "Our thoughts are from the stars, our emotions from the planets, and our forms from the earth."

Entering the chamber of the Mithraic rites the candidate found himself in a great cavern either formed by natural means or hewn from solid rock by the priests. In the center of the cavern stood a pyramid rising in seven steps, each of its levels painted a different color. In some cases the pyramid was divided into definite platforms; in others a narrow spiral pathway wound from base to summit as in the Chaldean ziggurats, or astronomical towers. From the flight of steps leading up the face of the pyramid access to the various planes or levels was had through low gates, each composed of a different metal. The description given by Celsus of these metals is probably a "blind," for the ancients followed a definite system which he has deviated from. Conducted by the hierophant who discoursed to him concerning the mysteries as he progressed, the neophyte ascended the steps of the pyramid, first entering through a silver gate onto the platform of the moon. Beyond was another gate resembling brass, which was that of Mercury, and still farther on a third gate of copper sacred to Venus. The fourth gate was of gold, the fifth of iron, the sixth of tin, and the seventh, and last, of lead. After passing through these gates the neophyte found himself upon a flat square area, and before him a triangular altar upon which burned three fires.

The master of the rite then explained that by this ascent was revealed the felicity of liberated souls—the joyous upward motion of lives toward their sovereign cause; that passing from one plane to another the candidate had recapitulated the afterdeath process by which his superphysical constitution verged away from matter and inclined itself toward the immaterial foundation which is in the heavens and concealed from the profane by the leaden ramparts of Saturn. In his climb the aspirant had actually stepped from planet to planet, leaving behind him the inferior spheres, finally to approach proximity to that threefold fire—the triform flame of unimaginable being that bums forever and a day upon the glorious altar of Universal Reality. "Learn, O my son," the master continued, "the mystery of the ever-burning fire whose triple wick dipped in an inexhaustible fuel burns with steady luminosity throughout all the Aions. The first flame is Universal Life, the second Universal Light, and the third Universal Motion, and these together are one flame. God is a blinding light and a consuming fire, for his light is eternal reason which renders all things visible and comprehensible. Light the lamp of your own mind upon this altar of Eternal Mind, that the reason which is in all things may call forth the reason that is in you. When the lamp of your reason is lighted, all things become evident; the dark mysteries of life are dissipated and the glow of realization causes all secrets to reveal thmselves and all hidden works to be made manifest. The base of this pyramid is square. It is your body. Its four elements combine to produce the mystic cube called man, The seven steps are your senses by which the within comes to know the without and which the without climbs, even as a ladder, to discover the within. Consciousness, ascending the ladder of the senses finally brings its message to the inner nature. The threefold flame here is the One, the Beautiful, and the Good, which together are the light of equality, the torch of r^son, and the magical fire the magician must carry if he would invoke the dread person of Deity."

Upon the other side of this pyramid the stairs descend into the darkness of the cavern below. The candidate follows his initiator down again into the darkness of the subterranean room. Having passed through the metallic gates and standing once more at the base of the pyramid, the initiator resumes:

"This descent signifies the soul departing from its state of felicity and, after passing downward through the gates of the Seven Spheres taking upon itself the sorrows of birth. In the gloomy cavern of the world uninitiated men and women struggle vainly against the inevitable reactions of their own ignorance. Seeking permanence in an impermanent sphere they suffer without respite and their lot is indeed desperate. But those who by rational procedure have discovered the pyramidal nature of creation and learned to know the order of divine procedure whereby man ascends and descends the steps of destiny—such can no longer be bound to the untranquil sphere, but abiding therein a little while and tolerating its sorrows, prepare themselves for a more auspicious day by inclining their minds to reason.

"By these mysteries, then, is arcanely revealed the order of life and by this pyramid the procedure of life. He who accepts the mystery into himself and ponders its meaning will be rewarded for his industry by the realization of sidereal order.

We are ever walking up and down the steps of space—descending either from a more blissful state into one of uncertainty, or ascending from an uncertain state into one of blessed felicity. He who comprehends the wisdom of this divine motion will realize that God is ever drawing lives to himself that they may partake of the fullness of his inspiration, and then casting them from him again that through great need they may learn to value the fullness of that inspiration. From the presence of the Unchanging One there pours ever downward through the substances of the invisible world a host of souls moving inevitably into birth, while from the world of visible and tangible physical things there comes a host of souls pouring into death. Those coming into life descend the ladder, and those coming into death ascend the ladder, for death brings the soul nearer to God than does birth. Through the Mysteries there pours still another stream—that exalted order which ascends the great pyramid to descend no more, who upon reaching the fiery altar upon its summit cast themselves into the eternal flame, and from their own natures feed its eternal hunger."

In his Chemical Marriage Christian Rosenkreutz describes the vision of C. R. C. as he slept shackled in the antechamber of the House of Initiation. In his dream C. R. C. beheld the strange sight of a multitude of persons suspended from heaven by cords. In an early Rosicrucian book which I examined some years ago the subject of these "hanging men" was elucidated in detail. The dangling figures are the sophists, those false learners who ever seek to climb to heaven upon their own suppositions. We are all supported by our beliefs, held up as it were by the strength of our premises and the sufficiency of our postulations. Yet in all too many instances how slender and inadequate is the thread of mortal reason to which we trust our weight. Among the Sons of Islam there is an ancient fable to the effect that there shall come forth a prophet who will stretch a hair from the Mount of Olives to the golden gate of Jerusalem, and using it for a bridge will walk across the Valley of Jehoshaphat, or the place of death. The hair, according to the Cabala, is the symbol of the glory of God and the countless diversity of his mercy. Taking this fable in its literal sense, a Mohammedan fanatic wove a rope of human hair and essayed the feat, but was killed.

In the legend of Christian Rosenkreutz it is further stated that an aged man (who represents Cronus, or Time, the justifier of all actions) flew in and out among the hanging sophists.

Wearing an hourglass tied to the top of his head and carrying In his hand a pair of sharp shears, the divine iconoclast would fly up behind any of the worldly-wise men who climbed too ambitiously up their swaying ropes and cut away their slender support. Another observation by the author of the Chemical Marriage is to the effect that the higher these false learners climbed, the harder and more disastrous was their fall, so that many were dashed to pieces. The more prudent ones, however, realizing the insecurity of their position, remained close to the earth and suffered comparatively little harm when their cords were cut, often alighting uninjured upon their feet. We all share in common the desire to climb to heaven up the ladder of our own convictions, and believing ourselves to be infallible, we set out to storm the gates of the Eternal. No spectacle is more pathetic than that of the individual who, led to false and dizzy heights by his egotism, has been dashed therefrom into the depths of misery and disillusionment. The more we depend upon the false the more we suffer when that falseness is exposed. The story of the hanging men is evidently concerned with the effort to ridicule those Aristotelian schoolmen whose fallacies were already apparent at the beginning of the 17th century. Elevated above their fellow men by vain assertions, and maintaining themselves by subterfuge and equivocation, these pedants preyed upon the credulity of an illiterate age. But time was finding them out, for science, rising out of this protest against intellectual pettifoggery, furnished Cronus with the shears wherewith to cut down the scholastic befogger of issues. In this allegory heaven is used to signify the sphere of the truly learned, for it was presumed that those whose knowledge was sufficient dwelt in a state of tranquillity far above the abode of ordinary mortals tormented by doubt and rendered impotent by ignorance. The light of tranquility, as the followers of Boehme might call it, radiates from the paradisaic sphere of the contented.

Humanity moves instinctively toward that tranquil state of the philosophic blest, for we incline toward that person or condition which radiates happiness. This instinct has been shamelessly exploited in the name of religion, but the age of empty promises is closed. Having vainly sought happiness among the dictums of faith and in the company of the so-called holy, the individual is coming to realize that peace lies only within himself. In Dryden's translation of the Aeneid are found several significant copper engravings, one particularly showing a genius cutting the slender thread of life connecting mortal man with his divine origin. A small plate also showing this thread issuing from the crown of the head and disappearing upward into a cloud of divine radiance is to be found in Michael Maier's Scrutinium Chymicum .

Various modifications of this idea constituted a favorite theme of the medieval emblem writers, especially such as were in touch with the Rosicrucian activities. This thread rising from the head is the Platonic cord—a fine hypothetical line which unites the personality to its own causal part. According to the Hermetic axiom of analogy, as the spirit and body of man are connected by a thread, so heaven and earth—the spirit and body of the solar man—are united by this swaying ladder which, lowered from above, becomes the way of souls descending into life. Cronus with his reaping scythe is the guardian of this rope, and at his will the line is severed and all the objective nature dissociated from its causal principle. This thread, then, is Btfrost, the bridge of the gods, over the immortals—like the Aesir of Scandinavia—crossed before its final severance when returning to their sacred castle. Like the builders of the fated Tower of Babel, the worldly-wise men of C. R. C.'s vision sought to elevate personality above principle and draw the body above its own source; hence their ultimate discomfiture. By attempting to elevate an impermanent nature to a divine state they attempted the impossible and so Death, the master of processes, cut down each one in turn; for that man does not exist who shall be empowered to reach heaven in his physical nature. The cords are the faith and power that sustain the individual during the prime of his life, but like life itself, power is a physical uncertainty, and neither wealth, position, nor physical knowledge can support the soul in that dread extremity which men are pleased to term death.

In his vision of the Apocalypse, the initiate, known to the Christians as St. John the Divine, experienced in his ascent to heaven the spiritual mystery of climbing upward through the seven congregations or churches "which are in Asia," finally coming to the door in the heavenly vault and passing through into the Empyrean to find himself in the presence of the Lord of the Cherubim and the Paschal Lamb. St. John is described as being "in the spirit," a good old Neoplatonic term. From this we are to infer that the Gnostic initiate had learned the mystery of the rope swinging from heaven, for according to tradition he had climbed his way hand over hand in approved nautical fashion. Mohammed, a prudent man of more portly build, overtaxed the meager facilities of a knotted rope and consequently employed (if we are to believe the accounts) a safer and more commodious rope ladder in his ascent. In substance, however, the experiences of the two initiates were practically identical, and though slight differences exist in the terminology of the symbolism, nevertheless the principle involved demonstrates that both men had been initiated—St. John presumably by the Gnostics and Mohammed by the Nestorian Christians. St. John the Divine employed seven great Asiatic cities to symbolize the spiritual knots or ganglia, which placed at intervals along the rope assisted the climber in his difficult task. Mohammed's rope ladder was of golden cords and its rungs presumably were fashioned from the substances of the seven worlds. He was forced, it is said, to stop at each of the seven gates to receive the adoration of the patriarchs, who had apparently waited since their demise for his coming.

There is also an East Indian fable of the goddess Kundalini who, being of an inquisitive mind and seeing a rope hanging from heaven with its lower end concealed in impenetrable gloom, decided to climb down this rope and investigate the unknown darkness below. Having descended the rope for an incalculable period, Kundalini discovered that its lower end rested upon an island that seemed to float in the midst of a great sea of darkness. While exploring this strange island the rope was cut from above, and Kundalini was left floating in the midst of a vast ocean. In terror the goddess ran and hid herself in a cave and refused to come out. In the secret teachings it is revealed that she could be induced to come forth from her asylum only by an aggregation of wise men who with offerings, supplications, and grave discoursings finally persuaded her to leave her gloomy retreat. The goddess Kundalini is the spirit fire that descends the mysterious ladder which is here emblematic of the umbilical cord. When this cord is cut the goddess is left stranded in the underworld. Alarmed, she hides in the great cavern of the sacral plexus, there to remain coiled up as a serpent (as her name implies) until the sage can lure her forth again by holy observances 4 .

Never should we lose sight of the relationship between the processes of the physical body and the universal orders. The umbilical cord is not only the divine ladder in the case of the goddess Kundalini, but is symbolic also of that spiritual cord by which man is ever suspended from his Divine Parent. While man's outer nature is nourished by physical food and drink,

his inner nature receives life from the Universal Parent transmitted by means of ethereal cords analogous to the umbilicus.

In the Shinto Mysteries of Japan the luring of an obstinate goddess from her pout was a grave problem. The Goddess of the Sun, Amaterasu O-mikami, had quarreled with the other celestials, and giving vent to her anger hied herself, light and all, into a dark cavern, thus leaving the heavenly world in a condition of deplorable gloom. Realizing that the temperament of the goddess was endangering the whole order of creation, the immortals finally lured her forth by a stratagem which appealed to her vanity. They fashioned a great mirror even

as the Titans polished the surface of the universe that Bacchus might see his face therein. Standing this mirror in front of the cavern they made a great ado as though in celebration of some fortuitous circumstance. Chagrined at the thought that the gods could be happy without her, Amaterasu came to the cavern entrance and peered out to discover the cause of their merriment. As she looked she saw her own face, surrounded by a halo of light, reflected in the mirror. Wondering who this radiant person could be and terrified by the possibility that the gods had somewhere discovered a new sun goddess, Amaterasu slowly approached the entrance of the cave, only to see the radiant figure in the mirror also increasing in splendor.

At last, overcome by her jealousy she dashed from the cave to discomfit the rival sun goddess, whereupon the other celestials who had gathered above the cavern entrance dropped a net over the irate goddess as she rushed forth, thereby preventing her escape and insuring that the sun should again light the world. Amaterasu and her mirror are household words in every Shinto home, and even the august imperial line regards the sun goddess as its founder, and her mirror is carried in the coronation ceremonials. The luring of the light out of darkness is an allegory frequently employed by many ancient writers on mysticism. It represents the effort of material man to evoke, by discipline and fetish, that lucid or rational part of himself which for some temperamental reason refuses to make itself known. Offended by the crassness of the outer life, the aesthetic and superphysical attributes of the soul retire into the uttermost recesses of the nature, there to await that more auspicious day when the awakening individual will concern himself with the nobler issues of life. The sages who ponder the problem of enticing the goddess from retirement signify the rational mind, the gods, and the intuitive instincts, while the priest represents the regenerated emotions. All these, holding solemn conclave together, finally lure the rational soul from its dark abode that its radiance may benefit the whole life. The invoking of the soul is possible only to those who have assumed the Great Work and resolved to live with the concerns of the spirit paramount. Through virtue, integrity, and aesthetics the soul life is thus caused to diffuse its power throughout the nature, thereby quickening the parts and rendering the whole more responsive to divine impulse. From a consideration of these various allegories it becomes evident that the ladder signifies the thread or cord from which the generating soul is suspended from its monadic, or ungenerated part. The God of the philosophic elect is not technically a being, but rather this monad, or universal self.

Approach to Deity is consequently, the elevation of the life to unity with its monadic cause. The abode of this monad is the true heaven world, for heaven merely signifies the state of the One divorced from all quality or condition whatsoever and abiding in the felicity of its own nature, without beginning and without end. Thus the ascent of the ladder and the climbing of the knotted cord are both emblematic of man's ceaseless climb toward Self. It is the retirement of life along the lines of its own first emanation—-the natural ascent of the wise to wisdom, the virtuous to virtue, the beautiful to beauty, and the good to the enduring state of good. The ladder, then, bridges that mysterious fourth-dimensional interval of quality described in Chapter X; it is the symbolic figure under which are concealed the tedious processes of crossing that vast interval between diversity and unity. The ladder is the bridge of reason, the way of the gods.

The stepped pyramid is significant of man's instinctive urge to build toward Cause, and all action which tends to elevate, ennoble, or perfect may be conceived of as pyramidal, dia- grammatically considered. Thus in his discourse to his son on initiation, Hermes declares that the heart was built like a pyramid in that the heart is the seat of aspiration, and aspiration is the universal building power. As the Unknown God dwelt within the deepest recesses of the Great Pyramid, so a mysterious spirit dwells within the heart—man's House of the Hidden Places. The pyramid builders differed from all other architects because of the purpose for which their edifices were constructed. All men are builders—a few in permanent things, the many in impermanent things. St. Paul calls himself a "master builder," by which he intimated that he had been initiated into that body of elect artisans banded together to the erection of everlasting houses. The pyramid thus became the symbol of those called together by an inner rationality who, moved by a divine intelligence, heaped up realities that they might form mountains, as it were, up which the aspiring soul could climb in its search for heaven. While many were cutters of stone, hewers of wood, and carriers of water, they were but apprentices of the noble art, not having heard as yet the call that inclines the soul away from temporal accomplishments to the building of those enduring monuments to qualities and convictions.

The mystic Masons, so we are told, built their lodges either upon the mountain tops or deep in the valleys, thus obscurely intimating that the Mysteries, while in their own nature lofty institutions, in the service of mankind descended into the depths of matter to effect the redemption of the human soul. God appeared to the patriarchs as a cloud over some lofty mountain top, and his voice thundered among the summits.

These sacred mountains—hovering places of the Most High— are the sanctified pyramids. These pyramids, in turn, are rationalized natures—the chief accomplishment of the master builders. They are altars set up in the wilderness to signify that integrity has been established in a sphere to which integrity was once foreign. An ancient fable, in describing the stature of one whom God has thus anointed and lifted up into the assemblage of the illumined, declares that his face shone like the sun, and all the brightness of the stars was in his eyes;

the flow of his hair was like the rippling waves of great rivers, and even his breath was as the soft breeze of spring sighing among the trees. Though his body was that of a man, his inner nature was as vast as the world, and his integrity rose like a mighty mountain whose summit is forever hidden by the clouds of meditation. The laughter of this perfected one sounded like the song of the waterfall, yet his sorrow was like the cool of evening among the shelter of the trees. All the beauties of the universe were invoked to define his virtues, and the immensities of space belittled his greatness. It follows that when such an illumined nature heaps together the stones of its accomplishment and forms therefrom the altar of its God—a high and holy place suitable for the reception of the Eternal—the rational soul, invoked by these accomplishments, lends its power to the convocation of perfected faculties. Then, like the awful hierophant of Revelation, the rational self stands in splendid majesty in the midst of the flaming candles.

Thus all natures are symbolic ladders, for by ascending the concatenated orders of his own intelligence man comes proximate to his own rational and enduring part. The allegory of Jack and the beanstalk, which like so many other children's fables has its origin in primitive folklore, well describes the mystery of the ladder. The beanstalk, which in a single night grew up to heaven, reminds one of the fabled mango tree of the elusive Hindu mahatma or the rope thrown into the air which does not fall. The miraculous growth of the magician's plant signifies the culturing of the soul. Every philosopher is a magician, for by the aid of his unfolded intellect he accomplishes that which to the ignorant appears impossible. The rope suspended from nothing, up to which the naked Hindu boy scampers out of sight, teaches a valuable lesson to such as will inquire into its meaning. The question is often asked by the incredulous: "But how can the rope stay there with nothing to hold it?" The magician may answer: "It is well-supported, only you do not see the support." The unenlightened behold the accomplishments of the wise, but the methods by which such ends are attained are incomprehensible. The great truths of life are, like the magician's rope, held in their proper place by an unseen agent. Those unable to pierce the magicians subterfuge have eyes but see not. The millions to whom the concerns of the spirit are of no importance, who though continually surrounded by manifestations of universal intelligence are still oblivious to the whole pageantry—these are the truly blind and their affliction is most grievous.

In the allegory of the beanstalk, Jack is the initiate climbing upward toward perfection. The beanstalk has two significances. First, it is the secret doctrine which may grow up to its fullness in a single night, if that night be regarded as the duration of a soul in the mortal state. The beanstalk is further symbolic of the soul itself, up which consciousness must climb to discover the divine sphere from which it was exiled. It is noteworthy that when Jack reaches the upper world, where one would naturally expect beauty and tranquillity to reign, he finds instead that his newly-discovered sphere is the dwelling place of a fierce ogre who has the distressing proclivity of using strangers to supply the requirements of his menu. This giant is the ancient demiurgus—the lord of the world, the royal autocrat, the vast tyrant who opposes all who would climb out of their materiality. He is selfishness, egotism, lust, and hate. He is the epitome of all physical attachment, and the appetites by which man is inclined toward the corporeal state. He is the giant of form, the hero of little minds, the fetish of the materialist, the god of those who worship through the senses alone, the supreme genius of the physical-minded, the magnificence to which fools bow down. Those who would escape the clutches of this giant must be wise indeed, for they must outwit themselves. In the ancient writings it is said that all will fail except a fortuitous destiny move with them, for skill will not suffice, prayers will be unavailing, and only the graciousness of the gods can in- sure success.

The subject of Providence, or fortuitous destiny, is worthy of amplification at this point. One of the symbolic aphorisms of Pythagoras enjoined the disciple to abstain from the eating of beans. In its literal sense there is seemingly no reason whatsoever for the admonition. Among the Greeks, however, beans were used in gambling and various games of chance, and the esoteric purpose of the admonition was to discharge man's reliance upon auspicious fortune; for he who consigns himself to the vagaries of chance in reality rests his fate upon his own integrity. This point is well made by Mephistopheles in Goethe's Faust:

"How closely linked are Luck and Merit Doth never to these fools occur;

Had they the Philosopher's Stone, I swear it, The Stone would lack the Philosopher I"

Man eternally struggles against the littleness that is himself, seeking to increase thereby the virtue of his own destiny. By such effort he frequently is able to maintain a higher footing than would otherwise be his natural right, for effort shall not be left unrewarded. If, however, man ceases his struggle and, doing nothing, trusts to Providence for an auspicious throw, that which is his own will know his face and his reward shall be according to the insufficiency of himself. He who trusts himself to himself is brave indeed! Luck is not what it seems, for it connives with Law to bring about the undoing of the foolish. The bit and bridle which Nemesis carries she slips over the head of the unwary. With blinders she takes away his vision, with checkrein lifts his head so high that he can no longer see the road, and then with loose rein drives him to destruction. But if the gods throw dice they cannot lose, for by reason of their very nature they are predestined to be the victors in every contest. Being as yet imperfect, however man may never relax his vigilance or cease his struggle lest the imperfections which he seeks to outdistance overtake and humiliate him.

What, then, is Providence? It is like flowing into like, a quality reproducing its kind. Providence is not what we desire but what we actually are, and when we open the floodgates of fortune we shall simply be inundated by the torrents of similars—drowned in the substances of ourselves. By confronting destiny with effort we aspire to reach the ideal state of the higher self; but by appealing to fortune we place ourselves in the keeping of an impersonal fate that tortures us with our every defect, and decrees us to abide by the measure of our smallest virtue. Thus only in the truly great is the appeal to fortune to be relied upon; for the rest the law of labor is the only certain way. When it is written that man can succeed only when the gods are auspicious it merely signifies that accomplishment depends upon the perfect mastery of self and the development of all parts, so that the flow of destiny brings to the disciple a propitious end to enterprise. Good fortune is not good to the foolish, nor is evil fortune evil to the wise. The foolish are incapable of benefiting from that which may in its own nature be good; conversely, the wise are incapable of being injured by evil, for understanding renders* all things usable. Thus the identical so-called evil serves the philosopher while it undoes the thoughtless.

The theory of evolution as expounded by the ancient sages does not agree with the Darwinian concept that life moves from one form or kind to another, but rather that life continually moves through the various states of itself. For example, plants do not move toward the perfection of man, nor does man incline toward the perfection of daemons. Each of these orders

is complete in itself, moving inevitably toward its own perfection in the perfect unfoldment of its own intrinsic characteristics. Growth, then, is that eternal procession of qualities marching to unity with themselves. Man, the personality, approaches Man, the idea, and achieves perfection by unity with his own paradigm. Man reaches completion when he perfectly fills the mold or pattern that exists in the transcendental spheres. Evolution, then, is the fitting of a nature into its own archetype, and its end is attained when no longer any point of difference remains between the object as a transitory body and the object as a permanent idea. By growth we learn to become our essential selves, ordered after the precise image of our own divine prototype.

That growth should be the process whereby man becomes reconciled to his own transcendental being may seem a strange thought, but to those who ponder the mystery, this truth becomes evident. Our path is rendered plain: we are destined by Eternal Providence to become the fullness of ourselves. Inclining to neither side nor departing from our persons, we shall find perfection in the consummation of the destiny for which we were first conceived. The imitator must fail, because departing from self he would assume the virtues of another rather than his own. Each individual is alloted an end peculiar to himself, and through uncounted milleniums moves inevitably toward that archetypal ideal patterned for him prior to his departure from Universal Self in quest of individuality. All creatures of a similar kind share a common origin and destiny. It is the peculiar purpose of men that they should become Man, and united in one nature constitute a complete being—that glorious assemblage of parts possessing three virtues, of which the first is completeness and the other two are the poles of this completeness, namely, rationality and permanence.

THE BIRD OF THE SOUL

While the body of the candidate lay in the stone sarcophagus, the soul, hovering in the air above it, assumed the form of a bird, and, passing upward out of the crypt through the vent or chimney of the planets, entered into the presence of the great Osiris, lord of decarnate souls. After remaining three days in the Fields of Amenti, the soul returns to its body amidst the rejoicing of the priests.

# XXXVIII

# Rosicrucian and Masonic Origins

REEMASONRY is a fraternity within a fraternity—an outer A organization concealing an inner brotherhood of the elect. Before it is possible to intelligently discuss the origin of the craft it is necessary to establish the existence of these two separate yet interdependent orders, the one visible and the other invisible. The visible society is a splendid camaraderie of "free and accepted" men enjoined to devote themselves to ethical, educational, fraternal, patriotic, and humanitarian concerns. The invisible society is a secret and most august fraternity whose members are dedicated to the service of a mysterious arcanum arcanorum . Those brethren who have essayed to write the history of their craft have not included in their disquisitions the story of that truly secret inner society which is to the body Freemasonic what the heart is to the body human. In each generation only a few are accepted into the inner sanctuary of the work, but these are veritable princes of truth, and their sainted names shall be remembered in future ages together with the seers and prophets of the elder world.

Though the great initiate-philosophers of Freemasonry can be counted upon one's fingers, yet their power is not to be measured by the achievements of ordinary men. They are dwellers upon the threshold of the innermost, masters of that secret doctrine which forms the invisible foundation of every great theological and rational institution.

The outer history of the Masonic order is one of noble endeavor, altruism, and splendid enterprise; the inner history one of silent conquest, persecution, and heroic martyrdom. The body of Masonry rose from the guilds of workmen who wandered the face of medieval Europe, but the spirit of Masonry walked with God before the universe was spread out or the scroll of the heavens unrolled. The enthusiasm of the young Mason is the effervescence of a pardonable pride. Let him extol the merits of his craft, reciting its steady growth, its fraternal spirit, and its worthy undertakings. Let him boast of splendid buildings and an ever-increasing sphere of influence. These are the tangible evidence of power, and should rightly set a-flutter the heart of the apprentice who does not fully comprehend as yet that great strength which abides in silence, or that unutterable dignity to be sensed only by those who have been "raised" into the contemplation of the inner mystery.

An obstacle well-nigh insurmountable is to convince the Mason that the secrets of his craft are worthy of his profound consideration. As St. Paul (so we are told) kicked against the "pricks" of conversion, so the rank and file of present-day Masons strenuously oppose any effort put forth to interpret Masonic symbols in the light of philosophy. They are seemingly obsessed by the fear that from their ritualism may be extracted a meaning more profound than is actually contained therein. For years it has been a moot question whether Freemasonry is actually a religious organization. "Masonry," writes Pike in the Legcnda for the Nineteenth Degree, "has and always had a religious creed. It teaches what it deems to be the truth in respect to the nature and attributes of God." The more studious-minded Mason regards the craft as an aggregation of thinkers concerned with the deeper mysteries of life.

The all-too prominent younger members of the fraternity, however, if not openly skeptical, are at least indifferent to these weightier issues. The champions of philosophic Masonry, alas, are a weak, small voice which grows weaker and smaller as time goes by. In fact, there are actual blocs among the brethren who would divorce Masonry from both philosophy and religion at any and all cost. If, however, we search the writings of eminent Masons, we find a unanimity of viewpoint, namely, that Masonry is a religious and philosophic body. Every effort

initiated to elevate Masonic thought to its true position has thus invariably emphasized the metaphysical and ethical aspects of the craft.

But a superficial perusal of available documents will demonstrate that the modern Masonic order is not united respecting the true purpose for its own existence. Nor will this factor of doubt be dispelled until the origin of the craft is established beyond all quibbling. The elements of Masonic history are strangely elusive; there are gaps which apparently cannot be bridged. "Who the early Freemasons really were," states Gould in A Concise History of Freemasonry, "and whence they came, may afford a tempting theme for inquiry to the speculative antiquary. But it is enveloped in obscurity, and lies far outside the domain of authentic history." Between modern Freemasonry with its vast body of ancient symbolism, and those original Mysteries which first employed these symbols, there is a dark interval of centuries. To the conservative Masonic historian the deductions of such writers as Higgins, Churchward, Vail, and Waite—though ingenious and fascinating—actually prove nothing. That Masonry is a body of ancient lore is self-evident, but the tangible "link" necessary to convince the recalcitrant brethren that their order is the direct successor of the pagan Mysteries, has unfortunately not been adduced to date. Of such problems as these is composed the "angel" with which the Masonic Jacob must wrestle throughout the night.

It is possible to trace Masonry back a few centuries with comparative ease, but then the thread suddenly vanishes from sight in a maze of secret societies and political enterprises.

Dimly silhouetted in the mists that becloud these tangled issues are such figures as Cagliostro, Comte de St.-Germain, and St. Martin, but even the connection between these individuals and the craft has never been clearly defined. The writings of early Masonic history is involved in such obvious hazard as to provoke the widespread conclusion that further search is futile. The average Masonic student is content, therefore, to trace his craft back to the workmen who chipped and chiselled the cathedrals and public buildings of medieval Europe. While such men as Albert Pike have realized this attitude to be ridiculous, it is one thing to declare it insufficient and quite another to prove the fallacy to an adamantine mind. So much has been lost and forgotten, so much ruled in and out by those unfitted for such legislative revision, that the modern rituals do not in every case represent the original rites of the craft. In his Symbolism, Pike (who spent a lifetime in the quest for Masonic secrets) declares that few of the original meanings of the symbols are known to the modern order, nearly all the so-called interpretations now given being superficial. Pike confessed that the original meanings of the very symbols he himself was attempting to interpret were irretrievably lost; that even such familiar emblems as the apron and the pillars were locked mysteries, whose "keys" had been thrown away by the uninformed. "The initiated," writes John Fellows, "as well as those without the pale of the order, are equally ignorant of their derivation and import." (See The Mysteries of Freemasonry .) Preston, Gould, Mackey, Oliver, and Pike—in fact, nearly every great historian of Freemasonry—have all admitted the possibility of the modern society being connected, indirectly at least, with the ancient Mysteries, and their descriptions of the modern society are prefaced by excerpts from ancient writings descriptive of primitive ceremonials. These eminent Masonic scholars have recognized in the legend of Hiram Abifi an adaptation of the Osiris myth; nor do they deny that the major part of the symbolism of the craft is derived from the pagan institutions of antiquity when the gods were venerated in secret places with strange figures and appropriate rituals.

Though cognizant of the exalted origin of their order, these historians—either through fear or uncertainty—have failed to drive home the one point necessary to establish the true purpose of Freemasonry: They did not realize that the Mysteries whose rituals Freemasonry perpetuates were the custodians of a secret philosophy of life of such transcendent nature that it can be entrusted to only an individual tested and proved beyond any possibility of human frailty. The secret schools of Greece and Egypt were neither fraternal nor political fundamentally, nor were their ideals similar to those of the modern craft. They were essentially philosophic and religious institutions, and all admitted into them were consecrated to the service of the sovereign good. Modern Freemasons, however, regard their craft as neither primarily philosophic nor religious, but rather as ethical. Strange as it may seem, the majority openly ridicule the very supernatural powers and agencies for which their symbols stand.

The secret doctrine that flows through Freemasonic symbols (and to whose perpetuation the invisible Masonic body is consecrated) has its source in three ancient and exalted orders.

The first is the Dionysiac artificers, the second the Roman collegia, and the third the Arabian Rosicrucians. The Dionysian s were the master builders of the ancient world. Originally founded to design and erect the theaters of Dionysus wherein were enacted the tragic dramas of the rituals, this order was repeatedly elevated by popular acclaim to greater dignity, until at last it was entrusted with the planning and construction of all public edifices concerned with the commonwealth or the worship of the gods and heroes. Hiram, King of Tyre, was the patron of the Dionysians, who flourished in Tyre and Sidon, and Hiram Abiff (if we may believe the sacred account) was himself a grand master of this most noble order erf pagan builders. King Solomon in his wisdom accepted the services of this famous craftsman, and thus at the instigation of Hiram, King of Tyre, Hiram Abiff, though himself a member of a different faith, journeyed from his own country to design and supervise the erection of the everlasting house to the true God on Mount Moriah. TTie tools of the builders' craft were first employed by the Dionysian as symbols under which to conceal the mysteries of the soul and the secrets of human regeneration. The Dionysians also first likened man to a rough ashlar which, trued into a finished block through the instrument of reason, could be fitted into the structure of that living and eternal Temple built without the sound of hammer, the voice of workman, or any tool of contention.

The Roman collegiate was a branch of the Dionysiacs and to it belonged those initiated artisans who fashioned the impressive monuments whose ruins still lend their immortal glory to the Eternal City, In his Ten Boofo on Architecture, Vitruvius, the initiate of the collegia, has revealed that which was permissible concerning the secrets of his holy order. Of the inner mysteries, however, he could not write, for these were reserved for such as had donned the leather apron of the craft. In his consideration of the books now available concerning the Mysteries the thoughtful reader should note the following words appearing in a 12th-century volume entitled Artephil Liber Secretus: "Is not this an art full of secrets? And believest thou, O fooll that we plainly teach this Secret of Secrets, taking our words according to their literal interpretation?" (See Sephar H ' Debarim.) Into the stones they trued, the adepts of the collegia deeply carved their gnostic symbols. From earliest times the initiated stonecutters marked their perfected works with the secret emblems of their crafts and degrees, that unborn generations might realize that the master builders of the first ages also labored for the same ends sought by men today.

The Mysteries of Egypt and Persia that had found a haven in the Arabian Desert reached Europe by way of the Knights Templars and the Rosicrucians. The Temple of the Rose Cross at Damascus had preserved the secret philosophy of the Rose of Sharon; the Druses of the Lebanon mountains still retain the mysticism of ancient Syria; and the dervishes, as they lean on their carved and crotched sticks, still meditate upon the secret instruction perpetuated from the days of the four caliphs. From the far places of Irak and the hidden retreats of the Sufi mystics, the Ancient Wisdom found its way into Europe. Was Jacques de Molay burned by the Holy Inquisition merely because he wore the red cross of the Templar? What were those secrets to which he was true even in death? Did his companion knights perish with him merely because they had amassed a fortune and exercised an unusual degree of temporal power? To the thoughtless these may constitute ample grounds, but to those who can pierce the film of the specious and the superficial they are assuredly insufficient. It was not the physical power of the Templars, but the knowledge which they had brought with them from the East, that the church feared. The Templars had discovered part of the great arcanum; they had become wise in those mysteries which had been celebrated in Mecca thousands of years before the advent of Mohammed; they had read a few pages from the dread book of the Anthropos, and for this knowledge they were doomed to die. What was the black magic of which the Templars were accused? What was Baphomet, the Goat of Mendes, whose mysteries they were declared to have celebrated ? All these are questions worthy of thoughtful consideration by every studious Mason.

Truth is eternal. The so-called revelations of truth that come in diiferent religions are actually but a re-emphasis of an ever-existing doctrine. Moses did not originate a new religion for Israel; he simply adapted the Mysteries of Egypt to the needs of Israel. The ark triumphantly borne by the twelve tribes through the wilderness was copied after the Isiac ark, which may still be traced in faint bas-relief upon the ruins of the Temple of Philac. Even the two brooding cherubim over the mercy scat are visible in the Egyptian carving, furnishing indubitable evidence that the secret doctrine of Egypt was the prototype of Israel's mystery religion. In his reformation of Indian philosophy, Buddha likewise did not reject the esoteri- cism of the Brahmins, but rather adapted this esotericism to the needs of the masses in India. The mystic secrets locked within the holy Vedas were disclosed in order that all men, irrespective of caste, might partake of wisdom and share in a common heritage of good. Jesus was a Rabbi of the Jews, a teacher of the holy law who discoursed in the synagogue, interpreting the Torah according to the teachings of his sect. He brought no new message nor were his reformations radical.

He merely tore away the veil from the temple in order that not only Pharisee and Sadducee, but also publican and sinner might together behold the glory of an ageless faith. In his cavern on Mount Hira, Mohammed prayed not for new truths, but for old truths to be restated in their original purity and simplicity in order that men might understand again the primitive religion: God's clear revelation to the first patriarchs. The Mysteries of Islam had been celebrated in the sanctuary of the Kaaba centuries before the holy pilgrimage. The prophet was but the reformer of a decadent pagandom, the smasher of idols, the purifier of defiled Mysteries. The dervishes, who patterned their garments after those of the prophet, still preserve that inner teaching of the elect, and for them the Axis of the Earth—the supreme hierophant- visible only to the faith still sits in meditation upon the flat roof of the Kaaba. Neither carpenter nor camel driver, as Abdul Baha might have said, can fashion a world religion from the substances of his own mind. Neither prophet nor savior preached a doctrine which was his own, but in language suitable to his time and race retold that Ancient Wisdom which has been preserved within the Mysteries since the dawning of human consciousness. So with the Masonic Mysteries of today. Each Mason has at hand those lofty principles of universal order upon whose certainties the faiths of mankind have ever been established.

Father C. R. C., the master of the Rosy Cross, was initiated into the great work at Damcar. Later at Fez further information was given him relating to the sorcery of the Arabians.

From these wizards of the desert he also secured the sacred book M , which is declared to have contained the accumulated knowledge of the world. He translated this volume into Latin for the edification of his order, but only the initiates know the present hidden repository of the Rosicrucian manuscripts, charters, and manifestoes. From the Arabians C. R. C. also learned of the elemental peoples and how, with their aid, it was possible to gain admission to the ethereal world where dwelt the genii and nature spirits. He thus discovered that the magical creatures of the Arabian "Nights Entertainment actually existed, though invisible to the ordinary mortal. From astrologers living in the desert far from the concourse of the marketplace he was further instructed concerning the mysteries of the stars, the virtues resident in the astral light, the rituals of magic and invocation, the preparation of therapeutic talismans, and the binding of the genii. He became an adept in the gathering of medicinal herbs, the transmutation of metals, and the manufacture, of precious gems by artificial means.

Even the secret of the elixir of life and the universal panacea were communicated to him. Enriched beyond the dreams of Croesus, the holy master returned to Europe and there established a house of wisdom which he called Domus Sancti Spirit™. This house he enveloped in clouds, it is said, so that men could not discover it. What arc these "clouds," but the rituals and symbols under which is concealed the great arcanum—that unspeakable mystery which every true Mason must seek if he would become in reality a "Prince of the Royal Secret"?

Paracelsus, the Swiss Hermes, was initiated into the secrets of alchemy in Constantinople and there beheld the consummation of the magnum opus. He is consequendy endded to be mentioned among those initiated by the Arabians into the Rosicrucian work. Cagliostro was also initiated by the Arabians, and because of the knowledge he had thus secured incurred the displeasure of the Holy See. From the unprobed depths of Arabian Rosicrucianism issued the illustrious Comte dc St.-Germain, over whose Masonic activities the veil of impenetrable mystery still hangs. The exalted body of initiates whom he represented, as well as the mission he came to accomplish, have both been concealed from the members of the craft at large, and are apparent only to those few discerning Masons who sense the supernal philosophic destiny of their fraternity.

The modern Masonic order can be traced back to a period in European history famous for its intrigue both political and sociological. Between the years 1600 and 1800, mysterious agents moved across the face of the Continent. The forerunner of modern thought was beginning to make its appearance, and all Europe was passing through the throes of internal dissension and reconstruction. Democracy was in its infancy, yet its potential power was already being felt. Thrones were beginning to totter. The aristocracy of Europe was like the old man on Sinbad's back; it was becoming more unbearable with every passing day. Although upon the surface national governments were seemingly able to cope with the situation, there was a definite undercurrent of impending change. Out of the masses, long patient under the yoke oppression, were rising up the champions of religious, philosophic, and political liberty. These led the factions of the dissatisfied; people with legitimate grievances against the intolerance of the church and the oppression of the crown. Out of this struggle for expression certain definite ideals materialized which have now come to be considered peculiarly Masonic.

The divine prerogatives of humanity were being crushed out by the three great powers of ignorance, superstition, and fear—ignorance, the power of the mob; superstition, the power of the church, and fear, the power of the despot. Between the thinker and personal liberty loomed the three "ruffians" or personifications of impediment—the torch, the crown, and the tiara. Brute force, kingly power, and ecclesiastical persuasion became the agents of a great oppression, the motive of a deep unrest, the deterrent to all progress. It was unlawful to think, well-nigh fatal to philosophize, rank heresy to doubt. To question the infallibility of the existing order was to invite the persecution of the church and the state. Together they incited the populace, which thereupon played the role of (executioner for these arch-enemies of human liberty. Thus the ideal of democracy assumed a definite form during these stormy periods of European history. This democracy was not only a vision, but a retrospection; not only a looking forward, but a gazing backward upon better days and the effort to project those better days into the unborn tomorrow. The ethical, political, and philosophical institutions of antiquity, with their constructive effect upon the whole structure of the state, were noble examples of possible conditions. It became the dream of the oppressed to re-establish a golden age upon the earth; an age in which the thinker could think in safety and the dreamer dream in peace; when the wise should lead and the simple follow, yet all dwell together in fraternity and industry.

During this period several books were in circulation, which to a certain degree registered the pulse of the time. One of these documents—More's Utopia —was the picture of a new age when heavenly conditions should prevail upon the earth. This ideal of establishing good in the world savored of blasphemy, for in that day it was assumed that heaven alone could be good. Men did not seek to establish heavenly conditions upon earth, but rather earthly conditions in heaven. According to popular concept, the more the individual suffered the torments of the damned upon earth, the more he would enjoy the blessedness in heaven. Life was a period of chastisement, and earthly happiness an unattainable mirage. More's Utopia thus came as a definite blow to autocratic pretensions and attitudes, giving impulse to the material emphasis which was to follow in succeeding centuries. Another prominent figure of this period was Sir Walter Raleigh, who paid with his life for high treason against the crown. Raleigh was tried, and though the charge was never proved he was executed. Before he went to trial it was known that he must die, and that no defense could save him. His treason against the crown was of a character very different, however, from that which history records. Raleigh was a member of a secret society, or body of men, which was already moving irresistibly forward under the banner of democracy, and for that affiliation he died a felon's death. The actual reason for his death sentence was his refusal to reveal the identity of that great political organization of which he was a member, or his confreres who were fighting the dogma of faith and the divine right of kings. On the title page of the first edition of Raleigh's History of the World , we accordingly find a mass of intricate emblems framed between two great columns. When the executioner sealed his lips forever, Raleigh's silence, while it added to the discomfiture of his persecutors, assured the safety of his colleagues.

One of the truly great minds of that secret fraternity—in fact, the moving spirit of the whole enterprise—was Sir Francis Bacon, whose prophecy of the coming age forms the theme in his New Atlantis, and whose vision of the reformation of knowledge finds expression in the Novum Organum. In the engraving at the beginning of the latter volume may be seen the little ship of progressivism sailing out between the pillars of Galenic and Avicennian philosophy venturing forth beyond the imaginary pillars of church and state upon the unknown sea of human liberty. It is significant that Bacon was appointed by the British Crown to protect its interests in the new American Colonies beyond the sea. We find him writing of this new land, dreaming of the day when a new world and a new government of the philosophic elect should be established there, and scheming to consummate that end when the right time came. Upon the title page of the 1640 edition of Bacon's Advancement of Learning is a Latin motto to the effect that he was the third great mind since Plato. Bacon was a member of the same group to which Sir Walter Raleigh belonged, but Bacon's position as lord chancellor protected him from Raleigh's fate. Every effort was made, however, to humiliate and discredit him. At last, in the sixty-sixth year of his life, he completed the work which held him in England. He feigned death and passed over into Germany, there to guide the destinies of his philosophic and political fraternity for nearly twenty-five years before his actual demise.

Other notable characters of the period are Montaigne, Ben Jonson, Marlowe, and the great Franz Joseph of Transylvania—the latter one of the most important as well as active figures in all this drama; a man who ceased fighting Austria and retired to a monastery in Transylvania from where he directed the activities of his secret society. One political upheaval followed another. The grand climax culminated in the French Revolution, which was directly precipitated by the attacks upon the person of Alessandro Cagliostro. The "divine" Cag- liostro, by far the most picturesque character of the time, has the distinction of being more maligned than any other person of history. Tried by the Inquisition for founding a Masonic lodge in the city of Rome, he was sentenced to die, a sentence later commuted by the Pope to life imprisonment in the old castle of San Leo. Shortly after his incarceration Cagliostro disappeared, and the story was circulated that he had been strangled in an attempt to escape from prison. In reality he was liberated and returned to his masters in the East. But Cagliostro—the idol of France, surnamed "the Father of the Poor,'* who never received anything from anyone and gave everything to everyone—was most adequately revenged. Though the people little understood this inexhaustible pitcher of bounty which poured forth benefits and never required replenishment, they remembered him in the day of their power. Cagliostro founded the Egyptian rite of Freemasonry, which received into its mysteries many of the French nobility and was regarded favorably by the most learned minds of Europe. Having established the Egyptian rite, Cagliostro declared himself to be an agent of the order of the Knights Templars, and to have received initiation from them on the Isle of Malta. (See Morals and Dogma in which Albert Pike quotes Eliphas Levi on Cagliostro's affiliation with the Templars.) Called upon the carpet by the supreme council of France, it was demanded of Cagliostro that he prove by what authority he had founded a Masonic lodge in Paris, independent of the Grand Orient. Of such surpassing mentality was Cagliostro that the supreme council found it difficult to secure an advocate qualified to discuss with him philosophic Masonry and the ancient Mysteries he claimed to represent. Court de Gebelin—the greatest Egyptologist of his day and an authority on ancient philosophies—was chosen as the outstanding scholar. A time was set and the brethren convened. Attired in an Oriental coat and a pair of violet-colored breeches, Cagliostro was haled before this council of his peers. Court de Gebelin asked three questions and then sat down, admitting himself disqualified to interrogate a man so much his superior in every branch of learning. Cagliostro then took the floor, revealing to the assembled Masons not only his personal qualifications, but prophesying the future of France. He foretold the fall of the French throne, the Reign of Terror, and the fall of the Bastille. At a later time he revealed the dates of the death of Marie Antoinette and the king, and also the advent of Napoleon. Having finished his address he made a spectacular exit, leaving the French Masonic lodge in consternation and utterly incapable of coping with the profundity of his reasoning. Though no longer regarded as a ritual in Freemasonry, the Egyptian rite is available, and all who read it will recognize its author to have been no more a charlatan than was Plato.

Then appears that charming "first American gentleman," Dr. Benjamin Franklin, who together with the Marquis de Lafayette, played an important role in this drama of empires. While in France Dr. Franklin was privileged to receive definite esoteric instruction. It is noteworthy that he was the first in America to reprint Anderson's Constitutions of the Vree-Masons, which is a most prized work on the subject though its accuracy is disputed. Through all this stormy period these impressive figures come and go, part of a definite organization of political and religious thought—a functioning body of philosophers represented in Spain by no less an individual than Cervantes, in France by Cagliostro and St.-Germain, in Germany by Gichtel and Andireae, in England by Bacon, More, and Raleigh, and in America by Washington and Franklin. Coincident with the Baconian agitation in England, the Varna Vraternitatis and Confessio Vraternitatis appeared in Germany, both of these works being contributions to the establishment of a philosophic government upon the earth. One of the outstanding links between the Rosicrucian Mysteries of the Middle Ages and modern Masonry is Elias Ash mole, the historian of the Order of the Garter and the first Englishman to compile the alchemical writings of the English chemists.

The foregoing may seem to be a useless recital of inanities, but its purpose is to impress upon the reader's mind the philosophical and political situation in Europe at the time of the inception of the Masonic order. A philosophic clan, as it were, which had moved across the face of Europe under such names as the "Illuminati" and the "Rosicrucians," had undermined in a subtle manner the entire structure of regal and sacerdotal supremacy. The founders of Freemasonry were all men who were more or less identified with the progressive tendencies of their day. Mystics, philosophers, and alchemists were all bound together with a secret tie, and dedicated to the emancipation of humanity from ignorance and oppression.

In my researches among ancient books and manuscripts I have pieced together a little story of probabilities which has a direct bearing upon the subject. Long before the establishment of Freemasonry as a fraternity, a group of mystics founded in Europe what was called the "Society of Unknown Philosophers." Prominent among the profound thinkers who formed the membership of this society were the alchemists, who were engaged in transmuting the political and religious "base metal" of Europe into ethical and spiritual "gold"; the Cabalists, who as investigators of the superior orders of nature sought to discover a stable foundation for human government; and lastly the astrologers who, from a study of the procession of the heavenly bodies, hoped to find therein the rational archetype for all mundane procedure. Here and there is to be found a character who contacted this society. By some it is believed that both Martin Luther and that great mystic, Philipp Melanchthon, were connected with it. The first edition of the King James Bible, which was edited by Francis Bacon and prepared under Masonic supervision, bears more Mason's marks than the Cathedral of Strasbourg. The same is true respecting the Masonic symbolism found in the first English edition of Flavius Josephus* The Antiquities of the Jews.

For some time the Society of Unknown Philosophers moved extraneous to the church. Among the fathers of the church, however, were a great number of scholarly and intelligent men who were keenly interested in philosophy and ethics, prominent among them being the German Jesuit Athanasius Kircher, who is recognized as one of the great scholars of his day.

A Rosicrucian, and also a member of the Society of Unknown Philosophers as revealed by the cryptograms in his writings, Kircher was in harmony with the program of philosophic reconstruction. Since learning was largely limited to churchmen, the body of philosophers soon developed an overwhelming preponderance of ecclesiastics in its membership. The original antiecclesiastical ideals of the society were speedily reduced to an innocuous state, and the organization gradually became an actual auxiliary of the church. A small portion of the membership, however, maintained an aloofness from the literati of the faith, for it represented an unorthodox class— the alchemists, Rosicrucians, Cabalists, and magicians. This latter group accordingly retired from the outer body of the society that had come to be known as the "Order of the Golden and Rose Cross" and whose adepts were elevated to the dignity of Knights of the Golden Stone. Upon the withdrawal of these initiated adepts, a powerful clerical body remained which possessed considerable of the ancient lore but in many instances lacked the "keys" by which this symbolism could be interpreted. As this body continued to increase in temporal power, its philosophical power grew correspondingly less.

The smaller group of adepts that had withdrawn from the order apparently remained inactive, having retired to what they termed the "House of the Holy Spirit," where they were enveloped by certain "mists" impenetrable to the eyes of the profane. Among these reclusive adepts must be included such well-known Rosicrucians as Robert Fludd, Eugenius Philalethes, John Heydon, Michael Maier, and Henri Khunrath. These adepts in their retirement constituted a loosely organized society which, though lacking the solidarity of a definite fraternity, occasionally initiated a candidate and met annually at a specified place. It was the Comte de Chazal, an initiate of this order, who "raised" Dr. Sigismund Bacstrom while the latter was on the Isle of Mauritius. In due time the original members of the order passed on, after first entrusting their secrets to carefully chosen successors. In the meantime a group of men in England, under the leadership of such mystics as Ash mole and Fludd, had resolved upon repopularizing the ancient learning and reclassifying philosophy in accordance with Bacon's plan for a world encyclopedia. These men had undertaken to reconstruct ancient Platonic and Gnostic mysticism, but were unable to attain their objective for lack of information. Elias Ashmolc may have been a member of the European order of Rosicrucians, and as such evidently knew that in various parts of Europe there were isolated individuals who were in possession of the secret doctrine handed down in unbroken line from the ancient Greeks and Egyptians through Boethius, the early Christian Church, and the Arabians. The efforts of the English group to contact such individuals were evidently successful. Several initiated Rosicrucians were brought from the mainland to England, where they remained for a considerable time designing the symbolism of Freemasonry and incorporating into the rituals of the order the same divine principles and philosophy that had formed the inner doctrine of all great secret societies from the time of the Eleusinia in Greece. In fact, the Eleusinian Mysteries themselves continued in the custody of the Arabians, as attested by the presence of Masonic symbols and figures upon early Mohammedan monuments. The adepts who were brought over from the Continent to sit in council with the English philosophers were initiates of the Arabian rites, and through them the Mysteries were ultimately returned to Christendom. Upon completion of the by-laws of the new fraternity the initiates retired again to Central Europe, leaving a group of disciples to develop the outer organization which was to function as a sort of screen to conceal the activities of the esoteric order. Such, in brief, is the story which we are able to piece together from the fragmentary bits of evidence available. The whole structure of Freemasonry is founded upon the activities of this secret society of Central European adepts, whom the studious Mason will find to be the definite "link" between the modern craft and the ancient wisdom. The outer body of Masonic philosophy was merely the veil of this cabalistic order whose members were the custodians of the true arcanum.

Does this inner and secret brotherhood of initiates still exist independent of the Freemasonic order? Evidence points to the fact that it does, for these august adepts are the actual preservers of those secret operative processes of the Greeks whereby the illumination and completion of the individual is effected. They are the veritable guardians of the "Lost Word" —the Keepers of the Inner Mystery—and the Mason who searches for and discovers them is rewarded beyond all mortal estimation.

In the preface to a book entitled Long-Livers, published in 1772, Eugenius Philalethes, the Rosicrucian initiate, thus addresses his Brethren of the Most Ancient and Most Honorable Fraternity of the Free Masons: "Remember that you are the Salt of the Earth, the Light of the World, and the Fire of the Universe. You are living Stones, built upon a Spiritual House, who believe and rely on the chief Lapis Angularis which the refractory and disobedient Builders disallowed. You are called from Darkness to Light; you are a chosen Generation, a royal Priesthood. This makes you, my dear Brethren, fit Companions for the greatest Kings; and no wonder, since the King of Kings hath condescended to make you so to himself, compared to whom the mightiest and most haughty Princess of the Earth are but as worms, and that not so much as we are all Sons of the same one Eternal Father, by whom all Things were made; but inasmuch as we do the Will of his and our Father which is in Heaven. You see now your high Dignity; you see what you are; act accordingly, and show yourselves (what you are) MEN, and walk worthy the high Profession to which you are called. • # # Remember, then, what the great End we all aim at is: Is it not to be happy here and hereafter? For they both depend on each other. The Seeds of that eternal Peace and Tranquillity and everlasting Repose must be sown in this Life; and he that would glorify and enjoy the Sovereign Good then must learn to do it now, and from contemplating the Creature gradually ascend to adore the Creator."

Of all obstacles to surmount in matters of rationality, the most difficult is that of prejudice. Even the casual observer must realize that the true wealth of Freemasonry lies in its mysticism. The average Masonic scholar is fundamentally opposed to a mystical interpretation of his symbols, for he shares the attitude of the modern mind in its general antipathy toward transcendentalism. A most significant fact, however, is that those Masons who have won signal honors for their contributions to the craft have been transcendentalists almost without exception. It is quite incredible that any initiated Brother, when presented with a copy of Morals and Dogma upon the conferment of his fourteenth degree, can read that volume and yet maintain that his order is not identical wth the Mystery schools of the first ages. Much of the writings of Albert Pike are extracted from the books of the French magician, Eliphas Levi, one of the greatest transcendentalists of modern times. Levi was an occultist, a metaphysician, a Platonic philosopher, who by the rituals of magic invoked even the spirit of Apollonius of Tyana, and yet Pike has inserted in his Morals and Dogma whole pages, and even chapters, practically verbatim. To Pike the following remarkable tribute was paid by Stirling Kerr, Jr., 33°, Deputy Inspector-General for the District of Columbia upon crowning with laurel the bust of Pike in the House of the Temple: "Pike was an oracle greater than that of Delphi. He was Truth's minister and priest. His victories were those of peace. Long may his memory live in the hearts of the Brethren." Affectionately termed "Albertus Magnus" by his admirers, Pike wrote of Hermetism and alchemy and hinted at the Mysteries of the Temple. Through his zeal and unflagging energy American Freemasonry was raised from comparative obscurity to become the most powerful organization in the land. Though Pike, a transcendental thinker, was the recipient of every honor that the Freemasonic bodies of the world could confer, the modern Mason is loath to admit that transcendentalism has any place in Freemasonry. This is an attitude filled with embarrassment and inconsistency, for whichever way the Mason turns he is confronted by these inescapable issues of philosophy and the Mysteries. Yet withal he dismisses the entire subject as being more or less a survival of primitive superstitions. The Mason who would discover the Lost Word must remember that in the first ages every neophyte was a man of profound learning and unimpeachable character, who for the sake of wisdom and virtue had faced death unafraid and had triumphed over those limitations of the flesh which bind most mortals to the sphere of mediocrity. In those days the rituals were not put on by degree teams who handled candidates as though they were perishable commodities, but by priests deeply versed in the lore of their cults. Not one Freemason out of a thousand could have survived the initiations of the pagan rites, for the tests were given in those strenous days when men were men and death the reward of failure. The neophyte of the Druid Mysteries was set adrift in a small boat to battle the stormy sea, and unless his knowledge of natural law enabled him to quell the storm as did Jesus upon the Sea of Galilee, he returned no more. In the Egyptian rites of Serapis it was required of the neophyte that he cross an unbridged chasm in the temple floor. In other words, if unable by magic to sustain himself in the air without visible support he fell headlong into a volcanic crevice, there to die of heat and suffocation. In one of the Mithraic rites the candidate seeking admission to the inner sanctuary was required to pass through a closed door by dematerialization. The philosopher who has authenticated the reality of ordeals such as these no longer entertains the popular error that the performance of "miracles" is confined solely to Biblical characters. "Do you still ask," writes Pike, "if it has its secrets and mysteries? It is certain that something in the Ancient Initiations was regarded as of immense value, by such Intellects as Herodotus, Plutarch and Cicero. The magicians of Egypt were able to imitate several of the miracles wrought by Moses; and the Science of the Hierophants of the Mysteries produced effects that to the Initiated seemed mysterious and supernatural " (See Legenda for the Twenty-eighth Degree.)

It is self-evident that he who passed successfully through these arduous tests involving both natural and also supernatural hazards was a man apart in his community. Such an initiate was deemed to be more than human, for he had achieved where countless ordinary mortals, having failed, had returned no more. Let us hear the words of Apuleius when admitted into the Temple of Isis, as recorded in The Metamorphosis, or Golden Ass: "Then also the priest, all the profane being removed, taking hold of me by the hand, brought me to the penetralia of the temple, clothed in a new linen garment. Perhaps, inquisitive reader, you will very anxiously ask me what was then said and done? I would tell you, if it could be lawfully told; you should know it, if it were lawful for you to hear it. But both ears and the tongue are guilty of rash curiosity. Nevertheless, I will not keep you in suspense with religious desire, nor torment you with long-continued anxiety. Hear, therefore, but believe what is true. I approached to the confines of death, and having trod on the threshold of Proser* pine, / returned from it, being carried through all the elements. At midnight I saw the sun shining with a splendid light; and I manifestly drew near to the Gods beneath, and the Gods above, and proximately adored them. Behold, I have narrated to you things, of which, though heard, it is nevertheless necessary that you should be ignorant. I will, therefore, only relate that which may be enunciated to the understanding of the profane without a crime" Kings and princes paid homage to the initiate—the "newborn" man, the favorite of the gods. The initiate had actually entered into the presence of the divine beings. He had "died" and been "raised" again into the radiant sphere of everlasting light. Seekers after wisdom journeyed across great continents to hear his words, and his sayings were treasured with the revelations of oracles. It was esteemed an honor to receive from such a one an inclination of the head, a kindly smile, or a gesture of approbation. Disciples gladly paid with their lives for the master's word of praise, and died of a broken heart at his rebuke. On one occasion Pythagoras became momentarily irritated because of the seeming stupidity of one of his students. The master's displeasure so preyed upon the mind of the humiliated youth that, drawing a knife from the folds of his garment, he committed suicide. So greatly moved was Pythagoras by the incident that never from that time on was he known to lose patience with any of his followers, regardless of the provocation. With a smile of paternal indulgence the venerable master who senses the true dignity of the mystic tie, should gravely incline the minds of the brethren toward the sublimer issues of the craft. The officer who would serve his lodge most effectively must realize that he is of an order apart from other men; that he is the keeper of an awful secret; that the chair upon which he sits is the seat of immortals; and that if he would be a worthy successor to those master Masons of other ages his thoughts must be measured by the profundity of Pythagoras and the lucidity of Plato. Enthroned in the radiant East, the worshipful master is the "Light" of his lodge—the representative of the gods, one of that long line of hierophants who, through the blending of their rational powers with the reason of the ineffable, have been accepted into the great school. This high priest after an ancient order must realize that those before him are not merely a gathering of properly tested men, but the custodians of an eternal lore, the guardians of a sacred truth, the perpetuators of an ageless wisdom, the consecrated servants of a living God, the wardens of a supreme mystery. A new day is dawning for Freemasonry. From the insufficiency of theology and the hopelessness of materialism, men are turning to seek the God of philosophy. In this new era wherein the old order of things is breaking down and the individual is rising triumphant above the monotony of the masses, there is much work to be accomplished. The "Temple Builder" is needed as never before. A great reconstruction period is at hand; the debris of a fallen culture must be cleared away; the old footings must be found again that a new Temple significant of a new revelation of law may be raised thereon.

This is the peculiar work of the builder; this is the high duty for which he was called out of the world; this is the noble enterprise for which he was "raised" and given the tools of his craft. By doing his part in the reorganization of society, the workman may earn his "wages" as all good Masons should. A new light is breaking in the East; a more glorious day is at hand. The rule of the philosophic elect—the dream of the ages—will yet be realized and is not far distant. To her loyal sons, Freemasonry sends this clarion call: "Arise ye, the day of labor is at hand; the great work awaits completion, and the days of man's life are few." Like the singing guildsman of bygone days, the craft of the builders marches victoriously down the broad avenues of time. Their song is of labor and glorious endeavor; their anthem is of toil and industry; they rejoice in their noble destiny, for they are builders of cities, the hewers of worlds, the master craftsmen of the universe.

THE PILLARS OF HERCULES

The city of the philosophic elect rises from the highest mountain peak of the earth, and here the gods of the wise dwell together in everlasting felicity. In the foreground are the symbolic Pillars of Hercules, which appear on the title page of Bacon's Novum Organum, and between them runs the path that leads upward from the uncertainties of earth to that perfect order which is established in the sphere of the enlightened.

# XXXIX

❦

# The Rosicrucian Mysteries by Max Heindel

Originally published: 1911

The Rosicrucian Mysteries is a concise and illuminating guide to the Western Mystery Tradition as presented by the Rosicrucian Order. Written by mystic and astrologer Max Heindel, a student of esoteric Christianity, this work offers profound insights into the soul's journey, the invisible worlds, spiritual evolution, and the path of initiation.

Heindel's clear and earnest voice makes complex metaphysical ideas accessible to the earnest seeker. Drawing from personal spiritual experiences and the wisdom of the Elder Brothers of the Rose Cross, he outlines the esoteric meaning behind birth, death, rebirth, karma, the constitution of man, and the inner workings of cosmic law.

Whether you're a newcomer to esotericism or a devoted student of the mysteries, The Rosicrucian Mysteries serves as a valuable stepping stone toward the deeper teachings found in Heindel's seminal work, The Rosicrucian Cosmo-Conception.

From the author:

"IN EVERY MAN THERE IS LATENT THE SAME WONDERFUL POWER WHICH MADE THE CHRIST. THE GREAT WORK OF EVOLUTION IS TO BRING THAT POWER OUT INTO THE OPEN AND TO UNFOLD IT INTO USEFULNESS."

— MAX HEINDEL

# XL

⁂

# The Rosicrucian Mysteries by Max Heindel

Chapter I. The Order of Rosicrucians and the Rosicrucian Fellowship Our Message And Mission

A Sane Mind A Soft Heart A Sound Body

Before entering upon an explanation of the teachings of the Rosicrucians, it may be well to say a word about them and about the place they hold in the evolution of humanity.

For reasons to be given later these teachings advocate the dualistic view; they hold that man is a spirit enfolding all the powers of God as the seed enfolds the plant, and that these powers are being slowly unfolded by a series of existences in a gradually improving earthy body; also that this process of development has been performed under the guidance of exalted beings who are yet ordering our steps, though in a decreasing measure, as we gradually acquire intellect and will. These exalted Beings, though unseen to the physical eyes, are nevertheless potent factors in all affairs of life, and give to the various groups of humanity lessons which will most efficiently promote the growth of their spiritual powers. In fact, the earth may be likened to a vast training school in which there are pupils of varying age and ability as we find it in one of our own schools. There are the savages, living and worshipping under most primitive conditions, seeing in stick or stone a God. Then, as man progresses onwards and upwards in the scale of civilization, we find a higher and higher conception of Deity, which has flowered here in our Western World in the beautiful Christian religion that now furnishes our spiritual inspiration and incentive to improve. These various religions have been given to each group of humanity by the exalted beings whom we know in the Christian religion as the Recording Angels, whose wonderful prevision enable them to view the trend of even so unstable a quantity as the human mind, and thus they are enabled to determine what steps are necessary to lead our enfoldment along the lines congruous to the highest universal good.

When we study the history of the ancient nations we shall find that at about six hundred years B. C. a great spiritual wave had its inception on the Eastern shores of the Pacific Ocean where the great Confucian Religion accelerated the progress of the Chinese nation, then also the Religion of the Buddha commenced to win its millions of adherents in India, and still further West we have the lofty philosophy of Pythagoras. Each system was suited to the needs of the particular people to whom it was sent. Then came the period of the Sceptics, in Greece, and later, traveling westward the same spiritual wave is manifested as the Christian religion of the so-called "Dark Ages" when the dogma of a dominant church compelled belief from the whole of Western Europe. It is a law in the universe that a wave of spiritual awakening is always followed by a period of doubting materialism, each phase is necessary in order that the spirit may receive equal development of heart and intellect without being carried too far in either direction. The Great Beings aforementioned, Who care for our progress, always take steps to safeguard humanity against that danger, and when they foresaw the wave of materialism which commenced in the sixteenth century with the birth of our modern Science, they took steps to protect the West as they had formerly safeguarded the East against the Sceptics who were held in check by the Mystery schools. In the thirteenth century there appeared in central Europe a great spiritual teacher whose symbolical name was Christian Rosenkreuz. or Christian Rose Cross. who founded the mysterious Order of the Rosy Cross, concerning which so many speculations have been made and so little has become known to the world at large, for it is the Mystery school of the West and is only open to those who have attained the stage of spiritual unfoldment necessary to be initiated in its secrets concerning the Science of Life and Being. If we are so far developed that we are able to leave our dense physical body and take a soul flight into interplanetary space we shall find that the ultimate physical atom is spherical in shape like our earth; it is a ball. When we take a number of balls of even size and group them around one, it will take just twelve balls to hide a thirteenth within. Thus the twelve visible and the one hidden are numbers revealing a cosmic relationship and as all Mystery Orders are based upon cosmic lines, they are composed of twelve members gathered around a thirteenth who is the invisible head.

There are seven colors in the spectrum: red, orange, yellow, green, blue, indigo and violet. But between the violet and the red there are still other five colors which are invisible to the physical eye but reveal themselves to the spiritual sight. In every Mystery Order there are also seven brothers who at times go out into the world and there perform whatever work may be necessary to advance the people among whom they serve, but five are never seen outside the temple. They work with and teach those alone who have passed through certain stages of spiritual unfoldment and are able to visit the temple in their spiritual bodies; a feat taught in the first initiation which usually takes place outside the temple as it is not convenient for all to visit that place physically. Let not the reader imagine that this initiation makes the pupil a Rosicrucian, it does not, any more than admission to a High School makes a boy a member of the faculty.  Nor does he become a Rosicrucian even after having passed through all the nine degrees of this or any other Mystery School. The Rosicrucians are Hierophants of the lesser Mysteries, and beyond them there are still schools wherein Greater Mysteries are taught. Those who have advanced through the lesser Mysteries and have become pupils of the Greater Mysteries are called Adepts, but even they have not reached the exalted standpoint of the twelve Brothers of the Rosicrucian Order or the Hierophants of any other lesser Mystery School any more than the freshman at college has attained to the knowledge and position of a teacher in the High school from which he has just graduated.

A later work will deal with initiation, but we may say here that the door of a genuine Mystery

School is not unlocked by a golden key, but is only opened as a reward for meritorious
service to humanity and any one who advertises himself as a Rosicrucian or makes a charge for
tuition, by either of those acts shows himself to be a charlatan. The true pupil of any Mystery
School is far too modest to advertise the fact, he will scorn all titles or honors from men, he will
have no regard for riches save the riches of love given to him by those whom it becomes his privilege to help and teach.

In the centuries that have gone by since the Rosicrucian Order was first formed they have worked
quietly and secretly, aiming to mould the thought of Western Europe through the works of
Paracelsus, Boehme, Bacon, Shakespeare, Fludd and others. Each night at midnight when the
physical activities of the day are at their lowest ebb, and the spiritual impulse at its highest flood
tide, they have sent out from their temple soul-stirring vibrations to counteract materialism and
to further the development of soul powers. To their activities we owe the gradual spiritualization
of our once so materialistic science.

With the commencement of the twentieth century a further step was taken. It was realized that
something must be done to make religion scientific as well as to make science religious, in order
that they may ultimately blend; for at the present time heart and intellect are divorced. The heart
instinctively feels the truth of religious teachings concerning such wonderful mysteries as the Immaculate Conception (the Mystic Birth), the Crucifixion (the Mystic Death), the cleansing blood,
the atonement, and other doctrines of the Church, which the intellect refuses to believe, as they
are incapable of demonstration, and seemingly at war with natural law. Material advancement
may be furthered when intellect is dominant and the longings of the heart unsatisfied, but soul
growth will be retarded until the heart also receives satisfaction.

In order to give the world a teaching so blended that it will satisfy both the mind and heart, a
messenger must be found and instructed. Certain unusual qualifications were necessary, and the
first one chosen failed to pass a certain test after several years had been spent to prepare him for
the work to be done.

It is well said that there is a time to sow, and a time to reap, and that there are certain times for
all the works of life, and in accordance with this law of periodicity each impulse in spiritual uplift
must also be undertaken at an appropriate time to be successful. The first and sixth decades of
each century are particularly propitious to commence the promulgation of new spiritual teachings. Therefore the Rosicrucians were much concerned at this failure, for only five years were left
of the first decade of the twentieth century.

Their second choice of a messenger fell upon the present writer, though he knew it not at the
time, and by shaping circumstances about him they made it possible for him to begin a period
of preparation for the work they desired him to do. Three years later, when he had gone to Germany, also because of circumstances shaped by the invisible Brotherhood, and was on the verge
of despair at the discovery that the light which was the object of his quest, was only a jack-o-
lantern, the Brothers of the Rosicrucian Order applied the test to see whether he would be a
faithful messenger and give the teachings they desired to entrust to him, to the world. And when
he had passed the trial they gave him the monumental solution of the problem of existence first
published in "The Rosicrucian Cosmo Conception" in November,

1909, more than a year before the expiration of the first decade
of the twentieth century. This book marked a new era in so-called "occult" literature, and the many editions which have since been published, as well as the thousands of letters which continue to come to the author, are speaking testimonies to the fact that people are finding in this teaching a satisfaction they have long sought elsewhere in vain.

The Rosicrucians teach that all great religions have been given to the people among whom they are found, by Divine Intelligences who designed each system of worship to suit the needs of the race or nation to whom it was given. A primitive people cannot respond to a lofty and sublime religion, and vice versa. What helps one race would hinder another, and in pursuance of the same policy there has been devised a system of soul-unfoldment suited specially to the Western people, who are racially and temperamentally unfit to undergo the discipline of the Eastern school, which was designed for the more backward Hindoos.

THE ROSICRUCIAN FELLOWSHIP

For the purpose of promulgating the Rosicrucian teachings in the Western World, the Rosicrucian Fellowship was founded in 1909. It is the herald of the Aquarian Age, when the Sun by its precessional passage through the constellation Aquarius will bring out all the intellectual and spiritual potencies in man which are symbolized by that sign. As heat from a fire warms all objects within the sphere of its radiations, so also the Aquarian ray will raise the earth's vibrations to a pitch we are as yet unable to comprehend, though we have demonstrations of the material workings of this force in the inventions which have revolutionized life within the memory of the present generation. We have wondered at the X-ray, which sees through the human body, but each one has a sense latent which when evolved will enable him to see through any number of bodies or to any distance. We marvel at the telephone conversations across the continent of America, but each has within a latent sense of speech and hearing that is far more acute; we are surprised at the exploits of ships under sea and in the sky, but we are all capable of passage under water or through the sky; nay, more, we may pass unscathed through the solid rock and the raging fire, if we know how, and lightning itself is slow compared to the speed

with which we may travel. This sounds like a fairy tale today, as did Jules Verne's stories a generation ago, but the Aquarian Age will witness the realization of these dreams, and ever so much more that we still do not even dream of. Such faculties will then be the possessions of large numbers of people who will have gradually evolved them as previously the ability to walk, speak, hear, and see, were developed.

Therein lies a great danger, for, obviously, anyone endowed with such faculties may use them to the greatest detriment of the world at large, unless restrained by a spirit of unselfishness and an all-embracing altruism. Therefore religion is needed today as never before, to foster love and fellow-feeling among humanity so that it may be prepared to use the great gifts in store for it wisely and well. This need of religion is specially felt in a certain class where the ether is more loosely knit to the physical atoms than in the majority, and on that account they are now beginning to sense the Aquarian vibrations.

This class is again divided in two groups. In one the intellect is dominant, and the people in that class therefore seek to grasp the spiritual mysteries out of curiosity from the viewpoint of cold reason. They pursue the path of knowledge for the sake of knowledge, considering that an end in itself. The idea that knowledge is of value only when put to practical constructive use does not seem to have presented itself to them. This class we may call occultists. The other group does not care for knowledge, but feels an inner urge God-ward, and pursues the path of devotion to the high ideal set before them in Christ, doing the deeds that He did as far their flesh will permit, and this in time results in an interior illumination which brings with it all the knowledge obtained by the other class, and much more. This class we may describe as mystics.

Certain dangers confront each of the two groups. If the occultist obtains illumination and evolves within himself the latent spiritual faculties, he may use them for the furtherance of his personal objects, to the great detriment of his fellow-men. That is black magic, and the punishment which it automatically calls down upon the head of the perpetrator is so awful that it is best to draw the veil over it. The mystic may also err because of ignorance, and fall into the meshes of nature's law, but being actuated by love, his mistakes will never be very serious, and as he grows in grace the soundless voice within his heart will speak more distinctly to teach him the way.

The Rosicrucian Fellowship endeavors to prepare the world in general, and the sensitives of the two groups in particular, for the awakening of the latent powers in man, so that all may be guided safely through the danger-zone and be as well fitted as possible to use these new faculties. Effort is made to blend the love without which Paul declared a knowledge of all mysteries worthless, with a mystic knowledge rooted and grounded in love, so that the pupils of this school may become living exponents of this blended soul-science of the Western Wisdom School, and gradually educate humanity at large in the virtues necessary to make the possession of higher powers safe.

Note:—

Pages 19 to 26 inclusive, describing Mt. Ecclesia, have been transferred to the back of the book. (Transcriber's Note: They are pages 191 through 200.)


Chapter II. The Problem of Life and Its Solution
THE PROBLEM OF LIFE.


Among all the vicissitudes of life, which vary in each individual's experience, there is one event which sooner or later comes to everyone—Death! No matter what our station in life, whether the life lived has been a laudable one or the reverse, whether great achievements have marked our path among men, whether health or sickness have been our lot, whether we have been famous and surrounded by a host of admiring friends or have wandered unknown through the years of our life, at some time there comes a moment when we stand alone before the portal of death and are forced to take the leap into the dark.

The thought of this leap and of what lies beyond must inevitably force itself upon every thinking person. In the years of youth and health, when the bark of our life sails upon seas of prosperity, when all appears beautiful and bright, we may put the thought behind us, but there will surely come a time in the life of every thinking person when the problem of life and death forces itself upon his consciousness and refuses to be set aside. Neither will it help him to accept the ready made solution of anyone else without thought and in blind belief, for this is a basic problem which every one must solve for himself or herself in order to obtain satisfaction.

Upon the Eastern edge of the Desert of Sahara there stands the world-famous Sphinx with its inscrutable face turned toward the East, ever greeting the sun as its rising rays herald the newborn day. It was said in the Greek myth that it was the wont of this monster to ask a riddle of each traveler. She devoured those who could not answer, but when Oedipus solved the riddle she destroyed herself.

The riddle which she asked of men was the riddle of life and death, a query which is as relevant today as ever, and which each one must answer or be devoured in the jaws of death. But when once a person has found the solution to the problem, it will appear that in reality there is no death, that what appears so, is but a change from one state of existence to another. Thus, for the man who finds the true solution to the riddle of life, the sphinx of death has ceased to exist, and he can lift his voice in the triumphant cry "Oh death where is thy sting, oh grave where is thy victory."

Various theories of life have been advocated to solve this problem of life. We may divide them into two classes, namely the monistic theory, which holds that all the facts of life can be explained by reference to this visible world wherein we live, and the dualistic theory, which refers part of the phenomenon of life to another world which is now invisible to us.

Raphael in his famous painting "the School of Athens" has most aptly pictured to us the attitude of these two schools of thought. We see upon that marvelous painting a Greek Court such as those wherein philosophers were once wont to congregate. Upon the various steps which lead into the building a large number of men are engaged in deep conversation, but in the center at the top of the steps stand two figures, supposedly of Plato and Aristotle, one pointing upwards, the other towards the earth, each looking the other in the face, mutely, but with deeply concentrated will. Each seeking to convince the other that his attitude is right for each bears the conviction in his heart. One holds that he is of the earth earthy, that he has come from the dust and that thereto he will return, the other firmly advocates the position that there is a higher something which has always existed and will continue regardless of whether the body wherein it now dwells holds together or not. The question who is right is still an open one with the majority of mankind. Millions of tons of paper and printer's ink have been used in futile attempts to settle it by argument, but it will always remain open to all who have not solved the riddle themselves, for it is a basic problem, a part of the life experience of every human being to settle that question, and therefore no one can give us the solution ready made for our acceptance. All that can be done by those who have really solved the problem, is to show to others the line along which they have found the solution, and thus direct the inquirer how he also may arrive at a conclusion.

That is the aim of this little book; not to offer a solution to the problem of life to be taken blindly, on faith in the author's ability of investigation. The teachings herein set forth are those handed down by the Great Western Mystery School of the Rosicrucian Order and are the result of the concurrent testimony of a long line of trained Seers given to the author and supplemented by his own independent investigation of the realms traversed by the spirit in its cyclic path from the invisible world to this plane of existence and back again.

Nevertheless, the student is warned that the writer may have misunderstood some of the teachings and that despite the greatest care he may have taken a wrong view of that which he believes to have seen in the invisible world where the possibilities of making a mistake are legion. Here in the world which we view about us the forms are stable and do not easily change, but in the world around us which is perceptible only by the spiritual sight, we may say that there is in reality no form, but that all is life. At least the forms are so changeable that the   metamorphosis recounted in fairy stories is discounted there to an amazing degree, and therefore we have the surprising revelations of mediums and other untrained clairvoyants who, though they may be perfectly honest, are deceived by illusions of form which is evanescent,because they are incapable of viewing the life that is the permanent basis of that form. We must learn to see in this world. The new-born babe has no conception of distance and will reach for things far, far beyond its grasp until it has learned to gauge its capacity. A blind man who acquires the faculty of sight, or has it restored by an operation, will at first be inclined to close his eyes when moving from place to place, and declare that it is easier to walk by feeling than by sight; that is because he has not learned to use his newly acquired faculty. Similarly the man whose spiritual vision has been newly opened requires to be trained, in fact he is in much greater need thereof than the babe and the blind man already mentioned. Denied that training he would be like a new-born babe placed in a nursery where the walls are lined with mirrors of different convex and concave curvatures, which would distort its own shape and the forms of its attendants. If allowed to grow up in such surroundings and unable to see the real shapes of itself and its nurses it would naturally believe that it saw many different and distorted shapes where in reality the mirrors were responsible for the illusion. Were the persons concerned in such an experiment and the child taken out of the illusory surroundings, it would be incapable of recognizing them until the matter had been properly explained. There are similar dangers of illusion to those who have developed spiritual sight, until they have been trained to discount the refraction and to view the life which is permanent and stable, disregarding the form which is evanescent and changeable. The danger of getting things out of focus always remains however and is so subtle that the writer feels an imperative duty to warn his readers to take all statements concerning the unseen world with the proverbial grain of salt, for he has no intention to deceive. He is therefore inclined rather to magnify than to minimize his limitations and would advise the student to accept nothing from the author's pen without reasoning it out for himself. Thus, if he is deceived, he will be self-deceived and the author is blameless.

Three Theories of Life.

Only three noteworthy theories have been offered as solutions to the riddle of existence and in order that the reader may be able to make the important choice between them, we will state briefly what they are and give some of the arguments which lead us to advocate the doctrine of Rebirth as the method which favors soul-growth and the ultimate attainment of perfection, thus offering the best solution to the problem of life.

1) THE MATERIALISTIC THEORY teaches that life is but a short journey from the cradle to the grave, that there is no higher intelligence in the universe than man; that his mind is produced by certain correlations of matter and that therefore death, and dissolution of the body terminate existence.

There was a day when the arguments of Materialistic philosophers seemed convincing, but as science advances it discovers more and more that there is a spiritual side to the universe. That life and consciousness may exist without beingable to give us a sign, has been amply proven in the cases where a person who was entranced and thought dead for days has suddenly awakened and told all that had taken place around the body. Such eminent scientists as Sir Oliver Lodge, Camille Flammarion, Lombroso and other men of highest intelligence and scientific training, have unequivocally stated as the result of their investigations, that the intelligence which we call man survives death of the body and lives on in our midst as independently of whether we see them or not as light and color exist all about the blind man regardless of the fact that he does not perceive them. These scientists have reached their conclusion after years of careful investigation. They have found that the so-called dead can, and under certain circumstances do, communicate with us in such a manner that mistake is out of the question. We maintain that their testimony is worth more than the argument of materialism to the contrary, for it is based upon years of careful investigation, it is in harmony with such well established laws as the law of conservation of matter and the law of conservation of energy. Mind is a form of energy, and immune from destruction as claimed by the materialist. Therefore we disbar the materialistic theory as unsound, because out of harmony with the laws of nature and with well established facts.

2) THE THEORY OF THEOLOGY claims that just prior to each birth a soul is created by God and enters into the world where it lives for a time varying from a few minutes to a few score of years; that at the end of this short span of life it returns through the portal of death to the invisible beyond, where it remains forever in a condition of happiness or misery according to the deeds done in the body during the few years it lived here.

Plato insisted upon the necessity of a clear definition of terms as a basis of argument and we contend that that is as necessary in discussing the problem of life from the Bible point of view as in arguments from the platonic standpoint. According to the Bible man is a composite being consisting of body, soul and spirit. The two latter are usually taken to be synonymous, but we insist that they are not interchangeable and present the following to support our dictum.

All things are in a state of vibration. Vibrations from objects in our surroundings are constantly impinging upon us and carry to our senses a cognition of the external world. The vibrations in the ether act upon our eyes so that we see, and vibrations in the air transmit sounds to the ear.

We also breathe the ether which is charged with pictures of our surroundings and the sounds in our environment, so that by means of the breath we receive at each moment of our life, internally an accurate picture of our external surroundings.

That is a scientific proposition. Science does not explain what becomes of these vibrations however, but according to the Rosicrucian Mystery teaching they are transmitted to the blood, and then etched upon a little atom in the heart as automatically as a moving picture is imprinted upon the sensitized film, and a record of sounds is engraven upon the phonographic disc. This breath-record starts with the first breath of the newborn babe and ends only with the last gasp of the dying man, and "soul" is a product of the breath. Genesis also shows the connection between breath and soul in the words: "And the Lord God formed man of the dust of the ground, and breathed into his nostrils the breath of life; and man became a living soul" (The same word:

nephesh, is translated breath and soul in the above quotation.)

In the post mortem existence the breath-record is disposed of. The good acts of life produce feelings of pleasure and the intensity of attraction incorporates them into the spirit as soul- power. Thus the breath-records of our good acts are the soul which is saved, for by the union with the spirit they become immortal. As they accumulate life after life, we become more soulful and they are thus also the basis of soulgrowth.

The record of our evil acts is also derived from our breath in the moments when they were committed. The pain and suffering they bring cause the spirit to expel the breath-record from its being in Purgatory. As that cannot exist independently of the life-giving spirit, the breath-record of our sins disintegrates upon expurgation, and thus we see that "the soul that sinneth, it shall die." The memory of the suffering incidental to expurgation however, remains with the spirit as conscience, to deter from repetition of the same evil in later lives.

Thus both our good and evil acts are recorded through the agency of the breath, which is therefore the basis of the soul, but while the breath-record of good acts amalgamates with the

spirit and lives on forever as an immortal soul, the breath-record of evil deeds is disintegrated; it is the soul that sinneth and dies. While the Bible teaches that immortality of the soul is conditional upon well-doing, it makes no distinction in respect of the spirit. The statement is clear and emphatic that when ... "The silver cord be loosed ... then shall the dust return to the earth as it was and the spirit shall return to God who gave it." Thus the Bible teaches that the body is made of dust and returns thereto, that a part of the soul generated in the breath is perishable, but that the spirit survives bodily death and persists forever. Therefore a "lost soul" in the common acceptance of that term is not a Bible teaching, for the spirit is uncreate and eternal as God Himself, and therefore the orthodox theory cannot be true.

3) THE THEORY OF REBIRTHS which teaches that each spirit is an integral part of God, that it enfolds all divine possibilities as the acorn enfolds the oak; that by means of many existences in an earthy body of gradually improving texture its latent powers are being slowly unfolded and become available as dynamic energy; that none can be lost but that all will ultimately attain to perfection and reunion with God, each bringing with it the accumulated experience which is the fruitage of its pilgrimage through matter.

Or, as we may poetically express it: WE ARE ETERNAL.On whistling stormcloud; on Zephyrus wing, The Spirit-choir loud the World-anthems sing

Hark! Lis't to their voice "we have passed through death's door

There's no Death; rejoice! life lives evermore."We are, have always been, will ever be. We are a portion of Eternity Older than Creation, a part of One Great Whole, Is each Individual and immortal Soul On Time's whirring loom our garments we've wrought Eternally weave we on network of Thought,

Our kin and our country, by Mind brought to birth, Were patterned in heaven ere molded on earth.

We have shone in the Jewel and danced on the Wave, We have sparkled in Fire defying the grave; Through shapes everchanging, in size, kind and name Our individual essence still is the same.

And when we have reached to the highest of all, The gradations of growth our minds shall recall So that link by link we may join them together And trace step by step the way we reached thither.

Thus in time we shall know, if only we do What lifts, ennobles, is right and true. With kindness to all; with malice to none, That in and through us God's will may be done. We venture to make the assertion that there is but one sin: Ignorance and but one salvation: Applied Knowledge. Even the wisest among us know but little of what may be learned, however, and no one has attained to perfection, or can attain in one single short life, but we note that everywhere in nature slow persistent unfoldment makes for higher and higher development of every thing and we call this process evolution.

One of the chief characteristics of evolution lies in the fact that it manifests in alternating periods of activity and rest. The busy summer, when all things upon earth are exerting themselves to bring forth, is followed by the rest and inactivity of winter. The busy day alternates with the quiet of night. The ebb of the ocean is succeeded by the flood-tide. Thus, as all other things move in cycles, the life that expresses itself here upon earth for a few years is not to be thought of as ended when death has been reached, but as surely as the sun rises in the morning after having set at night, will the life that was ended by the death of one body be taken up again in a new vehicle and in a different environment.

This earth may in fact be likened to a school to which we return life after life to learn new lessons, as our children go to school day after day to increase their knowledge. The child sleeps through the night which intervenes between two days at school and the spirit also has its rest from active life between death and a new birth. There are also different classes in this world-school which correspond to the various grades from kindergarten to college. In the lower classes we find spirits who have gone to the school of life but a few times, they are savages now, but in time they will become wiser and better than we are, and we ourselves shall progress in future lives to spiritual heights of which we cannot even conceive at the present. If we apply ourselves to learn the lessons of life, we shall of course advance much faster in the school of life than if we dilly-dally and idle our time away. This, on the same principle which governs in one of our own institutions of learning.

We are not here then, by the caprice of God. He has not placed one in clover and another in a desert nor has He given one a healthy body so that he may live at ease from pain and sickness, while He placed another in poor circumstances with never a rest from pain. But what we are, we are, on account of our own diligence or negligence, and what we shall be in the future depends upon what we will to be and not upon Divine caprice or upon inexorable fate. No matter what the circumstances, it lies with us to master them, or to be mastered, as we will. Sir Edwin Arnold puts the teaching most beautifully in his "Light of Asia."

"The Books say well, my Brothers! each man's life The outcome of his former living is;

The bygone wrongs bring forth sorrows and woes The bygone right breeds bliss. Each has such lordship as the loftiest ones Nay for with powers around, above, below As with all flesh and what-soever lives Act maketh joy or woe. Who toiled a slave may come anew a prince For gentle worthiness and merit won; Who ruled a king may wander earth in rags For things done or undone."

"One ship sails East and another sails West With the self same winds that blow.

Tis the set of the sail, and not the gale, Which determines the way they go. As the winds of the sea are the ways of fate As we voyage along through life.

'Tis the act of the soul, which determines the goal And not the calm or the strife." When we wish to engage someone to undertake a certain mission we choose some one whom we think particularly fitted to fulfill the requirements and we must suppose that a Divine Being would use at least as much common sense, and not choose anyone to go his errand who was not fitted therefor. So when we read in the Bible that Samson was foreordained to be the slayer of the Philistines and that Jeremiah was predestined to be a prophet, it is but logical to suppose that they must have been particularly suited to such occupation. John the Baptist also, was born to be a herald of the coming Savior and to preach the kingdom of God

which is to take the place of the kingdom of men.

Had these people had no previous training, how could they have developed such a fitness to fulfill their various missions, and if they had been fitted, how else could they have received their training if not in earlier lives?

The Jews believed in the Doctrine of Rebirth or they would not have asked John the Baptist if he were Elijah, as recorded in the first chapter of John. The Apostles of Christ also held the belief as we may see from the incident recorded in the sixteenth chapter of Matthew where the Christ asked them the question: "Whom do men say that I the Son of Man am?" The Apostles replied: "Some say that Thou art John the Baptist; some, Elias; and others Jeremias or one of the Prophets." Upon this occasion the Christ tacitly assented to the teaching of Rebirth because He did not correct the disciples as would have been His plain duty in His capacity as teacher, when the pupils entertained a mistaken idea.

But to Nicodemus He said unequivocally: "Except a man be born again, he cannot see the kingdom of God" and in the eleventh chapter of Matthew, the fourteenth verse, He said,

speaking of John the Baptist: "this is Elijah," in the seventeenth chapter of Matthew, the twelfth verse, He said: "Elijah has come already and they knew him not, but have done to him whatsoever they listed, ... then the disciples understood that he spoke to them of John the Baptist."

Thus we maintain that the Doctrine of Rebirth offers the only solution to the problem of life which is in harmony with the laws of nature, which answers the ethical requirements of the case and permits us to love God without blinding our reason to the inequalities of life and the varying circumstances which give to a few the ease and comfort, the health and wealth, which are denied to the many.

The theory of Heredity advanced by Materialists applies only to the form, for as a carpenter uses material from a certain pile of lumber to build a house in which he afterwards lives, so does the spirit take the substance wherewith to build its house from the parents. The carpenter cannot build a house of hard wood from spruce lumber and the spirit also must build a body which is like those from which the material was taken, but the theory of Heredity does not apply upon the moral plane, for it is a notorious fact, that in the rogues galleries of America and Europe there is no case where both father and son are represented. Thus the sons of criminals, though they have the tendencies to crime, keep out of the clutches of the law. Neither will Heredity hold good upon the plane of the intellect, for many cases may be cited where a genius and an idiot spring from the same stock. The great Cuvier, whose brain was of about the same weight, as Daniel Webster's, and whose intellect was as great, had five children who all died of paresis, the brother of Alexander the Great was an idiot, and thus we hold that another solution must be found to account for the facts of life.

The law of Rebirth coupled with its companion law, the law of Causation does that. When we die after one life, we return to earth later, under circumstances determined by the manner in which we lived before. The gambler is drawn to pool parlors and race tracks to associate with others of like taste, the musician is attracted to the concert halls and music studios, by congenial spirits, and the returning Ego also carries with it its likes and dislikes which cause it to seek parents among the class to which it belongs.

But then someone will point to cases where we find people of entirely opposite tastes living lives of torture, because grouped in the same family, and forced by circumstances to stay there contrary to their wills. But that does not vitiate the law in the slightest, in each life we contract certain obligations which cannot then be fulfilled. Perhaps we have run away from a duty such as the care of an invalid relative and have met death without coming to a realization of our mistake. That relative upon the other hand may have suffered severely from our neglect, and have stored up a bitterness against us before death terminates the suffering.  Death and the subsequent removal to another environment does not pay our debts in this life, any more than the removal from the city where we now live to another place will pay the debts we have contracted prior to our removal. It is therefore quite possible that the two who have injured each other as described, may find themselves members of the same family. Then, whether they remember the past grudge or not, the old enmity will assert itself and cause them to hate anew until the consequent discomfort forces them to tolerate each other, and perhaps later they may learn to love where they hated.

The question also arises in the mind of inquirers: If we have been here before why do we not remember? And the answer is, that while most people are not aware of how their previous existences were spent, there are others who have a very distinct recollection of previous lives. A friend of the writer's for instance, when living in France, one day started to read to her son about a certain city where they were then going upon a bicycle tour, and the boy exclaimed: you do not need to tell me about that mother. I know that city, I lived there and was killed! He then commenced to describe the city and also a certain bridge. Later he took his mother to that bridge and showed her the spot where he had met death centuries before. Another friend travelling in Ireland saw a scene which she recognized and she also described to the party the scene around the bend of the road which she had never seen in this life, so it must have been a memory from a previous life. Numerous other instances could be given where such minor flashes of memory reveal to us glimpses from a past life. The verified case in which a little three year old girl in Santa Barbara described her life and death has been given in the Rosicrucian Cosmo Conception. It is perhaps the most conclusive evidence as it hinges on the veracity of a child too young to have learned deception.

This theory of life does not rest upon speculation however, it is one of the first facts of life demonstrated to the pupil of a Mystery school. He is taught to watch a child in the act of dying, also, to watch it in the invisible world from day to day, until it comes to a new birth a year or two later.

Then he knows with absolute certainty that we return to earth to reap in a future life what we now sow.

The reason for taking a child to watch in preference to an adult, is, that the child is reborn very quickly, for its short life on earth has borne but few fruits and these are soon assimilated, while the adult who has lived a long life, and had much experience remains in the invisible worlds for centuries, so that the pupil could not watch him from death to rebirth. The cause of infant mortality will be explained later, here we merely desire to emphasize the fact that it is within the range of possibilities of every one without exception to become able to know at first hand that which is  here taught.

The average interval between two earth-lives is about a thousand years. It is determined by the movement of the sun known to astronomers as precession of the equinox, by which the sun moves through one of the signs of the Zodiac in about 2100 years. During that time the conditions upon earth have changed so much that the spirit will find entirely new experiences here, and therefore it returns.

The Great Leaders of evolution always obtain the maximum benefit from each condition designed by them, and as the experiences in the same social conditions are very different in the case of a man from what they are for a woman, the human spirit takes birth twice during the 2100 years measured by the precession of the equinox as already explained, it is born once as a man and another time as a woman. Such is the rule, but it is subject to whatever modifications may be necessary to facilitate reaping what the spirit has sown, as required under the law of Causation which works hand in hand with the law of Rebirth. Thus, at times a spirit may be brought to birth long ere the thousand years have expired, in order to fulfill a certain  mission, or it may be detained in the invisible worlds after the time when it should have come to birth according to the strict requirements of a blind law. The laws of nature are not that however. They are Great Intelligences who always subordinate minor considerations to higher ends, and under their beneficent guidance we are constantly progressing from life to life under conditions exactly suited to each individual, until in time we shall attain to a higher evolution and become Supermen.

Oliver Wendell Holmes has so beautifully voiced that aspiration and its consummation in the lines:

"Build thee more stately mansions Oh! my soul, As the swift seasons roll, Leave thy low-vaulted past; Let each new temple, nobler than the last, Shut thee from heaven with a dome more vast. Till thou at length art free, Leaving thy outgrown shell by life's unresting sea."

Chapter III. The Visible and the Invisible World

The Chemical Region.

If one who is capable of consciously using his spiritual body with the same facility that we now use our physical vehicles should glide away from the earth into interplanetary space, the earth and the various other planets of our solar system would appear to him to be composed of three kinds of matter, roughly speaking. The densest matter, which is our visible earth, would appear to him as being the center of the ball as the yolk is in the center of an egg. Around that nucleus he would observe a finer grade of matter similarly disposed in relation to the central mass, as the white of the egg is disposed outside the yolk. Upon a little closer investigation he would also discover that

this second kind of substance permeates the solid earth to the very center,
even as the blood percolates through the more solid parts of our flesh. Outside both of these mingling layers of matter he would observe a still finer, third layer corresponding to the shell of the egg, except that this third layer is the finest most subtile of the three grades of matter, and that it inter-penetrates both of the two inner layers. As already said, the central mass, spiritually seen, is our visible world, composed of solids, liquids and gases. They constitute the earth, its atmosphere, and also the ether, of which physical science speaks hypothetically as permeating the atomic substance of all chemical elements. The second layer of matter is called the Desire World and the outermost layer is called the World of Thought.

A little reflection upon the subject will make clear that just such a constitution is necessary to account for facts of life as we see them. All forms in the world about us are built from chemical substances: solids, liquids and gases, but in so far that they do move, these forms obey a separate and distinct impulse, and when this impelling energy leaves, the form becomes inert. The steam engine rotates under the impetus of an invisible gas called steam. Before steam filled its cylinder, the engine stood still, and when the impelling force is shut off its motion again ceases. The dynamo rotates under the still more subtile influence of an electric current which may also cause the click of a telegraph instrument or the ring of an electric bell, but the dynamo ceases its swift whirl and the persistent ring of the electric bell becomes mute when the invisible electricity is switched off. The form of the bird, the animal and the human being also cease their motion when the inner force which we call life has winged its invisible way.

All forms are impelled into motion by desire:—the bird and the animal roam land and air in their desire to secure food and shelter, or for the purpose of breeding, man is also moved by these desires, but has in addition other and higher incentives to spur him to effort, among them is desire for rapidity of motion which led him to construct the steam engine and other devices that move in obedience to his desire.

If there were no iron in the mountains man could not build machines. If there were no clay in the soil, the bony structure of the skeleton would be an impossibility, and if there were no Physical World at all, with its solids, liquids and gases, this dense body of ours could never have come into existence. Reasoning along similar lines it must be at once apparent that if there were no Desire World composed of desire-stuff, we should have no way of forming feelings, emotions and desires. A planet composed of the materials we perceive with our physical eyes and of no other substances, might be the home of plants which grow unconsciously, but have no desires to cause them to move. The human and animal kingdoms however, would be impossibilities.

Furthermore, there is in the world a vast number of things, from the simplest and most crude instruments, to the most intricate and cunning devices which have been constructed by the hand of man. These reveal the fact of man's thought and ingenuity. Thought must have a source as well as form and feeling. We saw that it was necessary to have the requisite material in order to build a steam engine or a body and we reasoned from the fact that in order to obtain material to express desire there must also be
a world composed of desire stuff. Carrying our argument to its logical conclusion, we also hold that unless a World of Thought provides a reservoir of mind stuff upon which we may draw, it

would be impossible for us to think and invent the things which we see in even the lowest civilization.

Thus it will be clear that the division of a planet into worlds is not based on fanciful metaphysical speculation, but is logically necessary in the economy of nature. Therefore it must be taken into consideration by any one who would study and aim to understand the inner nature of things. When we see the street cars moving along our streets, it does not explain to say that the motor is driven by electricity of so many amperes at so many volts. These names only add to our confusion until we have thoroughly studied the science of electricity and then we shall find that the mystery deepens, for while the street car belongs to the world of inert form perceptible to our vision, the electric current which moves it is indigenous to the realm of force, the invisible Desire World, and the thought which created and guides it, comes from the still more subtle World of Thought which is the home world of the human spirit, the Ego.

It may be objected that this line of argument makes a simple matter exceedingly intricate, but a little reflection will soon show the fallacy of such a contention. Viewed superficially any of the sciences seem extremely simple; anatomically we may divide the body into flesh and bone, chemically we may make the simple divisions between solid, liquid and gas, but to thoroughly master the science of anatomy it is necessary to spend years in close application and learn to know all the little nerves, the ligaments which bind articulations between various parts of the bony structure, to study the several kinds of tissue and their disposition in our system where they form the bones, muscles, glands, etc., which in the aggregate we know as the human body. To properly understand the science of chemistry we must study the valence of the atom which determines the power of combination of the various elements, together with other niceties, such as atomic weight, density, etc. New wonders are constantly opening up to the most experienced chemist, who understands best the immensity of his chosen science.

The youngest lawyer, fresh from law school knows more about the most intricate cases, in his own estimation, than the judges upon the Supreme Court bench who spend long hours, weeks and months, seriously deliberating over their decisions. But those who, without having studied, think they understand and are fitted to discourse upon the greatest of all sciences, the science of Life and Being, make a greater mistake. After years of patient study, of holy life spent in close application, a man is oftentimes perplexed at the immensity of the subject he studies. He finds it to be so vast in both the direction of the great and small that it baffles description, that language fails, and that the tongue must remain mute. Therefore we hold, (and we speak from knowledge gained through years of close study and investigation), that the finer distinctions which we have made, and shall make, are not at all arbitrary, but absolutely necessary as are divisions and distinctions made in anatomy or chemistry.

No form in the physical world has feeling in the true sense of that word. It is the indwelling life which feels, as we may readily see from the fact that a body which responded to the slightest touch while instinct with life, exhibits no sensation whatever even when cut to pieces after the life has fled. Demonstrations have been made by scientists, particularly by Professor Bose of Calcutta, to show that there is feeling in dead animal tissue and even in tin and other metal, but we maintain that the diagrams which seem to support his contentions in reality demonstrate only a response to impacts similar to the rebound of a rubber ball, and that must not be confused with such feelings as love, hate, sympathy and aversion. Goethe also, in his novel "Elective Affinities," (Wahlverwandtschaft), brings out some beautiful illustrations wherein he makes it seem as if atoms loved and hated, from the fact that some elements combine readily while other substances refuse to amalgamate, a phenomenon produced by the different rates of speed at which various elements vibrate and an unequal inclination of their axes. Only where there is sentient life can there be feelings of pleasure and pain, sorrow or joy.

The Etheric Region. In addition to the solids, liquids and gases which compose the Chemical Region of the Physical World there is also a finer grade  [062] of matter called Ether, which permeates the atomic structure of the earth and its atmosphere substantially as science teaches. Scientists have never seen, nor have they weighed, measured or analyzed this substance, but they infer that it must exist in order to account for transmission of light and various other phenomena. If it were possible for us to live in a room from which the air had been exhausted we might speak at the top of our voices, we might ring the largest bell or we might even discharge a cannon close to our ear and we should hear no sound, for air is the medium which transmits sound vibrations to the tympanum of our ear, and that would be lacking. But if an electric light were lighted, we should at once perceive its rays; it would illumine the room despite the lack of air. Hence there must be a substance, capable of being set into vibration, between the electric light and our eyes. That medium scientists call ether, but it is so subtle that no instrument has been devised whereby it may be measured or analyzed and therefore the scientists are without much information concerning it, though forced to postulate its existence.

We do not seek to belittle the achievements of modern scientists, we have the greatest admiration for them and we entertain high expectations of what ambitions they may yet realize, but we perceive a limitation in the fact, that all discoveries of the past have been made by the invention of wonderful instruments applied in a most ingenious manner to solve seemingly insoluble and baffling problems. The strength of science lies vested in its instruments, for the scientist may say to anyone: Go, procure a number of glasses ground in a certain manner, insert them in a tube, direct that tube toward a certain point in the sky where now nothing appears to your naked eye. You will then see a beautiful star called Uranus. If his directions are followed, anyone is quickly and without preparation, able to demonstrate for himself the truth of the scientist's assertion. But while the instruments of science are its tower of strength they also mark the end of its field of investigation, for it is impossible to contact the spirit world with physical instruments, so the research of occultists begins where the physical scientist finds his limit and are carried on by spiritual means.

These investigations are as thorough and as reliable as researches by material scientists, but not as easily demonstrable to the general public. Spiritual powers lie dormant within every human being, and when awakened, they compensate for both telescope and microscope, they enable their possessor to investigate, instanter, things beyond the veil of matter, but they are only developed by a patient application and continuance in well doing extended over years, and few are they who have faith to start upon the path to attainment or perseverance to go through with the ordeal. Therefore the occultist's assertions are not generally credited.

We can readily see that long probation must precede attainment, for a person equipped with spiritual sight is able to penetrate walls of houses as easily as we walk through the atmosphere, able to read at will the innermost thoughts of those about him; if not actuated by the most pure and unselfish motives, he would be a scourge to humanity. Therefore that power is safeguarded as we would withhold the dynamite bomb from an anarchist and from the well-intentioned but ignorant  person, or, as we withhold match and powder barrel from a child. In the hands of an experienced engineer the dynamite bomb may be used to open a highway of commerce, and an intelligent farmer may use gunpowder to good account in clearing his field of tree-stumps, but in the hands of an ill-intentioned criminal or ignorant child an explosive may wreck much property and end many lives. The force is the same, but used differently, according to the ability or intention of the user, it may produce results of a diametrically opposite nature. So it is also with spiritual powers, there is a time-lock upon them, as upon a bank safe, which keeps out all until they have earned the privilege and the time is ripe for its exercise.

As already said, the ether is physical matter and responsive to the same laws which govern other physical substances upon this plane of existence. Therefore it requires but a slight extension of physical sight to see ether, (which is disposed in four grades of density), the blue haze seen in mountain canyons is in fact ether of the kind known to occult investigators as "chemical ether." Many people who see this ether, are unaware that they are possessed of a faculty not enjoyed by all. Others, who have developed spiritual sight are not endowed with etheric vision, a fact which seems an anomaly until the subject of clairvoyance is thoroughly understood.

The reason is, that as ether is physical matter, etheric sight depends upon the sensitiveness of the optic nerve while spiritual sight is acquired by developing latent vibratory powers in two little organs situated in the brain: the Pituitary body and the Pineal gland. Nearsighted people even, may have etheric vision. Though unable to read the print in a book, they may be able to "see through a wall," owing to the fact that their optic nerve responds more rapidly to fine than to coarse vibrations.

When anyone views an object with etheric sight he sees through that object in a manner similar to the way an x-ray penetrates opaque substances. If he looks at a sewing machine, he will perceive, first an outer casing; then, the works within, and behind both, the casing furthest away from him.

If he has developed the grade of spiritual vision which opens the Desire World to him and he looks at the same object, he will  see it both inside and out. If he looks closely, he will perceive every little atom spinning upon its axis and no part or particle will be excluded from his perception.

But if his spiritual sight has been developed in such a measure that he is capable of viewing the sewing machine with the vision peculiar to the World of Thought, he will behold a cavity where he had previously seen the form.

Things seen with etheric vision are very much alike in color, they are nearly reddish-blue, purple or violet, according to the density of the ether, but when we view any object with the spiritual sight pertaining to the Desire World, it scintillates and coruscates in a thousand ever changing colors so indescribably beautiful that they can only be compared to living fire, and the writer therefore calls this grade of vision color sight, but when the spiritual vision of the World of Thought is the medium of perception, the seer finds that in addition to still more beautiful colors, there issues from the cavity described a constant flow of a certain harmonious tone. Thus this world wherein we now consciously live and which we perceive by means of our physical senses is preeminently the world of form, the Desire World is particularly the world of color and the World of Thought is the realm of tone. Because of the relative proximity or distance of these worlds, a statue, a form, withstands the ravages of time for millenniums, but the colors upon a painting fade in far shorter time, for they come from the Desire World, and music which is native to the World furthest removed from us, the World of Thought, is like a will-o-the-wisp which none may catch or hold, it is gone again as soon as it has made its appearance. But there is in color and music a compensation for this increasing evanescence.

The statue is cold and dead as the mineral of which it is composed and has attractions for but few though its form is a tangible reality.

The forms upon a painting are illusory yet they express life, on account of the color which has come from a region where nothing is inert and lifeless. Therefore the painting is enjoyed by many. Music is intangible and ephemeral, but it comes from the home world of the spirit and though so fleeting it is recognized by the spirit as a soul-speech fresh from the celestial realms, an echo from the home whence we are now exiled, and therefore it touches a cord in our being, regardless of whether we realize the true cause or not.

Thus we see that there are various grades of spiritual sight, each suited to the superphysical realm which it opens to our perception: Etheric vision, color vision and tonal vision.

The occult investigator finds that ether is of four kinds, or grades of density:

The Chemical Ether, The Life Ether,

The Light Ether,

The Reflecting Ether.

The Chemical Ether is the avenue of expression for forces promoting assimilation, growth and the maintenance of form.

The Life Ether is the vantage ground of forces active in propagation, or the building of new forms. The Light Ether transmits the motive power of the sun along the various nerves of living bodies and makes motion possible.

The Reflecting Ether receives an impression of all that is, lives and moves. It also records each change, in a similar manner as the film upon a moving picture machine. In this record mediums and psychometrists may read the past, upon the same principle as, under proper conditions, moving pictures are reproduced time and again.

We have been speaking of ether as an avenue of forces, a word which conveys no meaning to the average mind, because force is invisible. But to an occult investigator the forces are not merely names such as steam, electricity, etc. He finds them to be intelligent beings of varying grades, both sub and superhuman. What we call "laws of nature," are great intelligences which guide more elemental beings in accordance with certain rules designed to further their evolution.

In the Middle Ages, when many people were still endowed with a remnant of negative clairvoyance, they spoke of Gnomes and Elves or Fairies, which roamed about the mountains and forests.

These were the earth spirits. They also told of the Undine or water-sprite, which inhabited rivers and streams, of Sylphs which were said to dwell in the mists above moat and

moor, as air spirits, but not much was said of the Salamanders, as they are, fire spirits, and therefore not so easily detected, or so readily accessible to the majority of people.

The old folk stories are now regarded as superstitions, but as a matter of fact, one endowed with etheric vision may yet perceive the little gnomes building green chlorophyll into the leaves of plants and giving to flowers the multiplicity of delicate tints which delight our eyes.

Scientists have attempted time and again to offer an adequate explanation of the phenomenon of wind and storm but have failed signally, nor can they succeed while they seek a mechanical solution to what is really a manifestation of life. Could they see the hosts of sylphs winging their way hither and thither, they would know who and what is responsible for the fickleness of the wind; could they watch a storm at sea from the etheric view-point they would perceive that the saying "the war of the elements" is not an empty phrase, for the heaving sea is truly then a battlefield of sylphs and undines and the howling tempest is the war cry of spirits in the air.

Also the salamanders are found everywhere and no fire is lighted without their help, but they are mostly active underground. They are responsible for explosions and volcanic eruptions.

The classes of beings which we have mentioned are still sub-human, but will all at some time reach a stage in evolution corresponding to the human, though under different circumstances from those under which we evolve. But at present the wonderful intelligences we speak of as the laws of nature, marshall the armies of less evolved entities mentioned.

To arrive at a better understanding of what these various beings are, and their relation to us, we may take an illustration: Let us suppose that a mechanic is making an engine, and meanwhile a dog is watching him. It sees the man at his labor, and how he uses various tools to shape his materials, also how, from the crude iron, steel, brass and other metals the engine slowly takes shape. The dog is a being from a lower evolution and does not comprehend the purpose of the mechanic but it sees both the workman, his labor and the result thereof, which manifests as an engine.

Let us now suppose that the dog were able to see the materials which slowly change their shape, assemble and become an engine but that it is unable to perceive the workman and to see the work he does. The dog would then be in the same relation to the mechanic as we are to the great intelligences we call laws of nature, and their assistants, the nature spirits, for we behold the manifestations of their work as force moving matter in various ways but always under immutable conditions.

In the ether we may also observe the angels, whose densest body is made of that material, as our dense body is formed of gases, liquids and solids. These beings are one step beyond the human stage, as we are a degree in advance of the animal evolution. We have never been animals like our present fauna, however, but at a previous stage in the development of our planet we had an animal-like constitution. Then the angels were human, though they have never possessed a dense body such as ours, nor ever functioned in any material denser than ether. At some time, in a future condition, the earth will again become ethereal. Then man will be like the angels. Therefore the Bible tells us that man was made a little while lower than the angels (Paul's letter to the Hebrews, second chapter, seventh verse; see marginal reading.) As ether is the avenue of vital, creative forces, and as angels are such expert builders of ether, we may readily understand that they are eminently fitted to be warders of the propagative forces in plant, animal and man. All through the Bible we find them thus engaged: Two angels came to Abraham and announced the birth of Isaac, they promised a child to the man who had obeyed God. Later these same angels destroyed Sodom for abuse of the creative force. Angels foretold to the parents of Samuel and Samson, the birth of these giants of brain and brawn. To Elizabeth came the angel (not archangel) Gabriel and announced the birth of John, later he appeared also to Mary with the message that she was chosen to bear Jesus.

The Desire World.

When spiritual sight is developed so that it becomes possible to behold the Desire World, many wonders confront the newcomer, for conditions are so widely different from what they are here, that a description must sound quite as incredible as a fairy tale

to anyone who has not himself seen them. Many cannot even believe that such a world exists, and that other people can see that which is invisible to them, yet some people are blind to the beauties of this world which we see. A man who was born blind, may say to us: I know that this world exists, I can hear, I can smell, I can taste and above all I can feel but when you speak of light and of color, they are nonexistent to me. You say that you see these things, I cannot believe it for I cannot see myself. You say that light and color are all about me, but none of the senses at my command reveal them to me and I do not believe that the sense you call sight exists. I think you suffer from hallucinations. We might sympathize very sincerely with the poor man who is thus afflicted, but his scepticism, reasonings and objections and sneers notwithstanding we would be obliged to maintain that we perceive light and color.

The man whose spiritual sight has been awakened is in a similar position with respect to those who do not perceive the Desire World of which he speaks. If the blind man acquires the faculty of sight by an operation, his eyes are opened and he will be compelled to assert the existence of light and color which he formerly denied, and when spiritual sight is acquired by anyone, he also perceives for himself the facts related by others.

Neither is it an argument against the existence of spiritual realms that seers are at variance in their descriptions of conditions in the invisible world. We need but to look into books on travel, and compare stories brought home by explorers of China, India or Africa and we shall find them differing widely and often contradictory, because each traveler saw things from his own standpoint, under other conditions than those met by his brother authors, and we maintain that the man who has read most widely these varying tales concerning a certain Country and wrestled with the contradictions of narrators, will have a more comprehensive idea of the country or people of whom he has read, than the man who has only read one story assented to by all the authors. Similarly, the varying stories of visitors to the Desire World are of value, because giving a fuller view, and more rounded, than if all had seen things from the same angle.

In this world matter and force are widely different. The chief characteristic of matter here is inertia: the tendency to remain at rest until acted upon by a force which sets it in motion. In the Desire World, on the contrary, force and matter are almost indistinguishable one from the other. We might almost describe desire-stuff as force-matter, for it is in incessant motion, responsive to the slightest feeling of a vast multitude of beings which populate this wonderful world in nature. We often speak of the "teeming millions" of China and India, even of our vast cities, London, New York, Paris or Chicago, we consider them overcrowded in the extreme, yet even the densest population of any spot upon earth is sparsely inhabited compared with the crowded conditions of the Desire World. No inconvenience is felt by any of the denizens of that realm, however, for, while in this world two things cannot occupy the same space at the same time, it is different there. A number of people and things may exist in the same place at the same time and be engaged in most diverse activities, regardless of what others are doing, such is the wonderful elasticity of desire stuff. As an illustration we may mention a case where the writer while attending religious service, plainly perceived at the altar certain beings interested in furthering that service and working to achieve that end. At the same time there drifted through the room and the altar, a table at which four persons were engaged in playing cards. They were as oblivious to the existence of the beings engaged in furthering our religious service, as though these did not exist.

The Desire World is the abode of those who have died, for some time subsequent to that event, and we may mention in the above connection that the so-called "dead" very often stay for a long while among their still living friends. Unseen by their relatives they go about the familiar rooms. At first they are often unaware of the condition mentioned: "that two persons may be in the same place at the same time," and when they seat themselves in a chair or at the table, a living relative may take the supposedly vacant seat. The man we mistakenly call dead will at first hurry out of his seat to escape being sat upon, but he soon learns that being sat upon does not hurt him in his altered condition, and that he may remain in his chair regardless of the fact that his living relative is also sitting there.

In the lower regions of the Desire World the whole body of each being may be seen, but in the highest regions only the head seems to remain. Raphael, who like many other people in the middle ages was gifted with a so-called second sight, pictured that condition for us in his Sistine Madonna, now in the Dresden Art Gallery, where Madonna and the Christ-child are represented as floating in a golden atmosphere and surrounded by a host of genie-heads: conditions which the occult investigator knows to be in harmony with actual facts.

Among the entities who are, so to speak, "native" to that realm of nature, none are perhaps better known to the Christian world than the Archangels. These exalted Beings were human at a time in the earth's history when we were yet plant-like. Since then we have advanced two steps: through the animal and to the human stage of development. The present Archangels have also made two steps in progression; one, in which they were similar to what the angels are now, and another step which made them what we call Archangels.

Their densest body, though differing from ours in shape, and made of desire stuff, is used by them as a vehicle of consciousness in the same manner that we use our body. They are expert manipulators of forces in the Desire World, and these forces, as we shall see, move all the world to action. Therefore the Archangels work with humanity industrially and politically as arbitrators of the destiny of peoples and nations. The Angels may be said to be family-spirits whose mission is to unite a few spirits as members of a family, and cement them with ties of blood and love of kin, while the Archangels may be called race and national spirits, as they unite whole nations by patriotism or love of home and country. They are responsible for the rise and fall of nations, they give war or peace, victory or defeat as it serves the best interests of the people they rule. This we may see, for instance, from the book of Daniel, where the Archangel Michael (not to be confounded with the Michael, who is ambassador from the sun to the earth), is called the prince of the children of Israel. Another Archangel tells Daniel, (in the tenth chapter) that he intends to fight the prince of Persia by means of the Greeks.

There are varying grades of intelligence among human beings, some are qualified to hold high and lofty positions entirely beyond the ability of others. So it is also among higher beings, not all Archangels are fitted to govern a nation and rule the destiny of a race, people or tribe, some are not fitted to rule human beings at all, but as the animals also have a desire nature these lower grades of Archangels govern the animals as group-spirits and evolve to higher capacity thereby.

The work of the race spirits is readily observable in the people it governs. The lower in the scale of evolution the people, the more they show a certain racial likeness. That is due to the work of the race spirit. One national spirit is responsible for the swarthy complexion common to Italians, for instance, while another causes the Scandinavians to be blond. In the more advanced types of humanity there is a wider divergence from the common type, due to the individualized Ego, which thus expresses in form and feature its own particular idiosyncrasies. Among the lower types of humanity such as Mongolians, native African Negroes and South Sea Islanders, the resemblance of individuals in each tribe makes it almost impossible for civilized Westerners to distinguish between them. Among animals, where the separate spirit is not individualized and self-conscious, the resemblance is not only much more marked physically but extends even to traits and characteristics. We may write the biography of a man, for the experiences of each varies from that of others and his acts are different, but we cannot write the biography of an animal for members of each tribe all act alike under similar circumstances. If we desire to know the facts about Edward VII, it would profit us nothing to study the life of the Prince-Consort, his father, or of George V, his son, as both would be entirely different from Edward. In order to find out what manner of man he was, we must study his own individual life. If, on the other hand, we wish to know the characteristics of beavers, we may observe any individual of the tribe, and when we have studied its idiosyncrasies, we shall know the traits of the whole tribe of beavers. What we call "instinct," is in reality the dictates of group-spirits which govern separate individuals of its tribe telepathically, as it were.

The ancient Egyptians knew of these animal group spirits and sketched many of them, in a crude way, upon their temples and tombs. Such figures with a human body and an animal head actually live in the desire world. They may be spoken to, and will be found much more intelligent than the average human being.   That statement brings up another peculiarity of conditions in the Desire World in respect of language. Here in this World human speech is so diversified that there are countries where people who live only a few miles apart speak a dialect so different that they understand each other with great difficulty, and each nation has its own language that varies altogether from the speech of other peoples.

In the lower Regions of the Desire World, there is the same diversity of tongues as on earth, and the so-called "dead" of one nation find it impossible to converse with those who lived in another country. Hence linguistic accomplishments are of great value to the "Invisible Helpers", of whom we shall hear later, as their sphere of usefulness is enormously extended by that ability. Even apart from difference of language our mode of speech is exceedingly productive of misunderstandings. The same words often convey most opposite ideas to different minds. If we speak of a "body of water", one person may think we mean a lake of small dimensions, the thoughts of another may be directed to the great American Lakes and a third person's thoughts may be turned towards the Atlantic or Pacific Oceans. If we speak of a "light", one may think of a gas-light, another of an electric Arc-lamp, or if we say "red", one person may think we mean a delicate shade of pink and another gets the idea of crimson. The misunderstandings of what words mean goes even farther, as illustrated in the following.

The writer once opened a reading room in a large city where he lectured, and invited his audience to make use thereof. Among those who availed themselves of the opportunity was a gentleman who had for many years been a veritable "metaphysical tramp," roaming from lecture to lecture, hearing the teachings of everybody and practicing nothing. Like the Athenians on Mars' Hill, he was always looking for something "new," particularly in the line of phenomena, and his mind was in that seething chaotic state which is one of the most prominent symptoms of "mental indigestion."

Having attended a number of our lectures he knew from the program that: "The lecturer does not give readings, or cast horoscopes for pay." But seeing on the door of the newly opened reading room, the legend: "Free Reading Room," his erratic mind at once jumped to the conclusion that although we were opposed to telling fortunes for pay, we were now going to give free readings of the future in the Free Reading Room. He was much disappointed that we did not intend to tell fortunes, either gratis or for a consideration, and we changed our sign to "Free Library" in order to obviate a repetition of the error.

In the higher Regions of the Desire World the confusion of tongues gives place to a universal mode of expression which absolutely prevents misunderstandings of our meaning. There each of our thoughts takes a definite form and color perceptible to all, and this thought-symbol emits a certain tone, which is not a word, but it conveys our meaning to the one we address no matter what language he spoke on earth.

To arrive at an understanding of how such a universal language becomes possible and is at once comprehended by all, without preparation, we may take as an illustration the manner in which a musician reads music. A German or a Polish composer may write an opera. Each has his own peculiar terminology and expresses it in his own language. When that opera is to be played by an Italian band master, or by a Spanish or American musician, it need not be translated, the notes and symbols upon the page are a universally understood language of symbols which is intelligible to musicians of no matter what nationality. Similarly with figures, the German counts: ein, zwei, drei; the Frenchman says: un, deux, trois, and in English we use the words: one, two, three, but the figures: 1, 2, 3, though differently spoken, are intelligible to all and mean the same. There is no possibility of misunderstanding in the cases of either music or figures. Thus it is also with the universal language peculiar to the higher Regions of the Desire World and the still more subtle realms in nature, it is intelligible to all, an exact mode of expression.

Returning to our description of the entities commonly met with in the lower Desire World, we may note that other systems of religion than the Egyptian, already mentioned, have spoken of various classes of beings native to these realms. The Zoroastrian Religion, for instance, mentions Seven Ameshaspends and the Izzards as having dominion over certain days in the month and certain months in the year. The Christian religion speaks of Seven Spirits before the Throne, which are the same beings the Persians called Ameshaspends. Each of them rules over two months in the year while the seventh: Michael, the highest, is their leader, for he is ambassador from the sun to the earth, the others are ambassadors from the planets. The Catholic religion with its abundant occult information takes most notice of these "star-angels" and knows considerable about their influence upon the affairs of the earth.

The Ameshaspends, however, do not inhabit the lower Regions of the Desire World but influence the Izzards. According to the old Persian legend these beings are divisible into one group of twenty-eight classes, and another group of three classes. Each of these classes has dominion over, or takes the lead of all the other classes on one certain day of the month. They regulate the weather conditions on that day and work with animal and man in particular. At least the twenty-eight classes do that, the other group of three classes has nothing to do with animals, because they have only twenty-eight pair of spinal nerves, while human beings have thirty-one. Thus animals are attuned to

the lunar month of twenty-eight days, while man is correlated to the solar month of thirty or thirty-one days. The ancient Persians were astronomers but not physiologists, they had no means of knowing the different nervous constitution of animal and man, but they saw clairvoyantly these superphysical beings, they noted and recorded their work with animal and men and our own anatomical investigations may show us the reason for these divisions of the classes of Izzards recorded in that ancient system of philosophy.

Still another class of beings should be mentioned: those who have entered the Desire World through the gate of death and are now hidden from our physical vision. These so-called "dead" are in fact much more alive than any of us, who are tied to a dense body and subject to all its limitations, who are forced to slowly drag this clog along with us at the rate of a few miles an hour, who must expend such an enormous amount of energy upon propelling that vehicle that we are easily and quickly tired, even when in the best of health and who are often confined to a bed, sometimes for years, by the indisposition of this heavy mortal coil. But when that is once shed and the freed spirit can again function in its spiritual body, sickness is an unknown condition and distance is annihilated, or at least practically so, for though it was necessary for the Savior to liken the freed spirit to the wind which blows where it listeth, that simile gives but a poor description of what actually takes place in soul flights. Time is nonexistent there, as we shall presently explain, so the writer has never been able to time himself, but has on several occasions timed others when he was in the physical body and they speeding through space upon a certain errand. Distances such as from the Pacific Coast to Europe, the delivery of a short message there and the return to the body has been accomplished in slightly less than one minute. Therefore our assertion, that those whom we call dead are in reality much more alive than we, is well founded in facts.

We spoke of the dense body in which we now live, as a "clog" and a "fetter." It must not be inferred, however, that we sympathize with the attitude of certain people who, when they have learned with what ease soul-flights are accomplished, go about bemoaning the fact that they are now imprisoned. They are constantly thinking of, and longing for, the day when they shall be able to leave this mortal coil behind and fly away in their spiritual body. Such an attitude of mind is decidedly mistaken, the great and wise beings who are invisible leaders of our evolution have not placed us here to no purpose. Valuable lessons are to be learned in this visible world wherein we dwell, that cannot be learned in any other realm of nature, and the very conditions of density and inertia whereof such people complain, are factors which make it possible to acquire the knowledge this world is designed to give. This fact was so amply illustrated in a recent experience of the writer:—A friend had been studying occultism for a number of years but had not studied astrology.

Last year she became aroused to the importance of this branch of study as a key to self knowledge and a means of understanding the natures of others, also of developing the compassion for their errors, so necessary in the cultivation of love of one's neighbor. Love of our neighbor the Savior enjoined upon us as the Supreme Commandment which is the fulfillment of all laws, and as Astrology teaches us to bear and forbear, it helps as nothing else can in the development of the supreme virtue. She therefore joined one of the classes started in Los Angeles by the writer, but a sudden illness quickly ended in death and thus terminated her study of the subject in the physical body, ere it was well begun.

Upon one of many occasions when she visited the writer subsequent to her release from the body, she deplored the fact that it seemed so difficult to make headway in her study of astrology. The writer advised continued attendance at the classes, and suggested that she could surely get someone "on the other side" to help her study.

At this she exclaimed impatiently: "Oh yes! of course I attend the classes, I have done so right along; I have also found a friend who helps me here. But you cannot imagine how difficult it is to concentrate here upon mathematical calculations and the judgment of a horoscope or in fact upon any subject here, where every little thought-current takes you miles away from your study. I used to think it difficult to concentrate when I had a physical body, but it is not a circumstance to the obstacles which face the student here."

The physical body was an anchor to her, and it is that to all of us. Being dense, it is also to a great extent impervious to disturbing influences from which the more subtle spiritual bodies do not shield us. It enables us to bring our ideas to a logical conclusion with far less effort at concentration than is necessary in that realm where all is in such incessant and turbulent motion. Thus we are gradually developing the faculty of holding our thoughts to a center by existence in this world, and we should value our opportunities here, rather than deplore the limitations which help in one direction more than they fetter in another. In fact, we should never deplore any condition, each has its lesson. If we try to learn what that lesson is and to assimilate the experience which may be extracted therefrom, we are wiser than those who waste time in vain regrets.

We said there is no time in the Desire World, and the reader will readily understand that such must be the case from the fact, already mentioned, that nothing there is opaque.

In this world the rotation of the opaque earth upon its axis is responsible for the alternating conditions of day and night. We call it Day—when the spot where we live is turned towards the sun and its rays illumine our environment, but when our home is turned away from the sun and its rays obstructed by the opaque earth we term the resulting darkness: Night. The passage of the earth in its orbit around the sun produces the seasons and the year, which are our divisions of time. But in the Desire World where all is light there is but one long day. The spirit is not there fettered by a heavy physical body, so it does not need sleep and existence is unbroken. Spiritual substances are not subject to contraction and expansion such as arise here from heat and cold, hence summer and winter are also non-existent. Thus there is nothing to differentiate one moment from another in respect of the conditions of light and darkness, summer and winter, which mark time for us. Therefore, while the so-called "dead" may have a very accurate memory of time as regards the life they lived here in the body, they are usually unable to tell anything about the chronological relation of events which have happened to them in the Desire World, and it is a very common thing to find that they do not even know how many years have elapsed since they passed out from this plane of existence. Only students  of the Stellar Science are able to calculate the passage of time after their demise.

When the occult investigator wishes to study an event in the past history of man, he may most readily call up the picture from the memory of nature, but if he desires to fix the time of the incident, he will be obliged to count backwards by the motion of the heavenly bodies. For that purpose he generally uses the measure provided by the sun's precession: Each year the sun crosses the earth's equator about the twenty-first of March. Then day and night are of even length, therefore this is called the Vernal equinox. But on account of a certain wabbling motion of the earth's axis, the sun does not cross over at the same place in the Zodiac, it reaches the equator a little too early, it precedes, year by year it moves backwards a little. At the time of the birth of Christ, for instance, the Vernal Equinox was in about seven degrees of the Zodiacal sign Aries. During the two thousand years which intervene between that event and the present time, the sun has moved backwards about twenty-seven degrees, so that it is now in about ten degrees of the sign Pisces. It moves around the whole circle of the Zodiac in about 25,868 years. The occult investigator may therefore count back the number of signs, or whole circles, which the sun has preceded between the present day and the time of the event he is investigating. Thus he has by the use of the heavenly time keepers a very approximately correct measure of time even though he is in the Desire World and that is another reason for studying the Stellar Science.

The World of Thought.

When we have attained the spiritual development necessary to consciously enter the World of Thought and leave the Desire World, which is the realm of light and color, we pass through a condition which the occult investigator calls The Great Silence.

As previously stated, the higher Regions of the Desire World exhibit the marked peculiarity of blending form and sound, but when one passes through the Great Silence, all the world seems to disappear and the spirit has the feeling of floating in an ocean of intense light, utterly alone, yet absolutely fearless, since unimbued with a sense of its form or sound, nor past or future, but all is one eternal NOW. There seems to be neither pleasure nor pain and yet there is no absence of feeling but it all seems to center in the one idea:—"I am"! The human Ego stands face to face with itself as it were, and for the time being all else is shut out. This is the experience of anyone who passes that breach between the Desire World and the World of Thought, whether involuntarily, in the course of an ordinary cyclic pilgrimage of the soul, which we shall later elucidate when speaking of the post-mortem existence, or by an act of the will, as in the case of the trained occult investigator, all have the same experience in transition. There are two main divisions in the Physical World: the Chemical Region and the Etheric Region. The World of Thought also has two great subdivisions: The Region of concrete Thought and the Region of abstract Thought.

As we specialize the material of the Physical World and shape into a dense body, and as we form the force-matter of the Desire World into a desire body, so do we appropriate a certain amount of mindstuff from the Region of concrete Thought; but we, as spirits, clothe ourselves in spirit-substance from the Region of abstract Thought and thereby we become individual, separate Egos.

The Region of Concrete Thought.

The Region of concrete Thought is neither shadowy nor illusory. It is the acme of reality and this world which we mistakenly regard as the only verity, is but an evanescent replica of that Region.

A little reflection will show the reasonableness of this statement and prove our contention that all we see here is really crystallized thought. Our houses, our machinery, our chairs and tables, all that has been made by the hand of man is the embodiment of a thought. As the juices in the soft body of the snail gradually crystallize into the hard and flinty shell which it carries upon its back and which hides it, so everything used in our civilization is a concretion of invisible, intangible mind-stuff. The thought of James Watt in time congealed into a steam engine and revolutionized the world. Edison's thought was condensed into an electric generator which has turned night to day, and had it not been for the thought of Morse and Marconi, the telegraph would not have annihilated distance as it does today. An earthquake may wreck a city and demolish the lighting plant and telegraph station, but the thoughts of Watt, Edison and Morse remain, and upon the basis of their indestructible ideas new machinery may be constructed and operations resumed. Thus thoughts are more permanent than things.

The sensitive ear of the musician detects a certain musical note in every city which is different from that of another city. He hears in each little brook a new melody, and to him the sound of wind in the treetops of different forests give a varying sound. In the Desire World we noted the existence of forms similar to the shapes of things here, also that seemingly sound proceeds from form, but in the Region of concrete Thought it is different, for while each form occupies and obscures a certain space here, form is nonexistent when viewed from the standpoint of the Region of concrete Thought. Where the form was, a transparent, vacuous space is observable. From that empty void comes a sound which is the "keynote" that creates and maintains the form whence it appears to come, as the almost invisible core of a gas-flame is the source of the light we perceive. Sound from a vacuum cannot be heard in the Physical World, but the harmony which proceeds from the vacuous cavity of a celestial archetype is "the voice of the silence," and it becomes audible when all earthly sounds have ceased. Elijah heard it not while the storm was raging; nor was it in evidence during the turbulence of the earthquake, nor in the crackling and roaring fire, but when the destructive and inharmonious sounds of this world had melted into silence, "the still small voice" issued its commands to save Elijah's life.

That "keynote" is a direct manifestation of the Higher Self which uses it to impress and govern the Personality it has created. But alas, part of its life has been infused into the material side of its being, which has thus obtained a certain will of its own and only too often are the two sides of our nature at war.

At last there comes a time when the spirit is too weary to strive with the recalcitrant flesh, when "the voice of the silence" ceases.

The earthly nourishment we may seek to give, will not avail to sustain a form when this harmonious sound, this "word from heaven" no longer reverberates through the empty void of the celestial archetype, for "man lives not by bread alone," but by  the WORD, and the last sound-vibration of the "keynote" is the death-knell of the physical body.

In this world we are compelled to investigate and to study a thing before we know about it, and although the facilities for gaining information are in some respects much greater in the Desire World, a certain amount of investigation is necessary nevertheless to acquire knowledge. In the World of Thought, on the contrary, it is different. When we wish to know about any certain thing there, and we turn our attention thereto, then that thing speaks to us, as it were. The sound it emits at once gives us a most luminous comprehension of every phase of its nature. We attain to a realization of its past history; the whole story of its unfoldment is laid bare and we seem to have lived through all of those experiences together with the thing we are investigating.

Were it not for one enormous difficulty, the story thus obtained would be exceedingly valuable. But all this information, this life- picture, flows in upon us with an enormous rapidity in a moment, in the twinkling of an eye, so that it has neither beginning nor end, for, as said, in the World of Thought, all is one great NOW,  Time does not exist

Therefore, when we want to use the archetypal information in the Physical World, we must disentangle and arrange it in chronological order with beginning and ending before it becomes intelligible to beings living in a realm where Time is a prime factor. That rearrangement is a most difficult task as all words are coined with relation to the three dimensions of space and the evanescent unit of time, the fleeting moment, hence much of that information remains unavailable.

Among the denizens of this Region of concrete Thought we may note particularly two classes. One is called the powers of darkness by Paul and the mystic investigator of the Western World knows them as Lords of Mind. They were human at the time when the earth was in a condition of darkness such as worlds in the making go through before they become luminous and reach the firemist-stage. At that time we were in our mineral evolution. That is to say: The Human Spirit which has now awakened was encrusted in the ball of mindstuff, which was then the earth. At that time the present Human Spirits were as much asleep as is the life which ensouls our minerals of today, and as we are working with the mineral chemical constituents of the earth, molding them into houses, railways, steam-boats, chairs, etc, etc., so those beings, who are now Lords of Mind, worked with us when we were mineral-like. They have since advanced three steps, through stages similar to that of the Angels and Archangels, before they attained their present position and became creative intelligences. They are expert builders of mind stuff, as we are builders of the present mineral substances and therefore they have given us necessary help to acquire a mind which is the highest development of the human being.

According to the foregoing explanation it seems to be an anomaly when Paul speaks of them as evil and exhorts us to withstand them. The difficulty disappears, however, when we understand that good and evil are but relative qualities. An illustration will make the point clear:—Let us suppose that an expert organ builder has constructed a wonderful organ, a masterpiece. Then he has followed his vocation in the proper manner, and is therefore to be commended for the good which he has done. But if he is not satisfied to leave well enough alone, if he refuses to give up his product to the musician who understands how to play upon the instrument; if he intrudes his presence into the concert hall, he is out of place and to be censured as evil. Similarly the Lords of Mind did the greatest possible service to humanity when they helped us to acquire our mind, but many subtle thought influences come from them, and are to be resisted, as Paul very properly emphasizes.

The other class of beings which must be mentioned are called Archetypal Forces by the Western School of occultism. They direct the energies of the creative Archetypes native to this realm. They are a composite class of beings of many different grades of intelligences, and there is one stage in the cyclic journey of the Human Spirit when that also labors in, and is part of, that great host of beings. For the Human Spirit is also destined to become a great creative intelligence at some future time, and if there were no school wherein it could gradually learn to create, it would not be able to advance, for nothing in nature is done suddenly. An acorn planted in the soil does not become a majestic oak over night, but many years of slow, persistent growth are required before it attains to the stature of a giant of the forest. A man does not become an Angel by the mere fact of dying and entering a new world any more than an animal advances to be a man by the same process. But in time all that lives, mounts the ladder of Being from the clod to the God. There is no limitation possible to the spirit, and so at various stages in its unfoldment the Human Spirit works with the other nature forces, according to the stage of intelligence which it has attained. It creates, changes and remodels the earth upon which it is to live. Thus, under the great law of cause and effect, which we observe in every realm of nature, it reaps upon earth what it has sown in heaven, and vice versa. It grows slowly but persistently and advances continually.

The Region of Abstract Thought.

Various religious systems have been given to humanity at different times, each suited to meet the spiritual needs of the people among whom it was promulgated, and, coming from the same divine source:—God, all religions exhibit similar fundamentals or first principles.

All systems teach that there was a time when darkness reigned

supreme. Everything which we now perceive was then non- existent. Earth, sky and the heavenly bodies were uncreate, so were the multitudinous forms which live and move upon the various planets.—All, all, was yet in a fluidic condition and the Universal Spirit brooded quiescent in limitless Space as the One Existence.

The Greeks called that condition of homogeneity Chaos, and the state of orderly segregation which we now see; the marching orbs which illumine the vaulted canopy of heaven, the stately procession of planets around a central light, the majestic sun; the unbroken sequence of the seasons and the unvarying alternation of tidal ebb and flow;—all this aggregate of systematic order, was called Cosmos, and was supposed to have proceeded from Chaos.

The Christian Mystic obtains a deeper comprehension when he opens his Bible and ponders the first five verses of that brightest gem of all spiritual lore: the Gospel of St. John.

As he reverently opens his aspiring heart to acquire understanding of those sublime mystical teachings he transcends the form-side of nature, comprising various realms of which we have been speaking, and finds himself "in the spirit," as did the prophets in olden times. He is then in the Region of abstract Thought and sees the eternal verities which also Paul beheld in this, the third, heaven. For those among us who are unable to obtain knowledge save by reasoning upon the matter, however, it will be necessary to examine the fundamental meaning of words used by St. John to clothe his wonderful teaching, which was originally given in the Greek language, a much simpler matter than is commonly supposed, for Greek words have been freely introduced into our modern languages, particularly in scientific terms, and we shall show how this ancient teaching is supported by the latest discoveries of modern science.

The opening verse of the gospel of St. John is as follows: "In the beginning was the Word, and the Word was with God, and the Word was God." We will examine the words: "beginning," "Word" and "God." We may also note that in the Greek version the concluding sentence reads: "and God was the Word," a difference which makes a great distinction.

It is an axiomatic truth that "out of nothing, nothing comes," and it has often been asserted by scoffers that the Bible teaches generation "from nothing." We readily agree that translations into the modern languages promulgate this erroneous doctrine, but we have shown in The Rosicrucian Cosmo Conception (chapter on "the Occult Analysis of Genesis"), that the Hebrew text speaks of an ever-existing essence, as the basis whence all forms, the earth and the heavenly lights included, were first created, and John also gives the same teaching.

The Greek word arche, in the opening sentence of the gospel of St. John has been translated the beginning, and it may be said to have that meaning, but it also has other valid interpretations, vastly more significant of the idea John wished to convey. It means:—an elementary condition,—a chief source,—a first principle,—primordial matter.

There was a time when science insisted that the elements were immutable, that is to say, that an atom of iron had been an atom of iron since the earth was formed and would so remain to the end of time. The Alchemists were sneered at as fanciful dreamers or madmen, but since Professor J. J. Thomson's discovery of the electron, the atomic theory of matter, is no longer tenable. The principle of radio-activity has later vindicated the Alchemists.

Science and the Bible agree in teaching, that all that is, has been formed from one homogeneous substance.

It is that basic principle which John called arche:—primordial matter,—and the dictionary defines Archeology as: "the science of the origin (arche) of things." Masons style God the "Grand Architect," for the Greek word tektos means builder, and God is the Chief Builder (tektos) of arche: the primordial virgin matter which is also the chief source of all things.

Thus we see that when the opening sentence of St. John's gospel is properly translated, our Christian Religion teaches that once a virgin substance enfolded the divine Thinker:—God.

That is the identical condition which the earlier Greeks called Chaos. A little thought will make it evident that we are not arbitrary in finding fault with the translation of the gospel, for it is self-evident that a word cannot be the beginning, a thought must precede the word, and a thinker must originate thought before it can be expressed as a word.

When properly translated the teaching of John fully embodies that idea, for the Greek term logos means both the reasonable thought,—(we also say Logic),—and the word which expresses this (logical) thought.1)  In the primordial substance was thought, and the thought was with God And God was the word,

2)  THAT, [The Word], also was with God in the primal state. Later the divine WORD; the Creative Fiat, reverberates through space and segregates the homogeneous virgin substance into separate forms.

3)  Every thing has come into existence because of that prime fact, [The Word of God], and no thing exists apart from that fact.

4)  In that was Life.

In the alphabet we have a few elementary sounds from which words may be constructed. They are basic elements of expression, as bricks, iron and lumber are raw materials of architecture, or as a few notes are component parts of music.

  But a heap of bricks, iron and lumber, is not a house, neither is a jumbled mass of notes music, nor can we call a haphazard arrangement of alphabetical sounds a word.

These raw materials are prime necessities in construction of architecture, music, literature or poetry, but the contour of the finished product and the purpose it will serve depends upon the arrangement of the raw materials, which is subject to the constructor's design. Building materials may be formed to prison or palace; notes may be arranged as fanfare or funeral dirge; words may be indited to inspire passion or peace, all according to the will of the designer. So also the majestic rhythm of the Word of God has wrought the primal substance: arche, into the multitudinous forms which comprise the phenomenal world, according to His will.

Did the reader ever stop to consider the wonderful power of a human word. Coming to us in the sweet accents of love, it may lure us from paths of rectitude to shameful ignominy and wreck our life with sorrow and remorse, or it may spur us on in noblest efforts to acquire glory and honor, here or hereafter. According to the inflection of the voice a word may strike terror into the bravest heart or lull a timid child to peaceful slumber. The word of an agitator may rouse the passions of a mob and impel it to awful bloodshed, as in the French Revolution, where dictatorial mandates of mob-rule killed and exiled at pleasure,   or, the strain of "Home, Sweet Home" may cement the setting of a family-circle beyond possibility of rupture.

Right words are true and therefore free, they are never bound or fettered by time or space, they go to the farthest corners of the earth, and when the lips that spoke them first have long since mouldered in the grave, other voices take up with unwearying enthusiasm their message of life and love, as for instance the mystical "Come unto me" which has sounded from unnumbered tongues and brought oceans of balm to troubled hearts.

Words of Peace have been victorious, where war would have meant defeat, and no talent is more to be desired than ability to always say the right word at the auspicious time.

Considering thus the immense power and potency of the human word, we may perhaps dimly apprehend the potential magnitude of the Word of God, the Creative Fiat, when as a mighty dynamic force it first reverberated through space and commenced to form primordial matter into worlds, as sound from a violin bow moulds sand into geometrical figures. Moreover, the Word of God still sounds to sustain the marching orbs and impel them onwards in their circle paths, the Creative Word continues to produce forms of gradually increasing efficiency, as media expressing life and consciousness. The harmonious enunciation of consecutive syllables in the Divine Creative Word mark successive stages in evolution of the world and man. When the last syllable has been spoken and the complete word has sounded, we shall have reached perfection as human beings. Then Time will be at an end, and with the last vibration of the Word of God, the worlds will be resolved into their original elements. Our life will then be "hid with Christ in God," till the Cosmic Night:—Chaos,—is over, and we wake to do "greater things" in a "new heaven and a new earth."

According to the general idea Chaos and Cosmos are superlative antitheses of each other. Chaos being regarded as a past condition of confusion and disorder which has long since been entirely superseded by cosmic order which now prevails.

As a matter of fact, Chaos is the seed-ground of Cosmos, the basis of all progress, for thence come all IDEAS which later materialize as Railways, Steamboats, Telephones, etc.

We speak of "thoughts as being conceived by the mind," but as both father and mother are necessary in the generation of a child, so also there must be both idea and mind before a thought can be conceived. As semen germinated in the positive male organ is projected into the negative uterus at conception, so ideas are generated by a positive Human Ego in the spirit-substance of the Region of abstract Thought. This idea is projected upon the receptive mind, and a conception takes place. Then, as the spermatozoic nucleus draws upon the maternal body for material to shape a body appropriate to its individual expression, so does each idea clothe itself in a peculiar form of mindstuff. It is then a thought, as visible to the inner vision of composite man, as a child is to its parent.

Thus we see that ideas are embryonic thoughts, nuclei of spirit-substance from the Region of abstract Thought. Improperly conceived in a diseased mind they become vagaries and delusions, but when gestated in a sound mind and formed into rational thoughts they are the basis of all material, moral and mental  progress, and the closer our touch with Chaos, the better will be our Cosmos, for in that realm of abstract realities truth is not obscured by matter, it is self-evident.

Pilate was asked "what is Truth," but no answer is recorded. We are incapable of cognizing truth in the abstract while we live in the phenomenal world, for the inherent nature of matter is illusion and delusion, and we are constantly making allowances and corrections whether we are conscious of the fact or not. The sunbeam which proceeds for 90 millions of miles in a straight line, is refracted or bent as soon as it strikes our dense atmosphere, and according to the angle of its refraction, it appears to have one color or another. The straightest stick appears crooked when partly immersed in water, and the truths which are so self-evident in the Higher worlds are likewise obscured, refracted or twisted out of all semblance under the illusory conditions of this material world.

"The truth shall set you free," said Christ, and the more we turn our aspirations from material acquisitiveness and seek to lay up treasure above, the more we aim to rise, the oftener we "get in the spirit," the more readily we "shall know truth" and reach liberation from the fetter of flesh which binds us to a limited  environment, and attain to a sphere of greater usefulness.

 Study of philosophy and science has a tendency to further perception of truth, and as science has progressed it has gradually receded from its erstwhile crude materialism. The day is not far off when it will be more reverently religious than the church itself. Mathematics is said to be "dry," for it doesn't stir the emotions. When it is taught that "the sum of the angles of a triangle is 180 degrees," the dictum is at once accepted, because its truth is self-evident and no feeling is involved in the matter. But when a doctrine such as the Immaculate Conception is promulgated and our emotions are stirred, bloody war, or heated argument, may result, and still leave the matter in doubt. Pythagoras demanded that his pupils study mathematics, because he knew the elevating effect of raising their minds above the sphere of feeling, where it is subject to delusion, and elevating it towards the Region of abstract Thought which is the prime reality.

In this place we are dealing with worlds in particular, and will therefore defer comment upon the remainder of the first 5 verses of St. John's gospel:

 "And Life became Light in man,

5)  and Light shines in Darkness."

We have now seen that the earth is composed of three worlds which interpenetrate one another so that it is perfectly true when Christ said that "heaven is within you" or, the translation should rather have been among you. We have also seen that of these three realms two are subdivided. It has also been explained that each division serves a great purpose in the unfoldment of various forms of life which dwell in each of these worlds, and we may note in conclusion, that the lower regions of the Desire World constitute what the Catholic religion calls Purgatory, a place where the evil of a past life is transmuted to good, usable by the spirit as conscience in later lives. The higher regions of the Desire World are the first Heaven where all the good a man has done is assimilated by the spirit as soul power. The Region of concrete Thought is the second Heaven, where, as already said, the spirit prepares its future environment on earth, and the Region of abstract Thought is the third Heaven, but as Paul said,   it is scarcely lawful to speak about that.

Some will ask: is there then no hell?—No! The mercy of God tends as greatly towards the principle of GOOD as "the inhumanity of man" towards cruelty, so that he would consign his brother men to flames of hell during eternity for the puerile mistakes committed during a few years, or perhaps for a slight difference in belief. The writer has heard of a minister who wished to impress his "flock" with the reality of an eternity of hell flames, and to demonstrate the fallacy of a heretical notion entertained by some of his parishioners that when sinners come to hell they burn to ashes and that is the end.

He took with him an alcohol lamp and some asbestos into the pulpit and told his audience that God would turn their souls into a substance resembling asbestos. He showed them that though the asbestos were heated red hot it did not decompose into ashes. Fortunately the day of the hell preacher has gone by, and if we believe the Bible which says that "in God we live and move and have our being," we can readily understand that a lost soul would be an impossibility, for were

one single soul lost, then logically   a part of God Himself would be lost. No matter what our color, our race or our creed, we are all equally the children of God and in our various ways we shall obtain satisfaction. Let us therefore rather look to Christ and forget Creed.
Creed or Christ?

No man loves God who hates his kind, Who tramples on his Brother's heart and soul. Who seeks to shackle, cloud or fog the mind By fears of Hell has not perceived our goal.

God-sent are all religions blest;
And Christ, the Way, the Truth and Life, To give the heavy-laden rest,
And peace from Sorrow, Sin and Strife.
At his request the Universal Spirit came
To all the churches, not to one alone. On Pentecostal morn a tongue of flame
Round each apostle as a halo shone.
Since then, as vultures ravenous with greed, We oft have battled for an empty name,
And sought by Dogma, Edict, Creed, To send each other to the flame.
Is Christ then divided? Was Cephas or Paul Nailed to the deathly tree?
If not—then why these divisions at all? Christ's love doth embrace you and me.
His pure sweet love is not confined
By creeds which segregate and raise a wall; His love enfolds, embraces Humankind
No matter what ourselves or Him we call.
Then why not take Him at His word? Why hold to creeds which tear apart?
But one thing matters, be it heard, That brother-love fill every heart.
There is but one thing that the world has need to know; There is but one balm for all our human woe
There is but one way that leads to heaven above; That way is human sympathy and love.

Chapter IV. The Constitution of Man

Our chapter head, "the constitution of man," may surprise a reader who has not previously studied the Mystery teachings, or he may imagine that we intend to give an anatomical dissertation, but such is not our intention. We have spoken of the earth upon which we live as being composed of several invisible realms in addition to the world we perceive by means of our senses. We have also spoken of man as being correlated to these various divisions in nature, and a little thought upon the subject will quickly convince us that in order to function upon the various planes of existence described, it is necessary that a man should have a body composed of their substance, or at least have specialized for his own use, some of the material of each of these worlds We have said that finer matter, called desire stuff and mind stuff, permeates our atmosphere  and the solid earth, even as blood percolates through all parts of our flesh. But that is not a sufficient explanation to account for all facts of life. If that were all, then minerals, which are interpenetrated by the world of thought and the world of desire, would have thoughts and desires as well as man. This is not the case, so something more than mere interpenetration must be requisite to acquire the faculties of thought and feeling.

We know that in order to function in this world, to live as a physical being among other like beings, we must have a physical body all our own, built of the chemical constituents of this visible world. When we lose it at death, it profits us nothing that the world is full of just the very chemicals needed to build such a body. We cannot then specialize them, and therefore we are invisible to all others. Similarly, if we did not possess a special body made of ether, we should be unable to grow and to propagate. That is the case with the mineral. Had we no separate individual desire body, we should be unable to feel desires and emotions, there would be no incentive to move from one place

to another. We should then be stationary as plants, and did we not possess a mind, we should be incapable of thought, and act upon impulse and instinct as animals.

Some one may of course object to this last statement, and contend that animals do think. So far as our domesticated animals are concerned that is partially true, but it is not quite in the same way that we think and reason. The difference may perhaps best be understood if we take an illustration from the electrical field. When an electric current of high voltage is passed through a coiled copper wire, and another wire is placed in the center of the coils, that wire will become charged with electricity of a lower voltage. So also the animal, when brought within the sphere of human thoughts, evolves a mental activity of a lower order.

Paul, in his writings, also mentions the natural body and the spiritual body while the man himself is a spirit inhabiting those vehicles. We will briefly note the constitution of the various bodies of man invisible to the physical sight but as objective to spiritual sight as the dense body to ordinary vision.

The Vital Body.

That body of ours which is composed of ether is called the "vital body" in Western Mystery Schools, for, as we have already seen, ether is the avenue of ingress for vital force from the sun and the field of agencies in nature which promote such vital activities as assimilation, growth and propagation.

This vehicle is an exact counterpart of our visible body, molecule for molecule, and organ for organ, with one exception, which we shall note later. But it is slightly larger, extending about one and one-half inches beyond the periphery of our dense vehicle.

The spleen is the entrance gate of forces which vitalize the body. In the etheric counterpart of that organ solar energy is transmuted to vital fluid of a pale rose color. From thence it spreads all over the nervous system, and after having been used in the body it radiates in streams, much as bristles protrude from a porcupine.

The rays of the sun are transmitted either directly, or reflected by way of the planets and the moon. The rays directly from the sun give spiritual illumination, the rays received by way of the planets produce intelligence, morality, and soul growth, but the rays reflected by way of the moon make for physical growth, as seen in the case of plants which grow differently when planted in the light of the moon from what is the case when they are

planted when the moon is dark. There is also a difference in plants sown when the moon is in barren and fruitful signs of the Zodiac. The solar ray is absorbed by the human spirit which has its seat in the center of the forehead, the stellar ray is absorbed by the brain and spinal cord, and the lunar ray enters our system through the spleen.

The solar, stellar and lunar rays are three-colored, and in the lunar ray which supplies our vital force, the blue beam is the life of The Father, which causes germination, the yellow beam is the life of The Son, which is the active principle in nutrition and growth, and the red beam is the life of the Holy Spirit, which stimulates to action, dissipating the energy stored by the yellow force. This principle is particularly active in generation.

The various kingdoms absorb this life-force differently, according to their constitution. Animals have only 28 pairs of spinal nerves. They are keyed to the lunar month of 28 days and therefore dependent upon a Group spirit for an infusion of stellar rays necessary to produce consciousness. They are altogether incapable of absorbing the direct ray of the sun.

Man is in a transition stage, he has 31 pairs of spinal nerves which keys him to the solar month, but the nerves in the so-called cauda-equina—literally horse-tail—, at the end of our spinal cord, are still too undeveloped to act as avenues for the spiritual ray of the sun. In proportion as we draw our creative force upward by spiritual thought we develop these nerves and awaken dormant faculties of the spirit. But it is dangerous to attempt that development except under guidance of a qualified teacher, and the reader is earnestly warned not to use any method published in books, or sold, for their practice usually leads to dementia. The safe method is never sold for money or any earthly consideration however large or small; it is always freely given as a reward of merit. "Ask and ye shall receive, seek and ye shall find, knock and it shall be opened", said the Christ. If our life is a prayer for illumination, the search will not be uncertain, nor the knock without response.

When solar energy has been transmuted in the spleen it traverses the whole nervous system of the body glowing with a most beautiful color of a delicate rosy hue. It answers the same purpose as electricity in a telegraph system. We may string wires between cities, erect telegraph stations, install receivers and transmitters. We may even have operators ready at the keys, but until electric fluid is turned into our wires, the telegraph keys will refuse to click. So also in the body, the human spirit is operator, and from the central station of the brain, nerves ramify, go through the whole body to all the different muscles. When this vitalizing fluid of which we are speaking traverses the nervous system, the Ego may send his commands to the muscles and cause them to move but if the vital fluid for any reason does not flow into a certain part of the body such as an arm or a limb, then the spirit is powerless to move that part of the body and we say that it is paralyzed.

When we are in health, we specialize solar energy in such great quantities that we cannot use it all in the body and therefore it radiates through the pores of our skin in straight streams and serves a similar purpose as an exhaust fan. That machine drives the foul air out of a room or building and keeps the atmosphere within pure and sweet. The excessive vital force which radiates from the body drives out poisonous gases, deleterious microbes and effete matter thus tending to preserve a healthy condition. It also prevents armies of disease germs, which swarm about in the atmosphere, from entering; upon the same principle that a fly cannot wing its way into a building through the exhaust fan. Thus it serves a most beneficent purpose even after it has been utilized in our body and is returning to the free state.

It is a curious and most astounding sight when one first observes how, from exposed parts of the body such as hands and face, there suddenly commences to flow a stream of stars, cubes, pyramids and a variety of other geometrical forms. The writer has more than once rubbed his eyes when he first perceived the phenomenon, for it seemed that he must be suffering from hallucinations. The forms observed are chemical atoms however, which have served their purpose in the body and are expelled through the pores.

When one has eaten a meal, vital fluid is consumed by the body in great quantities, for it is the cement whereby nature's forces build our food into the body. Therefore the radiations
are weakest during the period of digestion. If the meal has been heavy, the outflow is very perceptibly diminished, and does not then cleanse our body as thoroughly as when the food has been digested, nor is it as potent in keeping out inimical germs. Therefore one is most liable to catch cold or other disease by overeating, a fault which should be avoided by all who wish to keep in good health.

During ill health the vital body specializes but little solar energy. Then, for a time, the visible body seems to feed upon the vital body as it were, so that the vehicle becomes more transparent and attenuated at the same rate as the visible body exhibits a state of emaciation. The cleansing odic radiations are almost entirely absent during sickness, therefore complications set in so easily. Though science has not directly observed this vital body of man, it has upon several occasions postulated the existence of such a vehicle as necessary to account for facts in life and the radiations have been observed by a number of scientists at different times and under varying conditions. Blondlot and Charpentier have called them N-rays after the city of Nantes where the radiations were observed by these scientists, others have named them "The Odic fluid". Scientific investigators who have conducted researches into psychic phenomena have even photographed it when it has been extracted through the spleen by materializing spirits. Dr. Hotz for instance obtained two photographs of a materialization through the German medium, Minna-Demmler. On one a cloud of ether is seen oozing out through the left side of the medium, shapeless and without form. The second picture, taken a few moments later, shows the materialized spirit standing at the medium's side. Other photographs obtained by scientists from the Italian medium Eusapio Palladino show a luminous cloud over-hanging her left side.

We said in the beginning of this description that the vital body is an exact counterpart of the dense body with one exception: it is of the opposite sex or perhaps we should rather say polarity. As the vital body nourishes the dense vehicle, we may readily understand that blood is its highest visible expression, and also that a positively polarized vital body would generate more blood than a negative one. Woman who is physically negative has a positive vital body, hence she generates a surplus of blood which is relieved by the periodical flow. She is also more prone to tears, which are white bleeding, than man, whose negative vital body does not generate more blood than he can comfortably take care of. Therefore it is not necessary for him to have the outlets which relieve excess of blood in woman.

The Desire Body.

In addition to the visible body and the vital body we also have a body made of desire stuff from which we form our feelings and emotions. This vehicle also impels us to seek sense gratification. But while the two instruments of which we have already spoken, are well organized, the desire body appears to spiritual sight as an ovoid cloud extending from sixteen to twenty inches beyond the physical body. It is above the head and below the feet so that our dense body sits in the center of this egg-shaped cloud as the yolk is in the center of an egg.

The reason for the rudimentary state of this vehicle is, that it has been added to the human constitution more recently than the bodies previously mentioned. Evolution of form may be likened to the manner in which the juices in the snail first condense into

flesh and later become a hard shell. When our present visible body first germinated in the spirit, it was a thought-form, but gradually it has become denser and more concrete until it is now a chemical crystallization. The vital body was next emanated by the spirit as a thought-form and is in the third stage of concretion which is etheric. The desire body is a still later acquisition. That also was a thought form at its inception, but has now condensed to desire stuff, and the mind, which we have only recently received, is still but a mere cloudy thought form. Arms and limbs, ears and eyes are not necessary to use the desire body, for it can glide through space more swiftly than wind without such means of locomotion as we require in this visible world.

When viewed by spiritual sight, it appears that there are in this desire body a number of whirling vortices. We have already explained that it is a characteristic of desire stuff to be in constant motion, and from the main vortex in the region of the liver there is a constant outwelling flow which radiates towards the periphery of this egg-shaped body and returns to the center through a number of other vortices. The desire body exhibits all the colors and shades which we know and a vast number of others which are indescribable in earthly language. Those colors vary in every person according to his characteristics and temperament and they also vary from moment to moment as passing moods, fancies or emotions are experienced by him. There is however in each one a certain basic color dependent upon the ruling star at the moment of his birth. The man in whose horoscope Mars is peculiarly strong usually has a crimson tint in his aura, where Jupiter is the strongest planet the prevailing tint seems to be a bluish tone, and so on with the other planets.

There was a time in the earth's past history when incrustation was not yet complete, and human beings of that time lived upon islands here and there, amid boiling seas. They had not yet evolved eyes or ears, but a little organ: the pineal gland, which anatomists have called the third eye, protruded through the back of the head and was a localised organ of feeling, which warned the man when he came too near a volcanic crater and thus enabled him to escape destruction. Since then the cerebral hemispheres have covered the pineal gland, and instead of a single organ of feeling, the whole body inside and out is sensitive to impacts, which of course is a much higher state of development.

In the desire body every particle is sensitive to vibrations similar to those which we call sight, sounds and feelings and every particle is in incessant motion rapidly swirling about so that in the same instant it may be at the top and bottom of the desire body and impart at all points to all the other particles a sensation of that which it has experienced thus every particle of desire stuff in this vehicle of ours will instantly feel any sensation experienced by any single particle. Therefore the desire body is of an exceedingly sensitive nature, capable of most intense feelings and emotions.

The Mind.

This is the latest acquisition of the human spirit, and in most people who have not yet accustomed themselves to orderly, consecutive thought, it is a mere inchoate cloud disposed particularly in the region of the head. When looking at a person clairvoyantly there appears to be an empty space in the center of the forehead just above and between the eyebrows. It looks like the blue part of a gas flame. That is mind stuff which veils the human spirit, or Ego, and the writer has been told that not even the most gifted seer can penetrate that veil which is said to have been spoken of in ancient Egypt as "the veil of Isis" which none may lift and live, for behind that veil is the Holy of Holies, the temple of our body, where the spirit is to be left secure from all intrusion. To those who have not previously studied the deeper philosophies the question may occur: But why all these divisions; even the Bible speaks only of soul and body, for most people believe soul and spirit to be synonymous terms. We can only answer that this division is not arbitrary but necessary, and founded upon facts in nature. Neither is it correct to regard the soul and the spirit as synonymous. Paul himself speaks of the natural body which is composed of physical substances: solids, liquids, gases and ethers; he mentions a spiritual body, which is the vehicle of the spirit composed of the mind and desire body, and the spirit itself, which is called Ego in Latin or "I" in English.

That term "I" is an appelation which can only be made by the human spirit of itself. We may all call a dog, dog; or we may call a table, table, and any one else may apply the same name tothe dog and to the table, but only a human being can be called "I" and only he himself can apply that most exclusive of all words, I, for this is the badge of self-consciousness, the recognition by the human spirit of itself as an entity, separate and apart from all others.

Thus we see that the constitution of man is more complex than appears upon the surface, and we will now proceed to note the effect upon this multiplex being of various conditions of life.


Chapter V. Life and Death
Invisible Helpers and Mediums.

There are two classes of people in the world. In one class the vital and dense bodies are so firmly cemented that the ethers cannot be extracted under any circumstances but remain with the dense body at all times and under all conditions from birth to death. Those people are insensible to any supersensuous sights or sounds. They are therefore usually exceedingly sceptic, and believe nothing exists but what they can see. There is another class of people in whom the connection between the dense and the vital bodies is more or less loose, so that the ether of their vital bodies vibrates at a higher rate than in the first class mentioned. These people are therefore more or less sensitive to the spiritual world.

This class of sensitives may again be divided. Some are weak characters, dominated by the will of others in a negative manner, as mediums, who are the prey of disembodied spirits desirous of obtaining a physical body when they have lost their own by death.

The other class of sensitives are strong positive characters, who act only from within, according to their own will. They may develop into trained clairvoyants, and be their own masters instead of slaves of a disembodied spirit. In some sensitives of both classes it is possible to extract part of the ether which forms the vital body. When a disembodied spirit obtains a subject of that nature, it develops the sensitive as a materializing medium. The man who is capable of extracting his own vital body by an act of will, becomes a citizen of two worlds, independent and free. Such are usually known as Invisible Helpers. There are certain other abnormal conditions where the vital body and the dense body are separated totally or in part, for instance if we place our limb in an uncomfortable position so that circulation of the blood ceases. Then we may see the etheric limb hanging down below the visible limb as a stocking. When we restore circulation and the etheric limb seeks to enter into place, an intense prickly sensation is felt, due to the fact that the little streams of force, which radiate all through the ether, seek to permeate the molecules of the limb and stir them into renewed vibration. When a person is drowning, the vital body also separates from the dense vehicle and the intense prickly pain incident to resuscitation is also due to the cause mentioned.

While we are awake and going about our work in the Physical World, the desire body and mind both permeate the dense and the vital bodies, and there is a constant war between the desire nature and the vital body. The vital body is continually engaged in building up the human organism, while the impulses of the desire body tend to tire and to break down tissue. Gradually, in the course of the day, the vital body loses ground before the onslaughts of the desire body, poisons of decay slowly accumulate and the flow of vital fluid becomes more and more sluggish, until at length it is incapable of moving the muscles. The body then feels heavy and drowsy. At last the vital body collapses, as it were, the little streams of force which permeate each atom seem to shrivel up, and the Ego is forced to abandon its body to the restorative powers of sleep.

When a building has become dilapidated and is to be restored and put in thorough repair, the tenants must move out to let the workmen have a free field. So also when the building of a spirit has become unfit for further use, it must withdraw therefrom. As the desire body caused the damage, it is a logical conclusion that that also must be removed. Every night when our body has become tired, the higher vehicles are withdrawn, only the dense and vital bodies are left upon the bed.

Then the process of restoration commences and lasts for a longer or a shorter time according to circumstances. At times however, the grip of the desire body upon our denser vehicles is so strong that it refuses to let go. When it has become so interested in the proceedings of the day, it continues to ruminate over them after the collapse of the physical body, and is perhaps only half extracted from that vehicle. Then it may transmit sights and sounds of the desire world to the brain. But as the connections are necessarily askew under such conditions, the most confused dreams result. Furthermore, as the desire body compels motion, the body is very apt to toss about when the desire body is not fully extracted, hence the restless sleep which usually accompanies dreams of a confused nature.

There are times of course when dreams are prophetic and come true, but such dreams result only after complete extraction of the desire body, under circumstances where the spirit has seen some danger perhaps, which may befall, and then impresses the fact upon the brain at the moment of awakening. It also happens that the spirit goes upon a soul flight and omits to perform its part of the work of restoration, then the body will not be fit to re-enter in the morning, so it sleeps on. The spirit may thus roam afield for a number of days, or even weeks, before it again enters its physical body and assumes the normal routine of alternating waking and sleep. This condition is called trance, and the spirit may remember upon its return what it has seen and heard in the super-physical realm, or it may have forgotten, according to the stage of its development and the depth of the trance condition. When the trance is very light, the spirit is usually present in the room where its body lies all the time, and upon its return to the body it will be able to recount to relatives all they said and did while its body lay unconscious. Where the trance is deeper, the returning spirit will usually be unconscious of what happened around its body, but may recount experiences from the invisible world.

A few years ago a little girl by the name of Florence Bennett in Kankakee, Illinois, fell into such a trance. She returned to the body every few days, but stayed within only a few hours each time, and the whole trance lasted three weeks, more or less. During the returns to her body she told relatives that in her absence she seemed to be in a place inhabited by all the people who died. But she stated that none of them spoke about dying and no one among them seemed to realize that they were dead. Among those she had seen was a locomotive engineer who had been accidentally killed. His body was mangled in the accident which caused death. The little girl perceived him there walking about minus arms, and with lesions upon his head, all of which is in line with facts usually seen by mystic investigators. Persons who have been hurt in accidents go about thus, until they learn that a mere wish to have their body made whole will supply a new arm or limb, for desire stuff is most quickly and readily molded by thought.

Death.

After a longer or shorter time there comes in each life a point where the experiences which a spirit can gain from its present environment have been exhausted, and life terminates in death. Death may be sudden and seemingly unexpected, as for instance by earthquake, upon the battle-field, or by accident, as we call it, but in reality, death is never accidental or unforeseen by Higher Powers. Not a sparrow falls to the ground without divine Will. There are along life's path partings of the way, as it were; on one side the main line of life continues onward, the other path leads into what we might call a blind alley. If the man takes that path, it soon ends in death. We are here in life for the sake of gaining experience and each life has a certain harvest to reap. If we order our life in such a manner that we gain the knowledge it is intended we should acquire, we continue in life, and opportunities of different kinds constantly come our way.

But if we neglect them, and the life goes into paths which are not congruous to our individual development it would be a waste of time to let us stay in such environment. Therefore the Great and Wise Beings, Who are behind the scene of evolution, terminate our life, that we may have a fresh start in a different sphere of influence. The law of conservation of energy is not confined to the Physical World, but operates in the spiritual realms also. There is nothing in life that has not its purpose. We do wrong to rail against circumstances, no matter how disagreeable, we should rather endeavor to learn the lessons which are contained therein, that we may live a long and useful life. Some one may object, and say: You are inconsistent in your teachings. You say there is really no death, that we go into a brighter existence, and that we have to learn other lessons there in a different sphere of usefulness! Why then aim to live a long life here?

It is very true that we make these claims, and they are perfectly consistent with the other assertions just mentioned, but there are lessons to be learned here which cannot be learned in the other worlds, and we have to bring up this physical body through the useless years of childhood, through hot and impulsive youth, to the ripeness of manhood or womanhood, before it becomes of true spiritual use. The longer we live after maturity has been attained, when we have commenced to look upon the serious side of life and started to truly learn lessons which make for soulgrowth, the more experience we shall gather and the richer our harvest will be. Then, in a later existence, we shall be so much more advanced, and capable of taking up tasks that would be impossible with less length of life and breadth of activity. Besides, it is hard to die for the man in the prime of life with a wife and growing family whom he loves; with ambitions of greatness unfulfilled; with hosts of friends about him, and with interests all centered upon the material plane of existence. It is sad for the woman whose heart is bound up in home and the little ones she has reared, to leave them, perhaps without anyone to care for them; to know that they have to fight their way alone through the early years when her tender care is needed, and perhaps to see those little ones abused, and she unable to lift a hand, though her heart may bleed as freely as it would in earth life. All these things are sad, and they bind the spirit to earth for a much longer time than ordinarily, they hinder it from reaping the experiences it should reap upon the other side of death, and they make it desirable along with other reasons already mentioned to live a long life before passing onwards.

The difference between those who pass out at a ripe old age, and one who leaves this earth in the prime of life, may be illustrated by the manner in which the seed clings to a fruit in an unripe state. A great deal of force is necessary to tear the stone from a green peach; it has such a tenacious hold upon the fruit that shreds of pulp adhere to it when forcibly removed, so also the spirit clings to the flesh in middle life and a certain part of its material interest remain and bind it to earth after death. On the other hand, when a life has been lived to the full, when the spirit has had time to realize its ambitions or to find out their futility, when the duties of life have been performed and satisfaction rests upon the brow of an aged man or woman; or when the life has been misspent and the pangs of conscience have worked upon the man and shown him his mistakes; when, in fact, the spirit has learned the lessons of life, as it must have to come to old age; then it may be likened to the seed of the ripe fruit which falls out clean, without a vestige of flesh clinging thereto, at the moment the encasing pulp is opened. Therefore we say, as before, that though there is a brighter existence in store for those who have lived well, it is nevertheless best to live a long life and to live it to the fullest extent possible. We also maintain, that no matter what may be the circumstances of a man's death, it is not accidental; it has either been brought about by his own neglect to embrace opportunities of growth, or else life has been lived to the ultimate possible. There is one exception to that rule, and that is due to man's exercise of his divine prerogative of interference. If we lived according to schedule, if we all assimilated the experiences designed for our growth by the Creative Powers, we should live to the ultimate length, but we ourselves usually shorten our lives by not taking advantage of opportunities, and it also happens that other men may shorten our lives and cut them off as suddenly as the so-called accident whereby the divine rulers terminate our life here. In other words, murder, or fatal accidents brought about by human carelessness, are in reality the only termination to life not planned by invisible leaders of humanity. No one is ever compelled to do murder or other evil, or there could not come to them a just retribution for their acts. The Christ said that evil must come but woe unto him by whom it cometh, and to harmonize that with the law of divine justice: "as a man soweth, so shall he also reap," there must at least be absolute free will in respect to evil acts.

There are also cases where a person lives such a full and good life of such vast benefit to humanity and to himself, that his days are lengthened beyond the ultimate, as they are shortened by neglect, but such cases are of course too few to allow of their being dwelt upon at length.

Where death is not sudden as in the case of accidents, but occurs at home after an illness, quietly and peacefully, dying persons usually experience a falling upon them as of a pall of great darkness shortly before termination of life. Many pass out from the body under that condition, and do not see the light again until they have entered the super-physical realms. There are many other cases however, where the darkness lifts before the final release from the body. Then the dying person views both worlds at once, and is cognizant of the presence of both dead and living friends. Under such circumstances it very often happens that a mother sees some of her children who have gone before, and she will exclaim joyously: Oh, there is Johnny standing at the foot of my bed; my but hasn't he grown! The living relatives may feel shocked and uneasy, thinking the mother suffering from hallucinations, while in reality she is more clear-sighted than they; she perceives those who have passed beyond the veil who have come to greet and help her to make herself at home in the new world she is entering.

Each human being is an individual, separate and apart from all others, and as experiences in the life of each differ from those of all others in the interval from the cradle to the grave, so we may also reasonably infer that the experiences of each spirit vary from those of every other spirit when it passes through the gates of birth and death. We print what purports to be a spirit message communicated by the late Professor James of Harvard at the Boston spirit temple, and in which he describes sensations

which he felt when passing through the gate of death. We do not vouch for its authenticity as we have not investigated the matter personally. Professor James had promised to communicate after death with his friends in this life, and the whole world of psychic research was and still is on watch for a word from him. Several mediums have claimed that Professor James has communicated through them, but the most remarkable are those given through the Boston spirit temple as follows:

"And this is death, only to fall asleep, only to awaken in the morning and to know that all is well. I am not dead, only arisen. "I only know that I experienced a great shock through my entire system, as if some mighty bond had been rent asunder. For a moment I was dazed and lost consciousness. When I awakened I found myself standing beside the old body which had served me faithfully and well. To say that I was surprised would only inadequately express the sensation that thrilled my very being, and I realized that some wonderful change had taken place. Suddenly I became conscious that my body was surrounded by many of my friends, and an uncontrollable desire took possession of me to speak and touch them that they might know that I still lived. Drawing a little nearer to that which was so like and yet unlike myself, I stretched forth my hand and touched them, but they heeded me not." "Then it was that the full significance of the great change that had taken place flashed upon my newly awakened senses; then it was that I realized that an impenetrable barrier separated me from my loved ones on earth, and that this great change which had taken place was indeed death. A sense of weariness and longing for rest took possession of me. I seemed to be transported through space, and I lost consciousness, to awaken in a land so different and yet so similar to the one which I had lately left. It was not possible for me to describe my sensations when I again regained consciousness and realized that, though dead, I was still alive.

"When I first became conscious of my new environment I was resting in a beautiful grove, and was realizing as never before what it was to be at peace with myself and all the world."

"I know that only with the greatest difficulty shall I be enabled to express to you my sensations when I fully realized that I had awakened to a new life. All was still, no sound broke the silence. Darkness had surrounded me. In fact, I seemed to be enveloped in a heavy mist, beyond which my gaze could not penetrate. Soon in the distance I discerned a faint glimmer of light, which slowly approached me, and then, to my wonder and joy, I beheld the face of her who had been my guiding star in the early days of my earth life." One of the saddest sights witnessed by the seer at a death-bed is the tortures to which we often subject our dying friends on account of ignorance of how to care for them in that condition. We have a science of birth; obstetricians who have been trained for years in their profession and have developed a wonderful skill, assist the little stranger into this world. We have also trained nurses attendant upon mother and child, the ingenuity of brilliant minds is focused upon the problem of how to make maternity easier, neither pains nor money are spared in these beneficent efforts for one whom we have never seen, but when the friend of a lifetime, the man who has served his kind well and nobly in profession, state, or church, is to leave the scene of his labors for a new field of activity, when the woman—who has labored to no less good purpose in bringing up a family to take its part in the world's work—has to leave that home and family, when one whom we have loved all our lives is about to bid us the final farewell, we stand by utterly at a loss how to help; perhaps we even do the very things most detrimental to the comfort and welfare of the departing one.

Probably there is no form of torture more commonly inflicted upon the dying than that which is caused by administering stimulants. Such potions have the effect of drawing a departing spirit into its body with the force of a catapult, to remain and to suffer for sometime longer. Investigators of conditions beyond have heard many complaints of such treatment. When it is seen that death must inevitably ensue, let not selfish desire to keep a departing spirit a little longer prompt us to inflict such tortures upon it. The death chamber should be a place of the utmost quiet, a place of peace and of prayer, for at that time, and for three and one-half days after the last breath, the spirit is passing through a Gethsemane and needs all the assistance that can be given. The value of the life that has just been passed depends greatly upon conditions which then prevail about the body; yes even the conditions of its future life are influenced by our attitude during that time, so that if ever we were our brother's keeper in life, we are a thousand times more so at death.

Post-mortem examinations, embalming and cremation during the period mentioned, not only disturb the passing spirit mentally, but are productive of a certain amount of pain, for there is still a slight connection with the discarded vehicle. If sanitary laws require us to prevent decomposition while thus keeping the body for cremation, it may be packed in ice till the three and one-half days have passed. After that time the spirit will not suffer, no matter what happens to the body.

The Panorama of a Past Life.

No matter how long we may keep the spirit from passing out however, at last there will come a time when no stimulant can hold it and the last breath is drawn. Then the silver cord, of which the Bible speaks, and which holds the higher and the lower vehicles together, snaps in the heart and causes that organ to stop. That rupture releases the vital body, and that with the desire body and mind float above the visible body for from one to three and one-half days while the spirit is engaged in reviewing the past life, an exceedingly important part of its post-mortem experience. Upon that review depends its whole existence from death to a new birth.

The question may arise in the student's mind: How can we review our past life from the cradle to the grave when we do not even remember what we did a month ago, and to form a proper basis for our future life, this record ought to be very accurate, but even the best memory is faulty? When we understand the difference between the conscious and sub-conscious memory and the manner in which the latter operates, the difficulty vanishes. This difference and the manner in which the sub-conscious memory keeps an accurate record of our life experiences may be best understood by an illustration, as follows: When we go into a field and view the surrounding landscape, vibrations in the ether carry to us a picture of everything within the range of our vision. It is as sad as it is true however, that "we have eyes and see not," as the Savior said. These vibrations impinge upon the retina of our eyes, even to the very smallest details, but they usually do not penetrate to our consciousness, and therefore are not remembered. Even the most powerful impressions fade in course of time so that we cannot call them back at will when they are stored in our conscious memory.

When a photographer goes afield with his camera the results which he obtains are different. The ether vibrations emanating from all things upon which his camera is focused, transmit to the sensitive plate an impression of the landscape true to the minutest detail, and, mark this well, this true and accurate picture is in no wise dependent upon whether the photographer is observant or not. It will remain upon the plate and may be reproduced under proper conditions. Such is the subconscious memory, and it is generated automatically by each of us during every moment of time, independently of our volition, in the following manner.

From the first breath which we draw after birth to our last dying gasp, we inspire air which is charged with pictures of our surroundings, and the same ether which carries that picture to the retina of our eye, is inhaled into our lungs where it enters the blood. Thus it reaches the heart in due time. In the left ventricle of that organ, near the apex, there is one little atom which is particularly sensitized, and which remains in the body all through life. It differs in this respect from all other atoms which come and go, for it is the particular property of God, and of a certain spirit.

This atom may be called the book of the Recording Angel, for as the blood passes through the heart, cycle after cycle, the pictures of our good and evil acts are inscribed thereon to the minutest detail. This record may be called the sub-conscious memory. It forms the basis of our future life when reproduced as a panorama just subsequent to death. By removal of the seed atom—which corresponds to the sensitized plate in a camera,—the reflecting ether of the vital body serves as a focus, and as the life unrolls slowly backwards from death to birth the pictures thereof are etched into the desire body which will be our vehicle during our sojourn in purgatory and the first heaven where evil is eradicated and good assimilated, so that in a future life the former may serve as conscience to withhold the man from repeating mistakes of the past, and the latter will spur us to greater good.

A phenomenon similar to the panorama of life usually takes place when a person is drowning. People who have been resuscitated speak of having seen their whole life in a flash. That is because under such conditions the vital body also leaves the dense body. Of course there is no rupture of the silver cord, or life could not be restored. Unconsciousness follows

quickly in drowning, while in the usual post-mortem review the consciousness continues until the vital body collapses in the same manner that it does when we go to sleep. Then consciousness ceases for a while and the panorama is terminated. Therefore also the time occupied by the panorama varies with different persons, according to whether the vital body was strong and healthy, or had become thin and emaciated by protracted illness. The longer the time spent in review, and the more quiet and peaceful the surroundings, the deeper will be the etching which is made in the desire body. As already said, that has a most important and far reaching effect, for then the sufferings which the spirit will realize in purgatory on account of bad habits and mis-deeds will be much more keen than if there is only a slight impression, and in a future life the still small voice of conscience will warn so much more insistently against mistakes which caused sufferings in the past.

When conditions are such at the time of death that the spirit is disturbed by outside conditions, for instance the din and turmoil of a battle, the harrowing conditions of an accident or the hys-terical wailings of relatives, the distraction prevents it from realizing an appropriate depth in the etching upon the desire  body. Consequently its post-mortem existence becomes vague and insipid, the spirit does not harvest fruits of experience as it should have done had it passed out of the body in peace and under normal conditions. It would therefore lack incentive to good in a future life, and miss the warning against evil which a deep etching of the panorama of life would have given. Thus its growth would be retarded in a very marked degree, but the beneficent pow-ers in charge of evolution take certain steps to compensate for our ignorant treatment of the dy-ing and other untoward circumstances mentioned. What these steps are, we shall discuss when considering the life of children in heaven, for the present let it be sufficient to say that in God's kingdom every evil is always transmuted to a greater good though the process may not be at once apparent.

Purgatory.

During life the collapse of the vital body at night terminates our view of the world about us, and causes us to lose ourselves in unconsciousness of sleep. When the vital body collapses just subsequent to death, and the panorama of life is terminated, we also lose consciousness for a time which varies according to the individual. A darkness seems to fall upon the spirit, then after a while it wakes up and begins dimly to perceive the light of the other world, but is only gradually accustomed to the altered conditions. It is an experience similar to that which we have when coming out of a darkened room into sunlight, which blinds us by its brilliancy, until the pupils of our eyes have contracted so that they admit a quantity of light bearable to our organism.

If under such a condition we turn momentarily from the bright sunlight and look back into the darkened room, objects there will be much more plain to our vision than things outside which are illumined by the powerful rays of the sun. So it is also with the spirit, when it has first been released from the body it perceives sights, scenes and sounds of the material world, which it has just left, much more readily than it observes the sights of the world it is entering. Wordsworth in his Ode to Immortality noted a similar condition in the case of new-born children, who are all clairvoyant and much more awake to the spiritual world than to this present plane of existence. Some lose the spiritual sight very early, others retain it for a number of years and a few keep it all through life, but as the birth of a child is a death in the spiritual world and it retains the spiritual sight for a time, so also death here is a birth upon the spiritual plane, and the newly dead retain a consciousness of this world for some time subsequent to demise.

When one awakes in the Desire World after having passed through aforementioned experiences, the general feeling seems to be one of relief from a heavy burden, a feeling perhaps akin to that of a diver encased in a heavy rubber suit, a weighty brass helmet upon his head, leaden soles under his feet and heavy weights of lead upon his breast and back, confined in his operations on the bottom of the ocean by a short length of air tube, and able only to move clumsily with difficulty. When after the day's work such a man is hauled to the surface, and divests himself of his heavy garments and he moves about with the facility we enjoy here, he must surely experience a feeling of great relief. Something like that is felt by the spirit when it has been divested of the mortal coil, and is able to roam all over the globe instead of being confined to the narrow environment which bound it upon earth.

There is also a feeling of relief for those who have been ill. Sickness, such as we know it, does not exist there. Neither is it necessary to seek food and shelter, for in that world there is neither heat nor cold. Nevertheless, there are many in the purgatorial regions who go to all bothers of housekeeping, eating and drinking just as we do here. George Du Maurier in his novel "Peter Ibbetson" gives a very good idea of this condition in the life lived between the hero and the Countess of Towers. This novel also illustrates splendidly what has been said of the sub-conscious memory, for Geo. Du Maurier has somewhere, somehow discovered an easy method which anyone may apply to do what he calls "dreaming true." By taking a certain position in going to sleep, it is possible, after a little practice, to compel the appearance, in a dream, of any scene in our past life which we desire to live over again. The book is well worth reading on that account.

When a fiery nebula has been formed in the sky and commences to revolve, a little matter in the center where motion is slowest commences to crystallize. When it has reached a certain density it is caught in the swirl, and whirled nearer and nearer to the outward extremity of what has, by that time, become the equator of a revolving globe. Then it is hurled into space and discarded from the economy of the revolving sun.

This process is not accomplished automatically as scientists would have us believe,—an assertion which has been proven in The Rosicrucian Cosmo Conception and other places in our literature. Herbert Spencer also rejected the nebular theory because it required a First Cause, which he denied, though unable to form a better hypothesis of the formation of solar systems,—but it is accomplished through the activity of a Great Spirit, which we may call God or by any other name we choose. As above, so below, says the Hermetic axiom. Man, who is a lesser spirit, also gathers about himself spirit-substance, which crystallizes into matter and becomes the visible body which the spiritual sight reveals as placed inside an aura of finer vehicles. The latter are in constant motion. When the dense body is born as a child it is extremely soft and flexible.

Childhood, youth, maturity and old age are but so many different stages of crystallization, which goes on until at last a point is reached where the spirit can no longer move the hardened body and it is thrown out from the spirit as the planet is expelled from the sun. That is death!—the commencement of a disrobing process which continues in purgatory. The low evil passions and desires we cultivated during life have crystallized the desire stuff in such a manner that that also must be expelled. Thus the spirit is purged of evil under the same law that a sun is purged of the matter which later forms a planet. If the life lived has been a reasonably decent one, the process of purgation will not be very strenuous nor will the evil desires thus expurgated persist for a long time after having been freed, but they quickly disintegrate. If, on the other hand, an extremely vile life has been led, the part of the expurgated desire nature may persist even to the time when the spirit returns to a new birth for further experience. It will then be attracted to him and haunt him as a demon, inciting him to evil deeds which he himself abhors. The story of Dr. Jekyll and Mr. Hyde is not a mere fanciful idea of Robert Louis Stevenson, but is founded upon facts well known to spiritual investigators. Such cases are extremes of course, but they are nevertheless possible and we have unfortunately laws which convert such possibilities to probabilities in the case of a certain class of so-called criminals. We refer to laws which decree capital punishment as penalty of murder.

When a man is dangerous he should of course be restrained, but even apart from the question of the moral right of a community to take the life of anyone—which we deny—society by its very act of retaliatory murder defeats the very end it would serve, for if the vicious murderer is restrained under whatever discipline is necessary in a prison for a number of years until his natural death, he will have forgotten his bitterness against his victim and against society, and when he stands as a free spirit in the Desire World, he may even by prayer have obtained forgiveness and have become a good Christian. He will then go on his way rejoicing, and will in the future life seek to help those whom he hurt here.

When society retaliates and puts him to a violent death shortly after he has committed the crime, he is most likely to feel himself as having been greatly injured, and not without cause. Then such a character will usually seek to "get even" as he calls it, he will go about for a long time inciting others to commit murder and other crimes. Then we have an epidemic of murders in a community, a condition not infrequent. The regicide in Servia shocked the Western World by wiping out an entire royal house in a most shockingly bloody manner, and the Minister of the Interior was one of the chief conspirators. Later he wrote his memoirs, and therein he writes that whenever the conspirators had tried to win anyone as a recruit, they always succeeded when they burned incense. He did not know why, but simply mentioned it as a curious coincidence. To the mystic investigator the matter is perfectly clear. We have shown the necessity of having a vehicle made of the materials of any world wherein we wish to function. We usually obtain a physical vehicle by going through the womb, or perhaps in a few special cases from a particularly good materializing medium, but where it is only necessary to work upon the brain and influence someone else to act, we need but a vehicle made of such ether as may be obtained from fumes of many different substances. Each kind attracts different classes of spirits, and there is no doubt that the incense burned at meetings where the conspirators were successful was of a low and sensual order and attracted spirits who had a grudge against humanity in general and the King of Servia in particular. These malcontents were unable to injure the King himself, but used a subtle influence which helped the conspirators in their work. The released murderer who has a grudge against society on account of his execution, may enter low gambling saloons where the fumes of liquor and tobacco furnish ample opportunity for working upon the class of people who congregate in such places, and the man whose spiritual sight has been developed is often sadly impressed when he sees the subtle influences to which those who frequent such places are exposed. It is a fact of course that a man must be of a low caliber to be influenced by low thoughts, and that it is as impossible to incite a person of benevolent character to do murder—unless we put him into a hypnotic sleep—as to make a tuning fork which vibrates to C sing by striking another attuned to the key of G, but the thoughts of both living and dead constantly surround us, and no man ever thought out a high spiritual philosophy under the influence of tobacco fumes or while imbibing alcoholic stimulants. Were capital punishment, newspaper notoriety of criminals, the manufacture of liquor and tobacco eliminated from society, the gun factories would soon cease to advertise and go out of business along with most of the locksmiths. The police force would decrease, so would jails and taxes would be correspondingly minimized.

When a person enters purgatory he is exactly the same person as before he died. He has just the same appetites, likes and dislikes, sympathies and antipathies, as before. There is one important difference, however, namely, that he has no dense body wherewith to gratify his appetites. The drunkard craves drink, in fact, far more than he did in this life, but has no stomach which can contain liquor and cause chemical combustion necessary to bring about the state of intoxication in which he delights. He may and does enter saloons, where he interpolates his body into the body of a physical drunkard, so that he may obtain his desires at second hand as it were, he will incite his victim to drink more and more. Yet there is no true satisfaction. He sees the full glass upon the counter but his spirit hand is unable to lift it. He suffers tortures of Tantalus until in time he realizes the impossibility of gratifying his base desire. Then he is free to go on so far as that vice is concerned. He has been purged from that evil without intervention of an angry deity or a conventional devil with hell's flames and pitchfork to administer punishment, but under the immutable law that as we sow so shall we reap, he has suffered exactly according to his vice. If his craving for drink was of a mild nature, he would scarcely miss the liquor which he cannot there obtain. If his desires were strong and he simply lived for drink, he would suffer veritable tortures of hell without need of actual flames. Thus the pain experienced in eradication of his vice would be exactly commensurate with the energy he had expended upon contracting the habit, as the force wherewith a falling stone strikes the earth is proportionate to the energy expended in hurling it upwards into the air.

Yet it is not the aim of God to "get even;" love is higher than law and in His wonderful mercy and solicitude for our welfare He has opened the way of repentance and reform whereby we may obtain forgiveness of sin, as taught by the Lord of Love: the Christ. Not indeed contrary to law, for His laws are immutable, but by application of a higher law, whereby we accomplish here that which would otherwise be delayed until death had forced the day of reckoning. The method is as follows:

In our explanation concerning the sub-conscious memory we noted that a record of every act, thought and word is transmitted by air and ether into our lungs, thence to the blood, and finally inscribed upon the tablet of the heart:—a certain little seedatom, which is thus the book of Recording Angels. It was later explained how this panorama of life is etched into the desire body and forms the basis of retribution after death. When we have committed a wrong and our conscience accuses us in consequence, and this accusation is productive of sincere repentance accompanied by reform, the picture of that wrong act will gradually fade from the record of our life, so that when we pass out at death it will not stand accusingly against us. We noted that the panorama of life unwinds backwards just after death. Later, in the purgatorial life it again passes before the spiritual vision of the man, who then experiences the exact feeling of those whom he has wronged. He seems to lose his own identity for the time being, and assumes the condition of his one time victim, he experiences all the mental and physical suffering himself which he inflicted upon others. Thus he learns to be merciful instead of cruel, and to do right instead of wrong in a future life. But if he awakens to a thorough realization of a wrong previous to his death, then, as said, the feeling of sorrow for his victim and the restitution or redress which he gives of his own free will, make the suffering after death unnecessary, hence—"his sin is forgiven."

The Rosicrucian Mystery teaching gives a scientific method whereby an aspirant to higher life may purge himself continually, and thus be able to entirely avoid existence in purgatory. Each night after retiring the pupil reviews his life during the past day in reverse order. He starts to visualize as clearly as possible the scene which took place just before retiring. He then endeavors to impartially view his actions in that scene examining them to see whether he did right or wrong. If the latter, he endeavors to feel and realize as vividly as possible that wrong. For instance, if he spoke harshly to someone, and upon later consideration finds it was not merited, he will endeavor to feel exactly as that one felt whom he wronged and at the very earliest opportunity to apologize for the hasty expression. Then he will call up the next scene in backward succession which may perhaps be the supper table. In respect of that scene he will examine himself as to whether he ate to live, sparingly and of foods prepared without suffering to other creatures of God, (such as flesh foods that cannot be obtained without taking life). If he finds that he allowed his appetite to run away with him and that he ate gluttonously, he will endeavor to overcome these habits, for to live a clean life we must have a clean body and no one can live to his highest possibilities while making his stomach a graveyard for the decaying corpses of murdered animals. In this respect there occurs to the writer a little poem by Ella Wheeler Wilcox:

"I am the voice of the voiceless; Through me the dumb shall speak,

Till a deaf world's ear Shall be made to hear

The wrongs of the wordless weak.

The same force formed the sparrow That fashioned man the king;

The God of the whole Gave a spark of soul

To furred and feathered thing.

And I am my brother's keeper And I will fight his fight,

And speak the word For beast and bird

Till the world shall set things right.

Thus the pupil will continue to review each scene in reverse order from night till morning, and to feel really sorry for whatever he has done amiss. He will not neglect to feel glad either when he comes to a scene where he has done well, and the more intensely he can feel, the more thoroughly he will eradicate the record upon the tablet of the heart and sharpen his conscience, so that as time goes on from year to year, he will find less cause for blame and enhance his soul power enormously. Thus he will grow in a measure impossible by any less systematic method, and there will be no necessity for his stay in purgatory after death.

This evening exercise and another, for the morning, if persistently performed day by day, will in time awaken the spiritual vision as they improve life. his matter has, however, been so thoroughly treated in number 11 of the lecture series: "Spiritual Sight and Insight; its safe culture and control," that it is unnecessary to dwell upon the matter further in this place.

The First Heaven.

In the first heaven, which is located in the higher regions of the Desire World, the panorama of life again unrolls and reveals every scene where we aimed to help or benefit others. They were not felt at the time the spirit was in the lower regions, for higher desires cannot express themselves in the coarse matter composing the lower regions of the Desire World, but when the spirit ascends to the first heaven it reaps from each scene all the good which it expressed in life. It will feel the gratitude poured out by those whom it helped; if it comes to a scene where itself received a favor from others and was grateful, it will experience the gratitude anew. The sum of all these feelings is there amalgamated into the spirit to serve in a future life as incentives to good.

Thus, the soul is purged from evil in purgatory, and strengthened in good in the first heaven. In one region the extract of sufferings become conscience to deter us from doing wrong, in the other region the quintessence of good is transmuted to benevolence and altruism which are the basis of all true progress. Moreover, purgatory is far from being a place of punishment, it is perhaps the most beneficent realm in nature, for because of purgation we are born innocent life after life. The tendencies to commit the same evil for which we suffered remain with us and temptations to commit the same wrongs will be placed in our path until we have consciously overcome the evil here; temptation is not sin, however, the sin is in yielding. Among the inhabitants of the invisible world there is one class which lives a particularly painful life, sometimes for a great many years, namely, the suicide who tried to play truant from the school of life. Yet it is not an angry God or a malevolent devil who administers punishment, but an immutable law which proportions the sufferings differently to each individual suicide. We learned previously, when considering the World of Thought, that each form in this visible world has its archetype there,—a vibrating hollow mold which emits a certain harmonious sound; that sound attracts and forms physical matter into the shape we behold, much in the same manner as when we place a little sand upon a glass plate and rub the edge with a violin bow, the sand is shaped into different geometrical figures which change as the sound changes.

The little atom in the heart is the sample and the center around which the atoms in our body gather. When that is removed at death, the center is lacking, and although the archetype keeps on vibrating until the limit of the life has been reached—as also previously explained,—no matter can be drawn into the hollow shape of the archetype and therefore the suicide feels a dreadful gnawing pain as if he were hollowed out, a torture which can only be likened to the pangs of hunger. In his case, the intense suffering will continue for exactly as many years as he should have lived in the body. At the expiration of that time, the archetype collapses as it does when death comes naturally. Then the pain of the suicide ceases, and he commences his period of purgation as do those who die a natural death. But the memory of sufferings experienced in consequence of the act of suicide will remain with him in future lives and deter him from a similar mistake.

In the first heaven there is a class who have not had any purgatorial existence and who lead a particularly joyous life: the children. Our homes may be saddened almost beyond endurance when the little flower is broken and the sunshine it brought has gone. But could we see the beautiful existence which these little ones lead, and did we understand the great benefits which accrue to a child from its limited stay there, our sorrow would be at least ameliorated in a great measure, and the wound upon our heart would heal more quickly. Besides, as nothing else in the world happens without a cause, so there is also a much deeper cause for infant mortality than we are usually aware of, and as we awake to the facts of the case, we shall be able to avoid in future the sorrow incident to loss of our little ones.

To understand the case properly we must revert to the experiences of the dying in the death hour. We remember that the panorama of the past life is etched upon the desire body during a period varying from a few hours to three and one-half days, just subsequent to demise. We recall also, that upon the depth of this etching depends the clearness of the picture, and that the more vivid this panorama of life, the more intensely will the spirit suffer in purgatory and feel the joys of heaven; also, that the greater the suffering in purgatory the stronger the conscience in the next life.

It was explained how the horrors of death upon the battlefield, in an accident or other untoward circumstances would prevent the spirit from giving all its attention to the panorama of life with the result that there would be a light etching in the desire body, followed by a vague and insipid existence in purgatory and the first heaven. It was also stated that hysterical lamentations in the death chamber would produce the same effect.

A spirit which had thus escaped suffering proportionate to its misdeeds, and which had not experienced the pleasure commensurate with the good it had done, would not in a future life have as well developed a conscience as it ought to have, nor would it be as benevolent as it ought to be, and therefore the life, terminated under conditions over which the spirit had no control, would be partly wasted. The Great Leaders of humanity therefore take steps to counteract such a calamity and prevent   an injustice. The spirit is brought to birth, caused to die in childhood, it re-enters the Desire World and in the first heaven it is taught the lessons of which it was deprived previously.

As the first heaven is located in the Desire World,—which is the realm of light and color,—where matter is shaped most readily by thought, the little ones are given wonderful toys impossible of construction here. They are taught to play with colors which work upon their moral character in exactly the manner each child requires. Anyone who is at all sensitive is affected by the color of his clothing and surroundings. Some colors have a depressing effect, while others inspire us with energy, and others again soothe and comfort us. In the Desire World the effect of colors is much more intense, they are much more potent factors of good and evil there than here, and in this color play, the child imbibes unconsciously the qualities which it did not acquire on account of accident or lamentations of relatives. Often it also falls to the lot of such relatives to care for a child in the invisible world, or perhaps to give it birth and see it die. Thus they receive just retribution for the wrong committed. As wars cease, and   man learns to be more careful of life, and also how to care for the dying, infant mortality, which now is so appalling, will decrease.

The Second Heaven.

When both the good and evil of a life has been extracted, the spirit discards its desire body and ascends to the second heaven. The desire body then commences to disintegrate as the physical body and the vital body have done, but it is a peculiarity of desire stuff, that once it has been formed and inspired with life, it persists for a considerable time. Even after that life has fled it lives a semi-conscious, independent life. Sometimes it is drawn by magnetic attraction to relatives of the spirit whose clothing it was, and at spiritualistic seances these shells generally impersonate the departed spirit and deceive its relatives. As the panorama of the past life is etched into the shells they have a memory of incidents in connection with these relatives, which facilitates the deception. But as the intelligence has fled, they are of course unable to give any true counsel, and that accounts for the inane, goody-goody nonsense of which these things deliver themselves.

When passing from the first to the second heaven, the spirit experiences the condition known and described previously as "The Great Silence," where it stands utterly alone conscious only of its divinity. When that silence is broken there floats in upon the spirit celestial harmonies of the world of tone where the second heaven is located. It seems then to lave in an ocean of sound and to experience a joy beyond all description and words, as it nears its heavenly home—for this is the first of the truly spiritual realms from which the spirit has been exiled during its earth life and the subsequent post-mortem existence. In the Desire World its work was corrective, but in the World of Thought the human spirit becomes one with the nature forces and its creative activity begins.

Under the law of causation we reap exactly what we sow, and it would be wrong to place one spirit in an environment where there is a scarcity of the necessities of life, where a scorching sun burns the crop and millions die from famine, or where the raging flood sweeps away primitive habitations not built to withstand its ravages, and to bring another  spirit to birth in a land of plenty, with a fertile soil which yields a maximum of increase with a minimum of labor, where the earth is rich in minerals that may be used in industry to facilitate transportation of products of the soil from one point to another. If we were thus placed without action or acquiescence upon our part, there would be no justice, but as our post-mortem existence in purgatory and the first heaven is based upon our moral attitude in this life so our activities in the second heaven are determined by our mental aspirations and they produce our future physical environment, for in the second heaven, the spirit becomes part of the nature forces which work upon the earth and change its climate, flora and fauna. A spirit of an indolent nature, who indulges in day dreams and metaphysical speculations here, is not transformed by death respecting its mental attitude any more than regarding its moral propensities. It will dream away time in heaven, glorying in its sights and sounds. Thus it will neglect to work upon its future country and return to a barren and arid land. Spirits, on the other hand, whose material aspirations lead them to desire so-called solid comforts of hearth and home, who aim to promote great industries and whose mind is concerned in trade and commerce, will build in heaven a land that will suit their purpose: fertile, immineralized, with navigable rivers and sheltered harbors. They will return in time to enjoy upon earth the fruits of their labors in the second heaven, as they reap the result of their life upon earth in purgatory and the first heaven.

The Third Heaven.

In the third heaven most people have very little consciousness for reasons explained in connection with the Region of Abstract Thought, for there the third heaven is located. It is therefore more of a place of waiting where the spirit rests between the time when its labors in the second heaven have been completed and the time when it again experiences the desire for rebirth. But from this realm inventors bring down their original ideas; there the philanthropist obtains the clearest vision of how to realize his utopian dreams and the spiritual aspirations of the saintly minded are given renewed impetus. In time the desires of the spirit for further experiences draws it back to rebirth, and the Great Celestial Beings who are known in the Christian Religion as Recording Angels, assist the spirit to come to birth in the place best suited to give it the experience necessary to further unfold its powers and possibilities.

We have all been here many times and in different families, we have had relations of varying nature with many different people and usually there are several families among whom we may seek re-embodiment to work out our self-generated destiny and reap what we have sown in former life. If there are no special reasons why we should take birth in any particular family among certain friends or foes, the spirit is allowed to choose its own place of birth. Thus it may be said that most of us are in our present places by our own prenatal choice.

In order to assist us in making that choice the Recording Angels call up before the spirit's vision a panorama in general outlines of each of the offered lives. This panorama will show what part of our past debts we are to pay, and what fruits we may be expected to reap in the coming life.

The spirit is left free to choose between the several lives offered. But once a choice has been made no evasion is possible during life. We have free will with regard to the future, but the past "mature" destiny we cannot escape, as shown by the incident recorded in The Rosicrucian Cosmo Conception, where the writer warned a well known Los Angeles lecturer that if he left his home upon a certain day, he would be injured by a conveyance, in head, neck, breast and shoulders. The gentleman believed and intended to heed our warning. Nevertheless he went to Sierra Madre to lecture upon the fateful day. He was injured in the places stated by a collision and later explained: "I thought the twenty-eighth was the twenty-ninth."

When the spirit has made its choice, it descends into the second heaven where it is instructed by the Angels and Archangels how to build an archetype of the body which it will later inhabit upon earth. Also here we note the operation of the great law of justice which decrees that we reap what we sow. If our tastes are coarse and sensual, we shall build an archetype which will express these qualities; if we are refined and of aesthetic taste, we shall build an archetype correspondingly refined, but no one can obtain a better body than he can build. Then, as the architect who builds a house in which he afterwards lives, will suffer discomfort if he neglects to properly ventilate it, so also the spirit feels disease in a poorly constructed body, and as the architect learns to avoid mistakes and remedy the short-comings of one house when building another, so also the spirit which suffers from defects in its body, learns in time to build better and better vehicles.

In the Region of Concrete Thought, the spirit also draws to itself materials for a new mind. As a magnet draws iron filings but leaves other substances alone, so also each spirit draws only the kind of mind-stuff which it used in its former life, plus that which it has learned to use in its present post-mortem state. Then it descends into the Desire World where it gathers material for a new desire body such as will express appropriately its moral characteristics, and later it attracts a certain amount of ether which is built into the mold of the archetype constructed in the second heaven and acts as cement between the solids, liquids and gaseous material from the bodies of parents which forms the dense physical body of a child, and in due time the latter is brought to birth.

Birth and Child Life.

It must not be imagined, however, that when the little body of a child has been born, the process of birth is completed. The dense physical body has had the longest evolution, and as a shoemaker who has worked at his trade for a number of years is more expert than an apprentice and can make better shoes and quicker, so also the spirit which has built many physical bodies produces them quickly, but the vital body is a later acquisition of the human being. Therefore we are not so expert in building that vehicle. Consequently it takes longer to construct that from the materials not used up in making the lining of the archetype, and the vital body is not born until the seventh year. Then the period of rapid growth commences. The desire body is a still later addition of composite man, and is not brought to birth until the fourteenth year when the desire nature expresses itself most strongly during so-called "hot" youth, and the mind, which makes man man, does not come to birth until the twenty-first year. In law that age is recognized as the earliest time he is fitted to exercise a franchise.

This knowledge is of the utmost importance to parents, as a proper understanding of the development which should take place in each of the septenary epochs enables the educator to work intelligently with nature and thus fulfill more thoroughly the trust of a parent than those who are ignorant of the Rosicrucian Mystery Teaching. We shall therefore devote the remaining pages to an elucidation of this matter and of the importance of the knowledge of astrology upon the part of the parent.

The Mystery of Light, Color and Consciousness.

"God is Light," says the Bible, and we are unable to conceive of a grander simile of His Omnipresence, or the mode of His manifestation. Even the greatest telescopes have failed to reach the boundaries of light, though they reveal to us stars millions of miles from the earth, and we may well ask ourselves, as did the Psalmist of old: Whither shall I flee from Thy Presence? If I ascend into heaven Thou art there, If I make my bed in the grave (the Hebrew word sheol means grave and not hell), Thou art there, If I take the wings of morning and dwell in the uttermost parts of the sea, even there shall thy hand lead me.

When, in the dawn of Being, God the Father enunciated The Word, and The Holy Spirit moved upon the sea of homogeneous Virgin Matter, primeval Darkness was turned to Light. That is therefore the prime manifestation of Deity, and a study of the principles of Light will reveal to the mystic intuition a wonderful source of spiritual inspiration. As it would take us too far afield from our subject we shall not enter into an elucidation of that theme here, except so far as to give an elementary idea of how divine Life energizes the human frame and stimulates to action. Truly, God is ONE and undivided, He enfolds within His Being all that is, as the white light embraces all colors. But He appears three-fold in manifestation, as the white light is refracted in three primary colors: Blue, Yellow and Red. Wherever we see these colors they are emblematical of the Father, Son and Holy Spirit. These three primary rays of divine Life are diffused or radiated through the sun and produce Life, Consciousness and Form upon each of the seven light-bearers, the planets, which are called "the Seven Spirits before the Throne." Their names are:

Mercury, Venus, Earth, Mars, Jupiter, Saturn and Uranus. Bode's law proves that Neptune does not belong to our solar system and the reader is referred to "Simplified Scientific Astrology" by the present writer, for mathematical demonstration of this contention. Each of the seven planets receives the light of the sun in a different measure, according to its proximity to the central orb and the constitution of its atmosphere, and the beings upon each, according to their stage of development, have affinity for some of the solar rays. They absorb the color or colors congruous to them, and reflect the remainder upon the other planets. This reflected ray bears with it an impulse of the nature of the beings with which it has been in contact.

Thus the divine Light and Life comes to each planet, either directly from the sun, or reflected from its six sister planets, and as the summer breeze which has been wafted over blooming fields carries upon its silent invisible wings the blended fragrance of a multitude of flowers, so also the subtle influences from the garden of God bring to us the commingled impulses of all the Spirits and in that varicolored light we live and move and have our being.

The rays which come directly from the sun are productive of spiritual illumination, the reflected rays from other planets make for added consciousness and moral development and the rays reflected by way of the moon give physical growth. But as each planet can only absorb a certain quantity of one or more colors according to the general stage of evolution there, so each being upon earth: mineral, plant, animal and man can only absorb and thrive upon a certain quantity of the various rays projected upon the earth. The remainder do not affect it or produce sensation, any more than the blind are conscious of light and color which exist everywhere around them. Therefore each being is differently affected by the stellar rays and the science of Astrology a fundamental truth in nature, of enormous benefit in the attainment of spiritual growth.

From a horoscopic figure in mystic script we may learn our own strength and weakness, with the path best suited to our development, or we may see the tendencies of those friends who come to us as children, and what traits are dormant in them. Thus we shall know clearly how to discharge our duty as parents, by repressing evil before it comes to birth and fostering good, so that it may bring forth most abundantly the spiritual potencies of the soul committed to our care.

As we have already said, man returns to earth to reap that which he has sown in previous lives and to sow anew the seeds which make for future experience. The stars are the heavenly time keepers which measure the year, the moon indicates the month when time will be propitious to harvest or to sow.

The child is a mystery to us all, we can only know its propensities as they slowly develop into characteristics, but it is usually too late to check when evil habits have been formed and the youth is upon the downward grade. A horoscope cast for the time of birth in a scientific manner shows the tendencies to good or evil in the child, and if a parent will take time and trouble necessary to study the science of the stars, he or she may do the child intrusted to his or her care an inestimable service by fostering tendencies to good and repressing the evil bent of a child ere it has crystallized into habit. Do not imagine that a superior mathematical knowledge is necessary to erect a horoscope. Many construct a horoscope in such an involved manner, so "fearfully and wonderfully made" that it is unreadable to themselves or others, while a simple figure easy of reading may be constructed by anyone who knows how to add and subtract. This method has been thoroughly elucidated in Simplified Scientific Astrology which is a complete text book, though small and inexpensive, and parents who have the welfare of their children thoroughly at heart should endeavor to learn for themselves, for even though their ability may not compare with that of a professional astrologer, their intimate knowledge of the child and their deep interest will more than compensate for such lack and enable them to see most deeply into the child's character by means of its horoscope.

Education of Children.

Respecting the birth of the various vehicles and the influence which that has upon life, we may say that during the time from birth to the seventh year the lines of growth of the physical body are determined, and as it has been noted that sound is builder both in the great and small, we may well imagine that rhythm must have an enormous influence upon the growing and sensitive little child's organism. The apostle John in the first chapter of his gospel expresses this idea mystically in the beautiful words: "In the beginning was the WORD ... and without it was not anything made that was made ... and the word became flesh;" the word is a rhythmic sound, which issued from the Creator, reverberated through the universe and marshaled countless millions of atoms into the multiplex variety of shapes and forms which we see about us. The mountain, the mayflower, the mouse and the man are all embodiments of that great Cosmic Word which is still sounding through the universe and which is still building and ever building though unheard by our insensitive ears. But though we do not hear that wonderful celestial sound, we may work upon the little child's body by terrestrial music, and though the nursery rhymes are without sense, they are nevertheless bearers of a wonderful rhythm, and the more a child is taught to say, sing and repeat them, to dance and to march to them, the more music is incorporated into a child's daily life, the stronger and healthier will be its body in future years.

There are two mottoes which apply during this period, one to the child and the other to the parent: Example and Imitation. No creature under heaven is more imitative than a little child, and its conduct in after years will depend largely upon the example set by its parents during its early life. It is no use to tell the child "not to mind," it has no mind wherewith to discriminate, but follows its natural tendency, as water flows down a hill, when it imitates. Therefore it behooves every parent to remember from morning till night that watchful eyes are upon him all the time waiting but for him to act in order to follow his example.

It is of the utmost importance that the child's clothing should be very loose, particularly the clothing of little boys, as chafing garments often produce vices which follow a man through life.

If anyone should attempt to forcibly extract a babe from the protecting womb of its mother, the outrage would result in death, because the babe has not yet arrived at a maturity sufficient to endure impacts of the Physical World. In the three septenary periods which follow birth, the invisible vehicles are still in the womb of mother nature. If we teach a child of tender years to memorize, or to think, or if we arouse its feelings and emotions, we are in fact opening the protecting womb of nature and the results are equally as disastrous in other respects as a forced premature birth. Child prodigies usually become men and women of less than ordinary intelligence. We should not hinder the child from learning or thinking of his own volition, but we should not goad them on as parents often do to nourish their own pride.

When the vital body is born at the age of seven a period of growth begins and a new motto, or relation rather, is established between parent and child. This may be expressed in the two words Authority and Discipleship. In this period the child is taught certain lessons which it takes upon faith in the authority of its teachers, whether at home or at school, and as memory is a faculty of the vital body it can now memorize what is learned. It is therefore eminently teachable; particularly because it is unbiased by pre-conceived opinions which prevent most of us from accepting new views. At the end of this second period: from about twelve to fourteen, the vital body has been so far developed that puberty is reached. At the age of fourteen we have the birth of the desire body, which marks the commencement of self-assertion. In earlier years the child regards itself more as belonging to a family and subordinate to the wishes of its parents than after the fourteenth year. The reason is this: In the throat of the fœtus and the young child there is a gland called the thymus gland, which is largest before birth, then gradually diminishes through the years of childhood and finally disappears at ages which vary according to the characteristics of the child. Anatomists have been puzzled as to the function of this organ and have not yet come to any settled conclusion, but it has been suggested that before development of the red marrow bones, the child is not able to manufacture its own blood, and that therefore the thymus gland contains an essence, supplied by the parents, upon which the child may draw during infancy and childhood, till able to manufacture its own blood. That theory is approximately true, and as the family blood flows in the child, it looks upon itself as part of the family and not as an Ego. But the moment it commences to manufacture its own blood, the Ego asserts itself, it is no longer Papa's girl or Mamma's boy, it has an "I"-dentity of its own. Then comes the critical age when parents reap what they have sown. The mind has not yet been born, nothing holds the desire nature in check, and much, very much, depends upon how the child has been taught in earlier years and what example the parents have set. At this point in life self-assertion, the feeling "I am myself", is stronger than at any other time and therefore authority should give place to Advice; the parent should practice the utmost tolerance, for at no time in life is a human being as much in need of sympathy as during the seven years from fourteen to twenty-one when the desire nature is rampant and unchecked.

It is a crime to inflict corporal punishment upon a child at any age. Might is never right, and as the stronger, parents should always have compassion for the weaker. But there is one feature of corporal punishment which makes it particularly dangerous to apply it to the youth: namely, that it wakens the passional nature which is already perhaps beyond the control of a growing boy.

If we whip a dog, we shall soon break its spirit and transform it into a cringing cur, and it is deplorable that some parents seem to regard it as their mission in life to break the spirit of their children with the rule of the rod. If there is one universal lack among the human race which is more apparent than any other, it is lack of will, and as parents we may remedy the evil in a large measure by guiding the wills of our children along such lines as dictated by our own more mature reason, so that we help them to grow a backbone instead of a wishbone with which unfortunately most of us are afflicted. Therefore, never whip a child; when punishment is necessary, correct by withholding favors or withdrawing privileges.

At the twenty-first year the birth of the mind transforms the youth into a man or a woman fully equipped to commence his own life in the school of experience. Thus we have followed the human spirit around a life cycle from death to birth and maturity, we have seen how immutable law governs his every step and how he is ever encompassed by the loving care of the Great and Glorious Beings who are the ministers of God. The method of his future development will be explained in a later work which will deal with "The Christian Mystic Initiation."

Mt. Ecclesia

(Transcriber's Note: This chapter is the series of pages which, earlier, the author said "had been transferred" to the back of the book.)

A DESCRIPTION OF THE HEADQUARTERS OF THE ROSICRUCIAN FELLOWSHIP

Work in the physical world requires physical means of accomplishment; therefore a tract of land was bought in 1911 in the town of Oceanside, ninety miles south of Los Angeles, California. Southern California was selected because of the abundance of ether in the atmosphere there, and this spot was found to be particularly favored in that respect.

On this commanding site having a wide view of the great Pacific Ocean, of snow capped mountains and smiling valleys, we began to establish our headquarters in the latter part of 1911. Soon after this we erected a sanctuary, the Pro-Ecclesia, where the Rosicrucian Temple Service is held at appropriate times. The Rose Cross Healing Circle holds its meetings there to help sufferers, and it is the place appointed for the united morning and evening devotions of the workers. In the latter half of 1920 we built an Ecclesia, which is designed to be a Temple of Healing. The building, a beautiful domed structure, is of steel and reinforced concrete. It is twelve sided in shape, corresponding to the twelve signs of the zodiac. At the present writing, January, 1921, the final work upon it is just being completed. The esoteric work of the Fellowship will be carried on here.

We have also built a two-story Administration Building to house the general office, the book department, the correspondence school in Christian Mysticism which links Headquarters with students all over the world, and the editorial offices of our monthly publications, notably the "Rosicrucian Fellowship Magazine—Rays from the Rose Cross." We have also an astrological department which conducts a correspondence school. Its offices are located on the second floor.

The whole first floor is occupied by a modern printing plant and book bindery required to furnish the immense amount of literature needed in this work. In the book department we publish all the standard works and text books of the Rosicrucian Philosophy written by Max Heindel. We are now in process of publishing in book form his former lessons to students.

In October, 1920, a Training School was established for the preparation of candidates for the lecture field. It is our intention to thereby maintain a Lecture Bureau, from which we will send our lecturers throughout the country to disseminate the teachings and carry the message of our philosophy to the people to a greater extent than has before been possible.

A Dining Hall with seating capacity for over one hundred people affords ample accommodation for workers, students, and patients. The scientific meatless diet served there preserves or restores health, as required in each case. Furthermore, it improves the vitality and mentality in an astonishing degree. A large dormitory, and a number of cottages and tents provide living quarters for all.

By the liberal use of water and the expenditure of much labor, Mount Ecclesia is gradually being transformed into a luxuriant tropical park. There is a deep spiritual purpose in this attempt to make the visible centre of the new world movement beautiful, for it fosters in the workers a poise and peace which are absolutely essential to the proper performance of their work. Without that they cannot escape being disturbed by the flood of sorrow and trouble which flows into Headquarters from members all over the world; without that they cannot continue to put heart into the letters of help, hope and cheer which continually go out to souls who are groaning under the burden of sickness, but by bathing their souls in the beauty of the surroundings, whether consciously or not, they gain in strength and grow in grace, they become better and better fitted for the Great Work in the Master's Vineyard. In order to aid those who feel the upward urge, to prepare intelligently and reverently for the unfoldment of their inner latent spiritual powers, the Rosicrucian Fellowship maintains two correspondence courses which furnish instruction to students all over the world. One deals with Astrology, the other with Christian Mysticism.

The Astrology to which we refer is not to be confounded with fortune-telling; it is a phase of the Mystic Religion, as sublime as the stars with which it deals, and to the Mystic they are not dead bodies moving in space in obedience to so-called blind natural law, but they are the embodiments of "The Seven Spirits before the Throne," mighty Star-Angels who use their benevolent influences to guide other less exalted beings, humanity included, upon the path of evolution.

There is a side of the moon which we never see, but that hidden half is as potent a factor in creating the ebb and flow, as the part of the moon which is visible. Similarly, there is an invisible part of man which exerts a powerful influence in life, and as the tides are measured by the motion of sun and moon, so also the eventualities of existence are measured by the circling stars, which may therefore be called "the Clock of Destiny," and knowledge of their import is an immense power, for to the competent Astrologer a horoscope reveals every secret of life.

Thus, when you have given an astrologer the data of your birth, you have given him the key to your innermost soul, and there is no secret that he may not ferret out. This knowledge may be used for good or ill, to help or hurt, according to the nature of the man. Only a friend should be trusted with this key to your soul, and it should never be given to anyone base enough to prostitute a spiritual science for material gain.

To the medical man Astrology is invaluable in diagnosing diseases and prescribing a remedy, for it reveals the hidden cause of all ailments, in a manner that has often perplexed the skeptic and dumbfounded the scoffer. The opinion of thousands is of great value, but it does not prove anything, for thousands may hold an opposite view; occasionally a single man may be right and the rest of the world wrong, as when Galileo maintained that the earth moves. Today the whole world has been converted to the opinion for which he suffered torture, and we assert that, as man is a composite being, cures are successful only in proportion as they remedy defects on the physical, moral and mental planes of Being. We also maintain that results may be obtained more easily at certain times when stellar rays are propitious to healing of a particular disease, or by treatment with remedies previously prepared under auspicious conditions.

If you are a parent the horoscope will aid you to detect the evil latent in your child and teach you how to apply the ounce of prevention. It will show you the good points also, that you may make a better man or woman of the soul entrusted to your care. It will reveal systemic weakness and enable you to guard the health of your child; it will show what talents are there, and how the life may be lived to a maximum of usefulness. Therefore, the message of the marching orbs is so important that you cannot afford to remain ignorant thereof. In order to aid those who are willing to help themselves we maintain a Correspondence Class in Astrology, but make no mistake, we do not teach fortune-telling; if that is what you are looking for, we have nothing for you.

OUR LESSONS ARE SERMONS

They embody the highest moral and spiritual principles, together with the loftiest system of ethics, for Astrology is, to us, a phase of religion; we never look at a horoscope without feeling that we are in a holy presence, face to face with an immortal soul, and our attitude is one of prayer for light to guide that soul aright.

WE DO NOT CAST HOROSCOPES

Despite all we can say, many people write enclosing money for horoscopes, forcing us to spend valuable time writing letters of refusal and giving us the trouble of returning their money. Please do not thus annoy us; it will avail you nothing.

THE COURSE IN CHRISTIAN MYSTICISM

Christ taught the multitude in parables, but explained the mysteries to His disciples. Paul gave milk to the babes, but meat to the strong. Max Heindel, the founder and leader of the Rosicrucian Fellowship, endeavored to follow in their steps and give to interested and devoted students a deeper teaching than that promulgated in public. For that purpose we conduct a correspondence course in Christian Mysticism. The General Secretary may admit applicants to the preliminary course, but advancement in the deeper degrees depends upon merit. It is for those alone who have been tried, and found true.

HOW TO APPLY FOR ADMISSION

Anyone who is not engaged in fortune-telling or similar methods of commercializing spiritual knowledge will, upon request, receive an application blank from the General Secretary, Rosicrucian Fellowship. When this blank is returned properly filled, he may admit the applicant to instruction in either or both correspondence courses.

THE COST OF THE COURSE

There are no fixed fees; no esoteric instruction is ever put in the balance against coin. At the same time, it cannot be given "free," "for nothing," for those who work to promulgate it must have the necessities of life. Type, paper, machinery and postage also cost money, and unless you pay your part someone else must pay for you. There are a few who cannot contribute, and who need these teachings as much or more than those who may take comfort from financial ease or affluence. If they make their condition known, they will receive as much attention as the largest contributors, but others are expected to contribute for their own good as well as for the good of the work. Remember, a closed hand that does not give cannot receive.

# XLI

❧

# The Goal of Philosophy

Today is the hope of the world. Here and now we are welding that great chain of tomorrows which extends from the instant to infinity. We live not for ourselves alone but for all futurity. Our accomplishments survive us, for long after we have descended into the earth the orders which we have established shall dominate the activities of men. The world is an ancestral shrine filled with the mortuary tablets of the honored dead. We bow before our illustrious progenitors. We are the substance of their aspirations, the consummation of their dreams, for today is the focal point of time. We are all that has been about to be projected into all that shall be.

Each human soul holds eternity in suspension. Recognizing this truth, several modern scientists have formulated the theory that immortality is achieved through a succession of lives— that the father achieves immortality in his son, the son in his progeny, and so on to the end of generation. The torch of life which each expiring personality hands on to another does not go out; it is immortal, but he who bears it must perish by the way. Men are but incidents in the flow of life, yet they have a strange power, for while they cannot cause the vital flame to blaze up from nothingness, they are empowered to snuff it out, and when generations cease the countless ages die together.

To be is to be immortal, for that which has been can never utterly cease. The past hovers in the air like a mirage. Men feel its presence; they breath it in, and enveloped by it live their little now. Upon the surface of their polished mirrors the ancient Magi caught faint visions of forgotten times. Within the next century we shall discover that history is written in the air; that so-called space itself is photographic, preserving as on a sensitized plate the varied activities of created things. Egypt as a physical empire has long since crumbled

into dust, but upon each minute particle of the atmosphere the glory of ancient Egypt is preserved for all time. Men speak words, and their words seemingly vanish into nothingness, but in the living substances of the universe these selfsame words are traced in everlasting characters to be read in some distant time by men as yet unborn. Thoughts unuttered are not wholly lost, nor do dreams perish because their dreamer dares not give them speech. Somewhere in the infinite vistas of space, impressed as it were upon the memory of the infinite and sharing together a common immortality, all aspirations, all visions, and all deeds await the day when men with unfolding reason will bind all time into a common now.

In his experiments with plants the late Luther Burbank found substantiation for the scientific concept of immortality through progeny. The doctrine of natural salvation, as it is called, was demonstrated to Burbank through phenomena arising from the cross-pollination of plants. For example, Burbank pollinated a variety of plants bearing white flowers with another variety bearing colored flowers, and as a result secured blossoms which were wholly white, some wholly colored, and still others of mixed colors. Taking a white plant from this cross-pollination test, Burbank pollinated it with another white plant, the result being a number of new plants all white. Taking one of the latter, he again pollinated it with white, and the result was again white. This experiment was repeated tentimes. In every case the flowers were entirely white, but the eleventh time several blossoms reverted to the original color of the plant, thereby proving that though latent for a considerable period the elements of the first cross-pollination survived to reappear again. The original colored shrub had died long before its activities reappeared among the white blossoms, but Burbank recognized in this phenomena the immortality of the colored flower which was reborn in its own progeny.

To Burbank man was but a human plant, and the great horticulturist solved the philosophic problem of his life by observing the habits of the growing things in his garden. If after the lapse of ten pollinations the identity of a distant progenitor was re-established, was it not reasonable to assume that men are born again to blossom forth in their descendants ? Is not immortality the carrying forward of a primitive trace, and is not the urge which we feel within ourselves the voice of some ancestral impulse? For the physical thinker, to whom the invisible universe is simply a vast mechanism, and spirit an unnecessary hypothesis, there can be no immortality other than that which is carried in the seed. How small a germ man springs from, yet how much that germ contains; for in each wriggling sperm is the man with character, personality, and individuality. From so slight a beginning, what great issues come; for in the single tiny germ are contained not only the epitome of all the past, but also all the greatness that is to follow.

The philosopher takes issue with the scientist not as to the accuracy of the conclusion, but rather as to the field to which the conclusion is applied. A fact is a fact, but for the clarification it may often seem half a lie. Recognizing only the physical universe the savant limits all his premises to physical concerns, with the result that his discoveries are rendered of little value by false emphasis. If man were actually a body, physical immortality would be his hope and he would indeed survive in his progeny. But since man is not a physical body the laws controlling the body are powerless over the intangible essence which resides within its innermost parts. Indwelling spirit is not to be measured wholly by its outer form. Body has hands and feet, but spirit has no need of such appendages except when functioning in the physical world. Body has parts and dimensions, but spirit is impartible and dimensionless. Thus, while the laws of physical generation produce the actual phenomena so carefully classified by Burbank, it does not necessarily follow that spirit, which is not material, is dependent upon generation for its survival. It is obvious that spirit depends upon generation for its manifestation in form, but such manifestation is merely a phase in the condition of spirit.

Heredity is limited to the sphere of generation; it is of the accidents and not the essence in man. While men may inherit physical tendencies—even physical attitudes and, under some conditions, physical thoughts—this shell of personality is soulless until he animates it with his own immortal principle and gradually shapes it into an appropriate destiny. Heredity only controls such as are incapable of controlling themselves. Steeped in the vibration of its previous states, the stuff from which bodies are made comes to each incarnating soul. The life into whose vehicles it was formerly incorporated set the minute atoms whirling at a definite speed, and imprinted upon each of them its own purposes and characteristics. The child coming into the world must battle with these strange vibrations, reorganizing the substances of its body into individual vehicles by overcoming the motion of past agencies, and revibrating the electrons according to its own needs. TTic plant is a victim of circumstances to a far greater extent than is man. To escape its environment the plant must either die or trust to the unlikelihood of some gardener transplanting it to a more ideal habitat.  Man, however, if his surroundings be incongenial, may move at will to an environment more propitious to his destiny.

The analogy may be projected into the invisible structures of both plants and men. The evolving plant life is still working through a vehicle too low in its organic quality to respond to the impulses of the inner agent. While man is empowered to resist the impulses of heredity as these incline his physical body in one direction or another, the plant must abide by the dictates of its formal part. The fallibility of the law of heredity has already been proved, and additional evidence of its inaccuracy will be accumulated as evolving man takes more of his destiny into his own hands and relies less upon the elements of chance and environment. As the stars impel yet do not compel, so man's hereditary impulses traced upon the fabric of his atomic nature urge him to follow in the old accustomed way. The self, however, declares otherwise, and one by one the impediments of heredity are overcome by the onward march of consciousness toward perfection. Whereas science fights to maintain the dignity of form and the supremacy of matter throughout the universe, philosophy would establish the excellence of life and the rulership of all creation by its rational part. If we come to worship matter and elevate the physical universe to first place among the spheres, we can never hope to establish well-being in the nature of men, or fellowship among the nations of the earth. The premise of material supremacy is wholly destructive of the moral sense and reduces ethics to a superstition and aesthetics to an artist's vagaries. All that is beautiful is thus sacrificed in the defense of a premise, and the sovereign good is martyr to a notion. More cruel than Moloch is the God of the materialist, for he would feed whole nations into the maw of greed. To remedy a condition we must discover its cause.

Man's boast of a godless age is his undoing, for he who destroys the concept of Deity destroys with it the sufficiency of his own internal nature. In his pride that he is now able to govern the universe unaided, the 20th-century thinker has given the divinities on high Olympus notice to gather up their belongings and depart. The gods have obliged him.

Their thrones are empty; they have left for some other sphere where mortals are less vain. But man is still unhappy. His boasted knowledge has brought him doubt, doubt has brought terror, and terror has sapped away his strength. Afraid that his worst conclusions may yet be true, the materialist clings to his little ball of dirt, shuddering in anticipation of that day when he will be hurled therefrom into the abyss he himself has postulated. The heart of the thinker cannot accept the soulless universe that his mind has declared. How strangely fickle is the mind that from pure imaginings fashions a universal order, and then dissatisfied with the fabric it has spun convicts high heaven of manmade inconsistencies!

In his New Atlantis, a work unfinished. Sir Francis Bacon recites the virtues of an ideal philosophic empire. This empire. which he calls Bensalem, "the sons of peace, or of the ladder," is ruled over by a mysterious institution designated "Solomon's House." This "House" is an order of men united in the quest of universal realities. They are patrons of the arts and sciences, and investigators of nature's lore. The whole story is founded upon Plato's empire of Poseidon—the lost Atlantides, or the Isles of the Sea. One cannot read this account of the perfect state without marveling at the scope of Bacon's vision. Herein is set forth the substance of things hoped for and the prophecy of that which must inevitably come to pass in that time the gods decree to be opportune. Bacon claims America to be the lost Atlantis, adding that the Greeks were mistaken as to the sinking of the ancient continent, which was not actually submerged but rather temporarily inundated by tidal waves and freshets in the mountains. The inhabitants of the valleys were drowned, but the more savage peoples who roamed the tangled highlands escaped. In this manner culture was destroyed, and only savagery left to re-establish the orders of nations. In his Holy Guide, John Hcydon reprints the Hew Atlantis as an alchemical allegory, definitely connecting the book with the Rosicrucian Mysteries and, through inference, with the symbols of Freemasonry. The discriminating Mason can hardly ignore the obvious fact that "Solomon's House" as described by Bacon is the temple of universal wisdom and education. Nor can he overlook "the several degrees of ascent, whereby men did climb up to the same, as if it had been a scala Coeli ." In its philosophy the New Atlantis sets forth an ideal government of the earth. It foretells that day when in the midst of men there shall rise up a vast institution composed of the philosophic elect—an order of illumined men banded together for the purpose of investigating the laws of life and the mysteries of the universe. In this labor will be employed the ancient disciplines reconstructed and restated by Bacon in the Novum Organum.

Fate decrees that empires must fall and states vanish from the earth, for, erected upon and maintained by selfishness, these shall ultimately be destroyed by the internal dissension generated through selfishness. The age of boundaries is closing, and we are approaching a nobler era when nations shall be no more; when the lines of race and caste shall be wiped out; when the whole earth shall be under one order, one government, one administrative body. As Asgard rose amid the fertile plains of earth and as the Aesir guided the destinies of mortal creatures from their lofty thrones upon the snow-capped peaks, so upon the earth there shall arise a noble institution destined to lead humanity toward the condition of knowledge. A great city shall be established like the Holy City of ancient fable, which shall be the capitol of the world, the seat of all power, the hub of world administration. Here an exalted legislative body shall be convened which will mete out the justice of the wise and guide the unfoldment of the indigent many. From the seats of their authority the various heads of human undertaking will direct the destinies of all enterprise. Being in agreement with each other, these enlightened executives will move in accordance with the principles of harmony and compatibility. No longer will the various divisions of society oppress each other, for when all the parts work toward a common end the excellence of one over another is without consequence.

The time has not yet arrived when the average man is strong enough or wise enough to rule himself. Even when unfolding destiny greatly magnifies the accomplishments of the many, there will not come a day when the wisdom of the mass will be equal to the wisdom of its wisest few. As men's minds increase in capacity and establish newer and nobler codes of ethics and morals, there will still be the exceptional intellect that by divine Providence excels, and by virtue of such excellence demonstrates its fitness for honor and responsibility. By an exceptional intellect we do not mean an individual who through scheme or subterfuge steals glory from the impotent. Such thieves of prestige have a special substratum reserved for them in the realm of retribution. We refer to those illumined philosophers and mystics who, marching ahead of the body of the race, arc the only ones actually fitted to directionalize human activities. Never will peace reign upon the earth until we are ruled by the fit; until he who possesses vision is permitted to see for the blind; until he who senses greatness is permitted to interpret its issues for those who are unresponsive to magnitudes. Men are truly free only when, governed by the wise, they are inclined gently toward the perfection of their own natures. Men are truly great only when, admitting the supremacy of the wise, they offer both life and chattel to the service of integrity.

Plato dreamed of that glorious day when the wranglings and contentions of mankind would cease; when people would turn from their petty tyranny to unite in a common destiny; when the needs of the many would be removed from exploitation by the few. He dreams in vain, however, who envisions a government of the people or by the people; but he is a seer indeed who can formulate the concept of a rational government for the people. That man is happy who can trust his lord; that state is fortunate whose prince is a philosopher.

Humanity turns toward wisdom when the fruits of wisdom are apparent to it. Having once beheld the rewards of integrity, all men will move joyously toward that state of concord wherein dwell the wise, conserving their resources and fulfilling the destiny of rational souls. We must learn that wisdom is neither book-learning nor empty pedantry. The sham studiousness of the sophists was facetiously termed "eyeglass believing" by the medieval mystics.

Our present educational system would be fundamentally opposed to this philosophic program, because the school is the servant of utility and our standards of utility are lamentably insufficient. We teach men to bargain, barter, and connive; we are unsparing of both time and money in our effort to fit them into a "system" obviously impractical. Centuries must pass before the body of society will be sufficiently sickened of the vanities it supports to be inclined toward integrity. Eventually the day of awakening must come, for man cannot suffer indefinitely, and the saturation point of human endurance must sometime reach its limit. The unnecessary burden which we carry and have borne through uncounted ages will then be cast aside, and turning to truth we shall find liberation.

Polemics is not necessarily the abode of the wise, nor is much hairsplitting to be confused with erudition. The elevation of a man to high position does not ipso facto improve the quality of his nature or increase his capacity to receive. True elevation is opportunity, but the innate characteristics of the one promoted must determine the use to be made of that opportunity. To remove politicians from power and replace them with scientists or philosophers trained according to our present concepts would not necessarily solve our problem. The sages of Plato's vision are the truly

wise—men initiated into the disciplines of the soul and deeply versed in the mysteries of life. In the senates of the philosophic elect, blocs of biologists would not combine to frustrate the legislation of the physicists, nor would astronomers hold out on technicalities against the geometricians. Savants would neither give a little of this for a little of that, nor arbitrate away the rights of men to prolong an ephemeral political prestige. Where the learned differ, it is evident there is no learning. In that city of the wise all the arts and sciences will complement each other, and the disciples of every branch of learning will mutually venerate each other's knowledge. Competition will cease, and co-operation will be reinstated as the true life of trade. The bartering of interests, the misappropriation of power, the malfeasance of office—all these are crimes possible only in a nonphilosophic age where the blind who follow are unable to discern the fallacies of the blind who lead. For thousands of years a devotee to the fetish of competition, man has devastated that Edenic garden over which the Lord designed him to be the keeper. A poor gardener he has made! He has torn up all the flowering plants which lend beauty to the spot, that in their place he might grow weeds for a little profit. The highest expression of wisdom on the part of the many involves, first, appreciation for the still greater wisdom of the few, and secondly, the high-minded- ness to waive the rights of personal privilege that thereby the
greatest good to the greatest number may be achieved.

Death is the invariable product of ignorance, but life is prolonged in conformity with intelligence. Heedless of our own destiny, in the vain struggle for possessions we often perish for lack of wisdom even as we reach out to grasp the substance of our desires. The plains of earth are broad, the resources of earth are incalculable, and on this globe there is ample to satisfy the needs of all. Through commerce and industry, through legitimate intercourse and exchange, and with reasonable effort man can enjoy those necessities which contribute to his well-being. Acceptance of the false principle of diversity, however, has been man's undoing, for the existence of contiguous states or nations has been the excuse for their exploitation. Boundary lines were originally set up that they might later become diplomatic technicalities, for it was presupposed that an invading horde should some day sweep them away. Nations consequently prey upon nations according to their presumptions of necessity. Strong peoples absorb weaker peoples into themselves, thereby depriving some of that which js necessary that others may have more than enough. Oppression by the invader and retaliatory wars by the oppressed are the inevitable products of such encroachments. Fighting for what he conceives to be his inherent rights, the patriot is a martyr to vain standards and hopeless issues. He opposes ignorance with ignorance, and thus the sorrows of the ages are compounded. Man destroys man that man may live; life lives by killing; freedom is achieved by intolerance; and, if we are to believe the pronouncements of the foolish, peace is preserved by the sword. Where, may we ask, is the beginning or the end of this vicious circle which survives by destroying and also destroys by surviving?

Occasionally we find an individual of such innate perversity that he will actually cheat himself in material things. In matters pertaining to the spirit, however, dishonesty is quite the common order. In our foragings we generally descend Assyrian-like upon the stranger, still reasoning with primitive caveman logic that that which is not already our own is legitimate prey. With the abolishment of political states and the unification of all peoples into one great nation, the misunderstanding directly due to national jealously and competition would be outlawed; for what people would be so foolish as to raise an army for the conquest of that which is already part of itself and co-operating for the sovereign good? Such a national attitude, when once established, would constitute a powerful moral deterrent to individual conduct. So far- reaching is the influence of our environment that in a comparatively short time the spirit of competition, as applied to individual concerns, would be broken, and men would build into the common pattern of public weal instead of striving to acquire a passing supremacy over the bodies of the dead.

To be a wholesale killer is no longer the hallmark of greatness, for no strength is stronger than that which, withholding the hand, prevents violence; no courage more courageous than that which, facing the problems of each passing day, fights the battles of peace. Upon first thought it may be difficult to visualize a world ruled by philosophy instead of politics. What is politics, however, but the philosophy of government? Is it not universal law applied to the government of men, and should not the one who is made a ruler over others be conversant also with those sidereal forces by which the order of creation is maintained?

If a knowledge of cosmogony and universal law were a prerequisite to rulership, how many of our present governors would occupy their official chairs? Yet, for the regulation of human affairs, what pattern is more sublime than the harmony of the celestial spheres or the innate orderliness of crystal formation? The science of mundane government has failed because interests. What is responsible for this perversion and misdirection of executive power? Simply the elevation of the unfit. We recall the words of that satirist who, philosophizing upon the effects of the French Revolution, declared that the reign of terror had taken the affairs of the state out of the hands of a despotic few and transferred them into the keeping of the unqualified many. Let us never forget the words of that great Jewish statesman, Disraeli, who said: "The world is weary of statesmen whom democracy has degraded into politicians." The theory of democracy is one of the noblest yet conceived by man. It is the aristocratic gesture of the proletarian. It fails, however, because at no time can man be more than himself; for man's government—like his God—perforce must be but a highly magnified reflection of himself. The true seat of government is in the home. In his Apophthegms of Kings and Grand Commanders, Plutarch describes a reformer who was discussing with Lycurgus the setting up of a democracy in Sparta. "Pray," retorted the Spartan lawgiver, "do you first set up a democracy in your own house?" Governments obviously cannot succeed where men fail, for we are the makers of government and our statutes unsparingly reflect both the depth and the shallowness of our own individual selves.

When the citizen is told to appoint a representative, he generally takes the advice too literally. If the leader resembles too faithfully his constituency he is unable to point out to his following any course of action which they could not have discovered by their own efforts. Hence, the interval of rationality should intervene between the governed and the governor. When this interval of superiority is insufficient, our vices and not our virtues become the rulers of the state. "Democracy," writes Lowell in the Bigelow Papers, "gives every man a right to be his own oppressor." Each faction of the people mistakenly assumes that its primal need is a representative who will interpret its whims and further its own particular ends at the expense of all other groups. Philosophy, however, corrects this attitude, declaring that the popular need is a virtuous mind strong enough to incline the populace toward a greater good. The spokesman of the masses seldom says anything, for the voice of the masses is the incoherent babble of many voices in which no single voice is intelligible. The political philosopher should be an idealist, not a realist. Not content with preserving things in their present state, he should desire to elevate them to the state of the ideal. Government is the science of leadership, the philosophy of administration, the art of reconciling the apparently irreconcilable viewpoints of the many. Of all the sciences, government demands the greatest measure of integrity. A position requiring a superlative quality of integrity and involving the widest sphere of influence should, by every rule of logic, be reserved for the wisest and best fitted. Only that man who is above personal interest is a safe politician, for the citizenry suffers when so-called public servants arc the servants of their own desires. Only when the world is ruled by its best balanced intellects can we expect it to be well-ruled. We have never had a sufficient number of illumined leaders to permit the smaller nations a proper and adequate form of government. Only by combining into a single people and choosing the wisest of men— regardless of race or creed—to directionalize the activities of the human race, can we approach that philosophic empire which Bacon, profoundly versed in the theory of government, advanced as the true solution of empire. When inferior intellects are chosen to administer governmental destinies, dissension is inevitable in the state. TTie true philosopher is the born ruler of men. Though now considered impractical because he lives in a world divorced from personal interest, in reality the philosopher dwells in the sphere of things-as-they-ought-to-be. Contemplating, as he does, the eternal verities of the universe, he is peculiarly fitted to ponder the affairs of government; for from such contemplation of eternal verities he has come to realize that if any institution is to endure it must be patterned after the enduring qualities of the universe. By incorporating universal truths into the social structure the philosopher effects the stabilization of society. The true ends of philosophy are not realized in the spinning of vain theories or fourth-dimensional woolgathering. Philosophy is the pondering of problems, the quest for solutions, the effort to organize life so that by conforming his life to the dictates of rationality man may come to enjoy the maximum of peace, efficiency, and individual completeness.

As each age comes into manifestation it brings with it a definite philosophic revelation designed to solve the problems peculiar to that age. These revelations are keynotes of thought, and by their aid we bridge the ethical intervals between generations. Racial systems of culture now dead are remembered chiefly for the words of power which they passed on to the civilizations that succeeded them. Through the tangled mystery of time we have wound our way, achieving according to the measure of our understanding. In philosophic history certain outstanding individuals have come to be regarded as the epitome of vast orders of learning. We regard these individualities as the formers and reformers of doctrines and orders of life.

Thus, all the elements of Hindu Brahmanism are gathered into one colossal personality—Manu, the giver of the law. As the embodiment of Egyptian culture, Hermes founded the mysteries of statecraft, giving to the world the doctrines of universal order and procedure. In ancient Greece the half mythical Orpheus established the cult of beauty, teaching men the gospel of rhythm. Then to Asia came the strong voice of Buddha, calling men to the way of renunciation and the noble eightfold path. Again in Greece, while pondering the science of numbers, Pythagoras revealed God to the world as the Great Geometrician, bidding men enter upon the mathematical life. Then Socrates, the immortal proletarian, affirmed

the necessary to be the greatest good, giving men the gospel of justice. In China, Confucius, the unapotheosized saint and utilitarian of the Celestial Empire, expounded the worship of the imminent and the service of the now. In Syria, Jesus, the Rabbi of the Essenes, preached the gospel of friendship, seeking to unite the diverse interests of mankind in the fellowship of the spirit. To Arabia, Mohammed, "the desired of all nations," holding high the sword of Islam, brought the philosophy of retribution and a righteous destiny. Modern religious and philosophic concepts thus comprise an intricate eclecticism, combining the reconcilable elements of these and various other revelations. The faith we live by is woven from many threads. We are the sons of the prophets of elder days, and half-heartedly we strive to keep the varied array of their commandments. But, behold, the dawn of a new era is at hand! Humanity has elevated itself in temporal things far above all previous states of power. National strength has become so dominating as to require a code more ample, a revelation more specific.

Ascendancy brings with it great responsibility, and the ethical structure of society must be rendered stable if integrity is to be preserved amid the temptations of pre-eminence. Never before has the lawgiver been faced with a problem involving humanity as a whole. Previous revelations have been addressed, for the most part, to single nations or "chosen peoples". TTie prophet of those days brought that which was necessary for the survival of his own clan and the well-being of that particular order of which he himself was a part. Thus, while each of these messages contains elements of truth that are imperishable, they are not wholly suitable to present needs. For this age we must have a doctrine of synthesis, a code actuated and dominated by the spirit of unification. The supreme need is to blend the diverse interests of men into a common purpose. The philosophy of this age must reveal the interdependence of the Chinaman and the Turk, the white man and the black, the great and the small. In other words, we have need of a common denominator, a fundamental premise upon which all will be agreed; for if we are to establish the government of the philosophic elect it must be erected upon the foundation of mutual understanding. Today we have one set of laws for men who live in the valleys, and another for those who dwell upon the hills. The diversified interests of a great populace require many representatives to interpret those needs at the seats of government; for the tiller of the soil is a stranger to the captain of industry, and the financier in the environment of his money world little senses those broad impulses animating the souls of poets and philosophers.

 Humanity has grown to be so strong that it is now dangerous to allow its parts to remain disunited. No longer can wc maintain our position of isolated individualism without endangering the rights of all men. The old truth that man cannot live by himself alone is still true. The ever-increasing strength of the individual confers upon him an ever-increasing capacity to injure, and unless the desire to hurt ceases within his own soul he is capable of infinite destructiveness. The same is true of nations on a grander scale. War has revealed the destructive potentialities resident in aggregations of people. Communities apparently benign and harmless can be metamorphosed over night into a death-dealing mechanism which, justifying its destructiveness, like the Macedonian phalanx from which it was derived can move across the face of the virgin earth and leave nothing but shattered hopes and smoldering ruins in its wake. This power to injure, inherent in human nature and now scientifically organized and trained to wreak the fullest measure of evil, is an impending menace against which the race must protect itself. The social structure is infected with the hereditary taint of war, and none is so wise that he can predict at just what point the plague will break out next. In such emergencies laws are impotent, preachments in vain, and moralizings futile; for intoxicated with the lust for power men will turn against all that

they formerly held dear, and in the name of patriotism march ruthlessly to their own ultimate destruction. When they have loosed the dogs of war, men study Napoleon, not Socrates.

When the blood-letting is over and men have turned from the gory altar of Ares, they seek solace not in Caesar's memoirs but in the words of Jesus or Buddha. But man's forethought always comes behind, for he keeps the power of devastation in his own name and invokes Deity only during the reconstruction periods. After the plenitude of destruction has been wrought, a repentant people like naughty children turn to their Eternal Parent for sympathy.

In those more placid moments when our emotions are at rest and the stagnant pools of our desires are left unstirred, we are indeed a noble race, striving for a heavenly crown 1 But when greed stirs up our bile we revert to a most barbarous and primitive type, eagerly trading our equity in a state of future bliss for a few square leagues of more substantial earth. From all of which it is apparent that as yet no spiritual revelation has come sufficiently strong to successfully withstand the inherent weakness of the flesh. The rewards promised for virtue arc so distant and ephemeral that they do not tempt mere sordid men as do the instantaneous compensations which are apparently the rewards of perversion. Centuries must yet pass before the human soul will be sufficiently liberated from the involvements of the material nature to dominate and direc- tionalize the activities of its objective nature. We have come to a day of intensive classifications, of vast industries and corporations, of factional organizations. Each individual is ambitiously striving to become a specialist in some department of the arts, sciences, or professions of living. Each one's goal is to attain a position of familiarity with his subject which will enable him to "corner" the field and exploit it to his own aggrandizement. It consequently follows that when men simply use each other as means to further their own selfish ends there must result an ever-decreasing bond of understanding between them, for their selfishness and divergence of interest inevitably segregates and eventually results in utter isolation. Like rays of light pouring from a radiant center, humanity today is traveling at an incalculable rate towards diversity, limited only by its innate capacity to diverge.

A new keynote must consequently be struck, a new word of power sounded, a new message brought which will warn men that in this mad dash toward diversity lies annihilation; that this senseless separateness of interests must ultimately result in a confusion of tongues and the obliteration of all effort.

The highest message of yesterday was the message of friendship—an effort to unite men in a common cause. But friendship has proved insufficient as a remedy, for friendship is capable of perversion. The undeveloped man is a natural abuser of privileges and a perverter of issues. Friendship has become the chosen institution of rogues, and thus the power of evil has been strengthened; for when thugs fraternize the entire social order is at hazard. It has been demonstrated that the powers of evil, unable to lean upon the Infinite which was presumably against them, have developed the pernicious habit of depending upon themselves and each other, with the result that virtue is a disorganized and vice a well-regulated institution.

Friendship has failed, first, because men could not understand it and hence degraded it to a tool of interest; secondly, because to the average individual it is an artificial relation established in an effort to create a condition which did not naturally exist. Men have mouthed the word until it has become obnoxious and synonymous with the vagaries of a decadent faith. As yet we have not reached that point in our spiritual unfoldment where universal friendship is apparent to us. When you tell a man that friendship exists in nature and that God has decreed his creations to live together jn amicable relations, he may point to the jungle law where every animal lurks behind a bush ready to devour the passerby. Or he may ask you to explain the earthquake or the storm, and the host of natural agencies which conceal their affinity for each other so successfully that only a theologian can hope to discover them.

The new message is the gospel of identity . It is not an effort to unite lives in a common interest, but a recognition of the fact that all forms are but manifestations of one indivisible agent. According to this concept there are no longer two who can be friends, but rather one that cannot be divided and in whom the sense of diversity is an illusion of form and not a reality of spirit. No longer must we conceive of that type of friendship in which several parts fraternize, and all too often patronize, but rather that indissoluble unity which is fundamental throughout the universe. To the wise, however, this is not one life working against another, but the parts of one life moving upon each other. Cataclysms possibly evidence a magnified form of those same inconsistencies which man manifests when he deliberately injures some part of his own body for the gratificaton of a whim. The gospel of identity is not one that can be thundered from the pulpits, preached from the housetops or harangued in the marketplace. It is something that must come to be realized, that must be felt within the nature itself. It is that fundamental unity of each with all; that power which discovers all things within the Self and the Self within all things. The gospel of tomorrow will be a gospel of one being. No longer will a million universes or billions of half-formed creatures struggle out the destiny of worms; no longer will there be a seemingly endless, crawling, seething mass of minute lives, for out of his Tushito heaven has come the Lord of Tomorrow, the Sovereign of Eternity, whose doctrine is that of identity , The star and the gnat will be united, suspended as it were from a single monad—one in essence, though several in aspect. No longer will there be the great and the small, but one spirit moving inevitably toward itself. No longer will there be a great order of evolving lives, but rather one ideating whole; an expression moving from itself outward to the inclusion of all.

Today we live in an involuting civilization, a civilization of separateness, a world dedicated to the concept of struggling with the parts of itself, a world obsessed with the illusion that the self has parts. We must overcome the belief that Self can rise up against its own nature, or that spirit is fragmentary; for that one man should compete with another is as senseless as that the fingers should fight the hands to which they are attached, or dissent from each other as ro their individual supremacy. From the condition of primitive isolation man has raised himself through successive revelations to a limited capacity to understand the issues of life. A few broad-minded, far-seeing individuals have recognized the fundamental equality of life, and have issued an emancipation proclamation declaring all creatures by right of their divine origin to be entitled to a place in the sun. From equality it is but a logical step to identity. So the enlightened man who has been elevated to that point where, when he meets another man, he says, "You are my friend," will tomorrow meet that same man and say, "You arc myself." No longer will complicated codes be necessary to administer human affairs when each man's interest becomes the interest of all the rest and each man's needs the needs of all. Laws are largely established to govern relationships, but when all relationships are done away with, laws will pass with them; for the one is always itself, and the intervals for which theoretical relationships are remedial agencies cannot exist in a united body.

An intellectual concept of the gospel of identity is not sufficient. In fact, intellectualism is the trap by which most minds are ensnared. A fact is not established by the intellect, but by a deeper power which we like to term realization. Hence the truth of identity is demonstrated by the realization of identity. Never will we have true equality until we realize that equality is based upon identity, for that which is Self is equal to Self, and upon the appreciation of this fact democracy is established. Democracy is not the condescending, patronizing attitude of the politician, nor is it the system whereby a hundred million folk of uncertain mind are empowered to elect one from their number as their leader. Democracy is the realization of the unity of life, and this realization shatters forever the competitive standard of civilization which is based upon the erroneous assumption that one part of life can survive without or at the expense of another. Competition was founded upon the dual-

istic theory—an ancient anthropomorphism in which two spirits wage an endless fight for supremacy. So wherever two individuals, institutions, or nations conceive a separate origin or a separate destiny, we have the boast that one will be holier than the other. As long as we conceive of separateness in origin and ultimate there will be grounds for competition, and upon the basis of competition is erected the whole structure of human sorrow.

We have an age, therefore, in which the parts struggle with each other, a world that thinks it has accomplished gready when it picks its right pocket to fill its left pocket. Diversity is simply the manifestation of those potentialities that are ever within the substance of unity. The universe is simply the objectification of a single causal agent. This does not imply that all things are alike, but rather that while they may differ in noncsscntials (as, for example, external composition), they are composed of the same agencies and essences. The gospel of identity includes the theory of difference, not difference from the standpoint of inequality but from the standpoint of condition. The philosopher does not infer that a gnat is a star, but that in their essential natures each is the manifestation of a common life, and that whatever may occur to one is registered in the single life principle that agitates them both. We have a civilization in which each part is attempting to include the whole within itself. Man as an individual dreams of the day when he can dominate men as a mass, failing to realize that such dominance is in appearance only, and that the individual can never be more than he is—one of the many. Through consciousness he may elevate himself to the point where he and the many are one, but having achieved this exalted goal he ceases to be himself and becomes the many—thinking in the terms of the many and serving the ends of the many. The gospel of identity shows man his true greatness; namely, that he possesses the power to interpret the whole and can actually come to realize his kinship with all. Through such realization he achieves philosophic liberation. He who escapes from the littleness which is his not-self, into the vastness which is his real Self, achieves greatly and serves the sovereign good.

There is but one cure for selfishness; namely, to realize that nothing can be added to us and nothing taken from us—that we are what we are and have what we have. We may temporarily possess a certain measure of opulence, but unless it is our own it will depart from us again. Yet in departing it is not gone, for that which is the possession of any one is ultimately the possession of all. What use, then, can there be for selfishness when he who believes that he takes from another really takes from himself? And why should not a man be generous when that which he gives to another he gives to himself? In philosophy there is consequently neither giver nor receiver, in that the gift, the giver, and the receiver are one.

The spirit in man is not merely a life enclosed within a frame.

Man is really a frame enclosed within a spirit. The thing in you that says "I am" is identical with the thing in me that says "I am." Then why should we not unite in common purpose? Why should we struggle for a little outer glory and battle with shadows in the service of our greeds? If he so desires, each individual by receding into his own divine nature may discover within himself the divine nature of all creatures. He may even become every other creature, for that part of himself which is real is every other creature.

In the annihilation of the sense of separateness we annihilate both life and death, for when we identify ourselves with the one life moving through all things how can we end ? As long as there is life we are that life; as long as a single star twinkles in the heavens we are that star; as long as a single blade of grass grows we are that blade of grass. We are not of the same race as those hands and feet which we have so long identified with ourselves; we are not that driveling creature, clutching at power—that mad thing of destruction which tears and rends in childish rage and harbors revenge within its heart. When we have recognized the universality of spirit we are one with the very fabric of life, and are no longer tortured with fears and premonitons. In our folly we have tried to be petty despots and establish empires of our own. We have desired the gold braid and tinsel of princes, and are peevish when someone takes away our principality. Let us turn from our petty despotism to behold that greater glory which is our natural right; for we are citizens of eternity; we are that very life that in the beginning moved upon the face of the deep; we are that shining power that walked in the garden with the Lord; we are the seraphim and the cherubim and the choirs of the ineffable. We are not gods—we arc God exiled for a little while into the forgetfulness of ourselves, yet soon to awaken to the full measure of our splendor.

O slumbering life, awake from your dreams of manyness and soar into the free air of concord. Turn from the wheels that you have set spinning in the building of an ephemeral empire. Depart from the unsubstantialness which you have come to love too well, and lift your eyes to the contemplation of a nobler state. You have given so much for a little power. You have become so weary in your fruitless quest of gain. The world asks so much for the little it can give, and that semblance of happiness which oppression has given you is so shallow and devoid of peace. Philosophy summons you to a greater calling, a more noble profession, a more excellent destiny. The sages of old would welcome you into the brotherhood of the elect, into the true ranks of the immortals where life flows on in broad full sweep throughout all eternity. Leave the half- built world which crumbles even as you raise its structures, for the Great Mother already has shaken countless civilizations from off her back. The very dust beneath our feet cries out with desire unfulfilled, for it is the powdered substance of ambition. Only in truth is there sufficiency, only in reality is there power. The unity of life is man's great truth upon which foundation he may build the empire of his soul. He is rich who is rich in truth; he is poor who is poor in truth. All else is of little moment. We are immortal, and that our soul tomorrow may be in peace let us rebuild our civilization. Let us establish our government of realities, our commonwealth of the wise. We as citizens of today arc also the citizens of tomorrow. We arc the life that shall throb in the communities yet to come; we arc the voice that shall speak in the senates of an unborn day. To that great life which is our true Self, to that tomorrow which to us must ever be the now, let us dedicate our inner selves and the achievements of our external natures.

Manly Palmer Hall (1901–1990) was one of the 20th century's most prolific and respected scholars of mysticism, comparative religion, and ancient philosophy. A philosopher, teacher, and author, Hall is best known for his monumental 1928 work The Secret Teachings of All Ages, an encyclopedic exploration of the world's esoteric traditions, which he completed at just 27 years old. This magnum opus established Hall as a preeminent voice in the fields of Hermeticism, alchemy, Kabbalah, Rosicrucianism, and the occult philosophies of the ancient world.

Born in Peterborough, Ontario, Canada, and raised in the United States, Hall developed an early interest in metaphysics and spiritual wisdom. He quickly gained recognition as a gifted orator and lecturer, drawing large audiences in Los Angeles and across the United States throughout the 1920s and beyond. In 1934, he founded the Philosophical Research Society (PRS) in Los Angeles—an enduring center for spiritual learning, personal transformation, and academic inquiry.

Hall's teachings emphasized the pursuit of self-knowledge, moral integrity, and the universal truths found within all religious and philosophical traditions. Over his lifetime, he authored more than 150 books and essays and delivered thousands of lectures—always returning to the central idea that wisdom is timeless, and that humanity thrives when it seeks harmony between the material and the spiritual.

Remaining active well into his late years, Hall continued to write, teach, and inspire seekers until his passing in 1990. Today, his works are considered essential reading for students of esotericism, symbolism, and the hidden currents of history and belief. His legacy endures through the continued work of the Philosophical Research Society and the countless readers and thinkers his insights have awakened.

About Adultbrain Publishing

Adultbrain Publishing is dedicated to reviving the timeless works of philosophy, mysticism, esotericism, and self-development for a modern audience. With a catalog spanning the great minds of antiquity to the revolutionary thinkers of the 20th century, Adultbrain curates and restores important texts that challenge, enlighten, and inspire.

Whether it's uncovering ancient mysteries, exploring forgotten philosophies, or reintroducing visionary thinkers like Manly P. Hall, Helena Blavatsky, Rudolf Steiner, or Charles Haanel, Adultbrain Publishing delivers carefully produced audiobooks, eBooks, and print editions designed to awaken the curious mind.

Start using your Adultbrain today—because deep thought, true wisdom, and inner power never go out of style.